The
Landscape of
Qualitative
Research

4
EDITION

The Landscape of Qualitative Research

4 EDITION

Norman K. Denzin
University of Illinois

Yvonna S. Lincoln
Texas A&M University

Editors

SAGE

Los Angeles | London | New Delhi
Singapore | Washington DC

Los Angeles | London | New Delhi
Singapore | Washington DC

FOR INFORMATION:

SAGE Publications, Inc.
2455 Teller Road
Thousand Oaks, California 91320
E-mail: order@sagepub.com

SAGE Publications Ltd.
1 Oliver's Yard
55 City Road
London EC1Y 1SP
United Kingdom

SAGE Publications India Pvt. Ltd.
B 1/I 1 Mohan Cooperative Industrial Area
Mathura Road, New Delhi 110 044
India

SAGE Publications Asia-Pacific Pte. Ltd.
3 Church Street
#10-04 Samsung Hub
Singapore 049483

Acquisitions Editor: Helen Salmon
Editorial Assistant: Kaitlin Perry
Production Editor: Laura Stewart
Typesetter: C&M Digitals (P) Ltd.
Proofreader: Stefanie Storholt
Indexer: Molly Hall
Cover Designer: Candice Harman
Marketing Manager: Nicole Elliott
Permissions Editor: Jason Kelley

Printed in the United States of America

Library of Congress Cataloging-in-Publication Data

The landscape of qualitative research/editors, Norman K. Denzin, University of Illinois, Urbana-Champaign, Yvonna S. Lincoln, Texas A&M University.—Fourth Edition.

pages cm
Includes bibliographical references and index.

ISBN 978-1-4522-5806-5 (pbk.)

1. Social sciences—Research. 2. Qualitative research. 3. Qualitative reasoning. I. Denzin, Norman K. II. Lincoln, Yvonna S.

H62.L274 2013
300.72´1—dc23   2012035578

This book is printed on acid-free paper.

SUSTAINABLE FORESTRY INITIATIVE
Certified Chain of Custody
Promoting Sustainable Forestry
www.sfiprogram.org
SFI-01268
SFI label applies to text stock

12 13 14 15 16 10 9 8 7 6 5 4 3 2 1

Contents

Preface

For nearly five decades, a quiet methodological revolution has been taking place in the social sciences. A blurring of disciplinary boundaries has occurred. The social sciences and humanities have drawn closer together in a mutual focus on an interpretive, qualitative approach to research and theory. Although these trends are not new, the extent to which the "qualitative revolution" has overtaken the social sciences and related professional fields has been nothing short of amazing.

Reflecting this revolution, a host of textbooks, journals, research monographs, and readers have been published in recent years. In 1994 we published the first edition of the *Handbook of Qualitative Research* in an attempt to represent the field in its entirety, to take stock of how far it had come and how far it might yet go. The immediate success of the first edition suggested the need to offer the *Handbook* in terms of three separate volumes. So in 1998 we published a three-volume set, *The Landscape of Qualitative Research: Theories and Issues*; *Strategies of Inquiry*; *Collecting and Interpreting Qualitative Materials*. In 2013 we offer a new three-volume set, based on the fourth edition of the handbook.[1]

By 2005 we had published the third edition of the *Handbook*. Although it became abundantly clear that the "field" of qualitative research is still defined primarily by tensions, contradictions, and hesitations—and that they exist in a less-than-unified arena—we believed that the handbook could and would be valuable for solidifying, interpreting, and organizing the field in spite of the essential differences that characterize it.

The first edition attempted to define the field of qualitative research. The second and third editions went one step further. Building on themes in the first edition we asked how the practices of qualitative inquiry could be used to address issues equity and of social justice. The fourth edition continues where the third edition ended. The transformations that were taking place in the first decade of this new century continue to gain momentum in the second decade.

---

[1]To review: the first three-volume set was offered in 1998, the second in 2003, and the third in 2008.

Not surprisingly, this quiet revolution has been met by resistance. In many quarters, a resurgent, scientifically based research paradigm has gained the upper hand. Borrowing form the field of biomedical research, the National Research Council (NRC) has appropriated neo-positivist, evidence-based epistemologies. Calls for Randomized Control Trials and mixed-methods designs are now common. Interpretive methods are read as being unsuitable for those who legislate social policy.

The days of value-free inquiry based on a God's-eye of reality are over. Today many agree that inquiry is moral, and political. Experimental, reflexive ways of writing and performing first-person autoethnographic texts are now commonplace. There continues to be a pressing need to show how the practices of qualitative research can help change the world in positive ways. It is necessary to reengage the promise of qualitative research as a form of radical democratic practice. At the same time there is an urgent need to train students in the new qualitative methodologies.

We have been enormously gratified and heartened by the response to the *Handbook* since its publication. Especially gratifying has been that it has been used and adapted by such a wide variety of scholars and graduate students in precisely the way we had hoped: as a starting point, a springboard for new thought and new work.

The Paperback Project

The fourth edition of the *Handbook of Qualitative Research* is virtually all new. Over half of the authors from the first edition have been replaced by new contributors. Indeed there are 33 new chapter authors or co-authors. There are fifteen totally new chapter topics, including contributions on: mixed methods, the sacred and the spiritual, critical humanism and queer theory, Asian depistemologies, disability communities and transformative research, performance ethnography, participatory action inquiry, oral history focus groups in feminist research, applied ethnography, and anthropological poetics. All returning authors have substantially revised their original contributions, in many cases producing a totally new and different chapter.

A handbook, we were told by our publisher, should ideally represent the distillation of knowledge of a field, a benchmark volume that synthesizes an existing literature, helping to define and shape the present and future of that discipline. In metaphoric terms, if you were to take one book on qualitative research with you to a desert island (or for a comprehensive graduate examination), a handbook would be the book.

It was decided that the part structure of the *Handbook* could serve as useful point of departure for the organization of the paperbacks. Thus Volume 1, titled

The Landscape of Qualitative Research: Theories and Issues, takes a look at the field from a broadly theoretical perspective, and is composed of the *Handbook*'s Parts I ("Locating the Field"), II ("Major Paradigms and Perspectives"), and VI ("The Future of Qualitative Research"). Volume 2, titled *Strategies of Qualitative Inquiry,* focuses on just that, and consists of Part III of the *Handbook.* Volume 3, titled *Collecting and Interpreting Qualitative Materials,* considers the tasks of collecting, analyzing, and interpreting empirical materials, and comprises the *Handbook*'s Parts IV ("Methods of Collecting and Analyzing Empirical Materials") and V ("The Art of Interpretation, Evaluation, and Presentation").

As with the first edition of the Landscape series, we decided that nothing should be cut from the original *Handbook.* Nearly everyone we spoke to who used the *Handbook* had his or her own way of using it, leaning heavily on certain chapters and skipping others altogether. But there was consensus that this reorganization made a great deal of sense both pedagogically and economically. We and Sage are committed to making this iteration of the *Handbook* accessible for classroom use. This commitment is reflected in the size, organization, and price of the paperbacks, as well as in the addition of end-of-book bibliographies.

It also became clear in our conversations with colleagues who used the *Handbook* that the single-volume, hard-cover version has a distinct place and value, and Sage will keep the original version available until a revised edition is published.

ORGANIZATION OF THIS VOLUME

The Landscape of Qualitative Research attempts to put the field of qualitative research in context. Part I locates the field, starting with history, then action research and the academy, research for whom?, and the politics and ethics of qualitative research. Part II isolates what we regard as the major historical and contemporary paradigms now structuring and influencing qualitative research in the human disciplines. The chapters move from competing paradigms (positivist, postpositivist, constructivist, critical theory) to specific interpretive perspectives, feminisms, racialized discourses, cultural studies, sexualities, and queer theory. Part III considers the future of qualitative research.

Acknowledgments

This *Handbook* would not be without its authors, and the editorial board members who gave freely, often on very short notice, of their time, advice and ever courteous suggestions. We acknowledge *en masse* the support of the authors, and the editorial board members, whose names are listed facing the title page. These individuals were able to offer both long-term, sustained commitments to the project and short-term emergency assistance.

There are other debts, intensely personal and closer to home. The *Handbook* would never have been possible without the ever present help, support, wisdom, and encouragement of our editors and publishers at Sage: Michele Sordi, Vicki Knight, Sean Connelly, and Lauren Habib Their grasp of this field, its history, and diversity is extraordinary. Their conceptions of what this project should look like were extremely valuable. Their energy kept us moving forward. Furthermore, whenever we confronted a problem Michele, Vicki and Lauren were there with their assistance and good natured humor.

We would also like to thank the following individuals, and institutions for their assistance, support, insights and patience: our respective universities, administrations and departments. In Urbana James Salvo, Melba Velez, Koeli Goel, and Katia Curbelo were the *sine qua non.* Their good-humor and grace kept our ever -growing files in order, and everyone on the same timetable. Without them, this project would never have been completed!

Laura Stewart at Sage Publications helped move this project through production. We are extremely grateful to her, as well as to Stefanie Storholt and Molly Hall for their excellent work during the proofreading and indexing phases of production. Our spouses, Katherine Ryan and Egon Guba, helped keep us on track, listened to our complaints, and generally displayed extraordinary patience, forbearance and support.

Finally, there is another group of individuals who gave unstintingly of their time and energy to provide us with their expertise and thoughtful reviews when we needed additional guidance. Without the help of these individuals we would often have found ourselves with less than complete understandings of the various traditions, perspectives and methods represented in this volume. We would also like to acknowledge the important contributions of the following special readers to this project: Bryant Alexander, Susan Chase, Michele Fine, Susan Finley, Andrea Fontana, Jaber Gubrium, James Holstein, Alison Jones, Stacy Holman Jones, Tony Kuzel, Luis Miron, Ron Pelias, John Prosser, Johnny Saldana, Harry Torrance.

Norman K. Denzin
University of Illinois at Urbana-Champaign

Yvonna S. Lincoln
Texas A & M University

24 April 2012

About the Editors

Norman K. Denzin is Distinguished Professor of Communications, College of Communications Scholar, and Research Professor of Communications, Sociology and Humanities, at the University of Illinois, Urbana-Champaign. He is the author, editor, or coeditor of numerous books, including *The Qualitative Manifesto; Qualitative Inquiry Under Fire; Flags in the Window: Dispatches From the American War Zone; Searching for Yellowstone: Identity, Politics and Democracy in the New West; Performance Ethnography: Critical Pedagogy and the Politics of Culture; Screening Race: Hollywood and a Cinema of Racial Violence; Performing Ethnography;* and *9/11 in American Culture.* He is past editor of *The Sociological Quarterly;* coeditor of *The SAGE Handbook of Qualitative Research,* Fourth Edition; coeditor of *Qualitative Inquiry;* editor of *Cultural Studies <=> Critical Methodologies;* editor of *International Review of Qualitative Research,* editor of *Studies in Symbolic Interaction,* and founding President of the International Association of Qualitative Inquiry.

Yvonna S. Lincoln is Ruth Harrington Chair of Educational Leadership and Distinguished Professor of Higher Education at Texas A&M University, where she also serves as Program Chair for the higher education program area. She is the coeditor, with Norman K. Denzin, of the journal *Qualitative Inquiry,* and of the first and second, third and now fourth editions of *the SAGE Handbook of Qualitative Research* and the *Handbook of Critical and Indigenous Methodologies.* As well, she is the coauthor, editor, or coeditor of more than a half dozen other books and volumes. She has served as the President of the Association for the Study of Higher Education and the American Evaluation Association, and as the Vice President for Division J (Postsecondary Education) for the American Educational Research Association. She is the author or coauthor of more than 100 chapters and journal articles on aspects of higher education or qualitative research methods and methodologies. Her research interests include development of qualitative methods and methodologies, the status and future of research libraries, and other issues in higher education. And, she's fun.

About the Contributors

Gaile S. Cannella holds the Velma E. Schmidt Endowed Chair in Early Childhood Studies in the Department of Teacher Education and Administration, University of North Texas, and focuses on critical social science and qualitative research methodologies in her teaching and research projects. She has written several books, including *Deconstructing Early Childhood Education: Social Justice and Revolution; Kidworld: Childhood Studies, Globalization and Education* (with J. Kincheloe); *Childhood and (Post)colonization* (with R. Viruru); and *Childhoods: A Handbook* (with L. Diaz Soto). Cannella is past Vice President of the International Association of Qualitative Inquiry.

Clifford G. Christians is a Research Professor of Communications Emeritus at the University of Illinois, Urbana-Champaign, where he was Director of the Institute of Communications for 16 years. He has been a visiting scholar in philosophical ethics at Princeton University, in social ethics at the University of Chicago, and a PEW fellow in ethics at Oxford University. He completed the third edition of Rivers and Schramm's *Responsibility in Mass Communication,* has coauthored *Jacques Ellul: Interpretive Essays* with Jay Van Hook, and has written *Teaching Ethics in Journalism Education* with Catherine Covert. Christians is also the coauthor, with John Ferre and Mark Fackler, of *Good News: Social Ethics and the Press.* Christians' *Media Ethics: Cases and Moral Reasoning,* with Mark Fackler, Kathy McKee, Peggy Kreshel, and Robert Woods, is now in its ninth edition. He has authored or coauthored *Communication Ethics and Universal Values, Handbook of Mass Media Ethics, Moral Engagement in Public Life: Theorists for Contemporary Ethics, Ethical Communication: Moral Stances in Human Dialogue,* and *Normative Theories of the Media.* He was editor of *Critical Studies in Media Communication* and currently edits *The Ellul Forum.*

Cynthia B. Dillard (Nana Mansa II of Mpeasem, Ghana, West Africa) is Professor of Multicultural Teacher Education in the School of Teaching and Learning at The Ohio State University. Her major research interests include critical multicultural education, spirituality in teaching and learning, and African/African American feminist studies. She has published numerous book chapters and articles in journals including *International Review of Qualitative Research; Race, Ethnicity and Education; The Journal of Teacher Education;* and *The International Journal of Qualitative Studies in Education and Urban Education.* Her first book, *On Spiritual Strivings: Transforming an African American Woman's Academic Life* was published in 2006 by SUNY Press and was selected for the 2008 Critics' Choice Book Award by the American Educational Studies Association (AESA). Most recently, her research and service is focused in Ghana, West Africa, where she has established a preschool, is building a new elementary school, and is enstooled/crowned Nana Mansa II, Queen Mother of Development, in the village of Mpeasem, Ghana.

Margaret A. Eisenhart is University Distinguished Professor and Charles Professor of Educational Anthropology and Research Methodology at the University of Colorado, Boulder. Her research focuses on culture and gender in education, and women in science and engineering. She has conducted research in elementary and secondary schools, colleges, universities, and workplaces. Her most important works include *Educated in Romance: Women, Achievement, and College Culture* (with Dorothy Holland); *Women's Science: Learning and Succeeding From the Margins* (with Elizabeth Finkel); and *Designing Classroom Research* (with Hilda Borko). In her current research project, "Female Recruits Explore Engineering" (the FREE Project), she developed and delivered a program to encourage high school minority girls' interest in engineering and IT and studied how the program and its goals fit into the context of the girls' lives. She is a fellow of the American Anthropological Association and the American Educational Research Association, and a member of the National Academy of Education.

Frederick Erickson is George F. Kneller Professor of Anthropology of Education and Professor of Applied Linguistics at the University of California, Los Angeles (UCLA). His contributions to the field of anthropology of education have earned him numerous honors and awards, including fellowships from the Spencer Foundation and Annenberg Institute for Public Policy, a Fulbright Award, the Spindler Award for Scholarly Contributions to Educational Anthropology from the American Anthropological Association, and a Lifetime Achievement Award for Research on the Social Context of Education from Division G of the American Educational Research Association (AERA). Erickson's writings on the video-based microethnographic study of classroom and family interaction, and on qualitative research methods more generally, are widely cited. His recent book, *Talk and Social Theory: Ecologies of Speaking and Listening in Everyday Life* (2004) received an Outstanding Book Award for 2005 from AERA. He serves on the editorial boards of *Research on Language and Social Interaction,*

Discourse and Communication, the International Review of Qualitative Research, and *Teachers College Record.* In 1998–1999 and again in 2006–2007, he was a fellow at the Center for Advanced Study in the Behavioral Sciences at Stanford University. In 2000, he was elected a member of the National Academy of Education, and in 2009, he was elected a fellow of the American Educational Research Association.

Michael D. Giardina (PhD, University of Illinois) is Assistant Professor in the College of Education at Florida State University, where he teaches courses on physical cultural studies, qualitative research methods, and popular media. He is the author of *Sporting Pedagogies: Performing Culture & Identity in the Global Arena* (2005), which received the 2006 Most Outstanding Book award from the North American Society for the Sociology of Sport, and *Sport, Spectacle, and NASCAR Nation: Consumption and the Cultural Politics of Neoliberalism* (2011, with Joshua I. Newman). Giardina is also the editor of *Youth Culture & Sport: Identity, Power, & Politics* (2007, with Michele K. Donnelly), *Globalizing Cultural Studies: Ethnographic Interventions in Theory, Method, and Policy* (2007, with Cameron McCarthy et al.), and a series of seven books with Norman K. Denzin on cultural studies and interpretive research in the post–9/11 era, including *Contesting Empire/Globalizing Dissent: Cultural Studies after 9/11* (2006) and *Qualitative Inquiry and Social Justice: Toward a Politics of Hope* (2009). His work has similarly appeared in such journals as *Qualitative Inquiry, American Behavioral Scientist, Harvard Educational Review, International Journal of Qualitative Studies in Education,* and *Cultural Studies <=> Critical Methodologies.* He is Associate Editor of the *Sociology of Sport Journal* and a member of the editorial board of *Cultural Studies <=> Critical Methodologies.*

Davydd J. Greenwood is the Goldwin Smith Professor of Anthropology at Cornell University where he has served as a faculty member since 1970. He was elected Corresponding Member of the Spanish Royal Academy of Moral and Political Sciences in 1996. He served as the John S. Knight Professor and Director of the Mario Einaudi Center from 1983 to 1995 and as Director of the Cornell Institute for European Studies from 2000 to 2008. His work centers on action research, political economy, ethnic conflict, community and regional development, and neoliberal reforms of higher education. He has worked in the Spanish Basque Country, Spain's La Mancha region, and the Finger Lakes region of Upstate New York. The author of 8 books and more than 40 articles on agricultural industrialization, the use of biological ideologies to support political economic regimes, industrial cooperatives, and action research, he is currently working on the role of action research in developing creative responses to neoliberal reforms in higher education.

Egon Guba (1924–2008) was Professor Emeritus of Education, Indiana University. He received his PhD from the University of Chicago in quantitative inquiry (education) in 1952, and thereafter served on the faculties of the University of Chicago, the University of Kansas, the Ohio State University, and Indiana University. Over a two-decade period, he studied paradigms alternative to the received view and espoused a personal commitment to one of these: constructivism. He was the coauthor of *Effective Evaluation* (1981), *Naturalistic Inquiry* (1985), and *Fourth Generation Evaluation* (1989), all with Yvonna S. Lincoln, and he is the editor of *The Paradigm Dialog* (1990), which explores the implications of alternative paradigms for social and educational inquiry. He is the author of more than 150 journal articles and more than 100 conference presentations, many of them concerned with elements of new-paradigm inquiry and methods.

A. Susan Jurow is an Assistant Professor of Educational Psychology and Research on Teaching and Teacher Education at the University of Colorado, Boulder. Her research focuses on the relations among learning, teaching, and communication. She has conducted research in elementary and middle schools, professional development programs, and universities. In these projects she has focused on (1) the development of practice-linked identities to describe how people identify with particular ways of knowing, acting, and valuing, and are positioned to participate in social practices, and (2) individuals' engagement in long-term projects of learning located in classrooms and out-of-school settings. Her multidisciplinary approach to studying learning and teaching draws on the learning sciences, anthropology, and discourse analysis.

Joe L. Kincheloe (1950–2008) was a researcher's researcher, a teacher's teacher, and the quintessential embodiment of critical pedagogy. A tireless champion for socially just pedagogy, he authored and edited over 60 books and hundreds of articles underpinned by his commitment to engagement, authenticity, and cultural work. His notions of teacher as researcher, critical constructivism, research bricolage, postformal thinking, and critical cultural studies are internationally recognized. Joe was the supervisor and chair for scores of doctoral students from Pennsylvania State University, CUNY Graduate Center, and McGill University. His work and legacy continue to make a difference in faculties, schools, and communities from Barcelona, Spain, to Utrecht, Netherlands, to Daejong, Korea, to Melbourne, Australia, to Winnipeg, Manitoba, and back to where his work was grounded, Sao Paulo, Brazil. Joe was a father, a husband, a musician, a teacher, a friend, and a researcher; his life was a bricolage of hyperreality, Tennessee Volunteers football, epistemological quandaries, and radical love. His curiosity and wonder informed his work, and he filled his life with questioning the unquestioned and naming the unnamed.

Morten Levin is a Professor at the Department of Industrial Economics and Technology Management, the Faculty of Social Sciences and Technology Management, at the Norwegian University of Science and Technology in Trondheim, Norway. He holds graduate degrees in engineering and in sociology. Throughout his professional life, he has worked as an action researcher with a particular focus on processes and structures of social change in the relationships between technology and organization. His action research has taken place in industrial contexts, in local communities, and in university teaching, where he has developed and directed three PhD programs in action research. He is author of a number of books and articles, including *Introduction to Action Research: Social Research for Social Change,* and serves on the editorial boards of *Systemic Practice and Action Research, Action Research International, Action Research,* and *The Handbook of Action Research.*

James H. Liu is Professor of Psychology at Victoria University of Wellington and Deputy Director of its Centre for Applied Cross Cultural Research. He was born in Taiwan and grew up in a small town in the midwestern United States. He obtained a bachelor's degree in computer science from the University of Illinois and worked as an aerospace engineer for Hughes Aircraft Space and Communications. He completed a PhD in social psychology in 1992 at University of California, Los Angeles, and a postdoctoral fellowship at Florida Atlantic University. He has been teaching at Victoria University of Wellington since 1994. His research is at the intersection of cross-cultural psychology and intergroup relations. He specializes in the study of social identity and representations of history. He has more than 100 academic publications, and his edited volumes include *New Zealand Identities: Departures and Destinations* (2005), *Restorative Justice and Practices in New Zealand* (2010), *Ages Ahead: Promoting Intergenerational Relationships* (1998), and *Progress in Asian Social Psychology,* Volumes 2 (1997) and 6 (2006). He was Secretary General of the Asian Association of Social Psychology from 2003 to 2007, Treasurer from 1999 to 2003, and is now editor of the *Asian Journal of Social Psychology.* A naturalized citizen of two countries, he describes himself as a "Chinese-American-New Zealander." He is married to Belinda Bonzon Liu, and they have a daughter who is even more hyphenated: a Chinese-American-Filipino-New Zealander. His father is an eminent neo-Confucian philosopher living in Taiwan.

Susan A. Lynham is Associate Professor in the Research Methodology, and Organizational Performance and Change PhD programs at Colorado State University. Her scholarship focuses on strategic human resource development, leadership in complex and diverse environments, and applied theory building research methods. A past board member of the Academy of Human Resource

Development, Susan serves as Editor-in-Chief of the *Advances in Developing Human Resources* journal. She obtained her PhD from the University of Minnesota, in May 2000.

Peter McLaren is Professor of Urban Schooling, the Graduate School of Education and Information Studies, University of California, Los Angeles. He is the author and editor of more than 45 books on various subjects within the pedagogy of liberation. His writings have been translated into 25 languages. McLaren has been honored in numerous countries for his international scholarship and political activism. Among these honors, a Catedra McLaren has been established at Bolivarian University, Venezuela, and La Fundacion McLaren and Instituto Peter McLaren have been created in Northern Mexico by teachers, researchers and activists. As an award-winning author and educational activist, McLaren lectures worldwide.

Donna M. Mertens is Professor of Research Methodology and Program Evaluation at Gallaudet University in Washington, D.C. Her work focuses on the development of transformative research and evaluation methodologies with a goal of increasing social justice and furthering human rights. Her publications include *Research and Evaluation in Education and Psychology: Integrating Diversity with Quantitative, Qualitative, and Mixed Methods* (3rd ed., 2010), *Transformative Research and Evaluation* (2009), and *The Handbook of Social Research Ethics* (edited with Pauline Ginsberg, 2009).

Joshua I. Newman (PhD, University of Maryland) lectures in the areas of sport and physical culture, qualitative research, cultural studies, and critical pedagogy at the University of Otago's (New Zealand) School of Physical Education. Broadly speaking, his research, teaching, and supervision are committed to interrogating the intersections of late capitalism, identity, and cultural politics of the body. In recent years, his work has focused on the politics of embodiment and enfleshed performance within the U.S. South. He is the author of *Embodying Dixie: Studies in the Body Pedagogics of Southern Whiteness* (2010) and *Sport, Spectacle, and NASCAR Nation: Consumption and the Cultural Politics of Neoliberalism* (2011, with Michael D. Giardina). Newman has also published numerous research articles in journals such as *Cultural Studies <=> Critical Methodologies; American Behavioral Scientist; The Review of Education, Pedagogy, and Cultural Studies; Sociology of Sport Journal;* and *International Review for the Sociology of Sport.*

Chinwe Okpalaoka is Director of Special Programs in the College of Arts and Sciences at The Ohio State University. In this position, she oversees the recruitment and retention of targeted student populations as well assists in the development and management of freshman seminar courses for the university. Her major research interests include immigrant education, immigrant ethnic identity development, and African/African American feminist studies. She is currently working with other scholars on a collaborative piece that forwards the notion of transnational Black feminisms and corresponding methodologies. The most recent focus of her work is an examination of how West African immigrant girls' experiences in the United States might be interpreted through a transnational Black feminist lens.

Virginia Olesen, Professor of Sociology (Emerita), Department of Social and Behavioral Sciences, University of California, San Francisco, continues her long time exploration of feminist qualitative research with writing on the temporal dynamics of critical interpretive research in an age of despair (*Critical Studies <=> Critical Methodologies*, Vol. 9, pp. 52–55, 2009), the limits of reflexivity in qualitative research ("Reflexive Anthropology and Research Ethics: Elvi Whittaker's Contributions" in *Ethnography, Epistemology, Ethics: Essays in Honour of Elvi Whittaker,* G. V. Loewen, Ed., forthcoming) and feminist qualitative research and grounded theory ("Feminist Qualitative Research and Grounded Theory: Complexities, Criticisms and Opportunities," pp. 417–435 in A. Bryant and K. Charmaz, Eds., *The SAGE Handbook of Grounded Theory,* Sage, 2007). A pioneer in feminist qualitative studies of women's health, she recently worked with an interdisciplinary group (nurses, physicians, anthropologists, sociologists, social workers) that examined issues around the health of incarcerated women ("Social Capital: A Lens for Examining Health of Incarcerated and Formerly Incarcerated Women," pp. 13–22 in D. C. Hatton and A. A. Fisher, Eds., *Women Prisoners and Health Justice, Perspectives, Issues and Advocacy for an International Hidden Population,* 2009).

Ken Plummer is Emeritus Professor of Sociology at the University of Essex. His first book was *Sexual Stigma* (1975) and his most recent is *Sociology: The Basics* (2010). He has written on critical humanism and life stories, gay and lesbian life, sexual storytelling, narrative work, labeling theory, symbolic interactionism, queer theory, inequalities, rights, and citizenship. He was the founder editor of the journal *Sexualities* in 1996.

Judith Preissle is the 2001 Distinguished Aderhold Professor for the College of Education at the University of Georgia (UGA) where she has taught since 1975. She is an affiliate faculty member of the Institute for Women's Studies, who honored her with the 2006 Women's Studies Faculty Award. As an interdisciplinary scholar, she studies qualitative research methods and design; the anthropology of education; and gender, ethnic, and immigration studies. Recently, she has been studying ethics and the philosophy of social science. Her chapter, "Feminist Research Ethics" appeared in 2007 in *The Handbook of Feminist Research: Theory and Praxis*. She is the coauthor of *Ethnography and Qualitative Design in Educational Research* (1984, 1993), translated into Spanish in 1988, and coeditor of *The Handbook of Qualitative Research in Education* (1992). Her most recent book, coauthored with Xue Lan Rong, is the second edition of *Educating Immigrant Students* (2009). In addition to numerous book chapters, she has authored articles in such journals as the *American Educational Research Journal*, the *Anthropology of Education Quarterly*, the *Journal of Contemporary Ethnography*, the *Review of Educational Research*, the *Educational Researcher*, the *International Journal of Qualitative Studies in Education*, and *The Elementary School Journal*. She e-manages QUALRS-L (Qualitative Research for the Human Sciences), established in 1991 and the oldest such forum online, and QualPage, a web page on qualitative research. She founded the qualitative research program at UGA that now offers a graduate certificate program. In 2009 she was made a Fellow of the American Educational Research Association.

Hilary Stace is a Research Fellow at the School of Government, Victoria University of Wellington, New Zealand. Her PhD research is on autism and public policy, specifically how the expertise of policy consumers—people with autism and their families—can be brought into the policy process. Her lived experience as a parent of an adult autistic son has fuelled her autism advocacy. She is also interested in collaborative approaches to disability research.

Shirley R. Steinberg is the incoming Director and Chair of the Werklund Foundation Youth Leadership Education, and Professor of Youth Studies in Education at the University of Calgary, and was Research Professor at The University of Barcelona. The author and editor of many books in critical pedagogy, urban and youth culture, and cultural studies, some of her recent books include *Critical Qualitative Research* (with Gaile Cannella, 2012); the third edition of *Kinderculture: The Corporate Construction of Childhood* (2011); *Teaching Against Islamophobia* (edited with Joe Kincheloe and Christopher Stonebanks, 2010); *19 Urban Questions: Teaching in the City* (2010); *Christotainment: Selling Jesus Through Popular Culture* (edited with Joe Kincheloe, 2009); and *Diversity and Multiculturalism: A Reader* (2009). With Joe Kincheloe, she founded The Paulo and Nita Freire International Project for Critical Pedagogy (freireproject. org). A regular columnist for CTV and CBC Radio, she speaks internationally on critical pedagogy, youth studies, leadership, qualitative research, and social justice.

Martin Sullivan, PhD, QSO, is a senior lecturer at the School of Health and Social Services, Massey University, Palmerston North, New Zealand, where he coordinates postgraduate programs in disability studies and social policy. He coedited with Patricia O'Brien *Allies in Emancipation. Shifting From Providing Service to Being of Support* (2005), was part of the expert panel that reviewed and set guidelines for the disability research funded by the Health Research Council of New Zealand, and was a ministerial appointment to the National Ethics Advisory Committee for 6 years. He is currently working on a longitudinal study into the first two years of transition from spinal unit to community for people with spinal cord injury.

1

Introduction

The Discipline and Practice of Qualitative Research

Norman K. Denzin and Yvonna S. Lincoln

The global community of qualitative researchers is midway between two extremes, searching for a new middle, moving in several different directions at the same time.[1] Mixed methodologies and calls for scientifically based research, on the one side, renewed calls for social justice inquiry from the critical social science tradition on the other. In the methodological struggles of the 1970s and 1980s, the very existence of qualitative research was at issue. In the new paradigm war, "every overtly social justice-oriented approach to research . . . is threatened with de-legitimization by the government-sanctioned, exclusivist assertion of positivism . . . as the 'gold standard' of educational research" (Wright, 2006, pp. 799–800).

The evidence-based research movement, with its fixed standards and guidelines for conducting and evaluating qualitative inquiry, sought total domination: one shoe fits all (Cannella & Lincoln, Chapter 5, this volume; Lincoln, 2010). The heart of the matter turns on issues surrounding the politics and ethics of evidence and the value of qualitative work in addressing matters of equity and social justice (Torrance, Chapter 11, volume 3).

In this introductory chapter, we define the field of qualitative research, then navigate, chart, and review the history of qualitative research in the human disciplines. This will allow us to locate this handbook and its contents within their historical moments. (These historical moments are somewhat artificial; they are socially constructed, quasi-historical, and overlapping conventions. Nevertheless, they permit a "performance" of developing ideas. They also facilitate an increasing sensitivity to and sophistication about the pitfalls and promises of ethnography and qualitative research.) A conceptual framework for reading the qualitative research act as a multicultural, gendered process is presented.

We then provide a brief introduction to the chapters, concluding with a brief discussion of qualitative research. We will also discuss the threats to qualitative human-subject research from the methodological conservatism movement, which was noted in our Preface. As indicated there, we use the metaphor of the bridge to structure what follows. This volume provides a bridge between historical moments, politics, the decolonization project, research methods, paradigms, and communities of interpretive scholars.

History, Politics, and Paradigms

To better understand where we are today and to better grasp current criticisms, it is useful to return to the so-called paradigm wars of the 1980s, which resulted in the serious crippling of quantitative research in education. Critical pedagogy, critical theorists, and feminist analyses fostered struggles to acquire power and cultural capital for the poor, non-whites, women, and gays (Gage, 1989).

Charles Teddlie and Abbas Tashakkori's history is helpful here. They expand the time frame of the 1980s war to embrace at least three paradigm wars, or periods of conflict: the postpositivist-constructivist war against positivism (1970–1990); the conflict between competing postpositivist, constructivist, and critical theory paradigms (1990–2005); and the current conflict between evidence-based methodologists and the mixed methods, interpretive, and critical theory schools (2005–present).[2]

Egon Guba's (1990a) *The Paradigm Dialog* signaled an end to the 1980s wars. Postpositivists, constructivists, and critical theorists talked to one another, working through issues connected to ethics, field studies, praxis, criteria, knowledge accumulation, truth, significance, graduate training, values, and politics. By the early 1990s, there was an explosion of published work on qualitative research; handbooks and new journals appeared. Special interest groups committed to particular paradigms appeared, some with their own journals.[3]

The second paradigm conflict occurred within the mixed methods community and involved disputes "between individuals convinced of the 'paradigm purity' of their own position" (Teddlie & Tashakkori, 2003b, p. 7). Purists extended and repeated the argument that quantitative and qualitative methods and postpositivism and the other "isms" cannot be combined because of the differences between their underlying paradigm assumptions. On the methodo-logical front, the incompatibility thesis was challenged by those who invoked triangulation as a way of combining multiple methods to study the same phe-nomenon (Teddlie & Tashakkori, 2003a, p. 7). This ushered in a new round of arguments and debates over paradigm superiority.

A soft, apolitical pragmatic paradigm emerged in the post-1990 period. Sud-denly, quantitative and qualitative methods became compatible, and researchers could use both in their empirical inquiries (Teddlie & Tashakkori, 2003a, p. 7). Proponents made appeals to a "what works" pragmatic argument, contending that "no incompatibility between quantitative and qualitative methods exists at either the level of practice or that of epistemology . . . there are thus no good reasons for educational researchers to fear forging ahead with 'what works'" (Howe, 1988, p. 16). Of course, what works is more than an empirical question. It involves the politics of evidence.

This is the space that evidence-based research entered. It became the battle-ground of the third war, "the current upheaval and argument about 'scientific' research in the scholarly world of education" (Clark & Scheurich, 2008; Scheu-rich & Clark, 2006, p. 401). Enter Teddlie and Tashakkori's third moment: Mixed methods and evidence-based inquiry meet one another in a soft center. C. Wright Mills (1959) would say this is a space for abstracted empiricism. Inquiry is cut off from politics. Biography and history recede into the back-ground. Technological rationality prevails.

RESISTANCES TO QUALITATIVE STUDIES

The academic and disciplinary resistances to qualitative research illustrate the politics embedded in this field of discourse. The challenges to qualitative research are many. To better understand these criticisms, it is necessary to "distinguish analytically the political (or external) role of [qualitative] methodol-ogy from the procedural (or internal) one" (Seale, Gobo, Gubrium, & Silverman, 2004, p. 7). Politics situate methodology within and outside the academy. Proce-dural issues define how qualitative methodology is used to produce knowledge about the world (Seale et al., 2004, p. 7).

Often, the political and the procedural intersect. Politicians and hard scien-tists call qualitative researchers *journalists* or "soft" scientists. Their work is termed unscientific, only exploratory, or subjective. It is called criticism and not theory, or it is interpreted politically, as a disguised version of Marxism or secu-lar humanism (see Huber, 1995; also Denzin, 1997, pp. 258–261).

These political and procedural resistances reflect an uneasy awareness that the interpretive traditions of qualitative research commit one to a critique of the positivist or postpositivist project. But the positivist resistance to qualitative research goes beyond the "ever-present desire to maintain a distinction between hard science and soft scholarship" (Carey, 1989, p. 99). The experimental (positivist) sciences (physics, chemistry, economics, and psychology, for example) are often seen as the crowning achievements of Western civilization, and in their practices, it is assumed that "truth" can transcend opinion and personal bias (Carey, 1989, p. 99; Schwandt, 1997b, p. 309). Qualitative research is seen as an assault on this tradition, whose adherents often retreat into a "value-free objectivist science" (Carey, 1989, p. 104) model to defend their position. The positivists seldom attempt to make explicit, and critique the "moral and political commitments in their own contingent work" (Carey, 1989, p. 104; Lincoln, Lynham, & Guba, Chapter 6, this volume).

Positivists further allege that the so-called new experimental qualitative researchers write fiction, not science, and have no way of verifying their truth statements. Ethnographic poetry and fiction signal the death of empirical science, and there is little to be gained by attempting to engage in moral criticism. These critics presume a stable, unchanging reality that can be studied with the empirical methods of objective social science (see Huber, 1995). The province of qualitative research, accordingly, is the world of lived experience, for this is where individual belief and action intersect with culture. Under this model, there is no preoccupation with discourse and method as material interpretive practices that constitute representation and description. This is the textual, narrative turn rejected by the positivists.

The opposition to positive science by the poststructuralists is seen, then, as an attack on reason and truth. At the same time, the positivist science attack on qualitative research is regarded as an attempt to legislate one version of truth over another.

THE LEGACIES OF SCIENTIFIC RESEARCH

Writing about scientific research, including qualitative research, from the vantage point of the colonized, a position that she chooses to privilege, Linda Tuhiwai Smith states that "the term 'research' is inextricably linked to European imperialism and colonialism." She continues, "the word itself is probably one of the dirtiest words in the indigenous world's vocabulary . . . It is "implicated in the worst excesses of colonialism" (p. 1), with the ways in which "knowledge about indigenous peoples was collected, classified, and then represented back to the West" (Smith, 1999, p. 1). This dirty word stirs up anger, silence, distrust. "It is so powerful that indigenous people even write poetry about research " (Smith, 1999, p. 1). It is one of colonialism's most sordid legacies, she says.

Frederick Erickson's Chapter 3 of this volume charts many key features of this painful history. He notes with some irony that qualitative research in sociology and anthropology was born out of concern to understand the exotic, often dark-skinned "other." Of course, there were colonialists long before there were anthropologists and ethnographers. Nonetheless, there would be no colonial—and now no neo-colonial—history, were it not for this investigative mentality that turned the dark-skinned other into the object of the ethnographer's gaze. From the very beginning, qualitative research was implicated in a racist project.[4]

Definitional Issues

Qualitative research is a field of inquiry in its own right. It crosscuts disciplines, fields, and subject matter.[5] A complex, interconnected family of terms, concepts, and assumptions surrounds the term. These include the traditions associated with foundationalism, positivism, postfoundationalism, postpositivism, post-structuralism, postmodernism, post-humanism, and the many qualitative research perspectives and methods connected to cultural and interpretive studies (the chapters in Part II of this volume take up these paradigms).[6] There are separate and detailed literatures on the many methods and approaches that fall under the category of qualitative research, such as case study, politics and ethics, participatory inquiry, interviewing, participant observation, visual methods, and interpretive analysis.

In North America, qualitative research operates in a complex historical field that crosscuts at least eight historical moments. These moments overlap and simultaneously operate in the present.[7] We define them as the traditional (1900–1950), the modernist or golden age (1950–1970), blurred genres (1970–1986), the crisis of representation (1986–1990), the postmodern, a period of experimental and new ethnographies (1990–1995), postexperimental inquiry (1995–2000), the methodologically contested present (2000–2010), and the future (2010–), which is now. The future, the eighth moment, confronts the methodological backlash associated with the evidence-based social movement. It is concerned with moral discourse, with the development of sacred textualities. The eighth moment asks that the social sciences and the humanities become sites for critical conversations about democracy, race, gender, class, nation-states, globalization, freedom, and community.[8]

The postmodern and postexperimental moments were defined in part by a concern for literary and rhetorical tropes and the narrative turn, a concern for storytelling, for composing ethnographies in new ways (Ellis, 2009; and in this volume, Hamera, Chapter 6, volume 2; Tedlock, Chapter 7, volume 2; Spry, Chapter 7, volume 3; Ellingson, Chapter 13, volume 3; St.Pierre, Chapter 14, volume 3; and Pelias, Chapter 17 volume 3).

Successive waves of epistemological theorizing move across these eight moments. The traditional period is associated with the positivist, foundational paradigm. The modernist or golden age and blurred genres moments are connected to the appearance of postpositivist arguments. At the same time, a variety of new interpretive, qualitative perspectives were taken up, including hermeneutics, structuralism, semiotics, phenomenology, cultural studies, and feminism.[9] In the blurred genre phase, the humanities became central resources for critical, interpretive theory and the qualitative research project broadly conceived. The researcher became a *bricoleur* (as discussed later), learning how to borrow from many different disciplines.

The blurred genres phase produced the next stage, the crisis of representation. Here researchers struggled with how to locate themselves and their subjects in reflexive texts. A kind of methodological diaspora took place, a two-way exodus. Humanists migrated to the social sciences, searching for new social theory and new ways to study popular culture and its local ethnographic contexts. Social scientists turned to the humanities, hoping to learn how to do complex structural and poststructural readings of social texts. From the humanities, social scientists also learned how to produce texts that refused to be read in simplistic, linear, incontrovertible terms. The line between a text and a context blurred. In the postmodern experimental moment, researchers continued to move away from foundational and quasifoundational criteria (in this volume, see Altheide & Johnson, Chapter 12, volume 3; St.Pierre, Chapter 14, volume 3). Alternative evaluative criteria were sought, ones that might prove evocative, moral, critical, and rooted in local understandings.

Any definition of qualitative research must work within this complex historical field. Qualitative research means different things in each of these moments. Nonetheless, an initial, generic definition can be offered. *Qualitative research* is a situated activity that locates the observer in the world. Qualitative research consists of a set of interpretive, material practices that make the world visible. These practices transform the world. They turn the world into a series of representations, including fieldnotes, interviews, conversations, photographs, recordings, and memos to the self. At this level, qualitative research involves an interpretive, naturalistic approach to the world. This means that qualitative researchers study things in their natural settings, attempting to make sense of or interpret phenomena in terms of the meanings people bring to them.[10]

Qualitative research involves the studied use and collection of a variety of empirical materials—case study, personal experience, introspection, life story, interview, artifacts, and cultural texts and productions, along with observational, historical, interactional, and visual texts—that describe routine and problematic moments and meanings in individuals' lives. Accordingly, qualitative researchers deploy a wide-range of interconnected interpretive practices, hoping always to get a better understanding of the subject matter at hand. It is understood, however, that each practice makes the world visible in a different way. Hence, there is frequently a commitment to using more than one interpretive practice in any study.

The Qualitative Researcher-as-Bricoleur and Quilt Maker

Multiple gendered images may be brought to the qualitative researcher: scientist, naturalist, fieldworker, journalist, social critic, artist, performer, jazz musician, filmmaker, quilt maker, essayist. The many methodological practices of qualitative research may be viewed as soft science, journalism, ethnography, *bricolage,* quilt making, or montage. The researcher, in turn, may be seen as a *bricoleur,* as a maker of quilts, or in filmmaking, a person who assembles images into montages (on montage, see Cook, 1981, pp. 171–177; Monaco, 1981, pp. 322–328; and discussion below; on quilting, see hooks, 1990, pp. 115–122; Wolcott, 1995, pp. 31–33).

Douglas Harper (1987, pp. 9, 74–75, 92); Michel de Certeau (1984, p. xv); Cary Nelson, Paula A. Treichler, and Lawrence Grossberg (1992, p. 2); Claude Lévi-Strauss (1962/1966, p. 17); Deena and Michael Weinstein (1991, p. 161); and Joe L. Kincheloe (2001) clarify the meaning of bricolage and bricoleur.[11] A bricoleur makes do by "adapting the bricoles of the world. Bricolage is 'the poetic making do'" (de Certeau, 1984, p. xv), with "such bricoles—the odds and ends, the bits left over" (Harper, 1987, p. 74). The bricoleur is a "Jack of all trades, a kind of professional do-it-yourself[er]" (Lévi-Strauss, 1962/1966, p. 17). In Harper's (1987) work, the bricoleur defines herself and extends herself (p. 75). Indeed, her life story, her biography, "may be thought of as bricolage" (Harper, 1987, p. 92).

There are many kinds of bricoleurs—interpretive, narrative, theoretical, political. The interpretive bricoleur produces a bricolage; that is, a pieced-together set of representations that are fitted to the specifics of a complex situation. "The solution (bricolage) which is the result of the bricoleur's method is an [emergent] construction" (Weinstein & Weinstein, 1991, p. 161), which changes and takes new forms as different tools, methods, and techniques of representation and interpretation are added to the puzzle. Nelson et al. (1992) describe the methodology of cultural studies "as a bricolage. Its choice of practice, that is, is pragmatic, strategic, and self-reflexive" (p. 2). This understanding can be applied, with qualifications, to qualitative research.

The qualitative-researcher-as-bricoleur or a maker of quilts uses the aesthetic and material tools of his or her craft, deploying whatever strategies, methods, or empirical materials are at hand (Becker, 1998, p. 2). If new tools or techniques have to be invented or pieced together, then the researcher will do this. The choice of which interpretive practices to employ is not necessarily set in advance. The "choice of research practices depends upon the questions that are asked, and the questions depend on their context" (Nelson et al., 1992, p. 2), what is available in the context, and what the researcher can do in that setting.

These interpretive practices involve aesthetic issues, an aesthetics of representation that goes beyond the pragmatic or the practical. Here the concept of *montage* is useful (see Cook, 1981, p. 323; Monaco, 1981, pp. 171–172). Montage is a method of editing cinematic images. In the history of cinematography, montage is associated with the work of Sergei Eisenstein, especially his film, *The Battleship Potemkin* (1925). In montage, a picture is made by superimposing several different images on one another. In a sense, montage is like *pentimento*, where something painted out of a picture (an image the painter "repented," or denied) now becomes visible again, creating something new. What is new is what had been obscured by a previous image.

Montage and pentimento, like jazz, which is improvisation, create the sense that images, sounds, and understandings are blending together, overlapping, and forming a composite, a new creation. The images seem to shape and define one another; an emotional gestalt effect is produced. Often, these images are combined in a swiftly run sequence. When done, this produces a dizzily revolving collection of several images around a central or focused picture or sequence; such effects signify the passage of time.

Perhaps the most famous instance of montage is given in the Odessa Steps sequence in *The Battleship Potemkin*.[12] In the climax of the film, the citizens of Odessa are being massacred by tsarist troops on the stone steps leading down to the city's harbor. Eisenstein cuts to a young mother as she pushes her baby's carriage across the landing in front of the firing troops. Citizens rush past her, jolting the carriage, which she is afraid to push down to the next flight of stairs. The troops are above her firing at the citizens. She is trapped between the troops and the steps. She screams. A line of rifles pointing to the sky erupts in smoke. The mother's head sways back. The wheels of the carriage teeter on the edge of the steps. The mother's hand clutches the silver buckle of her belt. Below her, people are being beaten by soldiers. Blood drips over the mother's white gloves. The baby's hand reaches out of the carriage. The mother sways back and forth. The troops advance. The mother falls back against the carriage. A woman watches in horror as the rear wheels of the carriage roll off the edge of the landing. With accelerating speed, the carriage bounces down the steps, past the dead citizens. The baby is jostled from side to side inside the carriage. The soldiers fire their rifles into a group of wounded citizens. A student screams, as the carriage leaps across the steps, tilts, and overturns (Cook, 1981, p. 167).[13]

Montage uses sparse images to create a clearly defined sense of urgency and complexity. Montage invites viewers to construct interpretations that build on one another as a scene unfolds. These interpretations are built on associations based on the contrasting images that blend into one another. The underlying assumption of montage is that viewers perceive and interpret the shots in a "montage sequence not *sequentially,* or one at a time, but rather *simultaneously*" (Cook, 1981, p. 172, italics in original). The viewer puts the sequences together into a meaningful emotional whole, as if at a glance, all at once.

The qualitative researcher who uses montage is like a quilt maker or a jazz improviser. The quilter stitches, edits, and puts slices of reality together. This process creates and brings psychological and emotional unity to an interpretive experience. There are many examples of montage in current qualitative research. Using multiple voices and different textual formations, voices, and narrative styles, Marcelo Diversi and Claudio Moreira (2009) weave a complex text about race, identity, nation, class, sexuality, intimacy, and family. As in quilt making and jazz improvisation, many different things are going on at the same time: different voices, different perspectives, points of views, angles of vision. Autoethnographic performance texts use montage simultaneously to create and enact moral meaning. They move from the personal to the political, the local to the historical and the cultural. These are dialogical texts. They presume an active audience. They create spaces for give and take between reader and writer. They do more than turn the other into the object of the social science gaze (in volume 3, see Spry, Chapter 7; Pelias, Chapter 17).

Of course, qualitative research is inherently multimethod in focus (Flick, 2002, pp. 226–227; 2007). However, the use of multiple methods, or triangulation, reflects an attempt to secure an in-depth understanding of the phenomenon in question. Objective reality can never be captured. We know a thing only through its representations. Triangulation is not a tool or a strategy of validation but an alternative to validation (Flick, 2002, p. 227; 2007). The combination of multiple methodological practices, empirical materials, perspectives, and observers in a single study is best understood, then, as a strategy that adds rigor, breadth complexity, richness, and depth to any inquiry (see Flick, 2002, p. 229; 2007, pp. 102–104).

Laura L. Ellingson (Chapter 13, volume 3; also 2009) disputes a narrow conception of triangulation, endorsing instead a postmodern form (2009, p. 190). It asserts that the central image for qualitative inquiry is the crystal—multiple lenses—not the triangle. She sees crystallization as embodying an energizing, unruly discourse, drawing raw energy from artful science and scientific artwork (p. 190). Mixed-genre texts in the postexperimental moment have more than three sides. Like crystals, Eisenstein's montage, the jazz solo, or the pieces in a quilt, the mixed-genre text combines "symmetry and substance with an infinite variety of shapes, substances, transmutations . . . crystals grow, change, alter . . . crystals are prisms that reflect externalities and refract within themselves, creating different colors, patterns, arrays, casting off in different directions" (Richardson, 2000, p. 934).

In the crystallization process, the writer tells the same tale from different points of view. Crystallized projects mix genres and writing formats, offering partial, situated, open-ended conclusions. In *Fires in the Mirror* (1993) Anna Deavere Smith presents a series of performance pieces based on interviews with people involved in a racial conflict in Crown Heights, Brooklyn, on August 19, 1991. Her play has multiple speaking parts, including conversations with gang members, the police, and anonymous young girls and boys. There is no correct telling of this event. Each telling, like light hitting a crystal, gives a different reflection of the racial incident.

Viewed as a crystalline form, as a montage, or as a creative performance around a central theme, triangulation as a form of, or alternative to, validity thus can be extended. Triangulation is the display of multiple, refracted realities simultaneously. Each of the metaphors "works" to create simultaneity rather than the sequential or linear. Readers and audiences are then invited to explore competing visions of the context, to become immersed in and merge with new realities to comprehend.

The methodological bricoleur is adept at performing a large number of diverse tasks, ranging from interviewing to intensive self-reflection and introspection. The theoretical bricoleur reads widely and is knowledgeable about the many interpretive paradigms (feminism, Marxism, cultural studies, constructivism, queer theory) that can be brought to any particular problem. He or she may not, however, feel that paradigms can be mingled or synthesized. If paradigms are overarching philosophical systems denoting particular ontologies, epistemologies, and methodologies, one cannot move easily from one to the other. Paradigms represent belief systems that attach the user to a particular worldview. Perspectives, in contrast, are less well developed systems, and it can be easier to move between them. The researcher-as-bricoleur-theorist works between and within competing and overlapping perspectives and paradigms.

The interpretive bricoleur understands that research is an interactive process shaped by one's personal history, biography, gender, social class, race, and ethnicity and those of the people in the setting. Critical bricoleurs stress the dialectical and hermeneutic nature of interdisciplinary inquiry, knowing that the boundaries between traditional disciplines no longer hold (Kincheloe, 2001, p. 683). The political bricoleur knows that science is power, for all research findings have political implications. There is no value-free science. A civic social science based on a politics of hope is sought (Lincoln, 1999). The gendered, narrative bricoleur also knows that researchers all tell stories about the worlds they have studied. Thus, the narratives or stories scientists tell are accounts couched and framed within specific storytelling traditions, often defined as paradigms (e.g., positivism, postpositivism, constructivism).

The product of the interpretive bricoleur's labor is a complex, quilt-like bricolage, a reflexive collage or montage; a set of fluid, interconnected images and representations. This interpretive structure is like a quilt, a performance text, or a sequence of representations connecting the parts to the whole.

Qualitative Research as a Site of Multiple Interpretive Practices

Qualitative research, as a set of interpretive activities, privileges no single methodological practice over another. As a site of discussion or discourse, qualitative research is difficult to define clearly. It has no theory or paradigm that is distinctly its own. As Part II of this volume reveals, multiple theoretical paradigms claim use of qualitative research methods and strategies, from constructivism to cultural studies, feminism, Marxism, and ethnic models of study. Qualitative research is used in many separate disciplines, as we will discuss below. It does not belong to a single discipline.

Nor does qualitative research have a distinct set of methods or practices that are entirely its own. Qualitative researchers use semiotics, narrative, content, discourse, archival, and phonemic analysis—even statistics, tables, graphs, and numbers. They also draw on and use the approaches, methods, and techniques of ethnomethodology, phenomenology, hermeneutics, feminism, rhizomatics, deconstructionism, ethnographies, interviews, psychoanalysis, cultural studies, survey research, and participant observation, among others.[14] All of these research practices "can provide important insights and knowledge" (Nelson et al., 1992, p. 2). No specific method or practice can be privileged over another.

Many of these methods or research practices are used in other contexts in the human disciplines. Each bears the traces of its own disciplinary history. Thus, there is an extensive history of the uses and meanings of ethnography and ethnology in education (Erickson, Chapter 3, this volume); of participant observation and ethnography in anthropology (Tedlock, Chapter 7, volume 2); sociology (Holstein & Gubrium, Chapter 8, volume 2); communications (Hamera, Chapter 6, volume 2; Spry, Chapter 7, volume 3;); cultural studies (Giardina & Newman, Chapter 10, this volume); textual, hermeneutic, feminist, psychoanalytic, arts-based, semiotic, and narrative analysis in cinema and literary studies (in this volume, Olesen, Chapter 7; Chase, Chapter 2, volume 3; Finley, Chapter 3 vol); and narrative, discourse, and conversational analysis in sociology, medicine, communications, and education (in volume 3, Chase, Chapter 2; Peräkylä & Ruusuvuori, Chapter 9).

The many histories that surround each method or research strategy reveal how multiple uses and meanings are brought to each practice. Textual analyses in literary studies, for example, often treat texts as self-contained systems. On the other hand, a cultural studies or feminist perspective reads a text in terms of its location within a historical moment marked by a particular gender, race, or class ideology. A cultural studies use of ethnography would bring a set of understandings from feminism, postmodernism, and poststructuralism to the project. These understandings would not be shared by mainstream postpositivist sociologists. Similarly, postpositivist and poststructural historians bring different understandings and uses to the methods and findings of historical research. These tensions and contradictions are evident in many of the chapters in this handbook.

These separate and multiple uses and meanings of the methods of qualitative research make it difficult to agree on any essential definition of the field, for it is never just one thing.[15] Still, a definition must be made. We borrow from and paraphrase Nelson et al.'s (1992, p. 4) attempt to define cultural studies:

> Qualitative research is an interdisciplinary, transdiciplinary, and sometimes counterdisciplinary field. It crosscuts the humanities, as well as the social and the physical sciences. Qualitative research is many things at the same time. It is multiparadigmatic in focus. Its practitioners are sensitive to the

value of the multimethod approach. They are committed to the naturalistic perspective and to the interpretive understanding of human experience. At the same time, the field is inherently political and shaped by multiple ethical and political positions.

Qualitative research embraces two tensions at the same time. On the one hand, it is drawn to a broad, interpretive, postexperimental, postmodern, feminist, and critical sensibility. On the other hand, it is drawn to more narrowly defined positivist, postpositivist, humanistic, and naturalistic conceptions of human experience and its analysis. Furthermore, these tensions can be combined in the same project, bringing both postmodern and naturalistic, or both critical and humanistic, perspectives to bear.

This rather awkward statement means that qualitative research is a set of complex interpretive practices. As a constantly shifting historical formation, it embraces tensions and contradictions, including disputes over its methods and the forms its findings and interpretations take. The field sprawls between and crosscuts all of the human disciplines, even including, in some cases, the physical sciences. Its practitioners are variously committed to modern, postmodern, and postexperimental sensibilities and the approaches to social research that these sensibilities imply.

POLITICS AND REEMERGENT SCIENTISM

In the first decade of this new century, the scientifically based research movement (SBR) initiated by the National Research Council (NRC) created a new and hostile political environment for qualitative research (Howe, 2009). Connected to the No Child Left Behind Act of 2001 (NCLB), SBR embodied a reemergent scientism (Maxwell, 2004), a positivist evidence-based epistemology. Researchers are encouraged to employ "rigorous, systematic, and objective methodology to obtain reliable and valid knowledge" (Ryan & Hood, 2004, p. 80). The preferred methodology has well-defined causal models using independent and dependent variables. Causal models are examined in the context of randomized controlled experiments, which allow replication and generalization (Ryan & Hood, 2004, p. 81).

Under this framework, qualitative research becomes suspect. There are no well-defined variables or causal models. Observations and measurements are not based on random assignment to experimental groups. Hard evidence is not generated by these methods. At best, case study, interview, and ethnographic methods offer descriptive materials that can be tested with experimental methods. The epistemologies of critical race, queer, postcolonial, feminist, and postmodern theories are rendered useless, relegated at best to the category of scholarship, not science (Ryan & Hood, 2004, p. 81; St.Pierre & Roulston, 2006, p. 132).

Critics of the evidence movement are united on the following points. The movement endorses a narrow view of science (Lather, 2004; Maxwell, 2004), celebrating a "neoclassical experimentalism that is a throwback to the Campbell-Stanley era and its dogmatic adherence to an exclusive reliance on quantitative methods" (Howe, 2004, p. 42). There is "nostalgia for a simple and ordered universe of science that never was" (Popkewitz, 2004, p. 62). With its emphasis on only one form of scientific rigor, the NRC ignores the need for and value of complex historical, contextual, and political criteria for evaluating inquiry (Bloch, 2004).

Neoclassical experimentalists extol evidence-based "medical research as the model for educational research, particularly the random clinical trial" (Howe, 2004, p. 48). But the random clinical trial—dispensing a pill—is quite unlike "dispensing a curriculum" (Howe, 2004, p. 48), nor can the "effects" of the educational experiment be easily measured, unlike a "10-point reduction in diastolic blood pressure" (Howe, 2004, p. 48).

Qualitative researchers must learn to think outside the box as they critique the NRC and its methodological guidelines (Atkinson, 2004). We must apply our critical imaginations to the meaning of such terms as *randomized design, causal model, policy studies,* and *public science* (Cannella & Lincoln, 2004; Weinstein, 2004). At a deeper level, we must resist conservative attempts to discredit qualitative inquiry by placing it back inside the box of positivism.

CONTESTING MIXED METHODS EXPERIMENTALISM

Kenneth R. Howe (2004) observes that the NRC finds a place for qualitative methods in mixed methods experimental designs. In such designs, qualitative methods may be "employed either singly or in combination with quantitative methods, including the use of randomized experimental designs" (Howe, 2004, p. 49; also Clark & Creswell, 2008; Hesse-Biber & Leavy, 2008). Clark, Creswell, Green, and Shope (2008) define mixed methods research "as a design for collecting, analyzing, and mixing both quantitative and qualitative data in a study in order to understand a research problem" (p. 364).[16] Mixed methods are direct descendants of classical experimentalism and the triangulation movement of the 1970s (Denzin, 1989b). They presume a methodological hierarchy, with quantitative methods at the top, relegating qualitative methods to "a largely auxiliary role in pursuit of the *technocratic* aim of accumulating knowledge of 'what works'" (Howe, 2004, pp. 53–54).

The *incompatibility thesis* disputes the key claim of the mixed methods movement, namely that methods and perspectives can be combined. Recalling the paradigm wars of the 1980s, this thesis argues that "compatibility between quantitative and qualitative methods is impossible due to incompatibility of the paradigms that underlie the methods" (Teddlie & Tashakkori 2003a, pp. 14–15; 2003b). Others disagree with this conclusion, and some contend that the incompatibility thesis has been largely discredited because researchers have demonstrated that it is possible to successfully use a mixed methods approach.

There are several schools of thought on this thesis, including the four identified by Teddlie and Tashakkori (2003a); that is, the complementary, single paradigm, dialectical, and multiple paradigm models. There is by no means consensus on these issues. Morse and Niehaus (2009) warn that ad hoc mixing of methods can be a serious threat to validity. Pragmatists and transformative emancipatory action researchers posit a dialectical model, working back and forth between a variety of tension points, such as etic–emic, value neutrality–value committed. Others (Guba & Lincoln, 2005; Lather, 1993) deconstruct validity as an operative term. Sharlene Nagy Hesse-Biber and Patricia Leavy's (2008) emphasis on emergent methods pushes and blurs the methodological boundaries between quantitative and qualitative methods.[17] Their model seeks to recover subjugated knowledges hidden from everyday view.

The traditional mixed methods movement takes qualitative methods out of their natural home, which is within the critical interpretive framework (Howe, 2004, p. 54; but see Teddlie and Tashakkori, 2003a, p. 15). It divides inquiry into dichotomous categories, exploration versus confirmation. Qualitative work is assigned to the first category, quantitative research to the second (Teddlie & Tashakkori, 2003a, p. 15). Like the classic experimental model, this movement excludes stakeholders from dialogue and active participation in the research process. Doing so weakens its democratic and dialogical dimensions and decreases the likelihood that previously silenced voices will be heard (Howe, 2004, pp. 56–57).

Howe (2004) cautions that it is not just

[the] "methodological fundamentalists" who have bought into [this] approach. A sizeable number of rather influential . . . educational researchers . . . have also signed on. This might be a compromise to the current political climate; it might be a backlash against the perceived excesses of postmodernism; it might be both. It is an ominous development, whatever the explanation. (p. 57; also 2009, p. 438; Lincoln, 2010, p. 7)

The hybrid dialogical model, in contrast, directly confronts these criticisms.

THE PRAGMATIC CRITICISMS OF
ANTI-FOUNDATIONALISM

Clive Seale et al. (2004) contest what they regard as the excesses of an anti-methodological, "anything goes," romantic postmodernism that is associated with our project. They assert that too often the approach we value produces "low quality qualitative research and research results that are quite stereotypical and close to common sense" (p. 2). In contrast they propose a practice-based, pragmatic approach that places research practice at the center. Research involves an engagement "with a variety of things and people: research materials . . . social theories, philosophical debates, values, methods, tests . . . research participants" (p. 2). (Actually this approach is quite close to our own, especially our view of the bricoleur and bricolage).

Their situated methodology rejects the antifoundational claim that there are only partial truths, that the dividing line between fact and fiction has broken down (Seale et al., 2004, p. 3). They believe that this dividing line has not collapsed and that we should not accept stories if they do not accord with the best available facts (p. 6). Oddly, these pragmatic procedural arguments reproduce a variant of the evidence-based model and its criticisms of poststructural performative sensibilities. They can be used to provide political support for the methodological marginalization of many of the positions advanced in this handbook.

This complex political terrain defines the many traditions and strands of qualitative research: the British and its presence in other national contexts; the American pragmatic, naturalistic, and interpretive traditions in sociology, anthropology, communications, and education; the German and French phenomenological, hermeneutic, semiotic, Marxist, structural, and poststructural perspectives; feminist, African American, Latino, and queer studies; and studies of indigenous and aboriginal cultures. The politics of qualitative research create a tension that informs each of the above traditions. This tension itself is constantly being reexamined and interrogated, as qualitative research confronts a changing historical world, new intellectual positions, and its own institutional and academic conditions.

To summarize, qualitative research is many things to many people. Its essence is two-fold: (1) a commitment to some version of the naturalistic, interpretive approach to its subject matter and (2) an ongoing critique of the politics and methods of postpositivism. We turn now to a brief discussion of the major differences between qualitative and quantitative approaches to research. We will then discuss ongoing differences and tensions within qualitative inquiry.

QUALITATIVE VERSUS QUANTITATIVE RESEARCH

The word *qualitative* implies an emphasis on the qualities of entities and on processes and meanings that are not experimentally examined or measured (if measured at all) in terms of quantity, amount, intensity, or frequency. Qualitative researchers stress the socially constructed nature of reality, the intimate relationship between the researcher and what is studied, and the situational constraints that shape inquiry. Such researchers emphasize the value-laden nature of inquiry. They seek answers to questions that stress *how* social experience is created and given meaning. In contrast, quantitative studies emphasize the measurement and analysis of causal relationships between variables, not processes. Proponents claim that their work is done from within a value-free framework.

RESEARCH STYLES: DOING THE SAME THINGS DIFFERENTLY?

Of course, both qualitative and quantitative researchers "think they know something about society worth telling to others, and they use a variety of forms, media, and means to communicate their ideas and findings" (Becker, 1986, p. 122). Qualitative research differs from quantitative research in five significant ways (Becker, 1996). These points of difference turn on different ways of addressing the same set of issues. They return always to the politics of research and who has the power to legislate correct solutions to these problems.

Using Positivism and Postpositivism: First, both perspectives are shaped by the positivist and postpositivist traditions in the physical and social sciences (see discussion below). These two positivist science traditions hold to naïve and critical realist positions concerning reality and its perception. Proponents of the positivist version contend that there is a reality out there to be studied, captured, and understood, whereas the postpositivists argue that reality can never be fully apprehended, only approximated (Guba, 1990a, p. 22). Postpositivism relies on multiple methods as a way of capturing as much of reality as possible. At the same time, emphasis is placed on the discovery and verification of theories. Traditional evaluation criteria like internal and external validity are stressed, as are the use of qualitative procedures that lend themselves to structured (sometimes statistical) analysis. Computer-assisted methods of analysis, which permit frequency counts, tabulations, and low-level statistical analyses, may also be employed.

The positivist and postpositivist traditions linger like long shadows over the qualitative research project. Historically, qualitative research was defined within the positivist paradigm, where qualitative researchers attempted to do good positivist research with less rigorous methods and procedures. Some mid-century qualitative researchers (Becker, Geer, Hughes, & Strauss, 1961) reported findings from participant observations in terms of quasi-statistics. As recently as 1999 (Strauss & Corbin, 1999), two leaders of the grounded theory approach to qualitative research attempted to modify the usual canons of good (positivistic) science to fit their own postpositivist conception of rigorous research (but see Charmaz, Chapter 9, volume 2; also see Glaser, 1992). Some applied researchers, while claiming to be atheoretical, often fit within the positivist or postpositivist framework by default.

Uwe Flick (2002, pp. 2–3) usefully summarizes the differences between these two approaches to inquiry. He observes that the quantitative approach has been used for purposes of isolating "causes and effects . . . operationalizing theoretical relations . . . [and] measuring and . . . quantifying phenomena . . . allowing the generalization of findings" (p. 3). But today, doubt is cast on such projects.

> Rapid social change and the resulting diversification of life worlds are increasingly confronting social researchers with new social contexts and perspectives . . . traditional deductive methodologies . . . are failing . . . thus research is increasingly forced to make use of inductive strategies instead of starting from theories and testing them . . . knowledge and practice are studied as local knowledge and practice. (Flick, 2002, p. 2)

George and Louise Spindler (1992) summarize their qualitative approach to quantitative materials.

> Instrumentation and quantification are simply procedures employed to extend and reinforce certain kinds of data, interpretations and test hypotheses across samples. Both must be kept in their place. One must avoid their premature or overly extensive use as a security mechanism. (p. 69)

While many qualitative researchers in the postpositivist tradition will use statistical measures, methods, and documents as a way of locating a group of subjects within a larger population, they will seldom report their findings in terms of the kinds of complex statistical measures or methods that quantitative researchers are drawn to (i.e., path, regression, log-linear analyses).

Accepting Postmodern Sensibilities: The use of quantitative, positivist methods and assumptions has been rejected by a new generation of qualitative researchers who are attached to poststructural or postmodern sensibilities. These researchers argue that positivist methods are but one way of telling a story about society or the social world. They may be no better or no worse than any other method; they just tell a different kind of story.

This tolerant view is not shared by everyone. Many members of the critical theory, constructivist, poststructural, and postmodern schools of thought reject positivist and postpositivist criteria when evaluating their own work. They see these criteria as being irrelevant to their work and contend that positivist and postpositivist research reproduces only a certain kind of science, a science that silences too many voices. These researchers seek alternative methods for evaluating their work, including verisimilitude, emotionality, personal responsibility, an ethic of caring, political praxis, multivoiced texts, dialogues with subjects, and so on. In response, positivist and postpositivists argue that what they do is good science, free of individual bias and subjectivity. As noted above, they see postmodernism and poststructuralism as attacks on reason and truth.

Capturing the Individual's Point of View: Both qualitative and quantitative researchers are concerned with the individual's point of view. However, qualitative investigators think they can get closer to the actor's perspective by detailed interviewing and observation. They argue that quantitative researchers are seldom able to capture the subject's perspective because they have to rely on more remote, inferential empirical methods and materials. Many quantitative researchers regard empirical materials produced by interpretive methods as unreliable, impressionistic, and not objective.

Examining the Constraints of Everyday Life: Qualitative researchers are more likely to confront and come up against the constraints of the everyday social world. They see this world in action and embed their findings in it. Quantitative researchers abstract from this world and seldom study it directly. They seek a nomothetic or etic science based on probabilities derived from the study of large numbers of randomly selected cases. These kinds of statements stand above and outside the constraints of everyday life. Qualitative researchers, on the other hand, are committed to an emic, ideographic, case-based position, which directs their attention to the specifics of particular cases.

Securing Rich Descriptions: Qualitative researchers believe that rich descriptions of the social world are valuable, whereas quantitative researchers, with their etic, nomothetic commitments, are less concerned with such detail. They are deliberately unconcerned with such descriptions because such detail interrupts the process of developing generalizations.

These five points of difference described above (using positivism and post-positivism, accepting postmodern sensibilities, capturing the individual's point of view, examining the constraints of everyday life, securing thick descriptions) reflect commitments to different styles of research, different epistemologies, and different forms of representation. Each work tradition is governed by a different set of genres, and each has its own classics and its own preferred forms of representation, interpretation, trustworthiness, and textual evaluation (see Becker, 1986, pp. 134–135). Qualitative researchers use ethnographic prose, historical narratives, first-person accounts, still photographs, life history, fictionalized "facts," and biographical and autobiographical materials, among others. Quantitative researchers use mathematical models, statistical tables, and graphs and usually write in an impersonal, third-person prose.

Tensions Within Qualitative Research

It is erroneous to presume that qualitative researchers share the same assumptions about these five points of difference. As the discussion below will reveal, positivist, postpositivist, and poststructural differences define and shape the discourses of qualitative research. Realists and postpositivists within the interpretive, qualitative research tradition criticize poststructuralists for taking the textual, narrative turn. These critics contend that such work is navel-gazing. It produces the conditions "for a dialogue of the deaf between itself and the community" (Silverman, 1997, p. 240). Those who attempt to capture the point of view of the interacting subject in the world are accused of naïve humanism, of reproducing a Romantic impulse that elevates the experiential to the level of the authentic (Silverman, 1997, p. 248).

Still others argue that lived experience is ignored by those who take the textual, performance turn. David Snow and Calvin Morrill (1995) argue that

> This performance turn, like the preoccupation with discourse and storytelling, will take us further from the field of social action and the real dramas of everyday life and thus signal the death knell of ethnography as an empirically grounded enterprise. (p. 361)

Of course, we disagree.

According to Martyn Hammersley (2008, p. 1), qualitative research is currently facing a crisis symbolized by an ill-conceived postmodernist image of qualitative research, which is dismissive of traditional forms of inquiry. He feels that "unless this dynamic can be interrupted the future of qualitative research is endangered" (p. 11).

Paul Atkinson and Sara Delamont (2006), two qualitative scholars in the traditional, classic Chicago School tradition,[18] offer a corrective. They remain committed to qualitative (and quantitative) research "*provided that they are conducted rigorously and contribute to robustly useful knowledge*" (p. 749, italics in original). Of course, these scholars are committed to social policy initiatives at some level. But, for them, the postmodern image of qualitative inquiry threatens and undermines the value of traditional qualitative inquiry. Atkinson and Delamont exhort qualitative researchers to "think hard about whether their investigations are the best social science they could be" (p. 749). Patricia and Peter Adler (2008) implore the radical postmodernists to "give up the project for the good of the discipline and for the good of society" (p. 23).

Hammersley (2008, pp. 134–136, 144), extends the traditional critique, finding little value in the work of ethnographic postmodernists and literary ethnographers.[19] This new tradition, he asserts, legitimates speculative theorizing, celebrates obscurity, and abandons the primary task of inquiry, which is to produce truthful knowledge about the world (p. 144). Poststructural inquirers get it from all sides. The criticisms, Carolyn Ellis (2009, p. 231) observes, fall into three overlapping categories. Our work (1) is too aesthetic and not sufficiently realistic; it does not provide hard data; (2) is too realistic and not mindful of poststructural criticisms concerning the "real" self and its place in the text; and (3) is not sufficiently aesthetic, or literary; that is, we are second-rate writers and poets (p. 232).

THE POLITICS OF EVIDENCE

The critics' model of science is anchored in the belief that there is an empirical world that is obdurate and talks back to investigators. This is an empirical science based on evidence that corroborates interpretations. This is a science that returns to and is lodged in the real, a science that stands outside nearly all of the turns listed above; this is Chicago School neo-postpositivism.

Contrast this certain science to the position of those who are preoccupied with the politics of evidence. Jan Morse (2006), for example, says: "Evidence is not just something that is out there. Evidence has to be produced, constructed, represented. Furthermore, the politics of evidence cannot be separated from the ethics of evidence" (pp. 415–416). Under the Jan Morse model, representations of empirical reality become problematic. Objective representation of reality is impossible. Each representation calls into place a different set of ethical questions regarding evidence, including how it is obtained and what it means. But surely a middle ground can be found. If there is a return to the spirit of the paradigm dialogues of the 1980s, then multiple representations of a situation should be encouraged, perhaps placed alongside one another.

Indeed, the interpretive camp is not antiscience, per se. We do something different. We believe in multiple forms of science: soft, hard, strong, feminist, interpretive, critical, realist, postrealist, and post-humanist. In a sense, the traditional and postmodern projects are incommensurate. We interpret, we perform, we interrupt, we challenge, and we believe nothing is ever certain. We want performance texts that quote history back to itself, texts that focus on epiphanies; on the intersection of biography, history, culture, and politics; on turning point moments in people's lives. The critics are correct on this point. We have a political orientation that is radical, democratic, and interventionist. Many postpositivists share these politics.

CRITICAL REALISM

For some, there is a third stream between naïve positivism and poststructuralism. Critical realism is an antipositivist movement in the social sciences closely associated with the works of Roy Bhaskar and Rom Harré (Danermark, Ekstrom, Jakobsen, & Karlsson, 2002). Critical realists use the word *critical* in a particular way. This is not Frankfurt School critical theory, although there are traces of social criticism here and there (Danermark et al., 2002, p. 201). *Critical*, instead, refers to a transcendental realism that rejects methodological individualism and universal claims to truth. Critical realists oppose logical positivist, relativist, and antifoundational epistemologies. Critical realists agree with the positivists that there is a world of events out there that is observable and independent of human consciousness. Knowledge about this world is socially constructed. Society is made up of feeling, thinking human beings, and their interpretations of the world must be studied (Danermark et al., 2002, p. 200). A correspondence theory of truth is rejected. Critical realists believe that reality is arranged in levels. Scientific work must go beyond statements of regularity to the analysis of the mechanisms, processes, and structures that account for the patterns that are observed.

Still, as postempiricist, antifoundational, critical theorists, we reject much of what is advocated here. Throughout the last century, social science and philosophy were continually tangled up with one another. Various "isms" and philosophical movements criss-crossed sociological and educational discourse, from positivism to postpositivism to analytic and linguistic philosophy, to hermeneutics, structuralism, and poststructuralism; to Marxism, feminism, and current post-post-versions of all of the above. Some have said that the logical positivists steered the social sciences on a rigorous course of self-destruction.

We do not think critical realism will keep the social science ship afloat. The social sciences are normative disciplines, always already embedded in issues of value, ideology, power, desire, sexism, racism, domination, repression, and control. We want a social science committed up front to issues of social justice, equity, nonviolence, peace, and universal human rights. We do not want a social science that says it can address these issues if it wants to do so. For us, this is no longer an option.

Qualitative Research as Process

Three interconnected, generic activities define the qualitative research process. They go by a variety of different labels, including theory, method, and analysis; or ontology, epistemology, and methodology. Behind these terms stands the personal biography of the researcher, who speaks from a particular class, gendered, racial, cultural, and ethnic community perspective. The gendered, multiculturally situated researcher approaches the world with a set of ideas, a framework (theory, ontology) that specifies a set of questions (epistemology), which are then examined (methodology, analysis) in specific ways. That is, empirical materials bearing on the question are collected and then analyzed and written about. Every researcher speaks from within a distinct interpretive community, which configures, in its special way, the multicultural, gendered components of the research act.

In this volume, we treat these generic activities under five headings or phases: the researcher and the researched as multicultural subjects, major paradigms and interpretive perspectives, research strategies, methods of collecting and analyzing empirical materials, and the art of interpretation. Behind and within each of these phases stands the biographically situated researcher. This individual enters the research process from inside an interpretive community. This community has its own historical research traditions, which constitute a distinct point of view. This perspective leads the researcher to adopt particular views of the "other" who is studied. At the same time, the politics and the ethics of research must also be considered, for these concerns permeate every phase of the research process.

The Other as Research Subject

From its turn-of-the-century birth in modern, interpretive form, qualitative research has been haunted by a double-faced ghost. On the one hand, qualitative researchers have assumed that qualified, competent observers could, with objectivity, clarity, and precision, report on their own observations of the social world, including the experiences of others. Second, researchers have held to the belief in a real subject or real individual who is present in the world and able, in some form, to report on his or her experiences. So armed, researchers could blend their own observations with the self-reports provided by subjects through interviews, life story, personal experience, and case study documents.

These two beliefs have led qualitative researchers across disciplines to seek a method that would allow them to record accurately their own observations while also uncovering the meanings their subjects brought to their life experiences. This method would rely on the subjective verbal and written expressions of meaning given by the individuals, which are studied as windows into the inner life of the person. Since Wilhelm Dilthey (1900/1976), this search for a method has led to a perennial focus in the human disciplines on qualitative, interpretive methods.

Recently, as noted above, this position and its beliefs have come under assault. Poststructuralists and postmodernists have contributed to the understanding that there is no clear window into the inner life of an individual. Any gaze is always filtered through the lenses of language, gender, social class, race, and ethnicity. There are no objective observations, only observations socially situated in the worlds of—and between—the observer and the observed. Subjects, or individuals, are seldom able to give full explanations of their actions or intentions; all they can offer are accounts or stories about what they did and why. No single method can grasp the subtle variations in ongoing human experience. Consequently, qualitative researchers deploy a wide-range of interconnected interpretive methods, always seeking better ways to make more understandable the worlds of experience that have been studied.

Table 1.1 depicts the relationships we see among the five phases that define the research process (the researcher; major paradigms; research strategies; methods of collecting and analyzing empirical materials; and the art, practices, and politics of interpretation). Behind all but one of these phases stands the biographically situated researcher. These five levels of activity, or practice, work their way through the biography of the researcher. We take them up in brief order here, for each phase is more fully discussed in the transition sections between the various parts of this volume.

Table 1.1 The Research Process

Phase 1: The Researcher as a Multicultural Subject	Historical method
	Action and applied research
History and research traditions	Clinical research
Conceptions of self and the other	
The ethics and politics of research	*Phase 4: Methods of Collection and Analysis*
Phase 2: Theoretical Paradigms and Perspectives	Interviewing
	Observing
Positivism, postpositivism	Artifacts, documents, and records
Interpretivism, constructivism, hermeneutics	Visual methods
	Autoethnography
Feminism(s)	Data management methods
Racialized discourses	Computer-assisted analysis
Critical theory and Marxist models	Textual analysis
Cultural studies models	Focus groups
Queer theory	Applied ethnography
Post-colonialism	
	Phase 5: The Art, Practices, and Politics of Interpretation and Evaluation
Phase 3: Research Strategies	
Design	Criteria for judging adequacy
Case study	Practices and politics of interpretation
Ethnography, participant observation, performance ethnography	Writing as interpretation
	Policy analysis
Phenomenology, ethnomethodology	Evaluation traditions
Grounded theory	Applied research
Life history, ***testimonio***	

PHASE 1: THE RESEARCHER

Our remarks above indicate the depth and complexity of the traditional and applied qualitative research perspectives into which a socially situated researcher enters. These traditions locate the researcher in history, simultaneously guiding and constraining work that will be done in any specific study. This field has been constantly characterized by diversity and conflict, and these are its most enduring traditions (see Levin & Greenwood, Chapter 2, this volume). As a carrier of this complex and contradictory history, the researcher must also confront the ethics and politics of research (Christians, Chapter 4, this volume). It is no longer possible for the human disciplines to research the native, the indigenous other, in a spirit of value-free inquiry. Today researchers struggle to develop situational and transsituational ethics that apply to all forms of the research act and its human-to-human relationships. We no longer have the option of deferring the decolonization project.

PHASE 2: INTERPRETIVE PARADIGMS

All qualitative researchers are philosophers in that "universal sense in which all human beings . . . are guided by highly abstract principles" (Bateson, 1972, p. 320). These principles combine beliefs about *ontology* (What kind of being is the human being? What is the nature of reality?), *epistemology* (What is the relationship between the inquirer and the known?), and *methodology* (How do we know the world or gain knowledge of it?) (see Guba, 1990a, p. 18; Lincoln & Guba, 1985, pp. 14–15; and Lincoln, Lynham, & Guba in Chapter 6 of this volume). These beliefs shape how the qualitative researcher sees the world and acts in it. The researcher is "bound within a net of epistemological and ontological premises which—regardless of ultimate truth or falsity—become partially self-validating" (Bateson, 1972, p. 314).

The net that contains the researcher's epistemological, ontological, and methodological premises may be termed a *paradigm* (Guba, 1990a, p. 17) or interpretive framework, a "basic set of beliefs that guides action" (Guba, 1990a, p. 17). All research is interpretive: guided by a set of beliefs and feelings about the world and how it should be understood and studied. Some beliefs may be taken for granted, invisible, or only assumed, whereas others are highly problematic and controversial. Each interpretive paradigm makes particular demands on the researcher, including the questions that are asked and the interpretations that are brought to them.

At the most general level, four major interpretive paradigms structure qualitative research: positivist and postpositivist, constructivist-interpretive, critical (Marxist, emancipatory), and feminist-poststructural. These four abstract paradigms become more complicated at the level of concrete specific interpretive communities. At this level, it is possible to identify not only the constructivist but also multiple versions of feminism (Afrocentric and poststructural),[20] as well as specific ethnic, feminist, endarkened, social justice, Marxist, cultural studies, disability, and non-Western-Asian paradigms. These perspectives or paradigms are examined in Part II of this volume.

The paradigms examined in Part II work against or alongside (and some within) the positivist and postpositivist models. They all work within relativist ontologies (multiple constructed realities), interpretive epistemologies (the knower and known interact and shape one another), and interpretive, naturalistic methods.

Table 1.2 presents these paradigms and their assumptions, including their criteria for evaluating research, and the typical form that an interpretive or theoretical statement assumes in the paradigm.[21]

Each paradigm is explored in considerable detail in chapters 6 through 10. The positivist and postpositivist paradigms were discussed above. They work from within a realist and critical realist ontology and objective epistemologies, and they rely on experimental, quasi-experimental, survey, and rigorously defined qualitative methodologies.

The *constructivist paradigm* assumes a relativist ontology (there are multiple realities), a subjectivist epistemology (knower and respondent co-create understandings), and a naturalistic (in the natural world) set of methodological procedures. Findings are usually presented in terms of the criteria of grounded theory or pattern theories (in this volume, see Lincoln, Lynham, & Guba, Chapter 6; Creswell, Chapter 3, volume 2; Teddlie & Tashakkori, Chapter 4, volume 2; Charmaz, Chapter 9, volume 2; Morse, Chapter 12, volume 2; Altheide & Johnson, Chapter 12, volume 3; and St.Pierre, Chapter 14, volume 3). Terms like credibility, transferability, dependability, and confirmability replace the usual positivist criteria of internal and external validity, reliability, and objectivity.

Feminist, ethnic, Marxist, cultural studies, queer theory, Asian, and disability models privilege a materialist-realist ontology; that is, the real world makes a material difference in terms of race, class, and gender. Subjectivist epistemologies and naturalistic methodologies (usually ethnographies) are also employed. Empirical materials and theoretical arguments are evaluated in terms of their emancipatory implications. Criteria from gender and racial communities (e.g., African American) may be applied (emotionality and feeling, caring, personal accountability, dialogue).

Poststructural feminist theories emphasize problems with the social text, its logic, and its inability to ever represent the world of lived experience fully. Positivist and postpositivist criteria of evaluation are replaced by other terms, including the reflexive, multivoiced text, which is grounded in the experiences of oppressed people.

The cultural studies and queer theory paradigms are multifocused, with many different strands drawing from Marxism, feminism, and the postmodern sensibility (in this volume, Giardina & Newman, Chapter 10; Plummer, Chapter 11; St.Pierre, Chapter 14, volume 3). There is a tension between a humanistic cultural studies, which

Table 1.2 Interpretive Paradigms

Paradigm/ Theory	Criteria	Form of Theory	Type of Narration
Positivist/ postpositivist	Internal, external validity	Logical-deductive, grounded	Scientific report
Constructivist	Trustworthiness, credibility, transferability, confirmability	Substantive-formal, standpoint	Interpretive case studies, ethnographic fiction
Feminist	Afrocentric, lived experience, dialogue, caring, accountability, race, class, gender, reflexivity, praxis, emotion, concrete grounding, embodied	Critical, standpoint	Essays, stories, experimental writing
Ethnic	Afrocentric, lived experience, dialogue, caring, accountability, race, class, gender	Standpoint, critical, historical	Essays, fables, dramas
Marxist	Emancipatory theory, falsifiability, dialogical, race, class, gender	Critical, historical, economic	Historical, economic, sociocultural analyses
Cultural studies	Cultural practices, praxis, social texts, subjectivities	Social criticism	Cultural theory-as-criticism
Queer theory	Reflexivity, deconstruction	Social criticism, historical analysis	Theory-as-criticism, autobiography

stresses lived experiences (meaning), and a more structural cultural studies project, which stresses the structural and material determinants and effects (race, class, gender) of experience. Of course, there are two sides to every coin; both sides are needed and are indeed critical. The cultural studies and queer theory paradigms use methods strategically, that is, as resources for understanding and for producing resistances to local structures of domination. Such scholars may do close textual readings and discourse analysis of cultural texts (in this volume, Olesen, Chapter 7; Chase, Chapter 2, volume 3), as well as local, online, reflexive, and critical ethnographies; open-ended interviewing; and participant observation. The focus is on how race, class, and gender are produced and enacted in historically specific situations.

Paradigm and personal history in hand, focused on a concrete empirical problem to examine, the researcher now moves to the next stage of the research process, namely working with a specific strategy of inquiry.

PHASE 3: STRATEGIES OF INQUIRY AND INTERPRETIVE PARADIGMS

Table 1.1 presents some of the major strategies of inquiry a researcher may use. Phase 3 begins with research design, which broadly conceived involves a clear focus on the research question, the purposes of the study, "what information most appropriately will answer specific research questions, and which strategies are most effective for obtaining it" (LeCompte & Preissle with Tesch, 1993, p. 30; see also Cheek, Chapter 2, volume 2). A research design describes a flexible set of guidelines that connect theoretical paradigms, first, to strategies of inquiry and, second, to methods for collecting empirical material. A research design situates researchers in the empirical world and connects them to specific sites, people, groups, institutions, and bodies of relevant interpretive material, including documents and archives. A research design also specifies how the investigator will address the two critical issues of representation and legitimation.

A strategy of inquiry refers to a bundle of skills, assumptions, and practices that researchers employ as they move from their paradigm to the empirical world. Strategies of inquiry put paradigms of interpretation into motion. At the same time, strategies of inquiry also connect the researcher to specific methods of collecting and analyzing empirical materials. For example, the case study relies on interviewing, observing, and document analysis. Research strategies implement and anchor paradigms in specific empirical sites or in specific methodological practices, for example, making a case an object of study. These strategies include the case study, phenomenological and ethnomethodological techniques, the use of grounded theory, and biographical, autoethnographic, historical, action, and clinical methods. Each of these strategies is connected to a complex literature; each has a separate history, exemplary works, and preferred ways for putting the strategy into motion.

PHASE 4: METHODS OF COLLECTING AND ANALYZING EMPIRICAL MATERIALS

The researcher has several methods for collecting empirical materials.[22] These methods are taken up in Part IV. They range from the interview to direct observation, the use of visual materials or personal experience. The researcher may also use a variety of different methods of reading and analyzing interviews or cultural texts, including content, narrative, and semiotic strategies. Faced with large amounts of qualitative materials, the investigator seeks ways of managing and interpreting these documents, and here data management methods and computer-assisted models of analysis may be of use. In volume 3, David L. Altheide and John M. Johnson (Chapter 12), Laura L. Ellingson (Chapter 13), and Judith Davidson and Silvana di Gregorio (Chapter 15) take up these techniques.

PHASE 5: THE ART AND POLITICS OF INTERPRETATION AND EVALUATION

Qualitative research is endlessly creative and interpretive. The researcher does not just leave the field with mountains of empirical materials and easily write up his or her findings. Qualitative interpretations are constructed. The researcher first creates a field text consisting of fieldnotes and documents from the field, what Roger Sanjek (1992, p. 386) calls "indexing" and David Plath (1990, p. 374) "filework." The writer-as-interpreter moves from this text to a research text; notes and interpretations based on the field text. This text is then re-created as a working interpretive document that contains the writer's initial attempts to make sense out of what has been learned. Finally, the writer produces the public text that comes to the reader. This final tale from the field may assume several forms: confessional, realist, impressionistic, critical, formal, literary, analytic, grounded theory, and so on (see Van Maanen, 1988).

The interpretive practice of making sense of one's findings is both artistic and political. Multiple criteria for evaluating qualitative research now exist, and those we emphasize stress the situated, relational, and textual structures of the ethnographic experience. There is no single interpretive truth. As argued earlier, there are multiple interpretive communities, each having its own criteria for evaluating an interpretation.

Program evaluation is a major site of qualitative research, and qualitative researchers can influence social policy in important ways. Applied, qualitative research in the social sciences has a rich history (discussed in this volume by Levin

& Greenwood, Chapter 2; Cheek, Chapter 2, volume 2; Brydon-Miller, Kral, Maguire, Noffke, & Sabhlok, Chapter 11, volume 2; Morse, Chapter 12, volume 2; Torrance, Chapter 11, volume 3; Abma & Widdershoven, Chapter 18, volume 3). This is the critical site where theory, method, praxis, action, and policy all come together. Qualitative researchers can isolate target populations, show the immediate effects of certain programs on such groups, and isolate the constraints that operate against policy changes in such settings. Action and clinically oriented qualitative researchers can also create spaces for those who are studied (the other) to speak. The evaluator becomes the conduit for making such voices heard.

BRIDGING THE HISTORICAL MOMENTS: WHAT COMES NEXT?

St.Pierre (2004) argues that we are already in the post "post" period—post-poststructuralism, post-postmodernism, post-experimental. What this means for interpretive, ethnographic practices is still not clear. But it is certain that things will never again be the same. We are in a new age where messy, uncertain multivoiced texts, cultural criticism, and new experimental works will become more common, as will more reflexive forms of fieldwork, analysis, and intertextual representation. In a complex space like this, pedagogy becomes critical—that is, How do we teach qualitative methods? Judith Preissle (Chapter 14) and Margaret Eisenhart and S. Jurow (Chapter 15) offer insights on the future. It is true, as the poet said, the center no longer holds. We can reflect on what should be in this new center.

Thus, we come full circle. And returning to our bridge metaphor, the chapters that follow take the researcher back and forth through every phase of the research act. Like a good bridge, the chapters provide for two-way traffic, coming and going between moments, formations, and interpretive communities. Each chapter examines the relevant histories, controversies, and current practices that are associated with each paradigm, strategy, and method. Each chapter also offers projections for the future, where a specific paradigm, strategy, or method will be 10 years from now, deep into the formative years of the next century.

In reading this volume, it is important to remember that the field of qualitative research is defined by a series of tensions, contradictions, and hesitations. This tension works back and forth between and among (1) the broad, doubting, postmodern sensibility; (2) the more certain, more traditional positivist, post-positivist, and naturalistic conceptions of this project; and (3) an increasingly conservative, neoliberal global environment. All of the chapters that follow are caught in and articulate these tensions.

Notes

1. The following paragraphs draw from Denzin (2010, pp. 19–25).

2. They contend that our second moment, the Golden Age (1950–1970), was marked by the debunking of positivism, the emergence of postpositivism, and the development of designs that used mixed quantitative and qualitative methods. Full-scale conflict developed throughout the 1970–1990 period, the time of the first "paradigm war."

3. Conflict broke out between the many different empowerment pedagogies: feminist, anti-racist, radical, Freirean, liberation theology, postmodernists, poststructuralists, cultural studies, and so on (see Guba & Lincoln, 2005; also, Erickson, Chapter 3, this volume).

4. Recall bell hooks's reading of the famous cover photo on *Writing Culture* (Clifford & Marcus, 1986), which consists of a picture of Stephen Tyler doing fieldwork in India. Tyler is seated some distance from three dark-skinned people. A child is poking its head out of a basket. A woman is hidden in the shadows of the hut. A male, a checkered white and black shawl across his shoulder, elbow propped on his knee, hand resting along the side of his face, is staring at Tyler. Tyler is writing in a field journal. A piece of white cloth is attached to his glasses, perhaps shielding him from the sun. This patch of whiteness marks Tyler as the white male writer studying these passive brown and black people. Indeed, the brown male's gaze signals some desire or some attachment to Tyler. In contrast, the female's gaze is completely hidden by the shadows and by the words in the book's title, which cross her face (hooks, 1990, p. 127).

5. Qualitative research has separate and distinguished histories in education, social work, communications, psychology, history, organizational studies, medical science, anthropology, and sociology.

6. Definitions: *positivism:* Objective accounts of the real world can be given; *postpositivism:* Only partially objective accounts of the world can be produced, for all methods are flawed; *foundationalism:* We can have an ultimate grounding for our knowledge claims about the world, and this involves the use of empiricist and positivist epistemologies (Schwandt, 1997a, p. 103); *nonfoundationalism:* We can make statements about the world without "recourse to ultimate proof or foundations for that knowing" (Schwandt, 1997a, p. 102); *quasifoundationalism:* Certain knowledge claims about the world based on neorealist criteria can be made, including the correspondence concept of truth. There is an independent reality that can be mapped.

7. Jameson (1991, pp. 3–4) reminds us that any periodization hypothesis is always suspect, even one that rejects linear, stage-like models. It is never clear to what reality a stage refers. What divides one stage from another is always debatable. Our seven moments are meant to mark discernible shifts in style, genre, epistemology, ethics, politics, and aesthetics.

8. See Denzin and Lincoln (2005, pp. 13–21) for an extended discussion of each of these phases. This model has been termed a progress narrative by Alasuutari (2004, pp. 599–600) and Seale, Gobo, Gubrium, and Silverman (2004, p. 2). The critics assert

that we believe that the most recent moment is the most up-to-date, the avant-garde, the cutting edge (Alasuutari, 2004, p. 601). Naturally, we dispute this reading. Teddlie and Tashakkori (2003a, pp. 5–8) have modified our historical periods to fit their historical analysis of the major moments in the emergence of mixed methods in the last century.

9. *Definitions: structuralism:* Any system is made up of a set of oppositional categories embedded in language; *semiotics:* the science of signs or sign systems—a structuralist project; *poststructuralism:* Language is an unstable system of referents, making it impossible to ever completely capture the meaning or an action, text, or intention; *postmodernism:* a contemporary sensibility, developing since World War II, which privileges no single authority, method, or paradigm; *hermeneutics:* An approach to the analysis of texts that stresses how prior understandings and prejudices shape the interpretive process; *phenomenology:* A complex system of ideas associated with the works of Edmund Husserl, Martin Heidegger, Jean-Paul Sartre, Maurice Merleau-Ponty, and Alfred Schutz; *cultural studies:* a complex, interdisciplinary field that merges with critical theory, feminism, and poststructuralism.

10. Of course, all settings are natural, that is, places where everyday experience takes place. Qualitative researchers study people doing things together in the places where these things are done (Becker, 1986). There is no field site or natural place where one goes to do this kind of work (see also Gupta & Ferguson, 1997, p. 8). The site is constituted through our interpretive practices. Historically, analysts have distinguished between experimental (laboratory) and field (natural) research settings; hence the argument that qualitative research is naturalistic. Activity theory erases this distinction (Keller & Keller, 1996, p. 20; Vygotsky, 1978).

11. "The meaning of *bricoleur* in French popular speech is 'someone who works with his (or her) hands and uses devious means compared to those of the craftsman . . . the *bricoleur* is practical and gets the job done" (Weinstein & Weinstein, 1991, p. 161). These authors provide a history of this term, connecting it to the works of the German sociologist and social theorist Georg Simmel, and by implication to Charles Baudelaire. Martyn Hammersley (2000) disputes our use of this term. Following Claude Lévi-Strauss, he reads the bricoleur as a myth maker. He suggests it be replaced with the notion of the boat builder. Hammersley also quarrels with our "moments" model of qualitative research, contending it implies some sense of progress.

12. Brian De Palma reproduces this baby carriage scene in his 1987 film, *The Untouchables*.

13. In the harbor, the muzzles of the Potemkin's two huge guns swing slowly into the camera. Words on screen inform us: "The brutal military power answered by guns of the battleship." A final famous three-shot montage sequence shows, first, a sculptured sleeping lion, then the lion rising from his sleep, and finally the lion roaring, symbolizing the rage of the Russian people (Cook, 1981, p. 167). In this sequence, Eisenstein uses montage to expand time, creating a psychological duration for this horrible event. By drawing out this sequence, by showing the baby in the carriage, the soldiers firing on the citizens, the blood on the mother's glove, the descending carriage on the steps, he suggests a level of destruction of great magnitude.

14. Here it is relevant to make a distinction between techniques that are used across disciplines and methods that are used within disciplines. Ethnomethodologists, for example, employ their approach as a method, whereas others selectively borrow that method-as-technique for their own applications. Harry Wolcott (in conversation) suggests this distinction. It is also relevant to make a distinction between topic, method, and resource. Methods can be studied as topics of inquiry; that is how a case study gets done. In this ironic, ethnomethodological sense, method is both a resource and a topic of inquiry.

15. Indeed any attempt to give an essential definition of qualitative research requires a qualitative analysis of the circumstances that produce such a definition.

16. They identify four major mixed methods designs: triangulation, embedded, explanatory, and exploratory (Clark et al., 2008, p. 371).

17. Their emergent model focuses on methods that break out of traditional frameworks and exploit new technologies and innovations; this is a process model that works between politics, epistemology, theory, and methodology.

18. There are several generations of the Chicago School, from Robert Park and Ernest Burgess, Herbert Blumer, and Everett Hughes (1920–1950) period, to second (Becker, Strauss, Goffman), to third (Hammersley, Atkinson, Delamont, Snow, Anderson, Fine, Adler and Adler, Prus, Maines, Flaherty, Sanders et al).

19. His blanket term for auto, performance, poststructural ethnography.

20. Olesen (Chapter 7, this volume) identifies three strands of feminist research: mainstream empirical; standpoint and cultural studies; and poststructural, postmodern; placing Afrocentric and other models of color under the cultural studies and postmodern categories.

21. These, of course, are our interpretations of these paradigms and interpretive styles.

22. *Empirical materials* is the preferred term for what are traditionally described as data.

References

Adler, P. A., & Adler, P. (2008). Of rhetoric and representation: The four faces of ethnography. *Sociological Quarterly, 49*(4), 1–30.

Alasuutari, P. (2004). The globalization of qualitative research. In C. Seale, G. Gobo, J. F. Gubrium, & D. Silverman (Eds.), *Qualitative research practice* (pp. 595–608). London: Sage.

Atkinson, E. (2004). Thinking outside the box: An exercise in heresy. *Qualitative Inquiry, 10*(1), 111–129.

Atkinson, P., & Delamont, S. (2006). In the roiling smoke: Qualitative inquiry and contested fields. *International Journal of Qualitative Studies in Education, 19*(6), 747–755.

Bateson, G. (1972). *Steps to an ecology of mind.* New York: Ballantine.

Becker, H. S. (1986). *Doing things together.* Evanston, IL: Northwestern University Press.

Becker, H. S. (1996). The epistemology of qualitative research. In R. Jessor, A. Colby, & R. A. Schweder (Eds.), *Ethnography and human development* (pp. 53–71). Chicago: University of Chicago Press.

Becker, H. S. (1998). *Tricks of the trade.* Chicago: University of Chicago Press.

Becker, H S., Geer, B., Hughes, E. C., & Strauss, A. L. (1961). *Boys in white.* Chicago: University of Chicago Press.

Bloch, M. (2004). A discourse that disciplines, governs, and regulates: On scientific research in education. *Qualitative Inquiry, 10*(1), 96–110.

Cannella, G. S. (2004). Regulatory power: Can a feminist poststructuralist engage in research oversight? *Qualitative Inquiry, 10*(2), 235–245.

Cannella, G. S., & Lincoln, Y. S. (2004a). Dangerous discourses II: Comprehending and countering the redeployment of discourses (and resources) in the generation of liberatory inquiry. *Qualitative Inquiry, 10*(2), 165–174.

Cannella, G. S., & Lincoln, Y. S. (2004b). Epilogue: Claiming a critical public social science—reconceptualizing and redeploying research. *Qualitative Inquiry, 10*(2), 298–309.

Carey, J. W. (1989). *Culture as communication.* Boston: Unwin Hyman.

Cicourel, A. V. 1964. *Method and measurement in sociology.* New York: Free Press.

Clark, C., & Scheurich, J. (2008). Editorial: The state of qualitative research in the early twenty-first century. *International Journal of Qualitative Research in Education, 21*(4), 313.

Clark, V. L. P., & Creswell, J. W. (2008). Introduction. In V. L. Plano Clark & J. W. Creswell (Eds.), *The mixed methods reader* (pp. xv–xviii). Thousand Oaks: Sage.

Clark, V. L. P., Creswell, J. W., Green, D. O., & Shope, R. J. (2008). Mixing quantitative and qualitative approaches: An introduction to emergent mixed methods research. In S. N. Hesse-Biber & P. Leavy (Eds.), *Handbook of emergent methods* (pp. 363–388). New York: Guilford.

Clifford, J. (1988). *Predicament of culture.* Cambridge: Harvard University Press.

Clifford, J. (1997). *Routes: Travel and translation in the late twentieth century.* Cambridge: Harvard University Press.

Clifford, J., & Marcus, G. E. (Eds.). (1986). *Writing culture.* Berkeley: University of California Press.

Clough, P. T. (1992). *The end(s) of ethnography.* Newbury Park, CA: Sage.

Clough, P. T. (1998). *The end(s) of ethnography* (2nd ed.). New York: Peter Lang.

Clough, P. T. (2000). Comments on setting criteria for experimental writing. *Qualitative Inquiry, 6,* 278–291.

Cook, D. A. (1981). *A history of narrative film.* New York: W. W. Norton.

Creswell, J. W. (1998). *Qualitative inquiry and research design: Choosing among five traditions.* Thousand Oaks, CA: Sage.

Danermark, B., Ekstrom, M., Jakobsen, L., & Karlsson, J. C. (2002). *Explaining society: Critical realism in the social sciences.* London: Routledge.

de Certeau, M. (1984). *The practice of everyday life*. Berkeley: University of California Press.

Denzin, N. K. (1970). *The research act*. Chicago: Aldine.

Denzin, N. K. (1978). *The research act* (2nd ed.). New York: McGraw-Hill.

Denzin, N. K. (1989a). *Interpretive interactionism*. Newbury Park, CA: Sage.

Denzin, N. K. (1989b). *The research act* (3rd ed.). Englewood Cliffs, NJ: Prentice Hall.

Denzin, N. K. (1997). *Interpretive ethnography*. Thousand Oaks, CA: Sage.

Denzin, N. K. (2003). *Performance ethnography: Critical pedagogy and the politics of culture*. Thousand Oaks, CA: Sage.

Denzin, N. K. (2009). *Qualitative inquiry under fire: Toward a new paradigm dialogue*. Walnut Creek, CA: Left Coast Press.

Denzin, N. K. (2010). *The qualitative manifesto: A call to arms*. Walnut Creek, CA: Left Coast Press.

Denzin, N. K., & Lincoln, Y. S. (2005). Introduction: The discipline and practice of qualitative research. In N. K. Denzin & Y. S. Lincoln (Eds.), *The SAGE handbook of qualitative research* (3rd ed., pp. 1–32). Thousand Oaks, CA: Sage.

Dilthey, W. L. (1976). *Selected writings*. Cambridge, UK: Cambridge University Press. (Original work published 1900)

Diversi, M. (1998). Glimpses of street life: Representing lived experience through short stories. *Qualitative Inquiry, 4,* 131–137.

Diversi, M., & Moreira, C. (2009). *Betweener talk: Decolonizing knowledge production, pedagogy, and praxis*. Walnut Creek, CA: Left Coast Press.

Ellingson, L. L. (2009). *Engaging crystallization in qualitative research*. Thousand Oaks, CA: Sage.

Ellis, C. (2009). *Revision: Autoethnographic reflections on life and work*. Walnut Creek, CA: Left Coast Press.

Ellis, C., & Bochner, A. P. (Eds.). (2000). *Ethnographically speaking: Autoethnography, literature, and aesthetics*. Walnut Creek, CA: AltaMira Press.

Filstead, W. J. (Ed.). (1970). *Qualitative methodology*. Chicago: Markham.

Flick, U. (1998). *An introduction to qualitative research*. London: Sage.

Flick, U. (2002). *An introduction to qualitative research* (2nd ed.). London: Sage.

Flick, U. (2007). *Designing qualitative research*. London: Sage

Gage, N. L. (1989). The paradigm wars and their aftermath: A "historical" sketch of research and teaching since 1989. *Educational Researcher, 18*(7), 4–10.

Geertz, C. (1973). *Interpreting cultures*. New York: Basic Books.

Geertz, C. (1983). *Local knowledge*. New York: Basic Books.

Geertz, C. (1988). *Works and lives*. Stanford, CA: Stanford University Press.

Geertz, C. (1995). *After the fact: Two countries, four decades, one anthropologist*. Cambridge: Harvard University Press.

Glaser, B. G. (1992). *Emergence vs. forcing: Basics of grounded theory*. Mill Valley, CA: Sociology Press.

Glaser, B., & Strauss, A. (1967). *The discovery of grounded theory*. Chicago: Aldine.

Goodall, H. L., Jr. (2000). *Writing the new ethnography*. Walnut Creek, CA: AltaMira.

Gordon, D. A. (1988). Writing culture, writing feminism: The poetics and politics of experimental ethnography. *Inscriptions, 3/4* (8), 21–31.

Gordon, D. A. (1995). Conclusion: Culture writing women: Inscribing feminist anthropology. In R. Behar & D. A. Gordon (Eds.), *Women writing culture* (pp. 429–441). Berkeley: University of California Press.

Greenblatt, S. (1997). The touch of the real. In S. B. Ortner (Ed.), The fate of "culture": Geertz and beyond [Special issue]. *Representations, 59,* 14–29.

Grossberg, L., Nelson, C., & Treichler, P. (Eds.) (1992). *Cultural studies.* New York: Routledge.

Guba, E. G. (1990a). The alternative paradigm dialog. In E. G. Guba (Ed.), *The paradigm dialog* (pp. 17–30). Newbury Park, CA: Sage.

Guba, E. G. (1990b). Carrying on the dialog. In Egon G. Guba (Ed.), *The paradigm dialog* (pp. 368–378). Newbury Park, CA: Sage.

Guba, E., & Lincoln, Y. S. (1989). *Fourth generation evaluation.* Newbury Park, CA: Sage.

Guba, E., & Lincoln, Y. S. (2005). Paradigmatic controversies and emerging confluences. In N. K. Denzin & Y. S. Lincoln (Eds.), *The SAGE handbook of qualitative research* (3rd ed., pp. 191–216). Thousand Oaks, CA: Sage.

Gupta, A., & Ferguson, J. (Eds.). (1997). Discipline and practice: "The field" as site, method, and location in anthropology. In A. Gupta & J. Ferguson (Eds.), *Anthropological locations: Boundaries and grounds of a field science* (pp. 1–46). Berkeley: University of California Press.

Hammersley, M. (1992). *What's wrong with ethnography?* London: Routledge.

Hammersley, M. (2000). Not bricolage but boatbuilding. *Journal of Contemporary Ethnography, 28,* 5.

Hammersley, M. (2008). *Questioning qualitative inquiry: Critical essays.* London: Sage.

Harper, D. (1987). *Working knowledge: Skill and community in a small shop.* Chicago: University of Chicago Press.

Hesse-Biber, S. N., & Leavy, P. (2008). Introduction: Pushing on the methodological boundaries: The growing need for emergent methods within and across the disciplines. In S. N. Hesse-Biber & P. Leavy (Eds.), *Handbook of emergent methods* (pp. 1–15). New York: Guilford Press.

Holman-Jones, S. H. (1999). Torch. *Qualitative Inquiry, 5,* 235–250.

hooks, b.(1990). *Yearning: Race, gender, and cultural politics.* Boston: South End Press.

Howe, K. (1988). Against the quantitative-qualitative incompatibility thesis (Or dogmas die hard). *Educational Researcher, 17*(8), 10–16.

Howe, K. R. (2004). A critique of experimentalism. *Qualitative Inquiry, 10*(1), 42–61.

Howe, K. R. (2009). Positivist dogmas, rhetoric, and the education science question. *Education Researcher, 38* (August/September), 428–440.

Huber, J. (1995). Centennial essay: Institutional perspectives on sociology. *American Journal of Sociology, 101,* 194–216.

Jackson, M. (1998). *Minima ethnographica.* Chicago: University of Chicago Press.

Jameson, F. (1991). *Postmodernism, or the cultural logic of late capitalism.* Durham, NC: Duke University Press.

Keller, C. M., & Keller, J. D. (1996). *Cognition and tool use: The blacksmith at work.* New York: Cambridge University Press.

Kincheloe, J. L. (2001). Describing the bricolage: Conceptualizing a new rigor in qualitative research. *Qualitative Inquiry, 7*(6), 679–692.

Lather, P. (1993). Fertile obsession: Validity after poststructuralism. *Sociological Quarterly, 35,* 673–694.

Lather, P. (2004). This *is* your father's paradigm: Government intrusion and the case of qualitative research in education. *Qualitative Inquiry, 10*(1), 15–34.

Lather, P., & Smithies, C. (1997). *Troubling the angels: Women living with HIV/AIDS.* Boulder, CO: Westview Press.

LeCompte, M. D., & Preissle, J. with R. Tesch. (1993). *Ethnography and qualitative design in educational research* (2nd ed.). New York: Academic Press.

Lévi-Strauss, C. (1966). *The savage mind.* Chicago: University of Chicago Press. (Original work published 1962)

Lincoln, Y. S. (1997). Self, subject, audience, text: Living at the edge, writing in the margins. In W. G. Tierney & Y. S. Lincoln (Eds.*), Representation and the text: Re-framing the narrative voice* (pp. 37–56). Albany: SUNY Press.

Lincoln, Y. S. (1999, June 3–6). *Courage, vulnerability, and truth.* Paper presented to the Reclaiming Voice II Conference, University of California-Irvine, Irvine, CA.

Lincoln, Y. S. (2010). What a long, strange trip it's been . . . : Twenty-five years of qualitative and new paradigm research. *Qualitative Inquiry, 16*(1), 3–9.

Lincoln, Y. S., & Cannella, G. S. (2004a). Dangerous discourses: Methodological conservatism and governmental regimes of truth. *Qualitative Inquiry, 10*(1), 5–14.

Lincoln, Y. S., & Cannella, G. S. (2004b). Qualitative research, power, and the radical right. *Qualitative Inquiry, 10*(2), 175–201.

Lincoln, Y. S., & Guba, E. G. (1985). *Naturalistic inquiry.* Beverly Hills, CA: Sage.

Lincoln, Y. S., & Tierney, W. G. (2004). Qualitative research and institutional review boards. *Qualitative Inquiry, 10*(2), 219–234.

Lofland, J. (1971). *Analyzing social settings.* Belmont, CA: Wadsworth.

Lofland, J. (1995). Analytic ethnography: Features, failings, and futures. *Journal of Contemporary Ethnography, 24,* 30–67.

Lofland, J., & Lofland, L. H. (1984). *Analyzing social settings.* Belmont, CA: Wadsworth.

Lofland, J., & Lofland, L. H. (1995). *Analyzing social settings* (3rd ed.). Belmont, CA: Wadsworth.

Lofland, L. (1980). The 1969 Blumer-Hughes talk. *Urban Life and Culture, 8,* 248–260.

Malinowski, B. (1948). *Magic, science and religion, and other essays.* New York: Natural History Press. (Original work published 1916)

Malinowski, B. (1967). *A diary in the strict sense of the term.* New York: Harcourt.

Marcus, G., & Fischer, M. (1986). *Anthropology as cultural critique.* Chicago: University of Chicago Press.

Maxwell, J. A. (2004). Reemergent scientism, postmodernism, and dialogue across differences. *Qualitative Inquiry, 10*(1), 35–41.

Mills, C. W. (1959). *The sociological imagination.* New York: Oxford University Press.

Monaco, J. (1981). *How to read a film: The art, technology, language, history and theory of film* (Rev. ed.). New York: Oxford University Press.

Morse, J. M. (2006). The politics of evidence. In N. Denzin & M. Giardina (Eds.), *Qualitative inquiry and the conservative challenge* (pp. 79–92). Walnut Creek, CA: Left Coast Press.

Morse, J. M., & Niehaus, L. (2009). *Mixed method design: Principles and procedures.* Walnut Creek, CA: Left Coast Press.

Nelson. C., Treichler, P. A., & Grossberg, L. (1992). Cultural studies. In L. Grossberg, C. Nelson, & P. A. Treichler (Eds.), *Cultural studies* (pp. 1–16). New York: Routledge.

Ortner, S. B. (1997). Introduction. In S. B. Ortner (Ed.), The fate of "culture": Clifford Geertz and beyond [Special issue]. *representations, 59,* 1–13.

Pelias, R. J. (2004). *A methodology of the heart: Evoking academic & daily life.* Walnut Creek, CA: AltaMira.

Plath, David. (1990). Fieldnotes, filed notes, and the conferring of note. In R. Sanjek (Ed.), *Fieldnotes* (pp. 371–384). Albany: SUNY Press.

Popkewitz, T. S. (2004). Is the National Research Council committee's report on scientific research in education scientific? On trusting the manifesto. *Qualitative Inquiry, 10*(1), 62–78.

Richardson, L. (1991). Postmodern social theory. *Sociological Theory, 9,* 173–179.

Richardson, L. (1992). The consequences of poetic representation: Writing the other, rewriting the self. In C. Ellis & M. G. Flaherty (Eds.), *Investigating subjectivity: Research on lived experience.* Newbury Park, CA: Sage.

Richardson, L. (1997). *Fields of play.* New Brunswick, NJ: Rutgers University Press.

Richardson, L. (2000). Writing: A method of inquiry. In N. K. Denzin & Y. S. Lincoln (Eds.), *Handbook of qualitative research* (2nd ed., pp. 923–948). Thousand Oaks, CA: Sage.

Richardson, L., & Lockridge, E. (2004). *Travels with Ernest: Crossing the literary/ sociological divide.* Walnut Creek, CA: AltaMira.

Roffman, P., & Purdy, J. (1981). *The Hollywood social problem film.* Bloomington: Indiana University Press.

Ronai, C. R. (1998). Sketching with Derrida: An ethnography of a researcher/erotic dancer. *Qualitative Inquiry, 4,* 405–420.

Rosaldo, R. (1989). *Culture & truth.* Boston: Beacon.

Ryan, K. E., & Hood, L. K. (2004). Guarding the castle and opening the gates. *Qualitative Inquiry, 10*(1): 79–95.

Sanjek, R. (1992). *Fieldnotes.* Albany: SUNY Press.

Scheurich, J. & Clark, M. C. (2006). Qualitative studies in education at the beginning of the twenty-first century. *International Journal of Qualitative Studies in Education, 19*(4), 401.

Schwandt, T. A. (1997a). *Qualitative inquiry.* Thousand Oaks, CA: Sage.

Schwandt, T. A. (1997b). Textual gymnastics, ethics, angst. In W. G. Tierney & Y. S. Lincoln (Eds.), *Representation and the text: Re-framing the narrative voice* (pp. 305–313). Albany: SUNY Press.

Seale, C., Gobo, G., Gubrium, J. F., & Silverman, D. (2004). Introduction: Inside qualitative research. In C. Seale, G. Gobo, J. F. Gubrium, & D. Silverman (Eds.), *Qualitative research practice* (pp. 1–11). London: Sage.

Semaili, L. M., & Kincheloe, J. L. (1999). Introduction: What is indigenous knowledge and why should we study it? In L. M. Semaili & J. L. Kincheloe (Eds.), *What is indigenous knowledge? Voices from the academy* (pp. 3–57). New York: Falmer Press.

Silverman, D. (1997). Towards an aesthetics of research. In D. Silverman (Ed.), *Qualitative research: Theory, method, and practice* (pp. 239–253). London: Sage.

Smith, A. D. (1993). *Fires in the mirror.* New York: Anchor Books.

Smith, L. T. (1999). *Decolonizing methodologies: Research and indigenous peoples.* Dunedin, NZ: University of Otago Press.

Snow, D., & Morrill, C. (1995). Ironies, puzzles, and contradictions in Denzin and Lincoln's vision of qualitative research. *Journal of Contemporary Ethnography, 22,* 358–362.

Spindler, G., & Spindler, L. (1992). Cultural process and ethnography: An anthropological perspective. In M. D. LeCompte, W. L. Millroy, & J. Preissle (Eds.), *The handbook of qualitative research in education* (pp. 53–92). New York: Academic Press.

Stocking, G. W., Jr. (1986). Anthropology and the science of the irrational: Malinowski's encounter with Freudian psychoanalysis. In *History of anthropology: Vol. 4. Malinowski, Rivers, Benedict, and others: Essays on culture and personality* (pp. 13–49). Madison: University of Wisconsin Press.

Stocking, G. W., Jr. (1989). The ethnographic sensibility of the 1920s and the dualism of the anthropological tradition. In *History of anthropology: Vol. 6. Romantic Motives: Essays on anthropological sensibility* (pp. 208–276). Madison: University of Wisconsin Press.

Stoller, P., & Olkes, C. (1987). *In sorcery's shadow.* Chicago: University of Chicago Press.

St.Pierre, E. A. (2004). Refusing alternatives: A science of contestation. *Qualitative Inquiry, 10*(1), 130–139.

St.Pierre, E. A., & Roulston, K. (2006). The state of qualitative inquiry: A contested science. *International Jouranl of Qualitative Studies in Education, 19*(6), 673–684.

Strauss, A. (1987). *Qualitative analysis for social scientists.* New York: Cambridge.

Strauss, A., & Corbin, J. (1999). *Basics of qualitative research* (2nd ed.). Thousand Oaks, CA: Sage.

Taylor, S. J., & Bogdan, R. (1998). *Introduction to qualitative research methods: A phenomenological approach to the social sciences* (3rd ed.). New York: Wiley.

Teddlie, C., & Tashakkori, A. (2003a). Major issues and controversies in the use of mixed methods in the social and behavioral sciences. In A. Tashakkori & C. Teddlie (Eds.), *Handbook of mixed-methods in social and behavioral research* (pp. 3–50). Thousand Oaks, CA: Sage.

Teddlie, C., & Tashakkori, A. (2003b). Preface. In A. Tashakkori & C. Teddlie (Eds.), *Handbook of mixed-methods in social and behavioral research* (pp. ix-xv). Thousand Oaks, CA: Sage.

Turner, V., & Bruner, E. (Eds.). (1986). *The anthropology of experience.* Urbana: University of Illinois Press.

Van Maanen, J. (1988). *Tales of the field.* Chicago: University of Chicago Press.

Vygotsky, L. S. (1978). *Mind in society.* Cambridge, MA: Harvard University Press.

Weinstein, D., & Weinstein, M. A. (1991). Georg Simmel: Sociological *flaneur bricoleur. Theory, Culture & Society, 8,* 151–168.

Weinstein, M. (2004). Randomized design and the myth of certain knowledge: Guinea pig narratives and cultural critique. *Qualitative Inquiry, 10*(2), 246–260.

West, C. (1989). *The American evasion of philosophy.* Madison: University of Wisconsin Press.

Wolcott, H. F. (1990). *Writing up qualitative research.* Newbury Park, CA: Sage.

Wolcott, H. F. (1992). Posturing in qualitative research. In M. D. LeCompte, W. L. Millroy, & J. Preissle (Eds.), *The handbook of qualitative research in education* (pp. 3–52). New York: Academic Press, Inc.

Wolcott, H. F. (1995). *The art of fieldwork.* Walnut Creek, CA: AltaMira Press.

Wolfe, M. (1992). *A thrice-told tale.* Stanford, CA: Stanford University Press.

Wright, H. K. (2006). Are we there yet? Qualitative research in education's profuse and contested present. *International Journal of Qualitative Studies in Education, 19*(6), 793–802.

Part I

Locating the Field

Part I of the *Handbook* begins by locating qualitative research within the academy. It then turns to the history of qualitative inquiry in social and educational research. The last two chapters take up the ethics, politics, and moral responsibilities of the qualitative researcher.

The Academy and the Participatory Action Tradition

The opening chapter, by Morten Levin and Davydd Greenwood, calls for a reinvention of the social sciences. Their chapter reveals the depth and complexity of the traditional and applied qualitative research perspectives that are consciously and unconsciously inherited by the researcher-as-interpretive-bricoleur.[1] These traditions locate the investigator in academic systems of historical (and organizational) discourse. This system guides and constrains the interpretive work that is done in any specific study. The academy is in a state of crisis. Traditional funding connections to stakeholders no longer hold. Radical change is required, and action research can help lead the way.

Levin and Greenwood argue that action researchers have a responsibility to do work that is socially meaningful and socially responsible. The relationship between researchers, universities, and society must change. Politically informed action research, inquiry committed to praxis and social change, is the vehicle for accomplishing this transformation.

Action researchers are committed to a set of disciplined, material practices that produce radical, democratizing transformations in the civic sphere. These practices involve collaborative dialogue, participatory decision-making, inclusive democratic deliberation, and the maximal participation and representation of all relevant parties (Ryan & Destefano, 2000, p. 1). Action researchers literally help transform inquiry into praxis or action. Research subjects become co-participants and stakeholders in the process of inquiry. Research becomes praxis—practical, reflective, pragmatic action—directed to solving problems in the world.

These problems originate in the lives of the research co-participants; they do not come down from on high by way of grand theory. Together, stakeholders and action researchers co-create knowledge that is pragmatically useful and grounded in local knowledge. In the process, they jointly define research objectives and political goals, co-construct research questions, pool knowledge, hone shared research skills, fashion interpretations and performance texts that implement specific strategies for social change, and measure validity and credibility by the willingness of local stakeholders to act on the basis of the results of the action research.

Academic science has a history of not being able to accomplish goals such as these consistently. Levin and Greenwood offer several reasons for this failure, including the inability of a so-called positivistic, value-free social science to produce useful social research; the increasing tendency of outside corporations to define the needs and values of the university; the loss of research funds to entrepreneurial and private-sector research organizations; and bloated, inefficient internal administrative infrastructures.

Levin and Greenwood are not renouncing the practices of science; rather, they are calling for a reformulation of what science and the academy are all about. Their model of pragmatically grounded action research is not a retreat from disciplined scientific inquiry.[2] This form of inquiry reconceptualizes science as a multiperspective, methodologically diverse, collaborative, communicative, communitarian, context-centered, moral project. Levin and Greenwood want to locate action research at the center of the contemporary university. Their chapter is a call for a civic social science, a pragmatic science that will lead to the radical reconstruction of the university's relationships with society, state, and community in this new century.

History

In their monumental chapter ("Qualitative Methods: Their History in Sociology and Anthropology"), reprinted in the second edition of the *Handbook,* Arthur Vidich and Stanford Lyman (2000) show how the ethnographic tradition extends from the Greeks through the 15th- and 16th-century interests of Westerners in the origins of primitive cultures; to colonial ethnology connected to the empires of Spain, England, France, and Holland; to several 20th-century transformations in the United States and Europe. Throughout this history, the users of qualitative research have displayed commitments to a small set of beliefs, including objectivism, the desire to contextualize experience, and a willingness to interpret theoretically what has been observed.

In Chapter 3 of this volume, Frederick Erickson shows that these beliefs supplement the positivist tradition of complicity with colonialism, the commitments to monumentalism, and the production of timeless texts. The colonial model located qualitative inquiry in racial and sexual discourses that privileged white patriarchy. Of course, as indicated in our Introduction, these beliefs have recently come under considerable attack.

Erickson, building on Vidich and Lyman, documents the extent to which early as well as contemporary qualitative researchers were (and remain) implicated in these systems of oppression. His history extends Vidich-Lyman's, focusing on five foundational footings: disciplinary perspectives on qualitative research—especially sociology and anthropology; the participant observer as observer/author; the people observed during fieldwork; the rhetorical and substantive content of the qualitative research report; and the audiences for such texts.

He offers a trenchant review of recent disciplinary efforts (by the American Educational Research Association) to impose fixed criteria of evaluation on qualitative inquiry. He carefully reviews recent criticisms of the classic ethnographic text. He argues that the realist ethnographic text—the text with its omniscient narrator—is no longer a genre of reporting that can be responsibly practiced.

The Ethics of Inquiry

Clifford Christians locates the ethics and politics of qualitative inquiry within a broader historical and intellectual framework. He first examines the Enlightenment model of positivism, value-free inquiry, utilitarianism, and utilitarian ethics. In a value-free social science, codes of ethics for professional societies become the conventional format for moral principles. By the 1980s, each of the major social science associations (contemporaneous with passage of federal laws and promulgation of national guidelines) had developed its own ethical code with an emphasis on several guidelines: informed consent, nondeception, the absence of psychological or physical harm, privacy and confidentiality, and a commitment to collecting and presenting reliable and valid empirical materials. Institutional review boards (IRBs) implemented these guidelines, including ensuring that informed consent is always obtained in human subject research. However, Christians notes that in reality IRBs protect institutions and not individuals.

Several events challenged the Enlightenment model, including the Nazi medical experiments, the Tuskegee syphilis study, Project Camelot in the 1960s, Stanley Milgram's deception of subjects in his psychology experiments, Laud Humphrey's deceptive study of homosexuals, and the complicity of social scientists with military initiatives in Vietnam. In addition, charges of fraud, plagiarism, data tampering, and misrepresentation continue to the present day.

Christians details the poverty of the Enlightenment model. It creates the conditions for deception, for the invasion of private spaces, for duping subjects, and for challenges to the subject's moral worth and dignity (see also Angrosino & Rosenberg, Chapter 5, volume 3; also Guba & Lincoln, 1989, pp. 120–141). Christians calls for its replacement with an ethics based on the values of a feminist communitarianism.

This is an evolving, emerging ethical framework that serves as a powerful antidote to the deception-based, utilitarian IRB system. The new framework presumes a community that is ontologically and axiologically prior to the person. This community has common moral values, and research is rooted in a concept of care, of shared governance, of neighborliness, or of love, kindness, and the moral good. Accounts of social life should display these values and be based on interpretive sufficiency. They should have sufficient depth to allow the reader to form a critical understanding about the world studied. These texts should exhibit an absence of racial, class, and gender stereotyping. These texts should generate social criticism and lead to resistance, empowerment, social action, and positive change in the social world.

In the feminist communitarian model, as with the model of participatory action research advocated by Levin and Greenwood, participants have a co-equal say in how research should be conducted, what should be studied, which methods should be used, which findings are valid and acceptable, how the findings are to be implemented, and how the consequences of such action are to be assessed. Spaces for disagreement are recognized, while discourse aims for mutual understanding and the honoring of moral commitments.

A sacred, existential epistemology places us in a noncompetitive, nonhierarchical relationship to the earth, to nature, and to the larger world (Bateson, 1972, p. 335). This sacred epistemology stresses the values of empowerment, shared governance, care, solidarity, love, community, covenant, morally involved observers, and civic transformation. As Christians observes, this ethical episte-mology recovers the moral values that were excluded by the rational Enlightenment science project. This sacred epistemology is based on a philo-sophical anthropology that declares that "all humans are worthy of dignity and sacred status without exception for class or ethnicity" (Christians, 1995, p. 129). A universal human ethic, stressing the sacredness of life, human dig-nity, truth telling, and nonviolence, derives from this position (Christians, 1997, pp. 12–15). This ethic is based on locally experienced, culturally pre-scribed protonorms (Christians, 1995, p. 129). These primal norms provide a defensible "conception of good rooted in universal human solidarity" (Christians, 1995, p. 129; also 1997, 1998). This sacred epistemology recognizes and interrogates the ways in which race, class, and gender operate as important systems of oppression in the world today.

In this way, Christians outlines a radical ethical path for the future. He tran-scends the usual middle-of-the-road ethical models, which focus on the prob-lems associated with betrayal, deception, and harm in qualitative research. Christians's call for a collaborative social science research model makes the researcher responsible, not to a removed discipline (or institution), but rather to those studied. This implements critical, action, and feminist traditions, which forcefully align the ethics of research with a politics of the oppressed. Christians's framework reorganizes existing discourses on ethics and the social sciences.[3]

Clearly the existing, Belmont and Common Rule definitions have little, if any-thing, to do with a human rights and social justice ethical agenda. Regrettably, these principles have been informed by notions of value-free experimentation and utilitarian concepts of justice. They do not conceptualize research in participatory terms. In reality, these rules protect institutions and not people, although they were originally created to protect human subjects from unethical biomedical research. The application of these regulations is an instance of mission or ethics creep, or the overzealous extension of IRB regulations to interpretive forms of social science research. This has been criticized by many, including Kevin Haggerty (2004), C. K. Gunsalus et al. (2007), Leon Dash (2007), and the American Association of University Professors (AAUP, 2001, 2002, 2006a, 2006b).[4]

Oral historians (see Shopes, Chapter 4, volume 3) have contested the narrow view of science and research contained in current reports (American Historical Association, 2008; Shopes & Ritchie, 2004). Anthropologists and archaeologists have challenged the concept of informed consent as it impacts ethnographic inquiry (see Fluehr-Lobban, 2003a, 2003b; also Miller & Bell, 2002). Journalists argue that IRB insistence on anonymity reduces the credibility of journalistic reporting, which rests on naming the sources used in a news account. Dash (2007, p. 871) contends that IRB oversight interferes with the First Amendment rights of journalists and the public's right to know. Indigenous scholars Marie Battiste (2008) and Linda Tuhiwai Smith (2005) assert that Western conceptions of ethical inquiry have "severely eroded and damaged indigenous knowledge" and indigenous communities (Battiste, 2008, p. 497).[5]

As currently deployed, these practices close down critical ethical dialogue. They create the impression that if proper IRB procedures are followed, then one's ethical house is in order. But this is ethics in a cul de sac.

Disciplining and Constraining Ethical Conduct

The consequence of these restrictions is a disciplining of qualitative inquiry that extends from granting agencies to qualitative research seminars and even the conduct of qualitative dissertations (Lincoln & Cannella, 2004a, 2004b). In some cases, lines of critical inquiry have not been funded and have not gone forward because of criticisms from local IRBs. Pressures from the right discredit critical interpretive inquiry. From the federal to the local levels, a trend seems to be emerging. In too many instances, there seems to be a move away from protecting human subjects to an increased monitoring, censuring, and policing of projects that are critical of the right and its politics.

Yvonna S. Lincoln and William G. Tierney (2004) observe that these policing activities have at least five important implications for critical social justice inquiry. First, the widespread rejection of alternative forms of research means that qualitative inquiry will be heard less and less in federal and state policy forums. Second, it appears that qualitative researchers are being deliberately excluded from this national dialogue. Consequently, third, young researchers trained in the critical tradition are not being heard. Fourth, the definition of research has not changed to fit newer models of inquiry. Fifth, in rejecting qualitative inquiry, traditional researchers are endorsing a more distanced form of research, one that is compatible with existing stereotypes concerning people of color.

These developments threaten academic freedom in four ways: (1) they lead to increased scrutiny of human subjects research and (2) new scrutiny of classroom research and training in qualitative research involving human subjects; (3) they connect to evidence-based discourses, which define qualitative research as unscientific; and (4) by endorsing methodological conservatism, they reinforce the status quo on many campuses. This conservatism produces new constraints on graduate training, leads to the improper review of faculty research, and creates conditions for politicizing the IRB review process, while protecting institutions and not individuals from risk and harm.

A Path Forward

Since 2004, many scholarly and professional societies have followed the Oral History and American Historical Associations in challenging the underlying assumptions in the standard campus IRB model. A transdisciplinary, global, counter-IRB discourse has emerged (Battiste, 2008; Christians, 2007; Ginsberg & Mertens, 2009; Lincoln, 2009). This discourse has called for the blanket exclusion of non-federally funded research from IRB review. The AAUP (2006a, 2006b) has gone so far as to recommend that

> exemptions based on methodology, namely research on autonomous adults whose methodology consists entirely of collecting data by surveys, conducting interviews, or observing behavior in public places should be exempt from the requirement of IRB review, with no provisos, and no requirement of IRB approval of the exemption. (p. 4)

The executive council of the Oral History Association endorsed the AAUP recommendations at its October 2006 annual meeting. They were quite clear: "Institutions consider as straightforwardly exempt from IRB review any 'research whose methodology consists entirely of collecting data by surveys, conducting interviews, or observing behavior in public places'" (Howard, 2006, p. 9). This recommendation can be extended: Neither the Office for Human Resource Protection, nor a campus IRB has the authority to define what constitutes legitimate research in any field, only what research is covered by federal regulations.

We agree.

Ethics and Critical Social Science

In Chapter 5, Gaile Cannella and Yvonna S. Lincoln, building on the work of Michel Foucault, argue that a critical social science requires a radical ethics, an "ethics that is always/already concerned about power and oppression even as it avoids constructing 'power' as a new truth" (p. 97). A critical ethical stance works outward from the core of the person. A critical social science incorporates feminist, postcolonial, and even postmodern challenges to oppressive power. It is aligned with a critical pedagogy and a politics of resistance, hope, and freedom.

A critical social science focuses on structures of power and systems of domination. It creates spaces for a decolonizing project. It opens the doors of the academy so that the voices of oppressed people can be heard and honored and so that others can learn from them.

Conclusion

Thus do the chapters in Part I of the *Handbook* come together over the topics of ethics, power, politics, social justice, and the academy. We endorse a radical, participatory ethic, one that is communitarian and feminist, an ethic that calls for trusting, collaborative nonoppressive relationships between researchers and those studied, an ethic that makes the world a more just place (Collins, 1990, p. 216).

Notes

1. Any distinction between applied and nonapplied qualitative research traditions is somewhat arbitrary. Both traditions are scholarly. Each has a long tradition and a long history, and each carries basic implications for theory and social change. Good theoretical research should also have applied relevance and implications. On occasion, it is argued that applied and action research are nontheoretical, but even this conclusion can be disputed.

2. We will develop a notion of a sacred science below and in our concluding chapter.

3. Given Christians's framework, there are primarily two ethical models: utilitarian and nonutilitarian. However, historically, and most recently, one of five ethical stances (absolutist, consequentialist, feminist, relativist, deceptive) has been followed, although often these stances merge with one another. The *absolutist* position argues that any method that contributes to a society's self-understanding is acceptable, but only conduct in the public sphere should be studied. The *deception* model says any method, including the use of lies and misrepresentation, is justified in the name of truth. The *relativist* stance says researchers have absolute freedom to study what they want; ethical standards are a matter of individual conscience. Christians's feminist-communitarian framework elaborates a *contextual-consequential framework*, which stresses mutual respect, noncoercion, nonmanipulation, and the support of democratic values (see Guba & Lincoln, 1989, pp. 120–141; Smith, 1990; also Collins, 1990, p. 216; Mitchell, 1993).

4. Mission creep includes these issues and threats: rewarding wrong behaviors, focusing on procedures and not difficult ethical issues, enforcing unwieldy federal regulations, and involving threats to academic freedom and the First Amendment (Becker, 2004; Gunsalus et al., 2007; also Haggerty, 2004). Perhaps the most extreme form of IRB

mission is the 2002 State of Maryland Code, Title 13—Miscellaneous Health Care Program, Subtitle 20—Human Subject Research § 13–2001, 13–2002: Compliance with Federal Regulations: A person may not conduct research using a human subject unless the person conducts the research in accordance with the federal regulations on the protection of human subjects (see Shamoo & Schwartz, 2007).

5. There is a large Canadian project on indigenous intellectual property rights—Intellectual Property Issues in Cultural Heritage. This project represents an international, interdisciplinary collaboration among more than 50 scholars and 25 partnering organizations embarking on an unprecedented and timely investigation of intellectual property (IP) issues in cultural heritage that represent emergent local and global interpretations of culture, rights, and knowledge. Their objectives are:

- to document the diversity of principles, interpretations, and actions arising in response to IP issues in cultural heritage worldwide;

- to analyze the many implications of these situations;

- to generate more robust theoretical understandings as well as exemplars of good practice; and

- to make these findings available to stakeholders—from Aboriginal communities to professional organizations to government agencies—to develop and refine their own theories, principles, policies, and practices.

Left Coast is their publisher. See their website: http://www.sfu.ca/ipinch/

References

American Association of University Professors. (2001). Protecting human beings: Institutional review boards and social science research. *Academe, 87*(3), 55–67.

American Association of University Professors. (2002). Should all disciplines be subject to the common rule? Human subjects of social science research. *Academe, 88*(1), 1–15.

American Association of University Professors, Committee A. (2006a). *Report on human subjects: Academic freedom and the institutional review boards.* Available at http://www.aaup.org/AAUP/About/committees/committee+repts/CommA/

American Association of University Professors (AAUP). (2006b). *Research on human subjects: Academic freedom and the institutional review board.* Available at www.aaup.org/AAUP/comm./rep/A/humansub.htm

American Historical Association. (2008, February). AHA statement on IRBs and oral history research. *Perspectives on History.*

Bateson, G. (1972). *Steps to an ecology of mind.* New York: Ballantine.

Battiste, M. (2008). Research ethics for protecting indigenous knowledge and heritage: Institutional and researcher responsibilities. In N. K. Denzin, Y. S. Lincoln, & L. T. Smith (Eds.), *Handbook of critical and indigenous methodologies* (pp. 497–510). Thousand Oaks, CA: Sage.

Christians, G. C. (1995). The naturalistic fallacy in contemporary interactionist-interpretive research. *Studies in Symbolic Interaction, 19,* 125–130.

Christians, G. C. (1997). The ethics of being in a communications context. In C. Christians & M. Traber (Eds.), *Communication ethics and universal values* (pp. 3–23). Thousand Oaks, CA: Sage.

Christians, G. C. (1998). The sacredness of life. *Media Development, 2,* 3–7.

Christians, C. G. (2007). Neutral science and the ethics of resistance. In N. K. Denzin & M. D. Giardina (Eds.), *Ethical futures in qualitative research* (pp. 47–66). Walnut Creek, CA: Left Coast Press.

Collins, P. H. (1990). *Black feminist thought.* New York: Routledge.

Dash, L. (2007). Journalism and institutional review boards. *Qualitative Inquiry, 13*(6), 871–874.

Fluehr-Lobban, C. (Ed.). (2003a). *Ethics and the profession of anthropology* (2nd ed.). Walnut Creek, CA: AltaMira.

Fluehr-Lobban C. (2003b). Informed consent in anthropological research. In C. Fluehr-Lobban (Ed.), *Ethics and the profession of anthropology* (2nd ed., pp. 159–177). Walnut Creek, CA: AltaMira.

Ginsberg, P. E., & Mertens, D. M. (2009). Frontiers in social research ethics: Fertile ground for evolution. In D. M. Mertens & P. E. Ginsberg (Eds.), *The handbook of social research ethics* (pp. 580–613). Thousand Oaks, CA: Sage.

Guba, E. S., & Lincoln, Y. S. (1989). *Fourth generation evaluation.* Newbury Park, CA: Sage.

Gunsalus, C. K., Bruner, E. M., Burbules, N. C., Dash, L., Finkin, M., Goldberg, J. P., Greenough, W. T., Miller, G. A., Pratt, M. G., Iriye, M., & Aronson, D. (2007). The Illinois white paper: Improving the system for protecting human subjects: Counteracting IRB "mission creep." *Qualitative Inquiry, 13*(5), 617–649.

Haggerty, K. D. (2004). Ethics creep: Governing social science research in the name of ethics. *Qualitative Sociology, 27*(4), 391–414.

Howard, J. (2006, November 10). Oral history under review. *Chronicle of Higher Education.* Available at http:///chronicle.com/free/v53/112/12a01401.htm

Lincoln, Y. S. (2009). Ethical practices in qualitative research. In D. M. Mertens & P. E. Ginsberg (Eds.), *The handbook of social research ethics* (pp. 150–170). Thousand Oaks, CA: Sage.

Lincoln, Y. S., & Cannella, G. S. (2004a). Dangerous discourses: Methodological conservatism and governmental regimes of truth. *Qualitative Inquiry, 10*(1), 5–14.

Lincoln, Y. S., & Cannella, G. S. (2004b). Qualitative research, power, and the radical right. *Qualitative Inquiry, 10*(2), 175–201.

Lincoln, Y. S., & Tierney, W. G. (2004). Qualitative research and institutional review boards. *Qualitative Inquiry, 10*(2), 219–234.

Miller, T., & Bell, L. (2002). Consenting to what? Issues of access, gate-keeping, and "informed consent." In M. Mauthner, M. Birtch, J. Jessop, & T. Miller (Eds.), *Ethics in qualitative research* (pp. 70–89). London: Sage.

Mitchell, Richard J. Jr. (1993). *Secrecy and fieldwork.* Newbury Park: Sage.

Ryan, K., & Destefano, L. (2000). Introduction. In K. Ryan & L. Destefano (Eds.), *Evaluation in a democratic society: Deliberation, dialogue, and inclusion* (pp. 1–20). New Directions in Evaluation Series. San Francisco: Jossey-Bass.

Shopes, L., & Ritchie, D. (2004, March). Exclusion of oral history from IRB review: An update. *Perspectives online.* Available at htttp://www.historians.org/Perspecxtives/Issues'2004/0403new1.cfn

Smith, L. M. (1990). Ethics, field studies, and the paradigm crisis. In E. G. Guba (Ed.), *The paradigm dialog* (pp. 139–157). Newbury Park, CA: Sage.

Smith, L. T. (2005). On tricky ground: Researching the native in the age of uncertainty. In N. K. Denzin & Y. S. Lincoln (Eds.), *The SAGE handbook of qualitative research* (3rd ed., pp. 85–107). Thousand Oaks, CA: Sage.

Vidich, A., & Lyman, S. (2000). Qualitative methods: Their history in sociology and anthropology. In N. K. Denzin & Y. S. Lincoln (Eds.), *Handbook of qualitative research* (2nd ed., pp. 37–84). Thousand Oaks, CA: Sage.

Revitalizing Universities by Reinventing the Social Sciences

Bildung *and Action Research*

Morten Levin and Davydd Greenwood

Doing social science is, among other things, a form of contextualized institutional social practice. This banality, taken to its obvious conclusion and set in the context of contemporary academic social science, yields a number of consequences that most academic social scientists will not like. One implication is that theoretical and methodological approaches must be interpreted within the institutional contexts and social practices where they are embedded and practiced. If the desire for theoretical and methodological development is genuine, then this means the social sciences cannot proceed without developing and advocating an understanding of how universities, research institutions, and disciplinary structures shape the contexts and practices of their activities. Academic social scientists' engagement in autopoetic theoretical and methodological efforts disconnects them from society at large. Research and teaching agendas are motivated more by what is fashionable in the professionalized arenas of institutionalized social science than by the aim of addressing pertinent societal problems. Since the larger organizational structures and processes of universities, campus administrative structures, national and international professional societies, and national and international ranking systems currently are inimical to the development of socially meaningful theories/practices in social sciences, then those structures have to be analyzed and changed as well.

We make a situated, pragmatist analysis that examines university organizational structures, power relations, discourses, and external relations as they affect social research methodologies and practices. Doing this creates an epistemological, political, methodological, theoretical, and ethical necessity to go beyond conventional organizational analyses of the academic professions and analyze actual social science behavior in concrete contexts. Academic social scientists have to confront existing choices about university organizational structures and the larger extra-university context in which social science research operates. Social scientists have the tools to reveal the contours of these problems and the obligation to use them in playing a role in the pro-social reform of those structures. Leaving the changes to professional administrators, their consultants, and outside policymakers has already undermined universities in significant ways.

We pretend no neutrality on these matters. We believe that universities as something more than vocational schools and research shops are in real jeopardy. Current methods, professional practices, and organizational structures make the academic social sciences almost impossible to justify to increasingly hostile publics, funders, and policymakers. Since the Tayloristic structures of university organization are inimical to more than cosmetic institutional reform (e.g., strategic planning without any significant organizational change), we challenge them directly. We believe that universities matter and are therefore worth reforming, but only as loci for the formation of citizens; the analysis of complex technical, social, and ethical issues; and the support of meaningful efforts toward the solution of society's most pressing problems. Such universities could thrive only by means of fluid, multidimensional relationships within their own structures and with the nonuniversity worlds that are the source of their legitimacy and funding. We believe that the social sciences should have a privileged position and a core responsibility in bringing about the necessary changes.

Four important elements in practicing social science emerge as fundamental issues to be addressed if social science were to regain a solid foothold at universities and in society as a whole.

Multiperspective research. Social science research at universities has to include relevant social science, humanistic, and scientific professional expertise in multiperspective research on key societal problems. This multiperspective cogeneration of knowledge is vital in mobilizing the array of expertise found within the existing disciplines to generate meaningful and useful social knowledge and reform and to develop valid theories and methods in the fields of the participating academic partners. Fundamental reforms in teaching are also required to engage students, early and often, in multidisciplinary team research on complex problems. Doing so requires a significant reorganization of university operations and a revised set of ways of connecting intra-university worlds.

Methodological diversity. We necessarily support disciplinary and methodological diversity. For example, we believe that qualitative and quantitative methods are mutually necessary in the study of any important social problem (See, e.g., Creswell, 2003; Creswell & Clark, 2007). Significant problems do not come neatly divided into quantitative and qualitative dimensions. It is up to the researchers to combine these dimensions whenever necessary in comprehensive and actionable frameworks.

Academic social scientists want to believe that theory and practice can be neatly separated and that they should be (Eikeland, 2008). We disagree, and we assert that theory can best be generated in practice and can be properly tested only in practice. This means that the comfortable campus office/library/laboratory life is an insufficient context for the practice and further development of the social sciences. This is problematic since many academic social scientists have become academics precisely to withdraw from direct encounters with the non-academic world.

Inclusiveness of stakeholders. While it increases both theoretical and methodological demands, nonuniversity stakeholders should be included in social science research. Contrary to the widespread view within academia, creating mutual learning opportunities between universities and nonacademic stakeholders does not lower the expectations for theoretical and methodological rigor in the social sciences. Rather, it increases those demands because the researchers are forced to deal with more complex, multidimensional problems than most academics want to address (and are rewarded professionally for studying), and they must do so in ways that are persuasive to nonacademic stakeholders whose personal well-being is at stake.

Changes in social science teaching. Much social science teaching has become anti-social. Lecturing on general theory and method to passive students, equating social science development with theoretical and methodological elaboration in the absence of practice, and privileging the critique of the latest journal articles rather than evaluating the substantive contributions to understanding and managing social problems are standard practices. They sever the connection between the social sciences and everyday social problems. Our own experiences have shown us that sustained linkages between social science theory and method and work on concrete social problems with local stakeholders help students and their teachers become more competent theorists and practitioners.

To achieve this, teaching must depart from the abstract presentations of lectures on theory and methods. Formal presentation has its place but must be accompanied by supervised social research practice in multidisciplinary team situations with multiple stakeholders who are internal and external to the university. Teaching must create learning opportunities built on real-life problems where theory and method are challenged and also used to broaden understandings.

These changes are directly opposed to the hegemonic Tayloristic logic of academic organizational structures. To meet the tests of complexity, applicability, and trustworthiness in social research requires multidisciplinary research and teaching that redefines departmental boundaries and professional identities and that recontextualizes the relationships between universities and extra-university stakeholders. This involves radical changes in universities, in the social sciences, and in the ways these interact with society at large.

Action Research

The changes proposed here form the core elements in the kind of social research we have practiced for decades, action research. We know that the approaches we recommend work. If they are possible and they work effectively, it is scientifically unacceptable to ignore them, particularly when the social sciences are at risk with all but their internal professional constituencies.

This chapter is our third contribution to the *Handbook of Qualitative Inquiry.* The main thrust in the previous two contributions was to argue that action research is a viable research strategy enabling a balance between rigor and relevance and that it has great transformative potential. In our first contribution, "Reconstructing the Relationships Between Universities and Society Through Action Research" (Greenwood & Levin, 2000, pp. 85–106), we began with a limited presentation of the problems created by the disconnectedness between social sciences and society at large and advocated addressing it through action research as the core approach to university social research. In doing this, we briefly laid out the basic elements in action research built on a pragmatic philosophical position.

In our second contribution, "Reform of the Social Sciences and of Universities Through Action Research" (Greenwood & Levin, 2005, pp. 43–64), we tightened the focus on what counts as scientific knowledge in universities and developed arguments for action research as a genuinely scientific practice. We claimed that action research could be institutionalized as the principal model for research and teaching in universities. Action research would, we believed, support a closer linkage between academic knowledge creation and enhancement of concrete problem solving for all engaged stakeholders. We argued that action research is a research and teaching strategy that both could reform social science knowledge production and create a closer link between social research and society. The core idea was the creation of a research and teaching praxis that integrated researchers (teachers) and relevant stakeholders in the same knowledge acquisition process.

During the time since our first contribution and especially since 1998, when we published a synthetic introduction to action research (Greenwood & Levin, 1998a, 2007), we noticed that these arguments about action research have had no visible effect on university social science behavior. Parochial academic professionalism, ranking by peer review within disciplinary specialties, the separation of qualitative and quantitative research as methodological specialties, the separation of theory and practice—all of these continue. An understanding of action research as a major alternative strategy for social research is nowhere visible. The current financial crises of higher education have resulted in even more bunkerism among the disciplines, subdisciplines, and specialties. The standard administrative approach to financial problems has been to distribute the cuts according to the strengths and weaknesses of different departments, which creates even fewer incentives for cooperation across disciplines. As a result, we are once again "introducing" action research before we can proceed to our core arguments about universities. However, we do so more briefly than in the previous contributions. The reader can turn to those or the second edition of our *Introduction to Action Research* (Greenwood & Levin, 2007) for a more extended treatment.

In our book, *Introduction to Action Research*, we defined action research as follows:

> AR is a set of self-consciously collaborative and democratic strategies for generating knowledge and designing action in which trained experts in social and other forms of research and local stakeholders work together. The research focus is chosen collaboratively between the local stakeholders and the action researchers and the relationships among the participants are organized as joint learning processes. AR centers on doing "with" rather than doing "for" stakeholders and credits local stakeholders with the richness of experience and reflective possibilities that long experience living in complex situations brings with it. (Greenwood & Levin, 2007, p. 1)

Action researchers link praxis and theory in social research. Social research that is not applied cannot meaningfully be called research, we believe, because theories not tested in context are merely speculations. We reject the notion that there can be applied research practices that are not explicitly connected to theories and methods. So action research rejects the theory/practice dichotomy on which most conventional social research relies (Greenwood & Levin, 1998a, 1998b, 2000, 2001a, 2001b; Levin & Greenwood, 1998).

To many social scientists, action research is "mere" activism and is viewed as a retreat from rigorous theories and methods. The justification given for this position is that greater relevance requires less rigor (an extensive counterposition is found in Argyris & Schön, 1978, 1996). Our experience shows us that this view is wrong, although it conveniently allows conventional social researchers to reside in their universities without the "rigors" of connecting with engaged social actors in the world beyond.

The philosophical foundations for our action research position come from the pragmatism of John Dewey, William James, Charles Sanders Peirce, and others (Diggins, 1994). We have laid out this position in other publications and will not repeat the arguments here. Pragmatism builds a direct link between theory and praxis. Reflection proceeds from acting in a real context, reflecting on the results, and then acting again. This is necessarily a group process involving diverse stakeholders with different experiences and knowledge of the problems at hand. Pragmatic inquiry results in "warranted" assertions that guide both action and theory/method developments.

Pragmatism is intimately connected to democracy; it is the social science approach to democratic deliberation and action. We take the betterment of democratic societies to be a core mission of the "social" sciences. We believe that action research is "scientific" (Greenwood & Levin, 2007, Chapter 5) because it leads to results tested in action and evaluated by professional social researchers and the relevant local stakeholders.

Central to action research is a collaborative relationship we call *cogenerative inquiry*. This brings the experience and training of professional social researchers together with the depth of experience and commitment of the local stakeholders for the benefit of all. Both the professional researchers and the local stakeholders have needed knowledge to contribute to the process.

Action research produces significant generalizations, methodological developments, and empirical findings, as a reading of any issue of the journals *Action Research, Systemic Practice and Action Research,* and the *International Journal of Action Research* will show.

CRITIQUE OF ACTION RESEARCH

In making these arguments, we realize that our perspectives are idealized. Our definitional arguments regarding the potential of action research do not pay attention to problems and pitfalls that assail the everyday practice of action research, both inside and outside the university. We have published a number of articles and papers that deal critically with action research as it is actually practiced. (Greenwood, 2002, 2004; Levin, 2003). Our critique centers on seeing how little action researchers have contributed to theoretical and methodological debates in the social sciences. Much action research writing involves endless case reporting without a sharp intellectual focus, often unlinked to any particular scientific discourse. These writings are often hard to distinguish from work done in any of the applied social science fields. We believe that, like the conventional social sciences, action research has not lived up to its potential for the same reason: a lack of integration between solving relevant practical problems and a well-developed theoretical and methodological agenda.

However, there are enough good examples of action research that bridge practical problem solving and have significant theoretical and methodological ambitions to make our positive case. (For examples, see Eikeland, 2008; Emery & Thorsrud, 1976; Emery & Trist, 1973; and these exemplary doctoral dissertations: Aslaksen, 1999; Crane, 2000; Hittleman, 2007; Kassam, 2005; Klemsdal, 2008; Raymer, 2007; Ruiz-Casares, 2006; Skule, 1994; Vasily, 2006.)

Action research is not reducible to "public scholarship." The notion that there are legitimate "public" and "private" spheres of scholarship runs directly against our understanding of social research as a process that engages simultaneous understanding and social action as the way to produce reliable theories, methods, and knowledge.

PEDAGOGY

Action research pedagogy runs directly against the passive "banking method" (Freire, 1970; Giroux & Giroux, 2004; McLaren & Farahmandpur, 2005; McLaren & Jaramillo, 2007). Training action researchers cannot be done from a lectern or in university seminars alone. Students need to work collaboratively with the faculty, with their fellow students, and on real projects in order to learn. They need to develop theoretical and methodological competencies but also organizational, coordinating, leadership, and ethnographic skills that arise from experience sharing responsibility for both their own learning and the learning and welfare of others.

This kind of pedagogy is possible. Morten Levin and Davydd Greenwood have both been able to practice it in their universities, and so have others (Levin & Martin, 2007). It is not common because of the hierarchical, compartmentalized, and authoritarian structures that dominate higher education. Paradoxically, it is more likely for advanced science, engineering, medical, and law students to learn these kinds of skills than for social scientists and humanists. In those fields, some teaching involves structured teamwork and the struggle to apply knowledge to concrete situations, which is rarely the case in the non-performance oriented humanities and the conventional social sciences.

Thus, we argue that the social sciences, including action research, all must be moved to address both the intellectual and practical challenges of social knowledge creation and competence development with and for the key stakeholders.

University Reform—The Balancing Act

The position on university reform we articulated in our prior contributions to this Handbook has shifted significantly. When we first wrote, we believed the possibilities of reform were sufficient to warrant our effort. Since then, we have watched the juggernaut of neoliberal policies; the vocationalization of higher education; the Bologna Process (the reform of European universities); and the deepening crisis of confidence in the value of university education as a source of social mobility, citizen formation, and meaningful social reform undermine the university systems of the world. In the current climate of economic panic, energy for much of anything other than cost-cutting Tayloristic exercises has dried up. We believe we understand how very significant reforms in universities could be undertaken, which would dramatically improve them as teaching, research, and social reform institutions, but we also believe that such reforms are unlikely. Rather, the crisis has emphasized the worst features of universities as organizations. So we have moved from writing in the voice of hopeful reformers to writing in the mode of "what if" arguments, the "what if" being "what if society and academics really wanted to recreate a meaningful university system"?

In our vision of the university, the core organizational processes are a multifaceted integration of the generation of research strategies, methods, and findings in social research; the reform of university organizational structures and processes; and the engagement of that research with the multidimensional, urgent, and dynamic problems in the world. This scholarship would depend on the collaborative engagement of students and teachers as learners and actors in these processes. Linking these tasks is a daunting challenge. After all, the conventional social sciences reject the linkage. For many academics, research has to be rigorous or relevant, theoretical or applied, and so on. No point of encounter seems to exist and it is a major challenge to support the creation of a different conceptualization.

Our proposed conceptualization is what we call the "balancing act." It might appear that such a concept is lame because it could suggest an uninteresting compromise in which every involved actor and conceptualization is juxtaposed within its previous frames of reference to create a compromise position, a common ground of "consensus" where issues and people involved give a little and get a little in return. But this is not at all what we mean. For us, the balancing act is a radical and transformative vision of the future of the social sciences and of universities because it involves creating new points of encounter arising as everyone involved moves away from their former positions and institutional bunkers, taking on new theoretical, methodological, and institutional positions.

Thus, our model is based on Jürgen Habermas's (1984) discourse ethics. The balancing act is a reasoned way to let arguments and positions confront each other, not in a win-lose competition, but in a collaborative learning process where good arguments support transformative learning for all (see, e.g., Freire, 1970; Mezirow, 1991). We also build on Ronald Barnett's (2003) arguments that the essence of academic life is to demand the exercise of reason to support or to reject any position. We assert not only that there is a middle ground but also that meaningful social research must take place precisely on that middle ground. By forcing us to strive both to be relevant for practical problem-solving and rigorous enough to make an intellectual contribution to the ongoing development of social research approaches, the balancing act requires us to stand on this middle ground and justify our work in both practical and epistemological terms and then to struggle to reorganize the work environments and the external links of universities to make this possible and sustainable. This is the first dimension of the balancing act.

We argue for multiperspective research and teaching as prerequisites for connected knowledge generation. In the research arenas where different disciplines must contribute, it is evident that a middle ground has to be shaped to facilitate transdisciplinary research and teaching (Gibbons et al., 1994; Nowotny, Scott, & Gibbons, 2001). This is the second dimension of the balancing act.

Action research embodies this middle ground because it accepts the challenge to serve two "masters"—the demand for practical solutions and the scientific demands for intellectual focus and linkages resulting in publications that expand the understandings of professional peers. To do so, social scientists must have integrity, as they can neither operate fully in the world of abstract academic communication nor in the world of practical solutions to social problems. The integrity of the action researcher, moving continuously between these potentially contradictory demands, is key. The action researcher's self-imposed demand to maintain integrity in searching for the best possible theoretical, methodological, and practical outcomes is the only guarantee.

Practicing this integrity, action researchers also model scientific and social integrity for their students. The integrity of the university as an institution depends on facilitating these processes and protecting all parties from internal or external coercion caused by sensitive issues involving multiple stakeholders. This is the third element of the balancing act.

Because action research is built on a commitment to democratic dialogue and social processes, the further obligation of action researchers is to weigh the fairness and democratic implications of their research and teaching processes and of the practical solutions they propose (Flood & Romm, 1996). The power and interests of the relevant stakeholders affect these processes, and the researchers seek to balance these interests through open processes characterized by integrity throughout.

Another balancing act within universities is an institutional challenge to mediate between the development and promotion of deep expertise and high skill levels in many fields and the deployment of that capability around important transdisciplinary projects within and beyond the university. This is the fourth element of the balancing act. Disciplinary silos and autonomy oppose such a change project, but doing away with the ongoing development and teaching of deep expert knowledge would also be destructive to the future of the university and society at large. As important as this is, we see little evidence of a meaningful role played by university management structures in achieving and protecting this balance. Current evidence points in the opposite direction, toward academic commodity production in a fee-for-service environment.

Action research teaching is the fifth element in the balancing act. This teaching balances conveying social theories and methods drawn from the social sciences and connecting these theories and methods practically with everyday social life. Telling students how to think and act is not successful in giving students the ability to evaluate theories and methods, gather and analyze social research data, and work with diverse actors to bring about social change. Nothing short of balancing theory and practice in the classroom and taking the professor and students out of the classroom in the company of other colleagues from other fields and nonuniversity stakeholders constitutes "teaching social science." If the teaching activity does not bridge theory and praxis, then the students are not learning social science. Instead, they are becoming experts in academic commodity production for the benefit of their own careers.

This kind of engaged reflective research is impossible in the conventional academic social sciences or in the existing organizational structures of universities, despite the depth of the crisis in the funding of higher education and the loss of public confidence in the academic social sciences. To explain this, we provide a perspective on Tayloristic organization and management in universities, organizational dynamics that create the disconnected social sciences, which cannot deliver meaningful social formation (*Bildung*) and which have created a marketized teaching system where "shopping" for courses substitutes for a well-reasoned course plan that creates personal formation (*Bildung*).

SOCIAL SCIENTISTS' ANTISOCIAL SELF-UNDERSTANDINGS

Deep expertise in particular topics and approaches is essential to research about and understanding of broader systemic relationships. Disciplinary specialization accompanied by the organizational isolation of disciplines does not promote good social research. It makes important social problems impossible to understand and resolve and promotes poor quality higher education. Students are forced to walk around from academic department to department to "get an education," while the faculty who are not in intellectual communication generally have only stereotypical ideas of fields outside their own.

The lack of understanding of the contexts of the social scientists' own practices is paralleled by social scientists' lack of understanding of universities' organizational dynamics and their uneasy position in society. After working for generations to separate universities as producers of social science from nonacademic stakeholders engaged in the problems under study, academic social scientists have made meaningful and valid social research difficult and often professionally suicidal.

We have long been struck that most of our academic social science colleagues, whose specialties involve understanding the pervasive, complexly structured ways humans live in institutional and cultural worlds, conduct themselves personally and academically as if they were suprasocial and supracultural individualists whose behavior is not subject to their own theories and analytical methods. This self-estrangement from local organizational life and from society results in an absence of individual and collective self-understanding among social scientists and humanists, who claim to understand society and culture better than nonprofessionals.

This shows that many academics do not really believe or have not reflected on the ways that their theories and methods apply to themselves. They intuitively place themselves in a suprasocial position, adopting a modernist view, even though generations of social theory and philosophy have demonstrated the impossibility and inadvisability of pretending to take such a superhuman position. Social scientists have positioned themselves as "spectator" analysts (Eikeland, 2008; Skjervheim, 1974) and not as participants in their institutions and society.

Many academic social scientists combine professional hyperindividualism as academic entrepreneurs with a lack of understanding of organizational contexts in which academic social science knowledge is generated and communicated. As these contexts are rapidly changing, even the most un-self-conscious academics now are aware of some changes. But this lack of organizational self-understanding and reflection leaves them unprepared to develop and defend their own narrow academic interests and those of their students in the emerging academic regimes of "marketized" global higher education.

Instead, there is collective self-denial regarding the impact of the changing institutional and societal environments. Disturbing signals from external stakeholders are often met by retrenching: continuing to teach as always, admitting graduate students and training them for nonexistent academic jobs, and doing research on subjects of interest only to immediate professional peers This is an example of single-loop learning and Model O-I behavior (Argyris & Schön, 1978, 1996). This historical naiveté and resistance to confronting the challenge of a critical examination of their own research and teaching practices, institutional working contexts, and the roles they could play in society means that they do not exhibit behavior that could result in greater interest and respect for the social sciences.

These regressive behaviors play directly into the hands of "marketizing" (Slaughter & Leslie, 1997) managerial ideologies, using professional ranking systems to measure excellence in academic fields, and attempting to convert higher education into a fee-for-service training enterprise rather than a research and education effort to improve the quality of democratic societies. Rather, universities are organized according to an antiquated, dysfunctional Tayloristic model of a hierarchical, bureaucratic division of labor resulting in managerialism, authoritarianism, internal competition, and alienation from key external constituencies.

For generations, the more qualitatively oriented and interpretivist social scientists have been freer of constraints other than a lack of financial resources. They were not free in the political economy of university life or free from political attacks on their theories. We think they have confused being marginal with being free. Now both the public who pays the bills and the policymakers expect academic research and teaching to deliver value for the money. Nonacademics logically imagine that the importance of the social sciences is the light they shed on how society works in order to improve our lives. The distance between this public view of the social sciences and the lifeworld of a great many academic social scientists is significant.

UNIVERSITY MANAGEMENT AS TAYLORISM

Tayloristic organization, with its hermetic organizational units and command and control structures, makes a bad situation worse by concentrating the communication with the outside world and strategic planning in the central administration. Senior administrators, while privy to the overall "bottom line" of the institutions, generally do not have a good understanding of what real activities and processes produce this bottom line or how the bottom line is likely to change as new discoveries are made, new demands emerge, and so on. Unaware of the details of the research, teaching, and other work contexts that many individual faculty members know far better, the administrators and accountants see the results of the work but do not understand the contexts that make these results positive or negative. They thus elaborate policies and plans that often obstruct or undermine important developments while favoring the interests of the incumbent players and organizations they already know.

These systems unleash dynamics by which senior administrators maintain their power by controlling access to certain kinds of information and causing those who report to them to compete. Those lieutenants, in turn, do the same down the chain. It is a recipe for the already visible disaster. Like the bosses in Tayloristic factories, they are remote from the point of value creation and increasingly surrounded by accountants, finance managers, human resource professionals, advertising and public relations experts, lawyers, and risk managers. Thus, senior administrators have authority without having the relevant information. Not surprisingly, they routinely make decisions that are either counterproductive or impossible to implement.

When administrators argue that the crucial role of universities now is to prepare students for the knowledge society of the 21st century, neither they nor the faculty have a clear idea what they are talking about because they are divorced from the real worlds of work outside the university. Only a small portion of the faculty on most university campuses have relevant or current experience of the extra-university world to which their educational and research supposedly links. Lacking this experience, they cannot teach or provide research of value to those whose lives will be lived mainly outside the university.

This problem is less acute in the sciences and engineering. In these fields, there is a more constant and fluid link between the private sector, the public sector, and the university and more opportunity for sensible compromises between basic and applied research, all supported by the process of gaining external funding. While the process is not perfect, there are more external linkages, and work organization takes account of them.

In the social sciences, opportunities abound for academics to engage in disciplinary debates and set priorities for research and teaching having little linkage to what happens outside their disciplinary structures. The modesty of funding for all but some forms of quantitative positivistic research "liberates" many academic social scientists to pursue whatever topics and methods interest them or are currently in vogue. Doing irrelevant research, they do not receive much funding, and this allows them to continue the irrelevant work.

Should anyone care? We believe so because, as counterproductive as this situation is, the current direction of university reform results in a society of even more narrowly professionalized people, who neither understand their societies nor how to play a social solidary and self-conscious role in them. What academic Taylorism and adversarial politics with the outside world undermines are theoretically ambitious, methodologically sophisticated, and socially relevant social sciences dealing with the interests of students, policymakers, scientists, engineers, humanists, and society at large.

There is nothing to recommend in current university organizational systems that are ineffectual, costly, isolated, and prey to neoliberal accountability pressures. Only a radical transformation will prevent universities from continuing down the path that is converting them into technical (vocational) training institutes and fee-for-service research shops under direct external control.

THE DISCONNECTED SOCIAL SCIENCES

University relationships with key external constituencies often are handled in pecuniary and selfish ways or in aggressive and self-destructive ways. Universities often claim a service mission or an expertise-producing mission. However, the lack of fluid communication between universities and the taxpayers and the irrelevance of much university social research and teaching to nonuniversity people suggests that this mission is not real. The decline of the public land grant universities in the United States is a harbinger of things to come for all universities.

Calling attention to the disconnection between the social sciences, their own organizational and cultural environments, and the larger society sounds like the tired cliché about the "ivory tower." What interests us is not the isolation of social scientists but the radical contradiction between the stated missions of the social sciences and the organizational behavior of most academic social scientists.

It is tempting to treat this tension between irrelevant ivory towers and the "real world" in a stereotypical and moralizing way, but this is not our purpose. Enough jeremiads do this already (Giroux & Giroux, 2004; Kirp, 2003; Washburn, 2005). Our purpose is to highlight how unsustainable the social science practices and methods of academic social scientists are.

THE ROLE OF NEOLIBERAL HIGHER EDUCATION REFORMS

The issues we describe are not endogenous to universities. They express broader processes of political economic change that go under the headings of neoliberalism and globalization. These processes are real and menacing to organizations producing public goods, which do not fully follow the supposed logic of commodity production market processes. Davydd Greenwood (2009) has published on neoliberal reforms in higher education elsewhere, and so we will be brief here.

Neoliberalism is not conservatism, which believes that some values are not market negotiable, and it is not liberalism, which believes that human beings have basic rights beyond those allocated by market processes. Neoliberalism is based on a utopian belief that the market will allocate all goods and services to those who deserve them and away from those who do not, if left to do its work. Since it has not been left to do its work, neoliberals intervene constantly claiming to free up the market by destroying public goods and reallocating them (energy production, environmental protection, education, etc.) to private actors. These private actors are generally the sponsors of the neoliberal politicians, and the charade results in a rapid increase in socioeconomic inequality accompanied by increased corporatist governmental bureaucracy.

Higher education is among the public goods neoliberal policies have focused on heavily. Beginning with the Thatcher reforms in Britain, followed by the Bologna Process, and the work of the Department of Education in the United States (starting with George W. Bush but continuing now under Barack Obama), neoliberal reforms are decimating the independence and finances of public higher education. The metrics applied are customer satisfaction of students, transparency and accountability for resources expended, and the "flexibilization" of the academic workforce.

The conventional social sciences and universities as organizations are not faring well under these conditions, except for neoliberal economics and other forms of quantitative research. Support for social science that does not seem to be about anything of importance to nonsocial scientists is evaporating. By not studying and illuminating problems of immediate interest to external constituencies, social scientists have separated themselves from sources of support. By not studying social world problems in context, they do not challenge themselves theoretically or methodologically with complex problems. They substitute complex language and baroque methodologies for engagement with real social and cultural complexity. And, without application, they rarely discover if the theories and methods they produce have any value.

The study of social problems in context is more challenging theoretically and methodologically than disciplinary work because social world problems are multidimensional, dynamic, and puzzling "messes" (Ackoff, 1974). These messes are part of large-scale systems that include dimensions relevant to all the social sciences and humanities. Studying them out of context and in bits to fit disciplinary boundaries yields academic commodity production but rarely actionable understandings. Studying pieces of messes allows social scientists to acquiesce to the Tayloristic organization of universities and avoid facing the urgent challenges of university reorganization.

Frustrated with the waste of resources and lack of attention to salient social issues, policymakers and administrators make these problems worse. Rather than demanding fundamental structural reorganizations of universities, these constituencies have been persuaded to demand accountability and transparency within existing structures. They impose discipline-based accountability and ranking schemes, deepening the antiquated Tayloristic organization of the academy and creating less rather than more change. The ranking systems by discipline and the beauty contest rankings of universities conserve existing structures because they take the disciplines and organizational structures of universities for granted.

ACADEMIC TAYLORISM

Looking at the mission statements of some of the professional associations in United States makes clear the autopoetic professional orientations of the academic social sciences (see, e.g., those of the American Anthropological Association, http://www.aaanet.org/about/WhatisAnthropology.cfm; the American Political Science Association, http://www.apsanet.org/content_4403.cfm?navID=733; or the American Economic Association, http://www.vanderbilt.edu/AEA/gen_info .htm).

They take for granted the existence and rationality of the boundaries of the disciplines and then proceed to occupy and protect those turfs, with bows in the direction of being socially valuable. A greater emphasis on social value is absent not because most academic social scientists don't believe what they do is valuable but because they view their value as being beyond debate. Until now, they have rarely been asked to defend what they do outside of their disciplinary confines.

Compatible with the broad Taylorism of academia, this results in the compartmentalization of knowledge and a unit-based command-and-control structure in which powerful central administrative figures distribute resources among disciplinary departments according to the politics of the institution, the ranking of the departments in national and international league tables, and the research monies they gather. No one asks if this overall organization makes any sense. In what way do a set of departments side-by-side add up to a university? How does travel to and between these units amount to an education? Occasionally, when at an event a president or provost is asked to say something generic about the overall university, the emptiness of their pronouncements is evident.

The kind of discussion we are promoting rarely finds its way into the arena of open debate. Anthropologists, for example, who, in their own internal discussions, routinely describe the methodological poverty and ethnocentrism of fields like economics and political science, rarely stand up in a university forum and state that political science or economics needs anthropology's help. The Tayloristic rules are live and let live: Compete for resources by fighting for enrollments and majors, office space, and budget allocations, and improve your ranking in the national and international ranking system. The rules are clear and the professional consequences of "coloring outside the lines" for all but a few great practitioners (e.g., Claude Lévi-Strauss, Clifford Geertz, Jürgen Habermas, Michel Foucault, etc.) are harsh—failed promotions, low salaries, few students, isolation, and opprobrium. The everydayness of these ways of living and thinking prevents them from becoming a subject of conversation and analysis.

Another dimension of this organizational dynamic is that academic faculty members generally are competitive, individualist entrepreneurs (see Wright, Brenneis, & Shore, 2005). The process of getting into a university, graduating, doing a postgraduate degree, getting an academic job, securing grants, publishing, teaching effectively, and providing sufficient institutional service is a calculated career process. The individual is engaged in building curricula vitae that will lead to permanent appointment, advancement through the ranks, salary increases, increased influence, and eventually greater personal autonomy.

The whole process is based on individualistic competition. Disciplinary solidarity may be asserted when competing with other disciplines, but within the disciplinary department, the ethos is competitive and individualistic. What one academic gets often is gained by doing better than other colleagues in the same unit.

People who spend their professional lives operating according to these rules are unlikely to think of themselves as deeply connected to the structures within which they operate except when they look up the chain of command. Those who succeed within their disciplines nationally and internationally do sometimes become senior statesmen locally, taking on tasks for the collectivity, but they rarely arrive at the position of senior statesmen without first having won a competition with colleagues in their earlier years within their departments.

This behavior is amply supported by the intellectual property regimes current in academia. The ownership of ideas and the authorship of manuscripts are taken for granted as the property of individuals and disciplinary research teams. Ideas are supposed to be original, and the fiction is that an academic's original ideas belong to her or him alone. He or she communicates them and tries to get others to use some of her or his language and to refer to her or his work in the process. If the ideas result in useful inventions, an all-out struggle between the faculty member and the university administration often ensues over the distribution of the rights to the profits between the individual and the university (Marginson & Considine, 2000; Kirp, 2003; Slaughter & Leslie, 1997; Washburn, 2005).

We could multiply examples and arguments, but we have said enough to show how the organizational environment of the social sciences encourages anti- or at least nonsocial thought and action. The relevant social life is within the discipline and department, and even there, it is generally competitive. It is rare for an academic social scientist to think of her- or himself as a part of a university collectivity with shared cultural norms, a worldview, and preferred methods and as a person whose behavior is largely explained by the social and cultural context in which he or she operates. Instead, it is the "others," the informants, the people the social scientists study outside the university, who have culture, roles, and values and who live in a sociocultural context, not the social scientists. Taylorism is firmly backed up by modernism.

We provide a concrete example from anthropology. For generations, it was assumed that the ability of anthropologists to see and understand the cultures of others was based on their unquestioned rationality and training as Western intellectuals. This was a perverse legacy. Culture and society are claimed to have a pervasive causal influence on the behavior of humans, but the anthropologists making this claim operated professionally as if this general human condition did not apply to them. In anthropology, this tension was long hidden by giving up the study of North America and Europe as part of anthropology. It is telling that the Society for the Anthropology of Europe was not founded until 1987 and that the Society for North American Anthropology was founded at nearly the same time. By not treating these areas as suitable for anthropology, anthropologists removed themselves from the study of their own societies (also reducing competition with economics, political science, and sociology) and steered clearer of political repression like that suffered in the era of the House Un-American Activities Committee and Senator Joseph McCarthy (Price, 2004). They could also engage the modernist fiction of the unquestioned superiority of Western knowledge systems.

This untenable position became more paradoxical when the combination of feminism and cultural studies made positionality, the impossibility of neutral stances, the politics of research, and other previously obscured issues open to discussion. Taking on these perspectives at a discursive level and representing them in the bibliographies of manuscripts and course syllabi, anthropologists and other social scientists still generally have resisted studying themselves, their own institutions, and their own practices. Talking about positionality and reflexivity is not the same as understanding one's positions and being reflexive.

Social science teaching shows the same kind of dynamic. Typically, the general introductory courses are taught as lectures, sometimes with discussion sections, but mainly as passive learning activities. The lecturers state their understanding of what the discipline is about, how professionals operate, and what the key lessons from generations of research are. Students do not learn how to act as social scientists, why the disciplines exist, how they are similar and different from each other, or how research is done. These practices change some in upper-level courses, where enrollments are smaller and more interaction is possible, but many social science majors after 3 years cannot conduct research nor explain how or why the discipline they majored in differs from other disciplines.

At the graduate level, at least in the United States, the situation is more extreme. Graduate students are mentored more individually and must learn to "talk the talk" and "walk the walk" of their professors as a condition for getting a PhD. Taking a particularly egregious example from anthropology, fewer than 10% of the graduate departments of anthropology in the United States require a methodology course as part of graduate training. Students who want to learn how to do anthropological field research often find themselves doing their doctoral research without training on how to proceed.

Other disciplines offer more methodological training. Graduates in sociology, political science, and economics know the main techniques associated with their disciplines. Are they trained, therefore, as researchers? Do they know what their discipline "is," why it exists, and how it relates to others? Our experience is that they do not. Nor do many of these students have practice collaborating with academics from other disciplines on joint research projects and/or as members of teams doing research outside the university. A few get this experience in fields like archaeology and landscape architecture, but it is a rare practice in the conventional core of the social sciences.

The market-competitive model exacerbates the worst features of these teaching situations. Universities are presented to beginning students as giant educational cafeterias. They are told to go down the line among the offered dishes, picking and choosing within the limits set by curricular requirements, administrative rules, and course enrollment limitations. Departments that attract many students get more university resources. Departments with popular majors get more university resources. Departments with lots of students get graduate teaching assistantships and so are able to admit more graduate students. Departments with large and highly ranked graduate programs get more university resources. The "business model" is clear.

This system already is based on the student market model, although the market language long remained hidden. Students are supposed to make choices according to how attractive they find the courses offered, the campus reputation of the lecturers, and what they take to be the market value of one discipline over another. It is no accident that fields like classics have low enrollments and applied economics and management have high ones.

The departments or disciplines compete rather than cooperate because the Tayloristic system demands it. How these fields relate to each other is a not question addressed in such systems, nor is it possible to make any serious analysis of the mix and relative sizes of the constituent units. What the students learn and why is much less relevant than how many students enroll. How the student as a whole person emerges changed from the exposure to multiple fields and agendas is a question not asked. Students graduate, are given a degree, and are defined as having an "education."

Research suffers a similar fate. Research topics commanding the most external resources contribute most to the internal prestige and power of a unit and a faculty member and to the ranking of the university at large. Universities play little or no role in setting these funding agendas. National governments, private foundations, national research councils, and private sector funders call the tune, and thus the research market is controlled by powerful nonacademic forces that channel research into their areas of military, industrial, and economic development. Most universities do not have their own means of linking to the external world, engaging important external groups, or working toward university activities that are both intellectually challenging and socially desired. Most such relationships pass through individual faculty members and the research groups and centers they create.

Some successful university researchers may work in teams, and these teams are driven by grants. Often the team leader spends most of her or his time, not in the laboratory or classroom, but writing and administering grants, applying for patents, and working out negotiations over the sharing of resources created by the research projects. Many well-funded university researchers barely teach at all, although they might have some students working in their labs and getting some valuable mentoring by observation and participation.

Poorly funded university researchers are either working on unpopular topics or are not very good at getting research funding. They cobble together modest resources or simply do research on weekends and evenings or during the summers. They are less likely to work in teams, and without funding, few work with students as apprentices. They also end up doing the bulk of the teaching at the university.

What is the research agenda of a given university? Every institution now has a research statement and mission statements, but most employees and students have no idea what they are or how they affect them. What the "mission" of the institution might be is a question not asked in a way to produce organizational innovation and change. Rather, it is mainly a public relations instrument.

The research agenda of most universities, like their teaching, is the sum total of the activity going on that year. Whether it adds up to anything, whether the whole is more than the sum of its parts, is mostly irrelevant. Senior administrators answer questions about the mission of their institutions either with vague statements about the "knowledge society," "environmental crisis," and so on or with a table showing the research rankings of their university vis-à-vis peers.

THE MISSING BILDUNG IN THE "MARKETIZED" MODEL OF ACADEMIC TEACHING AND RESEARCH

There are a host of attempts worldwide to use what are wrongly imagined to be conventional business management strategies to direct higher education institutions (Barnett, 2003; Birnbaum, 2000; Kirp, 2003; Newfield, 2008). Because this management approach has not been countered successfully at most universities, it threatens the public and private university systems around the world.

There are ideological antimarket thinkers in academia (McLaren & Farahmandpur, 2005; McLaren & Jaramillo, 2007), but antimarket ideology does not motivate our critique. We see that pseudo-market ideologies and management practices are imposed on universities with the justification of the need to "rationalize" operations for efficiency and improved quality. However, our observations and much of the analytical literature, both on the left (Ehrenberg, 2006; Kirp, 2003; Newfield, 2008; Slaughter & Leslie, 1997) and among conservatives (MacMahon, 2009), show that what is claimed as rational economic management is not economically rational. Sheila Slaughter and Larry L. Leslie call this pseudo-economic management "marketizing" higher education, by which they mean claiming economic rationality while actually imposing authoritarian command-and-control management systems on faculty, students, and staff members. The rational allocation of resources, efficiency, quality, and transparency are the supposed motives, but the results are authoritarianism, suppression of information, maladaptive behavior, lowering of quality and transparency, and the creation of scores of new administrative positions to run an unwieldy, inefficient system.

A powerful critique of this pseudo-economics of university management comes from a well-known conservative economist, William MacMahon, whose *Higher Learning, Greater Good* (2009) uses social capital theory to attack the neoliberal "new public management" of higher education. MacMahon shows that the neoliberal management models in higher education and higher education policy underestimate by at least half the value of the goods produced by higher education because half of these goods are "public goods" that accrue to individuals and society over longer periods. They are not simple academic commodities for sale at a given instant.

This argument is key because it shows that, by failing to count the public goods and failing to understand that universities are capable of producing vast stores of public goods, the current models of management by the numbers actually undermine the ability of higher education to produce public goods and drastically reduce their productivity and contribution to the economy and to positive social change. In effect, MacMahon (2009) argues that many higher education managers and policymakers actually have no idea of the breadth and complexity of the goods their institutions produce and thus make economically irrational decisions, undermining their institutions' ability to operate efficiently and effectively. A related argument has been made for conventional manufacturing businesses by H. Thomas Johnson and Robert S. Kaplan in *Relevance Lost* (1987).

Another way of framing this is to state that these managers *do not know what higher education is.* In the language of many, students are customers, faculty are employees, tuition is the payment of a fee-for-service, and research is a profit/loss effort to be analyzed according to cost-benefit criteria. While there are senses in which all this is true, such views miss a significant part of what goes on in higher education. The focus is on the vocational training, content transmission activities, and research profit/loss ratios that obtain, but these by themselves are not the defining characteristics of university teaching, research, and service. They do not constitute an acceptable definition of higher education.

University teaching and research efforts, while satisfying some preferences from the "customers," involve processes aimed at shaping and reshaping the preferences of students, colleagues, administrators, and external constituencies, that is, at *Bildung*. It is the way we link scientific approaches to the social functions of higher education (Prange, 2004).

No unified understanding of *Bildung* exists, but the concept is widely used. The central meanings focus on an ongoing process of formation, of enhancing the intellectual and ethical strengths of individuals and thus preparing them to play meaningful roles in democratic societies (Bruford, 1975). *Bildung* creates critical, well informed, and reflective intellectuals able to address societal problems with integrity. The effects of *Bildung* are precisely what MacMahon (2009) captures in accounting for the value of higher education. These are reasoned affirmations about values, definable processes with measurable outcomes.

Generations after the Manhattan Project and sending a man to the moon, we are still living off the public goods created in efforts that remade (for good and ill) our world (and the industrial economies) fundamentally. University research and education can do this, but proving it, as MacMahon (2009) points out, involves a longer temporal perspective and deeper analysis than the single-year balance sheet favored by university administrators and marketizing policymakers.

Promoting *Bildung* in university teaching, research, and service is demanding. It is much harder than having students read a number of classic texts (the approach favored in the Norwegian curricular debates and in the U.S. "great books" culture wars). It requires vision, an ability to take a long-term time perspective to achieve a greater gain or a greater good. It involves conceptualizing university teaching, research, and service as knowledge creation and transmission activities with outcomes that are both immediate and long-term and conceptualizing them in relationship to a concept of what education and knowledge are. To strengthen these processes requires the autonomy and support to permit students and faculty take up unpopular, divisive topics and to study complex, multisystem problems. It also requires flexible, open-minded administrators to allocate resources wisely in substantive terms rather than to paint by the numbers. In a word, it requires creative and reflective leadership.

This leadership is essential to the integrity of knowledge creation and transmission processes, but it is inhibited by the marketization of university teaching and research. In the case of social science research, inhibition means that social research is unlikely to occur if it involves examining controversial problems in their complex scope, in collaboration with important outsiders or over sustained periods of time without immediate results. The result has been the destruction of the classical *Bildung*, the conversion of education into vocational training, the disconnection of faculty teachers and researchers from the complexities of the real-world contexts, and the disconnection of most of the university from the ongoing core processes in democratic societies. These developments limit the academic freedom of both students and faculty to follow subjects wherever the teaching and research processes take them. Stated more briefly, the lack of collective reflective practice to address these challenges is a direct consequence of academic Taylorism. We argue for a new *Bildung* that includes individual formation and also collective efforts and shared responsibility.

We are not backward-looking romantics about *Bildung*. This notion was used to found the Humboldtian university and to justify the creation of the U.S. research universities. It is historically connected to the current dreary scene we portray. The conventional understanding of *Bildung* pointed to the formation of the individual in the perspective of accessing classical virtues of philosophy, history, and literature. Through reading Greek and Roman texts in philosophy, studying history, and seeking the beauty in poetry, prose, and theater, *Bildung* would automatically emerge in the mind and body of the student. But as Prange (2004) argues, "The concept of *Bildung* is a latecomer in a long line of spiritual independence versus material circumstances [tearing sic.] us down to considerations of earthly well-being. Education is for now, *Bildung* is forever" (p. 506). The eternal perspective is matched with the earlier argument that *Bildung* links the scientific ideal to the social impact of higher education. Our own understanding of the social function of education relates to the role of the academically trained person. We see genuine humanism as the expected consequence of a broader understanding of forces and processes that have created our societies and cultures.

But we believe that more than this is needed. As a consequence of our being members of society, *Bildung* has to deal with integrity, equality, and democracy. These virtues can be taught about, but basically they should emerge as a by-product of participating in a learning community, the university. Through active engagement in discourses among students, between students and teachers, and with citizens at large, integrity, equality, and democracy can be nourished. So, *Bildung* cannot simply be taught in class; it emerges as an effect of having joined the university's larger learning community, a community that is open to society itself.

The Role of Action Research in Addressing Reform of Universities

We argue that there must now be a *New Bildung*, one that readdresses the meaning of university education and knowledge in the 21st century, not one that looks backward. We have indicated a few meanings of *Bildung* in an age of globalization, marketization, and increasing inequality. How, then, do universities contribute to addressing these problems? Part of our answer is that action research itself can be a significant source of the *New Bildung*.

We have addressed some major challenges for social science in universities: antisocial behavior by academics, the Tayloristic leadership and organizational models, the disconnection from society at large, and the evaporation of *Bildung* as a unique mission of universities. What, then, would the application of action research to academic organization and behavior look like, and how could this lead to a positive change that could regenerate vigorous universities for the 21st century?

Almost all universities are subject to pressure related to economic resources, whether they are private or publicly funded. Clearly no university on either side of the Atlantic will see the glory years of the last century again soon. Universities also now face the dilution of the public trust in university education and research as a major driver of economic prosperity and trustworthy knowledge generation. Universities can either adapt passively by further tweaking of the Tayloristic organizational structure to streamline themselves as marketplaces for knowledge commodities, or they can fundamentally reorganize through collective, participative engagement (professors, students, administrators, and support staff).

Fundamental reorganization is the only feasible way out of this economic and social crisis. It involves both a bottom-up process and a top-down process because we must create a common space for collective reflection where different points of view and sources of expertise and experience are confronted and where the reflections that emerge can lead directly to changes. This involves a balancing act between what changes are possible and what forces are counteracting change processes.

The change process we describe is relevant both for teaching and research. In fact, we would argue that the same type of knowledge generation process permeates both arenas. Reflection and experimentation would form the kind of continuous learning spiral central to action research (Greenwood & Levin, 2007; Heron 1996; Kolb 1984; Reason, 1994). This reform process has to be multidisciplinary, multiperspective, and transorganizational. It is clear that no single branch of social science is capable of encapsulating the reform process.

What we advocate is controversial, and we know from long experience that this perspective is not welcome in the conventional practices of the social sciences. Among the central problems that would arise are several ontological, epistemological, and methodological clashes right on the horizon. The ontological and epistemological fractures between modernism, realism, positivism, hermeneutics, structuralism, and so on have divided the social sciences for many years. Discussions of ontology and epistemology are ongoing, but they have had little impact on daily life among social scientists, where methodological approaches are a constant source of debate and academic commodity production. This dynamic is already well known and has been well discussed in the theory of science literature (Berger & Luckmann, 1966; Skjervheim, 1974; Toulmin, 1990).

We prefer to concentrate on methodological clashes that would have to be dealt with in any process of linking the social sciences. Only when we engage in praxis in the social sciences do different perspectives productively confront each other, and we also know that any change activity in universities ultimately involves changes in work life as it is lived daily. To engage the change process, we believe it is necessary to confront the conventional social sciences with the direct challenge of creating a new and different social science praxis.

Action research, well practiced, offers a way to accomplish this because it links all disciplines, the university, and its external stakeholders in a cogenerative social research process that tests theories and methods for validity in the form of concrete solutions to problems in real-world contexts. Action research also involves collaborative research teams in which new learners from within and outside the university are welcome and contribute their energy and experiences to the process. In this way, action research necessarily develops the democratization of knowledge generation, transmission, and application.

The action research process is based on making concrete organizational and behavioral changes, and these change processes are used as a systematic tool for learning. As such, action research forms a spiral of experimentation and reflection where all involved take part in the learning activities. This is a democratic and engaged activity giving a voice to everyone involved; it is what we have labeled cogenerative learning.

Obviously, this runs counter to the disciplinary, proprietary, commodity view of research and teaching. In recommending action research, we are insisting that the way forward is to reconfigure universities, particularly public universities, as central institutions in the further development of democracy through participative processes.

What would such a change activity look like at universities? Action research activity would have to address the antisocial behavior of academics that we have alluded to earlier, the Tayloristic organizational structure and leadership systems of universities, and universities' disconnectedness from society; finally, it would be oriented around a core *Bildung* process for all involved parties.

Where is there both energy and possibility for such a process? It is fairly clear where it is not. Attacking the bunkers of the professionalized disciplines and departments directly is a recipe for failure. Making demands on senior administrators and policymakers to give up their Taylorist, marketized addictions is routinely advocated and ignored. Insisting that universities serve society democratically at a time when the only service that counts is service to powerful economic and political players is not promising.

In this challenging environment, we are left with the re-creation of the university as a center of *Bildung*. The one place where we think it might be possible to imagine reform through *Bildung* managed by action research is in teaching and research activities. For centuries, university teaching has meant learning that is a top-down, passive process, where the teacher knows what the students need to come to know. By contrast, in line with a long history in adult education and with the principles advocated by Dewey, we see learning as an active process in which the students are presented problems, raise questions, and are assisted in gaining the skills to seek answers for themselves. In this perspective, the teacher, who is also a learner, is a mentor and participant in the same learning process. We see the relationship between students and teachers as a genuine cogenerative process where each participant contributes her or his knowledge and insight as a collaborator in this joint learning activity.

But this kind of learning works only when the students and the teachers see the problems being dealt with as important. Thus, this kind of education can and should make solving practical problems its point of entry—for example, learning what it means to be "green" by working with multidisciplinary teams of inside and external stakeholders to clean up the local water supply, learning administrative skills by helping a local group set up a volunteer health clinic, and so on. Such projects, which work equally well at the beginning university level and the postgraduate level, connect universities to the outside society and necessarily include those who own the local problem in the same learning activity. Because the focus of learning is real problems that are too complex for single discipline approaches, such projects are necessarily multidisciplinary and multiperspective ones.

We are not advocating the impossible. The best way to prove that something is possible is to show that it has already been done somewhere. What we present here are two modest efforts to push the boundaries of what can be possible, even within the current *modus operandi* of universities.

Levin provides one example from a class in organizational development at the Norwegian University of Science and Technology (NTNU). When the class began, there was no clear problem focus. Instead, the students began by visiting a company and meeting with managers, trade union representatives, and workers. Students had the option of interviewing local people, or they could have access to videotaped interviews done by Levin that were later subjected to analysis. The next stage was for the students to interpret the situation and develop perspectives on a meaningful problem focus. In this phase, they met for the second time with the local company people. The students worked in groups of three to five members.

They created a plan for a developmental process in the company, which was presented in writing to the class, and they got feedback from Levin. This feedback shaped a dynamic that effectively simulates a real-life dynamic on organizational development processes. Finally, representatives from the company were invited to the presentation of the students' work, and the company people also participated in the grading process. The companies found this process useful in helping them think through organizational dilemmas, and it has been relatively easy to get companies to volunteer for it.

The *Bildung* elements are clear. Students are receiving formation by interacting with each other, with the professor, and with external stakeholders over real-world problems with real data and real consequences. They work with real people and experience the social responsibility involved in interacting with other human beings. What the students do in their activity can have real impact on people in the company. The stakes are high, and the problems are complex enough to require collaboration among the members of the class and the acquisition of relevant knowledge and coaching from other parts of the university as well. The students, the faculty member, and the company partners all improve their skills, knowledge, and understanding and learn to share their thinking in a cogenerative environment in which all are stakeholders.

Greenwood offers another example, this one drawn from an English composition class he teaches to a group of 14 students who are in their first year at Cornell University and are about 18 years old. This is part of a Cornell system for teaching freshman writing through small intensive writing seminars on topics of interest to faculty members in many disciplines. Greenwood's course focuses on the anthropological study of universities as its topic and introduces students to action research in the process.

This particular edition of the course began conventionally with a short essay from each student on the process of application to universities and the experiences he or she had. In addition to the writing corrections and revision, the course dealt with developing an ability to study and conceptualize organizational processes such as applications and admissions, residential living, dining, physical organization, structure of requirements, and many other topics through combined ethnographic work by the students (some in teams) and readings.

Early in the course, the students (with widely varied intellectual interests, ethnic backgrounds, and social interests) read Paolo Freire's (1970) *The Pedagogy of the Oppressed* and then began making connections to their experiences of the passive, banking model of education. One visionary student said that if they really believed what Freire wrote, they should convert the seminar into a group project and take their education into their own hands. After brief negotiations about the process and requirements, they developed a project to eliminate contaminants in the water coming from and passing through the university campus.

The class, including Greenwood, worked out an overall plan, and they divided up into teams according to interest and skills; they spread out all over the campus, dealing with the central administration, the water plant, the city's water treatment system, the conservation biologists who had ways of cleaning the water by means of the use of plants, among others. The dynamic was intense and resulted in a submission to a national competition for green campus projects sponsored by General Electric and MTV. Thousands of e-mails were exchanged, and the collaborative website grew to hundreds of pages.

Their motivation, work, solidarity, and sophistication grew beyond Greenwood's expectations, and he ended up spending time trying to prevent them from ignoring their other courses while they worked for a month on this project. Greenwood is convinced that these students developed the kinds of capacities summarized by the *Bildung* ideal, did so happily and willingly, and received support and approval from people around the university.

Thus, it is possible to work in existing universities within the action research mode. We also know from experience that such learning arenas often become pivotal in the development of individual students, whose academic and life choices thereafter are strongly affected by these experiences.

In previous versions of this Handbook, we have shown how research also can be re-organized on university campuses. Rather than recapitulate these here, we refer you to those chapters (Greenwood & Levin, 2000, 2005). The lesson from the examples is that both teaching and research can be based on the principles of action research. As the professors who engaged in those efforts, we could be in a state of great optimism because we see a way to make a modest contribution to students' *Bildung*. However, we are not because our experiments have shown that it is possible to reconstruct teaching and research, but we have seen little or no diffusion to other classes or research arenas. Business as usual prevails.

Conclusion

Our arguments about teaching in this chapter, as well as our arguments in earlier editions of this Handbook about the epistemology and methodology of action research, indicate that this is a superior way to link teaching, research, and real-world engagement. If this is true, why does it not dominate the research universities of the world? Most action research activities take place outside the boundaries of higher education.

What we recommend requires academic social scientists to change their behavior radically—away from hyperprofessional internal debates, away from individualism and entrepreneurialism, and toward multidisciplinary research and action that takes them beyond the university. It requires the Tayloristic organization of the university to be, if not abandoned, transformed to permit easy collaborative work across internal institutional boundaries and across the boundaries between the university and society without a commodity production view of external linkages. And it would require a recommitment of universities to *Bildung* and democracy as core values. All of these changes seem quite unlikely.

Action research disconnected from universities, as some advocate, breaks the link to educating and forming new generations of social scientists. This permits universities to continue training people who lack the knowledge and skills to make the contributions we advocate to democratic society. And, if future researchers are not trained in action research at universities, they are not likely to develop this capability after graduation. Equally important, the potential contribution of action research to the redevelopment of the social sciences is greatly hampered. Thus, we believe that universities as centers of *Bildung* cannot survive without reorganizing teaching and research along action research lines and that action research will not survive unless it develops a key position within *Bildung*-oriented higher education.

Is action research likely to achieve this key position any time soon? No. Still, we know that the fit between the problems we have identified and action research is real, and we know that it is possible because we have done it on an admittedly limited basis. We have seen the power of the results.

Perhaps the current crisis in higher education will create a propitious environment on a few campuses for the changes we advocate. If so, we have provided a map of one road toward a better future for both the university and democratic society.

References

Ackoff, R. L. (1974). *Redesigning the future: A systems approach to societal problems.* New York: John Wiley.

Argyris, C., & Schön, D. A. (1978). *Organizational learning: A theory of action perspective.* New York: Addison-Wesley.

Argyris, C., & Schön, D. A. (1996). *Organizational learning II: Theory, method, and practice.* New York: Addison-Wesley.

Aslaksen, K. (1999). *Strategies for change in corporate settings: A study of diffusion of organizational innovations in a Norwegian corporation.* Unpublished doctoral dissertation, Norwegian University of Science and Technology, Department of Industrial Economics and Technology Management, Trondheim.

Barnett, R. (2003). *Beyond all reason: Living with ideology in the university.* Buckingham, UK: Society for Research in Higher Education and Open University Press.

Berger, P., & Luckmann, T. (1966). *The social construction of reality.* Garden City, NY: Doubleday.

Birnbaum, R. (2000). *Management fads in higher education: Where they come from, what they do, why they fail.* San Francisco: Jossey-Bass.

Bruford, W. H. (1975). *The German tradition of self-cultivation: Bildung from Humboldt to Thomas Mann.* Cambridge, UK: Cambridge University Press.

Crane, B. (2000). *Building a theory of change and a logic model for an empowerment-based family support training and credentialing program.* Unpublished doctoral dissertation, Cornell University, Ithaca, NY.

Cresswell, J. W. (2003). *Research design: Qualitative, quantitative, and mixed methods approaches* (2nd ed.). Thousand Oaks, CA: Sage.

Cresswell, J. W., & Clark, V. L. P. (2007). *Mixed methods research.* Thousand Oaks, CA: Sage.

Diggins, J. (1994). *The promise of pragmatism.* Chicago: University of Chicago Press.

Ehrenberg, R. G. (Ed.). (2006). *What is happening to public higher education?* Westport, CT: American Council on Education and Praeger.

Eikeland, O. (2008). *The ways of Aristotle: Aristotelian phronesis, Aristotelian philosophy of dialogue, and action research.* Bern, Switzerland: Peter Lang.

Emery, F., & Thorsrud, E. (1976). *Democracy at work.* Leiden, Netherlands: Martinus Nijhoff.

Emery, F., & Trist, E. (1973). *Towards a social ecology.* London: Plenum Press.

Flood, R., & Romm, N. R. A. (1996). *Diversity management: Triple-loop learning.* Chichester, UK: Wiley.

Freire, P (1970). *The pedagogy of the oppressed.* New York: Herder & Herder.

Gibbons, M., Limoges, C., Nowotny, H., Schwartzman, S., Scott, P., & Trow, M. (1994). *The new production of knowledge: The dynamics of science and research in contemporary society.* London: Sage.

Giroux, H. A., & Giroux, S. S. (2004). *Take back higher education.* New York: Palgrave.

Greenwood, D. J. (2002). Action research: Unfulfilled promises and unmet challenges. *Concepts and Transformation, 7*(2), 117–139.

Greenwood, D. J. (2004). Action research: Collegial responses fulfilled. *Concepts and Transformation, 9*(1), 80–93.

Greenwood, D. J. (2009). Bologna in America: The Spellings Commission and neoliberal higher education policy. *Learning and Teaching, 2*(1), 1–38.

Greenwood, D. J., & Levin, M. (1998a). *Introduction to action research: Social research for social change.* Thousand Oaks, CA: Sage.

Greenwood, D. J., & Levin, M. (1998b). The reconstruction of universities: Seeking a different integration into knowledge development processes. *Concepts and Transformation, 21*(2), 145–163.

Greenwood, D. J., & Levin, M. (2000). Reconstructing the relationships between universities and society through action research. In N. K. Denzin & Y. S. Lincoln (Eds.), *Handbook of qualitative research* (2nd ed., pp. 85–106). Thousand Oaks, CA: Sage.

Greenwood, D. J., & Levin, M. (2001a). Pragmatic action research and the struggle to transform universities into learning communities. In P. Reason & H. Bradbury (Eds.), *Handbook of action research* (pp. 103–114). Thousand Oaks, CA: Sage.

Greenwood, D. J., & Levin, M. (2001b). Reorganizing universities and "knowing how": University restructuring and knowledge creation for the twenty-first century. *Organization, 8*(2), 433–440.

Greenwood, D. J., & Levin, M. (2005). Reform of the social sciences and of universities through action research. In N. K. Denzin & Y. S. Lincoln (Eds.), *The SAGE handbook of qualitative research* (3rd ed., pp. 43–64). Thousand Oaks, CA: Sage.

Greenwood, D. J., & Levin, M. (2007). *Introduction to action research: Social research for social change* (2nd ed.). Thousand Oaks, CA: Sage.

Habermas, J. (1984). *The theory of communicative action: Reason and the rationality of society.* Boston: Beacon.

Heron, J. (1996). *Co-operative inquiry: Research into the human condition.* London: Sage.

Hittleman, M. (2007). *Counting caring: Accountability, performance, and learning at the Greater Ithaca Activities Center.* Unpublished doctoral dissertation, Cornell University, Ithaca, NY.

Johnson, H. T., & Kaplan, R. (1987). *Relevance lost: The rise and fall of management accounting.* Cambridge, MA: Harvard Business Press.

Kassam, K.-A. (2005). *Diversity, ways of knowing, and validity—a demonstration of relations between the biological and the cultural among indigenous peoples of the circumpolar north.* Unpublished doctoral dissertation, Cornell University, Ithaca, NY.

Kirp, D. L. (2003). *Shakespeare, Einstein, and the bottom line: The marketing of higher education.* Cambridge, MA: Harvard University Press.

Klemsdal, L. (2008). *Making sense of the "new way of organizing": Managing the micro processes of planned change in a municipality.* Unpublished doctoral dissertation, Norwegian University of Science and Technology, Department of Industrial Economics and Technology Management, Trondheim.

Kolb, D. (1984). *Experiential learning.* Englewood Cliffs, NJ: Prentice Hall.

Levin, M. (2003). Action research and the research community. *Concepts and Transformation, 8*(3), 275–280.

Levin, M., & Greenwood, D. J. (1998). Action research, science, and co-optation of social research. *Studies in Cultures, Organizations, and Societies, 4*(2), 237–261.

Levin, M., & Martin, A. W. (Eds.). (2007). The praxis of education action researchers [Special issue]. *Action Research, 5,* 249–264.

MacMahon, W. W. (2009). *Higher learning, greater good: The private and social benefits of higher education.* Baltimore. Johns Hopkins University Press.

Marginson, S., & Considine, M. (2000). *The enterprise university: Power, governance, and reinvention in Australia.* Cambridge, UK: Cambridge University Press.

McLaren, P., & Farahmandpur, R. (2005). *Teaching against global capitalism and the new imperialism.* Lanham, MD: Rowman & Littlefield.

McLaren, P., & Jaramillo, N. (2007). *Pedagogy and praxis.* Boston: Sense Publishers.

Mezirow, J. (1991). *Transformative dimensions of adult learning.* San Francisco: Jossey-Bass.

Newfield, C. (2008). *Unmaking the public university: The forty-year assault on the middle class.* Cambridge, MA: Harvard University Press.

Nowotny, H., Scott, P., & Gibbons, M. (2001). *Re-thinking science: Knowledge and the public in the age of uncertainty.* London: Sage.

Prange, K. (2004, November). Bildung: A paradigm regained? *European Educational Research Journal, 3,* 501–509.

Price, D. (2004). *Threatening anthropology.* Durham, NC: Duke University Press.

Raymer, A. L. (2007). *Democratic places through democratic means with participatory evaluative action research (PEAR), a model of inquiry for habits and habitats where public life matters.* Unpublished doctoral dissertation, Cornell University, Ithaca, NY.

Reason, P. (Ed.). (1994). *Participation in human inquiry.* London: Sage.

Ruiz-Casares, M. (2006). *Strengthening the capacity of child-headed households in Namibia to meet their own needs: A social networks approach.* Unpublished doctoral dissertation, Cornell University, Ithaca, NY.

Skjervheim, H. (1974). *Objektivismen og studiet av mennesket* [Objectivity and the study of man]. Oslo, Norway: Gyldendal.

Skule, S. (1994). *From skills to organizational practice: A study of the relation between vocational education and organizational learning in the food-processing industry.* Unpublished doctoral dissertation, Norwegian University of Science and Technology, Department of Industrial Management and Work Science, Trondheim.

Slaughter, S., & Leslie, L. L. (1997). *Academic capitalism: Politics, policies, and the entrepreneurial university.* Baltimore: Johns Hopkins University Press.

Toulmin, S. (1990). *Cosmopolis: The hidden agenda of modernity.* Chicago: University of Chicago Press.

Vasily, L. (2006). *Reading one's life: A case study of an adult educational participatory action research curriculum development project for Nepali Dalit social justice.* Unpublished doctoral dissertation, Cornell University, Ithaca, NY.

Washburn, J. (2005). *University, Inc.: The corporate corruption of American higher education.* New York: Basic Books.

Wright, S., Brenneis, D., & Shore, C. (Eds.). (2005). Universities and the politics of accountability [Special issue]. *Anthropology in Action, 12*(1).

3

A History of Qualitative Inquiry in Social and Educational Research[1]

Frederick Erickson

Qualitative inquiry seeks to discover and to describe in narrative reporting what particular people do in their everyday lives and what their actions mean to them. It identifies meaning-relevant *kinds* of things in the world—kinds of people, kinds of actions, kinds of beliefs and interests—focusing on differences in forms of things that make a difference for meaning. (From Latin, *qualitas* refers to a primary focus on the qualities, the features, of entities—to distinctions in kind—while the contrasting term *quantitas* refers to a primary focus on differences in amount.) The qualitative researcher first asks, "What are the kinds of things (material and symbolic) to which people in this setting orient as they conduct everyday life?" The quantitative researcher first asks, "How many instances of a certain kind are there here?" In these terms, quantitative inquiry can be seen as always being preceded by foundational qualitative inquiry, and in social research, quantitative analysis goes haywire when it tries to shortcut the qualitative foundations of such research—it then ends up counting the wrong kinds of things in its attempts to answer the questions it is asking.

This chapter will consider major phases in the development of qualitative inquiry. Because of the scale of published studies using qualitative methods, the citations of literature present illustrative examples of work in each successive phase of qualitative inquiry's development rather than an exhaustive review of literature in any particular phase. I have referred the reader at various points to additional literature reviews and historical accounts of qualitative methods, and at the outset, I want to acknowledge the comprehensive historical chapter by Arthur Vidich and Stanford Lyman (1994, pp. 23–59), which was published in the first edition of this *Handbook*. Our discussion here takes a somewhat different perspective concerning the crisis in authority that has developed in qualitative inquiry over the last 30 years.

This chapter is organized both chronologically and thematically. It considers relationships evolving over time between five foundational "footings" for qualitative research: (1) disciplinary perspectives in social science, particularly in sociology and anthropology; (2) the participant-observational fieldworker as an observer/author; (3) the people who are observed during the fieldwork; (4) the rhetorical and substantive content of the qualitative research report as a text; and (5) the audiences to which such texts have been addressed. The character and legitimacy of each of these "footings," have been debated over the entire course of qualitative social inquiry's development, and these debates have increased in intensity in the recent past.

I. Origins of Qualitative Research

In the ancient world, there were precursors to qualitative social inquiry. Herodotus, a Greek scholar writing in the 5th century B.C.E., had interests that were cross-cultural as well as historical. Writing in the 2nd century C.E., the Greek skeptical philosopher Sextus Empiricus conducted a cross-cultural survey of morality, showing that what was considered right in one society was considered wrong in others. Both he and Herodotus worked from the accounts of travelers, which provided the primary basis for comparative knowledge about human lifeways until the late 19th century. Knowledge of nature also was reported descriptively, as in the physics of Aristotle and the medicine of Galen.

Descriptive reporting of everyday social practices flourished again in the Renaissance and Baroque eras in the publication of "how to do it books" such as Baldassar Castiglione's *The Book of the Courtier* and the writing of Thoinot Arbeau (*Orchésographie*) on courtly dancing, of Johann Comenius (*Didactica Magna*) on pedagogy, of Isaak Walton (*The Compleat Angler*) on fishing, and of John Playford (*The Division Viol*) on how to improvise in playing the viola da gamba. The treatises on dancing and music especially were descriptive accounts of very particular practices—step-by-step description at molecular grain size. Narrative descriptive reports were also written in broader terms, such as the accounts of the situation of Native Americans under early Spanish colonial rule in Latin America, written by Bartolomeo de las Casas in the 16th century, and the

17th-century reports French Jesuits submitted to superiors regarding their missionary work in North America (*Relations*). A tension between scope and specificity of description remains in contemporary qualitative inquiry and reporting.

Simultaneously with the 17th-century writing on everyday practices, the quantitative physics of Galileo Galilei and Isaac Newton was being established. As the Enlightenment developed, quantitatively based inquiry became the standard for physical science. The search was for general laws that would apply uniformly throughout the physical world and for causal relations that would obtain universally. Could there be an equivalent to this in the study of social life—a "social physics"—in which social processes were monitored by means of frequency tabulation and generalizations about social processes could be derived from the analysis of frequency data? In England, William Petty's *Political Arithmetic* was one such attempt, published in 1690. In France and Germany, the term *statistics* began to be used to refer to quantitative information collected for purposes of the state—information about finance, population, disease, and mortality. Some of the French Enlightenment philosophers of the 18th century saw the possibility that social processes could be mathematically modeled and that theories of the state and of political economy could be formulated and empirically verified in ways that would parallel physics, chemistry, and astronomy.

As time went on, a change of focus occurred in published narrative descriptive accounts of daily practices. In the 16th and 17th centuries, the activities of the leisured classes were described, while the lower classes were portrayed patronizingly at the edges of the action, as greedy, lascivious, and deceitful, albeit clever. (A late example can be found in the portrayal of the lusty, pragmatic countrymen and women in Picander's libretto for J. S. Bach's *Peasant Cantata*, written and performed in 1742.) By the end of the 18th century, the everyday lives of servants and rustics were being portrayed in a more sympathetic way. Pierre Beaumarchais's play, *The Marriage of Figaro*, is an example. Written in 1778, it was initially banned in both Paris and Vienna on the grounds that by valorizing its servant characters and satirizing its aristocratic characters, it was dangerously subversive and incited insubordination. By the early 19th century, the Brothers Grimm were collecting the tales of German peasants, and documentation of folklore and folklife of commoners became a general practice.

By the mid-19th century, attempts were being made to define foundations for the systematic conduct of social inquiry. A fundamental disagreement developed over what kind of a "science" the study of society should be. Should such inquiry be modeled after the physical sciences, as Enlightenment philosophers had hoped? That is what Auguste Comte (1822/2001) claimed as he developed a science of society he would come to call *sociology*; his contemporary, Adolphe

Quetelet (1835/2010) advocated the use of statistics to accomplish a "social physics." Early anthropologists with foundational interests in social and cultural evolution also aimed their inquiry toward generalization (e.g., Morgan, 1877; Tylor, 1871); they saw the comparative study of humans as aiming for general knowledge, in their case, an understanding of processes of change across time in physical and cultural ways of being human—of universal stages of development from barbarism to contemporary (European) civilization—comparative study that came to be called *ethnology*. Like Comte, they saw the purposes of social inquiry as the discovery of causal laws that applied to all cases, laws akin to those of physics and chemistry.

In contrast, the German social philosopher Wilhelm Dilthey (1883/1989) advocated an approach that differed from that of natural sciences (which he called *Naturwissenschaften*). He advocated conducting social inquiry as *Geisteswissenschaften*—literally "sciences of the spirit" and more freely translated as "human sciences" or, better, "human studies." Such inquiry was common to both the humanities and what we would now call the social sciences. It focused on the particulars of meaning and action taken in everyday life. The purpose of inquiry in the human sciences was understanding (*verstehen*) rather than proof or prediction. Dilthey's ideas influenced younger scholars—in particular Max Weber and Georg Simmel in sociology and early phenomenologists in philosophy such as Edmund Husserl and Martin Heidegger. His ideas became even more influential in the mid-20th century "hermeneutical turn" taken by philosophers such as Hans-Georg Gadamer and Jürgen Habermas and by anthropologists such as Ernest Gellner and Clifford Geertz.

The emergence of ethnography. In the last quarter of the 19th century, anthropologists began to use the term *ethnography* for descriptive accounts of the lifeways of particular local sets of people who lived in colonial situations around the world. These accounts, it was claimed, were more accurate and comprehensive than the reports of travelers and colonial administrators. In an attempt to improve the information quality and comprehensiveness of description in traveler's accounts, as well as to support the fieldwork of scholars in the emerging field of anthropology, the British Society for the Advancement of Science published in 1874 a manual to guide data collection in observation and interviewing, titled *Notes and Queries on Anthropology for the Use of Travelers and Residents in Uncivilized Lands* (available at http://www.archive.org/details/notesandqueries00readgoog). The editorial committee for the 1874 edition of *Notes and Queries* included George Lane-Fox Pitt-Rivers, Edward Tylor, and Francis Galton, the latter being one of the founders of modern statistics. The *Notes and*

Queries manual continued to be reissued in further editions by the Royal Anthropological Society, with the sixth and last edition appearing in 1951.

At 6 ½ by 4 inches, the book could be carried to field settings in a large pocket, such as that of a bush jacket or suit coat. Rulers in both inches and centimeters are stamped on the edge of the cover to allow the observer to readily measure objects encountered in the field. The volume contains a broad range of questions and observation topics for what later became the distinct branches of physical anthropology and social/cultural anthropology: topics include anatomical and medical observations, clothing, navigation, food, religion, laws, and "contact with civilized races," among others. The goal was an accurate collection of facts and a comprehensive description of the whole way of life of those who were being studied.

This encyclopedic approach to fieldwork and information collection characterized late 19th-century qualitative research, for example, the early fieldwork of Franz Boas on the northwest coast of North America and the two expeditions to the Torres Straits in Oceania led by Alfred Haddon. The second Haddon expedition involved fieldworkers who would teach the next generation of British anthropologists—for example, W. H. R. Rivers and C. G. Seligman, with whom A. R. Radcliffe Brown and B. Malinowski later studied. (For further discussion of the early history of field methods in anthropology, see Urrey, 1984, pp. 33–61.)

This kind of data collection and reporting in overseas settings was called *ethnography*, combining two Greek words: *graphein*, the verb for "to write," and *ethnoi*, a plural noun for "the nations—the others." For the ancient Greeks, the *ethnoi* were people who were not Greek—Thracians, Persians, Egyptians, and so on—contrasting with *Ellenoi* or Hellenes, as us versus them. The Greeks were more than a little xenophobic, so that ethnoi carries pejorative implications. In the Greek translation of the Hebrew scriptures, *ethnoi* was the translation for the Hebrew term for "them"—*goyim*—which is not a compliment. Given its etymology and its initial use in the 19th century for descriptive accounts of non-Western people, the best definition for ethnography is "writing about other people."

Perhaps the first monograph of the kind that would become modern realist ethnography was *The Philadelphia Negro*, by W. E. B. DuBois (1899). His study of a particular African American census tract combined demographic data, area maps, recent community history, surveys of local institutions and community groups, and some descriptive accounts of the conduct of daily life in the neighborhood. His purpose was to make visible the lives—and the orderliness in those lives—of people who had been heretofore invisible and voiceless in the discourses of middle class white society and academia. A similar purpose and descriptive approach, combining demography and health statistics with narrative accounts, was taken in the reports of working class life in East London by Charles Booth (1891), whose collaborators included Sidney and Beatrice Webb. Even more emphasis on narrative description was found in *How the Other Half Lives*, an account of the everyday life of immigrants on the lower East Side of New York City, written by the journalist Jacob Riis (1890) and illustrated with photographs. All of these authors—and especially Booth and DuBois—aimed for factual accuracy and holistic scope. Moreover, these authors were social reformers—Booth and the Webbs within the Fabian Socialist movement in England, Riis as a founder of "muckraking" journalism and popular sociology, and DuBois as an academic sociologist who turned increasingly to activism, becoming a leader of the early 20th-century African American civil rights movement. Beyond description for its own sake, their purpose was to advocate for and to inform social change.

None of these early practitioners claimed to be describing everyday life from the points of view of those who lived it. They were outsider observers. DuBois, although an African American, grew up in a small New England town, not Philadelphia, and he had a Harvard education. Booth and the Webbs were upper middle class, and so was Riis. They intended to provide accurate descriptions of "facts" about behavior, presented as self-evidently accurate and "objective," but not about their functional significance in use, or as Clifford Geertz (1973) said, what distinguishes an eye blink from a wink (p. 6). To use terms that developed later in linguistics and metaphorically applied to ethnography, their descriptions were *etic* rather than *emic* in content and epistemological status.

Adding point of view. Portraying social action (as wink) rather than behavior (as eye blink)—that is, describing the conduct of everyday life in ways that make contact with the subjective orientations and meaning perspectives of those whose conduct is being reported—is the fundamental shift in interpretive (hermeneutical) stance within ethnography that Bronislaw Malinowski claimed to have accomplished a generation later. In his groundbreaking monograph, *Argonauts of the Western Pacific* (Malinowski, 1922), he said that ethnographic description should not only be holistic and factually accurate, but should aim "to grasp the native's point of view, his relation to life, his vision of his world" (p. 25).

During World War I, Malinowski, a Pole who had studied anthropology in England, was interned by British colonial authorities during his fieldwork in the Trobriand Islands of Melanesia because they were concerned that, as a subject of the Austro-Hungarian Empire, he might be a spy. He was not allowed to return home until the war had ended. Malinowski later made a virtue of necessity and claimed that his 4 years of enforced fieldwork and knowledge of the local language enabled him to write a report that encompassed the system of everyday life in its entirety and accurately represented nuances of local meaning in its daily conduct. After Malinowski, this became a hallmark of ethnography in anthropology—reporting that included the meaning perspectives of those whose daily actions were being described.

Interpretively oriented (i.e., hermeneutic) realist ethnography presumed that *local meaning* is causal in social life and that local meaning varies fundamentally (albeit sometimes subtly) from one local setting to another. One way this manifested in anthropology was through cultural relativism—a position that Franz Boas had taken before Malinowski. By the late 1920s, anthropologists were presuming that because human societies were very different culturally, careful ethnographic case study documentation was necessary before valid ethnological comparison could take place—the previous armchair speculations of scholars like Edward Tylor and Lewis Henry Morgan were seen as having been premature.

What is implied in the overall emphasis on the distinctive differences in local meaning from one setting to another is a presumption that stands in sharp contrast to a basic presumption in natural science. There one assumes a fundamental *uniformity of nature* in the physical universe. For example, one can assume that a unit measurement of heat, or of force, or a particular chemical element is the same entity in Mexico City and Tokyo as it is in London—and also on the face of the sun and in a far distant galaxy. The presumption of uniformity of natural elements and processes permitted the statement of general laws of nature in physics, chemistry, and astronomy, and to a lesser extent in biology. In contrast, a human science focus on locally constructed meaning and its variability in construction presumes, in effect, a fundamental *nonuniformity of nature in social life.* That assumption was anathema to those who were searching for a social physics. But qualitative social inquiry is not aiming to be a social physics. Or is it? Within anthropology, sociology, and educational research, researchers disagreed about this, even as they did ethnographic case studies in traditional and modern societies.

A basic, mainstream approach was developing in qualitative social inquiry. We can see that approach as resting on five foundational grounds or footings: the disciplinary enterprise of social science, the social scientific observer, those who are observed, the research report as a text, and the research audience to which that text is addressed. Each of these five was considered as an entity whose nature was simple and whose legitimacy was self-evident. In current qualitative inquiry, the nature and the legitimacy of each of those footings have been called into question.

First, the *enterprise of social science.* By the late 19th century, sociology and anthropology were developing as new disciplines, beginning to achieve acceptance within universities. Physical sciences had made great progress since the 17th century, and social scientists were hoping for similar success.

Next, the *social scientist as observer*. His (and these were men) professional warrant for paying research attention to other humans was the social scientific enterprise in which he was engaged—that engagement gave him the right to watch other people and question them. It was assumed that he would and should be systematic and disinterestedly open-minded in the exercise of research attention. The process of looking closely and carefully at another human was seen as being no more ethically or epistemologically problematic than looking closely and carefully at a rock or a bird. Collecting specimens of human activity was justifiable because it would lead to new knowledge about social life. (Unlike the field biologist the social scientist was not justified to kill those he studied or to capture them for later observation in a zoological museum—although some non-Western people were exhibited at world expositions and the anthropologist Alfred Kroeber had housed a Native American, Ishi, at the anthropological museum of the University of California, Berkeley, making him available for observation and interview there—but artifact collecting and the writing of field-notes were the functional equivalent of the specimen collection and analysis methods of biologists and geologists.) Moreover, research attention in social inquiry was a one-way matter—just as the field biologist dissected an animal specimen and not the other way around, it was the researcher's watching and asking that counted in social inquiry, not the attending to and questioning of the researcher by the people whose daily lives were being studied.

Those who were observed as research objects (not as subjects but as objects) were thus considered as essentially passive participants in the research enterprise—patients rather than agents—there to be acted upon by observing and questioning, not there to affect the direction taken in the inquiry. Thus, in the division of labor within the process of qualitative social inquiry, a fundamental line of distinction and asymmetry was drawn between the observer and the observed, with control over the inquiry maximized for the observer and minimized for the observed.

That asymmetry extended to the process of *producing the text of a research report*, which was entirely the responsibility of the social scientist as author. Such reports were not written in collaboration with those whose lives were studied, nor were they accompanied by parallel reports produced by those who were studied (just as the finches of the Galapagos islands had not published a report of Darwin's visit to them). In reports of the results of social inquiry by means of firsthand participant observation, the portrayal of everyday life of the people studied was done by the researcher.

The asymmetry in text production extended further to text consumption. The written report of social inquiry was addressed to *an audience consisting of people other than those who had been studied*—the community of the researcher's fellow social scientists (and perhaps, of policymakers who might commission the research work). This audience had as its primary interests the substantive significance of the research topic and the technical quality of the conduct of the study. The success of the report (and of the author's status as a reporter) was a matter of judgment residing in the scholarly community. The research objects' existential experience of being scrutinized during the researcher's fieldwork and then described in the researcher's report was not a primary consideration for the readers of the report, nor for its author. Indeed those who had been studied were not expected to read the research report, since many were not literate.

For a time, each of these five footings had the stability of canonical authority in the "normal science" practice of qualitative inquiry. That was a period that could be called a "golden age," but with a twinge of irony in such a designation, given what we now know about the intense contestation that has developed recently concerning each of the footings.

II. A "Golden Age" of Realist Ethnography

From the mid 1920s to the early 1950s, the basic approach in qualitative inquiry was realist general ethnography—at the time it was just called *ethnography*. More recently, such work has been called *realist* because of its literary quality of "you are there" reporting, in which the narrator presents description as if it were plain fact, and *general* because it attempted a comprehensive description of a whole way of life in the particular setting that was being described—a setting (such as a village or an island or, later, an urban neighborhood or workplace within a formal organization) that was seen as being distinctly bounded. Typically, the narrator wrote in third person and did not portray him- or herself as being present in the scenes of daily life that were described. A slightly distanced authorial voice was intended to convey an impression of even-handedness—conveying "the native's point of view" without either overt advocacy of customary practices or explicit critique of them. (For a discussion of the stance of detachment, see Vidich & Lyman, 1994, p. 23.) Usually, the social theory perspective underlying such work was some form of functionalism, and this led authors to focus less on conflict as a driving force in society and more on the complementarity of various social institutions and processes within the local setting.

Ethnographic monographs in anthropology during this time followed the overall approach found in Bronislaw Malinowski's (1922) *Argonauts*, where he said that an adequate ethnography should report three primary bodies of evidence:

1. *The organisation of the tribe, and the anatomy of its culture* must be recorded in firm, clear outline. The method of *concrete, statistical documentation* is the means through which such an outline has to be given.

2. Within this frame *the imponderabilia of actual life*, and the *type of behaviour* must be filled in. They have to be collected through minute, detailed observations, in the form of some sort of ethnographic diary, made possible by close contact with native life.

3. A collection of ethnographic statements, characteristic narratives, typical utterances, items of folk-lore, and magical formulae has to be given as a *corpus inscriptionem*, as documents of native mentality. (p. 24)

What was studied was a certain village or region in which a named ethnic/linguistic group resided. The monograph usually began with an overall description of the physical setting (and often of subsistence activities). This was followed by a chapter on an annual cycle of life, one on a typical day, one on kinship and other aspects of "social organization," one on child rearing, and then chapters on certain features of the setting that were distinctive to it. (Thus, for example, Evans-Pritchard's 1940 monograph on a herding people, *The Nuer*, contains detailed description of the aesthetics of appreciation of color patterns in cowhide.) Narrative vignettes describing the actions of particular people in an actual event were sometimes provided, or typical actions were described more synoptically. These vignettes and quotes from informants were linked in the text by narrating commentary. Often maps, frequency tables, and analytic charts (including kinship diagrams) were included.

Notable examples in British and American anthropology during this period include volumes by students of Franz Boas, such as Margaret Mead's (1928) semipopular account, *Coming of Age in Samoa*. Raymond Firth, a student of Malinowski, produced *We the Tikopia* (1936/2004), E. E. Evans-Pritchard, a student of Malinowski's contemporary, Alfred Radcliffe-Brown (who himself had published a monograph *The Andaman Islanders* in the same year as Malinowski's *Argonauts*, 1922) published *The Nuer* in 1940. David Holmberg (1950) published a study of the Siriono, titled *Nomads of the Longbow*. In addition to American work on indigenous peoples of the Western Hemisphere, there were monograph series published on British colonial areas—from Australia, studies of New

Guinea, Micronesia, and Melanesia, and from England, studies of East Africa, West Africa, and South Africa.

In the United States, community studies in an anthropologically ethnographic vein were encouraged by Robert Park and Ernest Burgess at the department of sociology of the University of Chicago. On the basis of hunches about geographic determinism in the founding and maintenance of distinct social areas within cities, various Chicago neighborhoods were treated as if they were bounded communities, for example, Louis Wirth's (1928) study of the West Side Jewish ghetto and Harvey Warren Zorbaugh's (1929) study of contiguous working-class Italian and upper class "mainstream American" neighborhoods on the near North Side. A tradition of community study followed in American sociology. Robert and Helen Lynd (1929, 1937) conducted a two-volume study of a small Midwestern city, Muncie, Indiana, which they called Middletown. The anthropologist W. Lloyd Warner studied Newburyport, Massachusetts (1941), the Italian neighborhood of Boston's North End was described by William F. Whyte (1943/1955), and the anthropologists Conrad Arensberg and Solon Kimball studied a rural Irish village (1940).

The urban community studies efforts continued after World War II, with St. Clair Drake and Horace Cayton's (1945) description of the African American neighborhoods of Chicago's South Side and Herbert J. Gans's report (1962) on an Italian American neighborhood in New York, among others. Gerald Suttles (1968) revisited the "social areas" orientation of Chicago School sociology in a study of interethnic relations in a multi-ethnic neighborhood on Chicago's Near West Side, and Elijah Anderson (1992) described a multiracial West Philadelphia neighborhood in a somewhat similar vein. Some studies narrowed the scope of community studies from a whole neighborhood to a particular setting within it, as in the case of bars as sites for friendship networks among African American men in the reports (e.g., Liebow, 1967). Rural sociology in America during the 1930s had also produced ethnographic accounts. (For an extensive review and listing of American community studies, see the discussion in Vidich & Lyman, 1994.)

Institutional and workplace studies began to be done ethnographically, especially in the postwar era. Labor-management relations were studied by means of participant observation (e.g., Roy, 1959). Chris Argyris published descriptive accounts of daily work in a bank department (1954a, 1954b) and of the worklife of a business executive (1953). Ethnographic accounts of socialization into professions began to appear (e.g., Becker & Geer, 1961; Glaser & Strauss, 1965). Workplace accounts, as in community studies, began to focus more closely on immediate scenes of everyday social interaction, a trend that continued into the future (see, e.g., Vaught & Smith, 1980; Fine, 1990).

Journal-length reports of workplace studies (as well as accounts of overseas development interventions by applied anthropologists) appeared in the interdisciplinary journal *Human Organization,* which began publication under that title in 1948, sponsored by the Society for Applied Anthropology.

Ethnographic documentary film developed in the 1950s and 1960s as field recording of sound became easier, with more portable equipment—audiotape and the 16-mm camera. Boas had used silent film in the 1920s to document Kwakiutl life on the Northwest Coast of Canada, and Gregory Bateson and Mead used silent film in the late 1930s in their study of dance instruction in Bali. Robert Flaherty produced semifictional, partially staged films of Canadian Inuit in the 1920s, notably *Nanook of the North.*

The new ethnographic documentaries were shot in naturalistic field situations, using for the most part hand-held cameras and microphones in order to move with the action. John Marshall's film, *The Hunters,* featured Kalahari Bushmen of southern Africa; Napoleon Chagnon's "The Ax Fight" and Tim Asch's "The Feast" were filmed in the Amazon River Delta in Brazil, among the Yanomamo. John Adair and Sol Worth gave 16 mm hand-held cameras to Navaho informants in a project that tried to identify differences in ways of seeing between the Navaho and Western European cinematographers. They produced film footage and a monograph on the project titled, "Through Navaho Eyes" (Worth & Adair, 1972). John Collier Jr. shot extensive silent film footage showing Native American school classrooms in Alaska. He also published a book on the use of still photographs for ethnographic documentation (Collier, 1967)—a practice that Mead had pioneered a generation earlier (see Byers, 1966, 1968). The Society for Visual Anthropology, a network of ethnographic filmmakers and scholars of documentary film semiotics, was founded in 1984.

U.S. sociologists made institutionally focused documentary films during the same time period, notably the films produced in the 1960s and 1970s by Frederick Wiseman. These interpretive film essays, through the editing of footage of naturally occurring events, bridge fiction and more literal documentary depiction. They include "Titicut Follies" (1967), a portrayal of a mental hospital; "High School" (1968); "Hospital" (1970); and "Essene" (1972), a portrayal of conflict and community in a monastery (for further discussion, see Barnouw, 1993; Benson & Anderson 2002; deBrigard, 1995; Heider, 1982; Ruby, 2000).

III. Crises in Ethnographic Authority

A gathering storm. Even in the postwar heyday of realist ethnography, some cracks in its footings were beginning to appear. In American anthropology, a bitter controversy developed over accuracy and validity of competing ethnographic descriptions of a village on the outskirts of Mexico City, Tepoztlán. Robert Redfield (1930) at the University of Chicago had published an account of everyday life in Tepoztlán; in keeping with a functionalist perspective in social theory, he characterized the community as harmonious and internally consistent, a place where people led predictable, happy lives. Beginning fieldwork in the same village 17 years after Redfield and viewing everyday life in the community through a lens of Marxist conflict theory, Oscar Lewis (1951) saw life in Tepoztlán as fraught with tension and individual villagers as tending toward continual anger, jealousy, and anxiety; in his monograph, he harshly criticized Redfield's portrayal. Two fieldworkers had gone to the "same" place and collected very different evidence. Which one was right?

Concern was developing over texts that reported the general ethnography of a whole community—those reports seemed increasingly to be hazy in terms of evidence: Description flowed a mile wide but an inch deep. One way to address this limitation was to narrow the scope of research description and to focus on a particular setting within a larger community or institution. Another way was to become more careful in handling evidence. Within American anthropology, specialized "hyphenated" subfields of sociocultural study developed, such as cognitive anthropology, economic anthropology, anthropology of law, ethnography of communication, and interactional sociolinguistics. Studies in those subfields were often published as tightly focused journal-length articles in which evidence was presented deliberately and specifically. Careful elicitation techniques and increasing use of audio and audiovisual recording were used in attempts to get "better data." An interdisciplinary field called sociolinguistics developed across the disciplines of linguistics, anthropology, sociology, and social psychology.

In sociology first and then increasingly in anthropology, methods texts were published—becoming more explicit about methods of participant observation as another route to "better data." Notable examples are McCall and Simmons (1969), Glaser and Strauss (1967), Denzin (1970), Pelto and Pelto (1970), Hammersley and Atkinson (1983), Ellen (1984), and Sanjek (1990).

Autobiographical accounts of fieldwork also began to be published. The second edition of Whyte's *Street Corner Society* (1943/1955) and subsequent editions contained an extensive appendix in which Whyte described, in first person, his field experience. Hortense Powdermaker (1966) described her field experience in White and Black Southern U.S. rural communities in the 1930s. Even earlier, Laura Bohannon had published a fictionalized memoir of fieldwork, writing a quasi-novel under the pseudonym Elenore Smith Bowen (1954) because frank revelations of ambivalence, ethical dilemmas, the intense emotionality of fieldwork, and tendencies toward self-deception were not considered proper topics of "academic" discourse at the time. Rosalie Wax (1971) candidly recalled the difficulties of her fieldwork as a White woman in Japanese internment camps during World War II. These accounts showed that actual fieldwork was not so consistently guided by detached, means-ends rationality as ethnographic monographs had sometimes suggested. In 1967, Malinowski's Trobriand Island field diary was published posthumously. Over the next 15 years, the diary came to occupy a central place in what became a firestorm of criticism of realist general ethnography.

After World War II, the accuracy of ethnography began to draw challenges from the "natives" whose lives were portrayed in them. Thirty years after Malinowski left the Trobriands, Father Baldwin, a Roman Catholic missionary who succeeded him there, reported in a master's thesis how the "natives" had reacted to the text of *Argonauts*. Baldwin had lived on the island of Boyowa longer than Malinowski had done and learned the local language more thoroughly. To check the validity of Malinowski's portrayal of the "native's point of view," Father Baldwin translated large portions of *Argonauts* and read those texts with the Boyowans he knew, some of whom remembered Malinowski's presence among them:

> He seems to have left nothing unexplained and his explanations are enlightening, even to the people who live there. It is curious, then, that this exhaustive research, and patient, wise, and honest explanation, should leave a sense of incompleteness. But it does. I feel that his material is still not properly digested, that Malinowski would be regarded in some ways naive by the people he was studying . . .
>
> I was surprised at the number of times informants helping me with checking Malinowski would bridle. Usually when a passage has been gone over more than once, they would say it was not like that. They did not quarrel with facts or explanations, but with the coloring as it were. The sense expressed was not the sense they had of themselves or of things Boyowan. (Baldwin, n.d., pp. 17–18, as cited in Young, 1979, pp. 15–16)

Vine deLoria, a Native American, was more harsh in his criticism of American anthropologists, in a book evocatively titled *Custer Died for Your Sins* (1969). He characterized Amerindian studies done by American anthropologists as ethnocentric and implicitly colonialist. Sociological community studies also drew negative reactions from the "natives." Some small-town residents in rural New York were deeply offended by the monograph titled, *Small Town in Mass Society* (Vidich & Bensman, 1958; see Vidich's discussion of this reaction in Vidich &

Bensman, 2000, and in Young, 1996). They castigated the authors for inaccuracy, for taking sides in local disputes, and for violating the confidentiality of individuals (e.g., there being only one mayor, his anonymity was compromised even though his name was not used; this later became a classic example of ethical difficulties in the conduct of qualitative research and its reporting.) The rise of Black nationalism in African American communities in the late 1960s (and the reaction of African American scholars to the "blame the victim" tone of studies about inner-city families such as that of Moynihan, 1965) gave further impetus to the contention that only "insiders" could study fellow insiders in ways that would be unbiased and accurate.

This directly contradicted the traditional view that an outsider researcher, with enough time to develop close acquaintance, could accurately observe and interpret meaning, without being limited by the insider's tendency to overlook phenomena so familiar they were taken for granted and had become invisible. As the anthropologist Clyde Kluckhohn (1949) put it in a vivid metaphor: "It would hardly be fish who discovered the existence of water" (p. 11).

This was not only a matter of inaccurate conclusions—it also had to do with the power relations that obtained in the conduct of "participant observation" itself. Various feminist authors, in a distinct yet related critique of standard anthropology and sociology, pointed out that fieldworkers should attend to their own mentality/subjectivity as a perceiving *subject* trying to make sense of others' lives, especially when power relations between the observer and the observed were asymmetric. An early instantiation of these perspectives was Jean Briggs's (1970) study of her conflicting relationships with an Inuit (Canadian Eskimo) nuclear family with whom she lived during fieldwork. Titled *Never in Anger,* her monograph reported in first person and placed her self and her reactions to her "informants" centrally in the narrative picture her monograph presented.

The notion that the researcher always sees from within (and is also blinded by) the power relationships between her and those she studies was pointedly explicated in Dorothy Smith's 1974 essay "Women's Perspective as a Radical Critique of Sociology." That idea continues to evolve in feminist criticism (see, e.g., Harding, 1991; Lather, 1991) that advocates reflexivity regarding the personal standpoints, the positionality, through which the fieldworker perceives— gendered, classed, age-graded, and raced/ethnicized ways of seeing and feeling in the world, especially as these are in part mutually constructed in the interaction that takes place between the observer and observed.

George Marcus and James Clifford (1986; Clifford, 1988) extended this line of criticism in the mid 1980s, a period when Malinowski became a prime target for those who considered conventional "participant observation" to be deeply flawed. With the publication of his *Diary*, Malinowski had become an easy target. The diary had unmasked power relationships that his ethnographic reporting had disguised. Thus, Malinowski's portrayal of the "native's point of view" in *Argonauts* may have had to do with the power relationships of his fieldwork. He does not mention this in his discussion of his fieldwork method; rather, he portrays himself simply as a detective, a Sherlock Holmes searching avidly for clues concerning native customs and character (Malinowski, 1922, p. 51):

> It is difficult to convey the feelings of intense interest and suspense with which an ethnographer enters for the first time the district that is to be the future scene of his field work. Certain salient features characteristic of the place had once riveted attention and filled him with hopes or apprehensions. The appearance of the natives, their manner, their types of behavior, may augur well or ill for the possibilities of rapid and easy research. One is on the lookout for the symptoms of deeper sociological facts. One suspects many hidden and mysterious ethnographic phenomena behind the commonplace aspect of things. Perhaps that queer looking, intelligent native is a renowned sorcerer. Perhaps between those two groups of men there exists some important rivalry or vendetta, which may throw much light on the customs and character of the people if one can only lay a hand upon it.

From the diary (Malinowski, 1967), a very different voice sounds—boredom, frustration, hostility, lust.

> December 14, 1917: "When I look at women I think of their breasts and figure in terms of ERM [an Australian woman who he later married]." (pp. 151–152)
> December 17, 1917: "I was fed up with the niggers and with my work." (p. 154)
> December 18, 1917: "I thought about my present attitude toward ethnographic work and the natives, my dislike of them, my longing for civilization." (p. 154)

What went without mention was the asymmetry in power relationships between Malinowski and those he studied. He was the primary initiator of actions toward those around him. Years later, working with the same informants, Father Baldwin (n.d.) reported:

> It was a surprise to me to find that Malinowski was mostly remembered by the natives as a champion ass at asking damn fool questions, like "You bury

the seed tuber root end or sprout end down? . . . They said of him that he made of his profession a sacred cow. You had to defer though you did not see why. (p. 41, as cited in Young, 1979, p. 15)

In contrast, Malinowski's tone in the original monograph suggests a certain smugness and lack of self-awareness: "In fact, as they knew that I would thrust my nose into everything, even where a well-mannered native would not dream of intruding, they finished by regarding me as part and parcel of their life, unnecessary evil or nuisance, mitigated by donations of tobacco" (Malinowski, 1922, p. 8).

Admittedly, the alienation Malinowski revealed in the diary was not unique to him. As Young (1979) puts it,

It is only fair to point out that the chronic sense of alienation which permeates the diary is a common psychic experience of anthropologists in the field, and it is intensified by homesickness, nostalgia, loneliness, and sexual frustration, all of which Malinowski suffered in full measure. (p. 13)

That is humanly true, but it does not square with the popular image of the scientist—rather, it puts the professional social scientist on the same plane as the practical social actor, the "man in the street." Furthermore, it makes one distrust the dispassionate tenor of what Rosaldo (1989, p. 60) called "distanced normalizing description" in ethnographic research reporting.

Malinowski—and the overall credibility of ethnographic research reporting—was further undermined by similar criticism of Margaret Mead. Her first published study, titled *Coming of Age in Samoa* (Mead, 1928), had considered the experience of adolescence from the culturally relativist perspective of her teacher, Boas. Interviewing young Samoan girls and women, Mead concluded that their adolescent years were not emotionally turbulent and that, unlike American teenagers, they were able to engage in sexual experimentation without guilt. Her book attracted a wide popular audience and, together with subsequent popular writing, established Mead's reputation in the United States as a public intellectual. Derek Freeman (1983), an Australian anthropologist, waited until after Mead's death to publish a scathing critique of Mead's research in Samoa. He claimed that Mead had been naive in believing what her informants told her; that they had exaggerated their stories in the direction she had signaled that she wanted to hear. Subsequent consideration suggests that Mead's interpretation was correct overall (see, e.g., Shankman, 1996), but the highly authoritative style of Mead's text (and the lack of systematic presentation of evidence to support the claims she was making) left her vulnerable to the accusation that she had got her findings wrong.

Were all ethnographers self-deceived—or worse, were many of them "just making things up?" The Redfield-Lewis controversy—two vastly different descriptions of the same group—raised an even deeper question: Do the perspective, politics, and ideology of the observer so powerfully influence what he or she notices and reflects on that it overdetermines the conclusions drawn? Realist general ethnography was experiencing heavy weather indeed.

One line of response to these doubts was the "better evidence" movement already discussed. Somewhat earlier, another stream of work had developed that led to participatory action research or collaborative action research. In this approach, outside researchers worked with members of a setting to effect change that was presumed to be of benefit there—for example, improvements in public health, agricultural production, the formation of cooperatives for marketing, and the organization of work in factories. Research efforts accompanied attempts at instituting change, as in the study of local community health practices and beliefs within a project aimed to prevent cholera and dysentery by providing clean water. The social psychologist Kurt Lewin (1946) was one of the pioneers of these attempts, focusing especially on labor-management relations in England. The attempts in England spread through trade union channels into Scandinavia (see Emery & Thorsrud, 1969). Another pioneer was Whyte, working in industrial settings in the United States (see Whyte, Greenwood, & Lazes, 1989).

Also in the period immediately before and after World War II, anthropologists were undertaking change-oriented research overseas, and the Society for Applied Anthropology was founded in 1948. During the 1960s and 1970s, applied anthropologists and linguists worked in action projects in the United States and England in ethnic and racial minority communities (e.g., Gumperz, Roberts, & Jupp, 1979; Schensul & Schensul, 1992).

One line of justification for applied research harked back to the "better evidence" movement: Through a researcher's "involvement in the action" (Schensul, 1974), the accuracy and validity of evidence collection and analysis are tested in conditions of natural experimentation.

Another justification for applied research had to do with the explicit adoption of value positions by action researchers and their community partners. This is similar to the "critical" position in social research that especially took hold in the 1970s and 1980s, and as action research progressed, it combined increasingly with the various critical approaches discussed in the previous section (for elaboration, see Kemmis & McTaggart, 2005).

This aspect of action research led away from the stance of cultural relativism itself—from even the appearance of value neutrality—toward value affirmation. In research efforts to effect social change, explicit value commitments had to be adopted if the work was to make change in specific directions. This was called critical ethnography, related to the "critical theory" perspective articulated by the Frankfurt School. Theodor Adorno and Max Horkheimer had developed a critique, based in neo-Marxist social analysis, of both capitalism and fascism. The point was to criticize whatever material or cultural influences might lead people to take actions or support actions that resulted in limiting their own life chances—that is, their collusion in their own oppression. In Marxist terms one could say that critical theory made visible social processes that worked against the class interests of those being dominated—for example U.S. white workers supporting an oligarchy that oppressed both them and Black workers. Culturally relativist ethnography had not called domination by that name, nor had it named suffering as an object of attention and of description. Critical ethnography claimed to do just that, and in so doing, the ethnographer stepped out of a defended position of value neutrality to one of vulnerability, shifting from distanced relations with informants to relations of solidarity. This was to engage in social inquiry as ethnography "that breaks your heart" (Behar, 1996).

The adoption of an explicit value position created a fixed fulcrum from which analytic leverage could be exerted in distinguishing between which everyday practices led to increase or decrease in life chances (see Bredo & Feinberg 1982). As the critical ethnography movement developed, the focus shifted somewhat from careful explication of the value yardsticks used to judge habitual practices to claims about domination and oppression as if the inequity involved was self-evident. There was a push back from the earlier generation of scholars, who accused critical ethnographers of letting their values so drive their fieldwork that they were able to see only what they expected to see, ignoring disconfirming evidence.

As critical ethnographers identified more and more kinds of inequity, it became apparent that social criticism itself was relative depending on which dimension of superordination/subordination was the locus for analysis. If it was economic relations, then processes of class-based oppression appeared most salient; if gender relations, then patriarchal processes of domination; if postcolonial relations, the survivals of "colonized" status; if sexual identification, then heterosexual domination. And if race became the primary fulcrum for critical social analysis—race, as distinct from, yet as linked to class, gender, colonization, or sexuality—then racial privilege and disprivilege occupied the foreground of attention, with other dimensions of inequity less prominent. Arguments over whose oppression was more heinous or more fundamental—"oppresseder than thou"—took on a sectarian character.

There was also a new relativity in the considerations of the seats of power itself, its manifestations in various aspects or domains, and the ways in which existing patterns of life (including patterns of domination) are reproduced within and across successive generations. Marxism had explained social order as a forcefield of countervailing tensions that were the result of macro-social economic forces. Structural functionalism in anthropology and sociology had explained social order as the result of socialization of individuals, who followed systems of cultural rules. Structuralism in anthropology and linguistics had identified cultural rule systems, which appeared to operate according to inner logics that could be identified and specified by the social scientist. All these approaches treated macro-social structures as determining factors that constrained local social actors. Poststructuralist critiques of this top-down determinism developed. One line of critique stressed the opportunistic character of the everyday practices of local social actors, who as agents made choices of conduct within sets constrained by social processes (i.e. "structures") operating at the macro-social level (for example, Bourdieu's 1977 critique of Lévi-Strauss's structuralism). Another line of critique (Foucault, 1977) showed how power could be exercised over local social actors without physical coercion through the knowledge systems that were maintained discursively and through surveillance by secular "helping" professions—the modern successors of pre-modern religion—whose ideologically ratified purpose was to benefit the clients they "served" by controlling them—medicine, psychiatry, education, and modern prisons. Michel Foucault's notion of discourse as embodied in the conventional common sense of institutions is akin to Gramsci's (1988) notion of "cultural hegemony"—again, an ideological means by which control can be exercised nonviolently through commonsense rationalization justifying the exercise of such power. Power and social structure are thus seen to be strongly influential processes, even though the influence is partial, indirect, and contested—local actors are considered to be agents, not simply passive rule followers, yet they are agents who must swim in rivers that have strong currents.

At the same time, historians began to look away from the accounts of the past that were produced by the powerful (rich, literate, Caucasian, male, or any combination of those traits) and began to focus more centrally on the daily life practices of people whose subaltern "unwritten" lives could fly, as it were, below the radar of history. (This was a challenge to the accounts of orthodox historians who stuck to the conventional primary source materials.) An additional line of criticism of the authoritativeness of texts, which was once taken for granted, came from postmodern scholars (e.g., Derrida, Lyotard, Deleuze) who questioned the entire Enlightenment project of authoritative academic discourse concerning human activity, whether this discourse manifested in the arts, in history, or in social science. With roots in the early modernism of the Enlightenment, all these discourses attempted to construct "master narratives" whose credibility would be robust because they were based on reason and evidence. For the post-modernists, the rhetorical strategies that scholarly authors used to persuade readers of their text's accuracy and truthfulness could be unmasked through a textual analysis called *deconstruction*. Critical ethnography had challenged the authority of realist narrative accounts that left out explicit mention of processes of conflict and struggles over power; the postmodern line of criticism challenged the fundamental authoritativeness of texts per se. Moreover, lines of demarcation between qualitative social inquiry and scholarship in the humanities were dissolving. Approaches from literary criticism—outside the boundaries of mainstream social science—were used both in the interpretist (hermeneutic) orientation in ethnography and in the critical scrutiny of scholarly texts by means of deconstruction.

One of the ways to demystify the text of a qualitative research report is to include the author (and the author's "standpoint" perspectives) as an explicit presence in the fieldwork. The author becomes a character in the story being told—perhaps a primary one—and much or all of the text is written in first-person narration using past tense rather than the earlier ethnographic convention of present-tense narration, which to critics of realist ethnography seemed to connote timelessness—weightless social action in a gravitationless world outside history and apart from struggle. This autobiographical reporting approach came to be called *autoethnography*. Early examples of the approach have already been mentioned: the fiction of Bohannon (Bowen, 1954) and the first confessional ethnographic monograph by Jean Briggs (1970). Later examples of autoethnographic reporting include Rabinow (1977) and Kondo (1990)—see also the recent comprehensive discussion in Bochner and Ellis (2002).

Another approach toward alteration in the text of reports came from attempts to heighten the dramatic force of those texts, making full use of the rhetorics of performance to produce vivid kinds of narration, for example, breaking through from prose into poetry or adopting the means of "street theater," in which scripted or improvised dramatic performances were presented. Ethnographers have sometimes been invidiously called failed novelists and poets because their monographs typically did not make for compelling reading. By analogy with performance art, the new performance ethnography sought to employ more audience-engaging means of representation (see Conquergood, 1989, 2000; Denzin, 2003; Madison & Hamera, 2006.) Examples of arts-based representation approaches are also found in the recent work of Richardson (2004, 2007; see also the discussion in Richardson, 1999).

Classic and more innovative approaches to qualitative inquiry were extensively reviewed in the three successive handbooks on qualitative research methods edited by Denzin and Lincoln (1994, 2000, 2005).

Bent Flyvbjerg (2001), a member of the urban planning faculty at the University of Aalborg, Denmark, made an important statement in the edgily titled *Making social science matter: How social inquiry fails and how it can succeed again.* The book argued for the use of case study to address matters of value, power, and local detail, as these are pertinent to policy decision making. What policymakers need in making decisions is not general knowledge, says Flyvbjerg, but rather the specific circumstances of the local situation. He uses as an example the planning of auto parking and pedestrian mall arrangements in the city of Aalborg. To achieve the best traffic solution for Aalborg, one cannot make a composite of what was done in Limerick, Bruges, Genoa, Tokyo, and Minneapolis. To know what is good for Aalborg involves detailed understanding of Aalborg itself. Such understanding comes from a kind of knowledge that Flyvbjerg calls *phronesis,* action-oriented knowledge of a local social ecosystem.

Qualitative inquiry in educational research. The authority of realist ethnography was beginning to be challenged at the very time when qualitative research approaches developed in certain fields of human services delivery, especially in education. By the 1950s, a subfield of anthropology of education was forming (Spindler 1955, 1963). Henry (1963) published chapter-length accounts of elementary school classrooms that were highly critical of the practices used to encourage competition among students. The first book-length reports, modeled after the writing of ethnologists and anthropologists, were Smith and Geoffrey's (1968) *The Complexities of an Urban Classroom,* and Jackson's (1968) *Life in Classrooms.* Also in 1968, the Council on Anthropology and Education was founded within the American Anthropological Association. Its newsletter developed into a journal in 1973, the *Anthropology and Education Quarterly,* and for a time, this was the primary journal outlet for qualitative studies in education in the United States. Spindler became the editor of a series of overseas ethnographic studies of educational settings, published from the 1960s to the late 1980s by Holt, Rinehart, and Winston.

In England, qualitative inquiry was pioneered by educational evaluation researchers with an orientation from sociology and action research. At CARE, Laurence Stenhouse formed a generation of evaluators who studied schools and classrooms by means of participant observation and who wrote narrative research reports (see, for example, in chronological order, Walker & Adelman, 1975; Adelman, 1981; Kushner, Brisk, & MacDonald, 1982; Kushner, 1991;

Torrance, 1995). Various sociologists also engaged in qualitative educational research. In 1977, Willis published *Learning to Labour*. See also Delamont (1984, 1989, 1992) and Walkerdine (1998). Following in the tradition of Henry and Spindler in the United States and the "new sociology of education" in England, many of these studies focused on aspects of the "hidden curriculum" of social relations and values socialization in classrooms.

Because of the "objectivist" postpositivist tenor of mainstream educational research, this early work in education anticipated to some extent the criticisms of ethnographic authority that developed in anthropology in the late 1970s and early 1980s. In defense, the early qualitative researchers in education took pains to present explicit evidence; indeed, some of them had come out of the 'better data" and "hyphenated subfields" movements in anthropology or the ethnomethodological critique of mainstream work in sociology.

In the United States, qualitative approaches began to be adopted within research on subject matter instruction—initially in literacy studies (Heath, 1983) and social studies. Some of this work derived from the ethnography of communication/sociolinguistics work begun in the 1960s. As portable video equipment became available, classroom participant observation research was augmented by audiovisual recording (Erickson & Shultz, 1977/1997; McDermott, Gospodinoff, & Aron, 1978; Mehan, 1978). A literature on classroom discourse analysis developed, involving transcriptions of recordings of speech (see Cazden, 2001). Initially focused on literacy instruction, after the mid 1980s, this approach was increasingly used in studies of "teaching for understanding" in mathematics and science that were funded by the National Science Foundation in the United States, and that tendency has increased up to the present time.

Methods texts began to appear, explaining to postpositivist audiences of educational researchers how qualitative research could be rigorous and systematic: Guba (1978), Bogdan and Biklen (1982), and Guba and Lincoln (1985); see also Schensul, LeCompte, and Schensul (1999). Erickson's (1986) essay on interpretive qualitative research on teaching appeared in a handbook sponsored by the American Educational Research Association, and that discussion came to be widely cited in educational research. Preceded by a meeting in 1978 at which Mead was the keynote speaker, shortly before her death, and established as an annual meeting 2 years later, the Ethnography in Education conference at the University of Pennsylvania soon became the largest gathering of qualitative educational researchers in the world, surpassed in scale only recently by the International Congress of Qualitative Inquiry at the University of Illinois, Urbana. Also in the 1980s, a movement of practitioner research in education developed in the United States, principally as teachers began to write narrative accounts of their classroom practice (see Cochran-Smith & Lytle, 1993). This was related to participatory action research (see the discussion in Erickson, 2006).

By the early 1990s, qualitative research on subject areas in both the humanities and in science/mathematics had become commonplace, where 20 years earlier it had been very rare. Video documentation was especially useful in the study of "hands on" instruction in science and in the use of manipulables in teaching mathematics instruction (see Goldman, Barron, Pea, & Derry, 2007). Increasingly, the subject matter studies—especially those supported by NSF funds—focused on the "manifest curriculum" rather uncritically. This tendency was counterbalanced by the adoption of "critical ethnography" by some educational researchers (e.g., Fine, 1991; Kincheloe, 1993; Lather, 1991; McLaren, 1986).

In a number of ways qualitative inquiry in education anticipated and later ran in parallel with the shifts taking place within recent qualitative work in anthropology and sociology. From the outset of qualitative inquiry in education, its research subjects—school teachers, administrators, parents—were literate, fully able to read the research reports that were written about them, and capable of talking back to researchers using the researchers' own terms. The "gaze" of educational researchers—its potential for distorted perception and its status as an exercise of power over those observed—had been identified as problematic in qualitative educational inquiry before critics such as Clifford and Marcus (1986) had published on those matters. Also action research and practitioner research—involving "insiders" in studying and reflecting on their own customary practices—had been done by educational researchers before such approaches were attempted by scholars from social science disciplines.

Today there is a bifurcation in qualitative educational studies—with subject matter-oriented studies on the one hand and critical or postmodern studies on the other. In effect, this results in a split between attention to issues of manifest curriculum and hidden curriculum. Ironically, as the authority of realist ethnography was increasingly challenged within sociology and anthropology, "realist" work in applied research in education, medicine, nursing, and business came to be the most valued.

IV. The Current Scene

At this writing, there appear to be seven major streams of qualitative inquiry: a continuation of realist ethnographic case study, a continuation of "critical" ethnography, a continuation of collaborative action research, "indigenous" studies done by "insiders" (including practitioner research in education), auto-ethnography, performance ethnography, and further efforts along postmodern lines, including literary and other arts-based approaches.

The differences go beyond technique to basic assumptions. A question arises: Is it more useful to consider these as differing "paradigms," as Guba and Lincoln have done among many others (e.g., Guba 1990), or as a more mundane phenomenon? As Hammersley (2008) has put it, "differences among qualitative researchers are embedded in diverse forms of situated practices that incorporate characteristic ways of thinking and feeling about the research process" (p. 167). Whatever terms one uses to characterize this divergence, it is apparent that major differences in purposes, value positions, and ontological and epistemological assumptions obtain.

At the outset of this chapter, I mentioned five foundational "footings" for qualitative inquiry, each of which has been contested across the course of the development of such inquiry: (1) disciplinary perspectives in social science, (2) the participant-observational fieldworker as an observer/author, (3) the people who are observed during the fieldwork, (4) the rhetorical and substantive content of the research report, and (5) the audiences to which such reports have been addressed.

As the social sciences began to develop along lines of natural science models, its social theory orientations (social evolution, then functionalism combined with cultural relativism) were seen to justify data collection and analysis as a "value-neutral" enterprise. That stance was challenged by conflict-oriented social theory, with the research enterprise redefined as social criticism. Today the possibility of valid social critique is itself questioned by postmodern skepticism about the authoritativeness of scholarly inquiry in general, and core organizing notions taken from arts and humanities disciplines inform much new qualitative research. Sociology and anthropology are no longer the foundational "homes" for social and cultural studies.

Formerly, an "expert knowledge" model of the social scientist was seen as justifying long-term firsthand observation and interviewing—"fieldwork"—that was conducted autonomously by a researcher, who operated in ways akin to those of a field biologist. Today the adequacy and legitimacy of that researcher stance has been seriously challenged, with many researchers allying themselves as advocates (collaborators/joint authors/editors) with the people who are studied, or working with researchers coming from the ranks of the "studied." Thus, the roles of "researcher" and "researched" have been blended in recent work.

The research report was formerly considered to be an accurate, realistic, and comprehensive portrayal of the lifeways of those who were studied, with an underlying rhetoric of persuasion as to the realism of the account. Today qualitative research reports are often considered to be partial—renderings done from within the standpoints of the life experience of the researcher. The "validity" of these accounts can be compared to that of novels and poetry—a pointing toward "truths" that are not literal; fiction may be employed as a means of illuminating interpretive points in a report.

Initially, the audiences of such reports were the author's scholarly peers—fellow social scientists, and rarely those who were studied. Today those who are studied are expected to read the report—and they may also participate in writing it. Moreover, in action research and other kinds of advocacy research, research may also address popular audiences.

This is a story of decentering and jockeying for position as qualitative inquiry has evolved over the last 120 years. Today there is an uneven pattern of adoption and rejection of the newer approaches in qualitative inquiry. In applied fields, such as education, medicine, and business, "realist" ethnography has gained wide acceptance, while more recently developed approaches have sometimes been adopted (especially in education) and sometimes met with skepticism or with outright rejection. In anthropology, heroic "lone ethnographer" fieldwork and reporting, after the self-valorizing model of Malinowski, has generally gone out of fashion. In sociology, the detached stance of professional researcher has also been seriously questioned, together with the realist mode of research reporting.

Yet there has also been push back. In education, for example, while realist ethnography was officially accepted as legitimately scientific in an influential report issued by the National Research Council (Shavelson & Towne, 2002), postmodern approaches were singled out for harsh criticism. The report also took the position that science is a seamless enterprise, with social scientific inquiry being continuous in its fundamental aims and procedures with that of natural science. This position was reinforced by a statement by the primary professional society of researchers in education, the American Educational Research Association. Quoting from the AERA website:

> The following definition of scientifically based research (SBR) was developed by an expert working group convened by the American Educational Research Association (AERA) . . . AERA provided this definition in response to congressional staff requests for an SBR definition that was grounded in scientific standards and principles. The request derived from an interest in averting the inconsistencies and at times narrowness of other SBR definitions used in legislation in recent years.
>
> Alternate Definition of Scientifically Based Research (SBR) Supported by AERA Council, July 11, 2008.

The term "principles of scientific research" means the use of rigorous, systematic, and objective methodologies to obtain reliable and valid knowledge. Specifically, such research requires

development of a logical, evidence-based chain of reasoning;

methods appropriate to the questions posed;

observational or experimental designs and instruments that provide reliable and generalizable findings;

data and analysis adequate to support findings;

explication of procedures and results clearly and in detail, including specification of the population to which the findings can be generalized;

adherence to professional norms of peer review;

dissemination of findings to contribute to scientific knowledge; and

access to data for reanalysis, replication, and the opportunity to build on findings.

The statements by the NRC panel and the AERA Council claimed to provide a more broadly ecumenical definition of scientific research than that which some members of the U.S. Congress and their staffs were trying to insist on in developing criteria of eligibility for federal funding. Some legislators proposed that funding should be restricted to experimental designs with random assignment of subjects to treatment or control conditions. However, AERA's adoption of the "seamless" view of science means that many of the recent approaches to qualitative inquiry are declared beyond the boundaries of legitimate research. Moreover, the statements by the NRC and by AERA show no awareness of an intellectual history of social and cultural research in which, across many generations of scholars, serious doubts have been raised as to the possibility that inquiry in the human sciences should be, or could be, conducted in ways that were continuous with the natural sciences.

Geertz warned against the "broad umbrella" conception of science in his favorable review of Flyvbjerg's (2001) book, *Making Social Science Matter.*

Using the term "science" to cover everything from string theory to psychoanalysis is not a happy idea because doing so elides the difficult fact that the ways in which we try to understand and deal with the physical world and those in which we try to understand and deal with the social one are not altogether the same. The methods of research, the aims of inquiry, and the standards of judgment all differ, and nothing but confusion, scorn, and accusation—relativism! Platonism! reductionism! verbalism!—results from failing to see this. (Geertz, 2001, p. 53)

In addition to external critique from the advocates of social inquiry as "hard science," there is also a conservative reaction from within the community of qualitative researchers. One such statement appears in a recent collection of essays by Martin Hammersley (2008):

> I have argued that this postmodern approach is founded on some false assumptions that undermine the distinctive nature of social research . . . one consequence of this has been a legitimization of speculative theorizing; another has been a celebration of obscurity, and associated denunciations of clarity . . . [this] leads toward an abdication of the responsibility for clear and careful argument aimed at discovering what truths qualitative inquiry is capable of providing. (p. 144)

> We must work to overcome, or at least to reduce, methodological pluralism. It is not that all research can or should be done in the same standardised way. Rather, my point is that any approach to methodological thinking needs to engage with the same general issues. (p. 181)

> This postmodernist image of qualitative inquiry is not only ill-conceived but . . . its prominence at the present time, not least in arguments against what it dismisses as methodological conservatism, is potentially very damaging—not just to qualitative research but to social science more generally. (p. 11)

The postmodern range within the current spectrum of qualitative inquiry approaches was also criticized in a recent presidential address at the Midwest Sociological Society's annual meeting in 2006 (Adler & Adler, 2008). Reviewing past and current practices, Adler and Adler contrasted mainstream, realist interpretive ethnography and its literary tropes of verisimilitude with the postmodern approaches: "With its focus on the exploration of new forms, it [i.e., postmodern ethnography] offers great possibilities for continuing innovation. There is increasing unlikeliness, however, that it will ever be legitimized beyond its own rather narrow orbit" (p. 29).

In a response to these and other critics, Denzin (2009) wrote a rejoinder in the form of an imaginary play in which various characters—some of whom are scholars, living or dead, some of whom are fictional—engage in dispute on either side of this argument. Many of the lines the characters "speak" come from published work by the various scholars, and the form of the rejoinder as a performance text—a blending of scholarly quotation with novelistic creation of new utterances—mocks the high seriousness of the critics.

Mark Twain is said to have said, "History doesn't repeat itself—at best it sometimes rhymes." If he was correct, then the proponents of postpositivist social science are in serious trouble. Such inquiry, grounded in what is assumed to be a seamless whole of science, aims to discover general laws of social process that are akin to the laws of physics, that is, an enterprise firmly grounded in prose and in literal meanings of things. It will continue to be controverted by the stubborn poetics of everyday social life—its rhyming, the nonliteral, labile meanings inherent in social action, the unexpected twists and turns that belie prediction and control. It may well be that social science will at last give up on its perennially failing attempts to assume that history actually repeats itself and therefore can be studied as if it did. One might think that contemporary qualitative social inquiry would be better equipped than such a prosaic social physics to take account of the poetics of social and cultural processes, and yet qualitative social inquiry expends considerable energy on internecine dispute, with "classical" and "anticlassical" approaches vying for dominance. It seems too soon to know whether this situation is more an opportunity than a liability.

Let me conclude in first person. It seems to me that the full-blown realist ethnographic monograph, with its omniscient narrator speaking to the reader with an apparent neutrality as if from nowhere and nowhen, is no longer a genre of reporting that can responsibly be practiced, given the duration and force of the critique that has been leveled against it. Some adaptation, some deviation from the classic form seems warranted. It also seems to me that there should be a viable place within qualitative inquiry between harsh critique and self-satisfied nostalgia—and that this need not involve what Hammersley (2008) has called overcoming methodological pluralism. But it does require adopting a certain degree of humility as we consider what any of our work is capable of accomplishing.

It is only 86 years since Malinowski set foot in the Trobriand Islands. I want to say that Malinowski's overall aim for ethnography was a noble one, especially as amended in the words that follow: "to grasp the points of view of those who are studied and of those who are studying, their relations to life, their visions of their worlds." I think it is fair to say that we have learned over the past 60 years how hard it is to achieve such an aim partially, even to move in the direction of that aim. We know now that this is far more difficult than Malinowski and his contemporaries had anticipated. Yet it could still orient our continuing reach.

Note

1. Some discussion here is adapted from my own previous writing on these topics, drawing especially on Erickson 1986 and 2006. Because the literature on qualitative research methods is huge, the reader is also referred to Vidich and Lyman (1994) for an extensive review of classic realist ethnography in American sociology and anthropology; to Urrey (1994) for an extensive review of field research methods, primarily in British social anthropology; and to Heider (1982) for an extensive review of ethnographic film.

References

Adelman, C. (1981). *Uttering, muttering: Collecting, using, and reporting talk for social and educational research.* London: McIntyre.

Adler, P., & Adler, P. (2008). Of rhetoric and representation: The four faces of ethnography. *Sociological Quarterly, 49*(1), 1–30.

Anderson, E. (1992). *Streetwise: Race, class, and change in an urban community.* Chicago: University of Chicago Press.

Arensberg, C., & Kimball, S. (1940). *Family and community in Ireland.* Cambridge MA: Harvard University Press.

Argyris, C. (1953). *Executive leadership: An appraisal of a manager in action.* New York: Harper.

Argyris, C. (1954a). Human relations in a bank. *Harvard Business Review, 32*(5), 63–72.

Argyris, C. (1954b). *Organization of a bank: A study of the nature of organization and the fusion process.* New Haven, CT: Yale University Labor and Management Center.

Baldwin, B. (n.d.). Traditional and cultural aspects of Trobriand Island chiefs. Unpublished MS thesis. Canberra: Australia National University, Anthropology Department, Royal Society of Pacific Studies.

Barnouw, E. (1993). *Documentary: A history of the non-fiction film* (2nd Rev. ed.). New York: Oxford University Press.

Becker, H., & Geer, B. (1961). *Boys in white: Student culture in medical school.* Chicago: University of Chicago Press.

Behar, R. (1996). *The vulnerable observer: Anthropology that breaks your heart.* Boston: Beacon.

Benson, T., & Anderson C. (2002). *Reality fictions: The films of Frederick Wiseman* (2nd ed.). Carbondale: Southern Illinois University Press.

Bochner, A., & Ellis, C. (Eds.). (2002). *Ethnographically speaking: Autoethnography, literature, and aesthetics.* Walnut Creek, CA: Alta Mira.

Bogdan, R., & Biklen, S. (1982). *Qualitative research for education: An introduction to theory and methods.* Boston: Allyn & Bacon.

Booth, C. (1891). *Labour and life of the people of London.* London and Edinburgh: Williams and Nargate.

Bourdieu, P. (1977). *Outline of a theory of practice* (R. Nice, Trans.). Cambridge, UK: Cambridge University Press.

Bowen, E. (1954). *Return to laughter.* Garden City, NY: Doubleday.

Bredo, E., & Feinberg, W. (1982). *Knowledge and values in social and educational research.* Philadelphia: Temple University Press.

Briggs, J. L. (1970). *Never in anger: Portrait of an Eskimo family.* Cambridge, MA: Harvard University Press.

Byers, P. (1966). Cameras don't take pictures. *The Columbia University Forum, 9*(1), Winter. Reprinted in *Afterimage,* Vol. 4, No. 10, April 1977.

Byers, P. (with Mead, M.). (1968). *The small conference: An innovation in communication.* The Hague: Mouton.

Cazden, C. (2001). *Classroom discourse: The language of teaching and learning.* Portsmouth, NH: Heineman.

Clifford, J. (1988). *The predicament of culture: Twentieth century ethnography, literature, and art.* Cambridge, MA: Harvard University Press.

Clifford, J., & Marcus, G. (1986). *Writing culture: The poetics and politics of ethnography.* Berkeley: University of California Press.

Cochran-Smith, M., & Lytle, S. (1993). *Inside/outside: Teacher research and knowledge.* New York: Teachers College Press.

Collier, J., Jr. (1967). *Visual anthropology: Photography as a research method.* New York: Holt, Rinehart, & Winston.

Comte, A. (2001). *Plan des travaux scientifiques necessaires pour reorganizer la societe.* Paris: L'Harmattan. (Original work published 1822)

Conquergood, D. (1989). *I am a shaman: A Hmong life story with ethnographic commentary.* Minneapolis: University of Minnesota, Center for Urban and Regional Affairs.

Conquergood, D. (2000). Rethinking elocution: The trope of the talking book and other figures of speech. *Text and Performance Quarterly, 20*(4), 325–341.

deBrigard, E. (1995). The history of ethnographic film. In P. Hockings (Ed.), *Principles of visual anthropology* (2nd ed., pp. 13–44). New York: Mouton de Gruyter.

deLoria, V. (1969). *Custer died for your sins: An Indian manifesto.* New York: Macmillan.

Delamont, S. (1984). The old girl network. In R. Burgess (Ed.), *The research process in educational settings.* London: Falmer.

Delamont, S. (1989). *Knowledgeable women: Structuralism and the reproduction of elites.* London: Routledge.

Delamont, S. (1992). *Fieldwork in educational settings: Methods, pitfalls, and perspectives.* London: Falmer.

Denzin, N. (1970). *The research act in sociology: A theoretical introduction to sociological methods.* London: Butterworths.

Denzin, N. (2003). *Performance ethnography: Critical pedagogy and the politics of culture.* Thousand Oaks, CA: Sage.

Denzin, N. K. (2009). Apocalypse now: Overcoming resistances to qualitative inquiry. *International Review of Qualitative Inquiry, 2*(3), 331–344.

Denzin, N. K., & Lincoln, Y. S. (Eds.). (1994). *The handbook of qualitative research.* Thousand Oaks, CA: Sage.

Denzin, N. K., & Lincoln, Y. S. (Eds.). (2000). *The handbook of qualitative research* (2nd ed.). Thousand Oaks, CA: Sage.

Denzin, N. K., & Lincoln, Y. S. (Eds.). (2005). *The SAGE handbook of qualitative research* (3rd ed.). Thousand Oaks, CA: Sage.

Dilthey, W. (1989). *Einleitung in die Geisteswissenschaften—Introduction to the human sciences* (R. Makkreel & F. Rodi, Ed. & Trans.). Princeton, NJ: Princeton University Press. (Original work published 1883)

Drake, S. C., & Cayton, H. (1945). *Black metropolis: A study of Negro life in a northern city.* Chicago: University of Chicago Press.

DuBois, W. E. B. (1899). *The Philadelphia negro: A social study.* New York: Schocken.

Ellen, R. (1984). *Ethnographic research: A guide to general conduct.* London and San Diego: Academic Press.

Emery, F., & Thorsrud, E. (1969). *Form and content of industrial democracy: Some experiments from Norway and other European countries.* Assen, The Netherlands: Van Gorcum.

Erickson, F. (1986). Qualitative methods in research on teaching. In M. C. Wittrock (Ed.), *Handbook of research on teaching* (3rd ed., pp. 119–161). New York: Macmillan.

Erickson, F. (2006). Studying side by side: Collaborative action ethnography in educational research. In G. Spindler & L. Hammond (Eds.), *New horizons for ethnography in education* (pp. 235–257). Mahwah, NJ: Lawrence Erlbaum.

Erickson, F., & Shultz, J. (1997). When is a context?: Some issues and methods in the analysis of social competence. Reprinted in M. Cole, M. Engeström, & O. Vasquez (Eds.), *Mind, culture, and activity: Seminal papers from the Laboratory of Comparative Human Cognition* (pp. 22–31). Cambridge, UK: Cambridge University Press. (Original work published 1977)

Evans-Pritchard, E. (1940). *The Nuer: A description of the modes of livelihood and political institutions of a Nilotic people.* Oxford, UK: Oxford University Press.

Fine, G. (1990). Organizational time: Temporal demands and the experience of work in restaurant kitchens. *Social Forces, 69*(1), 95–114.

Fine, M. (1991). *Framing dropouts.* Albany: SUNY Press.

Firth, R. (2004). *We the Tikiopia.* New York: Routledge. (Original work published 1936)

Flyvbjerg, B. (2001). *Making social science matter: How social inquiry fails and how it can succeed again.* Cambridge and New York: Cambridge University Press.

Flyvbjerg, B. (2006). Five misunderstandings about case-study research. *Qualitative Inquiry, 12*(2), 219–245.

Foucault, M. (1977). *Discipline and punish: The birth of the prison.* London: Penguin Books.

Freeman, D. (1983). *Margaret Mead and Samoa.* Cambridge, UK: Harvard University Press.

Gans, H. (1962). *The urban villagers.* New York: The Free Press.

Geertz, C. (1973). *The interpretation of cultures: Selected essays.* New York: Basic Books.

Geertz, C. (2001). Empowering Aristotle. *Science, 293,* 53.

Glaser, B., & Strauss, A. (1965). *Awareness of dying.* Chicago: Aldine.

Glaser, B., & Strauss, A. (1967). *The discovery of grounded theory: Strategies for qualitative research.* Chicago: Aldine.

Goldman, R., Barron, B., Pea, R., & Derry, S. (Eds.). (2007). *Video research in the learning sciences.* Mahwah, NJ: Lawrence Erlbaum.

Gramsci, A. (1988). *A Gramsci reader.* London: Lawrence & Wishart.

Guba, E. (1978). *Toward a methodology of naturalistic inquiry in educational evaluation.* Los Angeles: UCLA, Center for the Study of Evaluation.

Guba, E. (1990). *The paradigm dialogue.* Thousand Oaks, CA: Sage.

Guba, E., & Lincoln, Y. (1985). *Naturalistic inquiry.* Beverly Hills, CA: Sage.

Gumperz, J., Roberts, C., & Jupp, T. (1979). *Culture and communication: Background and notes to accompany the BBC film "Crosstalk."* London: British Broadcasting Company.

Hammersley, M. (2008). *Questioning qualitative inquiry: Critical essays.* London: Sage.

Hammersley, M., & Atkinson, P. (1983). *Ethnography: Principles in practice.* London: Tavistock.

Harding, S. (1991). *Whose science? Whose knowledge? Thinking from women's lives.* Ithaca, NY: Cornell University Press.

Heath, S. (1983). *Ways with words: Language, life, and work in communities and classrooms.* Cambridge: Cambridge University Press.

Heider, K. (1982). *Ethnographic film* (3rd ed.). Austin: University of Texas Press.

Henry, J. (1963). *Culture against man.* New York: Random House.

Hollingshead, A. (1949). *Elmtown's youth: The impact of social classes on adolescents.* New York: John Wiley.

Holmberg, A. (1950). *Nomads of the long bow: The Siriono of Eastern Bolivia.* Garden City, NY: Natural History Press.

Jackson, P. (1968). *Life in classrooms.* New York: Holt, Rinehart, & Winston.

Kemmis, S., & McTaggart, R. (2005). Participatory action research: Communicative action and the public sphere. In N. K. Denzin & Y. S. Lincoln (Eds.), *The SAGE handbook of qualitative research* (3rd ed., pp. 559–603). Thousand Oaks, CA: Sage.

Kincheloe, J. (1993). *Toward a critical politics of teacher thinking.* S. Hadley, MA: Bergin & Garvey.

Kluckhohn, C. (1949). *Mirror for man.* New York: McGraw-Hill.

Kondo, D. (1990). *Crafting selves: Power, gender, and discourses of identity in a Japanese workplace.* Chicago: Chicago University Press.

Kushner, S. (1991). *The children's music book: Performing musicians in schools.* London: Calouste Gulbenkian Foundation.

Kushner, S., Brisk, M., & MacDonald, B. (1982). *Bread and dreams: A case study of bilingual schooling in the U.S.* Norwich, UK: University of East Anglia, Centre for Applied Research in Education.

Lather, P. (1991). *Getting smart: Feminist research and pedagogy with/in the postmodern.* New York: Routledge.

Latour, B., & Woolgar, S. (1979). *Laboratory life: The social construction of scientific facts.* Beverly Hills: Sage.

Lewin, K. (1946). Action research and minority problems. *Journal of Social Issues, 24*(1), 34–46.

Lewis, O. (1951). *Life in a Mexican village: Tepoztlán restudied.* Urbana: University of Illinois Press.

Liebow, E. (1967). *Tally's corner: A study of Negro streetcorner men.* Boston: Little, Brown.

Lynch, M. (1993). *Scientific practice and ordinary action: Ethnomethodology and social studies of science.* Cambridge, UK: Cambridge University Press.

Lynd, R., & Lynd, H. (1929). *Middletown: A study in contemporary American culture.* New York: Harcourt, Brace.

Lynd, R., & Lynd, H. (1937). *Middletown in transition: A study in cultural conflicts.* New York: Harcourt, Brace.

Madison, D. S., & Hamera, J. (Eds.). (2006). *The SAGE handbook of performance studies.* Thousand Oaks, CA: Sage.

Malinowski, B. (1922). *Argonauts of the Western Pacific: An account of native enterprise and adventure in the archipelagoes of Melanesian New Guinea.* London and New York: G. Routledge and E. P. Dutton.

Malinowski, B. (1967). *A diary in the strict sense of the term.* New York: Harcourt, Brace.

McCall, G., & Simmons, J. (1969). *Issues in participant observation: A text and reader.* Reading, MA: Addison-Wesley.

McLaren, P. (1986). *Schooling as a ritual performance.* London: Routledge and Kegan Paul.

McDermott, R., Gospodinoff, K., & Aron, J. (1978). Criteria for an ethnographically adequate description of concerted activities and their contexts. *Semiotica, 24*(3–4), 245–276.

Mead, M. (1928). *Coming of age in Samoa: A psychological study of primitive youth for Western civilization.* New York: William Morrow.

Mehan, H. (1978). *Learning lessons: Social organization in the classroom.* Cambridge, MA: Harvard University Press.

Morgan, L. H. (1877). *Ancient society: Researches in the lines of human progress from savagery through barbarism to civilization.* New York: MacMillan.

Moynihan, D. (1965). *The Negro family: The case for national action.* Washington, DC: U.S. Department of Labor, Office of Policy Planning and Research.

Munhall, P. (Ed.). (2001). *Nursing research: A qualitative perspective.* Sudbury MA: Jones and Bartlett.

Nash, J. (1979). *We eat the mines and the mines eat us.* New York: Columbia University Press National Research Council.

Pelto, P. J., & Pelto, G. H. (1970). *Anthropological research: The structure of inquiry.* New York: Harper & Row.

Powdermaker, H. (1966). *Stranger and friend: The way of an anthropologist.* New York: W. W. Norton.

Quetelet, L. A. (2010). *A treatise on man and the development of his faculties* (T. Smibert, Ed). Charlestown, SC: Nabu Press. (Original work published 1835)

Rabinow, P. (1977). *Reflections on fieldwork in Morocco.* Berkeley: University of California Press.

Radcliffe-Brown, A. (1922). *The Andaman islanders: A study in social anthropology.* Cambridge, UK: Cambridge University Press.

Redfield, R. (1930). *Tepoztlán, a Mexican village: A study in folk life.* Chicago: University of Chicago Press.

Richardson, L. (1999). Feathers in our CAP. *Journal of Contemporary Ethnography, 28,* 660–668.

Richardson, L. (2004). *Travels with Ernest: Crossing the literary/sociological divide.* Walnut Creek, CA: AltaMira.

Richardson, L. (2007). Last writes: A daybook for a dying friend. Thousand Oaks, CA: Left Coast Press.

Riis, J. (1890). *How the other half lives: Studies among the tenements of New York.* New York: Charles Scribner's Sons.

Rosaldo, R. (1989). *Culture and truth: The remaking of social analysis.* Boston: Beacon.

Roy, D. (1959). "Banana Time": Job satisfaction and informal interaction. *Human Organization, 18*(04), 158–168.

Ruby, J. (2000). *Picturing culture: Explorations of film and anthropology.* Chicago: University of Chicago Press.

Sanjek, R. (1990). *Fieldnotes: The makings of anthropology.* Ithaca, NY: Cornell University Press.

Schensul, J., LeCompte, M., & Schensul, S. (1999). *The ethnographer's toolkit* (Vols. 1–5). Walnut Creek, CA: AltaMira Press.

Schensul, J., & Schensul, S. (1992). Collaborative research: Methods of inquiry for social change. In M. LeCompte, W. Milroy, & J. Preissle (Eds.), *The handbook of qualitative research in education.* San Diego and New York: Academic Press.

Schensul, S. (1974). Skills needed in action anthropology: Lessons learned from El Centro de la Causa. *Human Organization, 33,* 203–209.

Shankman, P. (1996). The history of Samoan sexual conduct and the Mead-Freeman controversy. *American Anthropologist, 98*(3), 555–567.

Smith, D. (1974). Women's perspective as a radical critique of sociology. *Sociological Inquiry, 44,* 7–13.

Smith, L., & Geoffrey, W. (1968). *The complexities of an urban classroom.* New York: Holt, Rinehart, & Winston.

Spindler, G. (1955). *Education and anthropology.* Stanford, CA: Stanford University Press.

Spindler, G. (1963). *Education and culture: Anthropological approaches.* New York: Holt, Rinehart, & Winston.

Stenhouse, L. (1975). *An introduction to curriculum research and development.* London: Heineman.

Torrance, H. (1995). *Evaluating authentic assessment: Problems and possibilities in new approaches to assessment.* Buckingham, UK: Open University Press.

Tylor, E. B. (1871). *Primitive culture.* London: John Murray.

Urrey, J. (1984). A history of field methods. In R. Ellen (Ed.), *Ethnographic research: A guide to general conduct* (pp. 33–61). London and San Diego: Academic Press.

Van Maanen, J. (1988). *Tales of the field: On writing ethnography.* Chicago: University of Chicago Press.

Van Maanen, J. (2006). Ethnography then and now. *Qualitative Research in Organizations and Management: An International Journal, 1*(1), 13–21.

Vaught, C., & Smith, D. L. (1980). Incorporation & mechanical solidarity in an underground coal mine. *Sociology of Work and Occupations, 7*(2), 159–187.

Vidich, A., & Bensman, J. (1958). *Small town in mass society: Class, power, and religion in a rural community.* Garden City, NY: Doubleday.

Vidich, A., & Bensman, J. (2000). *Small town in mass society: Class, power, and religion in a rural community* (Rev. ed.). Urbana: University of Illinois Press.

Vidich, A., & Lyman, S. (1994). Qualitative methods: Their history in sociology and anthropology. In N. K. Denzin & Y. S. Lincoln (Eds.), *Handbook of qualitative research* (pp. 23–59). Thousand Oaks, CA: Sage.

Walker, R., & Adelman, C. (1975). *A guide to classroom observation.* London: Routledge.

Walkerdine, V. (1998). *Counting girls out: Girls and mathematics.* London: Falmer.

Warner, W. L. (1941). *Yankee city.* New Haven, CT: Yale University Press.

Wax, R. (1971). *Doing fieldwork: Warnings and advice.* Chicago: University of Chicago Press.

Whyte, W. F. (1955). *Street corner society: The social structure of an Italian slum.* Chicago: University of Chicago Press. (Original work published 1943)

Whyte, W. F., Greenwood, D. J., & Lazes, P. (1989). Participatory action research: Through practice to science in social research. *American Behavioral Scientist, 32*(5), 513–551.

Willis, P. (1977). *Learning to labour: How working class kids get working class jobs.* Westemead, UK: Saxon House.

Wirth, L. (1928). *The ghetto.* Chicago: University of Chicago Press.

Worth, S., & Adair, J. (1972). *Through Navaho eyes: An exploration of film communication and anthropology.* Bloomington: Indiana University Press.

Young, F. (1996). Small town in mass society revisited. *Rural Sociology, 61*(4), 630–648.

Young, M. (1979). *The ethnography of Malinowski: The Trobriand Islands 1915–18.* London: Routledge and K. Paul.

Zorbaugh, H. (1929). *The gold coast and the slum: A sociological study of Chicago's Near North Side.* Chicago: University of Chicago Press.

4

Ethics and Politics in Qualitative Research

Clifford G. Christians

Getting straight on ethics in qualitative research is not an internal matter only. Putting ethics and politics together is the right move intellectually, but it engages a major agenda beyond adjustments in qualitative theory and methods. The overall issue is the Enlightenment mind and its progeny. Only when the Enlightenment's epistemology is contradicted will there be conceptual space for a moral-political order in distinctively qualitative terms. The Enlightenment's dichotomy between freedom and morality fostered a tradition of value-free social science and, out of this tradition, a means-ends utilitarianism. Qualitative research insists on starting over philosophically, without the Enlightenment dualism as its foundation. The result is an ethical-political framework that is multicultural, gender inclusive, pluralistic, and international in scope.

Enlightenment Dualisms

The Enlightenment mind clustered around an extraordinary dichotomy. Intellectual historians usually summarize this split in terms of subject/object, fact/value, or material/spiritual dualisms. All three of these are legitimate interpretations of the cosmology inherited from Galileo Galilei, René Descartes, and Isaac Newton. None of them puts the Enlightenment into its sharpest focus, however. Its deepest root was a pervasive autonomy. The cult of human personality prevailed in all its freedom. Human beings were declared a law unto themselves, set loose from every faith that claimed their allegiance. Proudly self-conscious of human autonomy, the 18th-century mind saw nature as an arena of limitless possibilities in which human sovereignty is master over the natural order. Release from nature spawned autonomous individuals, who considered themselves independent of any authority. The freedom motif was the deepest driving force, first released by the Renaissance and achieving maturity during the Enlightenment.

Obviously, one can reach autonomy by starting with the subject/object dualism. In constructing the Enlightenment worldview, the prestige of natural science played a key role in setting people free. Achievements in mathematics, physics, and astronomy allowed humans to dominate nature, which formerly had dominated them. Science provided unmistakable evidence that by applying reason to nature and human beings in fairly obvious ways, people could live progressively happier lives. Crime and insanity, for example, no longer needed repressive theological explanations but were deemed capable of mundane empirical solutions.

Likewise, one can get to the autonomous self by casting the question in terms of a radical discontinuity between hard facts and subjective values. The Enlightenment pushed values to the fringe through its disjunction between knowledge of what is and what ought to be. And Enlightenment materialism in all its forms isolated reason from faith, knowledge from belief. As Robert Hooke insisted three centuries ago, when he helped found London's Royal Society: "This Society will eschew any discussion of religion, rhetoric, morals, and politics." With factuality gaining a stranglehold on the Enlightenment mind, those regions of human interest that implied oughts, constraints, and imperatives simply ceased to appear. Certainly those who see the Enlightenment as separating facts and values have identified a cardinal difficulty. Likewise, the realm of the spirit can easily dissolve into mystery and intuition. If the spiritual world contains no binding force, it is surrendered to speculation by the divines, many of whom accepted the Enlightenment belief that their pursuit was ephemeral.

But the Enlightenment's autonomy doctrine created the greatest mischief. Individual self-determination stands as the centerpiece, bequeathing to us the universal problem of integrating human freedom with moral order. In struggling with the complexities and conundrums of this relationship, the Enlightenment, in effect, refused to sacrifice personal freedom. Even though the problem had a particular urgency in the 18th century, its response was not resolution but a categorical insistence on autonomy. Given the despotic political regimes and oppressive ecclesiastical systems of the period, such an uncompromising stance for freedom at this juncture is understandable. The Enlightenment began and ended with the assumption that human liberty ought to be cut away from the moral order, never integrated meaningfully with it (cf. Taylor, 2007, Chapter 10).

Jean-Jacques Rousseau was the most outspoken advocate of this radical freedom. He gave intellectual substance to free self-determination of the human personality as the highest good. Rousseau is a complicated figure. He refused to be co-opted by Descartes' rationalism, Newton's mechanistic cosmology, or John Locke's egoistic selves. He was not content merely to isolate and sacralize freedom either, at least not in his *Discourse on Inequality* or in the *Social Contract,* where he answers Thomas Hobbes.

Rousseau represented the romantic wing of the Enlightenment, revolting against its rationalism. He won a wide following well into the 19th century for advocating immanent and emergent values rather than transcendent and given ones. While admitting that humans were finite and limited, he nonetheless promoted a freedom of breathtaking scope—not just disengagement from God or the church, but freedom from culture and from any authority. Autonomy became the core of the human being and the center of the universe. Rousseau's understanding of equality, social systems, axiology, and language were anchored in it. He recognized the consequences more astutely than those comfortable with a shrunken negative freedom. The only solution that he found tolerable was a noble human nature that enjoyed freedom beneficently and therefore, one could presume, lived compatibly in some vague sense with a moral order.

Value-Free Experimentalism

Typically, debates over the character of the social sciences revolve around the theory and methodology of the natural sciences. However, the argument here is not how they resemble natural science, but their inscription into the dominant Enlightenment worldview. In political theory, the liberal state as it developed in 17th- and 18th-century Europe left citizens free to lead their own lives without obeisance to the church or the feudal order. Psychology, sociology, and economics—known as the human or moral sciences in the 18th and 19th centuries—were conceived as "liberal arts" that opened minds and freed the imagination. As the social sciences and liberal state emerged and overlapped historically, Enlightenment thinkers in Europe advocated the "facts, skills, and techniques" of experimental reasoning to support the state and citizenry (Root, 1993, pp. 14–15).

Consistent with the presumed priority of individual liberty over the moral order, the basic institutions of society were designed to ensure "neutrality between different conceptions of the good" (Root, 1993, p. 12). The state was prohibited "from requiring or even encouraging citizens to subscribe to one religious tradition, form of family life, or manner of personal or artistic expression over another" (Root, 1993, p. 12). Given the historical circumstances in which shared conceptions of the good were no longer broad and deeply entrenched, taking sides on moral issues and insisting on social ideals were considered counterproductive. Value neutrality appeared to be the logical alternative "for a society whose members practiced many religions, pursued many different occupations, and identified with many different customs and traditions" (Root, 1993, p. 11). The theory and practice of mainstream social science reflect liberal Enlightenment philosophy, as do education, science, and politics. Only a reintegration of autonomy and the moral order provides an alternative paradigm for the social sciences today.[1]

MILL'S PHILOSOPHY OF SOCIAL SCIENCE

For John Stuart Mill,

> neutrality is necessary in order to promote autonomy. . . . A person cannot be forced to be good, and the state should not dictate the kind of life a citizen should lead; it would be better for citizens to choose badly than for them to be forced by the state to choose well. (Root, 1993, pp. 12–13)

Planning our lives according to our own ideas and purposes is sine qua non for autonomous beings in Mill's *On Liberty* (1859/1978): "The free development of individuality is one of the principal ingredients of human happiness, and quite the chief ingredient of individual and social progress" (p. 50; see also Copleston, 1966, p. 303, note 32). This neutrality, based on the supremacy of individual autonomy, is the foundational principle in Mill's *Utilitarianism* (1861/1957) and in *A System of Logic* (1843/1893) as well. For Mill, "the principle of utility demands that the individual should enjoy full liberty, except the liberty to harm others" (Copleston, 1966, p. 54). In addition to bringing classical utilitarianism to its maximum development and establishing with Locke the liberal state, Mill delineated the foundations of inductive inquiry as social scientific method. In terms of the principles of empiricism, he perfected the inductive techniques of Francis Bacon as a problem-solving methodology to replace Aristotelian deductive logic.

According to Mill, syllogisms contribute nothing new to human knowledge. If we conclude that because "all men are mortal," the Duke of Wellington is mortal by virtue of his manhood, then the conclusion does not advance the premise (see Mill, 1843/1893, II.3.2, p. 140). The crucial issue is not reordering the conceptual world but discriminating genuine knowledge from superstition. In the pursuit of truth, generalizing and synthesizing are necessary to advance inductively from the known to the unknown. Mill seeks to establish this function of logic as inference from the known, rather than certifying the rules for formal consistency in reasoning (Mill, 1843/1893, III). Scientific certitude can be approximated when induction is followed rigorously, with propositions empirically derived and the material of all our knowledge provided by experience.[2] For the physical sciences, Mill establishes four modes of experimental inquiry: agreement, disagreement, residues, and the principle of concomitant variations (1843/1893, III.8, pp. 278–288). He considers them the only possible methods of proof for experimentation, as long as one presumes the realist position that nature is structured by uniformities.[3]

In Book 6 of *A System of Logic,* "On the Logic of the Moral Sciences," Mill (1843/1893) develops an inductive experimentalism as the scientific method for studying "the various phenomena which constitute social life" (VI.6.1, p. 606). Although he conceived of social science as explaining human behavior in terms of causal laws, he warned against the fatalism of full predictability. "Social laws are hypothetical, and statistically-based generalizations that by their very nature admit of exceptions" (Copleston, 1966, p. 101; see also Mill, 1843/1893, VI.5.1, p. 596). Empirically confirmed instrumental knowledge about human behavior has greater predictive power when it deals with collective masses than when it concerns individual agents.

Mill's positivism is obvious throughout his work on experimental inquiry.[4] Based on Auguste Comte's *Cours de Philosophie Positive* (1830), he defined matter as the "permanent possibility of sensation" (Mill, 1865b, p. 198) and believed that nothing else can be said about the metaphysical.[5] Social research is amoral, speaking to questions of means only. Ends are outside its purview. In developing precise methods of indication and verification, Mill established a theory of knowledge in empirical terms. Truth is not something in itself but "depends on the past history and habits of our own minds" (Mill, 1843/1893, II, Vol. 6, p. 181). Methods for investigating society must be rigorously limited to the risks and benefits of possible courses of action. With David Hume and Comte, Mill insisted that metaphysical substances are not real; only the facts of sense phenomena exist. There are no essences or ultimate reality behind sensations; therefore, Mill (1865/1907, 1865a, 1865b) and Comte (1848/1910) argued that social scientists should limit themselves to particular data as a factual source out of which experimentally valid laws can be derived. For both, this is the only kind of knowledge that yields practical benefits (Mill, 1865b, p. 242); in fact, society's salvation is contingent on such scientific knowledge (p. 241).[6]

Like his consequentialist ethics, Mill's philosophy of social science is built on a dualism of means and ends. Citizens and politicians are responsible for articulating ends in a free society and science for providing the know-how to achieve them. Science is amoral, speaking to questions of means but with no wherewithal or authority to dictate ends. Methods in the social sciences must be disinterested regarding substance and content. Protocols for practicing liberal science "should be prescriptive, but not morally or politically prescriptive and should direct against bad science but not bad conduct" (Root, 1993, p. 129). Research cannot be judged right or wrong, only true or false. "Science is political only in its applications" (Root, 1993, p. 213). Given his democratic liberalism, Mill advocates neutrality "out of concern for the autonomy of the individuals or groups" social science seeks to serve. It should "treat them as thinking, willing, active beings who bear responsibility for their choices and are free to choose" their own conception of the good life by majority rule (Root, 1993, p. 19).

VALUE NEUTRALITY IN MAX WEBER

When 21st-century mainstream social scientists contend that ethics is not their business, they typically invoke Max Weber's essays written between 1904 and 1917. Given Weber's importance methodologically and theoretically for sociology and economics, his distinction between political judgments and scientific neutrality is given canonical status.

Weber distinguishes between value freedom and value relevance. He recognizes that in the discovery phase, "personal, cultural, moral, or political values cannot be eliminated; . . . what social scientists choose to investigate . . . they choose on the basis of the values" they expect their research to advance (Root, 1993, p. 33). But he insists that social science be value-free in the presentation phase. Findings ought not to express any judgments of a moral or political character. Professors should hang up their values along with their coats as they enter their lecture halls.

"An attitude of moral indifference," Weber (1904/1949b) writes, "has no connection with scientific objectivity" (p. 60). His meaning is clear from the value-freedom/value-relevance distinction. For the social sciences to be purposeful and rational, they must serve the "values of relevance."

> The problems of the social sciences are selected by the value relevance of the phenomena treated. . . . The expression "relevance to values" refers simply to the philosophical interpretation of that specifically scientific "interest" which determines the selection of a given subject matter and problems of empirical analysis. (Weber, 1917/1949a, pp. 21–22)

In the social sciences the stimulus to the posing of scientific problems is in actuality always given by practical "questions." Hence, the very recognition of the existence of a scientific problem coincides personally with the possession of specifically oriented motives and values.. . . .

Without the investigator's evaluative ideas, there would be no principle of selection of subject matter and no meaningful knowledge of the concrete reality. Without the investigator's conviction regarding the significance of particular cultural facts, every attempt to analyze concrete reality is absolutely meaningless. (Weber, 1904/1949b, pp. 61, 82)

Whereas the natural sciences, in Weber's (1904/1949b, p. 72) view, seek general laws that govern all empirical phenomena, the social sciences study those realities that our values consider significant. Whereas the natural world itself indicates what reality to investigate, the infinite possibilities of the social world are ordered in terms of "the cultural values with which we approach reality" (1904/1949b, p.78).[7] However, even though value relevance directs the social sciences, as with the natural sciences, Weber considers the former value-free. The subject matter in natural science makes value judgments unnecessary, and social scientists by a conscious decision can exclude judgments of "desirability or undesirability" from their publications and lectures (1904/1949b, p. 52). "What is really at issue is the intrinsically simple demand that the investigator and teacher should keep unconditionally separate the establishment of empirical facts . . . and his own political evaluations" (Weber, 1917/1949a, p. 11).

Weber's opposition to value judgments in the social sciences was driven by practical circumstances (Brunn, 2007). Academic freedom for the universities of Prussia was more likely if professors limited their professional work to scientific know-how. With university hiring controlled by political officials, only if the faculty refrained from policy commitments and criticism would officials relinquish their control.

Few of the offices in government or industry in Germany were held by people who were well trained to solve questions of means. Weber thought that the best way to increase the power and economic prosperity of Germany was to train a new managerial class learned about means and silent about ends. The mission of the university, on Weber's view, should be to offer such training.[8] (Root, 1993, p. 41; see also Weber, 1973, pp. 4–8)

Weber's practical argument for value freedom and his apparent limitation of it to the reporting phase have made his version of value neutrality attractive to 21st-century social science. He is not a positivist like Comte or a thoroughgoing empiricist in the tradition of Mill. He disavowed the positivist's overwrought disjunction between discovery and justification and developed no systematic epistemology comparable to Mill's. His nationalism was partisan compared to Mill's liberal political philosophy. Nevertheless, Weber's value neutrality reflects Enlightenment autonomy in a fundamentally similar fashion. In the process of maintaining his distinction between value relevance and value freedom, he separates facts from values and means from ends. He appeals to empirical evidence and logical reasoning rooted in human rationality. "The validity of a practical imperative as a norm," he writes, "and the truth-value of an empirical proposition are absolutely heterogeneous in character" (Weber, 1904/1949b, p. 52). "A systematically correct scientific proof in the social sciences" may not be completely attainable, but that is most likely "due to faulty data" not because it is conceptually impossible (1904/1949b, p. 58).[9] For Weber, like Mill, empirical science deals with questions of means, and his warning against inculcating political and moral values presumes a means-ends dichotomy (see Weber, 1917/1949a, pp. 18–19; 1904/1949b, p. 52; cf. Lassman, 2004).

As Michael Root (1993) concludes, "John Stuart Mill's call for neutrality in the social sciences is based on his belief" that the language of science "takes cognizance of a phenomenon and endeavors to discover its laws." Max Weber likewise "takes it for granted that there can be a language of science—a collection of truths—that excludes all value-judgments, rules, or directions for conduct" (p. 205). In both cases, scientific knowledge exists for its own sake as morally neutral. For both, neutrality is desirable "because questions of value are not rationally resolvable" and neutrality in the social sciences is presumed to contribute "to political and personal autonomy" (p. 229). In Weber's argument for value relevance in social science, he did not contradict the larger Enlightenment ideal of scientific neutrality between competing conceptions of the good.

UTILITARIAN ETHICS

In addition to its this-worldly humanism, utilitarian ethics has been attractive for its compatibility with scientific thought. It fit the canons of rational calculation as they were nourished by the Enlightenment's intellectual culture.

In the utilitarian perspective, one validated an ethical position by hard evidence. You count the consequences for human happiness of one or another course, and you go with the one with the highest favorable total. What counts as human happiness was thought to be something conceptually unproblematic, a scientifically establishable domain of facts. One could abandon all the metaphysical or theological factors which made ethical questions scientifically undecidable. (Taylor, 1982, p. 129)

Utilitarian ethics replaces metaphysical distinctions with the calculation of empirical quantities, reflecting the inductive processes Mill delineated in his *System of Logic.* Utilitarianism favors specific actions or policies based on evidence. It follows the procedural demand that if "the happiness of each agent counts for one . . . the right course of action should be what satisfies all, or the largest number possible" (Taylor, 1982, p. 131). Autonomous reason is the arbiter of moral disputes.

With moral reasoning equivalent to calculating consequences for human happiness, utilitarianism presumes there is "a single consistent domain of the moral, that there is one set of considerations which determines what we ought morally to do" (Taylor, 1982, p. 132). This "epistemologically-motivated reduction and homogenization of the moral" marginalizes the qualitative languages of admiration and contempt—integrity, healing, liberation, conviction, dishonesty, and self-indulgence, for example (Taylor, 1982, p. 133). In utilitarian terms, these languages designate subjective factors that "correspond to nothing in reality. . . . They express the way we feel, not the way things are" (Taylor, 1982, p. 141).[10] This single-consideration theory not only demands that we maximize general happiness, but considers irrelevant other moral imperatives that conflict with it, such as equal distribution. One-factor models appeal to the "epistemological squeamishness" of value-neutral social science, which "dislikes contrastive languages." Moreover, utilitarianism appealingly offers "the prospect of exact calculation of policy through . . . rational choice theory" (Taylor, 1982, p. 143). "It portrays all moral issues as discrete problems amenable to largely technical solutions" (Euben, 1981, p. 117). However, to its critics, this kind of exactness represents "a semblance of validity" by leaving out whatever cannot be calculated (Taylor, 1982, p. 143).[11]

Another influential critique of utilitarianism was developed earlier by W. David Ross.[12] Ross (1930) argued against the utilitarian claim that others are morally significant to us only when our actions impact them pro or con (pp. 17–21). We usually find ourselves confronting more than one moral claim at the same time involving different ethical principles. Asking only what produces the most good is too limiting. It does not cover the ordinary range of human relationships and circumstances. People recognize promise-keeping, equal distribution, nonviolence, and prevention of injury as moral principles. In various situations, any of them might be the most stringent.

Ordinary moral sensitivities suggest that when someone fulfills a promise because he thinks he ought to do so, it seems clear that he does so with no thought of its total consequences. . . . What makes him think it's right to act in a certain way is the fact that he has promised to do so—that and, usually, nothing more. (Ross, 1930, p. 17)

For both Taylor and Ross, the domain of the good in utilitarian theory is extrinsic. Given its dualism of means and ends, all that is worth valuing is a function of the consequences. Prima facie duties are literally inconceivable. "The degree to which my actions and statements" truly express what is important to someone does not count. Ethical and political thinking in consequentialist terms legislate[s] intrinsic valuing out of existence" (Taylor, 1982, p. 144). The exteriority of ethics is seen to guarantee the value neutrality of experimental procedures.[13]

CODES OF ETHICS

In value-free social science, codes of ethics for professional and academic associations are the conventional format for moral principles. By the 1980s, each of the major scholarly associations had adopted its own code, with an overlapping emphasis on four guidelines for directing an inductive science of means toward majoritarian ends.

1. *Informed consent.* Consistent with its commitment to individual autonomy, social science in the Mill and Weber tradition insists that research subjects have the right to be informed about the nature and consequences of experiments in which they are involved. Proper respect for human freedom generally includes two necessary conditions. Subjects must agree voluntarily to participate—that is, without physical or psychological coercion. In addition, their agreement must be based on full and open information. "The Articles of the Nuremberg Tribunal and the Declaration of Helsinki both state that subjects must be told the duration, methods, possible risks, and the purpose or aim of the experiment" (Soble, 1978, p. 40).

The self-evident character of this principle is not disputed in rationalist ethics. Meaningful application, however, generates ongoing disputes. As Punch (1998) observes, "In much fieldwork there seems to be no way around the predicament that informed consent—divulging one's identity and research purpose to all and sundry—will kill many a project stone dead" (p. 171). True to the privileging of means in a means-ends model, Punch reflects the general conclusion that codes of ethics should serve as a guideline prior to fieldwork but not intrude directly on the research process itself. "A strict application of codes" may "restrain and restrict" a great deal of "innocuous" and "unproblematic" research (p. 171).

2. *Deception.* In emphasizing informed consent, social science codes of ethics uniformly oppose deception. Even paternalistic arguments for possible deception of criminals, children in elementary schools, or the mentally incapacitated are no longer credible. The ongoing exposé of deceptive practices since Stanley Milgram's experiments have given this moral principle special status; that is, deliberate misrepresentation is not ethically justified. In Kai Erikson's (1967) classic formulation:

> The practice of using masks in social research compromises both the people who wear them and the people for whom they are worn, and in doing so violates the terms of a contract which the sociologist should be ready to honor in his dealings with others. (pp. 367–368)

The straightforward application of this principle suggests that researchers design experiments free of active deception. But with ethical constructions exterior to the scientific enterprise, no unambiguous application is possible. Within both psychological experimentation and medical research, some information cannot be obtained without at least deception by omission. Given that the search for knowledge is obligatory and deception is codified as morally unacceptable, in some situations, both criteria cannot be satisfied. The standard resolution for this dilemma is to permit a modicum of deception when there are explicit utilitarian reasons for doing so. Opposition to deception in the codes is de facto redefined in these terms: "The crux of the matter is that some deception, passive or active, enables you to get at data not obtainable by other means" (Punch, 1998, p. 172). As Bulmer (2008) contends,

> As a general principle, the use of deception in research has been condemned. But there are many situations in which it is not possible to be completely open to all participants and sometimes a full explanation of one's purposes would overwhelm the listener. (p. 154)

The general exhortations of codes are considered far removed from the interactional complexities of the field.

3. *Privacy and confidentiality*. Codes of ethics insist on safeguards to protect people's identities and those of the research locations. Confidentiality must be assured as the primary safeguard against unwanted exposure. All personal data ought to be secured or concealed and made public only behind a shield of anonymity. Professional etiquette uniformly concurs that no one deserves harm or embarrassment as a result of insensitive research practices. "The single most likely source of harm in social science inquiry" is the disclosure of private knowledge considered damaging by experimental subjects (Reiss, 1979, p. 73).

As Enlightenment autonomy was developed in philosophical anthropology, a sacred innermost self became essential to the construction of unique personhood. Already in Locke, this private domain received nonnegotiable status. Democratic life was articulated outside these atomistic units, a secondary domain of negotiated contracts and problematic communication. In the logic of social science inquiry revolving around the same understanding of autonomy, invading people's fragile but distinctive privacy is intolerable.

Despite the signature status of privacy protection, watertight confidentiality has proved to be impossible. Pseudonyms and disguised locations are often recognized by insiders. What researchers consider innocent is perceived by participants as misleading or even betrayal. What appears neutral on paper is often conflictual in practice. When government agencies or educational institutions or health organizations are studied, what private parts ought not be exposed? And who is blameworthy if aggressive media carry the research further? Encoding privacy protection is meaningless when there is no distinction between public and private that has consensus any longer (Punch, 1998, p. 175).

4. *Accuracy*. Ensuring that data are accurate is a cardinal principle in social science codes as well. Fabrications, fraudulent materials, omissions, and contrivances are both nonscientific and unethical. Data that are internally and externally valid are the coin of the realm, experimentally and morally. In an instrumentalist, value-neutral social science, the definitions entailed by the procedures themselves establish the ends by which they are evaluated as moral.

Accuracy defined in scientist terms and included in codes of ethics represents a version of Alfred North Whitehead's fallacy of misplaced concreteness. The moral domain becomes equivalent to the epistemological. The unspecifiable abstract is said to have existence in the rigorous concrete. A set of methodological operations becomes normative, and this confusion of categories is both illogical and stale.

INSTITUTIONAL REVIEW BOARDS

As a condition of funding, government agencies in various countries have insisted that review and monitoring bodies be established by institutions engaged in research involving human subjects. Institutional review boards (IRBs) embody the utilitarian agenda in terms of scope, assumptions, and procedural guidelines.

In 1978, the U.S. National Commission for the Protection of Human Subjects in Biomedical and Behavioral Research was established. As a result, three principles, published in what became known as the Belmont Report, were developed as the moral standards for research involving human subjects: respect for persons, beneficence, and justice.

1. The commitment to respect for persons reiterates the codes' demands that subjects enter the research voluntarily and with adequate information about the experiment's procedures and possible consequences. On a deeper level, respect for persons incorporates two basic ethical tenets: "First, that individuals should be treated as autonomous agents, and second, that persons with diminished autonomy [the immature and incapacitated] are entitled to protection" (University of Illinois, *Investigator Handbook,* 2009).

2. Under the principle of beneficence, researchers are enjoined to secure the well-being of their subjects. Beneficent actions are understood in a double sense as avoiding harm altogether and, if risks are involved for achieving substantial benefits, minimizing as much harm as possible:

> In the case of particular projects, investigators and members of their institutions are obliged to give forethought to the maximization of benefits and the reduction of risks that might occur from the research investigation. In the case of scientific research in general, members of the larger society are obliged to recognize the longer term benefits and risks that may result from the improvement of knowledge and from the development of novel medical, psychotherapeutic, and social procedures. (University of Illinois, *Investigator Handbook,* 2009)

3. The principle of justice insists on fair distribution of both the benefits and burdens of research. An injustice occurs when some groups (e.g., welfare recipients, the institutionalized, or particular ethnic minorities) are overused as research subjects because of easy manipulation or their availability. When research supported by public funds leads to "therapeutic devices and procedures, justice demands that these not provide advantages only to those who can afford them" (University of Illinois, *Investigator Handbook,* 2009).

These principles reiterate the basic themes of value-neutral experimentalism—individual autonomy, maximum benefits with minimal risks, and ethical ends exterior to scientific means. The policy procedures based on them reflect the same guidelines that dominate the codes of ethics: informed consent, protection of privacy, and nondeception. The authority of IRBs was enhanced in 1989 when Congress passed the NIH Revitalization Act and formed the Commission on Research Integrity. The emphasis at that point was on the invention, fudging, and distortion of data. Falsification, fabrication, and plagiarism continue as federal categories of misconduct, with a revised report in 1996 adding warnings against unauthorized use of confidential information, omission of important data, and interference (that is, physical damage to the materials of others).

With IRBs, the legacy of Mill, Comte, and Weber comes into its own. Value-neutral science is accountable to ethical standards through rational procedures controlled by value-neutral academic institutions in the service of an impartial government. Consistent with the way anonymous bureaucratic regimes become refined and streamlined toward greater efficiency, the regulations rooted in scientific and medical experiments now extend to humanistic inquiry. Protecting subjects from physical harm in laboratories has grown to encompass human behavior, history, and ethnography in natural settings. In Jonathon Church's (2002) metaphor, "a biomedical paradigm is used like some threshing machine with ethnographic research the resulting chaff" (p. 2). Whereas Title 45/Part 46 of the Code of Federal Regulations (45 CFR 46) designed protocols for research funded by 17 federal agencies, at present, most universities have multiple project agreements that consign all research to a campus IRB under the terms of 45 CFR 46 (cf. Shopes & Ritchie, 2004).

While this bureaucratic expansion has gone on unremittingly, most IRBs have not changed the composition of their membership. Medical and behavioral scientists under the aegis of value-free neutrality continue to dominate. And the changes in procedures have generally stayed within the biomedical model also. Expedited review under the common rule, for social research with no risk of physical or psychological harm, depends on enlightened IRB chairs and organizational flexibility. Informed consent, mandatory before medical experiments, is simply incongruent with interpretive research that does not reduce humans to subjects but sees itself as collaboration among human beings (Denzin & Giardina, 2007, pp. 20–28).[14] Despite technical improvements,

Intellectual curiosity remains actively discouraged by the IRB. Research projects must ask only surface questions and must not deviate from a path approved by a remote group of people. . . . Often the review process seems to be more about gamesmanship than anything else. A better formula for stultifying research could not be imagined. (Blanchard, 2002, p. 11)

In its conceptual structure, IRB utilitarian policy is designed to produce the best ratio of benefits to costs (McIntosh & Morse, 2009, pp. 99–100). IRBs ostensibly protect the subjects who fall under the protocols they approve. However, given the interlocking utilitarian functions of social science, the academy, and the state that Mill identified and promoted, IRBs in reality protect their own institutions rather than subject populations in society at large (see Vanderpool, 1996, Chapters 2 to 6). Only when professional associations like the American Anthropological Association create their own best practices for ethnographic research is the IRB structure pushed in the right direction. Such renovations, however, are contrary to the centralizing homogeneity of closed systems such as the IRBs.

CURRENT CRISIS

Mill and Comte, each in his own way, presumed that experimental social science benefited society by uncovering facts about the human condition. Durkheim and Weber believed that a scientific study of society could help people come to grips with the development of big-business monopolies and industrialism. The American Social Science Association was created in 1865 to link "real elements of the truth" with "the great social problems of the day" (Lazarsfeld & Reitz, 1975, p. 1). This myth of beneficence was destroyed with "the revelations at the Nuremberg trials (recounting the Nazis' 'medical experiments' on concentration camp inmates) and with the role of leading scientists in the Manhattan Project" (Punch, 1998, pp. 166–167).

The crisis of confidence multiplied with the exposure of actual physical harm in the Tuskegee Syphilis Study and the Willowbrook Hepatitis Experiment. In the 1960s, Project Camelot, a U.S. Army attempt to use social science to measure and forecast revolutions and insurgency, was bitterly opposed around the world and had to be canceled. Milgram's (1974) deception of unwitting subjects and Laud Humphreys's (1970, 1972) deceptive research on homosexuals in a public toilet and later in their homes, were considered scandalous for psychologically abusing research subjects. Noam Chomsky (1969/2002) exposed the complicity of social scientists with military initiatives in Vietnam.

Vigorous concern for research ethics since the 1980s, support from foundations, and the development of ethics codes and the IRB apparatus are credited by their advocates with curbing outrageous abuses. However, the charges of fraud, plagiarism, and misrepresentation continue on a lesser scale, with dilemmas, conundrums, and controversies unabated over the meaning and application of ethical guidelines. Entrepreneurial faculty competing for scarce research dollars are generally compliant with institutional control, but the vastness of social science activity in universities and research entities makes full supervision impossible.[15]

Underneath the pros and cons of administering a responsible social science, the structural deficiencies in its epistemology have become transparent (Mantzavinos, 2009). A positivistic philosophy of social inquiry insists on neutrality regarding definitions of the good, and this worldview has been discredited. The understanding of society it entails and promotes is inadequate (Winch, 2007). The dominant Enlightenment model, setting human freedom at odds with the moral order, is bankrupt. Even Weber's weaker version of contrastive languages rather than oppositional entities is not up to the task. Reworking the ethics codes so that they are more explicit and less hortatory will make no fundamental difference. Requiring ethics workshops for graduate students and strengthening government policy are desirable but of marginal significance. Refining the IRB process and exhorting IRBs to account for the pluralistic nature of academic research are insufficient.

In utilitarianism, moral thinking and experimental procedures are homogenized into a unidimensional model of rational validation. Autonomous human beings are clairvoyant about aligning means and goals, presuming that they can objectify the mechanisms for understanding themselves and the social world surrounding them (see Winch, 2007, Chapters 3 and 4).[16] This restrictive definition of ethics accounts for some of the goods we seek, such as minimal harm, but those outside a utility calculus are excluded. "Emotionality and intuition" are relegated "to a secondary position" in the decision-making process, for example, and no attention is paid to an "ethics of caring" grounded in "concrete particularities" (Denzin, 1997, p. 273; see also Ryan, 1995, p. 147). The way power and ideology influence social and political institutions is largely ignored. Under a rhetorical patina of deliberate choice and the illusion of autonomous creativity, a means-ends system operates in fundamentally its own terms.

This constricted environment no longer addresses adequately the complicated issues we face in studying the social world. But failure in the War on Poverty, contradictions over welfare, ill-fated studies of urban housing, and the thinness of medical science in health care reform have dramatized the limitations of a utility calculus that occupies the entire moral domain. Certainly, levels of success and failure are open to dispute even within the social science disciplines themselves.

More unsettling and threatening to the empirical mainstream than disappointing performance is the recognition that neutrality is not pluralistic but imperialistic. Reflecting on past experience, disinterested research under presumed conditions of value freedom is increasingly seen as de facto reinscribing the agenda in its own terms. Empiricism is procedurally committed to equal reckoning, regardless of how research subjects may constitute the substantive ends of life. But experimentalism is not a neutral meeting ground for all ideas; rather, it is a "fighting creed" that imposes its own ideas on others while uncritically assuming the very "superiority that powers this imposition" (Taylor et al., 1994, pp. 62–63).[17] In Foucault's (1979, pp. 170–195) more decisive terms, social science is a regime of power that helps maintain social order by normalizing subjects into categories designed by political authorities. A liberalism of equality is not neutral but represents only one range of ideals and is itself incompatible with other goods.

This noncontextual, nonsituational model that assumes "a morally neutral, objective observer will get the facts right" ignores "the situatedness of power relations associated with gender, sexual orientation, class, ethnicity, race, and nationality" (Denzin, 1997, p. 272). It is hierarchical (scientist-subject) and biased toward patriarchy. "It glosses the ways in which the observer-ethnographer is implicated and embedded in the 'ruling apparatus' of the society and the culture" (p. 272). Scientists "carry the mantle" of university-based authority as they venture out into "local community to do research" (Denzin, 1997, p. 272; see also Ryan, 1995, pp. 144–145).[18] There is no sustained questioning of expertise itself in democratic societies that belong in principle to citizens who do not share this specialized knowledge (Pacey, 1996, Chapter 3).

Feminist Communitarianism

SOCIAL ETHICS

Over the past decade, social and feminist ethics have made a radical break with the individual autonomy and rationalist presumption of canonical ethics (see Koehn, 1998). The social ethics of Agnes Heller (1988, 1990, 1996, 1999, 2009), Charles Taylor (1989, 1991, 1995, 2007; Taylor et al., 1994), Carole Pateman (1985, 1988, 1989; Pateman & Mills, 2007), Edith Wyschogrod (1985, 1990, 1998, 2002), Kwasi Wiredu (1996), and Cornel West (1989, 1991, 1993/2001) and the feminist ethics of Carol Gilligan (1982, 1983; Gilligan, Ward,

& Taylor, 1988), Nel Noddings (1984, 1989, 1990, 2002), Virginia Held (1993), and Seyla Benhabib (1992, 1994, 2002, 2008) are fundamentally reconstructing ethical theory (see Code, 1991; Steiner, 2009). Rather than searching for neutral principles to which all parties can appeal, social ethics rests on a complex view of moral judgments as integrating into an organic whole everyday experience, beliefs about the good, and feelings of approval and shame, in terms of human relations and social structures. This is a philosophical approach that situates the moral domain within the general purposes of human life that people share contextually and across cultural, racial, and historical boundaries (Christians, Glasser, McQuail, Nordenstreng, & White, 2009, Chapters 2 and 3). Ideally, it engenders a new occupational role and normative core for social science research (Gunzenhauser, 2006; White, 1995).

Carol Gilligan (1982, 1983; Gilligan et al., 1988) characterizes the female moral voice as an ethic of care. This dimension of moral development is rooted in the primacy of human relationships. Compassion and nurturance resolve conflicting responsibilities among people, standards totally opposite of merely avoiding harm.[19] In *Caring,* Nel Noddings (1984) rejects outright the "ethics of principle as ambiguous and unstable" (p. 5), insisting that human care should play the central role in moral decision making. Feminism in Linda Steiner's work critiques the conventions of impartiality and formality in ethics while giving precision to affection, intimacy, nurturing, egalitarian and collaborative processes, and empathy. Feminists' ethical self-consciousness also identifies subtle forms of oppression and imbalance and teaches us to "address questions about whose interests are regarded as worthy of debate" (Steiner, 1989, p. 158; see also Steiner, 1997).

> Feminist approaches to ethics challenge women's subordination, prescribe morally justifiable ways of resisting oppressive practices, and envision morally desirable alternatives that promote emancipation. . . . Fully feminist ethics, far more than their feminine and maternal counterparts, are distinctively political. . . . A feminist approach to ethics asks questions about power even before it asks questions about good and evil, care and justice, or maternal and paternal thinking. With feminism's persuasive critique of the disembodied ethical subject generating a healthy respect for difference, a multiculturalist feminism may yet construct a non-sexist theory that respects difference of all sorts. (Steiner, 2009, p. 377)

While sharing in the turn away from an abstract ethics of calculation, Charlene Seigfried (1996) argues against the Gilligan-Noddings tradition (cf. Held, 2006). Linking feminism to pragmatism, in which gender is socially constructed, she contradicts "the simplistic equation of women with care and nurturance and men with justice and autonomy" (Seigfried, 1996, p. 206). Gender-based moralities de facto make one gender subservient to another. In her social ethics, gender is replaced with engendering: "To be female or male is not to instantiate an unchangeable nature but to participate in an ongoing process of negotiating cultural expectations of femininity and masculinity" (p. 206). Seigfried challenges us to a social morality in which caring values are central but contextualized in webs of relationships and constructed toward communities with "more autonomy for women and more connectedness for men" (p. 219). Heller and Wyschogrod are two promising examples of proponents of social ethics that meet Seigfried's challenge while confronting forthrightly today's contingency, mass murder, conceptual upheavals in ethics, and hyperreality (cf. Noddings, 2002).

Heller is a former student of Georg Lukács and a dissident in Hungary, who became the Hannah Arendt Professor of Philosophy (Emerita) at the New School for Social Research. Her trilogy developing a contemporary theory of social ethics (Heller, 1988, 1990, 1996) revolves around what she calls the one decisive question: "Good persons exist—how are they possible?" (1988, p. 7). She disavows an ethics of norms, rules, and ideals external to human beings. Only exceptional acts of responsibility under duress and predicaments, each in its own way, are "worthy of theoretical interest" (1996, p. 3). Accumulated wisdom, moral meaning from our own choices of decency, and the ongoing summons of the Other together reintroduce love, happiness, sympathy, and beauty into a modern, nonabsolutist, but principled theory of morals.

In *Saints and Postmodernism,* Edith Wyschogrod (1990) asserts that anti-authority struggles are possible without assuming that our choices are voluntary. She represents a social ethics of self and Other in the tradition of Emmanuel Levinas (see Wyschogrod, 1974).[20] "The other person opens the venue of ethics, the place where ethical existence occurs" (Wyschogrod, 1990, p. xxi). The Other, "the touchstone of moral existence, is not a conceptual anchorage but a living force." Others function "as a critical solvent;" their existence carries "compelling moral weight" (p. xxi). As a professor of philosophy and religious thought at Rice University, with a commitment to moral narrative, Wyschogrod believes that one venue for Otherness is the saintly life, defined as one in "which compassion for the Other, irrespective of cost to the saint, is the primary trait." Saints put their own "bodies and material goods at the disposal of the Other. . . . Not only do saints contest the practices and beliefs of institutions, but in a more subtle way they contest the order of narrativity itself" (1990, pp. xxii–xxiii).

In addition to the Other, directed across a broad spectrum of belief systems who have "lived, suffered, and worked in actuality," Wyschogrod (1990, p. 7) examines historical narratives for illustrations of how the Other's self-manifestation is depicted. Her primary concern is the way communities shape shared experience in the face of cataclysms and calamities, arguing for historians who situate themselves "in dynamic relationship to them" (1998, p. 218). The overriding challenge for ethics, in Wyschogrod's view, is how researchers enter into communities that create and sustain hope in terms of immediacy—"a presence here and now" but "a presence that must be deferred" to the future (1998, p. 248). Unless it is tangible and actionable, hope serves those in control. Hope that merely projects a future redemption obscures abuses of power and human need in the present.

Martin Buber (1958) calls the human relation a primal notion in his famous lines, "in the beginning is the relation" and "the relation is the cradle of life" (pp. 69, 60). Social relationships are preeminent. "The one primary word is the combination I-Thou" (p. 3). This irreducible phenomenon—the relational reality, the in-between, the reciprocal bond, the interpersonal—cannot be decomposed into simpler elements without destroying it.[21] Given the primacy of relationships, unless we use our freedom to help others flourish, we deny our own well-being (cf. Verlinden, 2008, pp. 201–210).

Rather than privileging an abstract rationalism, the moral order is positioned close to the bone, in the creaturely and corporeal rather than the conceptual. "In this way, ethics . . . is as old as creation. Being ethical is a primordial movement in the beckoning force of life itself" (Olthuis, 1997, p. 141). The ethics of Levinas is one example:

> The human face is the epiphany of the nakedness of the Other, a visitation, a meeting, a saying which comes in the passivity of the face, not threatening, but obligating. My world is ruptured, my contentment interrupted. I am already obligated. Here is an appeal from which there is no escape, a responsibility, a state of being hostage. It is looking into the face of the Other that reveals the call to a responsibility that is before any beginning, decision or initiative on my part. (Olthuis, 1997, p. 139)

Humans are defined as communicative beings within the fabric of everyday life. Through dialogic encounter, subjects create life together and nurture one another's moral obligation to it. Levinas's ethics presumes and articulates a radical ontology of social beings in relation (see, e.g., Levinas, 1985, 1991).

Moreover, in Levinasian terms, when I turn to the face of the Other, I not only see flesh and blood, but a third party arrives—the whole of humanity. In responding to the Other's need, a baseline is established across the human race. For Benhabib (1992, cf. 1994), this is interactive universalism.[22] Our universal solidarity is rooted in the principle that "we have inescapable claims on one another which cannot be renounced except at the cost of our humanity" (Peukert, 1981, p. 11).

A FEMINIST COMMUNITARIAN MODEL

Feminist communitarianism is Norman Denzin's (1997, pp. 274–287; 2003, pp. 242–258; 2009, pp. 155–162) label for the ethical theory to lead us forward at this juncture (Christians, 2002b).[23] This is a normative model that serves as an antidote to individualist utilitarianism. It presumes that the community is onto-logically and axiologically prior to people. Human identity is constituted through the social realm, and human bonding is the epicenter of social formation. We are born into a sociocultural universe where values, moral commitments, and exis-tential meanings are negotiated dialogically. Feminist communitarianism "embodies a sacred, existential epistemology that locates persons in a noncom-petitive, nonhierarchical relationship to the larger moral universe" (Denzin, 2009, p. 158). Moral reasoning does not depend on formal consensus but goes forward because reciprocal care and understanding make moral discourse pos-sible. Every communal act is measured against the ideals of a universal respect for the dignity of all human beings, regardless of gender, age, race, or religion (see Benhabib, 1992, Chapter 1).

For communitarians, the liberalism of Locke and Mill confuses an aggregate of individual pursuits with the common good (Christians, Ferre, & Fackler, 1993, Chapter 1). Moral agents need a context of social commitments and community ties for assessing what is valuable. What is worth preserving as a good cannot be self-determined in isolation; it can be ascertained only within specific social situ-ations where human identity is nurtured. The public sphere is conceived as a mosaic of particular communities, a pluralism of ethnic identities and world-views intersecting to form a social bond but each seriously held and competitive as well. Rather than pay lip service to the social nature of the self while presum-ing a dualism of two orders, communitarianism interlocks personal autonomy with communal well-being. Morally appropriate action intends community. Common moral values are intrinsic to a community's ongoing existence and identity.

Therefore, the mission of social science research is enabling community life to prosper—equipping people to come to mutually held conclusions. The aim is not fulsome data per se, but community transformation. The received view assumes that research advances society's interests by feeding our individual capacity to reason and make calculated decisions. Instead of moving forward with IRB approval of human subjects, research is intended to be collaborative in its design and participatory in its execution. Rather than having their concerns defined by ethics codes in the files of academic offices and distributed in research reports prepared for clients, the participants themselves are given a forum to activate the polis mutually. In contrast to utilitarian experimentalism, the substantive conceptions of the good that drive the problems reflect the conceptions of the community rather than the expertise of researchers or funding agencies.

In the feminist communitarian model, participants have a say in how the research should be conducted and are involved in actually conducting it. Participants offer "a voice or hand in deciding which problems should be studied, what methods should be used to study them, whether the findings are valid or acceptable, and how the findings are to be used or implemented" (Root, 1993, p. 245). This research is rooted in "community, shared governance . . . and neighborliness." Given its cooperative mutuality, it serves "the community in which it is carried out, rather than the community of knowledge producers and policymakers" (Lincoln, 1995, pp. 280, 287). It finds its genius in the maxim that "persons are arbitrators of their own presence in the world" (Denzin, 1989, p. 81).

For feminist communitarians, research becomes "a civic, participatory, collaborative project. It uses democratically arrived at, participant-driven criteria of evaluation" (Denzin, 2009, p. 158). Researchers and subjects become "coparticipants in a common moral project." Ethnographic inquiry is "characterized by shared ownership of the research project, community-based analyses, an emancipatory, dialectical, and transformative commitment" to social action (Denzin, 2009, p. 158; see also Denzin, 1984, p. 145; Reinharz, 1993). This collaborative research model "makes the researcher responsible not to a removed discipline (or institution), but to those he or she studies." It aligns the ethics of research "with a politics of resistance, hope and freedom" (Denzin, 2003, p. 258).

Interpretive Sufficiency

Within a feminist communitarian model, the mission of social science research is interpretive sufficiency. In contrast to an experimentalism of instrumental efficiency, this paradigm seeks to open up the social world in all its dynamic dimensions. The thick notion of sufficiency supplants the thinness of the technical, exterior, and statistically precise received view. Rather than reducing social issues to financial and administrative problems for politicians, social science research enables people to come to terms with their everyday experience themselves.

Interpretive sufficiency means taking seriously lives that are loaded with multiple interpretations and grounded in cultural complexity. Ethnographic accounts should, therefore, "possess that amount of depth, detail, emotionality, nuance, and coherence that will permit a critical consciousness to be formed by the reader. Such texts should also exhibit representational adequacy, including the absence of racial, class, and gender stereotyping" (Denzin, 1997, p. 283; see 1989, pp. 77–81).

From the perspective of a feminist communitarian ethics, interpretive discourse is authentically sufficient when it fulfills three conditions: represents multiple voices, enhances moral discernment, and promotes social transformation. Consistent with the community-based norms advocated here, the focus is not on professional ethics per se but on the general morality. When feminist communitarianism is integrated with non-Enlightenment communal concepts such as *ubuntu* (from the Zulu maxim *umuntu ngumuntu ngabantu,* "a person is a person through other persons" or "I am because of others"), a dialogic ethics is formed that expands the general morality to the human race as a whole (Christians, 2004).

MULTIVOCAL AND CROSS-CULTURAL REPRESENTATION

Within social and political entities are multiple spaces that exist as ongoing constructions of everyday life. The dialogical self is situated and articulated within these decisive contexts of gender, race, class, and religion. In contrast to contractarianism, where tacit consent or obligation is given to the state, promises are made and sustained to one another. Research narratives reflect a community's multiple voices through which promise-keeping takes place.

In Carole Pateman's communitarian philosophy, sociopolitical entities are not to be understood first of all in terms of contracts. Making promises is one of the basic ways in which consenting human beings "freely create their own social relationships" (Pateman, 1989, p. 61; see also Pateman, 1985, pp. 26–29). We assume an obligation by making a promise. When individuals promise, they are obliged to act accordingly. But promises are primarily made not to authorities through political contracts, but to fellow citizens. If obligations are rooted in promises, obligations are owed to other colleagues in institutions and to participants in community practices. Therefore, only under conditions of participatory democracy can there be self-assumed moral obligation.

Pateman understands the nature of moral agency. We know ourselves primarily in relation and derivatively as thinkers withdrawn from action. Only by overcoming the traditional dualisms between thinker and agent, mind and body, reason and will, can we conceive of being as "the mutuality of personal relationships" (MacMurray, 1961a, p. 38). Moral commitments arise out of action and return to action for their incarnation and verification. From a dialogical perspective, promise-keeping through action and everyday language is not a supercilious pursuit because our way of being is not inwardly generated but socially derived.

> We become full human agents, capable of understanding ourselves, and hence of defining our identity, through . . . rich modes of expression we learn through exchange with others. . . .
>
> My discovering my own identity doesn't mean that I work it out in isolation, but that I negotiate it through dialogue, partly overt, partly internal, with others. My own identity crucially depends on my dialogical relations with others. . . .
>
> In the culture of authenticity, relationships are seen as the key loci of self-discovery and self-affirmation. (Taylor et al., 1994, pp. 32, 34, 36)

If moral bondedness flows horizontally and obligation is reciprocal in character, the affirming and sustaining of promises occurs cross-culturally. But the contemporary challenge of cultural diversity has raised the stakes and made easy solutions impossible. One of the most urgent and vexing issues on the democratic agenda at present is not just how to meet the moral obligation to treat ethnic differences with fairness but how to recognize explicit cultural groups politically (Benhabib, 2002, 2008).

Communitarianism as the basis for ethnic plurality rejects melting pot homogeneity and replaces it with the politics of recognition. The basic issue is whether democracies are discriminating against their citizens in an unethical manner when major institutions fail to account for the identities of their members (Taylor et al., 1994, p. 3). In what sense should the specific cultural and social features of African Americans, Asian Americans, Native Americans, Buddhists, Jews, the physically disabled, or children matter publicly? Should not public institutions ensure only that democratic citizens share an equal right to political liberties and due process without regard to race, gender, or religion? Beneath the rhetoric is a fundamental philosophical dispute that Taylor calls the "politics of recognition." As he puts it, "Nonrecognition or misrecognition can inflict harm, can be a form of oppression, imprisoning someone in a false, distorted, and reduced mode of being. Due recognition is not just a courtesy we owe people. It is a vital human need" (Taylor et al., 1994, p. 26). This foundational issue regarding the character of cultural identity needs to be resolved for cultural pluralism to come into its own. Feminist communitarianism is a nonassimilationist framework in which such resolution can occur.

However, liberal proceduralism cannot meet this vital human need. Emphasizing equal rights with no particular substantive view of the good life "gives only a very restricted acknowledgement of distinct cultural identities" (Taylor et al., 1994, p. 52). Insisting on neutrality, and without collective goals, produces at best personal freedom, safety, and economic security understood homogeneously. As Bunge (1996) puts it, "Contractualism is a code of behavior for the powerful and the hard—those who write contracts, not those who sign on the dotted line" (p. 230). However, in promise-based communal formation the flourishing of particular cultures, religions, and ethnic groups is the substantive goal to which we are morally committed as human beings.

Denzin (2002) demonstrates how multicultural representation ought to operate in the media's construction of the American racial order. An ethnic cinema that honors racial difference is not assimilationist, nor does it "celebrate exceptional blackness" supporting white values; and it refuses to pit "the ethnic other against a mainstream white America" as well as "dark skin against dark skin" (p. 6). Rather than "a didactic film aesthetic based on social problems realism"—one that is "trapped by the modernist agenda"—Denzin follows Hal Foster and bell hooks in arguing for an anti-aesthetic or postmodern aesthetic that is cross-disciplinary, is oriented to the vernacular, and denies "the idea of a privileged aesthetic realm" (pp. 11, 180). A "feminist, Chicana/o and black performance-based aesthetic" creates "a critical counter-hegemonic race consciousness" and implements critical race theory (p. 180).

In feminist communitarian terms, this aesthetic is simultaneously political and ethical. Racial difference is imbricated in social theories and in conceptions of the human being, of justice, and the common good. It requires an aesthetic that "in generating social criticism . . . also engenders resistance" (p. 181). It is not a "protest or integrationist initiative" aimed at "informing a white audience of racial injustice," but instead "offers new forms of representation that create the space for new forms of critical race consciousness" (p. 182). The overarching standard made possible by this aesthetic is enhancing moral agency, that is, serving as a catalyst for moral discernment (Christians, 2002a, p. 409).

With the starting hypothesis that all human cultures have something important to say, social science research recognizes particular cultural values consistent with universal human dignity (Christians, 1997, pp. 11–14; 2008, pp. 16–17). Interpretive sufficiency in its multicultural dimension helps people in their home territory see how life could be different. This framework "imagines new forms of human transformation and emancipation" (Denzin, 2009, p. 158). These transformations are enacted "through dialogue. If necessary, it sanctions nonviolent forms of civil disobedience." In its "asking that interpretive work provide the foundations for social criticism and social action, this ethic represents a call to action" (Denzin, 2009, p. 158).

MORAL DISCERNMENT

Societies are embodiments of institutions, practices, and structures recognized internally as legitimate. Without allegiance to a web of ordering relations, society becomes, as a matter of fact, inconceivable. Communities not only constitute linguistic entities but also require at least a minimal moral commitment to the common good. Because social entities are moral orders and not merely functional arrangements, moral commitment constitutes the self-in-relation. Our identity is defined by what we consider good or worth opposing. Only through the moral dimension can we make sense of human agency. As Stephen Mulhall and Adam Swift (1996) write:

> Developing, maintaining and articulating [our moral intuitions and reactions] is not something humans could easily or even conceivably dispense with. . . . We can no more imagine a human life that fails to address the matter of its bearings in moral space than we can imagine one in which developing a sense of up and down, right and left is regarded as an optional human task. . . . A moral orientation is inescapable because the questions to which the framework provides answers are themselves inescapable. (pp. 106–108; see also Taylor, 1989, pp. 27–29)

A self exists only within "webs of interlocution," and all self-interpretation implicitly or explicitly "acknowledges the necessarily social origin of any and all their conceptions of the good and so of themselves" (Mulhall & Swift, 1996). Moral frameworks are as fundamental for orienting us in social space as the need to establish ourselves in physical space. The moral dimension must, therefore, be considered intrinsic to human beings, not a system of rules, norms, and ideals external to society. Moral duty is nurtured by the demands of social linkage and not produced by abstract theory.

The core of a society's common morality is pretheoretical agreement. However, "what counts as common morality is not only imprecise but variable . . . and a difficult practical problem" (Bok, 1995, p. 99). Moral obligation must be articulated within the fallible and irresolute voices of everyday life. Among disagreements and uncertainty, we look for criteria and wisdom in settling disputes and clarifying confusions; and normative theories of an interactive sort can invigorate our common moral discourse. But generally accepted theories are not necessary for the common good to prosper. The common good is not "the complete morality of every participant . . . but a set of agreements among people who typically hold other, less widely shared ethical beliefs" (Bok, 1995, p. 99). Instead of expecting more theoretical coherence than history warrants, Reinhold Niebuhr inspires us to work through inevitable social conflicts while maintaining "an untheoretical jumble of agreements" called here the common good (Barry, 1967, pp.190–191). Through a common morality, we can approximate consensus on issues and settle disputes interactively. In Jürgen Habermas's (1993) terms, discourse in the public sphere must be oriented "toward mutual understanding" while allowing participants "the communicative freedom to take positions" on claims to final validity (p. 66; see also Habermas, 1990).

Communitarians challenge researchers to participate in a community's ongoing process of moral articulation. Conceptions of the good are shared by researchers and subjects, both of them self-reflexive and collaborating to bring moral issues to clarity. In fact, culture's continued existence depends on this type of identification and defense of its normative base (Fackler, 2009, pp. 312–315). Therefore, ethnographic texts must enable us "to discover moral truths about ourselves"; narratives ought to "bring a moral compass into readers' lives" by accounting for things that matter to them (Denzin, 1997, p. 284). Feminist communitarianism seeks to engender moral reasoning internally. Communities are woven together by narratives that invigorate their common understanding of good and evil, happiness and reward, the meaning of life and death. Recovering and refashioning moral vocabulary helps to amplify our deepest humanness. Researchers are not constituted as ethical selves antecedently, but moral discernment unfolds dialectically between researchers and the researched who collaborate with them.

Our widely shared moral convictions are developed through discourse within a community. These communities, where moral discourse is nurtured and shared, are a radical alternative to the utilitarian individualism of modernity. But in feminist communitarianism, communities are entered from the universal. The total opposite of an ethics of individual autonomy is universal human solidarity. Our obligation to sustain one another defines our existence. The primal sacredness of all without exception is the heart of the moral order and the new starting point for our theorizing (Christians, 1998, 2008).

The rationale for human action is reverence for life on earth. Living nature reproduces itself as its very character. Embedded in the animate world is the purposiveness of bringing forth life. Therefore, within the natural order is a moral claim on us for its own sake and in its own right. Nurturing life has a taken-for-granted character outside subjective preferences. Reverence for life on earth is a pretheoretical given that makes the moral order possible. The sacredness of life is not an abstract imperative but the ground of human action.[24] It is a primordial generality that underlies reification into ethical principles, an organic bond that everyone shares inescapably. In our systematic reflection on this protonorm, we recognize that it entails such basic ethical principles as human dignity and nonviolence (Christians, Rao, Ward, & Wasserman, 2009, pp. 143–145).

Reverence for life on earth establishes a level playing floor for cross-cultural collaboration in ethics. It represents a universalism from the ground up. Various societies articulate this protonorm in different terms and illustrate it locally, but every culture can bring to the table this fundamental norm for ordering political relationships and social institutions. We live out our values in a community setting where the moral life is experienced and a moral vocabulary articulated. Such protonorms as reverence for life can be recovered only locally. Language situates them in history. The sacredness of life reflects our common condition as a species, but we act on it through the immediate reality of geography, ethnicity, and ideology (Fackler, 2003). But according to feminist communitarianism, if we enter this communal arena not from individual decision making but from a universal commonness, we have the basis for believing that researchers and the researched can collaborate on the moral domain. Researchers do not bring a set of prescriptions into which they school their subjects. Instead they find ways interactively to bring the sacredness of life into its own—each culture and all circumstances providing an abundance of meaning and application.

How the moral order works itself out in community formation is the issue, not, first of all, what researchers consider virtuous. The challenge for those writing culture is not to limit their moral perspectives to their own generic and neutral principles but to engage the same moral space as the people they study. In this perspective, research strategies are not assessed, first of all, in terms of statistical sophistication, but for their vigor in illuminating how communities can flourish.

POLITICS OF RESISTANCE

Ethics in the feminist communitarian mode generates social criticism, leads to resistance, and empowers to action those who are interacting (see Habermas,

1971, pp. 301–317). Thus a basic norm for interpretive research is enabling the humane transformation of the multiple spheres of community life, such as religion, politics, ethnicity, and gender.

From his own dialogic perspective, Paulo Freire speaks of the need to reinvent the meaning of power:

> For me the principal, real transformation, the radical transformation of society in this part of the century demands not getting power from those who have it today, or merely to make some reforms, some changes in it. . . . The question, from my point of view, is not just to take power but to reinvent it. That is, to create a different kind of power, to deny the need power has as if it were metaphysics, bureaucratized, and anti-democratic. (quoted in Evans, Evans, & Kennedy, 1987, p. 229)

Certainly, oppressive power blocs and monopolies—economic, technological, and political—need the scrutiny of researchers and their collaborators. Given Freire's political-institutional bearing, power for him is a central notion in social analysis. But, in concert with him, feminist communitarian research refuses to deal with power in cognitive terms only. The issue is how people can empower themselves instead.

The dominant understanding of power is grounded in nonmutuality; it is interventionist power, exercised competitively and seeking control. In the communitarian alternative, power is relational, characterized by mutuality rather than sovereignty. Power from this perspective is reciprocity between two subjects, a relationship not of domination but of intimacy and vulnerability—power akin to that of Alcoholics Anonymous, in which surrender to the community enables the individual to gain mastery. In these terms, Cannella and Lincoln (2009) challenge us to "construct critical research that does not simultaneously create new forms of oppressive power for itself or for its practitioners" (p. 54). The indigenous Kaupapa Maori approach to research meets this standard: "The researcher is led by the members of the community and does not presume to be a leader, or to have any power that he or she can relinquish" (Denzin, 2003, p. 243).

Dialogue is the key element in an emancipatory strategy that liberates rather than imprisons us in manipulation or antagonistic relationships. Although the control version of power considers mutuality weakness, the empowerment mode maximizes our humanity and thereby banishes powerlessness. In the research process, power is unmasked and engaged through solidarity as a researched-researcher team. There is certainly no monologic "assumption that the researcher is giving the group power" (Denzin, 2003, p. 243). Rather than play semantic games with power, researchers themselves are willing to march against the barricades. As Freire insists, only with everyone filling his or her own political space, to the point of civil disobedience as necessary, will empowerment mean anything revolutionary (in McLaren & Leonard, 1993, Chapters 8, 10).

What is nonnegotiable in Freire's theory of power is participation of the oppressed in directing cultural formation (Stefanos, 1997). If an important social issue needs resolution, the most vulnerable will have to lead the way: "Revolutionary praxis cannot tolerate an absurd dichotomy in which the praxis of the people is merely that of following the [dominant elite's] decisions" (Freire, 1970a, p.120; see also Freire, 1978, pp. 17ff.).[25] Arrogant politicians—supported by a bevy of accountants, lawyers, economists, and social science researchers—trivialize the nonexpert's voice as irrelevant to the problem or its solution. On the contrary, transformative action from the inside out is impossible unless the oppressed are active participants rather than a leader's object. "Only power that springs from the weakness of the oppressed will be sufficiently strong to free both" (Freire, 1970b, p. 28).[26]

In Freire's (1973) terms, the goal is conscientization, that is, a critical consciousness that directs the ongoing flow of praxis and reflection in everyday life. In a culture of silence, the oppressor's language and way of being are fatalistically accepted without contradiction. But a critical consciousness enables us to exercise the uniquely human capacity of "speaking a true word" (Freire, 1970b, p. 75). Under conditions of sociopolitical control, "the vanquished are dispossessed of their word, their expressiveness, their culture" (1970b, p. 134). Through conscientization, the oppressed gain their own voice and collaborate in transforming their culture (1970a, pp. 212–213). Therefore, research is not the transmission of specialized data but, in style and content, a catalyst for critical consciousness. Without what Freire (1970b, p. 47) calls "a critical comprehension of reality" (that is, the oppressed "grasping with their minds the truth of their reality"), there is only acquiescence in the status quo.

The resistance of the empowered is more productive at the interstices—at the fissures in social institutions where authentic action is possible. Effective resistance is nurtured in the backyards, the open spaces, and voluntary associations, among neighborhoods, schools, and interactive settings of mutual struggle without elites. Since only nonviolence is morally acceptable for sociopolitical change, there is no other option except an educational one—having people movements gain their own voice and nurturing a critical conscience through dialogic means. People-based development from below is not merely an end in itself, but a fundamental condition of social transformation. "We are no longer called to just interpret the world"; rather than be limited to this mandate of traditional ethnography, "we are called to change the world and to change it in ways that resist injustice" (Denzin & Giardina, 2009, p. 23). In seeking research strategies of this kind, Guba (1990) insists correctly on a dialogic framework, a conversation of peace and hope "that will move us to new, more informed, and more sophisticated empowerment paradigms" (p. 27).

Conclusion

As Guba and Lincoln (1994) argue, the issues in social science ultimately must be engaged at the worldview level. "Questions of method are secondary to questions of paradigm, which we define as the basic belief system or worldview that guides the investigator, not only in choices of method but in ontologically and epistemologically fundamental ways" (p. 105). The conventional view, with its extrinsic ethics, gives us a truncated and unsophisticated paradigm that needs to be ontologically transformed. This historical overview of theory and practice points to the need for an entirely new model of research ethics in which human action and conceptions of the good are interactive.

"Since the relation of persons constitutes their existence as persons, . . . morally right action is [one] which intends community" (MacMurray, 1961b, p. 119). In feminist communitarianism, personal being is cut into the very heart of the social universe. The common good is accessible to us only in personal form; it has its ground and inspiration in a social ontology of the human.[27] "Ontology must be rescued from submersion in things by being thought out entirely from the viewpoint of person and thus of Being" (Lotz, 1963, p. 294). "Ontology is truly itself only when it is personal, and persons are truly themselves only as ontological" (Lotz, 1963, p. 297).

When rooted in a positivist or postpositivist worldview, explanations of social life are considered incompatible with the renderings offered by the participants themselves. In problematics, lingual form, and content, research production presumes greater mastery and clearer illumination than the nonexperts who are the targeted beneficiaries. Protecting and promoting individual autonomy has been the philosophical rationale for value neutrality since its origins in Mill. But the incoherence in that view of social science is now transparent. By limiting the active involvement of rational beings or judging their self-understanding to be false, empiricist models contradict the ideal of rational beings who "choose between competing conceptions of the good" and make choices "deserving of respect" (Root, 1993, p. 198). The verification standards of an instrumentalist system "take away what neutrality aims to protect: a community of free and equal rational beings legislating their own principles of conduct" (Root, 1993, p. 198). The social ontology of feminist communitarianism escapes this contradiction by reintegrating human life with the moral order.

Freed from neutrality and a superficial instrumentalism, the ethics of feminist communitarianism participates in the revolutionary social science advocated by Cannella and Lincoln (2009):

> Research conceptualizations, purposes, and practices would be grounded in critical ethical challenges to social (therefore science) systems, supports for egalitarian struggle, and revolutionary ethical awareness and activism from within the context of community. Research would be relational (often as related to community) and grounded within critique of systems, egalitarian struggle, and revolutionary ethics. (p. 68)

In this form, the positivist paradigm is turned upside down intellectually, and qualitative research advances social justice and is grounded in hope (Denzin & Giardina, 2009, pp. 41–42). Denzin, Yvonna Lincoln, and Linda Tuhiwai Smith (2008) correctly locate the politics and ethics of this chapter in global terms. For them, Occidental social scientists advocating alternative interpretive research "and indigenous communities alike have been moving toward the same goals." They both "seek a set of ethical principles that are feminist, caring, communitarian, holistic, respectful, mutual (rather than power imbalanced), sacred, and ecologically sound" (p. 569).

Notes

1. Michael Root (1993) is unique among philosophers of the social sciences in linking social science to the ideals and practices of the liberal state on the grounds that both institutions "attempt to be neutral between competing conceptions of the good" (p. xv). As he elaborates: "Though liberalism is primarily a theory of the state, its principles can be applied to any of the basic institutions of a society; for one can argue that the role of the clinic, the corporation, the scholarly associations, or professions is not to dictate or even recommend the kind of life a person should aim at. Neutrality can serve as an ideal for the operations of these institutions as much as it can for the state. Their role, one can argue, should be to facilitate whatever kind of life a student, patient, client, customer, or member is aiming at and not promote one kind of life over another" (p. 13). Root's interpretations of Mill and Weber are crucial to my own formulation.

2. Although committed to what he called "the logic of the moral sciences" in delineating the canons or methods for induction, Mill shared with natural science a belief in the uniformity of nature and the presumption that all phenomena are subject to cause-and-effect relationships. His five principles of induction reflect a Newtonian cosmology.

3. Utilitarianism in John Stuart Mill was essentially an amalgamation of Jeremy Bentham's greatest happiness principle, David Hume's empirical philosophy and concept of utility as a moral good, and Comte's positivist tenets that things-in-themselves cannot be known and knowledge is restricted to sensations. In his influential *A System of Logic,* Mill (1843/1893) is typically characterized as combining the principles of French positivism (as developed by Comte) and British empiricism into a single system.

4. For an elaboration of the complexities in positivism—including reference to its Millian connections—see Lincoln and Guba (1985, pp. 19–28).

5. Mill's realism is most explicitly developed in his *Examination of Sir William Hamilton's Philosophy* (1865b). Our belief in a common external world, in his view, is rooted in the fact that our sensations of physical reality "belong as much to other human or sentient beings as to ourselves" (p. 196; see also Copleston, 1966, p. 306, note 97).

6. Mill (1873/1969) specifically credits Comte for his use of the inverse deductive or historical method: "This was an idea entirely new to me when I found it in Comte; and but for him I might not soon (if ever) have arrived at it" (p. 126). Mill explicitly follows Comte in distinguishing social statics and social dynamics. He published two essays on Comte's influence in the *Westminster Review,* which were reprinted as *Auguste Comte and Positivism* (Mill, 1865a; see also Mill, 1873/1969, p. 165).

7. Emile Durkheim is more explicit and direct about causality in both the natural and the social worlds. While he argues for sociological over psychological causes of behavior and did not believe intention could cause action, he unequivocally sees the task of social science as discovering the causal links between social facts and personal behavior (see, e.g., Durkheim, 1966, pp. 44, 297–306).

8. As one example of the abuse Weber resisted, Root (1993, pp. 41–42) refers to the appointment of Ludwig Bernhard to a professorship of economics at the University of Berlin. Although he had no academic credentials, the Ministry of Education gave Bernhard this position without a faculty vote (see Weber, 1973, pp. 4–30). In Shils's (1949) terms, "A mass of particular, concrete concerns underlies [his 1917] essay—his recurrent effort to penetrate to the postulates of economic theory, his ethical passion for academic freedom, his fervent nationalist political convictions, and his own perpetual demand for intellectual integrity" (p. v).

9. The rationale for the Social Science Research Council in 1923 is multilayered, but in its attempt to link academic expertise with policy research, and in its preference for rigorous social scientific methodology, the SSRC reflects and implements Weber.

10. In *Utilitarianism,* Chapter 4, Mill (1861/1957) drew an analogy between visibility and desirability to prove the utilitarian moral standard. He argued that the proof an object is visible is the fact that people in real life actually see it. By analogy, the proof that something is desirable is people actually desiring it. Therefore, since people do in fact desire happiness, happiness must be desirable or good. As Harris (2006, p. 142) and others

have argued, although visibility/desirability illustrates Mill's empiricism, his intended proof is not convincing. Insisting that something is actually desired by people does not mean it should be desired. People often desire what they should not. My desiring happiness does not itself make the promotion of happiness a moral obligation for me or in general.

11. Often in professional ethics at present, we isolate consequentialism from a full-scale utilitarianism. We give up on the idea of maximizing happiness, but "still try to evaluate different courses of action purely in terms of their consequences, hoping to state everything worth considering in our consequence-descriptions" (Taylor, 1982, p. 144). However, even this broad version of utilitarianism, in Taylor's terms, "still legislates certain goods out of existence" (p. 144). It is likewise a restrictive definition of the good that favors the mode of reasoned calculation and prevents us from taking seriously all facets of moral and normative political thinking (p. 144). As Lincoln observes, utilitarianism's inescapable problem is that "in advocating the greatest good for the greatest number, small groups of people (all minority groups, for example) experience the political regime of the 'tyranny of the majority.'" She refers correctly to "liberalism's tendency to rein-scribe oppression by virtue of the utilitarian principle" (personal communication, February 16, 1999).

12. John Rawls's (1971) justice-based moral theory is also a compelling critique of utilitarianism. Utilitarianism is a teleological theory and Rawls's justice-as-fairness is deontological. Rawls needs to be elaborated in debates over moral theory itself. Taylor and Ross are included here since they are more explicitly epistemological, interlacing Mill's empiricism and utilitarianism.

13. Given the nature of positivist inquiry, Jennings and Callahan (1983) conclude that only a short list of ethical questions are considered, and they "tend to merge with the canons of professional scientific methodology.... Intellectual honesty, the suppression of personal bias, careful collection and accurate reporting of data, and candid admission of the limits of the scientific reliability of empirical studies—these were essentially the only questions that could arise. And, since these ethical responsibilities are not particularly controversial (at least in principle), it is not surprising that during this period [the 1960s] neither those concerned with ethics nor social scientists devoted much time to analyzing or discussing them" (p. 6).

14. Most biomedical research occurs in a laboratory. Researchers are obliged to inform participants of potential risk and obtain consent before the research takes place. Ethnographic research occurs in settings where subjects live, and informed consent is a process of "ongoing interaction between the researcher and the members of the community being studied.... One must establish bonds of trust and negotiate consent ... taking place over weeks or months—not prior to a structured interview" (Church, 2002, p. 3).

15. As Taylor (1982) puts it, "The modern dispute about utilitarianism is not about whether it occupies some of the space of moral reason, but whether it fills the whole space." "Comfort the dying" is a moral imperative in contemporary Calcutta, even

though "the dying are in an extremity that makes [utilitarian] calculation irrelevant" (p. 134).

16. While rejecting this utilitarian articulation of means to ends, a philosophical critique of the means-ends trajectory is necessary for this rejection to have long-term credibility. Drescher (2006, pp. 183–188) represents a recent review of the means-ends relation, establishing criteria in rationalist terms.

17. This restates the well-known objection to a democratic liberalism of individual rights: "Liberalism is not a possible meeting ground for all cultures, but is the political expression of one range of cultures, and quite incompatible with other ranges. Liberalism can't and shouldn't claim complete cultural neutrality. Liberalism is also a fighting creed. Multiculturalism as it is often debated today has a lot to do with the imposition of some cultures on others, and with the assumed superiority that powers this imposition. Western liberal societies are thought to be supremely guilty in this regard, partly because of their colonial past, and partly because of their marginalization of segments of their populations that stem from other cultures" (Taylor et al., 1994, pp. 62–63).

18. Denzin in this passage credits Smith (1987, p. 107) with the concept of a "ruling apparatus."

19. Gilligan's research methods and conclusions have been debated by a diverse range of scholars. For this debate and related issues, see Brabeck (1990), Card (1991), Tong (1989, pp. 161–168; 1993, pp. 80–157), Seigfried (1996), and Wood(1994).

20. Levinas (b. 1905) was a professor of philosophy at the University of Paris (Nanterre) and head of the Israelite Normal School in Paris. In Wyschogrod's (1974) terms, "He continues the tradition of Martin Buber and Franz Rosenweig" and was "the first to introduce Husserl's work into . . . the French phenomenological school" (pp. vii–viii). Although Wyschogrod is a student of Martin Heidegger, Georg Wilhelm Friedrich Hegel, and Edmund Husserl (see, e.g., Wyschogrod, 1985)—and engages Jacques Derrida, Jean-François Lyotard, Michel Foucault, and Gilles Deleuze—her work on ethics appeals not to traditional philosophical discourse but to concrete expressions of self-Other transactions in the visual arts, literary narrative, historiography, and the normalization of death in the news.

21. Levinas sees the irreducibility of the I-Thou relation as a critical contribution to the history of ideas: "The dialogical relation and its phenomenological irreducibility . . . will remain the unforgettable contribution of Martin Buber's philosophical labours. . . . Any reflection of the alterity of the others in his or her irreducibility to the objectivity of objects and the being of beings must recognize the new perspective Buber opened" (Levinas, as cited in Friedman, 2002, p. 338).

22. Martha Nussbaum (1993) argues for a version of virtue ethics in these terms, contending for a model rooted in Aristotle that has cross-cultural application without being detached from particular forms of social life. In her model, various spheres of human experience that are found in all cultures represent questions to answer and choices to make—attitudes toward the ill or good fortune of others, how to treat strangers, management of property, control over bodily appetites, and so forth. Our experiences in

these areas "fix a subject for further inquiry" (p. 247), and our reflection on each sphere will give us a "thin or nominal definition" of a virtue relevant to this sphere. On this basis, we can talk across cultures about behavior appropriate in each sphere (see Nussbaum, 1999).

23. Root (1993, Chapter 10) also chooses a communitarian alternative to the dominant paradigm. In his version, critical theory, participatory research, and feminist social science are three examples of the communitarian approach. This chapter offers a more complex view of communitarianism developed in political philosophy and intellectual history, rather than limiting it to social theory and practical politics. Among the philosophical communitarians (Sandel, 1982/1998; Taylor, 1989; Walzer, 1983, 1987), Pateman (1985, 1989) is explicitly feminist, and her promise motif forms the axis for the principle of multivocal representation outlined below. In this chapter's feminist communitarian model, critical theory is integrated into the third ethical imperative—empowerment and resistance. In spite of that difference in emphasis, I agree with Root's (1993) conclusion: "Critical theories are always critical for a particular community, and the values they seek to advance are the values of that community. In that respect, critical theories are communitarian. . . . For critical theorists, the standard for choosing or accepting a social theory is the reflective acceptability of the theory by members of the community for whom the theory is critical" (pp. 233–234). For a review of communitarian motifs in terms of Foucault, see Olssen (2002).

24. The sacredness of life as a protonorm differs fundamentally from the Enlightenment's monocultural ethical rationalism in which universal imperatives were considered obligatory for all nations and epochs. Cartesian foundationalism and Immanuel Kant's formalism presumed noncontingent starting points. Universal human solidarity does not. Nor does it flow from Platonism, that is, the finite participating in the infinite and receiving its essence from it (see Christians, 2008, pp. 10–12). In addition to the sacredness of life as a protonorm, there are other appeals to universals that are not Western or do not presume a Newtonian cosmology; for a summary, see Cooper & Christians (2008, pp. 296–300).

25. Mutuality is a cardinal feature of the feminist communitarian model generally and therefore crucial to the principle of empowerment. For this reason, critical theory is inscribed into the third principle here, rather than following Root (see note 18, above), allowing it to stand by itself as an illustration of communitarianism. Root (1993, p. 238) himself observes that critical theorists often fail to transfer the "ideals of expertise" to their research subjects or give them little say in the research design and interpretation. Without a fundamental shift to communitarian interactivity, research in all modes is prone to the distributive fallacy.

26. Because of his fundamental commitment to dialogue, empowering for Freire avoids the weaknesses of monologic concepts of empowerment in which researchers are seen to free up the weak and unfortunate (summarized by Denzin, 2003, pp. 242–245, citing Bishop, 1998). While Freire represents a radical perspective, he does not claim, "as more radical theorists" do, that "only they and their theories can lead" the researched into freedom (Denzin, 2003, p. 246; citing Bishop, 1998).

27. Michael Theunissen (1984) argues that Buber's relational self (and therefore its legacy in Levinas, Freire, Heller, Wyschogrod, and Taylor) is distinct from the subjectivity of continental existentialism. The subjective sphere of Husserl and Jean-Paul Sartre, for example, "stands in no relation to a Thou and is not a member of a We" (p. 20; see also p. 276). "According to Heidegger the self can only come to itself in a voluntary separation from other selves; according to Buber, it has its being solely in the relation" (p. 284).

References

Barry, B. (1967). Justice and the common good. In A. Quinton (Ed.), *Political philosophy* (pp. 190–191). Oxford, UK: Oxford University Press.

Benhabib, S. (1992). *Situating the self: Gender, community, and postmodernism in contemporary ethics.* Cambridge, UK: Polity.

Benhabib, S. (1994). *Feminist contentions: A philosophical exchange.* New York: Routledge.

Benhabib, S. (2002). *The claims of culture: Equality and diversity in the global era.* Princeton, NJ: Princeton University Press.

Benhabib, S. (2008). *Democracy and difference.* New York: Oxford University Press.

Bishop, R. (1998). Freeing ourselves from neo-colonial domination in research: A Maori approach to creating knowledge. *International Journal of Qualitative Studies in Education, 11,* 199–219.

Blanchard, M. A. (2002, January). *Should all disciplines be subject to the common rule?* Washington, DC: U.S. Department of Health and Human Services.

Bok, S. (1995). *Common values.* Columbia: University of Missouri Press.

Brabeck, M. M. (Ed.). (1990*). Who cares? Theory, research, and educational implications of the ethic of care.* New York: Praeger.

Brunn, H. H. (2007). *Science, values, and politics in Max Weber's methodology.* Surrey, UK: Ashgate.

Buber, M. (1958). *I and thou* (2nd ed.; R. G. Smith, Trans.). New York: Scribner's.

Bulmer, M. (2008). The ethics of social research. In N. Gilbert (Ed.), *Researching social life* (3rd ed., pp. 145–161). London: Sage.

Bunge, M. (1996*). Finding philosophy in social science.* New Haven, CT: Yale University Press.

Cannella, G. S., & Lincoln, Y. S. (2009). Deploying qualitative methods for critical social purposes. In N. K. Denzin & M. D. Giardina (Eds.), *Qualitative inquiry and social justice* (pp. 53–72). Walnut Creek, CA: Left Coast Press.

Card, C. (Ed.). (1991). *Feminist ethics.* Lawrence: University of Kansas Press.

Chomsky, N. (2002). *American power and the new mandarins.* New York: The Free Press. (Original work published 1969)

Christians, C. G. (1997). The ethics of being. In C. G. Christians & M. Traber (Eds.), *Communication ethics and universal values* (pp. 3–23). Thousand Oaks, CA: Sage.

Christians, C. G. (1998). The sacredness of life. *Media Development, 45*(2), 3–7.

Christians, C. G. (2002a). Introduction. In C. G. Christians (Ed.), Ethical theorists and qualitative research [Special issue]. *Qualitative Inquiry, 8*(1), 407–410.

Christians, C. G. (2002b). Norman Denzin's feminist communitarianism. *Studies in Symbolic Interactionism, 25,* 167–177.

Christians, C. G. (2004). *Ubuntu* and communitarianism in media ethics. *Ecquid Novi, 25*(2), 235–256.

Christians, C. G. (2008). The ethics of universal being. In S. J. A. Ward & H. Wasserman (Eds.), *Media ethics beyond borders: A global perspective* (pp. 6–23). Johannesburg, South Africa: Heinemann.

Christians, C., Ferre, J., & Fackler, M. (1993). *Good news: Social ethics and the press.* New York: Oxford University Press.

Christians, C. G., Glasser, T. L., McQuail, D., Nordenstreng, K., & White, R. (2009). *Normative theories of the media: Journalism in democratic societies.* Urbana: University of Illinois Press.

Christians, C., Rao, S., Ward, S. J. A., & Wasserman, H. (2009). Toward a global media ethics: Theoretical perspectives. *Ecquid Novi: African Journalism Studies, 29*(2), 135–172.

Church, J. T. (2002, January). *Should all disciplines be subject to the common rule?* Washington, DC: U. S. Department of Health and Human Services.

Code, L. (1991). *What can she know? Feminist theory and the construction of knowledge.* Ithaca, NY: Cornell University Press.

Comte, A. (1830). *Cours de Philosophie Positive.* Paris: Bachelier Librarie pour les Mathematiques.

Comte, A. (1910). *A general view of positivism* (J. H. Bridges, Trans.). London: Routledge. (Original work published 1848)

Cooper, T. W., & Christians, C. G. (2008). On the need and requirements for a global ethic of communication. In J. V. Ciprut (Ed.), *Ethics, politics, and democracy: From primordial principles to prospective practices* (pp. 293–318). Cambridge, MA: MIT Press.

Copleston, F. (1966). *A history of philosophy: Vol. 8. Modern philosophy: Bentham to Russell.* Garden City, NY: Doubleday.

Denzin, N. K. (1984). *On understanding emotion.* San Francisco: Jossey-Bass.

Denzin, N. K. (1989). *Interpretive biography.* Newbury Park, CA: Sage.

Denzin, N. K. (1997). *Interpretive ethnography: Ethnographic practices for the 21st century.* Thousand Oaks, CA: Sage.

Denzin, N. K. (2002). *Reading race: Hollywood and the cinema of racial violence.* Thousand Oaks, CA: Sage.

Denzin, N. K. (2003). *Performance ethnography: Critical pedagogy and the politics of culture.* Thousand, Oaks, CA: Sage.

Denzin, N. K. (2009). *Qualitative inquiry under fire: Toward a new paradigm dialogue.* Walnut Creek, CA: Left Coast Press.

Denzin, N. K., & Giardina, M. D. (Eds.). (2007). *Ethical futures in qualitative research*, Walnut Creek, CA: Left Coast Press.

Denzin, N. K., & Giardina, M. D. (Eds.). (2009). *Qualitative inquiry and social justice*. Walnut Creek, CA: Left Coast Press.

Denzin, N. K., Lincoln, Y. S., & Smith, L. T. (Eds.). (2008). *Handbook of critical and indigenous methodologies*. Thousand Oaks, CA: Sage.

Drescher, G. L. (2006). *Good and real: Demystifying paradoxes from physics to ethics*. Cambridge, MA: MIT Press.

Durkheim, E. (1966). *Suicide: A study of sociology*. New York: Free Press.

Erikson, K. (1967). Disguised observation in sociology. *Social Problems, 14,* 366–373.

Euben, J. P. (1981). Philosophy and the professions. *Democracy, 1*(2), 112–127.

Evans, A. F., Evans, R. A., & Kennedy, W. B. (1987). *Pedagogies for the non-poor*. Maryknoll, NY: Orbis.

Fackler, M. (2003). Communitarian theory with an African flexion. In J. Mitchell & S. Marriage (Eds.), *Mediating religion: Conversations in media, religion, and culture* (pp. 317–327). London: T & T Clark.

Fackler, M. (2009). Communitarianism. In L. Wilkins & C. Christians (Eds.), *The handbook of mass media ethics* (pp. 305–316). New York: Routledge.

Foucault, M. (1979). *Discipline and punish: The birth of the prison* (A. Sheridan, Trans.). New York: Random House.

Freire, P. (1970a). *Education as the practice of freedom: Cultural action for freedom*. Cambridge, MA: Harvard Educational Review/Center for the Study of Development.

Freire, P. (1970b). *Pedagogy of the oppressed*. New York: Seabury.

Freire, P. (1973). *Education for critical consciousness*. New York: Seabury.

Freire, P. (1978). *Pedagogy in process: The letters of Guinea-Bissau*. New York: Seabury.

Friedman, M. S. (2002). *Martin Buber: The life of dialogue*. New York: Routledge.

Gilligan, C. (1982). *In a different voice: Psychological theory and women's development*. Cambridge, MA: Harvard University Press.

Gilligan, C. (1983). Do the social sciences have an adequate theory of moral development? In N. Haan, R. N. Bellah, P. Rabinow, & W. N. M. Sullivan (Eds.), *Social science as moral inquiry* (pp. 33–51). New York: Columbia University Press.

Gilligan, C., Ward, J. V., & Taylor, J. M. (1988). *Mapping the moral domain*. Cambridge, MA: Harvard University, Graduate School of Education.

Guba, E. G. (1990). The alternative paradigm dialog. In E. Guba (Ed.), *The paradigm dialog* (pp. 17–30). Thousand Oaks, CA: Sage.

Guba, E. G., & Lincoln, Y. S. (1994). Competing paradigms in qualitative research. In N. K. Denzin & Y. S. Lincoln (Eds.), *Handbook of qualitative research* (pp.105–117). Thousand Oaks, CA: Sage.

Gunzenhauser, M. G. (2006). A moral epistemology of knowing subjects: Theorizing a relational turn for qualitative research. *Qualitative Inquiry, 12*(3), 621–647.

Habermas, J. (1971). *Knowledge and human interests* (J. J. Shapiro, Trans.). Boston: Beacon.

Habermas, J. (1990). *Moral consciousness and communicative action* (C. Lenhardt & S. W. Nicholson, Trans.). Cambridge, MA: MIT Press.

Habermas, J. (1993). *Justification and application: Remarks on discourse ethics* (C. Cronin, Trans.). Cambridge, MA: MIT Press.

Harris, C. E. (2006). *Applying moral theories* (5th ed.). Stamford, CT: Wadsworth.

Held, V. (1993). *Feminist morality: Transforming culture, society, and politics.* Chicago: University of Chicago Press.

Held, V. (2006). *The ethics of care: Personal, political, and global.* New York: Oxford University Press.

Heller, A. (1988). *General ethics.* Oxford, UK: Blackwell.

Heller, A. (1990). *A philosophy of morals.* Oxford, UK: Blackwell.

Heller, A. (1996). *An ethics of personality.* Oxford, UK: Blackwell.

Heller, A. (1999). *A theory of modernity.* Oxford, UK: Blackwell.

Heller, A. (2009). *A theory of feelings* (2nd ed.). Lanham, MD: Lexington Books.

Humphreys, L. (1970). *Tearoom trade: Impersonal sex in public places.* Chicago: Aldine.

Humphreys, L. (1972). *Out of the closet.* Englewood Cliffs, NJ: Prentice Hall.

Jennings, B., & Callahan, D. (1983, February). Social science and the policy-making process. *Hastings Center Report,* pp. 3–8.

Koehn, D. (1998). *Rethinking feminist ethics: Care, trust, and empathy.* New York: Routledge.

Lassman, P. (2004). Political theory in an age of disenchantment: The problem of value pluralism—Weber, Berlin, Rawls. *Max Weber Studies, 4*(2), pp. 251–269.

Lazarsfeld, P., & Reitz, J. G. (1975). *An introduction to applied sociology.* New York: Elsevier.

Levinas, E. (1985). *Ethics and infinity* (R. A. Cohen, Trans.). Pittsburgh, PA: Duquesne University Press.

Levinas, E. (1991). *Otherwise than being or beyond essence* (A. Lingis, Trans.). Dordrecht, Netherlands: Kluwer Academe.

Lincoln, Y. S. (1995). Emerging criteria for quality in qualitative and interpretive inquiry. *Qualitative Inquiry, 1,* 275–289.

Lincoln, Y. S., & Guba, E. G. (1985). *Naturalistic inquiry.* Beverly Hills, CA: Sage.

Lotz, J. B. (1963). Person and ontology. *Philosophy Today, 7,* 294–297.

MacMurray, J. (1961a). *The form of the personal: Vol. 1. The self as agent.* London: Faber & Faber.

MacMurray, J. (1961b). *The form of the personal: Vol. 2. Persons in relation.* London: Faber & Faber.

Mantzavinos, C. (Ed.). (2009). *Philosophy of the social sciences: Philosophical theory and scientific practice.* Cambridge, UK: Cambridge University Press.

McIntosh, M. J., & Morse, J. M. (2009). Institutional review boards and the ethics of emotion. In N. K. Denzin & M. D. Giardina (Eds.), *Qualitative inquiry and social justice* (pp. 81–107). Walnut Creek, CA: Left Coast Press.

McLaren, P., & Leonard, P. (Eds.). (1993). *Paulo Freire: A critical encounter.* London: Routledge.

Milgram, S. (1974). *Obedience to authority.* New York: Harper & Row.

Mill, J. S. (1865a). *Auguste Comte and positivism.* London.

Mill, J. S. (1865b). *Examination of Sir William Hamilton's philosophy and of the principal philosophical questions discussed in his writings*. London: Longman, Green, Roberts & Green.

Mill, J. S. (1893). *A system of logic, ratiocinative and inductive: Being a connected view of the principles of evidence and the methods of scientific investigation* (8th ed.). New York: Harper & Brothers. (Original work published 1843)

Mill, J. S. (1957). *Utilitarianism*. Indianapolis, IN: Bobbs-Merrill. (Original work published 1861)

Mill, J. S. (1969). *Autobiography*. Boston: Houghton Mifflin. (Original work published posthumously 1873)

Mill, J. S. (1978). *On liberty*. Indianapolis: Hackett. (Original work published 1859)

Mulhall, S., & Swift, A. (1996). *Liberals and communitarians* (2nd ed.). Oxford, UK: Blackwell.

Noddings, N. (1984). *Caring: A feminine approach to ethics and moral education*. Berkeley: University of California Press.

Noddings, N. (1989). *Women and evil*. Berkeley: University of California Press.

Noddings, N. (1990). Ethics from the standpoint of women. In D. L. Rhode (Ed.), *Theoretical perspectives on sexual difference* (pp. 160–173). New Haven, CT: Yale University Press.

Noddings, N. (2002). *Starting at home: Caring and social policy*. Berkeley: University of California Press.

Nussbaum, M. (1993). Non-relative virtues: An Aristotelian approach. In M. Nussbaum & A. Sen (Eds.), *The quality of life* (pp. 242–269). Oxford, UK: Clarendon.

Nussbaum, M. (1999). *Sex and social justice*. New York: Oxford University Press.

Olssen, M. (2002). Michel Foucault as "thin" communitarian: Difference, community, democracy." *Cultural Studies <=> Critical Methodologies, 2*(4), 483–513.

Olthuis, J. (1997). Face-to-face: Ethical asymmetry or the symmetry of mutuality? In J. Olthuis (Ed.), *Knowing other-wise* (pp. 134–164). New York: Fordham University Press.

Pacey, A. (1996). *The culture of technology*. Cambridge, MA: MIT Press.

Pateman, C. (1985). *The problem of political obligation: A critique of liberal theory*. Cambridge, UK: Polity.

Pateman, C. (1988). *The sexual contract*. Stanford, CA: Stanford University Press.

Pateman, C. (1989). *The disorder of women: Democracy, feminism and political theory*. Stanford, CA: Stanford University Press.

Pateman, C., & Mills, C. W. (2007). *Contract and domination*. Cambridge, UK: Polity Press.

Peukert, H. (1981). Universal solidarity as the goal of ethics. *Media Development, 28*(4), 10–12.

Punch, M. (1998). Politics and ethics in qualitative research. In N. K. Denzin & Y. S. Lincoln (Eds.), *The landscape of qualitative research* (pp. 156–184). Thousand Oaks, CA: Sage.

Rawls, J. (1971). *A theory of justice*. Cambridge, MA: Harvard University Press.

Reinharz, S. (1993). *Social research methods: Feminist perspectives*. New York: Elsevier.

Reiss, A. J., Jr. (1979). Governmental regulation of scientific inquiry: Some paradoxical consequences. In C. B. Klockars & F. W. O'Connor (Eds.), *Deviance and decency: The ethics of research with human subjects* (pp. 61–95). Beverly Hills, CA: Sage.

Root, M. (1993). *Philosophy of social science: The methods, ideals, and politics of social inquiry.* Oxford, UK: Blackwell.

Ross, W. D. (1930). *The right and the good.* Oxford, UK: Clarendon.

Ryan, K. E. (1995). Evaluation ethics and issues of social justice: Contributions from female moral thinking. In N. K. Denzin (Ed.), *Studies in symbolic interaction: A research annual* (Vol. 19, pp. 143–151). Greenwich, CT: JAI.

Sandel, M. J. (1998). *Liberalism and the limits of justice* (2nd ed.). Cambridge, UK: Cambridge University Press. (Original work published 1982)

Seigfried, C. H. (1996). *Pragmatism and feminism: Reweaving the social fabric.* Chicago: University of Chicago Press.

Shils, E. A. (1949). Foreword. In M. Weber, *The methodology of the social sciences* (pp. iii-x). New York: Free Press.

Shopes, L., & Ritchie, D. (2004). Exclusion of oral history from IRB review: An update. *Perspectives on History.* Available at http://www.historians.org/Perspectives/Issues/2004/0403/0403new1.cfm

Smith, D. E. (1987). *The everyday world as problematic: A feminist sociology.* Boston: Northeastern University Press.

Soble, A. (1978, October). Deception in social science research: Is informed consent possible? *Hastings Center Report,* pp. 40–46.

Stefanos, A. (1997). African women and revolutionary change: A Freirian and feminist perspective. In P. Freire (Ed.), *Mentoring the mentor: A critical dialogue with Paulo Freire* (pp. 243–271). New York: Peter Lang.

Steiner, L. (1989). Feminist theorizing and communication ethics. *Communication, 12*(3), 157–174.

Steiner, L. (1997). A feminist schema for analysis of ethical dilemmas. In F. L. Casmir (Ed.), *Ethics in intercultural and international communication* (pp. 59–88). Mahwah, NJ: Lawrence Erlbaum.

Steiner, L. (2009). Feminist media ethics. In L. Wilkins & C. Christians (Eds.), *The handbook of mass media ethics* (pp. 366–381). New York: Routledge.

Taylor, C. (1982). The diversity of goods. In A. Sen & B. Williams (Eds.), *Utilitarianism and beyond* (pp. 129–144). Cambridge, UK: Cambridge University Press.

Taylor, C. (1989). *Sources of the self: The making of the modern identity.* Cambridge, MA: Harvard University Press.

Taylor, C. (1991). *The ethics of authenticity.* Cambridge, MA: Harvard University Press.

Taylor, C. (1995). *Philosophical arguments.* Cambridge, MA: Harvard University Press.

Taylor, C. (2007). *A secular age.* Cambridge, MA: Harvard University Press.

Taylor, C., Appiah, K. A., Habermas, J., Rockefeller, S. C., Walzer, M., & Wolf, S. (1994). *Multiculturalism: Examining the politics of recognition* (A. Gutmann, Ed.). Princeton, NJ: Princeton University Press.

Theunissen, M. (1984). *The other: Studies in the social ontology of Husserl, Heidegger, Sartre, and Buber* (C. Macann, Trans.). Cambridge: MIT Press.

Tong, R. (1989). *Feminist thought.* Boulder, CO: Westview.

Tong, R. (1993). *Feminine and feminist ethics.* Belmont, CA: Wadsworth.

University of Illinois at Urbana-Champaign, Institutional Review Board. (2009). Part I: Fundamental principles for the use of human subjects in research. In *Investigator handbook.* Available at http://irb.illinois.edu/?q=investigator-handbook/index.html

Vanderpool, H. Y. (Ed.). (1996). *The ethics of research involving human subjects: Facing the 21st century.* Frederick, MD: University Publishing Group.

Verlinden, A. (2008). Global ethics as dialogism. In M. S. Comers, W. Vanderkerchove, & A. Verlinden (Eds.), *Ethics in an era of globalization* (pp. 187–215). Aldershot, UK: Ashgate.

Walzer, M. (1983). *Spheres of justice: A defense of pluralism and equality.* New York: Basic Books.

Walzer, M. (1987). *Interpretation and social criticism.* Cambridge, MA: Harvard University Press.

Weber, M. (1949a). The meaning of ethical neutrality in sociology and economics. In M. Weber, *The methodology of the social sciences* (E. A. Shils & H. A. Finch, Eds. & Trans.). New York: Free Press. (Original work published 1917)

Weber, M. (1949b). Objectivity in social science and social policy. In M. Weber, *The methodology of the social sciences* (E. A. Shils & H. A. Finch, Eds. & Trans.). New York: Free Press. (Original work published 1904)

Weber, M. (1973). *Max Weber on universities* (E. A. Shils, Ed. & Trans.). Chicago: University of Chicago Press.

West, C. (1989). *The American evasion of philosophy: A genealogy of pragmatism.* Madison: University of Wisconsin Press.

West, C. (1991). *The ethical dimensions of Marxist thought.* New York: Monthly Review Books.

West, C. (2001). *Race matters.* Boston: Beacon. (Original work published 1993)

White, R. (1995). From codes of ethics to public cultural truth. *European Journal of Communication, 10,* 441–460.

Winch, P. (2007). *The idea of a social science and its relation to philosophy* (2nd ed.). New York: Routledge. (Original work published 1958)

Wiredu, K. (1996). *Cultural universals: An African perspective.* Bloomington: Indiana University Press.

Wood, J. T. (1994). *Who cares? Women, care, and culture.* Carbondale: Southern Illinois University Press.

Wyschogrod, E. (1974). *Emmanuel Levinas: The problem of ethical metaphysics.* The Hague: Martinus Nijhoff.

Wyschogrod, E. (1985). *Spirit in ashes: Hegel, Heidegger, and man-made death.* Chicago: University of Chicago Press.

Wyschogrod, E. (1990). *Saints and post-modernism: Revisioning moral philosophy.* Chicago: University of Chicago Press.

Wyschogrod, E. (1998). *An ethics of remembering: History, heterology, and the nameless others.* Chicago: University of Chicago Press.

Wyschogrod, E. (2002). *Emmanuel Levinas: The problem of ethical metaphysics* (2nd ed.). New York: Fordham University Press.

5

Ethics, Research Regulations, and Critical Social Science

Gaile S. Cannella and Yvonna S. Lincoln

The social, intellectual, and even political positions from which the notion of research ethics can be defined have certainly emanated from diverse knowledges and ways of experiencing the world, as well as from a range of historical locations. The regulation of research ethics (especially legislated regulation) has, however, most often been influenced by traditional, postpositivist orientations. Clifford G. Christians (2005) discusses the histories of research ethics, from a value-free scientific neutrality that constructs science as "political only in its application" (Mill, 1859/1978; Root, 1993, p. 129; Weber, 1904/1949) to communitarian perspectives that challenge researchers to join with communities in new forms of moral articulation (Benhabib, 1992; Denzin, 1997, 2003).

In 2007, in a special issue of *Qualitative Inquiry* dedicated to research ethics and regulation, we discussed these multiple locations as well as contemporary power orientations from which diverse perspectives emanate. We focused on legislation imposed on researchers regarding the ethical conduct of research; ethical perspectives practiced, taught, or denied by those who teach and perform research methods; contemporary concerns that research is legitimated through market philosophies; and voices of the marginalized, created as the Other by or through research practices. Intertwined throughout our discussion was the recognition that regulation in its multiple forms results in an illusion of ethical practice and that any universalist ethic would be "catastrophic" (Foucault, 1985, p. 12). Furthermore, diversity of theoretical positions and perspectives within the field of qualitative inquiry has already generated rich and profound possibilities for reflexive ethics. From within these diverse perspectives, authors in the special issue reconceptualized research ethics as particularized, infused throughout inquiry, and requiring a continued moral dialogue—as calling for the development of a critical consciousness that would challenge the contemporary predatory ethical policies facilitated through neoliberalism (Christians, 2007; Clark & Sharf, 2007).

We who identify ourselves as *critical* in some form (whether hybrid–other–subject–feminist–scholar) have attempted to engage with the multiplicities embedded within notions of ethical scholarship. Being critical requires a radical ethics, an *ethics that is always/already concerned about power and oppression even as it avoids constructing 'power' as a new truth.* The intersection of power, oppression, and privilege with issues of human suffering, equity, social justice, and radical democracy results in a critical ethical foundation. Furthermore, ethical orientations are believed to be played out within the personal core of the researcher as she or he examines and makes decisions about the conceptualization and conduct of research as either oppressive or emancipatory practice.

A conceptualization of what some have called a *critical social science* incorporates the range of feminist, postcolonial, and even postmodern challenges to oppressive power, as well as the various interpretations of critical theory and critical pedagogies that are radically democratic, multilogical, and publicly, centrally concerned with human suffering and oppression. Traditional social science tends to address research ethics as following particular methodological rules in practices that are designed in advance and would reveal universalist results identified as ethical from within an imperative that would generalize to "save" humankind. For criticalists, however, this "will to save" is an imperialist imperative. Rather, critical radical ethics is relational and collaborative; it aligns with resistance and marginality. In *Ethical Futures in Qualitative Research,* Norman K. Denzin and Michael D. Giardina (2007) describe the range of scholars who have called for a collaborative critical social science model that "aligns the ethics of research with a politics of the oppressed, with a politics of resistance, hope, and freedom" (p. 35).

A critical social science literally requires that the researcher reconstruct the purposes of inquiry to engage with the struggle for equity and justice, while at the same time examining (and countering) individual power created for the researcher within the context of inquiry. The ethics of critical social science require that scholars "take up moral projects that decolonize, honor, and reclaim indigenous cultural practices" (Denzin & Giardina, 2007, p. 35), as well as engage with research that mobilizes collective actions that result in "a radical politics of possibility, of hope, of love, care, and equality for all humanity" (p. 35).[1] Researcher actions must avoid the perpetuation or maintenance of inquirer-oriented power (as savior, decolonizer, or one that would empower).

A critical social science reconceptualizes everything, from the embeddedness of ethics (and what that means) to the role of ethics in constructing research questions, methodologies, and possibilities for transformation. The major focus of this chapter is to examine the complexities of creating an ethical critical social science within our contemporary sociopolitical condition, a condition that has reinvigorated the privilege of empire through neoliberal Western discourses and regulatory technologies that would intervene into the lives of and literally create the Other and that continues redistribution of resources for neoliberal purposes (even from within a new administration in the United States that we believe is concerned with equity, anti-oppression, and social justice). We have previously discussed the positions from which research ethics tend to have been drawn, ranging from government regulation to voices of peoples who have not benefited and have often been damaged by research (Cannella & Lincoln, 2007; Cannella & Manuelito, 2008; Viruru & Cannella, 2006). In this chapter, we use these various standpoints to further explore a radical ethics as necessary for critical social science. We focus on constructing dialogic critical foundations (that we hope are anticolonial and even countercolonial) as well as reconceptualizing inquiry and forms of research (and researcher) regulation. Critical perspectives are located in the continuous alliance (and attempts at solidarity) with countercolonial positions and bodies and with the always/already historical acknowledgment of intersecting forms of privilege/oppression within contemporary contexts.

Furthermore, an evolving critical pedagogy (Kincheloe, 2007, 2008) is employed as a lens from which to generate forms of critical ethics that would transform academic (and public) spaces. This evolving criticality reconfigures the purposes of inquiry to focus on the dynamics and intersections of power relations between competing interests. Inquiry becomes the examination of contemporary forms of domination, as well as studies of what "could be"—of equitable and socially just futures. In addition, governmentality is addressed as produced by and producing forms of regulation interwoven with individual technologies of desire and accepted institutional practices. Finally, research regulation as ethical construct is rethought as reconfigured through the voices of those who have been traditionally marginalized as well as through the deployment of a critical social science whose purposes are to "join with," rather than "know and save."

Constructing Critical Ways of Being

Although not without conflicting beliefs, the range of critical perspectives (whether feminisms, poststructuralist work, queer theories, postcolonial critique, or other forms of knowledge that would address power) all tend to recognize the ways that particular groups of people have historically and continually been denied access to sites of power and have been systematically disenfranchised. These critical viewpoints have increasingly identified with marginalized peoples and have recognized the need to avoid forms of representation that maintain power in traditional locations. Furthermore, critical perspectives have called for the formation of alliances and attempts to join the struggle for solidarity with those who have been oppressed and inequitably treated. Patriarchal, racist, and colonializing forms of power are understood as historically grounded and recognized as never independent of cultural, political, and social context. For these reasons, we begin with a discussion of the need for critical ethical alliances that are always cognizant of the historical grounding and dominant power structures within the present.

Ethics and countercolonial alliance. An ethical perspective that would always address human suffering and life conditions, align with politics of the oppressed, and move to reclaim multiple knowledges and ways of being certainly involves complexity, openness to uncertainty, fluidity, and continued reflexive insight. Diverse conceptualizations of critical social science have reintroduced multiple knowledges, logics, ways of being in the world, and ethical orientations that have been historically marginalized and brutally discredited, facing violent attempts at erasure. As examples, Linda Tuhiwai Smith (1999) proposes four research processes that represent Maori collective ethics—decolonization, healing, transformation, and mobilization. Lester-Irabinna Rigney recommends that research methods privilege indigenous voices, resistance, and political integrity (1999). Sandy Grande (2007) puts forward Red pedagogy, an indigenous methodology that requires critique of democracy and indigenous sovereignty, functions as a pedagogy of hope that is contingent with the past, cultivates collective agency, is concerned with the dehumanizing effects of colonization on both the colonized and the colonizer, and is boldly and unabashedly political. Using Emmanuel Levinas's focus on the primacy of the well-being of the Other (1988), Jenny Ritchie and Cheryl Rau (2010) construct a countercolonial ethics, labeled an *ethics of alterity,* which would shift the focus from "us" or "them" to "a collective reconfiguring of who 'we' are" (p. 364). Corrine Glesne (2007) even suggests that the purpose of research should be solidarity: "If you want to research us, you can go home. If you have come to accompany us, if you think our struggle is also your struggle, we have plenty of things to talk about" (p. 171). Critical pedagogues focus on the underpinnings of power in whatever context they find themselves and the ways that power performs or is performed to create injustice.

These are just a few of the ethical locations from which a critical social science has been proposed, introducing multiplicities, complexities, and ambiguities that would be part of any moral conceptualization and practice of research focusing on human suffering and oppression, radical democracy, and the struggle for equity and social justice. Furthermore, those of us who have been privileged through our connection with the dominant (e.g., education, economic level, race, gender) and may at least appear as the face of the oppressor must always avoid actions or interpretations that appropriate. We must struggle to "join with," and "learn from" rather than "speak for" or "intervene into." Voices from the margins demonstrate the range of knowledges, perspectives, languages, and ways of being that should become foundational to our actions, that should become a new center.

At various points, we have attempted to stand for a critical, transformative social science, for example: with Viruru (Viruru & Cannella, 2006) the critique of the construction of the ethnographic subject and the examination of privilege created by language in research practices; with Manuelito (Cannella & Manuelito, 2008) in proposing that social science be constructed in ways that are egalitarian, anticolonial, and ethically embedded within the nonviolent revolutionary consciousness proposed by hooks (1990). Recognizing that ethics as a construct is always and already essentializing, we have suggested that a revolutionary ethical conscience would be anticolonial and ask questions like: How are groups being used politically to perpetuate power within systems? How can we enlarge the research imaginary (e.g., regarding gender, race, childhood) to reveal the possibilities that our preoccupations have obscured? Can we cultivate ourselves as those who can desire and inhabit unthought spaces regarding research (about childhood, diverse views of the world)? (Lincoln & Cannella, 2007). Can we critique our own privilege? Can we join the struggle for social justice in ways that support multiple knowledges and multiple logics? These diverse perspectives and the underlying moral foundations from which they are generated are basic to the construction of an ethical, critical, even anticolonial social science. The ethics and the science must be understood as complex, must always be fluid, and must continually employ self-examination.

Furthermore, using the scholarship of Michel Foucault, Frantz Fanon, Judith Butler, and Gayatri Chakravorty Spivak, Anthony C. Alessandrini (2009) calls for an ethics without subjects that is a new concept of ethical relationships, a responsible ethics that can be considered "after" humanism (p. 78). This postcolonial ethics would not be between people; rather in its future-oriented construction, an ethical relationship would occur with "would-be subjects that have not yet come into existence" (p. 78). The ethical relations would address contemporary political and power orientations by recognizing that the investigator and investigated (whether people, institutions, or systems) are subjects of the presence or aftermath of colonialism (Spivak, 1987). The tautology of humanist piety that would "save" others through science, religion, or politics would be avoided (Fanon, 1967; Foucault, 1984a). Yet, the Enlightenment blackmail that insists on a declaration of acceptance or rejection would be circumvented, while at the same time a critical flexibility is maintained (Butler, 2002; Foucault, 1984b). Ethics would involve being responsive and responsible to, while both trusting and avoiding construction of the Other. Ethical responsibility would be to a future, which can be accepted as unknowable (Attridge, 1994).

Drawing from Ritchie and Rau (2010), we would also support a *critical research ethics* that would counter colonialism. This critical ethics would value and recognize the need to

- Expose the diversity of realities
- Engage with the webs of interaction that construct problems in ways that lead to power/privilege for particular groups
- Reposition problems and decisions toward social justice
- Join in solidarity with the traditionally oppressed to create new ways of functioning

The magnitude and history of contemporary power. The ethics of a critical social science cannot avoid involvement with contemporary, everyday life and dominant societal discourses influencing that life. Research that would challenge oppression and foster social justice must acknowledge the gravity of context and the history of power within that context.

In the 21st century, this life has been constructed by the "Imperial Court of Corporate Greed and Knowledge Control" (Kincheloe, 2008, p. 15). Interpretations of knowledge and literally all human activity have been judged as valid and reliable if they fit the entrepreneurial imperative, if they foster privatization, competition, corporatization, and profiteering. In recent years, many of us have expressed outrage regarding this hypercapitalist influence, the free market illusion, over everything from definitions of public and higher education as benchmarked and measureable to privatization of services for the public good, to war mongering as a vehicle for corporatization to technologies that produce human desires that value self and others only as economic, measured, and entrepreneurial performers (Cannella & Miller, 2008; Cannella & Viruru, 2004; Chomsky, 1999; Horwitz, 1992).

Many of us would hope that a different administration in Washington, D.C., combined with the current financial crisis around the world, would result in confrontation with and transformation of capitalist imperialism. However, contemporary corporate fundamentalism is so foundational to dominant discourses that questioning failing corporations is not at all synonymous with contesting corporate forms of intellectual colonization. Examples abound in the early 21st century, like the discourse that labeled AIG as "too big" to fail, attempts to convince European governments to create stimulus packages, or presidential admonitions regarding "raising standards" in public schools (rather than the recognition of structural inequities in the system and taking actions to broaden definitions of public education as related to critical democracy and social justice).

Actually, the economic crisis may have created a new urgency within which critical scholars and others must take action. Living within a context in which "corporate-produced images" (Kincheloe, 2007, p. 30) have created new ideological templates for both affect and intellect, the need to accept corporate constructs and align with business interests is assumed. Corporate discourses have been so infused into the fabric of everyday life that most are not even recognized as such (for example, the construction of elitist public schools, which had been previously denied as not equitable or benefiting the common good—for example, by Lusher (Klein, 2007) and others—immediately following Hurricane Katrina in New Orleans). This illustrates what Klein (2007) has identified as "disaster capitalism." In the current economic crisis, even as big business is criticized, an unquestioned language of hypercapitalism (e.g., competition, free market, choice) results in further depoliticization of corporate colonization of the mind (both the mind of society and the mind of the individual) and of societal institutions (e.g., acceptance of privatized public services, education, even the armed forces). The Obama administration's unquestioned implementation of the Bush administration's charter school agenda for public education in the United States is an excellent example. The charter school concept has been used to reawaken the "free market" notion of public school choice (which was originally rejected when put forward as vouchers) and reinvigorate the power of the business roundtable, corporate turnaround models, and profiteering in public education.

"Western knowledge producers" (Kincheloe, 2008, p. 10) have held that their various forms of information were universal and enlightened (and as the progress that all should embrace, whether tied to the Christian religion or Cartesian science), in all conditions a risky circumstance for those who do not produce that knowledge. However, the politics of knowledge is even more dangerous when embedded within hypercapitalism and the power generated by capital and those that control resources. The acceptance of corporate perspectives that would invoke capitalist accountability constructs like evidenced-based research or scores on particular achievement tests (created by multinational companies) decontextualize and further subjectify and objectify students and children, their teachers, and their families. Human beings are treated as if their bodies (defined as achievement test scores) were the measure of "what works" within a particular discourse, just as financial success is used as the measure of a supposedly free-market, competitive, successful enterprise. Definitions are not questioned because the measured and measurement language and discourses of neoliberalism are accepted as correct, efficient, indisputable, universal, and even just. This contemporary condition constructs particular views of morality and equity, and thus expectations for what can be defined as ethical. From within this context, conceptualizing ethics and ethical practices as independent from (and necessary challenges to) hypercapitalism is very difficult but absolutely necessary.

The ethics of a critical social science requires the cultivation of a consciousness that is aware of both the sociopolitical condition of the times and one's own self-productive reactions to dominant disciplinary and regulatory technologies. This awareness involves engaging with the complexities of power and how it operates in the social order. Critical ethics would recognize the dominant (in our contemporary condition economics) but would never accept the truth of a superstructure (like economics) as always dictating human existence. Finally, a critical immanence would be necessary to move beyond ethnocentrism or ego-centrism and construct new, previously unthought-of relationships and societal possibilities (Kincheloe, 2007).

Ethics, Critical Social Science, and Institutionalized Forms of Governmentality

In recent years, research ethics have been most often tied to one of the following:

- An ethics of entitlement (Glesne, 2007) that legitimizes engagement in research and the right to "know" the other
- Qualitative research methods, which require and employ ethical considerations like reflexive ethics (Guilleman & Gillam, 2004)
- Communitarian ethics through which values and moral commitments are negotiated socially (Christians, 2007; Denzin, 1997, 2003)
- Forms of legislated research regulation (e.g., institutional reviews of projects) that create an illusion of ethical concern (Lincoln & Tierney, 2004)

All are embedded within the notion of governmentality, either the construction of technologies that govern by producing control of populations (regulatory power) or the internalized discipline of bodies of individuals (researchers) based on the desire (from a range of value perspectives) to construct a particular self within the context (Foucault, 1978). The reader can consider *govern* as the action and *mentality* as the way people think about accepting control, the internalization of beliefs that allow regulation (Dean, 1999).

Research regulation that is legislated is most often recognized (and critiqued) as an institutionalized form of governmentality, a technology of power that constructs, produces, and limits and is thus tied to the generation of intersecting oppressions. However, Foucault (1986) also discusses the construction of self-governance, "political technologies of individuals" (p. 87), that are entirely internalized. There is a range of examples of this individual governmentality, from technologies of the "free citizen" (Rose, 1999), to the "well-educated person," to the "good teacher," even to the "transformative activist" or the "dialogically engaged researcher." We believe that our discussion of ethics within critical social science can be interpreted as a form of governmentality; most likely, any construction of ethics (however flexible) represents a form of governance. To construct a critical ethics regarding research is to address mentality. Any belief structure, however emergent or flexible, certainly serves as discipline and regulation of the self.

Since research has traditionally been a predominantly individual project and research regulation is legislated practice, both forms of governmentality (self and researcher population) must be considered in constructing an ethical critical social science. While a critical social science would always examine and challenge the notion of governmentality as "truth structure," the construction of a critical desire for countercolonial solidarity, the embeddedness within institutional expectations regarding research, and the contemporary regulatory context within which research is practiced cannot be denied as themselves forms of governmentality.

Individual desire and forms of governmentality. Critical and qualitative researchers have for some time critiqued the power orientations of research methods, have discussed practices that facilitate a reflexive ethical orientation throughout the research process, and have certainly rethought the purposes of research as construct. As examples, Walkerdine (1997) warns against the "voyeuristic thrill" of observation that constructs researcher as expert in what people are "really like" (p. 67). Feminists, poststructuralists, constructivists, and other scholars associated with postmodern concerns with oppression and power have engaged in principled struggles concerning the conceptualization of research itself, from the purposes of research, to forms of representation (Fine, Weis, Weseen, & Wong, 2000; Tedlock, 2005), to the role of the researcher. Questions like the following have been asked: "How are forms of exclusion being produced? Is transformative and liberatory research possible that also examines its own will to emancipate? . . . How does the practice of research reinscribe our own privilege?" (Cannella & Lincoln, 2007, p. 321). These ethical positions and concerns are certainly being incorporated into constructions of research projects and publications, as well as in new forms of education and coursework for graduate students. These positions are critical forms of governmentality.

However, the interconnected structures that characterize the dominant (noncritical) research community and the institutions that support research are not critical and tend to support modernist forms of governmentality. Ethics are likely to be legislated or constructed by individual researchers from within value structures that either maintain that science can solve all problems, therefore legitimating intervention into the lives of others in the name of science, or that free-market capitalism will improve life conditions for all, also used as the ethical justification for research choices and actions. These conceptualizations of ethics (for individuals and institutions) remain modernist, male-oriented, and imperialist (especially as related to labeling individuals, supporting particular forms of knowledge, and underpinning the dominance of neoliberal economics generally). These structures are interconnected (Collins, 2000) and invasive, have a long history, and will likely dominate into the foreseeable future.

Even though we support a critical social science that would be relational, collaborative, and less individualistically oriented, the contemporary context continues to be oriented toward power for the individual researcher. Therefore, while we would continually critique the privileging of the individual as construct, we also believe that perspectives that avoid universalist ethical codes yet address individual ethical frameworks are necessary. We hope that from the perspective of an ethical critical social science, individual governmentality as construct can always be challenged. However, we would also avoid the Enlightenment blackmail (Butler, 2002; Foucault, 1984b) that either accepts or rejects individualism and would submit that the individual is conceptually a useful master's tool (Lorde, 1984) as well as a critical agent. We would, therefore, propose the development of the desire to be critical, of a form of doubled individual governmentality through which the researcher is both instrument in the critique of power and collaborative agent in joining with traditionally marginalized communities.

The work of Foucault (1985), which challenges the individual to counter his or her own fascist orientations that would yield to the love of power and domination, is an illustration of this doubled conceptualization, even a doubled identity. An ethical framework is proposed that avoids the inscription of universalist moral codes but rather constructs "an intensification of the relation to oneself by which one constitutes oneself as the subject of one's acts" (Foucault, 1986, p. 41). The purpose of this use of the individually oriented master's tools is to suggest a critical framework through which self-absorption could be avoided, as the researcher conducts a continuous genealogy of the self along the axes of truth, power, and ethics (Foucault, 1985; Rabinow, 1994). Our focus in this discussion is on the ethical axis through which the self acts on itself, although the self's construction of both truth and power are not unrelated. Four components are included within the ethical axis of self: (1) ethical substance, (2) mode of subjectification, (3) ethical work, and (4) *telos* or disassembly of oneself. These components can be pondered from an individualistic rationalist perspective that also attempts to incorporate critical pedagogies and postcolonial critique.

Ethical substance is the way in which the researcher legitimates self morally. This substance is not a given but is constituted as relational to the self as a creative agent. To some extent, we can describe ethical substance as that which is important to the researcher, as that which facilitates or disallows self-deception and is the grounding for ethics. The ethical substance is "that which enables one to get free from oneself" (Foucault, 1985, p. 9), and it varies for everyone. As examples, the unification of pleasure and desire served as the ethical substance for many in ancient Greece; for some, collective existence and communal decision making is ethical substance (Ritchie & Rau, 2010); for some, addressing equity and social justice in solidarity with those who have most likely been oppressed may be the ethical substance. Foucault (1985) suggests genealogical questions to determine the substance of the self that we believe can be applied to the researcher, focusing on circumstances in which research is constituted as a moral activity—whether circumstances related to research as construct, interpretation of the meaning of research, or circumstances under which the researcher defines his or her scholarship as a moral or ethical act.

We propose (and we are not the first) that the belief in critical social science that would address oppression and construct alliances and solidarity with those who have traditionally been excluded constitutes ethical substance. Recognizing that governmentality and technologies of the self are more often subconscious (but acknowledging conscious possibilities), we would further suggest that those who choose such critical mentalities join in the broader reconceptualizations that are literally creating a new ethical substance for research. An example of this is the work of critical pedagogues. In describing the "ever-evolving conceptual matrix" of criticality, Joe Kincheloe (2007, p. 21) provides us with content for both ethical substance and the further creation of domains of critical social science that can be the content of ethical substance. These critical domains can even construct the foundations for research. They include:

1. Analysis of the dynamics of competing power interests

2. Exposure of forces that inhibit the ability of individuals and groups to determine the direction of their own lives

3. Research into the intersection of various forms of domination

4. Analysis of contemporary forms of technical rationality and the impact on diverse forms of knowledge and ways of being

5. Examination of forms of self-governmentality, always recognizing the sociopolitical and sociocultural context

6. Inquiry into what "could be," into ways of constructing a critical immanence that moves toward new, more equitable relationships between diverse peoples (yet always avoids utopian, humanist rationalities)

7. Exploration of the continually emerging, complex exercise of power, as hegemonic, ideological, or discursive

8. Examination of the role of culture in the contested production and transmission of knowledge(s)

9. Studies of interpretation, perception, and diverse vantage points from which meaning is constructed

10. Analysis of the role of cultural pedagogy as education, as producing hegemonic forms of interpretation

As ethical substance, this critical content can lead to specific inquiry like historical problematizations (of the present) that refuse to either blame or endorse; examinations of policy discourses, networks, or resources; or research that exposes power while refusing to co-opt the knowledge(s), skills, and resources of the other.

The *mode of subjectification* is probably the ethical component most illustrative of governmentality. The notion that the individual submits the self to particular rules and obligations is included; the rules are constructed and accepted dependent on the ethical substance. For example, Immanuel Kant (whose ethical substance focused on intention as embedded within reason) valued the obligation to know and the use of reason as the method of self-governance (Foucault, 1985). Critical social scientists may construct an ethical obligation (and resultant related rules) to a critical, historical disposition that is flexible and responds to issues of oppression. As Glesne (2007) implies, this critical mode of subjectification would most likely reject the sense of entitlement that would "know" others and would further recognize the alienation created when one is placed under the observational gaze of the researcher. A criticalist's ethical rules might be more likely to accept communal decision making rather than rationalist forms of negotiation.

From within the ethical axis, researchers can ask questions of themselves related to the rules that are constructed within particular constructions of ethical substance and used to determine the existence of moral activity. "How are these rules acted on in research activities to conceptualize/legitimate and implement moral obligations" (e.g., for an individual researcher in choice of study, in choice of population, in collaborations with others, as I educate other researchers) (Cannella & Lincoln, 2007, p. 325)?

Ethical work is the method used to transform self into the form that one defines as ethical. Foucault (1994) proposes that this work requires a self-criticism that historically examines the constitution of the self. The work is expected to reveal the conditions under which one questions the self, invents new ways of forming relationships, and constructs new ways of being. This form of self-governance involves examination of the ways one can change oneself (as person and/or as researcher). An evolving critical pedagogy can be used to illustrate the ethics of an ontological transformation that goes beyond Western constructions of the self. Kincheloe (2007) illustrates the central critical features that can be related to ethical identity development. These features include constructs like socioindividual imagination, challenges to the boundaries of abstract individualism, socioindividual analysis of power, alternatives to the alienation of the individual, mobilizing desire, and critical consciousness that acknowledges self-production. To illustrate, socioindividual imagination is the ability to conceptualize new forms of collaboration, rethinking subjectivities and acknowledging that the professional and personal are critical social projects; institutions like education are thus constructed as emphasizing social justice and democratic community as the facilitator of human development. Another example, mobilizing desire, is constructed as a radical democratization, joining continued efforts of the excluded to gain access and input into civic life.

Finally, *telos* is the willingness to disassemble self, to deconstruct one's world (and one's research practices if a researcher) in ways that demonstrate commitment to an ethical practice that would avoid the construction of power over any individual or group of others (even unpredictable, yet to be determined others located in the future). Telos is a form of self-bricolage, slowly elaborating and establishing a self that is committed to think differently, that welcomes the unknown and can function flexibly (Foucault, 1994). As critical pedagogy again suggests, alternatives to alienation of the individual are created, forms of domination that construct isolation are rejected, and unthought-of ways to be with and for others are constructed (Kincheloe, 2007). Furthermore, telos can construct new pathways through which individual researchers, as well as groups of scholars, can consider notions like an ethics without subjects that combines critical and postcolonial perspectives that are committed to the future and to avoiding the continued colonialist construction of the Other (Alessandrini, 2009).

Although certainly consistent with modernist approaches to individual rationality, the examination of an individual ethical axis demonstrates the ways that even the master's tools can be used for critique and transformation.

Currently, researchers must both engage in their own individual ethical decisions regarding research and function within institutional forms of regulation. From a range of critical locations, we are continuously reminded that different disciplinary strategies are enacted by institutions dependent on the historical moment and context (Foucault, 1977). Certainly, individual critically ethical selves (in our modernist academic community, which privileges the scientific individual) will be more prepared to engage with the conflicting ethical messages within institutions, whether academic expectations or legislated regulation; to take hold of our own existence as researchers, to transform academic spaces, and to redefine discourses (Denzin & Giardina, 2007).

Transforming Regulations: Redefining the Technologies That Govern Us

Qualitative and critical qualitative researchers have continued to "take hold" of their academic spaces as they have clashed with legislated research regulation (especially, for example, as practiced by particular institutional review boards in the United States). This conflict has been much discussed and will not end any time soon. This work has demonstrated not only that legislated attempts to regulate research ethics are an illusion, but that regulation is culturally grounded and can even lead to ways of functioning that are damaging to research participants and collaborators. As examples, Marzano (2007) demonstrates the ways that following Anglo-Saxon ethical research regulation in an Italian setting with medical patients involved in qualitative research can be detrimental to the participant patients. Susan Tilley and Louise Gormley (2007) illustrate the ways that the construction of confidentiality represents challenges to understandings of individual integrity in a Mexican setting. Furthermore, a range of scholarship demonstrates that research ethics is particularized, must be infused throughout the process, and requires a continued dialogue with self (Christians, 2007; Clark & Sharf, 2007). Legislated forms of governmentality can certainly not address these particulars.

If researchers accompany communities, rather than "test/know/judge" them, perhaps community members will want to address review boards and legislators themselves concerning collaborative practices. In describing the Mi'kmaw Ethics Watch, Marie Battiste and James (Sa'ke'j) Youngblood Henderson (2000; Battiste, 2008) demonstrate just such a practice, as Mi'kmaw people have constructed research guidelines in which research is always to be an equal partnership in which the Mi'kmaw people are the guardians and interpreters of their intellectual and cultural property and review research conclusions for accuracy and sensitivity.

Aligned with the ethics of the traditionally marginalized, which could ultimately reconceptualize the questions and practices of research, a critical social science would no longer accept the notion that one group of people can "know" and define (or even represent) "others." This perspective would certainly change the research purposes and designs that are submitted for human subjects review, perhaps even eliminating the need for "human subjects" in many cases. This change could result in research questions and forms of data collection that do not require researchers to interpret the meaning making or constructions of participants. Rather, research questions could address the intersections of power across systems, institutions, and societal practices. As examples, assumptions underlying the conceptualizations of public policy, dominant knowledges, and dominant ideologies (in particular areas); actions that would protect and celebrate diverse knowledges; and analyses of forms of representation privileged by those in power, can all become research purposes without constructing human subjects as objects of data collection. If societal structures, institutions, and oppressions become the subjects of our research (rather than human beings), perhaps we can avoid further creation and subjectification of an or the Other. Denzin (2009) even suggests that we "abandon the dirty word called research" and take up a "critical, interpretive approach to the world" (p. 298), a practice that could benefit us all and would require major forms of activism within our academic settings.

This section on the legislated regulation of research is noticeably and purposely brief. We would suggest that, first, critical qualitative researchers make all efforts to move to the center the reconceptualized, broad-based critical social science that addresses institutionalized, policy-based, intersecting forms of power. This critical social science can even include studies of regulation from an ethics-without-subjects perspective. And, it would undoubtedly include alliances with countercolonial positions, as well as critical historical recognitions of context and ethical examinations of the researcher self. Until this critical social science is accepted as an important form of practice (perhaps even vital enough to be threatening to the mainstream), modernist research regulation will most likely change very little. We will simply (although it is not at all simple, or any less important) continue our attempts to educate those who have not learned about qualitative research as a field or the methods associated with it. However, if a critical social science aligns with the oppressed, demonstrating solidarity with the traditionally marginalized and constructing research that addresses power, our constructions of and concerns about legislated research regulations will be of a different nature. Perhaps our critical research ethics can anticipate and facilitate that change.

Note

1. Recognizing that we could be accused of assuming that postpositivist science has no ethical base, we must absolutely acknowledge that we understand that researchers from a range of philosophical perspectives believe that their research questions and practices are grounded in the ethical attempt to improve life for everyone, and following an Enlightenment, rational science orientation, we would agree. However, very often, these postpositivist forms of legitimation and scientific intentions do not acknowledge embeddedness within the Euro American "error" (Jaimes, 1992). This error is the unquestioned belief in modernist, progressive (both U.S. liberal and conservative) views of the world that would "unveil" universalist interpretations of all human experience; it assumes the omnipotent ability (and right) to "know" and interpret "others." Unfortunately, these ethical good intentions have most often denied the multiple knowledges, logics, and ways of being in the world that have characterized a large number of human beings. Furthermore, focusing on the individual and the discovery of theories and universals has masked societal, institutional, and structural practices that perpetuate injustices. Finally, an ethics that would help others "be like us" has created power for "us." This ethics of good intentions has tended to support power for those who construct the research and the furthering of oppressive conditions for the subjects of that research.

References

Alessandrini, A. C. (2009). The humanism effect: Fanon, Foucault, and ethics without subjects. *Foucault Studies, 7,* 64–80.
Attridge, D. (1994). Trusting the other: Ethics and politics in J. M. Coetzee's Age of Iron. *South Atlantic Quarterly, 93,* 70–71.

Battiste, M. (2008). Research ethics for protecting indigenous knowledge and heritage: Institutional and researcher responsibilities. In N. K. Denzin, Y. S. Lincoln, & L. T. Smith (Eds.), *Handbook of critical indigenous methodologies* (pp. 600–625). Thousand Oaks, CA: Sage.

Battiste, M., & Youngblood Henderson, J. (Sa'ke'j). (2000). *Protecting indigenous knowledge and heritage.* Saskatoon, Saskatchewan, Canada: Purich.

Benhabib, S. (1992). *Situating the self: Gender, community, and postmodernism in contemporary ethics.* Cambridge, UK: Polity.

Butler, J. (2002). What is critique? An essay on Foucault's virtue. In D. Ingram (Ed.), *The political* (pp. 212–227). Cambridge, MA: Blackwell.

Cannella, G. S., & Lincoln, Y. S. (2007). Predatory vs. dialogic ethics: Constructing an illusion or ethical practice as the core of research methods. *Qualitative Inquiry, 13*(3), 315–335.

Cannella, G. S., & Manuelito, K. (2008). Feminisms from unthought locations: Indigenous worldviews, marginalized feminisms, and revisioning an anticolonial social science. In N. K. Denzin, Y. S. Lincoln, & L. T. Smith (Eds.), *Handbook of critical and indigenous methodologies* (pp. 45–59). Thousand Oaks, CA: Sage.

Cannella, G. S., & Miller, L. L. (2008). Constructing corporatist science: Reconstituting the soul of American higher education. *Cultural Studies <=> Critical Methodologies, 8*(1), 24–38.

Cannella, G. S., & Viruru, R. (2004). *Childhood and postcolonization: Power, education, and contemporary practice.* New York: RoutledgeFalmer.

Chomsky, N. (1999). *Profit over people: Neoliberalism and global order.* New York: Seven Stories Press.

Christians, C. G. (2007). Cultural continuity as an ethical imperative. *Qualitative Inquiry, 13*(3), 437–444.

Clark, M. C., & Sharf, B. F. (2007). The dark side of truth(s): Ethical dilemmas in researching the personal. *Qualitative Inquiry, 13*(3), 399–416.

Collins, P. H. (2000). *Black feminist thought: Knowledge, consciousness, and the politics of empowerment.* New York: Routledge.

Dean, M. (1999). *Governmentality: Power and rule in modern society.* London: Sage.

Denzin, N. K. (1997). *Interpretive ethnography: Ethnographic practices for the 21st century.* Thousand Oaks, CA: Sage.

Denzin, N. K. (2003). *Performance ethnography: Critical pedagogy and the politics of culture.* Thousand Oaks, CA: Sage.

Denzin, N. K. (2009). *Qualitative inquiry under fire: Toward a new paradigm dialogue.* Walnut Creek, CA: Left Coast Press.

Denzin, N. K., & Giardina, M. D. (2007). Introduction: Ethical futures in qualitative research. In N. K. Denzin & M. D. Giardina (Eds.), *Ethical futures in qualitative research: Decolonizing the politics of knowledge* (pp. 9–44). Walnut Creek, CA: Left Coast Press.

Fanon, F. (1967). *Black skin, white masks* (C. L Markmann, Trans.). New York: Grove.

Fine, M., Weis, L., Weseen, S., & Wong, L (2000). For whom? Qualitative research, representation, and social responsibilities. In N. K. Denzin & Y. S. Lincoln (Eds.), *Handbook of qualitative research* (2nd ed., pp. 107–131). Thousand Oaks, CA: Sage.

Foucault, M. (1977). *Discipline and punish: The birth of the prison.* London: Allen Lane.

Foucault, M. (1978). Governmentality. In B. Burchell, C. Gordon, & P. Miller (Eds.), *The Foucault effect: Studies in governmentality* (pp. 87–104). Chicago: University of Chicago Press.

Foucault, M. (1984a). Nietzsche, genealogy, history (D. F. Bouchard & S. Simon, Trans.). In P. Rabinow (Ed.), *The Foucault reader* (pp. 76–100). New York: Vintage.

Foucault, M. (1984b). What is enlightenment? (C. Porter, Trans.). In P. Rabinow (Ed.), *The Foucault reader* (pp 32–50). New York: Vintage.

Foucault, M. (1985). *History of sexuality: Vol. 2. The use of pleasure* (R. Hurley, Trans.). New York: Pantheon.

Foucault, M. (1986). *History of sexuality: Vol. 3. The care of the self* (R. Hurley, Trans.). New York: Pantheon.

Foucault, M. (1994). On the genealogy of ethics: An overview of work in progress. In P. Rabinow (Ed.). *Michel Foucault: Ethics, subjectivity, and truth, 1954–1984* (Vol. 1, pp. 253–280). New York: The New York Press.

Glesne, C. (2007). Research as solidarity. In N. K. Denzin & M. D. Giardina (Eds.), *Ethical futures in qualitative research: Decolonizing the politics of knowledge* (pp. 169–178). Walnut Creek, CA: Left Coast Press.

Grande, S. (2007). Red pedagogy: Indigenizing inquiry or the un-methodology. In N. K. Denzin & M. D. Giardina (Eds.), *Ethical futures in qualitative research: Decolonizing the politics of knowledge* (pp. 133–144). Walnut Creek, CA: Left Coast Press.

Guilleman, M., & Gillam, L. (2004). Ethics, reflexivity, and "ethically important moments" in research. *Qualitative Inquiry, 10*(2), 261–280.

hooks, b. (1990). *Yearning: Race, gender, and cultural politics.* Boston: South End Press.

Horwitz, M. (1992). *The transformation of American law, 1870–1960.* Cambridge, MA: Harvard University Press.

Jaimes, M. A. (1992). La raza and indigenism: Alternatives to autogenocide in North America. *Global Justice, 3*(2–3), 4–19.

Kincheloe, J. L (2007). Critical pedagogy in the twenty-first century. In P. McLaren & J. L. Kincheloe (Eds.), *Critical pedagogy: Where are we now?* (pp. 9–42). New York: Peter Lang.

Kincheloe, J. L. (2008). Critical pedagogy and the knowledge wars of the twenty-first century. *International Journal of Critical Pedagogy, 1*(1), 1–22.

Klein, N. (2007). *The shock doctrine: The rise of disaster capitalism.* New York: Metropolitan Books.

Levinas, E. (1988). Useless suffering. In R. Bernasconi & D. Wood (Eds.), *The provocation of Levinas: Rethinking the Other* (pp. 156–167). London & New York: Routledge.

Lincoln, Y. S., & Cannella, G. S. (2007). Ethics and the broader rethinking/ reconceptualization of research as construct. In N. K. Denzin & M. D. Giardina (Eds.), *Ethical futures in qualitative research: Decolonizing the politics of knowledge* (pp. 67–84). Walnut Creek, CA: Left Coast Press.

Lincoln, Y. S., & Tierney, W. G. (2004). Qualitative research and institutional review boards. *Qualitative Inquiry, 10,* 219–234.

Lorde, A. (1984). *Sister outsider.* Langhorne, PA: Crossing Press.

Marzano, M. (2007). Informed consent, deception, and research freedom in qualitative research: A cross-cultural comparison. *Qualitative Inquiry, 12*(3), 417–436.

Mill, J. S. (1978). *On liberty.* Indianapolis, IN: Hackett. (Original work published 1859)

Rabinow, P. (1994). *Michel Foucault: Ethics, subjectivity, and truth, 1954–1984* (Vol. 1). New York: The New York Press.

Rigney, L.-I. (1999). Internationalization of an indigenous anticolonial cultural critique of research methodologies. *Wicazo Sa Review, 14*(2), 109–121.

Ritchie, J., & Rau, C. (2010). Kia mau ki te wairuatanga: Counter narratives of early childhood education in Aotearoa. In G. S. Cannella & L. D. Soto (Eds.), *Childhoods: A handbook* (pp. 355–373). New York: Peter Lang.

Root, M. (1993). *Philosophy of social science: The methods, ideals, and politics of social inquiry.* Oxford, UK: Blackwell.

Rose, N. (1999). *Powers of freedom: Reframing political thought.* Cambridge, UK: Cambridge University Press.

Smith, L. T. (1999). *Decolonizing methodologies: Research and indigenous peoples.* London: Zed Books.

Spivak, G. C. (1987). *In other worlds: Essays in cultural politics.* New York: Routledge.

Tedlock, B. (2005). The observation of participation and the emergence of public ethnography. In N. K. Denzin & Y. S. Lincoln (Eds.), *The SAGE handbook of qualitative research* (3rd ed., pp. 467–482), Thousand Oaks, CA: Sage.

Tilley, S., & Gormley, L. (2007). Canadian university ethics review: Cultural complications translating principles into practice. *Qualitative Inquiry, 13*(3), 368–387.

Viruru, R., & Cannella, G.S. (2006). A postcolonial critique of the ethnographic interview: Research analyzes research. In N. K. Denzin & M. D. Giardina (Eds.), *Qualitative inquiry and the conservative challenge* (pp. 175–192). Walnut Creek, CA: Left Coast Press.

Walkerdine, V. (1997). *Daddy's girl: Young girls and popular culture.* Cambridge, MA: Harvard University Press.

Weber, M. (1949). Objectivity in social science and social policy. In E. A. Shils & H. A. Finch (Eds. & Trans.), *The methodology of the social sciences* (pp. 50–112). New York: Free Press. (Original work published 1904)

Part II

Paradigms and Perspectives in Contention

In our introductory chapter, following Egon G. Guba (1990, p. 17), we defined a paradigm as a basic set of beliefs that guide action. Paradigms deal with first principles or ultimates. They are human constructions. They define the world-view of the researcher-as-interpretive-*bricoleur*. These beliefs can never be established in terms of their ultimate truthfulness. Perspectives, in contrast, are not as solidified nor as well unified as paradigms, although a perspective may share many elements with a paradigm, for example, a common set of methodological assumptions or a particular epistemology.

A paradigm encompasses four terms: ethics (axiology), epistemology, ontology, and methodology. Ethics ask, "How will I be as a moral person in the world?" Epistemology asks, "How do I know the world?" "What is the relationship between the inquirer and the known?" Every epistemology, as Christians indicates (Chapter 4, this volume) implies an ethical-moral stance toward the world and the self of the researcher. Ontology raises basic questions about the nature of reality and the nature of the human being in the world. Methodology focuses on the best means for gaining knowledge about the world.

Part II of the *Handbook* examines the major paradigms and perspectives that now structure and organize qualitative research. These paradigms and perspectives are positivism, postpositivism, critical theory, constructivism, and participatory action frameworks. Alongside these paradigms are the perspectives of feminism (in its multiple forms), critical race theory, critical pedagogy, cultural studies, queer theory, Asian epistemologies, and disability theories, coupled with transformative, social justice paradigms. Each of these perspectives has developed its own criteria, assumptions, and methodological practices. These practices are then applied to disciplined inquiry within that framework. The tables in Chapter 6 by Guba & Yvonna Lincoln, with Susan A. Lynham outline the major differences between the positivist, postpositivist, critical theory (feminism + race), constructivism, and participatory (+ postmodern) paradigms.

We provided a brief discussion of each paradigm and perspective in Chapter 1; here we elaborate them in somewhat more detail. However, before turning to this discussion, it is important to note three interconnected events. Within the last decade, the borders and boundary lines between these paradigms and perspectives have begun to blur. As Lincoln and Guba observe, the "pedigrees" of various paradigms are themselves beginning to "interbreed." However, although the borders have blurred, perceptions of differences between perspectives have hardened. Even as this occurs, the discourses of methodological conservatism, discussed in our Preface and in Chapter 1, threaten to narrow the range and effectiveness of qualitative research practices. Hence, the title of this part, Paradigms and Perspectives in Contention.

Major Issues Confronting All Paradigms

In Chapter 6, Lincoln, Lynham, and Guba suggest that, in the present moment, all paradigms must confront seven basic, critical issues. These issues involve (1) axiology (ethics and values), (2) accommodation and commensurability (can paradigms be fitted into one another), (3) action (what the researcher does in the world), (4) control (who initiates inquiry, who asks questions), (5) foundations of truth (foundationalism vs. anti- and nonfoundationalism), (6) validity (traditional positivist models vs. poststructural-constructionist criteria), and (7) voice, reflexivity, and postmodern representation (single vs. multivoiced).

Each paradigm takes a different stance on these topics. Of course, the positivist and postpositivist paradigms provide the backdrop against which these other paradigms and perspectives operate. Lincoln and Guba analyze these two traditions in considerable detail, including their reliance on naive realism; their dualistic epistemologies; their verificational approach to inquiry; and their emphasis on reliability, validity, prediction, control, and a building block approach to knowledge. Lincoln and Guba discuss the inability of these paradigms to address adequately issues surrounding voice, empowerment, and praxis. They also allude to the failure to satisfactorily address the theory- and value-laden nature of facts, the interactive nature of inquiry, and the fact that the same set of "facts" can support more than one theory.

Constructivism, Interpretivism and Hermeneutics

According to Lincoln and Guba, constructivism adopts a relativist ontology (relativism), a transactional epistemology, and a hermeneutic, dialectical methodology. Users of this paradigm are oriented to the production of reconstructed understandings of the social world. The traditional positivist criteria of internal and external validity are replaced by such terms as trustworthiness and authenticity. Constructivists value transactional knowledge. Their work overlaps with the several different participatory action approaches discussed by Morten Levin and Davydd Greenwood (Chapter 2), and Mary Brydon-Miller, Michael Kral, Patricia Maguire, Susan Noffke, and Anu Sabhlok (Chapter 11, volume 2) in this volume. Constructivism connects action to praxis and builds on antifoundational arguments, while encouraging experimental and multivoiced texts.

In the third edition of the *Handbook*, Douglas Foley and Angela Valenzuela (2005) offered a history and analysis of critical ethnography, giving special attention to critical ethnographers who study applied policy and also involve themselves in political movements. Foley and Valenzuela observe that post-1960s critical ethnographers began advocating cultural critiques of modern society. These scholars revolted against positivism and sought to pursue a politically progressive agenda using multiple standpoint epistemologies. Various approaches were taken up in this time period, including action anthropology; global, neo-Marxist, Marxist feminist, and critical ethnography; and participatory action research.

The Feminisms

In Chapter 7, Virginia Olesen observes that feminist qualitative research, at the dawn of the second decade of this new century, is a highly diversified and contested site. Already we see multiple articulations of gender and its enactment in post-9/11 spaces. Competing models blur together on a global scale. But beneath the fray and the debate, there is agreement that feminist inquiry in the new millennium is committed to action in the world. Feminists insist that a social justice agenda address the needs of men and women of color because gender, class, and race are intimately interconnected. Olesen's is an impassioned feminism. "Rage is not enough," she exclaims. We need "incisive scholarship to frame, direct, and harness passion in the interests of redressing grievous problems in the many areas of women's health" (Olesen, 2000, p. 215).

In 1994, Olesen identified three major strands of feminist inquiry (standpoint epistemology, empiricist, postmodernism-cultural studies). A decade later, these strands continued to multiply. Today separate feminisms are associated with specific disciplines and with the writings of women of color; women problematizing whiteness; postcolonial, transnational discourse; decolonizing arguments of indigenous women; lesbian research and queer theory; disabled women; standpoint theory; and postmodern and deconstructive theory. Two critical trends emerge from these developments: (1) endarkening, decolonizing, indigenizing inquiry and (2) an expanding and maturing intersectionality as a critical approach. This complexity has made the researcher-participant relationship more complicated. It has destablized the insider-outsider model of inquiry. Within indigenous spaces, it has produced a call for the decolonization of the academy. This is linked to a deconstruction of such traditional terms as experience, difference, and gender.

A gendered decolonizing discourse focuses on the concepts of experience, difference, bias and objectivity, validity and trustworthiness, voice, performance, and feminist ethics. On this last point, Olesen's masterful chapter elaborates the frameworks presented by Cannella and Lincoln (Chapter 5) and Christians (Chapter 4) in Part I.

The Endarkened Feminist Praxis

In their chapter in the third edition of the *Handbook*, Gloria Ladson-Billings and Jamel Donnor presented an activist version of critical race theory (CRT) committed to social justice and a revolutionary habitus. They focused their analysis on the meaning of the "call," those epiphanic moments when people of color are reminded that they are locked into a hierarchical racial structure. Critical race theorists experiment with multiple interpretive strategies, ranging from storytelling to autoethnography, case studies, textual and narrative analyses, traditional fieldwork, and most important, collaborative, action-based inquiries and studies of race, gender, law, education, and racial oppression in daily life. Inquiry for social justice is the goal. For justice to happen, the academy must change; it must embrace the principles of decolonization. A reconstructed university will become a home for racialized others, a place where indigenous, liberating empowering pedagogies have become commonplace.

In Chapter 8, Cynthia B. Dillard and Chinwe Okpalaoka radically extend the spaces of CRT by opening up a paradigm that embodies cultural and spiritual understandings. Their endarkened framework foregrounds spirituality, with links to Africa and the African diaspora. An endarkened feminist epistemology intersects with the historical and contemporary contexts of oppression for African ascendant woman. Under this model, research is a moral responsibility. It honors the wisdom, spirituality, and critical interventions of transnational Black women. These are powerful recipes for action.

Critical Pedagogy and Critical Theory

Multiple critical theories and Marxist or neo-Marxist models now circulate within the discourses of qualitative research In Lincoln and Guba's (2000) framework, this paradigm, in its many formulations, articulates an ontology based on historical realism, an epistemology that is transactional and a methodology that is both dialogic and dialectical. In Chapter 9, Joe L. Kincheloe, Peter McLaren, and Shirley Steinberg trace the history of critical research (and Marxist theory) from the Frankfurt School through more recent transformations in poststructural, postmodern, feminist, critical pedagogy, and cultural studies theory.

They outline a critical theory, a bricolage, which they call *critical humility,* an evolving criticality for the new millennium, beginning with the assumption that the societies of the West are not unproblematically democratic and free. Their version of critical theory rejects economic determinism and focuses on the media, culture, language, power, desire, critical enlightenment, and critical emancipation. Their framework embraces a critical hermeneutics. They read instrumental rationality as one of the most repressive features of contemporary society. Building on Paulo Freire, Karl Marx, Max Weber, Mikhail Bakhtin, and Jürgen Habermas, they present a critical, pragmatic approach to texts and their relationships to lived experience. This leads to a "resistance" version of critical theory, a version connected to critical ethnography, and partisan, critical inquiry committed to social criticism and the empowerment of individuals. As bricoleurs, critical theorists seek to produce practical, pragmatic knowledge, a bricolage that is cultural and structural, judged by its degree of historical situatedness and its ability to produce praxis or action.

Like Olesen's Chapter 7, this chapter is a call to arms. Getting mad is no longer enough. We must learn how to act in the world in ways that allow us to expose the workings of an invisible empire that leaves even more children behind.

Cultural Studies

Cultural studies cannot be contained within a single framework. There are multiple cultural studies projects, including those connected to the Birmingham School and the work of Stuart Hall and his associates (see Hall, 1996). Cultural studies research is historically self-reflective, critical, interdisciplinary, conversant with high theory, and focused on the global and the local; it takes into account historical, political, economic, cultural, and everyday discourses. It focuses on "questions of community, identity, agency, and change" (Grossberg & Pollock, 1998).

In its generic form, cultural studies involves an examination of how the history people live is produced by structures that have been handed down from the past. Each version of cultural studies is joined by a three-fold concern with cultural texts, lived experience, and the articulated relationship between texts and everyday life. Within the cultural text tradition, some scholars examine the mass media and popular culture as sites where history, ideology, and subjective experiences come together. These scholars produce critical ethnographies of the audience in relation to particular historical moments. Other scholars read texts as sites where hegemonic meanings are produced, distributed, and consumed. Within the ethnographic tradition, there is a postmodern concern for the social text and its production.

The disciplinary boundaries that define cultural studies keep shifting, and there is no agreed upon standard genealogy of its emergence as a serious academic discipline. Nonetheless, there are certain prevailing tendencies, including feminist understandings of the politics of the everyday and the personal; disputes between proponents of textualism, ethnography, and autoethnography; and continued debates surrounding the dreams of modern citizenship.

The open-ended nature of the cultural studies project leads to a perpetual resistance against attempts to impose a single definition over the entire project. There are critical-Marxist, constructionist, and postpositivist paradigmatic strands within the formation, as well as emergent feminist and ethnic models. Scholars within the cultural studies project are drawn to historical realism and relativism as their ontology, to transactional epistemologies and dialogic methodologies, while remaining committed to a historical and structural framework that is action-oriented.

In Chapter 10, Michael D. Giardina and Josh L. Newman outline a performative, embodied, poststructural, contextualist, and globalized cultural studies project. They locate the bodies of cultural studies within a post-9/11 militarization of culture, a destabilized Middle East, and endless wars in Iraq and Afghanistan. Cultural studies' bodies are under duress, assailed by heteronormative logics of consumption, racism, and gender oppression. Drawing on their own research, Giardina and Newman outline a methodological program for a radically embodied cultural studies that is defined by its interest in lived, discursive, and contextual dimensions of reality, weaving back and forth between culturalist and realist agendas.

Theirs is a historically embodied, physical cultural studies. It works outward from the politically located body, locating that body in those historical structures that overdetermine meaning, identity, and opportunity. They seek a performative cultural studies that makes the world visible in ways that implement the goals of social justice and radical, progressive democracy. Thus do they move back and forth between the local and the global, the cultural and the real, the personal and the political, the embodied and the performative.

Critical Humanism and Queer Theory

Critical race theory brought race and the concept of a complex racial subject squarely into qualitative inquiry. It remained for queer theory to do the same; namely, to question and deconstruct the concept of a unified sexual (and racialized) subject. In Chapter 11, Ken Plummer takes queer theory in a new direction. He writes from his own biography, a post-gay humanist, a sort of feminist, a little queer, a critical humanist who wants to move on. He thinks that in the postmodern moment certain terms, like *family* and much of our research methodology language, are obsolete. He calls them zombie categories. They are no longer needed. They are dead.

With the arrival of queer theory, the social sciences are in a new space. This is the age of postmodern fragmentation, globalization, and post-humanism. This is a time for new research styles, styles that take up the reflexive queer, polyphonic, narrative, ethical turn. Plummer's critical humanism, with its emphasis on symbolic interactionism, pragmatism, democratic thinking, storytelling, moral progress, and social justice, enters this space. It is committed to reducing human suffering, to an ethics of care and compassion, a politics of respect, and the importance of trust.

His queer theory is radical. It encourages the postmodernization of sexual and gender studies. It deconstructs all conventional categories of sexuality and gender. It is transgressive, gothic, and romantic. It challenges the heterosexual/homosexual binary; the deviance paradigm is abandoned. His queer methodology takes the textual turn seriously, endorses subversive ethnographies, scavenger methodologies, ethnographic performances, and queered case studies.

By troubling the place of the homo-heterosexual binary in everyday life, queer theory has created spaces for multiple discourses on gay, bisexual, transgendered, and lesbian subjects. This means researchers must examine how any social arena is structured, in part, by this homo-hetero dichotomy. They must ask how the epistemology of the closet is central to the sexual and material practices of everyday life. Queer theory challenges this epistemology, just as it deconstructs the notion of unified subjects. Queerness becomes a topic and a resource for investigating the way group boundaries are created, negotiated, and changed. Institutional and historical analyses are central to this project, for they shed light on how the self and its identities are embedded in institutional and cultural practices.

In a short postscript to his 2005 chapter, Plummer asks, in this current moment, "Is a global critical humanism possible—Is it possible to generate a transnational queer studies?" And, if so, what would it look like? He calls for a cosmopolitan methodology, a methodological open mindedness, a respect, and a willingness to listen, learn, and dialogue across the spaces of intimate citizenship.

Asian Epistemologies

In Chapter 12, James H. Liu analyzes Asian epistemologies and their influence on contemporary social psychological research in Asia and elsewhere. He thus extends the qualitative research project into non-Western cultures, noting that the social sciences in Asia continue to be shaped by an imported Western logical positivism.

Recently, there has been a rise of indigenous Asian epistemologies and indigenous psychologies—from Japan to China, India, Taiwan, the Philippines, and Korea. Chinese indigenous psychology, for example, has its own journal, regular conferences, and preferred research methods. A highly pragmatic approach, rooted in research practices rather than epistemology, characterizes the modal Asian indigenous psychology. Hermeneutic and empiricist schools of thought compete for attention.

Much of Asian ontology is holistic; culture is embedded within the processes and objects of inquiry. Culture is understood to be historically constructed.

Culture is constitutive of mind. People develop a theory of mind and construe themselves in and through language.

Tensions persist, and the positivist paradigm is still in ascendency. Asian scholars are in a transition period, and an epistemological breakthrough may be imminent. Even if the breakthrough does not occur, as Professor Liu observes, "even if the sky does not fall down, it may still be useful to work on the margins to connect the centers of an increasingly interconnected world of parallel and distributed cultural values" (p. 224).

Disability Communities: Transformative Research for Social Justice

In Chapter 13, Donna Mertens, Martin Sullivan, and Hilary Stace outline the major interpretive contours of a social disability paradigm. Following the examples set by antiracist, feminist, and gay rights movements of the 1960s, disabled people throughout the Western world began to organize to challenge the oppressive stereotypes of disabled people and to propose ways to conduct nonoppressive, empowering disability research. Positivist, emancipatory, and transformative inquiry paradigms are compared and contrasted. The transformative model focuses, not on disability per se (as in the emancipatory model), but on the historical, cultural contexts surrounding disability, gender, race, sexual orientation, and social class. Interpretive and mixed methods of inquiry are employed under both paradigms. The transformative paradigm is activist, critical, and constructivist, embedded in social justice and human rights agendas. It combines the transformative lens with the arguments of disability rights theorists. Examples from work with indigenous peoples are offered, understanding that there is no single, homogenous, indigenous or disability community. Mertens et al. end on a powerful note: "The pathway to full realization of human rights and social justice for people with disability is not smooth . . . the transformative paradigm provides a way forward" (p. 237).

Conclusion

The researcher-as-interpretive-bricoleur cannot afford to be a stranger to any of the paradigms and perspectives discussed in Part II of the *Handbook*. The researcher must understand the basic ethical, ontological, epistemological, and methodological assumptions of each and be able to engage them in dialogue. The differences between paradigms and perspectives have significant and important implications at the practical, material, everyday level. The blurring of paradigm differences is likely to continue, as long as proponents continue to come together to discuss their differences, while seeking to build on those areas where they are in agreement.

It is also clear that there is no single "truth." All truths are partial and incomplete. There will be no single conventional paradigm, as Lincoln and Guba (2000) argue, to which all social scientists might ascribe. We occupy a historical moment marked by multivocality, contested meanings, paradigmatic controversies, and new textual forms. This is an age of emancipation, freedom from the confines of a single regime of truth, emancipation from seeing the world in one color.

References

Foley, D., & Valenzuela, A. (2005). Critical ethnography: The politics of collaboration. In N. K. Denzin & Y. S. Lincoln (Eds.), *The SAGE handbook of qualitative research* (3rd ed., pp. 217–234). Thousand Oaks, CA: Sage.

Grossberg, L., & Pollock, D. (1998). Editorial statement. *Cultural Studies, 12*(2), 114.

Guba, E. (1990). The alternative paradigm dialog. In E. Guba (Ed.), *The paradigm dialog* (pp. 17–30). Newbury Park, CA: Sage.

Hall, S. (1996). Gramsci's relevance for the study of race and ethnicity. In D. Morley & K.-H. Chen (Eds.), *Stuart Hall: Critical dialogues in cultural studies* (pp. 411–444). London: Routledge.

Ladson-Bilings, G., & Donner, J. (2005). The moral activist role of critical race theory scholarship. In N. K. Denzin & Y. S. Lincoln (Eds.), *The SAGE handbook of qualitative research* (3rd ed., pp. 279–302). Thousand Oaks, CA: Sage.

Lincoln, Y. S., & Guba, E. (2000). Paradigmatic controversies, contradictions, and emerging confluences. In N. K. Denzin & Y. S. Lincoln (Eds.), *Handbook of qualitative research* (2nd ed., pp. 163–188). Thousand Oaks, CA: Sage.

6

Paradigmatic Controversies, Contradictions, and Emerging Confluences, Revisited

Yvonna S. Lincoln, Susan A. Lynham, and Egon G. Guba

In our chapter for the first edition of the *Handbook of Qualitative Research* (Guba & Lincoln, 1994), we focused on the contention among various research paradigms for legitimacy and intellectual and paradigmatic hegemony. The postmodern paradigms that we discussed (postmodernist, critical theory, and constructivism)[1] were in contention with the received positivist and postpositivist paradigms for legitimacy and with one another for intellectual legitimacy. In the 15 years that have elapsed since that chapter was published, substantial changes have occurred in the landscape of social scientific inquiry. On the matter of legitimacy, we observe that readers familiar with the literature on methods and paradigms reflect a high interest in ontologies and epistemologies that differ sharply from those undergirding conventional social science, including, but not limited to, feminist theories, critical race and ethnic studies, queer theory, border theories, postcolonial ontologies and epistemologies, and poststructural and postmodern work. Second, even those established professionals trained in quantitative social science (including the two of *us)* want to learn more about qualitative approaches because new professionals being mentored in graduate schools are asking serious questions about and looking for guidance in qualitatively oriented studies and dissertations. Third, the number of qualitative texts, research papers, workshops, and training materials has exploded. Indeed, it would be difficult to miss the distinct turn of the social sciences toward more interpretive, postmodern, and critical practices and theorizing (Bloland, 1989, 1995). This nonpositivist orientation has created a context (surround) in which virtually no study can go unchallenged by proponents of contending paradigms. Furthermore, it is obvious that the number of practitioners of new paradigm inquiry is growing daily. The legitimacy of postpositivist and postmodern paradigms is well established and at least equal to the legitimacy of received and conventional paradigms (Denzin & Lincoln, 1994).

On the matter of hegemony, or supremacy, among postmodern paradigms, it is clear that Clifford Geertz's (1988, 1993) prophecy about the "blurring of genres" is rapidly being fulfilled. Inquiry methodology can no longer be treated as a set of universally applicable rules or abstractions.

Methodology is inevitably interwoven with and emerges from the nature of particular disciplines (such as sociology and psychology) and particular perspectives (such as Marxism, feminist theory, and queer theory). So, for instance, we can read feminist critical theorists such as Virginia Olesen (2000; Chapter 7, this volume) and Patricia Lather (2007) or queer theorists such as Joshua Gamson (2000), or we can follow arguments about teachers as researchers (Kincheloe, 1991) while we understand the secondary text to be teacher empowerment and democratization of schooling practices. Indeed, the various paradigms are beginning to "interbreed" such that two theorists previously thought to be in irreconcilable conflict may now appear, under a different theoretical rubric, to be informing one another's arguments. A personal example is our own work, which has been heavily influenced by action research practitioners and postmodern and poststructural critical theorists. Consequently, to argue that it is paradigms that are in contention is probably less useful than to probe where and how paradigms exhibit confluence and where and how they exhibit differences, controversies, and contradictions. As the field or fields of qualitative research mature and continue to add both methodological and epistemological as well as political sophistication, new linkages will, we believe, be found, and emerging similarities in interpretive power and focus will be discovered.

Major Issues Confronting All Paradigms

In our chapter in the first edition of this *Handbook,* we presented two tables that summarized our positions, first, on the axiomatic nature of paradigms (the paradigms we considered at that time were positivism, postpositivism, critical theory, and constructivism; Guba & Lincoln, 1994, p. 109, Table 6.1); and second, on the issues we believed were most fundamental to differentiating the four paradigms (p. 112, Table 6.2). These tables are reproduced here in slightly different form as a way of reminding our readers of our previous statements. The axioms defined the ontological, epistemological, and methodological bases for both established and emergent paradigms; these are shown here in Table 6.1. The issues most often in contention were inquiry aim, nature of knowledge, the way knowledge is accumulated, goodness (rigor and validity) or quality criteria, values, ethics, voice, training (the nature of preparatory work that goes into preparing a researcher to engage in responsible and reflective fieldwork), accommodation, and hegemony; these are shown in Table 6.2. An examination of these two tables will reacquaint the reader with our original *Handbook* treatment; more detailed information is, of course, available in our original chapter. Readers will notice that in the interim, Susan Lynham has joined us in creating a new and more substantial version of one of the tables, one that takes into account both our own increasing understandings and her work with us and students in enlarging the frames of reference for new paradigm work.

Since publication of that chapter, at least one set of authors, John Heron and Peter Reason, has elaborated on our tables to include the *participatory/cooperative* paradigm (Heron, 1996; Heron & Reason, 1997, pp. 289–290). Thus, in addition to the paradigms of positivism, postpositivism, critical theory, and constructivism, we add the participatory paradigm in the present chapter (this is an excellent example, we might add, of the hermeneutic elaboration so embedded in our own view, constructivism; see, e.g., Guba 1990, 1996). Our aim here is to extend the analysis further by building on Heron and Reason's additions and by rearranging the issues to reflect current thought. The issues we have chosen include our original formulations and the additions, revisions, and amplifications made by Heron and Reason (1997) as well as by Lynham, and we have also chosen what we believe to be the issues most important today. We should note that *important* means several things to us. An important topic may be one that is widely debated (or even hotly contested)—validity is one such issue. An important issue may be one that bespeaks a new awareness (an issue such as recognition of the role of values). An important issue may be one that illustrates the influence of one paradigm on another (such as the influence of feminist, action research, critical theory, and participatory models on researcher conceptions of action within and with the community in which research is carried out). Or issues may be important because new or extended theoretical or field-oriented treatments for them are newly available—voice and reflexivity are two such issues. Important may also indicate that new or emerging treatments contradict

Table 6.1 Basic Beliefs (Metaphysics) of Alternative Inquiry Paradigms

Item	Positivism	Postpositivism	Critical Theory et al.	Constructivism
Ontology	Naïve realism—"real" reality but apprehendible	Critical realism—"real" reality but only imperfectly and probabilistically apprehendible	Historical realism—virtual reality shaped by social, political, cultural, economic, ethnic, and gender values; crystallized over time	Relativism—local and specific constructed and co-constructed realities
Epistemology	Dualist/objectivist; findings true	Modified dualist/ objectivist; critical tradition/ community; findings probably true	Transactional/ subjectivist; value-mediated findings	Transactional/ subjectivist; created findings
Methodology	Experimental/ manipulative; verification of hypotheses; chiefly quantitative methods	Modified experimental/ manipulative; critical multiplism; falsification of hypotheses; may include qualitative methods	Dialogic/dialectical	Hermeneutical/ dialectical

earlier formulations in such a way that debates about method, paradigms, or ethics take the forefront once again, resulting in rich and fruitful conversations about what it means to do qualitative work. *Important* sometimes foregrounds larger social movements that undermine qualitative research in the name of science or that declare there is only one form of science that deserves the name (National Research Council, 2002).

Table 6.3 reprises the original Table 8.3 but adds the axioms of the participatory paradigm proposed by Heron and Reason (1997). Table 6.4 deals with seven issues and represents an update of selected issues first presented in the old Table 8.4. *Voice* in the 1994 version of Table 6.2 has been renamed *inquirer posture,* and we have inserted a redefined *voice* in the current table.

In all cases except inquirer posture, the entries for the participatory paradigm are those proposed by Heron and Reason; in the one case not covered by them, we have

Table 6.2 Paradigm Positions on Selected Practical Issues

Item	Positivism		Postpositivism	Critical Theory et al.	Constructivism
Inquiry aim	Explanation: prediction and control			Critique and transformation; restitution and emancipation	Understanding; reconstruction
Nature of knowledge	Verified hypotheses established as facts or laws		Nonfalsified hypotheses that are probable facts or laws	Structural/historical insights	Individual or collective reconstructions coalescing around consensus
Knowledge accumulation	Accretion—"building blocks" adding to "edifice of knowledge"; generalizations and cause-effect linkages			Historical revisionism; generalization by similarity	More informed and sophisticated reconstructions; vicarious experience
Goodness or quality criteria	Conventional benchmarks of "rigor": internal and external validity, reliability, and objectivity			Historical situatedness; erosion of ignorance and misapprehension; action stimulus	Trustworthiness and authenticity, including catalyst for action
Values	Excluded—influence denied			Included—formative	Included—formative
Ethics	Extrinsic: tilt toward deception			Intrinsic: moral tilt toward revelation	Intrinsic: process tilt toward revelation; special problems
Voice	"Disinterested scientist" as informer of decision makers, policy makers, and change agents			"Transformative intellectual" as advocate and activist	"Passionate participant" as facilitator of multivoice reconstruction
Training	Technical and quantitative; substantive theories		Technical; quantitative and qualitative; substantive theories	Resocialization; qualitative and quantitative; history; values of altruism, empowerment, and liberation	
Accommodation	Commensurable			Incommensurable with previous two	
Hegemony	In control of publication, funding, promotion, and tenure			Seeking recognition and input; offering challenges to predecessor paradigms, aligned with postcolonial aspirations	

Table 6.3 Basic Beliefs of Alternative Inquiry Paradigms—Updated

Issue	Positivism	Postpositivism	Critical Theory et al.	Constructivism	Participatory[a]
Ontology	Naïve realism—"real" reality but apprehendible	Critical realism—"real" reality but only imperfectly and probabilistically apprehendible	Historical realism—virtual reality shaped by social, political, cultural, economic, ethnic, and gender values; crystallized over time	Relativism—local and specific co-constructed realities	Participative reality—subjective-objective reality, co-created by mind and given cosmos
Epistemology	Dualist/objectivist; findings true	Modified dualist/objectivist; critical tradition/community; findings probably true	Transactional/subjectivist; value-mediated findings	Transactional/subjectivist; co-created findings	Critical subjectivity in participatory transaction with cosmos; extended epistemology of experiential, propositional, and practical knowing; co-created findings
Methodology	Experimental/manipulative; verification of hypotheses; chiefly quantitative methods	Modified experimental/manipulative; critical multiplism; falsification of hypotheses; may include qualitative methods	Dialogic/dialectical	Hermeneutical/dialectical	Political participation in collaborative action inquiry; primacy of the practical; use of language grounded in shared experiential context

a. Entries in this column are based on Heron and Reason (1997).

Table 6.4 Paradigm Positions on Selected Issues—Updated

Issue	Positivism	Postpositivism	Critical Theories	Constructivism	Participatory[a]
Nature of knowledge	Verified hypotheses established as facts or laws	Nonfalsified hypotheses that are probable facts or laws	Structural/historical insights	Individual and collective reconstructions sometimes coalescing around consensus	Extended epistemology: primacy of practical knowing; critical subjectivity; living knowledge
Knowledge accumulation	Accretion—"building blocks" adding to "edifice of knowledge"; generalizations and cause-effect linkages		Historical revisionism; generalization by similarity	More informed and sophisticated reconstructions; vicarious experience	In communities of inquiry embedded in communities of practice
Goodness or quality criteria	Conventional benchmarks of "rigor": internal and external validity, reliability, and objectivity		Historical situatedness; erosion of ignorance and misapprehensions; action stimulus	Trustworthiness and authenticity including catalyst for action	Congruence of experiential, presentational, propositional, and practical knowing; leads to action to transform the world in the service of human flourishing

(Continued)

Table 6.4 (Continued)

Issue	Positivism	Postpositivism	Critical Theories	Constructivism	Participatory[a]
Values	Excluded—influence denied		Included—formative		
Ethics	Extrinsic—tilt toward deception		Intrinsic—moral tilt toward revelation	Intrinsic—process tilt toward revelation	
Inquirer posture	"Disinterested scientist" as informer of decision makers, policy makers, and change agents		"Transformative intellectual" as advocate and activist	"Passionate participant" as facilitator of multivoice reconstruction	Primary voice manifest through aware self-reflective action; secondary voices in illuminating theory, narrative, movement, song, dance, and other presentational forms
Training	Technical and quantitative; substantive theories	Technical; quantitative and qualitative; substantive theories	Resocialization; qualitative and quantitative; history; values of altruism, empowerment and liberation		Coresearchers are initiated into the inquiry process by facilitator/ researcher and learn through active engagement in the process; facilitator/ researcher requires emotional competence, democratic personality and skills

a. Entries in this column are based on Heron and Reason (1997), except for "ethics" and "values."

added a notation that we believe captures their intention. We make no attempt here to reprise the material well discussed in our earlier handbook chapter. Instead, we focus primarily on the issues in Table 6.4: axiology; accommodation and commensurability; action; control; foundations of truth and knowledge; validity; and voice, reflexivity, and postmodern textual representation. In addition, we take up the issues of cumulation and mixed methods since both prompt some controversy and friendly debate within the qualitative camp. We believe these issues to be the most important at this time. While we believe these issues to be the most contentious, we also believe they create the intellectual, theoretical, and practical space for dialogue, consensus, and confluence to occur. There is great potential for interweaving of viewpoints, for the incorporation of multiple perspectives, and for borrowing, or *bricolage,* where borrowing seems useful, richness-enhancing, or theoretically heuristic. For instance, even though we are ourselves social constructivists or constructionists, our call to action embedded in the authenticity criteria we elaborated in *Fourth Generation Evaluation* (Guba & Lincoln, 1989) reflects strongly the bent to action embodied in critical theorists' and participatory action research perspectives well outlined in the earlier editions (Kemmis & McTaggart, 2000; Kincheloe & McLaren, 2000). And although Heron and Reason have elaborated a model they call the *cooperative paradigm,* careful reading of their proposal reveals a form of inquiry that is post-postpositive, postmodern, and criticalist in orientation.

As a result, the reader familiar with several theoretical and paradigmatic strands of research will find that echoes of many streams of thought come together in the extended table. What this means is that the categories, as Laurel Richardson (personal communication, September 12, 1998) has pointed out, "are fluid, indeed what should be a category keeps altering, enlarging." She notes that "even as [we] write, the boundaries between the paradigms are shifting." This is the paradigmatic equivalent of the Geertzian "blurring of genres" to which we referred earlier, and we regard this blurring and shifting as emblematic of a dynamism that is critical if we are to see qualitative research begin to have an impact on policy formulation or on the redress of social ills.

Our own position is that of the constructionist camp, loosely defined. We do not believe that criteria for judging either "reality" or validity are absolutist (Bradley & Schaefer, 1998); rather, they are derived from community consensus regarding what is "real": what is useful and what has meaning (especially meaning for action and further steps) within that community, as well as for that particular piece of research (Lather, 2007; Lather & Smithies, 1997). We believe that a goodly portion of social phenomena consists of the meaning-making activities of groups and individuals around those phenomena. The meaning-making

(Text Continued on page 237)

Table 6.5 Themes of Knowledge: An Heuristic Schema of Inquiry, Thought, and Practice*

	Positivism	Postpositivism	Critical	Constructivism	Participatory
THEMES OF KNOWLEDGE: Inquiry Aims, Ideals, Design, Procedures, and Methods					
	Realists, "hard science" researchers	A modified form of positivism	(+ Feminism + Race)	(or Interpretivist)	(+ Postmodern)
			Create change, to the benefit of those oppressed by power	Gain understanding by interpreting subject perceptions	Transformation based on democratic participation between researcher and subject
A: BASIC BELIEFS (METAPHYSICS) OF ALTERNATIVE INQUIRY PARADIGMS					
Ontology	Belief in a single identifiable reality. There is a single truth that can be measured and studied. The purpose of research is to predict and control nature (Guba & Lincoln, 2005; Merriam, 1991; Merriam,	Recognize that nature can never fully be understood. There is a single reality, but we may not be able to fully understand what it is or how to get to it because of the hidden variables and a lack of absolutes in nature (Guba & Lincoln,	Human nature operates in a world that is based on a struggle for power. This leads to interactions of privilege and oppression that can be based on race or ethnicity, socioeconomic class, gender, mental or	Relativist: Realities exist in the form of multiple mental constructions, socially and experientially based, local and specific, dependent for their form and content on the persons who hold them (Guba, 1990, p. 27). Relativism: local and specific constructed and co-constructed realities (Guba & Lincoln, 2005, p. 193).	Participative reality: subjective-objective reality, co-created by mind and the surrounding cosmos (Guba & Lincoln, 2005, p. 195). Freedom from objectivity with a new understanding of relation between self and other (Heshusius, 1994, p. 15).
The worldviews and assumptions in which researchers operate in their search for new knowledge (Schwandt, 2007, p. 190). *The study of things that exist and the study of what exists (Latsis, Lawson, & Martins, 2007).*					

What is the nature of reality? (Creswell, 2007).	Caffarella, & Baumgartner, 2007).	2005; Merriam, 1991; Merriam et al., 2007).	physical abilities, or sexual preference (Bernal, 2002; Giroux, 1982; Kilgore, 2001).	"Our individual personal reality—the way we think life is and the part we are to play in it is—*self-created. We put together our own personal reality*" (Guba & Lincoln, 1985, p. 73). Multiple realities exist and are dependent on the individual (Guba, 1996). "Metaphysics that embraces relativity" (Josselson, 1995, p. 29). "We practice inquiries that make sense to the public and to those we study" (Preissle, 2006, p. 636). Assumes that reality as we know it is constructed intersubjectively through the meanings and	Socially constructed: similar to constructive, but do not assume that rationality is a means to better knowledge (Kilgore, 2001, p. 54). Subjective–objective reality: Knowers can only be knowers when known by other knowers. Worldview based on participation and participative realities (Heron & Reason, 1997).

(Continued)

Table 6.5 (Continued)

				understandings developed socially and experientially (Guba & Lincoln, 1994). *To me this means that we construct knowledge through our lived experiences and through our interactions with other members of society. As such, as researchers, we must participate in the research process with our subjects to ensure we are producing knowledge that is reflective of their reality.*	
Epistemology *The process of thinking. The relationship between what we know and what we see. The truths we seek and believe as*	Belief in total objectivity. There is no reason to interact with who or what researchers study. Researchers should value only	Assume we can only approximate nature. Research and the statistics it produces provide a way to make a decision using incomplete data. Interaction with	Research is driven by the study of social structures, freedom and oppression, and power and control. Researchers believe that the knowledge that	Subjectivist: Inquirer and inquired into are fused into a single entity. Findings are literally the creation of the process of interaction between the two (Guba, 1990, p. 27). Transactional/subjectivist: co-created findings (Guba & Lincoln, 2005, p. 195).	Holistic: "Replaces traditional relation between 'truth' and 'interpretation' in which the idea of truth antedates the idea of interpretation" (Heshusius, 1994, p. 15).

researchers (Bernal, 2002; Guba & Lincoln, 2005; Lynham & Webb-Johnson, 2008; Pallas, 2001). What is the relationship between the researcher and that being researched? (Creswell, 2007).	the scientific rigor and not its impact on society or research subjects (Guba & Lincoln, 2005; Merriam, 1991; Merriam et al., 2007).	research subjects should be kept to a minimum. The validity of research comes from peers (the research community), not from the subjects being studied (Guba & Lincoln, 2005; Merriam, 1991; Merriam et al., 2007).	is produced can change existing oppressive structures and remove oppression through empowerment (Merriam, 1991).	The philosophical belief that people construct their own understanding of reality; we construct meaning based on our interactions with our surroundings (Guba & Lincoln, 1985). "Social reality is a construction based upon the actor's frame of reference within the setting" (Guba & Lincoln, 1985, p. 80). Findings are due to the interaction between the researcher and the subject (Guba, 1996). "We cannot know the real without recognizing	Critical subjectivity in participatory transaction with cosmos; extended epistemology of experiential, propositional, and practical knowing; co-created findings (Guba & Lincoln, 2005, p. 195). Critical subjectivity: Understanding how we know what we know and the knowledge's consumating relations. Four ways of knowing: (1) experiential, (2) presentational,

(Continued)

Table 6.5 (Continued)

(3) propositional, and (4) practical (Heron & Reason, 1997).
our own role as knowers" (Flax, 1990). "Simultaneously empirical, intersubjective, and process-oriented" (Flax, 1990). "We are studying ourselves studying ourselves and others" (Preissle, 2006, p. 691). Assumes that we cannot separate ourselves from what we know. The investigator and the object of investigation are linked such that who we are and how we understand the world is a central part of how we understand ourselves, others, and the world (Guba & Lincoln, 1994). *This means we are shaped by our lived experiences, and these will always come out in the knowledge we generate as researchers and in the data generated by our subjects.*

Methodology					
The process of how we seek out new knowledge. The principles of our inquiry and how inquiry should proceed (Schwandt, 2007, p. 190). *What is the process of research?* (Creswell, 2007).	Belief in the scientific method. Value a "gold standard" for making decisions. Grounded in the conventional hard sciences. Belief in the falsification principle (results and findings are true until disproved). Value data produced by studies that can be replicated (Merriam, 1991).	Researchers should attempt to approximate reality. Use of statistics is important to visually interpret our findings. Belief in the scientific method. Research is the effort to create new knowledge, seek scientific discovery. There is an attempt to ask more questions than positivists	Dialogic/ Dialectical (Guba & Lincoln, 2005) Search for participatory research, which empowers the oppressed and supports social transformation and revolution (Merriam, 1991, p. 56).	Hermeneutic, dialectic: Individual constructions are elicited and refined hermeneutically, and compared and contrasted dialectically, with aim of generating one or a few constructions on which there is substantial consensus (Guba, 1990, p. 27). Hermeneutical; dialectical (Guba & Lincoln, 1985, p. 195). Hermeneutical discussion (Geertz, 1973).	Political participation in collaborative action inquiry, primacy of the practical; use of language grounded in shared experiential context (Guba & Lincoln, 2005, p. 195). Use deconstruction as a tool for questioning prevailing representations of learners and learning in the adult education literature; this discredits the false binaries that structure a

(Continued)

Table 6.5 (Continued)

| | because of the unknown variables involved in research.

There is a unifying method.

Distance the researcher to gain objectivity. Use the hypothetical deductive method—hypothesize, deduce, and generalize (Guba & Lincoln, 2005; Merriam, 1991; Merriam et al., 2007). | Hermeneutics (interpretation, i.e., recognition and explanation of metaphors) and comparing and contrasting dialectics (resolving disagreements through rational discussion) (Guba, 1996).

"Everyday consciousness of reality and its chameleonlike quality pervade politics, the media, and literature" (Guba & Lincoln, 1985, p. 70).

"The construction of realities must depend on some form of consensual language" (Guba & Lincoln, 1985, p. 71).

"Stock taking and speculations regarding the future nevertheless help us comprehend the past and the present and aid our choices for the futures we desire" (Preissle, 2006, p. 686). | communication and challenges the assertions of what is to be included or excluded as normal, right, or good (Kilgore, 2001, p. 56).

Experiential knowing is through face-to-face learning, learning new knowledge through the application of the knowledge.

Democratization and co-creation of both content and method.

Engage together in democratic dialogue as co-researchers and as co-subjects |
| | | | |

Interpretive approaches rely heavily on naturalistic methods (interviewing and observation and analysis of existing texts (Angen, 2000). These methods ensure an adequate dialog between the researchers and those with whom they interact in order to collaboratively construct a meaningful reality (Angen, 2000). Generally, meanings are emergent from the research process (Angen, 2000). Typically, qualitative methods are used (Angen, 2000). *Hermeneutic Cycle: Actions lead to collection of data, which leads to interpretation of data which spurs action based on data. (Class notes, 2008)*	(Heron & Reason, 1997).

(Continued)

Table 6.5 (Continued)

	Positivism	Postpositivism	Critical (+ Feminist + Race)	Constructivism (or Interpretivist)	Participatory (+ Postmodern)
THEMES OF KNOWLEDGE: Inquiry Aims, Ideals, Design, Procedures, and Methods					
B: PARADIGM POSITIONS ON SELECTED PRACTICAL ISSUES					
Inquiry aim *The goals of research and the reason why inquiry is conducted. What are the goals and the knowledge we seek?* (Guba & Lincoln, 2005).	Research should be geared toward the prediction and control of natural phenomena. Demonstrate laws that can be applied to natural order.	Researchers attempt to get as close to the answer as possible. Cannot fully attain reality but can approximate it.	Aim of inquiry is to find the social power structure in an attempt to discover the truth as it relates to social power struggles (Giroux, 1982; Merriam, 1991). Transformation (Guba & Lincoln, 2005). Stimulate oppressed people to rationally scrutinize all aspects of their lives to reorder their collective existence on	To understand and interpret through meaning of phenomena (obtained from the joint construction/ reconstruction of meaning of lived experience); such understanding is sought to inform praxis (improved practice). Understanding/ reconstruction (Guba & Lincoln, 2005, p. 194). Consensus toward understanding of culture (Geertz, 1973). Scientific generalizations may not fit in solving all problems (Guba, 1996). An approach needed to fill in the gaps between theory and practice (Guba, 1996).	What is the form and nature of reality and, therefore, what is there that can be known about it? What is the relationship between the knower or would-be knower and what can be known? How can the inquirer . . . go about finding out whatever he or she believes can be known about? What is intrinsically valuable in human life, in particular what sort of

			the basis of the understanding it provides, which will ultimately change social policy and practice (Fay, 1987).	The essential message of hermeneutics is that to be human is to mean, and only by investigating the multifaceted nature of human meaning can we approach the understanding of people (Josselson, 1995).	knowledge, if any, is intrinsically valuable? (Heron & Reason, 1997).
Nature of knowledge *How researchers view the knowledge that is generated through inquiry research* (Guba & Lincoln, 2005).	Hypothesis is verified as fact.	There is a correct single truth, which may have multiple hidden values and variables that prevent ever fully knowing the answer.	Knowledge is viewed as "subjective, emancipatory, and productive of fundamental social change" (Merriam, 1991, p. 53). Rationality is a means to better knowledge. Knowledge is a logical outcome of human interests (Kilgore, 2001). Structural/ historical insights (Guba & Lincoln, 2005).	The constructed meanings of actors are the foundation of knowledge. Individual and collective reconstructions sometimes coalescing around consensus (Guba & Lincoln, 2005, p. 196). Collective reconstruction coalescing around consensus on meaning of culture (Geertz, 1973). People construct their own understanding of reality (Guba, 1990).	Believe knowledge is socially constructed and takes the form in the eyes of the knower rather than being formulated from an existing reality (Kilgore, 2001, p. 51). Extended epistemology: primacy of practical knowing; critical subjectivity; living knowledge (Guba & Lincoln, 2005, p. 196).

(Continued)

Table 6.5 (Continued)

Believe knowledge is socially constructed and takes the form in the eyes of the knower rather than being formulated from an existing reality (Kilgore, 2001, p. 51).	"Realities are taken to exist in the form of multiple mental constructions that are socially and experientially based, local and specific, and dependent for their form and content on the persons who hold them" (Guba, 1990, p. 27). Knowledge is cognitively constructed from experience and interaction of the individual with others and the environment (Class Notes, 2008). Subjective and co-created through the process of interaction between the *inquirer* and the *inquired into* (Class Notes, 2008). Knowledge is socially constructed, not discovered (Class Notes, 2008).	Experiential participation. Propositional knowing. Subjective-objective reality. Practical knowing is knowing how to do something, demonstrated in a skill or competence (Heron & Reason, 1997). The constructed meanings of actors are the foundation of knowledge. Individual and collective reconstructions sometimes coalescing around consensus (Guba & Lincoln, 2005, p. 196). Collective reconstruction

"Observing dialogue allows us to construct a meta-narrative of whole people, not reducing people to parts, but recognizing in the interplay of parts the essence of wholeness. Only then can we begin to imagine the real" (Josselson, 1995, p. 42).

coalescing around consensus on meaning of culture (Geertz, 1973).

People construct their own understanding of reality (Guba, 1990).

"Realities are taken to exist in the form of multiple mental constructions that are socially and experientially based, local and specific, and dependent for their form and content on the persons who hold them" (Guba, 1990, p. 27).

Knowledge is cognitively constructed from experience and interaction of the individual with others and the environment (Epistemology Class Notes).

(Continued)

Table 6.5 (Continued)

					Subjective and co-created through the process of interaction between the inquirer and the inquired into (Epistemology Class Notes) Knowledge is socially constructed, not discovered (Epistemology class notes)
					In communities of inquiry embedded in communities of practice (Guba & Lincoln, 2005, p. 196). "Mind's conceptual articulation of the world is grounded in its experiential participation in what is present, in what there is" . . . Experiential
Knowledge accumulation *How does knowledge build off prior knowledge to develop a better understanding of the subject or field?* (Guba & Lincoln, 2005).	Seek to find cause-and-effect linkages that can build into a better understanding of the field. This can become law over time through use of the scientific method (Merriam, 1991).	Use statistics and other techniques to get as close as possible to reality. Although it can never be attained, approximations of reality can be made to develop further understanding.	Knowledge accumulation is based on historical perspective and revision of how history is viewed so that it no longer serves as an oppressive tool by those with structural power (Guba & Lincoln, 2005).	More informed and sophisticated reconstructions; vicarious experience (Guba & Lincoln, 2005, p. 196). "Since the 1980s, for example, qualitative inquiry has been much influenced by the poststructural and postmodern developments from the arts and the humanities. These bring a sensitivity to language, especially to linguistic	

Goodness or quality criteria				
How researchers judge the quality of inquiry (Guba & Lincoln, 2005).	Rigorous data produced through scientific research.	Statistical confidence level and objectivity in data produced through inquiry.	The value is found in the erosion of unearned privileges and its ability to impart action for the creation of a more fair society (Giroux, 1982; Guba & Lincoln, 2005).	assumptions embedded in disciplinary terminology (e.g. Scheurich, 1996) that has challenged scholars working in post-positivist, interpretive, and critical traditions" (Preissle, 2006, p. 688). Intersubjective agreement and reasoning among actors, reached through dialogue; shared conversation and construction. Trustworthiness and authenticity, including catalyst for action (Guba & Lincoln, 2005, p. 196). Credibility, transferability, dependability, and confirmability (Guba & Lincoln, 2005). "To interrogate objectivity and subjectivity and their relationship to one another" (Preissle, 2006, p. 691).	knowing consists of symbolic frameworks of conceptual, propositional knowing" (Heron & Reason, 1997, pp. 277–278). Congruence of experiential, presentational, and practical knowing; leads to action to transform the world in the service of human flourishing (Guba & Lincoln, 2005, p. 196). Intersubjective agreement and reasoning among actors, reached through dialogue; shared conversation and construction.

(Continued)

Table 6.5 (Continued)

				Trustworthiness and authenticity, including catalyst for action (Guba & Lincoln, 2005, p. 196). Credibility, transferability, dependability, and confirmability (Guba & Lincoln, 2005). "To interrogate objectivity and subjectivity and their relationship to one another" (Preissle, 2006, p. 691)	Included, formative (Guba & Lincoln, 2005, p. 196). Values are personally relative and need to be understood (Epistemology Class Notes).
Values *What do researchers seek as important products within inquiry research?* (Guba & Lincoln, 2005).	Standards-based research. Value is found in the scientific method. Gold standard is scientific rigor.	Can find useful information even if data are incomplete and contain hidden values.	Included, formative (Guba & Lincoln, 2005). Researchers seek data that can be transformative and useful in imparting social justice (Giroux, 1982). Value is found in the reasoned reflection and the change in practice	Are personally relative and need to be understood. Inseparable from the inquiry and outcomes. (Class Notes, 2008). Included, formative (Guba & Lincoln, 2005, p. 194).

THEMES OF KNOWLEDGE: Inquiry Aims, Ideals, Design, Procedures, and Methods

	Positivism	Postpositivism	Critical (+ Feminist + Race)	Constructivism (or Interpretivist)	Participatory (+ Postmodern)
			(Creswell, 2007). Values of research produced should include: rational self-clarity, collective autonomy, happiness, justice, bodily pleasure, play, love, aesthetic self-expression, and other values within these primary values (Fay, 1987).		

B: PARADIGM POSITIONS ON SELECTED PRACTICAL ISSUES continued

	Positivism	Postpositivism	Critical (+ Feminist + Race)	Constructivism (or Interpretivist)	Participatory (+ Postmodern)
Ethics *The interaction and relationship between the researcher and the subject as well as the effect inquiry research has on*	Belief that the data drive the side effects of any research. The effort is to study nature, not to influence how nature	Attempt to be as statistically accurate in their interpretation of reality as possible. Effect on others is not taken into	Frankfurt School of thought: Research is tied to a specific interest in the development	Intrinsic: process tilt toward revelation; special problems (Guba & Lincoln, 2005, p. 196). Included in all aspects of inquiry and examination of culture (Geertz, 1973).	Intrinsic: process tilt toward revelation (Guba & Lincoln, 2005, p. 196). Included in all aspects of inquiry and examination

(Continued)

Table 6.5 (Continued)

populations (Schwandt, 2007).	affects populations (Guba & Lincoln, 2005).	account because research is driven to gain accuracy, not influence populations.	of a society without injustice (Giroux, 1982).		of culture (Geertz, 1973).
Voice					
Who narrates the research that is produced? Qualitative approach: The ability to present the researcher's material along with the story of the research subject (Guba & Lincoln, 2005). *What is the language of research?* (Creswell, 2007).	The data speak for themselves. Consistent findings from inquiry leads to the researcher being disinterested in effect (Guba & Lincoln, 2005).	Researchers are to inform populations using the data produced through their inquiry (Guba & Lincoln, 2005).	The data are created with the intent of producing social change and imparting a social justice that leads to equal rights for all (Giroux, 1982). (Advocate/ Activist).	"Passionate participant" as facilitator of multivoice reconstruction (Guba & Lincoln, 2005). Facilitator of multivoice reconstruction of culture (Geertz, 1973). *This means that while critical theorists attempt to get involved in their research to change the power structure, researchers in this paradigm attempt to gain increased knowledge regarding their study and subjects by interpreting how the subjects perceive and interact within a social context.*	"Passionate participant" as facilitator of multivoice reconstruction (Guba & Lincoln, 2005). Facilitator of multivoice reconstruction of culture (Geertz, 1973).

Training					
How are researchers prepared to conduct inquiry research?	Researchers are trained in a technical and very quantitative way (Guba & Lincoln, 2005). Prescribe scientific method.	Researchers are trained in a technical and very quantitative way but also have the ability to conduct mixed-methods research (Guba & Lincoln, 2005).	Researchers are trained using both qualitative and quantitative approaches. They study history and social science to understand empowerment and liberation (Guba & Lincoln, 2005).	Resocialization; qualitative and quantitative; history, values of altruism, empowerment, and liberation (Guba & Lincoln, 2005, p. 196).	Co-researchers are initiated into the inquiry process by facilitator/researcher and learn through active engagement in the process; facilitator/researcher requires emotional competence, democratic personality, and skills (Guba & Lincoln, 2005, p. 196).

(Continued)

225

Table 6.5 (Continued)

Inquirer posture				
The point of view in which the researcher operates. How does the researcher approach the inquiry process? (Guba & Lincoln, 2005).	Disinterested scientist. Researchers should remain distant from the change process and should not attempt to influence decisions (Guba & Lincoln, 2005).	Researchers are removed from the process, but concerned about its results (Guba & Lincoln, 2005).	The researcher serves as an activist and a transformative intellectual. The researcher understands a way of producing a fair society through social justice (Bernal, 2002; Giroux, 1982; Guba & Lincoln, 2005; Merriam, 1991).	A co-constructor of knowledge, of understanding and interpretation of the meaning of lived experiences (Guba & Lincoln, 2005, p. 196).	Primary voice manifested through aware self-reflective action; secondary voices in illuminating theory, narrative, movement, song, dance, and other presentational forms (Guba & Lincoln, 2005, p. 196).

Can include alternative forms of data representation including film and ethnography (Eisner, 1997). |

Accommodation			
What needs are provided by the inquiry research? (Guba & Lincoln, 2005).	Commensurable: Research has a common unit for study and analysis (Guba & Lincoln, 2005, p. 194).	Commensurable: Research has a common unit for study and analysis (Guba & Lincoln, 2005, p. 194).	Incommensurable: Data produced do not have to be from a common unit of measurement. Approaches research with different styles and methods that can produce multiple forms of data (Guba & Lincoln, 2005).
		Incommensurable: Data produced do not have to be from a common unit of measurement. Approaches research with different styles and methods that can produce multiple forms of data (Guba & Lincoln, 2005).	Incommensurable with positivism and postpositivism; commensurable with critical and participatory inquiry (Guba & Lincoln, 2005, p. 194). Some accommodation with criticalist and participatory methods of examining culture (Geertz, 1973).
			Incommensurable: Data produced do not have to be from a common unit of measurement. Approaches research with different styles and methods that can produce multiple forms of data (Guba & Lincoln, 2005).
			Incommensurable: Data produced does not have to be from a common unit of measurement. Approaches research with different styles and methods that can produce multiple forms of data (Guba, & Lincoln, 2005). Some accommodation with criticalist and participatory methods of examining culture (Geertz, 1973).

Table 6.5 (Continued)

	Positivism	Postpositivism	Critical (+ Feminist + Race)	Constructivism (or Interpretivist)	Participatory (+ Postmodern)
Hegemony *The influence researchers have on others. Who has the power in inquiry and what is inquired. Presenting definition of reality (Kilgore, 2001).*	Belief that research should have the influence – not the person conducting the inquiry. Aim is to produce truth, not provide ways for that reality to affect others.	Statistical analysis of reality will produce data from which decisions can be made. Ultimately, the researcher is in charge of the inquiry process (Guba & Lincoln, 2005, p. 194).	Research demonstrates the interactions of privilege and oppression as they relate to race/ethnicity, gender, class, sexual orientation, physical or mental ability, and age (Kilgore, 2001).	Seeks recognition and input; offers challenges to predecessor paradigms, aligned with postcolonial aspirations (Guba & Lincoln, 2005, p. 196). *Postcolonial is in reference to theories that deal with the cultural legacy of colonial rule (Gandhi, 1998).*	Power is a factor in what and how we know (Kilgore, 2001, p. 51).
THEMES OF KNOWLEDGE: Inquiry Aims, Ideals, Design, Procedures, and Methods					
C: CRITICAL ISSUES OF THE TIME					
Axiology *How researchers act based on the research they produce—also the criteria of values and value judgments especially in ethics (Merriam-Webster, 1997).*	Researchers should remain distant from the subject so their actions are to not have influence on populations—only the laws their inquiry produces (Guba & Lincoln, 2005).	Researchers should attempt to gain a better understanding of reality and as close as possible to truth through the use of statistics that explains and describes what is known as	Researchers seek to change existing education as well as other social institutions' policies and practice (Bernal, 2002).	Propositional, transactional knowing is instrumentally valuable as a means to social emancipation, which is an end in itself, is intrinsically valuable (Guba & Lincoln, 2005, p. 198).	Practical knowing how to flourish with a balance of autonomy, co-operation and hierarchy in a culture is an end in itself, is intrinsically valuable (Heron & Reason, 1997).

What is the role of values? (Creswell, 2007).				
	reality (Guba & Lincoln, 2005).	Attempt to conduct research to improve social justice and remove barriers and other negative influences associated with social oppression (Giroux, 1982).	Emancipatory, but longer term, more reflective versus critical theory's desire for immediate results. "Intellectual digestion"	What is the purpose for which we create reality? To change the world or participation implies engagement, which implies responsibility. In terms of human flourishing, social practices and institutions need to enhance human associations by integration of these three principles; deciding for others with others and for ones self (Heron & Reason, 1997).

(Continued)

Table 6.5 (Continued)

Accommodation and commensurability *Can the paradigm accommodate other types of inquiry?* (Guba & Lincoln, 2005). Can the results of inquiry accommodate each other? (Guba & Lincoln, 1989). Can the paradigms be merged together to make an overarching paradigm? (Guba & Lincoln, 1989).	According to Guba and Lincoln, all positivist forms are commensurable. The data produced are equal in measure to all other data created (Guba & Lincoln, 2005).	According to Guba and Lincoln, all positivist forms are commensurable. The data produced are equal in measure to all other data created (Guba & Lincoln, 2005).	There is a priority or rank order to data created by different forms of research. Because critical researchers want to transform society, critical theory data must come before all other forms. (Incommensurable with empirical-analytical epistemologies and accommodates different forms of research paradigms) (Guba & Lincoln, 2005; Skrtic, 1990).	Incommensurable with positivistic forms; some commensurability with constructivist, criticalist, and participatory approaches, especially as they merge in liberationist approaches outside the West (Guba & Lincoln, 2005, p. 198). Commensurable with other modern paradigms; exception: attempt to understand a problem, but not transform (effect a change). Accommodates critical and participatory approaches to understanding of culture (Geertz, 1973). "Qualitative inquiry is composed of multiple and overlapping communities of practice. Many qualitative inquirers are members of several of these communities" (Preissle, 2006, p. 692).	Incommensurable with positivistic forms; some commensurability with constructivist, criticalist, and participatory approaches, especially as they merge in liberationist approaches outside the West (Guba & Lincoln, 2005, p. 198).

Action					
What is produced as a result of the inquiry process beyond the data? How does society use the knowledge generated? (Guba & Lincoln, 2005).	Researchers are to remain strictly objective, therefore do not concern themselves with the action that is produced as a result of inquiry research (Guba & Lincoln, 2005, p. 198).	Researchers are to remain strictly objective, therefore do not concern themselves with the action that is produced as a result of inquiry research (Guba & Lincoln, 2005, p. 198).	The research produced is to impart social change, change how people think, or serve as an examination of human existence (Creswell, 2007).	Intertwined with validity; inquiry often incomplete without action on the part of participants; constructivist formulation mandates training in political action if participants do not understand political systems (Guba & Lincoln, 2005, p. 198). Must act to be valid or trustworthy. If do not educate participants to act appropriately politically, could actually cause harm to them (accountability in research). Encourages readers to consider the findings presented and understanding of culture that is offered (Geertz, 1973).	Intertwined with validity; inquiry often incomplete without action on the part of participants; constructivist formulation mandates training in political action if participants do not understand political systems (Guba & Lincoln, 2005, p. 198).

(Continued)

Table 6.5 (Continued)

			Shared between inquirer and participants (Guba & Lincoln, 2005, p. 198). Without equal or co-equal control, research cannot be carried out. Knowledge is an expression of power (Kilgore, 2001, p. 59).
		According to my understanding of the readings, researchers must understand the social context and the culture in which the data are produced to accurately reflect what the data actually mean to the study.	Shared between inquirer and participants (Guba & Lincoln, 2005, p. 198). Without equal or co-equal control, research cannot be carried out.
		Critical race theory and critical raced-gendered epistemologies demonstrate that within the critical paradigm, control can be shared by the researcher and the subject, and ultimately the subject can have a say in how the research is conducted (Bernal, 2002).	
	According to Guba and Lincoln (2005), the control is conducted by the researchers without the input and/or concern of the participants and/or society as a whole.		
Control	According to Guba and Lincoln (2005), the control is conducted by the researchers without the input and/or concern of the participants and/or society as a whole.		
Who dictates how the research is produced and used? (Guba & Lincoln, 2005).			

	Positivism	Postpositivism	Critical (+ Feminist + Race)	Constructivism (or Interpretivist)	Participatory (+ Postmodern)
THEMES OF KNOWLEDGE: Inquiry Aims, Ideals, Design, Procedures, and Methods					
		C: CRITICAL ISSUES OF THE TIME continued			
Relationships to foundations of truth and knowledge Helps make meaning and significance of components explicit (Guba & Lincoln, 2005).	Positivists believe there is only one truth or reality. Knowledge is the understanding and control over nature.	Postpositivists believe in a single reality; however, they also believe it will never fully be understood. Knowledge is the attempt to approximate reality and get as close to truth as possible.	The foundation of the critical paradigm is found in the struggle for equality and social justice, and social science demonstrates the oppression of people. Knowledge is an attempt to emancipate the oppressed and improve human condition (Fay, 1987).	Antifoundational (Guba & Lincoln, 2005, p. 198). Refusal to adopt any permanent standards by which truth can be universally known. *According to the readings, to approach inquiry from a constructivist viewpoint is to yield to multiple perspectives of the same data.*	Knowledge is founded in transformation and experience as demonstrated through shared research inquiry between the researcher and subject(s) (Epistemology Class Notes). Knowledge is tentative, multifaceted, not necessarily rational (Kilgore, 2001, p. 59).

(Continued)

Table 6.5 (Continued)

Extended considerations of validity (goodness criteria)				
Bringing ethics and epistemology together (the moral trajectory) (Guba & Lincoln, 2005).	Validity is found in "gold standard" data, data that can be proven and replicated.	Validity is found in data that can be analyzed and studied using statistical tests. Data can be an approximation of reality.	Validity is found when research creates action (or action research) or participatory research, which creates the capacity for positive social change and emancipatory community action (Guba, & Lincoln, 2005; Merriam, 1991)	Extended constructions of validity (Guba & Lincoln, 2005, p. 198). Validity is a construct of the development of consensus. Based on participants and inquirer. "Assessment of any particular piece of research, then, may depend on very general expectations, on criteria tailored to the subcategory of approach and on emergent expectations that vary in all areas as the methodology itself changes" (Preissle, 2006, p. 691). *Based on this assessment of validity, can it be argued that all data are valid because what may not have meaning to one person could be the foundation of all truth to another? Taking this*	Extended constructions of validity (Guba & Lincoln, 2005, p. 198). Validity is found in the ability of the knowledge to become transformative according to the findings of the experiences of the subjects (Epistemology Class Notes).

Voice, reflexivity, postmodern textural representations Voice: Can include the voice of the author, the voice of the respondents (subjects), and the voice of the researcher through their inquiry (Guba & Lincoln, 2005). Reflexivity: The process of reflecting critically on the self as researcher, "the human instrument" (Guba & Lincoln, 2005).	Only the researcher has a voice; any effort to include the voice of the participants would impact objectivity (Guba & Lincoln, 2005).	Only the researcher has a voice; any effort to include the voice of the participants would impact objectivity (Guba & Lincoln, 2005).	The researcher has a voice, but also imparts the voice of the subjects. The researcher is careful to present knowledge through his or her own paradigm while being sensitive to the views of others (Bernal, 2002; Guba & Lincoln, 2005).	*approach, could we say that there is no such thing as invalidity of data or method if someone can find it to be an accurate reflection of their interpretation of reality?* Voices mixed with participants' voices sometimes dominant; reflexivity serious and problematic; textual representation and extended issue (Guba & Lincoln, 2005, p. 198). Voices mixed, with participants' voices sometimes dominant. Reflexivity is serious and problematic. Researchers do not wish to give direction to study. Must use reflection as a researcher: "A few issues seem to be perennial:	Voices mixed; textual representation rarely discussed but problematic; reflexivity relies on critical subjectivity and self-awareness (Guba & Lincoln, 2005, p. 199). Textural: Must be within the context of who or what (for institutions or organizations) is being studied. The subject(s) voice must be present in the research

(Continued)

Table 6.5 (Continued)

		(Epistemology Class Notes).
Postmodern textual representations: The approach researchers take in understanding how social science is written and presented to avoid "dangerous illusions" which may exist in text (Guba & Lincoln, 2005). *Whose voices are heard in the research produced through the inquiry process? Whose views are presenting and/or producing the data?* (Guba & Lincoln, 2005).	combining research approaches, assessing research quality, and the researcher's relationship to theory and philosophy, on the one hand, and participants and the public, on the other hand" (Preissle, 2006, p. 689).	

* Table originally developed by Guba and Lincoln, later expanded and extended by Susan A. Lynham as a teaching tool. The columns were filled in by David Byrd, a Ph.D. student in Dr. Lynham's epistemology class, 2008 Texas A&M University.

activities themselves are of central interest to social constructionists and constructivists simply because it is the meaning-making, sense-making, attributional activities that shape action (or inaction). The meaning-making activities themselves can be changed when they are found to be incomplete, faulty (e.g., discriminatory, oppressive, or nonliberatory), or malformed (created from data that can be shown to be false). We have tried, however, to incorporate perspectives from other major nonpositivist paradigms. This is not a complete summation; space constraints prevent that. What we hope to do in this chapter is to acquaint readers with the larger currents, arguments, dialogues, and provocative writings and theorizing, the better to see perhaps what we ourselves do not even yet see: where and when confluence is possible, where constructive rapprochement might be negotiated, where voices are beginning to achieve some harmony.

Axiology

Earlier, we placed values on the table as an "issue" on which positivists or phenomenologists might have a "posture" (Guba & Lincoln, 1989, 1994; Lincoln & Guba, 1985). Fortunately, we reserved for ourselves the right to either get smarter or just change our minds. We did both. Now, we suspect that *axiology* should be grouped with basic beliefs. In *Naturalistic Inquiry* (Lincoln & Guba, 1985), we covered some of the ways in which values feed into the inquiry process: choice of the problem, choice of paradigm to guide the problem, choice of theoretical framework, choice of major data-gathering and data-analytic methods, choice of context, treatment of values already resident issue within the context, and choice of format(s) for presenting findings. We believed those were strong enough reasons to argue for the inclusion of values as a major point of departure between positivist, conventional modes of inquiry and interpretive forms of inquiry. A second reading of the burgeoning literature and subsequent rethinking of our own rationale have led us to conclude that the issue is much larger than we first conceived. If we had it to do all over again, we would make values or, more correctly, axiology (the branch of philosophy dealing with ethics, aesthetics, and religion) a part of the basic foundational philosophical dimensions of paradigm proposal. Doing so would, in our opinion, begin to help us see the embeddedness of ethics within, not external to, paradigms (see, e.g., Christians, 2000) and would contribute to the consideration of and dialogue about the role of spirituality in human inquiry. Arguably, axiology has been "defined out" of scientific inquiry for no larger a reason than that it also concerns religion. But defining religion broadly to encompass spirituality would move constructivists closer to participative inquirers and would move critical theorists closer to both (owing to their concern with liberation from oppression and freeing of the human spirit, both profoundly spiritual concerns). The expansion of basic issues to include axiology, then, is one way of achieving greater confluence among the various interpretivist inquiry models. This is the place, for example, where Peter Reason's (1993) profound concerns with "sacred science" and human functioning find legitimacy; it is a place where Richardson's (1994) "sacred spaces" become authoritative sites for human inquiry; it is a place—or *the* place—where the spiritual meets social inquiry, as Reason (1993), and later Lincoln and Denzin (1994), proposed some years earlier.

Accommodation, Commensurability, and Cumulation

Positivists and postpositivists alike still occasionally argue that paradigms are, in some ways, commensurable; that is, they can be retrofitted to each other in ways that make the simultaneous practice of both possible. We have argued that at the paradigmatic or philosophical level, commensurability between positivist and constructivist worldviews is not possible, but that within each paradigm, mixed methodologies (strategies) may make perfectly good sense (Guba & Lincoln, 1981, 1982, 1989, 1994; Lincoln & Guba, 1985). So, for instance, in *Effective Evaluation* (Guba & Lincoln, 1981), we argued:

> The guiding inquiry paradigm most appropriate to responsive evaluation is . . . the naturalistic, phenomenological, or ethnographic paradigm. It will be seen that qualitative techniques are typically most appropriate to support this approach. There are times, however, when the issues and concerns voiced by audiences require information that is best generated by more conventional methods, especially quantitative methods. . . . In such cases, the responsive conventional evaluator will not shrink from the appropriate application. (p. 36)

As we tried to make clear, the "argument" arising in the social sciences was *not about method,* although many critics of the new naturalistic, ethnographic, phenomenological, or case study approaches assumed it was.[2] As late as 1998, Weiss could be found to claim that "some evaluation theorists, notably Guba and Lincoln (1989), hold that it is impossible to combine qualitative and quantitative approaches responsibly within an evaluation" (p. 268), even though we stated early on in *Fourth Generation Evaluation* (1989) that those claims, concerns, and issues that have *not* been resolved become the advance organizers for information collection by the evaluator: "The information may be quantitative or qualitative. Responsive evaluation does not rule out quantitative modes, as is mistakenly believed by many, but deals with whatever information is responsive to the unresolved claim, concern, or issue" (p. 43).

We had also strongly asserted earlier, in *Naturalistic Inquiry* (1985), that

> qualitative methods are stressed within the naturalistic paradigm not because the paradigm is antiquantitative but because qualitative methods come more easily to the human-as-instrument. *The reader should particularly note the absence of an antiquantitative stance,* precisely because the naturalistic and conventional paradigms are so often—mistakenly— equated with the qualitative and quantitative paradigms, respectively. Indeed, *there are many opportunities for the naturalistic investigator to utilize quantitative data—probably more than are appreciated.* (pp. 198–199, emphases added)

Having demonstrated that we were not then (and are not now) talking about an antiquantitative posture or the exclusivity of *methods,* but rather about the philosophies of which paradigms are constructed, we can ask the question again regarding commensurability: Are paradigms commensurable? Is it possible to blend elements of one paradigm into another, so that one is engaging in research that represents the best of both worldviews? The answer, from our perspective, has to be a cautious *yes.* This is so if the models (paradigms, integrated philosophical systems) share axiomatic elements that are similar or that resonate strongly. So, for instance, *positivism* and *postpositivism* (as proposed by Phillips, 2006) are clearly commensurable. In the same vein, elements of *interpretivist/ postmodern,* critical theory, constructivist, and participative inquiry fit comfortably together. Commensurability is an issue only when researchers want to "pick and choose" among the axioms of positivist and interpretivist models because the axioms are contradictory and mutually exclusive. Ironically enough, the National Research Council's 2002 report, when defining their take on science, made this very point clearly and forcefully for us. Positivism (their stance) and interpretivism (our stance) are not commensurable.

Cumulation. The argument is frequently made that one of the problems with qualitative research is that it is not cumulative, that is, it cannot be aggregated in such a way as to make larger understandings or policy formulations possible. We would argue this is not the case. Beginning with the Lucas (1974, 1976) case study aggregation analyses, developed at Rand Corporation in the 1970s, researchers have begun to think about ways in which similar studies, carried out via qualitative methods with similar populations or in similar contexts, might be cumulated into meta-analyses, especially for policy purposes. This is now a far more readily available methodology with the advent of large databases manageable on computers. Although the techniques have not, we would argue, been tested extensively, it would seem that cumulation of a growing body of qualitative research is now within our grasp. That makes the criticisms of the noncumulativeness of qualitative research less viable now, or even meaningless.

The Call to Action

One of the clearest ways in which the paradigmatic controversies can be demonstrated is to compare the positivist and postpositivist adherents, who view action as a form of contamination of research results and processes, and the interpretivists, who see action on research results as a meaningful and important outcome of inquiry processes. Positivist adherents believe action to be either a form of advocacy or a form of subjectivity, either or both of which undermine the aim of objectivity. Critical theorists, on the other hand, have always advocated varying degrees of social action, from the overturning of specific unjust practices to radical transformation of entire societies (Giroux, 1982). The call for action—whether in terms of internal transformation, such as ridding oneself of false consciousness, or of external social transformation (in the form, for instance, of extended social justice)—differentiates between positivist and postmodern criticalist theorists (including feminist and queer theorists). The sharpest shift, however, has been in the constructivist and participatory phenomenological models, where a step beyond interpretation and *verstehen,* or understanding, toward social action is probably one of the most conceptually interesting of the shifts (Lincoln, 1997, 1998a, 1998b).

For some theorists, the shift toward action came in response to widespread nonutilization of evaluation findings and the desire to create forms of evaluation that would attract champions who might follow through on recommendations with meaningful action plans (Guba & Lincoln, 1981, 1989). For others, embracing action came as both a political and an ethical commitment (see, e.g., Carr & Kemmis, 1986; Christians, 2000; Greenwood & Levin, 2000; Schratz & Walker, 1995; Tierney, 2000). Whatever the source of the problem to which inquirers were responding, the shift toward connecting action with research, policy analysis, evaluation, and social deconstruction (e.g., deconstruction of the patriarchal forms of oppression in social structures, which is the project informing much feminist theorizing, or deconstruction of the homophobia embedded in public policies) has come to characterize much new-paradigm inquiry work, both at the theoretical and at the practice and *praxis-oriented* levels. Action has become a major controversy that limns the ongoing debates among practitioners of the various paradigms. The mandate for social action, especially action designed and created by and for research participants with the aid and cooperation of researchers, can be most sharply delineated between positivist/postpositivist and new-paradigm inquirers. Many positivist and postpositivist inquirers still consider action the domain of communities other than researchers and research participants: those of policy personnel, legislators, and civic and political officials. Hard-line foundationalists presume that the taint of action will interfere with or even negate the objectivity that is a (presumed) characteristic of rigorous scientific method inquiry.

Control

Another controversy that has tended to become problematic centers on *control* of the study: Who initiates? Who determines salient questions? Who determines what constitutes findings? Who determines how data will be collected? Who determines in what forms the findings will be made public, if at all? Who determines what representations will be made of participants in the research? Let us be very clear: The issue of control is deeply embedded in the questions of voice, reflexivity, and issues of postmodern textual representation, which we shall take up later, *but only for new-paradigm inquirers.* For more conventional inquirers, the issue of control is effectively walled off from voice, reflexivity, and issues of textual representation because each of those issues in some way threatens claims to rigor (particularly objectivity and validity). For new-paradigm inquirers who have seen the preeminent paradigm issues of ontology and epistemology effectively folded into one another, and who have watched as methodology and axiology logically folded into one another (Lincoln, 1995, 1997), control of an inquiry seems far less problematic, except insofar as inquirers seek to obtain participants' genuine participation (see, e.g., Guba & Lincoln, 1981, on contracting and attempts to get some stakeholding groups to do more than stand by while an evaluation is in progress). Critical theorists, especially those who work in community organizing programs, are painfully aware of the necessity for members of the community or research participants to take control of their futures (see, e.g., Lather, 2007). Constructivists desire participants to take an increasingly active role in nominating questions of interest for any inquiry and in designing outlets for findings to be shared more widely within and outside the community. Participatory inquirers understand action controlled by the local context members to be the aim of inquiry within a community. For none of these paradigmatic adherents is control an issue of advocacy, a somewhat deceptive term usually used as a code within a larger metanarrative to attack an inquiry's rigor, objectivity, or fairness.

Rather, for new-paradigm researchers, control is a means of fostering emancipation, democracy, and community empowerment and of redressing power imbalances such that those who were previously marginalized now achieve voice (Mertens, 1998) or "human flourishing" (Heron & Reason, 1997). Control as a controversy is an excellent place to observe the phenomenon that we have always termed "Catholic questions directed to a Methodist audience:" We use this description—given to us by a workshop participant in the early 1980s—to refer to the ongoing problem of illegitimate questions: questions that have no meaning because the frames of reference are those for which they were never intended. (We could as well call these "Hindu questions to a Muslim" to give another sense of how paradigms, or overarching philosophies—or theologies—are incommensurable, and how questions in one framework make little, if any, sense in another.) Paradigmatic formulations interact such that control becomes inextricably intertwined with mandates for objectivity. Objectivity derives from the Enlightenment prescription for knowledge of the physical world, which is postulated to be separate and distinct from those who would know (Polkinghorne, 1989). But if knowledge of the social (as opposed to the physical) world resides in meaning-making mechanisms of the social, mental, and linguistic worlds that individuals inhabit, then knowledge cannot be separate from the knower but rather is rooted in his or her mental or linguistic designations of that world (Polkinghorne, 1989; Salner, 1989).

Foundations of Truth and Knowledge in Paradigms

Whether or not the world has a "real" existence outside of human experience of that world is an open question. For modernist (i.e., Enlightenment, scientific method, conventional, positivist) researchers, most assuredly there is a "real" reality "out there," apart from the flawed human apprehension of it. Furthermore, that reality can be approached (approximated) only through the utilization of methods that prevent human contamination of its apprehension or comprehension. For foundationalists in the empiricist tradition, the foundations of scientific truth and knowledge about reality reside in rigorous application of testing phenomena against a template as devoid as instrumentally possible of human bias, misperception, and other "idols" (Francis Bacon, cited in Polkinghorne, 1989). As Donald Polkinghorne (1989) makes clear:

> The idea that the objective realm is independent of the knower's subjective experiences of it can be found in Descartes's dual substance theory, with its distinction between the objective and subjective realms. . . . In the splitting of reality into subject and object realms, what can be known "objectively" is only the objective realm. True knowledge is limited to the objects and the relationships between them that exist in the realm of time and space. Human consciousness, which is subjective, is not accessible to science, and thus not truly knowable. (p. 23)

Now, templates of truth and knowledge can be defined in a variety of ways—as the end product of rational processes, as the result of experiential sensing, as the result of empirical observation, and others. In all cases, however, the referent is the physical or empirical world: rational engagement with it, experience of it, and empirical observation of it. Realists, who work on the assumption that there is a "real" world "out there" may in individual cases also be foundationalists, taking the view that all of these ways of defining are rooted in phenomena existing outside the human mind.

Although we can think about them, experience them, or observe them, the elements of the physical world are nevertheless transcendent, referred to but beyond direct apprehension. Realism is an ontological question, whereas foundationalism is a criterial question. Some foundationalists argue that having real phenomena necessarily implies certain final, ultimate criteria for testing them as truthful (although we may have great difficulty in determining what those criteria are); nonfoundationalists tend to argue that there are no such ultimate criteria, only those that we can agree on at a certain time, within a certain community (Kuhn, 1967) and under certain conditions. Foundational criteria are discovered; nonfoundational criteria are negotiated. It is the case, however, that most realists are also foundationalists, and many nonfoundationalists or antifoundationalists are relativists.

An ontological formulation that connects realism and foundationalism within the same "collapse" of categories that characterizes the ontological-epistemological collapse is one that exhibits good fit with the other assumptions of constructivism. That state of affairs suits new-paradigm inquirers well. Critical theorists, constructivists, and participatory/cooperative inquirers take their primary field of interest to be precisely that subjective and intersubjective, critical social knowledge and the active construction and co-creation of such knowledge by human agents, which is produced by human consciousness. Furthermore, new-paradigm inquirers take to the social knowledge field with zest, informed by a variety of social, intellectual, and theoretical explorations. These theoretical excursions include

- Saussurian linguistic theory, which views all relationships between words and what those words signify as the function of an internal relationship within some linguistic system;

- Literary theory's deconstructive contributions, which seek to disconnect texts from any *essentialist* or transcendental meaning and resituate them within both author's and reader's historical and social contexts (Hutcheon, 1989; Leitch, 1996);

- Feminist (Addelson, 1993; Alpern, Antler, Perry, & Scobie, 1992; Babbitt, 1993; Harding, 1993), race and ethnic (Kondo, 1990, 1997; Trinh, 1991), and queer theorizing (Gamson, 2000), which seeks to uncover and explore varieties of oppression and historical colonizing between dominant and subaltern genders, identities, races, and social worlds;

- The postmodern historical moment (Michael, 1996), which problematizes truth as partial, identity as fluid, language as an unclear referent system, and method and criteria as potentially coercive (Ellis & Bochner, 1996); and

- Criticalist theories of social change (Carspecken, 1996; Schratz & Walker, 1995).

The realization of the richness of the mental, social, psychological, and linguistic worlds that individuals and social groups create and constantly re-create and co-create gives rise, in the minds of new-paradigm postmodern and poststructural inquirers, to endlessly fertile fields of inquiry rigidly walled off from conventional inquirers. Unfettered from the pursuit of transcendental scientific truth, inquirers are now free to resituate themselves within texts, to reconstruct their relationships with research participants in less constricted fashions, and to create representations (Tierney & Lincoln, 1997) that grapple openly with problems of inscription, reinscription, metanarratives, and other rhetorical devices that obscure the extent to which human action is locally and temporally shaped. The processes of uncovering forms of inscription and the rhetoric of metanarratives are *genealogical*—"*expos[ing]* the origins of the view that have become *sedimented and accepted as truths*" (Polkinghorne, 1989, p. 42; emphasis added)—or *archaeological* (Foucault, 1971; Scheurich, 1997).

New-paradigm inquirers engage the foundational controversy in quite different ways. Critical theorists, particularly critical theorists who are more positivist in orientation, who lean toward Marxian interpretations, tend toward foundational perspectives, with an important difference. Rather than locating foundational truth and knowledge in some external reality "out there," such critical theorists tend to locate the foundations of truth in specific historical, economic, racial, gendered, and social infrastructures of oppression, injustice, and marginalization. Knowers are not portrayed as *separate from* some objective reality, but they may be cast as unaware actors in such historical realities ("false consciousness") or as aware of historical forms of oppression but unable or unwilling, because of conflicts, to act on those historical forms to alter specific conditions in this historical moment ("divided consciousness"). Thus, the "foundation" for critical theorists is a duality: social critique tied in turn to raised consciousness of the possibility of positive and liberating social change. Social critique may exist apart from social change, but both are necessary for most critical perspectives.

Constructivists, on the other hand, tend toward the antifoundational (Lincoln, 1995, 1998b; Schwandt, 1996). *Antifoundational* is the term used to denote a refusal to adopt any permanent, unvarying (or "foundational") standards by which truth can be universally known. As one of us has argued, truth—and any agreement regarding what is valid knowledge—arises from the relationship between members of some stakeholding community (Lincoln, 1995). Agreements about truth may be the subject of community *negotiations* regarding what will be accepted as truth (although there are difficulties with that formulation as well; Guba & Lincoln, 1989). Or agreements may eventuate as the result of a *dialogue* that moves arguments about truth claims or validity past the warring camps of objectivity and relativity toward "a communal test of validity through the argumentation of the participants in a discourse" (Bernstein, 1983; Polkinghorne, 1989; Schwandt, 1996). This "communicative and pragmatic concept" of validity (Rorty, 1979) is never fixed or unvarying. Rather, it is created by means of a community narrative, itself subject to the temporal and historical conditions that gave rise to the community. Thomas A. Schwandt (1989) has also argued that these discourses, or community narratives, can and should be bounded by moral considerations, a premise grounded in the emancipatory narratives of the critical theorists, the philosophical pragmatism of Richard Rorty, the democratic focus of constructivist inquiry, and the "human flourishing" goals of participatory and cooperative inquiry.

The controversies around foundationalism (and, to a lesser extent, essentialism) are not likely to be resolved through dialogue between paradigm adherents. The likelier event is that the "postmodern turn" (Best & Kellner, 1997), with its emphasis on the social construction of social reality, fluid as opposed to fixed identities of the self, and the partiality of all truths, will simply overtake modernist assumptions of an objective reality, as indeed, to some extent, it has already done in the physical sciences. We might predict that, if not in our lifetimes, at some later time, the dualist idea of an objective reality suborned by limited human subjective realities will seem as quaint as flat-earth theories do to us today.

Validity: An Extended Agenda

Nowhere can the conversation about paradigm differences be more fertile than in the extended controversy about validity (Howe & Eisenhart, 1990; Kvale, 1989, 1994; Ryan, Greene, Lincoln, Mathison, & Mertens, 1998; Scheurich, 1994, 1996). Validity is not like objectivity. There are fairly strong theoretical, philosophical, and pragmatic rationales for examining the concept of objectivity and finding it wanting. Even within positivist frameworks, it is viewed as conceptually flawed. But validity is a more irritating construct, one neither easily dismissed nor readily configured by new-paradigm practitioners (Angen, 2000; Enerstvedt, 1989; Tschudi, 1989). Validity cannot be dismissed simply because it points to a question that has to be answered in one way or another: Are these findings sufficiently authentic (isomorphic to some reality, trustworthy, related to the way others construct their social worlds) that I may trust myself in acting on their implications? More to the point, would I feel sufficiently secure about these findings to construct social policy or legislation based on them? At the same time, radical reconfigurations of validity leave researchers with multiple, sometimes conflicting, mandates for what constitutes rigorous research. One of the issues around validity is the conflation between method and interpretation. The postmodern turn suggests that no method can deliver on ultimate truth and, in fact, "suspects all methods," the more so the larger their claims to delivering on truth (Richardson, 1994). Thus, although one might argue that some methods are more suited than others for conducting research on human construction of social realities (Lincoln & Guba, 1985), no one would argue that a single method—or collection of methods—is the royal road to ultimate knowledge. In new-paradigm inquiry, however, it is not merely method that promises to deliver on some set of local or context-grounded truths; it is also the processes of interpretation.

Thus, we have two arguments proceeding simultaneously. The first, borrowed from positivism, argues for a kind of rigor in the application of method, whereas the second argues for both a community consent and a form of rigor-defensible reasoning, plausible alongside some other reality that is known to author and reader in ascribing salience to one interpretation over another and in framing and bounding the interpretive study itself. Prior to our understanding that there were, indeed, two forms of rigor, we assembled a set of methodological criteria, largely borrowed from an earlier generation of thoughtful anthropological and sociological methodological theorists. Those methodological criteria are still useful for a variety of reasons, not the least of which is that they ensure that such issues as prolonged engagement and persistent observation are attended to with some seriousness.

It is the second kind of rigor, however, that has received the most attention in recent writings: Are we *interpretively* rigorous? Can our co-created constructions be trusted to provide some purchase on some important human phenomenon? Do our findings point to action that can be taken on the part of research participants to benefit themselves or their particular social contexts?

Human phenomena are themselves the subject of controversy. Classical social scientists would like to see *human phenomena* limited to those social experiences from which (scientific) generalizations may be drawn. New-paradigm inquirers, however, are increasingly concerned with the single experience, the individual crisis, the epiphany or moment of discovery, with that most powerful of all threats to conventional objectivity, feeling, and emotion and to action. Social scientists concerned with the expansion of what count as social data rely increasingly on the experiential, the embodied, the emotive qualities of human experience, which contribute the narrative quality to a life. Sociologists such as Carolyn Ellis and Arthur P. Bochner (2000) and Richardson (2000), qualitative researchers such as Ronald Pelias (1999, 2004), and psychologists such as Michelle Fine (see Fine, Weis, Weseen, & Wong, 2000) and Ellis (2009) concern themselves with various forms of autoethnography and personal experience and performance methods, both to overcome the abstractions of a social science far gone with quantitative descriptions of human life and to capture those elements that make life conflictual, moving, and problematic. For purposes of this discussion, we believe the adoption of the most radical definitions of social science is appropriate because the paradigmatic controversies are often taking place at the edges of those conversations. Those edges are where the border work is occurring, and accordingly, they are the places that show the most promise for projecting where qualitative methods will be in the near and far future.

WHITHER AND WHETHER CRITERIA

At those edges, several conversations are occurring around validity. The first and most radical is a conversation opened by Schwandt (1996), who suggests that we say "farewell to criteriology" or the "regulative norms for removing doubt and settling disputes about what is correct or incorrect, true or false" (p. 59); this has created a virtual cult around criteria. Schwandt does not, however, himself say farewell to criteria forever; rather, he resituates and resuscitates social inquiry, with other contemporary philosophical pragmatists, within a framework that transforms professional social inquiry into a form of practical philosophy, characterized by "aesthetic, prudential, and moral considerations as well as more conventionally scientific ones" (p. 68). When social inquiry becomes the practice of a form of practical philosophy—a deep questioning about how we shall get on in the world and what we conceive to be the potentials and limits of human knowledge and functioning—then we have some preliminary understanding of what entirely different criteria might be for judging social inquiry.

Schwandt (1996) proposes three such criteria. First, he argues, we should search for a social inquiry that "generate[s] knowledge that complements or supplements rather than displac[ing] lay probing of social problems," a form of knowledge for which we do not yet have the *content,* but from which we might seek to understand the aims of practice from a variety of perspectives, or with different lenses. Second, he proposes a "social inquiry as practical philosophy" that has as its aim "enhancing or cultivating *critical* intelligence in parties to the research encounter," critical intelligence being defined as "the capacity to engage in moral critique." And finally, he proposes a third way in which we might judge social inquiry as practical philosophy: We might make judgments about the social inquirer-as-practical-philosopher. He or she might be "evaluated on the success to which his or her reports of the inquiry enable the training or calibration of human judgment" (p. 69) or "the capacity for practical wisdom" (p. 70). Schwandt is not alone, however, in wishing to say "farewell to criteriology," at least as it has been previously conceived. Scheurich (1997) makes a similar plea, and in the same vein, Smith (1993) also argues that validity, if it is to survive at all, must be radically reformulated if it is ever to serve phenomenological research well (see also Smith & Deemer, 2000).

At issue here is not whether we shall have criteria, or whose criteria we as a scientific community might adopt, but rather what the nature of social inquiry ought to be, whether it ought to undergo a transformation, and what might be the basis for criteria within a projected transformation. Schwandt (1989; also personal communication, August 21, 1998) is quite clear that both the transformation and the criteria are rooted in dialogic efforts. These dialogic efforts are quite clearly themselves forms of "moral discourse:" Through the specific connections of the dialogic, the idea of practical wisdom, and moral discourses, much of Schwandt's work can be seen to be related to, and reflective of, critical theorist and participatory paradigms, as well as constructivism, although Schwandt specifically denies the relativity of truth. (For a more sophisticated explication and critique of forms of constructivism, hermeneutics, and interpretivism, see Schwandt, 2000. In that chapter, Schwandt spells out distinctions between realists and nonrealists and between foundationalists and nonfoundationalists far more clearly than it is possible for us to do in this chapter.) To return to the central question embedded in validity: How do we know when we have specific social inquiries that are faithful enough to some human construction that we may feel safe in acting on them, or, more important, that members of the community in which the research is conducted may act on them? To that question, there is no final answer. There are, however, several discussions of what we might use to make both professional and lay judgments regarding any piece of work. It is to those versions of validity that we now turn.

VALIDITY AS AUTHENTICITY

Perhaps the first nonfoundational criteria were those we developed in response to a challenge by John K. Smith (see Smith & Deemer, 2000). In those criteria, we attempted to locate criteria for judging the processes and *outcomes* of naturalistic or constructivist inquiries (rather than the application of methods; see Guba & Lincoln, 1989). We described five potential outcomes of a social constructionist inquiry (evaluation is one form of disciplined inquiry, alongside research and policy analyses; see Guba & Lincoln, 1981), each grounded in concerns specific to the paradigm we had tried to describe and construct and apart from any concerns carried over from the positivist legacy. The criteria were instead rooted in the axioms and assumptions of the constructivist paradigm, insofar as we could extrapolate and infer them. Those authenticity criteria—so called because we believed them to be hallmarks of authentic, trustworthy, rigorous, or "valid" constructivist or phenomenological inquiry—were fairness, ontological authenticity, educative authenticity, catalytic authenticity, and tactical authenticity (Guba & Lincoln, 1989, pp. 245–251). *Fairness* was thought to be a quality of balance; that is, all stakeholder views, perspectives, values, claims, concerns, and voices should be apparent in the text. Omission of stakeholder or participant voices reflects, we believe, a form of bias.

This bias, however, was and is not related directly to the concerns of objectivity that flow from positivist inquiry and that are reflective of inquirer blindness or subjectivity. Rather, this fairness was defined by deliberate attempts to prevent marginalization, to act affirmatively with respect to inclusion, and to act with energy to ensure that all voices in the inquiry effort had a chance to be represented in any texts and to have their stories treated fairly and with balance. *Ontological and educative authenticity* were designated as criteria for determining a raised level of awareness, in the first instance, by individual research participants and, in the second, by individuals about those who surround them or with whom they come into contact for some social or organizational purpose. Although we failed to see it at that particular historical moment (1989), there is no reason these criteria cannot be—at this point in time, with many miles under our theoretic and practice feet—reflective also of Schwandt's (1996) "critical intelligence," or capacity to engage in moral critique. In fact, the authenticity criteria we originally proposed had strong moral and ethical overtones, a point to which we later returned (see, e.g., Lincoln, 1995, 1998a, 1998b). It was a point to which our critics strongly objected before we were sufficiently self-aware to realize the implications of what we had proposed (see, e.g., Sechrest, 1993).

Catalytic and tactical authenticities refer to the ability of a given inquiry to prompt, first, action on the part of research participants and, second, the involvement of the researcher/evaluator in training participants in specific forms of social and political action if participants desire such training. It is here that constructivist inquiry practice begins to resemble forms of critical theorist action, action research, or participative or cooperative inquiry, each of which is predicated on creating the capacity in research participants for positive social change and forms of emancipatory community action. It is also at this specific point that practitioners of positivist and postpositivist social inquiry are the most critical because any action on the part of the inquirer is thought to destabilize objectivity and introduce subjectivity, resulting in bias. The problem of subjectivity and bias has a long theoretical history, and this chapter is simply too brief for us to enter into the various formulations that either take account of subjectivity or posit it as a positive learning experience, practical, embodied, gendered, and emotive. For purposes of this discussion, it is enough to say that we are persuaded that objectivity is a chimera: a mythological creature that never existed, save in the imaginations of those who believe that knowing can be separated from the knower.

VALIDITY AS RESISTANCE AND AS POSTSTRUCTURAL TRANSGRESSION

Richardson (1994, 1997) has proposed another form of validity, a deliberately "transgressive" form, the *crystalline*. In writing experimental (i.e., nonauthoritative, nonpositivist) texts, particularly poems and plays, Richardson (1997) has sought to "problematize reliability, validity, and truth" (p. 165) in an effort to create new relationships: to her research participants, to her work, to other women, to herself (see also Lather, who seeks the same ends, 2007). Richardson says that transgressive forms permit a social scientist to "conjure a different kind of social science . . . [which] means changing one's relationship to one's work, *how* one knows and tells about the sociological" (p. 166). To see "how transgression looks and how it feels," it is necessary to "find and deploy methods that allow us to uncover the hidden assumptions and life-denying repressions of sociology; resee/refeel sociology. Reseeing and retelling are inseparable" (p. 167). The way to achieve such validity is by examining the properties of a crystal in a metaphoric sense. Here we present an extended quotation to give some flavor of how such validity might be described and deployed:

I propose that the central imaginary for "validity" for postmodernist texts is not the triangle—a rigid, fixed, two-dimensional object. Rather the central imaginary is the crystal, which combines symmetry and substance with an infinite variety of shapes, substances, transmutations, multidimensionalities, and angles of approach. Crystals grow, change, alter, but are not amorphous. Crystals are prisms that reflect externalities *and* refract within themselves, creating different colors, patterns, arrays, casting off in different directions. What we *see* depends upon our angle of repose. Not triangulation, crystallization. In postmodernist mixed-genre texts, we have moved from plane geometry to light theory, where light can be *both* waves *and* particles. Crystallization, without losing structure, deconstructs the traditional idea of "validity" (we feel how there is no single truth, we see how texts validate themselves); and crystallization provides us with a deepened, complex, thoroughly partial understanding of the topic. Paradoxically, we know more and doubt what we know. (Richardson, 1997, p. 92)

The metaphoric "solid object" (crystal/text), which can be turned many ways, which reflects and refracts light (light/multiple layers of meaning), through which we can see both "wave" (light wave/human currents) and "particle" (light as "chunks" of energy/elements of truth, feeling, connection, processes of the research that "flow" together) is an attractive metaphor for validity. The properties of the crystal-as-metaphor help writers and readers alike see the interweaving of processes in the research: discovery, seeing, telling, storying, representation.

OTHER "TRANSGRESSIVE" VALIDITIES

Richardson is not alone in calling for forms of validity that are "transgressive" and disruptive of the status quo. Patti Lather (1993) seeks "an incitement to discourse," the purpose of which is "to rupture validity as a regime of truth, to displace its historical inscription . . . via a dispersion, circulation and proliferation of counterpractices of authority that take the crisis of representation into account" (p. 674). In addition to catalytic validity (Lather, 1986), Lather (1993) poses *validity as simulacra/ironic validity; Lyotardian paralogy/neopragmatic validity,* a form of validity that "foster[s] heterogeneity, refusing disclosure" (p. 679); *Derridean rigor/rhizomatic validity,* a form of behaving "via relay, circuit, multiple openings" (p. 680); and *voluptuous/situated validity,* which "embodies a situated, partial tentativeness" and "brings ethics and epistemology together . . . via practices of engagement and self reflexivity" (p. 686). Together, these form a way of interrupting, disrupting, and transforming "pure" presence into a disturbing, fluid, partial, and problematic presence—a poststructural and decidedly postmodern form of discourse theory, hence textual revelation (see also Lather, 2007, for further reflections and disquisitions on validity).

VALIDITY AS AN ETHICAL RELATIONSHIP

As Lather (1993) points out, poststructural forms for validities "bring ethics and epistemology together" (p. 686); indeed, as Parker Palmer (1987) also notes, "every way of knowing contains its own moral trajectory" (p. 24). Alan Peshkin reflects on Nel Noddings's (1984) observation that "the search for justification often carries us farther and farther from the heart of morality" (p. 105; quoted in Peshkin, 1993, p. 24). The *way* in which we know is most assuredly tied up with both *what* we know and our *relationships with our research participants.*

Accordingly, one of us worked on trying to understand the ways in which the ethical intersects both the interpersonal and the epistemological (as a form of authentic or valid knowing; Lincoln, 1995). The result was the first set of understandings about emerging criteria for quality that were also rooted in the epistemology/ ethics nexus. Seven new standards were derived from that search: positionality, or standpoint, judgments; specific discourse communities and research sites as arbiters of quality; voice, or the extent to which a text has the quality of polyvocality; critical subjectivity (or what might be termed intense self-reflexivity; see, for instance, Heron & Reason, 1997); reciprocity, or the extent to which the research relationship becomes reciprocal rather than hierarchical; sacredness, or the profound regard for how science can (and does) contribute to human flourishing; and sharing of the perquisites of privilege that accrue to our positions as academics with university positions. Each of these standards was extracted from a body of research, often from disciplines as disparate as management, philosophy, and women's studies (Lincoln, 1995).

Voice, Reflexivity, and Postmodern Textual Representation

Texts have to do a lot more work these days than in the past. Even as they are charged by poststructuralists and postmodernists to reflect on their representational practices, those practices become more problematic. Three of the most engaging, but painful issues are voice, the status of reflexivity, and postmodern/ poststructural textual representation, especially as those problematics are displayed in the shift toward narrative and literary forms that directly and openly deal with human emotion.

VOICE

Voice is a multilayered problem, simply because it has come to mean many things to different researchers. In former eras, the only appropriate voice was the "voice from nowhere"—the "pure presence" of representation, as Lather (2007) terms it. As researchers became more conscious of the abstracted realities their texts created (Lather 2007), they became simultaneously more conscious of having readers "hear" their informants—permitting readers to hear the exact words (and, occasionally, the paralinguistic cues, the lapses, pauses, stops, starts, and reformulations) of the informants. Today, especially in more participatory forms of research, voice can mean not only having a real researcher—and a researcher's voice—in the text, but also letting research participants speak for themselves, either in text form or through plays, forums, "town meetings," or other oral and performance-oriented media or communication forms designed by research participants themselves (Bernal, 1998, 2002). Performance texts, in particular, give an emotional immediacy to the voices of researchers and research participants far beyond their own sites and locales (see McCall, 2000). Rosanna Hertz (1997) describes voice as

> a struggle to figure out how to present the author's self while simultaneously writing the respondents' accounts and representing their selves. Voice has multiple dimensions: First, there is the voice of the author. Second, there is the presentation of the voices of one's respondents within the text. A third dimension appears when the self is the subject of the inquiry. . . . Voice is how authors express themselves within an ethnography. (pp. xi–xii)

But knowing how to express ourselves goes far beyond the commonsense understanding of "expressing ourselves." Generations of ethnographers trained in the "cooled-out, stripped-down rhetoric" of positivist inquiry (Firestone, 1987) find it difficult, if not nearly impossible, to "locate" themselves deliberately and squarely within their texts (even though, as Geertz, 1988, has demonstrated finally and without doubt, the authorial voice is rarely genuinely absent, or even hidden).

Specific textual experimentation can help; that is, composing ethnographic work in various literary forms—Richardson's poetry and plays are good examples, or Lather and Chris Smithies's (1997) *Troubling the Angels*—can help a researcher to overcome the tendency to write in the distanced and abstracted voice of the disembodied "I." But such writing exercises are hard work. This is also work that is embedded in the practices of reflexivity and narrativity, without which achieving a voice of (partial) truth is impossible.

REFLEXIVITY

Reflexivity is the process of reflecting critically on the self as researcher, the "human as instrument" (Guba & Lincoln, 1981). It is, we would assert, the critical subjectivity discussed early on in Peter Reason and John Rowan's edited volume, *Human Inquiry* (1981). It is a conscious experiencing of the self as both inquirer and respondent, as teacher and learner, as the one coming to know the self within the processes of research itself. Reflexivity forces us to come to terms not only with our choice of research problem and with those with whom we engage in the research process, but with ourselves and with the multiple identities that represent the fluid self in the research setting (Alcoff & Potter, 1993). Shulamit Reinharz (1997), for example, argues that we not only "*bring* the self to the field . . . [we also] *create* the self in the field" (p. 3). She suggests that although we all have many selves we bring with us, those selves fall into three categories: research-based selves, brought selves (the selves that historically, socially, and personally create our standpoints), and situationally created selves (p. 5). Each of those selves comes into play in the research setting and consequently has a distinctive voice.

Reflexivity—as well as the poststructural and postmodern sensibilities concerning quality in qualitative research—demands that we interrogate each of our selves regarding the ways in which research efforts are shaped and staged around the binaries, contradictions, and paradoxes that form our own lives. We must question ourselves, too, regarding how those binaries and paradoxes shape not only the identities called forth in the field and later in the discovery processes of writing, but also our interactions with respondents, in who we become to them in the process of *becoming* to ourselves (Mayan, 2009). Someone once characterized qualitative research as the twin processes of "writing up" (fieldnotes) and "writing down" (the narrative). But D. Jean Clandinin and F. Michael Connelly (1994) have made clear that this bitextual reading of the processes of qualitative research is far too simplistic. In fact, many texts are created in the process of engaging in fieldwork.

As Richardson (1994, 1997, 2000) makes clear, writing is not merely the transcribing of some reality. Rather, writing—of all the texts, notes, presentations, and possibilities—is also a process of discovery: discovery of the subject (and sometimes of the problem itself) and discovery of the self.[3]

There is good news and bad news with the most contemporary of formulations. The good news is that the multiple selves—ourselves and our respondents—of postmodern inquiries may give rise to more dynamic, problematic, open-ended, and complex forms of writing and representation. The bad news is that the multiple selves we create and encounter give rise to more dynamic, problematic, open-ended, and complex forms of writing and representation. Among the various proposals for textual presentations, it is occasionally difficult to know to which proposals we should be attending; while it is often a matter of specific model (e.g., critical feminist studies, queer theories, hybrid theorists, postcolonial theorists, and the like) to which we are theoretically, philosophically, and morally inclined, it is nevertheless a buffet of wildly rich fare, and some choices must be made. Often such choices are made on the basis of both the needs of our research participants and coresearchers and the needs of our intended audiences.

POSTMODERN TEXTUAL REPRESENTATIONS

There are two dangers inherent in the conventional texts of scientific method: They may lead us to believe the world is rather simpler than it is, and they may reinscribe enduring forms of historical oppression. Put another way, we are confronted with a crisis of authority (which tells us the world is "this way" when perhaps it is some other way, or many other ways) and a crisis of representation (which serves to silence those whose lives we appropriate for our social sciences, and which may also serve subtly to re-create *this* world, rather than some other, perhaps more complex, but just one; Eisner, 1997). Catherine Stimpson (1988) has observed:

> Like every great word, "representation/s" is a stew. A scrambled menu, it serves up several meanings at once. For a representation can be an image visual, verbal, or aural. . . . A representation can also be a narrative, a sequence of images and ideas. . . . Or, a representation can be the product of ideology, that vast scheme for showing forth the world and justifying its dealings. (p. 223)

One way to confront the dangerous illusions (and their underlying ideologies) that texts may foster is through the creation of new texts that break boundaries; that move from the center to the margins to comment on and decenter the center; that forgo closed, bounded worlds for those more open-ended and less conveniently encompassed; that transgress the boundaries of conventional social science; and that seek to create a social science about human life rather than *on* subjects.

Experiments with how to do this have produced "messy texts" (Marcus & Fischer, 1986). Messy texts are not typographic nightmares (although they may be typographically nonlinear); rather, they are texts that seek to break the binary between science and literature; to portray the contradiction and truth of human experience; to break the rules in the service of showing, even partially (Flax, 1990), how real human beings cope with both the eternal verities of human existence and the daily irritations and tragedies of living that existence. Postmodern representations search out and experiment with narratives that expand the range of understanding, voice, and storied variations in human experience.

As much as they are social scientists, inquirers also become storytellers, poets, and playwrights, experimenting with personal narratives, first-person accounts, reflexive interrogations, and deconstruction of the forms of tyranny embedded in representational practices (see Richardson, 2000; Tierney & Lincoln, 1997).

Representation may be arguably the most open-ended of the controversies surrounding phenomenological research today because the ideas of what constitutes legitimate inquiry are expanding and, at the same time, the forms of narrative, dramatic, and rhetorical structure are far from being either explored or exploited fully and because we know that there is extensive slippage between life as lived and experienced and our ability to cast that life into words that exhibit perfect one-to-one correspondence with that experience. Words, and therefore any and all representations, fail us. Because, too, each inquiry, each inquirer, brings a unique perspective to our understanding, the possibilities for variation and exploration are limited only by the number of those engaged in inquiry and the realms of social and intrapersonal life that become interesting to researchers. The only thing that can be said for certain about postmodern representational practices is that they will proliferate as forms and they will seek and demand much of audiences, many of whom may be outside the scholarly and academic world. In fact, some forms of inquiry may never show up in the academic world because their purpose will be use in the immediate context, for the consumption, reflection, and use of local or indigenous audiences. Those that are produced for scholarly audiences will, however, continue to be untidy, experimental, and driven by the need to communicate social worlds that have remained private and "nonscientific" until now.

A Glimpse of the Future

The issues raised in this chapter are by no means the only ones under discussion for the near and far future. But they are some of the critical ones, and discussion, dialogue, and even controversies are bound to continue as practitioners of the various new and emergent paradigms continue either to look for common ground or to find ways in which to distinguish their forms of inquiry from others.

Some time ago, we expressed our hope that practitioners of both positivist and new-paradigm forms of inquiry might find some way of resolving their differences, such that all social scientists could work within a common discourse—and perhaps even several traditions—once again. In retrospect, such a resolution appears highly unlikely and would probably even be less than useful. This is not, however, because neither positivists nor phenomenologists will budge an inch (although that, too, is unlikely), or because the reinscription of stern positivist "science" abounds, with even more rancorous pronouncements about qualitative research than we have heard in previous decades. Rather, it is because, in the postmodern (and post-postmodern) moment, and in the wake of poststructuralism, the assumption that there is no single "truth"—that all truths are but partial truths; that the slippage between signifier and signified in linguistic and textual terms creates representations that are only and always shadows of the actual people, events, and places; that identities are fluid rather than fixed—leads us ineluctably toward the insight that there will be no single "conventional" paradigm to which all social scientists might ascribe in some common terms and with mutual understanding. Rather, we stand at the threshold of a history marked by multivocality, contested meanings, paradigmatic controversies, and new textual forms. At some distance down this conjectural path, when its history is written, we will find that this has been the era of emancipation: emancipation from what Hannah Arendt calls "the coerciveness of Truth," emancipation from hearing only the voices of Western Europe, emancipation from generations of silence, and emancipation from seeing the world in one color.

We may also be entering an age of greater spirituality within research efforts. The emphasis on inquiry that reflects ecological values, on inquiry that respects communal forms of living that are not Western, on inquiry involving intense reflexivity regarding how our inquiries are shaped by our own historical and gendered locations, and on inquiry into "human flourishing," as Heron and Reason (1997) call it, may yet reintegrate the sacred with the secular in ways that promote freedom and self-determination. Egon Brunswik, the organizational theorist, wrote of "tied" and "untied" variables—variables that are linked, or clearly not linked, with other variables—when studying human forms of organization. We may be in a period of exploring the ways in which our inquiries are both tied and untied, as a means of finding where our interests cross and where we can both be and promote others' being, as whole human beings.

Notes

1. There are several versions of critical theory, just as there are several varieties of postmodernism, including classical critical theory, which is most closely related to neo-Marxist theory; postpositivist formulations, which divorce themselves from Marxist theory but are positivist in their insistence on conventional rigor criteria; and

postmodernist, poststructuralist, or constructivist-oriented varieties. See, for instance, Fay (1987), Carr and Kemmis (1986), and Lather (1991). See also Kemmis and McTaggart (2000) and Kincheloe and McLaren (2000).

2. For a clearer understanding of how methods came to stand in for paradigms, or how our initial (and, we thought, quite clear) positions came to be misconstrued, see Lancy (1993) or, even more currently, Weiss (1998, esp. p. 268).

3. For example, compare this chapter with, say, the work of Richardson (2000) and Ellis and Bochner (2000), where the authorial voices are clear, personal, vocal, and interior, interacting subjectivities. Although some colleagues have surprised us by correctly identifying which chapters each of us has written in given books, nevertheless, the style of this chapter more closely approximates the more distanced forms of "realist" writing rather than the intimate, personal "feeling tone" (to borrow a phrase from Studs Terkel) of other chapters. Voices also arise as a function of the material being covered. The material we chose as most important for this chapter seemed to demand a less personal tone, probably because there appears to be much more "contention" than calm dialogue concerning these issues. The "cool" tone likely stems from our psychological response to trying to create a quieter space for discussion around controversial issues. What can we say?

References

Addelson, K. P. (1993). Knowers/doers and their moral problems. In L. Alcoff & E. Potter (Eds.), *Feminist epistemologies* (pp. 265–294). New York: Routledge.

Alcoff, L., &Potter, E. (Eds.). (1993). *Feminist epistemologies.* New York: Routledge.

Alpern, S., Antler, J., Perry, E. I., & Scobie, I. W. (Eds.). (1992). *The challenge of feminist biography: Writing the lives of modern American women.* Urbana: University of Illinois Press.

Angen, M. J. (2000). Evaluating interpretive inquiry: Reviewing the validity debate and opening the dialogue. *Qualitative Health Research, 10*(3), 378–395.

Babbitt, S. (1993). Feminism and objective interests: The role of transformation experiences in rational deliberation. In L. Alcoff & E. Potter (Eds.), *Feminist epistemologies* (pp. 245–264). New York: Routledge.

Bernal, D. D. (1998). Using a Chicana feminist epistemology in educational research. *Harvard Educational Review, 68*(4), 1–19.

Bernal, D. D. (2002). Critical race theory, Latino critical theory, and critical race-gendered epistemologies; Recognizing students of color as holders and creators of knowledge. *Qualitative Inquiry, 9*(1), 105–126.

Bernstein, R. J. (1983). *Beyond objectivism and relativism: Science, hermeneutics, and praxis.* Oxford, UK: Blackwell.

Best, S., & Kellner, D. (1997). *The postmodern turn.* New York: Guilford.

Bloland, H. (1989). Higher education and high anxiety: Objectivism, relativism, and irony. *Journal of Higher Education, 60,* 519–543.

Bloland, H. (1995). Postmodernism and higher education. *Journal of Higher Education, 66,* 521–559.

Bradley, J., & Schaefer, K. (1998). *The uses and misuses of data and models.* Thousand Oaks, CA: Sage.

Carr, W. L., & Kemmis, S. (1986). *Becoming critical: Education, knowledge, and action research.* London: Falmer.

Carspecken, P. F. (1996). *Critical ethnography in educational research: A theoretical and practical guide.* New York: Routledge.

Christians, C. G. (2000). Ethics and politics in qualitative research. In N. K. Denzin & Y. S. Lincoln (Eds.), *Handbook of qualitative research* (2nd ed., pp. 133–155). Thousand Oaks, CA: Sage.

Clandinin, D. J., & Connelly, F. M. (1994). Personal experience methods. In N. K. Denzin & Y. S. Lincoln (Eds.), *Handbook of qualitative research* (pp. 413–427). Thousand Oaks, CA: Sage.

Creswell, J. W. (2007). *Qualitative inquiry and research design: Choosing among five approaches.* Thousand Oaks, CA: Sage.

Denzin, N. K., & Lincoln, Y. S. (Eds.). (1994). *Handbook of qualitative research.* Thousand Oaks, CA: Sage.

Eisner, E. W. (1997). The promise and perils of alternative forms of data representation. *Educational Researcher, 26*(6), 4–10.

Ellis, C. (2009). *Autoethnographic reflections on life and work.* Walnut Creek, CA: Left Coast Press.

Ellis, C., & Bochner, A. P. (Eds.). (1996). *Composing ethnography: Alternative forms of qualitative writing.* Walnut Creek, CA: AltaMira.

Ellis, C., & Bochner, A. P. (2000). Autoethnography, personal narrative, reflexivity: Researcher as subject. In N. K. Denzin & Y. S. Lincoln (Eds.), *Handbook of qualitative research* (2nd ed., pp. 733–768). Thousand Oaks, CA: Sage.

Enerstvedt, R. (1989). The problem of validity in social science. In S. Kvale (Ed.), *Issues of validity in qualitative research* (pp. 135–173). Lund, Sweden: Studentlitteratur.

Fay, B. (1987). *Critical social science.* Ithaca, NY: Cornell University Press.

Fine, M., Weis, 1., Weseen, S., & Wong, 1. (2000). For whom? Qualitative research, representations, and social responsibilities. In N. K. Denzin & Y. S. Lincoln (Eds.), *Handbook of qualitative research* (2nd ed., pp. 107–131). Thousand Oaks, CA: Sage.

Firestone, W. (1987). Meaning in method: The rhetoric of quantitative and qualitative research. *Educational Researcher, 16*(7), 16–21.

Flax, J. (1990). *Thinking fragments.* Berkeley: University of California Press.

Foucault, M. (1971). *The order of things: An archaeology of the human sciences.* New York: Pantheon.

Gamson, J. (2000). Sexualities, queer theory, and qualitative research. In N. K. Denzin & Y. S. Lincoln (Eds.), *Handbook of qualitative research* (2nd ed., pp. 347–365). Thousand Oaks, CA: Sage.

Gandhi, L. (1998). *Postcolonial theory: A critical introduction.* St. Leonards, N.S.W.: Allen & Unwin.

Geertz, C. (1973). Thick description: Toward an interpretive theory of culture. In C. Geertz, *The interpretation of cultures* (pp. 2–30). New York: Basic Books.

Geertz, C. (1988). *Works and lives: The anthropologist as author.* Cambridge, UK: Polity.

Geertz, C. (1993). *Local knowledge: Further essays in interpretive anthropology.* London: Fontana.

Giroux, H. A. (1982). *Theory and resistance in education: A pedagogy for the opposition.* Boston: Bergin & Garvey.

Greenwood, D. J., &Levin, M. (2000). Reconstructing the relationships between universities and society through action research. In N. K. Denzin & Y. S. Lincoln (Eds.), *Handbook of qualitative research* (2nd ed., pp. 85–106). Thousand Oaks, CA: Sage.

Guba, E. G., (1990). *The paradigm dialog.* Newbury Park, CA: Sage.

Guba, E. G., (1996). What happened to me on the road to Damascus. In L. Heshusius & K. Ballard (Eds.), *From positivism to interpretivism and beyond: Tales of transformation in educational and social research* (pp. 43–49). New York: Teachers College Press.

Guba, E. G., & Lincoln, Y. S. (1981). *Effective evaluation: Improving the usefulness of evaluation results through responsive and naturalistic approaches.* San Francisco: Jossey-Bass.

Guba, E. G., & Lincoln, Y. S. (1982). Epistemological and methodological bases for naturalistic inquiry. *Educational Communications and Technology Journal, 31,* 233–252.

Guba, E. G., & Lincoln, Y. S. (1985). *Naturalistic inquiry.* Newbury Park, CA: Sage.

Guba, E. G., & Lincoln, Y. S. (1989). *Fourth generation evaluation.* Newbury Park, CA: Sage.

Guba, E. G., & Lincoln, Y. S. (1994). Competing paradigms in qualitative research. In N. K. Denzin & Y. S. Lincoln (Eds.), *Handbook of qualitative research* (pp. 105–117). Thousand Oaks, CA: Sage.

Guba, E. G., & Lincoln, Y. S. (2005). Paradigmatic controversies, contradictions, and emerging confluences. In N. K. Denzin & Y. S. Lincoln (Eds.), *The SAGE handbook of qualitative research* (3rd ed., pp. 191–215). Thousand Oaks, CA: Sage.

Harding, S. (1993). Rethinking standpoint epistemology: What is "strong objectivity"? In L. Alcoff & E. Potter (Eds.), *Feminist epistemologies* (pp. 49–82). New York: Routledge.

Heron, J. (1996). *Cooperative inquiry: Research into the human condition.* London: Sage.

Heron, J., & Reason, P. (1997). A participatory inquiry paradigm. *Qualitative Inquiry, 3,* 274–294.

Hertz, R. (1997). Introduction: Reflexivity and voice. In R. Hertz (Ed.), *Reflexivity and voice.* Thousand Oaks, CA: Sage.

Heshusius, L. (1994). Freeing ourselves from objectivity: Managing subjectivity or turning toward a participatory mode of consciousness? *Educational Researcher, 23*(3), 15–22.

Howe, K., & Eisenhart, M. (1990). Standards for qualitative (and quantitative) research: A prolegomenon. *Educational Researcher, 19*(4), 2–9.

Hutcheon, L. (1989). *The politics of postmodernism.* New York: Routledge.

Josselson, R. (1995). Imagining the real. *Interpreting experience. The narrative study of lives* (Vol. 3.). Thousand Oaks, CA: Sage.

Kemmis, S., & McTaggart, R. (2000). Participatory action research. In N. K. Denzin & Y. S. Lincoln (Eds.), *Handbook of qualitative research* (2nd ed., pp. 567–605). Thousand Oaks, CA: Sage.

Kilgore, D. W. (2001). Critical and postmodern perspectives in learning. In S. Merriam (Ed.), *The new update of education theory: New directions in adult and continuing education.* San Francisco: Jossey-Bass.

Kincheloe, J. L. (1991). *Teachers as researchers: Qualitative inquiry as a path to empowerment.* London: Falmer.

Kincheloe, J. L., & McLaren, P. (2000). Rethinking critical theory and qualitative research. In N. K. Denzin & Y. S. Lincoln (Eds.), *Handbook of qualitative research* (2nd ed., pp. 279–313). Thousand Oaks, CA: Sage.

Kondo, D. K. (1990). *Crafting selves: Power, gender, and discourses of identity* in *a Japanese workplace.* Chicago: University of Chicago Press.

Kondo, D. K. (1997). *About face: Performing race in fashion and theater.* New York: Routledge.

Kuhn, T. (1967). *The structure of scientific revolutions* (2nd ed.). Chicago: University of Chicago Press.

Kvale, S. (Ed.). (1989). *Issues of validity in qualitative research.* Lund, Sweden: Studentlitteratur.

Kvale, S. (1994, April). *Validation as communication and action.* Paper presented at the annual meeting of the American Educational Research Association, New Orleans.

Lancy, D. F. (1993). *Qualitative research in education: An introduction to the major traditions.* New York: Longman.

Lather, P. (1986). Issues of validity in openly ideological research: Between a rock and a soft place. *Interchange, 17*(4), 63–84.

Lather, P. (1991). *Getting smart: Feminist research and pedagogy within the postmodern.* New York: Routledge.

Lather, P. (1993). Fertile obsession: Validity after poststructuralism. *Sociological Quarterly, 34,* 673–693.

Lather, P. (2007). *Getting lost: Feminist efforts toward a double(d) science.* Albany: State University of New York Press.

Lather, P., & Smithies, C. (1997). *Troubling the angels: Women living with HIV/AIDS.* Boulder, CO: Westview/HarperCollins.

Latsis, J., Lawson, C., & Martins, N. (2007). Introduction: Ontology, philosophy, and the social sciences. In C. Lawson, J. Latsis, & N. Martins (Eds.), *Contributions to social ontology.* New York: Routledge.

Leitch, V. B. (1996). *Postmodern: Local effects, global flows.* Albany: State University of New York Press.

Lincoln, Y. S. (1995). Emerging criteria for quality in qualitative and interpretive research. *Qualitative Inquiry, 1,* 275–289.

Lincoln, Y. S. (1997). What constitutes quality in interpretive research? In C. K. Kinzer, K. A. Hinchman, & D. J. Leu (Eds.), *Inquiries in literacy: Theory and practice* (pp. 54–68). Chicago: National Reading Conference.

Lincoln, Y. S. (1998a). The ethics of teaching qualitative research. *Qualitative Inquiry, 4,* 305–317.

Lincoln, Y. S. (1998b). From understanding to action: New imperatives, new criteria, new methods for interpretive researchers. *Theory and Research in Social Education, 26*(1), 12–29.

Lincoln, Y. S., & Denzin, N. K. (1994). The fifth moment. In N. K. Denzin & Y. S. Lincoln (Eds.), *Handbook of qualitative research* (pp. 575–586). Thousand Oaks, CA: Sage.

Lincoln, Y. S., & Guba, E. G. (1985). *Naturalistic inquiry.* Beverly Hills, CA: Sage.

Lucas, J. (1974, May). *The case survey and alternative methods for research aggregation.* Paper presented at the Conference on Design and Measurement Standards in Political Science, Delavan, WI.

Lucas, J. (1976). *The case survey method: Aggregating case experience* (R-1515-RC). Santa Monica, CA: The Rand Corporation.

Lynham, S. A., & Webb-Johnson, G. W. (2008). Models of Epistemology and Inquiry Class Notes. Texas A&M University.

Marcus, G. E., & Fischer, M. M. J. (1986). *Anthropology as cultural critique: An experimental moment in the human sciences.* Chicago: University of Chicago Press.

Mayan, M. J. (2009). *Essentials of qualitative inquiry.* Walnut Creek, CA: Left Coast Press.

McCall, M. M. (2000). Performance ethnography: A brief history and some advice. In N. K. Denzin & Y. S. Lincoln (Eds.), *Handbook of qualitative research* (2nd ed., pp. 421–433). Thousand Oaks, CA: Sage.

Merriam, S. B. (1991). How research produces knowledge. In J. M. Peters & P. Jarvis (Eds.), *Adult education.* San Francisco: Jossey-Bass.

Merriam, S. B., Caffarella, R. S., & Baumgartner, L. M. (2007). *Learning in adulthood: A comprehensive guide.* San Francisco: Jossey-Bass.

Mertens, D. (1998). *Research methods* in *education and psychology: Integrating diversity with quantitative and qualitative methods.* Thousand Oaks, CA: Sage.

Michael, M. C. (1996). *Feminism and the postmodern impulse: Post-World War II fiction.* Albany: State University of New York Press.

Noddings, N. (1984). *Caring: A feminine approach to ethics and moral education.* Berkeley: University of California Press.

Olesen, Y. L. (2000). Feminisms and qualitative research at and into the millennium. In N. K. Denzin & Y. S. Lincoln (Eds.), *Handbook of qualitative research* (2nd ed., pp. 215–255). Thousand Oaks, CA: Sage.

Pallas, A. M. (2001). Preparing education doctoral students for epistemological diversity. *Educational Researcher, 30*(5), 6–11.

Palmer, P. J. (1987, September-October). Community, conflict, and ways of knowing. *Change, 19,* 20–25.

Pelias, R. J. (1999). *Writing performance: Poeticizing the researcher's body.* Carbondale: Southern Illinois University Press.

Pelias, R. J. (2004). *A methodology of the heart.* Walnut Creek, CA: AltaMira Press.

Peshkin, A. (1993). The goodness of qualitative research. *Educational Researcher, 22*(2), 24–30.

Phillips, D. C. (2006). A guide for the perplexed: Scientific educational research, methodolatry, and the gold versus the platinum standards. *Educational Research Review, 1*(1), 15–26.

Polkinghorne, D. E. (1989). Changing conversations about human science. In S. Kvale (Ed.), *Issues of validity in qualitative research* (pp. 13–46). Lund, Sweden: Studentlitteratur.

Preissle, J. (2006). Envisioning qualitative inquiry: A view across four decades. *International Journal of Qualitative Studies in Education 19*(6), 685–695.

Reason, P. (1993). Sacred experience and sacred science. *Journal of Management Inquiry, 2,* 10–27.

Reason, P., & Rowan, J. (Eds.). (1981). *Human inquiry.* London: John Wiley.

Reinharz, S. (1997). Who am I? The need for a variety of selves in the field. In R. Hertz (Ed.), *Reflexivity and voice* (pp. 3–20). Thousand Oaks, CA: Sage.

Richardson, L. (1994). Writing: A method of inquiry. In N. K. Denzin & Y. S. Lincoln (Eds.), *Handbook of qualitative research* (pp. 516–529). Thousand Oaks, CA: Sage.

Richardson, L. (1997). *Fields of play: Constructing an academic life.* New Brunswick, NJ: Rutgers University Press.

Richardson, L. (2000). Writing: A method of inquiry. In N. K. Denzin & Y. S. Lincoln (Eds.), *Handbook of qualitative research* (2nd ed., pp. 923–948). Thousand Oaks, CA: Sage.

Rorty, R. (1979). *Philosophy and the mirror of nature.* Princeton, NJ: Princeton University Press.

Ryan, K. E., Greene, J. C., Lincoln, Y. S., Mathison, S., & Mertens, D. (1998). Advantages and challenges of using inclusive evaluation approaches in evaluation practice. *American Journal of Evaluation, 19,* 101–122.

Salner, M. (1989). Validity in human science research. In S. Kvale (Ed.), *Issues of validity in qualitative research* (pp. 47–72). Lund, Sweden: Studentlitteratur.

Scheurich, J. J. (1994). Policy archaeology. *Journal of Educational Policy, 9,* 297–316.

Scheurich, J. J. (1996). Validity. *International Journal of Qualitative Studies in Education, 9,* 49–60.

Scheurich, J. J. (1997). *Research method in the postmodern.* London: Falmer.

Schratz, M., & Walker, R. (1995). *Research as social change: New opportunities for qualitative research.* New York: Routledge.

Schwandt, T. A. (1989). Recapturing moral discourse in evaluation. *Educational Researcher, 18*(8), 11–16, 34.

Schwandt, T. A. (1996). Farewell to criteriology. *Qualitative Inquiry, 2,* 58–72.

Schwandt, T. A. (2000). Three epistemological stances for qualitative inquiry: Interpretivism, hermeneutics, and social constructionism. In N. K. Denzin & Y. S. Lincoln (Eds.), *Handbook of qualitative research* (2nd ed., pp. 189–213). Thousand Oaks, CA: Sage.

Schwandt, T. A. (2007). *The SAGE dictionary of qualitative inquiry* (3rd ed.). Thousand Oaks, CA: Sage.

Sechrest, 1. (1993). *Program evaluation: A pluralistic enterprise.* San Francisco: Jossey-Bass.

Skrtic, T. M. (1990). Social accommodation: Toward a dialogical discourse in educational inquiry. In E. Guba (Ed.), *The paradigm dialog.* Newbury Park, CA: Sage.

Smith, J. K. (1993). *After the demise of empiricism: The problem of judging social and educational inquiry.* Norwood, NJ: Ablex.

Smith, J. K., & Deemer, D. K. (2000). The problem of criteria in the age of relativism. In N. K. Denzin & Y. S. Lincoln (Eds.), *Handbook of qualitative research* (2nd ed., pp. 877–896). Thousand Oaks, CA: Sage.

Stimpson, C. R. (1988). Nancy Reagan wears a hat: Feminism and its cultural consensus. *Critical Inquiry, 14,* 223–243.

Tierney, W. G. (2000). Undaunted courage: Life history and the postmodern challenge. In N. K. Denzin & Y. S. Lincoln (Eds.), *Handbook of qualitative research* (2nd ed., pp. 537–553). Thousand Oaks, CA: Sage.

Tierney, W. G., & Lincoln, Y. S. (Eds.). (1997). *Representation and the text: Re-framing the narrative voice.* Albany: State University of New York Press.

Trinh, T. M. (1991). *When the moon waxes red: Representation, gender, and cultural politics.* New York: Routledge.

Tschudi, F. (1989). Do qualitative and quantitative methods require different approaches to validity? In S. Kvale (Ed.), *Issues of validity in qualitative research* (pp. 109–134). Lund, Sweden: Studentlitteratur.

Weiss, C. H. (1998). *Evaluation* (2nd ed.). Upper Saddle River, NJ: Prentice Hall.

Feminist Qualitative Research in the Millennium's First Decade

Developments, Challenges, Prospects[1]

Virginia Olesen

There are many discourses of feminism in circulation, and we need, at times, to deploy them all.

—Susanne Gannon and Bronwyn Davies (2007, p. 100)

Feminisms and qualitative research practices continue to be highly diversified, contentious, dynamic, and challenging. Disparate orientations to both theoretical issues and research practices exist as new ideas and practices emerge, old ones ossify or fade (Fonow & Cook, 2005). Amid the multiple complexities, maturing and deepened developments in theory and research on intersectionality, participatory action research and transnational feminist work, insights, and practices expand, even as they destabilize some foundations. Energizing these developments is the growing importance of "endarkened"/decolonized feminist research. These position feminist qualitative researchers to address enduring and emergent questions of gendered social justice. This does not assume a global, homogeneous feminism. Feminists draw from different theoretical and pragmatic orientations that reflect national contexts where feminist agendas differ widely (Evans, 2002; Franks, 2002; Howard & Allen, 2000). Ideas of once dominant groups in the northern hemisphere are no longer the standard (Alexander, 2005; Arat-Koc, 2007; Harding & Norberg, 2005; Mohanty, 2003). Replicating whiteness is a major concern (Evans, Hole, Berg, Hutchinson, & Sookraj, 2009).

This chapter derives from the sharpening and focusing of my own research sensibilities since my 1975 chapter, "Rage Is Not Enough." That chapter called for incisive feminist scholarship relevant for policy to frame and harness passion to challenge injustice around women's health, one of my enduring concerns. Feminist postcolonial and deconstructive thought later substantially expanded my groundedness in constructionist symbolic interaction. Postmodern research that addresses social justice issues has also influenced me, as has the work of feminists of color and lesbian feminists.

A brief review of diverse feminist qualitative research will introduce a discussion of transformative themes and developments. A short exploration follows of some enduring concerns. A review of unresolved and emergent issues introduces discussion of new opportunities and an examination of realizing social justice in difficult times.

BREADTH

Feminist qualitative researchers continue to explore topics that range from interpersonal issues, that is, domestic violence (Jiwani, 2005; Renzetti, 2005), body and health (Dworkin & Wachs, 2009), health and illness (Schulz & Mullings, 2006), medical knowledge (Shim, 2000), and social movements (Bell, 2009; Klawiter, 2008; Kuumba, 2002).

Policy research, once erroneously thought impossible with qualitative approaches, increasingly draws feminist attention (Fonow & Cook, 2005), although the area is a challenge (Campbell, 2000; Harding & Norberg, 2005; Mazur, 2002; Priyadharshini, 2003).

If there is a dominant theme in feminist qualitative research, it is the issue of knowledges. Whose knowledges? Where and how obtained, by whom, from whom, and for what purposes? It moved feminist research from the lack of or flawed attention to marginalized women, usually nonwhite, homosexual, or disabled, to recognition of differences among women and within the same groups of women and the recognition that multiple identities and subjectivities are constructed in particular historical and social contexts. It opened discussion of critical epistemological issues, the researcher's characteristics and relationships to the research participants.

TRANSFORMATIVE DEVELOPMENTS

Transformative developments continue to emerge from approaches (post-colonial, globalization, transnational feminism), conceptual and theoretical shifts (standpoint theory, poststructural thought) and research by and about specific groups of women (gay, lesbian, and queer; disabled; women of color).

Postcolonial feminist thought. If the criticisms of an unremitting whiteness in feminist research in Western, industrialized societies unsettled feminist research frames, powerful and sophisticated research and feminist thought from postco-lonial theorists continued to shift grounds of feminist research with regard to "woman" and "women," the very definitions of feminism itself, and construc-tions of color. Feminism takes many different forms depending on the context of contemporary nationalism. Concerned about the invidious effects of "othering" (invidious, oppressive definitions of the people with whom research is done), postcolonial feminists claimed that Western feminist models were inappropriate for thinking of research with women in postcolonial sites.

Postcolonial feminists raised incisive questions whether subordinates can speak or are forever silenced by virtue of representation within elite thought (Mohanty, 1988, 2003; Spivak, 1988). They also asked whether all women could be conceptualized as unified subjectivities located in the category of woman. They argued that subjectivity and identity are constructed in many different ways in any historical moment (Kim, 2007) and undercut the concept of woman, the assumptions of subjectivity and objectivity, and the utility of the interview (Trinh, 1989, 1992). Postcolonial feminist thought demands decolonizing self and other (Kim, 2007).

Globalization and transnational feminism. Globalization, the relentless, neoliberal flow of capitalism across national borders, destabilizes labor markets, induces movements of workers (Kim-Puri, 2005, pp. 139–142), and creates new sites of inquiry beyond the nation-state and new interpretations of power as multisited and shifting (Mendez & Wolf, 2007, pp. 652). Feminists have complicated the nature and characteristics of globalization (Desai, 2007). Globalization is rife with contradictions and the potential to produce multiple subjectivities (Kim-Puri, 2005; Naples, 2002a, 2002b). Research examines the tension between the domi-nance of the state and economic forces and women's potential resistance (Thayer, 2001) and dialectic between "new" opportunities and oppressions (Chang, 2001; Lan, 2006).

Others have examined women's lives and working conditions in diverse international contexts: sex workers (Gulcur & Ilkkaracan, 2002; Katsulis, 2009); the international sex trade (Dewey, 2008; Hanochi, 2001); care work (Zimmerman, Litt, & Bose, 2006); domestic servants (Parrenas, 2008); and laborers (Keough, 2009) as well as how governments create "heroic" migrant labor (Guevarra, 2009).

This work invokes the efficacy of postmodern thinking (Lacsamana, 1999); the risk of reproducing Eurocentric concepts of feminism (Grewal & Kaplan, 1994; Kempadoo, 2001); questions of female agency (Doezema, 2000); and the inadequacies of cultural analyses to understand oppressions rooted in material conditions under globalization (Fraser, 2005; Kim-Puri, 2005; Mendoza, 2002).

Closely related, transnational feminism analyzes national and cross-national feminist organizing and action (Davis, 2007; Mendez & Wolf, 2007; Mendoza, 2002). This work examines bases of feminist mobilization, for example, class, race, ethnicity, religion, and regional struggles; it sidesteps imposing a Westernized version of feminism. It poses substantial critical challenges (Mendez & Wolf, 2007).

Transnational feminists also examine sex trafficking (DeRiviere, 2006; Firdous, 2005; Stout, 2008), violence against women (Jiwani, 2005), and reproductive technologies (Gupta, 2006).

Standpoint research. Standpoint research flourishes in the early years of the millennium (Harding, 2008). Sociologist Dorothy Smith,[2] sociologist Patricia Hill Collins,[3] philosopher Sandra Harding,[4] and political scientist Nancy Hartsock[5] replaced the concept of essentialized, universalized woman with the idea of a situated woman with experiences and knowledge specific to her place in the material division of labor and the racial stratification systems. Standpoint theorists are not identical; they offer divergent approaches for qualitative researchers.[6] Moreover, feminist qualitative researchers must read these theorists in their latest version—for example, Harding's plea to start with women's lives in households (2008)—if they are to avoid misinterpretation. Standpoint theories came in for extensive criticisms,[7] which evoked vigorous responses (Collins, 1997; Harding, 1997; Hartsock, 1997; D. E. Smith, 1997).

Regarding the relationship of standpoint theory to postmodern and poststructural thinking, "poststructural approaches have been especially helpful in enabling standpoint theories systematically to examine critically pluralities of power relations" (Harding, 1996, p. 451). Collins (1998b) warns about the corrosive effects of postmodern and deconstructive thought for Black women's group authority and social action, but she also argues that postmodernism's

Table 7.1

I. Transformative Developments		
Approaches	Postcolonial feminist thought	Kim, 2007; Mohanty, 1988, 2003; Spivak, 1988; Trinh, 1989, 1992
	Globalization	Chang, 2001; Dewey, 2008; Fraser, 2005; Guevara, 2009; Kim-Puri, 2005; Lan, 2006; Naples, 2002a,b; Parrenas, 2008; Zimmerman, Litt, & Bose, 2006
	Transnational feminism	Davis, 2007; DeRiviere, 2006; Firdous, 2005; Mendez & Wolf, 2007; Stout, 2008
	Standpoint theory	Collins, 1992, 1998 a,b; Haraway, 1991; Harding, 1987, 1993, 2008; Hartsock, 1983, 1997; Naples, 2007; Smith, 1987, 1997; Weeks, 2004
	Postmodern and poststructural deconstructive theory	Clough, 2000; Collins, 1998b; Flax, 1987, 1990; Gannon & Davies, 2007; Haraway, 1991; Hekman, 1990; Lacsamana, 1999; Lather, 2007; Mazzei, 2003, 2004; Pillow, 2003; St.Pierre, 1997b, 2009
Work By and About Specific Groups of Women	Lesbian research	Anzaldúa, 1987, 1990; Connolly, 2006; Kennedy & Davis, 1993; Lewin, 1993, 2009; Mamo, 2007; Merlis & Linville, 2006; Mezey, 2008; Weston, 1991
	Queer theory	Butler, 1990, 1993, 2004; Rupp & Taylor, 2003
	Disabled women	Fine, 1992; Garland-Thompson, 2005; Lubelska & Mathews, 1997; Meekosha, 2005; Mertens, 2009; Petersen, 2006 ; Tregaskis & Goodley, 2005
	Women of color	Acosta, 2008; Anzaldúa, 1990; Chow, 1987; Collins, 1986; Cummins & Lehman, 2007; Davis, 1981; Dill, 1979; Espiritu, 2007; Few, 2007; Glenn, 2002; Green, 1990; hooks, 1990; Majumdar, 2007; Mihesuah, 2003 ; Moore, 2008; Tellez, 2008
	Problematizing unremitting whiteness	Frankenberg, 1994; Hurtado & Stewart, 1997

(Continued)

Table 7.1 (Continued)

II. Critical Trends		
Endarkening, Decolonizing, Indigenizing Feminist Research		Anzaldúa, 1987; Battiste, 2008; Collins, 2000; Dillard, 2008; Gardiner & Meyer, 2008a; Saavedra & Nymark, 2008; Segura & Zavella, 2008; Smith, 1999, 2005
Intersectionality		Andersen 2005, 2008; Bhavnani, 2007; Bowleg, 2008; Brah & Phoenix, 2004; Collins, 2000, 2008, 2009; Crenshaw, 1989, 1991; Davis, 2008; Denis, 2008; Dill, McLaughlin, & Nieves, 2007; Dill & Zambrana, 2009; Glenn, 2002; Hancock, 2007a,b; McCall, 2005; Risman, 2004; Shields, 2008; Stewart & McDermott, 2004; Warner, 2008; Yuval-Davis, 2006
III. Continuing Issues		
Problematizing Researcher and Participant		Kahn, 2005; Lather & Smithies, 1997; Lather, 2007; Lincoln, 1993, 1997
Destabilizing Insider-Outsider		Kondo, 1990; Lewin, 1993; Naples, 1996; Narayan, 1997; Ong, 1995; Weston, 1991; Zavella, 1996
Troubling Traditional Concepts	Experience	Scott, 1991
	Difference	Felski, 1997; hooks, 1990
	Gender	Baravosa-Carter, 2001; Butler, 1990, 1993, 2004; Jurik & Siemsen, 2009; Lorber, 1994; West & Zimmerman, 1987
IV. Enduring Concerns		
"Bias" and Objectivity	Diaz, 2002; Fine, 1992; Harding, 1993, 1996, 1998; Phoenix, 1994; Scheper-Hughes, 1983	
Reflexivity	Few, 2007; Guilleman & Gillam, 2004; Hesse-Biber & Piatelli, 2007; Pillow, 2003	

"Validity" and Trustworthiness	Lather, 1993, 2007; Manning, 1997; Richardson, 1993; St.Pierre (Ch. 14, volume 3)	
Participants' Voices	Behar, 1993; Ellis & Bochner, 1996, 2000; Fine, 1992; Gray & Sinding, 2002; Kincheloe, 1997; Kondo, 1995; Lather & Smithies, 1997; Lincoln, 1993, 1997; Phoenix, 1994; Richardson, 1997; Stacey, 1998	
Deconstructing Voice	Jackson, 2003; MacLure, 2009; Mazzei, 2009; Mazzei & Jackson, 2009; Lather & Smithies, 1997	
Performance Ethnography	Alexander, 2005; Battacharya, 2009; Case & Abbitt, 2004; Cho & Trent, 2009; Denzin, 2005; Gray & Sinding, 2002; Kondo, 1995; Madison, 2005, 2006; Valentine, 2006	
Ethics in Feminist Research	Battacharya, 2007; Battiste, 2008; Corrigan, 2003; Edwards & Mauthner, 2002; Ellis, 2009a; Fine, Weis, Weseem, & Wong, 2000; Guilleman & Gillam, 2004; Halsey & Honey, 2005; Lincoln, 2005; Llewelyn, 2007; Mauthner, Birch, Jessop, & Miller, 2002; Miller & Bell, 2002; Morse, 2005, 2007; L. T. Smith, 1999, 2005; Stacey, 1988; Thapar-Bjorkert & Henry, 2004; Wolf, 1996	
Participatory Action Research	Cancian, 1996; Etowa, Bernard, Oynisan, & Clow, 2007; Evans, Hole, Berg, Hutchinson, & Sookraj, 2009; Fine & Torre, 2006; Reid, Tom, & Frisby, 2008	
V. Influences on Feminist Work		
Contexts	The Academy	Dever, 2004; Laslett & Brenner, 2001; Messer-Davidow, 2002; Shields, 2008
	Publishing and Eurocentric Parochialism	Messer-Davidow, 2002
VI. Into the Future		
Challenges: Making Feminist Work Count	Cook & Fonow, 2007; Davis & Craven, 2011; Hesse-Biber, 2007; Laslett & Brenner, 2001; Stacey, 2003	

powerful analytic tools can challenge dominant discourses and the very rules of the game. Nancy A. Naples (2007) argues for a multidimensional approach to standpoint research, which recognizes both the embodied aspects and the multiplicity of researcher and participant perspectives.

POSTSTRUCTURAL POSTMODERN THOUGHT

Postmodern and poststructural/deconstructive thinking continues to be controversial, yet energizes other feminist researchers (Gannon & Davies, 2007; Lather, 2007).

Concerned that it is impossible to produce more than a partial story of women's lives in oppressive contexts, postmodern feminists regard "truth" as a destructive illusion. They see the world as a series of stories or texts that sustain the integration of power and oppression and actually "constitute us as subjects in a determinant order" (Hawkesworth, 1989, p. 549). Influenced by French feminists (Luce Irigaray, Hélène Cixous) and theorists (Michel Foucault, Gilles Deleuze, Jean-François Lytoard, Jacques Derrida, and Jean Baudrillard) and American theorist Judith Butler, postmodern/deconstructive feminist research studies focus on representation and text. Some scholars also use Marxist theory from Louis Althusser, and psychoanalytic views (Flax, 1987, 1990; Gannon & Davies, 2007).

Taking the position that text is central to incisive analysis as a fundamental mode of social criticism, these inquiries typically analyze cultural objects (film, etc.) and their meanings (Balsamo, 1993; Clough, 2000; deLauretis, 1987; Denzin, 1992; Morris, 1998). Included are textual analyses of these objects and the discourses surrounding them (Denzin, 1992) and the "study of lived cultures and experiences which are shaped by the cultural meanings that circulate in everyday life" (Denzin, 1992, p. 81).

Here, too, will be found sophisticated feminist work in gender and science, wherein science is deconstructed to reveal its practices, discourses, and implications for control of women's lives (Haraway, 1991; Martin, 1999), including their health (Clarke & Olesen, 1999), and to suggest avenues for resistance or intervention. Research about women's reproductive issues also moved into this area (Clarke, 1998; Mamo, 2007; Rapp, 1999). These productions discomfort not only male-dominated institutions, such as science, but feminism itself by complicating where and how "women" are controlled, how multiple, shifting identities and selves are produced.

In particular, poststructural deconstructive feminists question the very nature and limits of qualitative research (Lather, 1991, 2007; St.Pierre, 2009). They argue that traditional empirical research, imbedded in regimes of power, merely replicates oppressive structures while fruitlessly seeking the impossible, namely a full, complete account of whatever is investigated with inadequate strategies. They do not seek "a method" but attempt to exploit these shortcomings with centripetal strategies that reach outward, "strategies, approaches, and tactics that defy definition or closure" (Gannon & Davies, 2007, p. 81), rather than centrifugal (leaning inward toward one, stable interpretation).

Poststructural deconstructive feminists question taken-for-granted terms such as data, arguing for "transgressive data" (emotional, dreams, sensual response) (St.Pierre, 1997b) and for analysis of silences (Mazzei, 2003, 2004). They have also deconstructed validity (Lather, 1993), reflexivity (Pillow, 2003), and voice, to be discussed shortly. They but point to "a less comfortable science" (Lather, 2007, p. 4) wherein researchers trouble their own categories, while recognizing the uncertainties and the absence of absolute frames of reference (Lather, 2007).

Critics of the postmodern/poststructural position alleged that it left no grounds for reform-oriented research, reinforced the status quo, erased structural power, and failed to address problems or to represent a cultural system.[8] However, as already noted, standpoint theorists Collins and Harding see the possibility of deconstructing power and opening new spaces for social action.

Poststructural feminist work offers the potential for thinking differently about obdurate problems (Gannon & Davies, 2007), which appears useful for feminist policy research. These feminists have done work oriented to social justice (Lather & Smithies, 1997; Mazzei, 2004; Scheurich & Foley, 1997; St.Pierre, 1997a). Transformative developments continue in work by and about groups of women.

Lesbian research. Research dissolved homogeneous views of lesbians (Lewin, 1993; Weston, 1991).[9] Other work revealed multiple bases of lesbian identity to further differentiate these views and destabilize notions of heteronormativity (Anzaldúa, 1987, 1990; Kennedy & Davis, 1993). Early millennial lesbian research continued this trend (Connolly, 2006; Lewin, 2009; Mamo, 2007; Merlis & Linville, 2006; Mezey, 2008). *Queer theory*, loosely used as a cover term for gay and lesbian studies, also refers to a more precise political stance and the push against "disciplinary legitimation and rigid categorization" (Adams & Jones, 2008, p. 381). Disruption of normalizing ideologies is the key to queer theory, which is oriented to a politics of change (Alexander, 2008).

Research shows how gay and lesbian marriage ceremonies simultaneously reflect accommodation and subversion (Lewin, 1998), and it questions the very stability of "man" and "woman" (Rupp & Taylor, 2003).

Disabled women. Disabled women were depersonalized and degendered, sometimes even, regrettably, within feminist circles (Lubelska & Mathews, 1997), when researchers overlooked their multiple statuses and viewed them solely in terms of their disability (Asch & Fine, 1992). Feminist scholars, both disabled and abled, began to problematize disability (Garland-Thompson, 2005).

In the new millennium, their work ranges widely (Meekosha, 2005; Mertens, 2009; Mertens, Sullivan, & Stace, Chapter 13, this volume; Petersen, 2006; Tregaskis & Goodley, 2005).

Women of color. That there *are* multiple knowledges, that women of color were frequently overlooked or interpreted in terms of white women has been forcefully argued (Anzaldúa, 1987, 1990; Chow, 1987; Collins, 2000; Davis, 1981; Dill, 1979; Green, 1990; hooks, 1990). This continues with exploration of Black families (Few, 2007; Moore, 2008), AIDS and Black women (Foster, 2007); Latino critical theory (Delgado Bernal, 2002), diversities among American Indian women (Mihesuah, 2003), Asian American men and women (Espiritu, 2007), eating disorders among Asian women (Cummins & Lehman, 2007), marriage among Southeast Asian women (Majumdar, 2007), and Chicana experiences on the U.S.-Mexican border (Acosta, 2008; Tellez, 2008). Important theoretical contributions examined interlocking influences of gender and race on citizenship (Glenn, 2002) and the argument that Blacks are a monolithic group (Collins, 2008).

Parallel investigations problematized the construction of women of color in relationship to whiteness (Puar, 1996) and whiteness itself (Frankenberg, 1994; Hurtado & Stewart, 1997). As Yen Le Espiritu has noted, "Racism affects not only people of color but organizes and shapes experiences of all women" (personal communication, September 15, 2003). To untangle whiteness and the existence of a global color line, Chandra Mohanty (2003) noted the necessity to think relationally about questions of power, equality, and justice, to make thinking and organizing contextual, and to root questions of history and experience.

CRITICAL TRENDS

Two critical trends emerged from these developments: (1) "endarkening," decolonizing, indigenizing feminist research and (2) expansion and maturing intersectionality as a critical approach.

Endarkening, Decolonizing, Indigenizing Feminist Research

Feminist scholars of color deepened thought and research to move away from colonial legacies, wherever found, and stressed the critical nature of subordinated women's (and men's) knowledge as legitimate foundations for attempts to realize social justice. Influential work on decolonizing methodologies (L. T. Smith, 1999, 2005) and on protecting indigenous knowledge (Battiste, 2008) spurred these developments, as did writing by African American and Mexican American feminists (Cannella & Manuelito, 2008).

Anzaldúa's (1987) experimental writing and work decenters Western thinking and theorizing to emphasize decolonizing research (Saavedra & Nymark, 2008). More specifically, her conceptualization of borderlands posed "dynamic processes deployed for specific purposes—fluctuating, permeable, and rife with possibilities and consequences" (Gardiner & Meyer, 2008b, p. 10). (See Gardiner & Meyer, 2008a; Segura & Zavella, 2008).

Anzaldúa's innovative thinking also emphasized spirituality as requisite to the political (Gardiner & Meyer, 2008a). A similar proposal, but more specifically directed to feminist research and action, is Dillard's (2008) call to locate spirituality and qualitative research in endarkening feminist research (see also Dillard and Okpalaoka, Chapter 8, this volume).

Intersectionality. Intersectionality (Crenshaw, 1989, 1991) denotes how social divisions are constructed and intermeshed with one another in specific historical conditions to contribute to the oppression of women not in mainstream white, heterosexual, middle-class, able-bodied America. By the early years of the new millennium, intersectional analysis had spread to numerous disciplines and professions (Brah & Phoenix, 2004; Davis, 2008; Denis, 2008; Yuval-Davis, 2006) and prompted special journal issues (Phoenix & Pettynama, 2006).

Not surprisingly, different views emerged. Some preferred interconnections, which configure one another, to intersectionality, which was seen as too static and at risk of overlooking agency (Bhavnani, 2007). Other worries include that intersectionality applies to all groups, not just the marginalized (Warner, 2008); is empirically weak (Nash, 2008); and does not attend to narrative accounts (Prins, 2006). Working only within an intersectional framework fails to acknowledge how structural mechanisms produce different inequalities (Risman, 2004). Feminists should not overlook "the broader, political, economic, and social processes that constitute and buttress inequality" (Acker, 2006; Andersen, 2008, p. 121). However, others claim that intersectionality addresses the very meaning of power (Collins, 2009; Dill & Zambrana, 2009; Hancock, 2007a) and is useful in political struggles (Davis, 2008).

Although there is agreement that categories are not additive but interactive and mutually constructed (Acker, 2008; Andersen, 2005; Collins, 2009; Hancock, 2007b; Shields, 2008; Yuval-Davis, 2006), debates about which combinations to use continue. Related is the criticism that intersectionality courts problems of "infinite regress" of categories (Hancock, 2007b). Three observations responded to this: (1) Judgments *can* be made about which categories to use (Stewart & McDermott, 2004); (2) researchers must be explicit as to which are chosen (Warner, 2008); and (3) in specific situations and for specific people, some social divisions are more important than others (Dill & Zambrana, 2009).

Running through these arguments are questions of dynamic interactions between individual identities and institutional factors (Hancock, 2007a, 2007b) that locate any group in socially stratified systems. This pushes feminist researchers to articulate ways to analyze simultaneously identities at structural and political levels (Dill, McLaughlin, & Nieves, 2007) and necessitates placing "social structural and narrative/interpretive approaches to social reality in dialogue with one another" (Collins, 2009, p. xi). This daunting challenge implicates research design, methods (Hancock, 2007b), and interpretation (Bowleg, 2008).

It also questions how complexity in categories is viewed: Anticategorical complexity holds that the completeness of any category can be challenged; for example, sexuality is no longer merely gay or straight but more complicated (McCall, 2005). Intracategorical complexity posits range of diversity and experiences within the same social category, for example, working-class men and working-class women (McCall, 2005).

Intercategorical complexity centers comparison of groups across analytical categories (McCall, 2005). Intersectionality analysis is a "field of cognitive land mines" (Collins, 2008, p. 73), one that is "typically partial" (one cannot handle race, class, gender, sexuality, able-bodiness, and age simultaneously) and is inherently comparative (Collins, 2008).

How, then, to do manageable intersectionality analyses? Collins (2008) finds dynamic centering and relational thinking useful. Dynamic centering places two or more entities at the center of analysis to get a closer look at their mutual construction (Collins, 2008). Relational thinking asks how categories mutually construct one another as systems of power.

Intersectional research promises to address complex feminist issues (Bredstrom, 2006; Dworkin, 2005; Morgen, 2006) to yield new insights, but much remains to be done to handle earlier criticisms (Luft & Ward, 2009). Thanks to new developments in qualitative analysis (Clarke, 2004) and the maturing of institutional ethnography (Smith, 2006), feminist qualitative research *in its own right* is well positioned to undertake these challenges. Blended with quantitative research approaches, it is a powerful way to analyze mechanisms of intersectionality in play (Weber, 2007).

Continuing Issues

Problematizing researcher and participants. Recognition grew that the researcher's attributes also enter the research interaction. History and context position both researcher and participant (Andrews, 2002). The subjectivity of the researcher, as much as that of the researched, became foregrounded, blurring phenomenological and epistemological boundaries between the researcher and the researched. This questioned whether being an "insider" gave feminist researchers access to inside knowledge (Collins, 1986; Kondo, 1990; Lewin, 1993; Naples, 1996; Narayan, 1997; Ong, 1995; Williams, 1996; Zavella, 1996). Also questioned were the views that insider knowledge and insider/outsider positions are fixed and unchanging (Kahn, 2005).

Troubling traditional concepts. Also under critical scrutiny were concepts key to feminist thought and research, experience, difference, and the workhorse concept, gender.

Experience. Recognition continues to grow that merely focusing on experience does not account for how that experience emerged (Scott, 1991) and the characteristics of the material, historical, and social circumstances. (For early millennial feminist research that does attend to those circumstances, see Garcia-Lopez, 2008; Higginbotham, 2009). Taking experience in an unproblematic way replicates rather than criticizes oppressive systems and carries a note of essentialism. Moreover, personal experience is not a self-authenticating claim to knowledge (O'Leary, 1997).

Difference. The recognition of difference pulled feminist thinkers and researchers away from the view of a shared gynocentric identity but gave way to concerns about the nature of the concept and whether its use led to an androcentric or imperialistic "othering" (Felski, 1997; hooks, 1990). Some wanted it replaced by such concepts as *hybridity, creolization,* and *metissage,* which "not only recognize differences within the subject but also address connections between subjects" (Felski, 1997, p. 12). Others argued that identity cannot be dropped entirely (hooks, 1990). They see differences as autonomous, not fragmented, producing knowledge that accepts "the existence of and possible solidarity with knowledges from other standpoints" (O'Leary, 1997, p. 63).

Gender. Influential reformulations of gender as performative rather than static (Butler, 1990, 1993; West & Zimmerman, 1987) or wholly constructed (Lorber,

1994) have shifted views away from gender as an individual attribute or biological characteristic. Gender is conceptualized as "done" and "undone" in everyday social interaction (Butler, 2004).[10]

Vigorous criticisms highlight conceptual problems. Some argued that Butler's performative conceptualizations draw attention away from practical interventions (Barvosa-Carter, 2001, p. 129), a point echoed in some criticisms of Candace West and Don Zimmerman (Jurik & Siemsen, 2009). Another critique examines whether the "doing gender" perspective obscures inequality in social relations (Smith, 2009).

Enduring Concerns

Concerns about bias, validity, voice, the text, and ethical conduct, well explored in an earlier era, continue to produce thoughtful uneasiness. Feminist empiricists and standpoint researchers share these worries, while deconstructionists focus on voice and text. All feminist researchers worry about replicating oppression and privilege.

Bias. Foregoing rigid ideas about objectivity, feminist theorists and researchers earlier opened new spaces around the enduring question of bias. Sandra Harding suggested "strong objectivity," which takes researchers as well as those researched as the focus of critical, causal, scientific explanations (1993, 1996, 1998) Donna Haraway (1997) urged going beyond strong objectivity to diffracting, which turns the researchers' lenses to show fresh combinations and possibilities of phenomena.

Reflexivity. This recognizes that both participants and researcher produce interpretations that are "the data" (Diaz, 2002) and goes beyond mere reflection on the conduct of the research. Reflexivity demands steady, uncomfortable assessment about the interpersonal and interstitial knowledge-producing dynamics of qualitative research, in particular, acute awareness as to what unrecognized elements in the researchers' background contribute (Gorelick, 1991; Scheper-Hughes, 1983).

Some have reservations; for example, reflexivity may only generate a rehearsal of the familiar, which reproduces hegemonic structures (Pillow, 2003). However, others argue that it facilitates preventing perpetuation of racial and ethnic stereotypes (Few, 2007). Finally, there remain difficult questions of how much and what kinds of reflexivity are possible and how they are realized (Hesse-Biber & Piatelli, 2007).

Validity. Feminist qualitative researchers address validity, also called "trustworthiness," in different ways depending on how they frame their approaches. Those who work in a traditional vein, reflecting the positivist origins of social science (there is a reality to be discovered), will use established techniques. Others disdain positivistic origins and use techniques that reflect their postpositivist views but do not hold out hard and fast criteria for according "authenticity" (Lincoln & Guba, 1985; Manning, 1997). Other feminist qualitative researchers "challenge different kinds of validity and call for different kinds of science practices" (Richardson, 1993, p. 65).

Lather's (1993) transgressive validity remains the most completely worked out feminist model; it calls for a subversive move, "retaining the term to circulate and break with the signs that code it" (p. 674) in a feminist deconstuctionist mode. This formulation and the articulation of a transgressive validity checklist (Lather, 2007, pp. 128–129) firmly retain a feminist emancipatory stance while working out problems in validity.

Voice(s) and text. How to avoid exploiting or distorting women's voices has long worried feminists (Hertz, 1997). In the new millennium, poststructural feminists raise critical questions about the very nature of voice.

Researchers earlier explored ideology, hegemonic pressures, or interpretation (Fine, personal communication). In the end, whoever writes up the account also has responsibility for the text, selects the audience that shapes voice (Kincheloe, 1997; Lincoln, 1993), and remains in a powerful position (Lincoln, 1997; Phoenix, 1994; Stacey, 1998).

To address this, researchers have outlined various strategies: using voice-centered relational methods (Mauthner & Doucet, 1998) or reconstructed research narratives (Birch, 1998), writing the less powerful voices (Standing, 1998), and presenting versions of voices (Wolf, 1992). Feminist researchers should articulate how, how not, and within what limits voices are framed and used (Fine, 1992).

Other feminist researchers blend respondent voices with their own in various formats: a doubled-voice ethnographic text (Behar, 1993), split-page textual format (Lather & Smithies, 1997), or sociological poetry and tales (Richardson, 1997). Autoethnography foregrounds deeply personal researcher experiences and participants' voices interwoven with political and social issues (Ellingson, 1998, 2009a, 2009b; Ellis, 1995; Ellis & Bochner, 1996, 2000; Gatson, Chapter 8, volume 3; Holman Jones 2005). Autoethnographic work links the personal and the political to refute criticisms that such personal reflections are merely solipsistic.

Autoethnography is a way to understand and change the world (Ellis, 2009a). Reflecting that it unsettles ideas of research, social scientists and poststructural feminists and scholars with literary perspectives have criticized the approach (Ellis, 2009a). There are ways to evaluate it (Richardson, 2000).

Deconstructing voice. Poststructural feminists question what constitutes voice (Jackson, 2003, 2009; Mazzei & Jackson, 2009). Their research problematizes voice to yield examples for others: laughter, silence, irony (MacLure, 2009); silent narratives (Mazzei, 2009); and HIV-positive women (Lather & Smithies, 1997).

Performance ethnography. Performance ethnography shifts from conventional prose and reporting findings to dramatic representations (Kondo, 1995). These pieces dramatize feminist subversions (Case & Abbitt, 2004): the experience of metastatic breast cancer (Gray & Sinding, 2002), lives of imprisoned women (Valentine, 2006), and issues of human rights (Madison, 2006). (See also Alexander, 2005; Denzin, 2005; Madison, 2005). Performance ethnography could be useful in taking feminist research public (Stacey, 2003). Work continues on how to evaluate these inquiries (Alexander, 2005, pp. 428–430; Battacharya, 2009; Cho & Trent, 2009; Madison, 2005, 2006).

Ethics. Feminist research ethics moved beyond universalist positions in moral philosophy (duty ethics of principles, utilitarian ethics of consequences) to recognize relationships with research participants as an ethical issue, called *relational ethics* (Edwards & Mauther, 2002; Ellis, 2009a; Mauthner, Birch, Jessop, & Miller, 2002; Preissle, 2007). This necessitates critical reflection to recognize, analyze, and act on ethically important research moments (Guilleman & Gillam, 2004; Halsey & Honey, 2005; Llewelyn, 2007).

Indigenous scholars continue to raise critical elements in feminist ethics. They see the dreary history of research as "a corporate, deeply colonial institution" (L. T. Smith, 2005, p. 101) that exploits indigenous peoples and commodifies indigenous knowledge (Battiste, 2008; Smith, 1999). They conceptualize indigenous research as a seedbed for ethical standards that reference not just the individual but the collective (Battiste, 2008; L. T. Smith, 2005) and, above all, stress respectful relationships and reflect mutual understanding (L. T. Smith, 2005).

Scrutiny of informed consent, destabilized as unproblematic, continues (Battacharya, 2007; Corrigan, 2003; Fine, Weis, Weseem, & Wong, 2000; Miller & Bell, 2002). Carolyn Ellis proposes *process consent,* the practice of continually checking with participants to accommodate changing research relationships and respondents' willingness to continue participating since what is outlined on an institutional review board (IRB) protocol will not necessarily reflect later events (2009a).

Other ethical dilemmas abound (Bell & Nutt 2002; Kirsch, 2005; Morse, 2005, 2007; Stacey, 1988). The view that the researcher occupies a more powerful position has been tempered by realization that the researcher's power is often partial (Ong, 1995), tenuous (Stacey, 1998; Wolf, 1996), and confused with researcher responsibility (Bloom, 1998); also, respondents manipulate or exploit shifts of power (Thapar-Bjorkert & Henry, 2004.)

Feminist qualitative researchers face, along with all qualitative researchers, a pinched, conservative era in which many IRB review practices are not sympathetic to even the most traditional qualitative research, never mind the complex approaches discussed in this chapter (Lincoln, 2005). The restrictive effects of "these politics of evidence" (Morse, 2005, 2006) add another level of struggle to the feminist qualitative search for social justice (Lincoln, 2005) and reflect an enduring climate of positivism. The challenge is to influence local IRBs and to seek changes in legislation and policy (Lincoln, 2005).

Feminists have also examined ethics qua ethics as a research topic. The view shifted from ethical or moral behavior as inherent in gender to the position that an ethics of caring emerges from an interaction between the individual and the milieu (Seigfried, 1996). These positions reach to concerns with the just community (Seigfried, 1996) and the potential to transform society in the public sphere (DesAutels & Wright, 2001; Fiore & Nelson, 2003). Long-standing concerns about ethical (or nonethical) treatment of women in health care systems carried into inquiries on new technologies, such as assisted reproduction, genetic screening and the regrettably enduring problems of equitable care for elderly, poor, deprived women in all ethnic groups.

Participatory action research. In participatory action research (PAR), "researchers" and "participants" fully share aspects of the research process to undertake emancipatory projects. Earlier PAR explored research-related matters: power (Cancian, 1996; Lykes, 1989); data (Acker, Barry, & Esseveld, 1991); and corrections of researchers' and participants' distortions (Skeggs, 1994). These continue with inquiries into participant vulnerability (Fine & Torre, 2006), risks for marginalized individuals (Reid, Tom, & Frisby, 2008), and ethical questions (Rice, 2009). In the new millennium, PAR examined health issues (Etowa, Bernard, Oyinsan, & Clow, 2007; Evans, Hole, Berg, Hutchinson, & Sookraj, 2009) and imprisoned women (Fine & Torre, 2006).

Contexts' Influence on Qualitative Feminist Work, Agendas

Academic sites. Structures of traditional academic life—at least in the United States—have influenced feminist qualitative research and not always to transform the university or realize reform more generally (Dever, 2004; Messer-Davidow,

2002). Continued emphasis on positivism in the social and behavioral sciences has also blunted reform efforts, but feminist scholars continue to argue for transformative scholarship (Shields, 2008).

To realize transformative scholarship, feminist researchers need to recognize the way higher education institutions work while generating "new strategies that correspond to new opportunities as well as the difficulties of these times" (Laslett & Brenner 2001, pp. 1233–1234). (For analyses of difficulties with Black women's scholarship and transformation of the academy, see "Black Women's Studies," 2010).

Publishing and Anglo/Eurocentric parochialism. Publishers bring out increasing numbers of feminist works—theoretical, empirical, experimental, and methodological (Messer-Davidow, 2002). More international scholars are being published, but in English because of translation difficulties and marketing pressures (Meaghan Morris, personal communication). Fortunately, these publications foreground different perspectives and postcolonial, endarkened feminist research, to undercut Westernizing and homogenizing assumptions about "women" anywhere and everywhere. Feminist talk lists and websites offer information about international feminist work, conferences, and publications, for example, those run by the Sociologists for Women in Society and the Anthropology Feminist Association. Some that are outside the United States or Britain, for instance, http://www.qualitative-research.net/, agi-feministafrica@act.cu.za, regularly cite international researchers.

Feminist research has yet to extensively explore Internet communication resources such as Twitter and Facebook, but their growing popularity has implications for dissemination of reform-oriented inquiries.

Into the Future

Challenges. Challenges to feminist qualitative research in all its complexity, diversity, and contentiousness will continue. Notable among these is deeper exploration and extension of intersectionality, using mature methodological approaches (Choo & Ferree, 2010). These explorations position feminist efforts to examine more incisively the interplay of multiple factors in all women's lives. They sharpen understandings of and the potential to generate action and policy in the pursuit of social justice. They link to emergent methods and new knowledge from critical work in "borderlands" and endarkening feminist research.

Also necessary is continued close attention to representation, voice, and text to avoid replication of the researcher and hidden or not so hidden oppressions and instead display participants' representations.

Feminist qualitative research grows stronger because theorists and researchers critically examine foundations; try new research approaches, experimental and traditional; and search for unexamined equity issues. They are more self-conscious and aware of and sensitive to issues in the formulation and conduct of research, as well as the nature of a feminist science. More sophisticated approaches position feminists to examine material social and cultural dynamics, for example, globalization and neoliberalism, which shape women's lives and their contexts (see Davis & Craven, 2011). The hope is for, if not emancipation, at least modest intervention and transformation without replicating oppression.

Making feminist work count. Feminist researchers have articulated thoughtful and realistic suggestions for change or transformation. "We must take our work public with extraordinary levels of reflexivity, caution, and semiotic and rhetorical sophistication" (Stacey, 2003, p. 28). Sociologists for Women in Society (www.socwomen.org) reports mainstream critical feminist research on urgent topics. Feminists have yet to explore the potential of cyberspace to intervene for social justice or disseminate research findings.

I believe that "it is important to recognize that knowledge production is continually dynamic—new frames open which give way to others which in turn open again and again. Moreover, knowledges are only partial" (Olesen & Clarke, 1999, p. 356). (See Cook & Fonow, 2007; Hesse-Biber, 2007.) Early millennial feminist qualitative research, outlined far too sketchily here, lays foundations to realize social justice in different feminist versions: "Our mission . . . must be nothing short of rethinking and reworking our future" (Randall, 2004, p. 23).

Recalling my 1975 paper, "Rage Is Not Enough" (1975), I contend that rage is *still* not enough, but developments in feminist qualitative scholarship, in whatever style or framework, are harnessing passion to realize social justice in more incisive ways. Much more, however, remains to be done to grapple with enduring and emerging issues of equity and social justice.

Notes

1. I am grateful for incisive criticisms from Norman Denzin, Yvonna Lincoln, Patricia Clough, Michelle Fine, Meaghan Morris, and Yen Le Espiritu and to Adele Clarke for continuing, stimulating feminist dialogue.

2. Dorothy Smith conceptualizes the everyday world as problematic, continually created, shaped, and known by women within it; its organization is shaped by external material factors or textually mediated relations (1987). She has fully explicated this approach, *institutional ethnography* (Smith, 2005, 2006), which she and others are developing (Campbell, 2002; Campbell & Gregor, 2002).

3. Collins (2000) grounds her Black women's standpoint in Black women's material circumstances and political situation. She refuses to abandon situated standpoints and links the standpoint of Black women with intersectionality, while she amplifies standpoint theory (1998a) *always* with keen consideration for power and structural relations (1998a).

4. Harding, a philosopher, early recognized three types of feminist inquiry (1987): (1) *Feminist empiricism*, which is of two types: (a) "spontaneous feminist empiricism" (rigorous adherence to existing research norms and standards) and (b) "contextual empiricism" (recognition of the influence of social values and interests in science) (1993); (2) *standpoint theory*, which recognizes that all knowledge attempts are socially situated and that some of these objective social locations are better than others for knowledge projects" (1993, 1998); and (3) *postmodern theories*, which void the possibility of a feminist science in favor of the many and multiple stories women tell about the knowledge they have (1987).

5. Key to Hartsock's (1983) Marxist standpoint theory is her view that women's circumstances in the material order provide them with experiences that generate particular and privileged knowledge, which both reflects oppression and women's resistance. Such knowledge is not innately essential nor do all women have the same experiences or the same knowledge. Rather, there is the possibility of a "concrete multiplicity" of perspectives (1990). "The subjects who matter are not individual subjects, but collective subjects, or groups" (Hartsock, 1997, p. 371).

6. See Harding, 1997; Weeks, 2004; Naples, 2003, 2007; Ramazanoglu and Holland, 2002.

7. See Clough, 1993a, 1993b, 1994; Collins, 1992; Harding, 1987; Hawkesworth, 1987; Hekman, 1990, 1997a 1997b; Kim, 2007; Maynard, 1994; Scott, 1997; Smith, 1992, 1993; Welton, 1997.

8. See Benhabib, 1995; Collins, 1998b; Ebert 1996.

9. It is useful to differentiate studies that focus on sexuality as an object of study from those that make sexuality a central concept (Yen Le Espiritu, personal communication, September 15, 2003). The former includes research that dissolved a homogeneous view of lesbians just noted in text. Alexander's work in the second category conceptualizes sexuality as fundamental to gender inequality and as a salient marker of otherness that has been central to racist and colonial ideologies (Alexander & Mohanty, 1997).

10. Differences among women as well as similarities between men and women were acknowledged (Brabeck, 1996; Lykes, 1994). For gender as causal explanation and analytic category and research implications for research, see Connell, 1997; Hawkesworth, 1997a, 1997b; McKenna & Kessler, 1997; S. G. Smith, 1997).

References

Acker, J. (2006). Inequality regimes: Gender, class and race in organizations. *Gender & Society, 4,* 441–464.

Acker, J. (2008). Feminist theory's unfinished business. *Gender & Society, 22,* 104–108.

Acker, J., Barry, K., & Esseveld, J. (1991). Objectivity and truth: Problems in doing feminist research. In M. M. Fonow & J. A. Cook (Eds.), *Beyond methodology: Feminist scholarship as lived research* (pp. 133–153). Bloomington: University of Indiana Press.

Acosta, K. L. (2008). Lesbians in the borderlands: Shifting identities and imagined communities. *Gender & Society, 22,* 639–659.

Adams, T. E., & Jones, S. H. (2008). Autoethnography is queer. In N. K. Denzin, Y. S. Lincoln, & L. T. Smith (Eds.), *Handbook of critical and indigenous methodologies* (pp. 373–390). Thousand Oaks, CA: Sage.

Alexander, B. K. (2005). Performance ethnography: The reenacting and citing of culture. In N. K. Denzin & Y. S. Lincoln (Eds.), *The SAGE handbook of qualitative research* (3rd ed., pp. 411–442). Thousand Oaks, CA: Sage.

Alexander, B. K. (2008). Queer(y)ing the post-colonial through the West(ern). In N. K. Denzin, Y. L. Lincoln, & L. T. Smith (Eds.), *Handbook of critical and indigenous methodologies* (pp. 101–134). Thousand Oaks, CA: Sage.

Alexander, M. J., & Mohanty, C. T. (1997). *Feminist geneaologies, colonial legacies, democratic futures.* New York: Routledge.

Andersen, M. L. (2005). Thinking about women: A quarter century's view. *Gender & Society, 19,* 437–455.

Andersen, M. L. (2008). Thinking about women some more: A new century's view. *Gender & Society, 22,* 120–125.

Andrews, M. (2002). Feminist research with non-feminist and anti-feminist women: Meeting the challenge. *Feminism and Psychology, 12,* 55–77.

Anzaldúa, G. (1987). *Borderlands/La frontera.* San Francisco: Aunti Lute Books.

Anzaldúa, G. (1990). *Making soul, Haciendo caras.* San Francisco: Aunti Lute Books.

Arat-Koc, S. (2007). (Some) Turkish transnationalisms in an age of capitalist globalization and empire: "White Turk" discourse, the new geopolitics and implications for feminist transnationalism. *Journal of Middle East Women's Studies, 3,* 35–57.

Asch, A., & Fine, M. (1992). Beyond the pedestals: Revisiting the lives of women with disabilities. In M. Fine (Ed.), *Disruptive voices: The possibilities of feminist research* (pp.139–174). Ann Arbor: University of Michigan Press.

Balsamo A. (1993). On the cutting edge: Cosmetic surgery and the technological production of the gendered body. *Camera Obscura, 28,* 207–237.

Barvosa-Carter, E. (2001). Strange tempest: Agency, structuralism and the shape of feminist politics to come. *International Journal of Sexuality and Gender Studies, 6,* 123–137.

Battacharya, K. (2007). Consenting to the consent form: What are the fixed and fluid understandings between the researcher and the researched. *Qualitative Inquiry, 13,* 1095–1115.

Battacharya, K. (2009). Negotiating shuttling between transnational experiences: A de/colonizing approach to performance ethnography. *Qualitative Inquiry, 15,* 1061–1083.

Battiste, M. (2008). Research ethics for protecting indigenous knowledge and heritage, In N. K. Denzin, Y. S. Lincoln, & L. T. Smith (Eds.), *Handbook of critical and indigenous methodologies* (pp. 497–510). Thousand Oaks, CA: Sage.

Behar, R. (1993). *Translated woman: Crossing the border with Esparanza's story.* Boston: Beacon.

Bell, L., & Nutt, L. (2002). Divided loyalties, divided expectations: Research ethics, professional and occupational responsibilities. In M. Mauthner, M. Birch, J. Jessop, & T. Miller (Eds.), *Ethics in qualitative research* (pp. 70–90). Thousand Oaks, CA: Sage.

Bell, S. E. (2009). *DES daughters, embodied knowledge, and the transformation of women's health politics.* Philadelphia: Temple University Press.

Benhabib, S. (1995). Feminism and post-modernism: An uneasy alliance. In S. Benhabib, J. Butler, D. Cornell, & N. Fraser (Eds.), *Feminist contentions: A philosophical exchange* (pp. 17–34). New York: Routledge.

Bhavnani, K.-K. (2007). Interconnections and configurations: Toward a global feminist ethnography, In S. N. Hesse-Biber (Ed.), *Handbook of feminist research: Theory and praxis* (pp. 639–650). Thousand Oaks, CA: Sage.

Birch, M. (1998). Reconstructing research narratives: Self and sociological identity in alternative settings. In J. Ribbens & R. Edwards (Eds.), *Feminist dilemmas in qualitative research: Public knowledge and private lives* (pp. 171–185). Thousand Oaks, CA: Sage.

Black women's studies and the transformation of the academy [Symposium]. (2010). *Signs, 35*(4).

Bloom, L. R. (1998). *Under the sign of hope: Feminist methodology and narrative interpretation.* Albany: State University of New York Press.

Bowleg, L. (2008). When Black + lesbian + woman = Black lesbian woman: The methodological challenges of qualitative and quantitative intersectionality research, *Sex Roles, 59,* 312–325.

Brabeck, M. M. (1996). The moral self, values, and circles of belonging. In K. F. Wyche & F. J. Crosby (Eds.), *Women's ethnicities: Journeys through psychology* (pp. 145–165). Boulder, CO: Westview Press.

Brah, A., & Phoenix, A. (2004). Ain't I a woman? Revisiting intersectionality. *International Journal of Women's Studies, 5,* 75–86.

Bredstrom, A. (2006). Intersectionality: A challenge for feminist HIV/AIDS Research? *European Journal of Women's Studies, 13,* 229–243.

Butler, J. (1990). *Gender trouble: Feminism and the subversion of identity.* London: Routledge.

Butler, J. (1993). *Bodies that matter: On the discursive limits of "sex."* London: Routledge.

Butler, J. (2004). *Undoing gender.* New York: Routledge.

Campbell, N. D. (2000). *Using women: Gender, policy, and social justice.* New York: Routledge.

Campbell, N. D. (2002). Textual accounts, ruling action: The intersection of knowledge and power in the routine conduct of nursing work. *Studies in Cultures, Organizations and Societies, 7,* 231–250.

Campbell, N. D., & Gregor, F. (2002). *Mapping social relations: A primer in doing institutional ethnography.* Toronto: Garamond.

Cancian, F. M. (1996). Participatory research and alternative strategies for activist sociology. In H. Gottfried (Ed.), *Feminism and social change* (pp. 187–205). Urbana: University of Illinois Press.

Cannella, G. S., & Manuelito, K. D. (2008). Indigenous world views, marginalized feminisms and revisioning an anticolonial social science. In N. K. Denzin, Y. S. Lincoln, & L. T. Smith (Eds.), *Handbook of critical and indigenous methodologies* (pp. 45–59). Thousand Oaks, CA: Sage.

Case, S-E., & Abbitt, E. S. (2004). Disidentifications, diaspora, and desire: Questions on the future of the feminist critique of performance. *Signs, 29,* 925–938.

Casper, M. J., & Talley, H. L. (2007). Feminist disability studies. In G. Ritzer (Ed.), *Blackwell encyclopedia of sociology* (pp. 15–30). London: Blackwell.

Chang, G. (2001). *Disposable domestics: Immigrant women workers in the global economy.* Cambridge, MA: South End Press.

Cho, J., & Trent, A. (2009). Validity criteria for performance-related qualitative work: Toward a reflexive, evaluative, and co-constructive framework for performance in/as. *Qualitative Inquiry, 15,* 1013–1041.

Choo, H. Y., & Ferree, M. M. (2010). Practicing intersectionality in sociological research: A critical analysis of inclusions, interactions and institutions in the study of inequalities. *Sociological Theory, 28,* 129–149.

Chow, E. N. (1987). The development of feminist consciousness among Asian American women. *Gender & Society, 1,* 284–299.

Clarke, A. (1998). *Disciplining reproduction: Modernity, American life sciences, and the problems of "sex."* Berkeley: University of California Press.

Clarke, A. (2004). *Grounded theory after the postmodern turn: Situational maps and analyses.* Thousand Oaks, CA: Sage.

Clarke, A., & Olesen, V. L. (Eds.). (1999). *Revisioning women, health, and healing. Feminist, cultural, and technoscience perspectives.* New York: Routledge.

Clough, P. T. (1993a). On the brink of deconstructing sociology: Critical reading of Dorothy Smith's standpoint epistemology. *The Sociological Quarterly, 34,* 169–182.

Clough, P. T. (1993b). Response to Smith's response. *The Sociological Quarterly, 34,* 193–194.

Clough, P. T. (1994). *Feminist thought: Desire, power, and academic discourse.* London: Basil Blackwell.

Clough, P. T. (2000). *Autoaffection: The unconscious in the age of teletechnology.* Minneapolis: University of Minnesota Press.

Collins, P. H. (1986). Learning from the outsider within: The sociological significance of Black feminist thought. *Social Problems, 33,* 14–32.

Collins, P. H. (1992). Transforming the inner circle: Dorothy Smith's challenge to sociological theory. *Sociological Theory, 10,* 73–80.

Collins, P. H. (1997). Comment on Hekman's "Truth and method: Feminist standpoint theory revisited." *Signs, 22,* 375–381.

Collins, P. H. (1998a). *Fighting words: Black women and the search for justice.* Minneapolis: University of Minnesota Press.

Collins, P. H. (1998b). What's going on? Black feminist thought and the politics of postmodernism. In P. H. Collins, *Fighting words, Black women and the search for justice* (Ch. 4, pp. 124–154). Minneapolis: University of Minnesota Press.

Collins, P. H. (2000). *Black feminist thought. Knowledge, consciousness and the politics of empowerment* (2nd ed.). Boston: Unwin Hyman.

Collins, P. H. (2008). Reply to commentaries: *Black sexual politics* revisited. *Studies in Gender and Sexuality, 9,* 68–85.

Collins, P. H. (2009). Foreword: Emerging intersections—Building knowledge and transforming institutions. In B. T. Dill & R. E. Zambrana (Eds.), *Emerging intersections. Race, class, and gender in theory, policy, and practice,* (pp. vii–xiii). New Brunwsick, NJ: Rutgers University Press.

Connell, R. W. (1997). Comment on Hawkesworth's "Confounding Gender." *Signs, 22,* 702–706.

Connolly, C. M. (2006). A feminist perspective of resilience in Lesbian couples, *Journal of Family Therapy, 18,* 137–162.

Cook, J. A., & Fonow, M. M. (2007). A passion for knowledge: The teaching of feminist methodology. In S. N. Hesse-Biber (Ed.), *Handbook of feminist research, theory, and praxis* (pp. 705–712). Thousand Oaks, CA: Sage.

Corrigan, O. (2003). Empty ethics: The problem with informed consent. *Sociology of Health and Illness, 25,* 768–792.

Crenshaw, K. (1989). Demarginalizing the intersection of race and sex: A Black feminist critique of antidiscrimination doctrine, feminist theory, and antiracist politics. *University of Chicago Legal Forum,* pp. 139–167.

Crenshaw, K. (1991). Mapping the margins: Intersectionality, identity politics, and violence against women of color. *Stanford Law Review, 43,* 1241–1299.

Cummins, L. H., & Lehman, J. (2007). Eating disorders and body image concerns in Asian American women: Assessment and treatment from a multi-cultural and feminist perspective. *Eating Disorders: The Journal of Treatment And Prevention, 15,* 217–230.

Davis, A. Y. (1981). *Women, race and class.* London: The Women's Press.

Davis, D.-A., & Craven, C. (2011). Revisiting feminist ethnography: Methods and activism at the intersection of neoliberal policy in the U.S. *Feminist Formations, 23.*

Davis, K. (2007). *The making of* Our Bodies, Ourselves*: How feminism travels across borders.* Durham, NC: Duke University Press.

Davis, K. (2008). Intersectionality as buzzword: A sociology of science perspective on what makes a feminist theory successful. *Feminist Theory, 9,* 67–85.

deLauretis, T. (1987). *Technologies of gender: Essays on theory, film, and fiction.* Bloomington: Indiana University Press.

Delgado Bernal, D. (2002). Critical race theory, Latino critical theory, and critical raced-gendered epistemologies: Recognizing students as creators and holders of knowledge. *Qualitative Inquiry, 8,* 105–126.

Denis, A. (2008). Intersectional analysis: A contribution of feminism to sociology, *International Sociology, 23,* 677–694.

Denzin, N. K. (1992). *Symbolic interaction and cultural studies.* Oxford, UK: Basil Blackwell.

Denzin, N. K. (2005). *Performance ethnography: Critical pedagogy and the politics of culture.* Thousand Oaks, CA: Sage.

DeRiviere, L. (2006). A human capital methodology for estimating the lifelong personal costs of young women leaving the sex trade. *Feminist Economics, 12,* 367–402.

Desai, M. (2007). The messy relationship between feminisms and globalization. *Gender & Society, 21,* 797–803.

DesAutels, P., & Wright, J. (2001). *Feminists doing ethics.* Boulder, CO: Rowan & Littlefield.

Dever, C. (2004). *Skeptical feminism, activist theory, activist practice.* Minneapolis: University of Minnesota Press.

Dewey, S. (2008). *Hollow bodies: Institutional responses to the traffic in women in Armenia, Bosnia, and India.* Sterling, VA: Kumarian Press.

Diaz, C. (2002). Conversational heuristic as a reflexive method for feminist research. *International Review of Sociology, 2,* 249–255.

Dill, B. T. (1979). The dialectics of Black womanhood. *Signs, 4,* 543–555.

Dill, B. T., McLaughlin, A. E., & Nieves, A. D. (2007). Future directions of feminist research: Intersectionality. In S. N. Hesse-Biber (Ed.), *Handbook of feminist research, theory and praxis* (pp. 629–638). Thousand Oaks, CA: Sage.

Dill, B. T., & Zambrana, R. E. (2009). Critical thinking about inequality: An emerging lens. In B. T. Dill & R. E. Zambrana (Eds.), *Emerging intersections: Race, class, and gender in theory, policy, and practice* (pp. 1–22). New Brunswick, NJ: Rutgers University Press.

Dillard, C. B. (2008). When the ground is black, the ground is fertile. In N. K. Denzin, Y. S. Lincoln, & L. T. Smith (Eds.), *Handbook of critical and indigenous methodologies* (pp. 277–292). Thousand Oaks, CA: Sage.

Doezema, J. (2000). Loose women or lost women? The re-emergence of the myth of white slavery in contemporary discourses in trafficking in women. *Gender Issues, 18,* 23–50.

Dworkin, S. L. (2005). Who is epidemiologically fathomable in the HIV-AIDS epidemic? Gender, sexuality, and intersectionality in public health. *Culture, Health, & Sexuality, 7,* 615–623.

Dworkin, S. L., & Wachs, F. L. (2009). *Body panic: Gender, health and the selling of fitness.* New York: New York University Press.

Ebert, T. (1996). *Ludic feminism and after: Postmodernism, desire and labor in late capitalism.* Ann Arbor: University of Michigan Press.

Edwards, R., & Mauthner, M. (2002). Ethics and feminist research: Theory and practice. In M. Mauthner, M. Birch, J. Jessop, & T. Miller (Eds.), *Ethics in qualitative research* (pp. 14–31). Thousand Oaks, CA: Sage.

Ellingson, L. L. (1998). Then you know how I feel: Empathy, identity, and reflexivity in fieldwork. *Qualitative Inquiry, 4,* 492–514.

Ellis, C. (1995). *Final negotiations: A story of love, loss and chronic illness.* Philadelphia: Temple University Press.

Ellis, C. (2009a). Fighting back or moving on: An autoethnographic response to critics. *International Review of Qualitative Research, 3*(2).

Ellis, C. (2009b). *Revision: Autoethnographic reflections on life and work.* Walnut Creek, CA: Left Coast Press.

Ellis, C., & Bochner, A. P. (1996). *Composing ethnography, Alternative forms of qualitative writing.* Walnut Creek, CA: AltaMira Press.

Ellis, C., & Bochner, A. P. (2000). Autoethnography, personal narrative, reflexivity: Researcher as subject. In N. K. Denzin & Y. S. Lincoln (Eds.), *Handbook of qualitative research* (2nd ed., pp. 733–768). Thousand Oaks, CA: Sage.

Espiritu, Y. L. (2007). *Asian American women and men: Labor, laws, and love.* Thousand Oaks, CA: Sage.

Etowa, J. B., Bernard, W. T., Oyinsan, B., & Clow, B. (2007). Participatory action research (PAR): An approach for improving Black women's health in rural and remote communities. *Journal of Transcultural Nursing, 18,* 349–357.

Evans, M., Hole, R., Berg, L. C., Hutchinson, P., & Sookraj, D. (2009). Common insights, differing methodologies: Toward a fusion of indigenous methodologies, participatory action research, and white studies in an urban aboriginal research agenda. *Qualitative Inquiry, 15,* 893–910.

Evans, S. M. (2002). Re-viewing the second wave. *Feminist Studies, 28,* 259–267.

Felski, R. (1997). The doxa of difference. *Signs, 23,* 1–22.

Few, A. L. (2007). Integrating Black consciousness and critical race feminism into family studies research. *Journal of Family Issues, 28,* 452–473.

Fine, M. (1992). Passions, politics, and power: Feminist research possibilities. In M. Fine (Ed.), *Disruptive voices* (pp. 205–232). Ann Arbor: University of Michigan Press.

Fine, M., Weis, L., Weseem, S., & Wong, L. (2000). For whom? Qualitative research, representations and social responsibilities. In N. K. Denzin & Yvonna S. Lincoln (Eds.), *Handbook of qualitative research* (2nd ed., pp. 107–132). Thousand Oaks, CA: Sage.

Fine, M., & Torre, M. E. (2006). Intimate details. Participatory research in prison. *Action Research, 4,* 253–269.

Fiore, R. N., & Nelson, H. L. (2003). *Recognition, responsibility, and rights: Feminist ethics and social theory.* Boulder, CO: Rowan & Littlefield.

Firdous, A. (2005). Feminist struggles in Bangladesh. *Feminist Review, 80,* 194–197.

Flax, J. (1987). Postmodernism and gender relations in feminist theory. *Signs, 14,* 621–643.

Flax, J. (1990). *Thinking fragments: Psychoanalysis, feminism, and postmodernism in the contemporary West.* Berkeley: University of California Press.

Fonow, M. M., & Cook, J. A. (2005). Feminist methodology: New applications in the academy and public policy. *Signs, 30,* 2211–2236.

Foster, N. (2007). Reinscribing Black women's position within HIV and AIDS discourses. *Feminism and Psychology, 17,* 323–329.

Frankenberg, R. (1994). *White women, race matters: The social construction of whiteness.* Minneapolis: University of Minnesota Press.

Franks, M. (2002). Feminisms and cross ideological feminist social research: Standpoint, situatedness, and positionality: Developing cross-ideological feminist research. *Journal of International Women's Studies, 3.* Available at http://www.bridgew.edu/SoAS/jiws/

Fraser, N. (2005). Mapping the feminist imagination: From redistribution to recognition to representation. *Constellations, 12,* 295–307.

Gannon, S., & Davies, B. (2007). Postmodern, poststructural, and critical theories. In S. N. Hesse-Biber (Ed.), *Handbook of feminist research: Theory and praxis* (pp. 71–106). Thousand Oaks, CA: Sage.

Garcia-Lopez, G. (2008). "*Nunca te toman en cuenta* [They never take you into account]": The challenges of inclusion and strategies for success of Chicana attorneys. In B. T. Dill & R. E. Zambrana (Eds.), *Emerging intersections: Race, class, and gender in theory, policy, and practice* (pp. 22–49). New Brunswick, NJ: Rutgers University Press.

Gardiner, J. K., & Meyer, L. D. (Eds.). (2008a). *Chicana studies* [Special issue] *34*(1),

Gardiner, J. K., & Meyer, L. D., for the editorial collective. (2008b). Preface, Chicana Studies. *Feminist Studies, 34,* 10–22.

Garland-Thomson, R. (2005). Feminist disability studies. *Signs, 30,* 1557–1587.

Glenn, E. N. (2002). *Unequal freedom. How race and gender shaped American citizenship and labor.* Cambridge, MA: Harvard University Press.

Gorelick, S. (1991). Contradictions of feminist methodology. *Gender & Society, 5,* 459–477.

Gray, R., & Sinding, C. (2002). *Standing ovation, Performing social science research about cancer.* Boulder, CO: Rowan & Littlefield.

Green, R. (1990). The Pocahontas perplex: The image of Indian women in American culture. In E. C. DuBois & V. L. Ruiz (Eds.), *Unequal sisters: A multi-cultural reader in U.S. women's history* (pp. 15–21). London: Routledge.

Grewal, I., & Caplan, K. (1994). *Scattered hegemonies: Postmodernity and trans-national practices.* Minneapolis: University of Minnesota Press.

Guevarra, A. (2009). *Marketing dreams, manufacturing heroes: The transnational labor brokering of Filipino workers.* New Brunswick, NJ: Rutgers University Press.

Guilleman, M., & Gillam, L. (2004). Ethics, reflexivity, and "ethically important" moments in research. *Qualitative Inquiry, 10,* 261–280.

Gulcur, L., & Ilkkaracan, P. (2002). The 'Natasha' experience: Migrant sex workers from the former Soviet Union and Eastern Europe in Turkey. *Women's Studies International Forum, 25,* 411–421.

Gupta, J. S. (2006). Toward transnational feminisms: Some reflections and concerns in relation to the globalization of reproductive technologies. *European Journal of Women's Studies, 13,* 23–38.

Halsey, C., & Honey, A. (2005). Unravelling ethics: Illuminating the moral dilemmas of research. *Signs, 30,* 2141–2162.

Hancock, A.-M. (2007a). Intersectionality as a normative and empirical paradigm. *Politics and Gender, 3,* 248–254.

Hancock, A.-M. (2007b). When multiplication doesn't equal quick addition: Examining intersectionality as a research paradigm. *Perspectives on Politics, 5,* 63–78.

Hanochi, S. (2001). Japan and the global sex industry. In R. M. Kelly, J. H. Hayes, M. H. Hawkesworth, & B. Young (Eds.), *Gender, globalization, and democratization.* Lanham, MD: Rowan & Littlefield.

Haraway, D. J. (1991). *Simians, cyborgs, and women. The reinvention of nature.* London: Routledge.

Haraway, D. J. (1997). Modest_witness@second millenium.FemaleMan©_ Meets_On coMouse™. New York: Routledge.

Harding, S. (1987). Conclusion: Epistemological questions. In S. Harding (Ed.), *Feminism and methodology* (pp. 181–90). Bloomington: University of Indiana Press.

Harding, S. (1993). Rethinking standpoint epistemology: What is "strong objectivity?" In L. Alcoff & E. Potter (Eds.), *Feminist epistemologies* (pp. 49–82). New York: Routledge.

Harding, S. (1996). Gendered ways of knowing and the "epistemological crisis" of the West. In N. R. Goldberger, J. M. Tarule, B. M. Clinchy, & M. F. Belenky (Eds.), *Knowledge, difference, and power: Essays inspired by women's ways of knowing* (pp. 431–454). New York: Basic Books.

Harding, S. (1997). Comment on Hekman's "Truth and method: Feminist standpoint theory revisited." *Signs, 22,* 382–391.

Harding, S. (1998). *Is science multicultural? Postcolonialisms, feminisms, and epistemologies.* Bloomington: Indiana University Press.

Harding, S. (2008). *Sciences from below: Feminisms, postcolonialities, and modernities.* Durham, NC: Duke University Press.

Harding, S., & Norberg, K. (2005). New feminist approaches to social science methodologies: An introduction. *Signs, 30,* 2009–2019.

Hartsock, N. (1983). The feminist standpoint: Developing the ground for a specifically feminist historical materialism. In S. Harding & M. B. Hintikka (Eds.), *Discovering reality* (pp. 283–310). Amsterdam: D. Reidel.

Hartsock, N. (1997). Comment on Hekman's "Truth and method: Feminist standpoint theory revisited": Truth or justice? *Signs, 22,* 367–374.

Hawkesworth, M. E. (1987). Feminist epistemology: A survey of the field. *Women and Politics, 7,* 115–127.

Hawkesworth, M. E. (1989). Knowing, knowers, known: Feminist theory and claims of Truth. *Signs, 14,* 553–557.

Hawkesworth, M. E. (1997a). Confounding gender. *Signs, 22,* 649–686.

Hawkesworth, M. E. (1997b). Reply to McKenna and Kessler, Smith, Scott and Connell: Interrogating gender. *Signs, 22,* 707–713.

Hekman, S. (1990). *Gender and knowledge: Elements of a post-modern feminism.* Boston: Northeastern University Press.

Hekman, S. (1997a). Truth and method: Feminist standpoint theory revisited. *Signs, 22,* 341–365.

Hekman, S. (1997b). Reply to Hartsock, Collins, Harding and Smith. *Signs, 22,* 399–402.

Hertz, R. (Ed.). (1997). *Reflexivity and voice.* Thousand Oaks, CA: Sage.

Hesse-Biber, S. N. (2007). Dialoguing about future directions in feminist theory, research, and pedagogy. In S. N. Hesse-Biber (Ed.), *Handbook of feminist research: Theory and praxis* (pp. 535–545). Thousand Oaks, CA: Sage.

Hesse-Biber, S. N., & Piatelli, D. (2007). Holistic reflexivity: The feminist practice of reflexivity. In S. N. Hesse-Biber (Ed.), *Handbook of feminist research: Theory and praxis* (pp. 493–544). Thousand Oaks, CA: Sage.

Higginbotham, E. (2009). Entering a profession: Race, gender, and class in the lives of black women attorneys. In B. T. Dill & R. E. Zambrana (Eds.), *Emerging intersections: Race, class, and gender in theory, policy, and practice* (pp. 22–49). New Brunswick, NJ: Rutgers University Press.

Holman Jones, S. (2005). Autoethnography: Making the personal political. In N. K. Denzin & Y. S. Lincoln (Eds.), *The SAGE handbook of qualitative research* (3rd ed., pp. 763–791). Thousand Oaks, CA: Sage.

hooks, b. (1990). Culture to culture: Ethnography and cultural studies as critical intervention. In b. hooks (Ed.), *Yearning: Race, gender, and cultural politics* (pp. 123–133). Boston: South End Press.

Howard, J. A., & Allen, C. (Eds.). (2000). Women at a millennium [Special issue]. *Signs, 25*(4).

Hurtado, A., & Stewart, A. J. (1997). Through the looking glass: Implications of studying whiteness for feminist methods. In M. Fine, L. Weis, L. C. Powell, & L. M. Wong (Eds.), *Off white: Readings on race, power, and society* (pp. 297–311). New York: Routledge.

Jackson, A. Y. (2003). Rhizovocality. *Qualitative Studies in Education, 16,* 693–710.

Jackson, A. Y. (2009). "What am I doing when I speak of this present?" Voice, power, and desire in truth-telling, In A. Y. Jackson & L. A. Mazzei (Eds.), *Voice in qualitative inquiry: Challenging conventional, interpretive, and critical consequences in qualitative research* (pp. 165–174). New York: Routledge.

Jiwani, Y. (2005). Walking a tightrope: The many faces of violence in the lives of immigrant girls and young women. *Violence Against Women, 11,* 846–875.

Jurik, N. C., & Siemsen, C. (2009). "Doing gender" as canon or agenda: A symposium on West and Zimmerman. *Gender & Society, 23,* 72–75.

Kahn, S, (2005). Reconfiguring the native informant: Positionality in the golden age. *Signs, 30,* 2017–2055.

Katsulis, Y. (2009). *Sex work and the city: The social geography of health and safety in Tijuana, Mexico.* Austin: University of Texas.

Kempadoo, K. (2001). Women of color and the global sex trade: Transnational feminist perspectives. *Meridians: Feminism, Race, Transnationalism, 1,* 28–51.

Kennedy, E. L., & Davis, M. (1993). *Boots of leather, slippers of gold: The history of a lesbian community.* New York: Routledge.

Keough, L. J. (2009). "Driven women": Gendered moral economies of women's migrant labor in postsocialist Europe's peripheries. *Dissertation Abstracts International, Section A: Humanities and Social Sciences, 69*(9-A), p. 3602.

Kim, H. S. (2007). The politics of border crossings: Black, postcolonial, and transnational feminist perspectives. In S. N. Hesse-Biber (Ed.), *Handbook of feminist research: Theory and praxis* (pp. 107–122). Thousand Oaks, CA: Sage.

Kim-Puri, H. J. (2005). Conceptualizing gender-sexuality-state-nation, An introduction. *Gender & Society, 19,* 137–159.

Kincheloe, J. (1997). Fiction formulas: Critical constructivism and the representation of reality. In W. G. Tierney & Y. S. Lincoln (Eds.), *Representation and the text: Reframng the narrative voice* (pp. 57–80). Albany: State University of New York Press.

Kirsch, G. E. (2005). Friendship, friendliness, and feminist fieldwork. *Signs, 30,* 2162–2172.

Klawiter, M. (2008). *The biopolitics of breast cancer: Changing cultures of disease and activism.* Minneapolis: University of Minnesota Press.

Kondo, D. K. (1990). *Crafting selves, power, gender, and discourses of identity in a Japanese workplace.* Chicago: University of Chicago Press.

Kondo, D. K. (1995). Bad girls: Theater, women of color, and the politics of representation. In R. Behar & D. Gordon (Eds.), *Women writing culture* (pp. 49–64). Berkeley: University of California Press.

Kuumba, M. B. (2002). "You've struck a rock": Comparing gender, social movements, and transformation in the United States and South Africa. *Gender & Society, 4,* 504–523.

Lacsamana, A. E. (1999). Colonizing the South: Postmodernism, desire, and agency, *Socialist Review, 27,* 95–106.

Lan, P-C. (2006). *Global Cinderellas: Migrant domestics and newly rich employers in Taiwan.* Durham, NC: Duke University Press.

Laslett, B., & Brenner, B. (2001). Twenty-first academic feminism in the United States: Utopian visions and practical actions. *Signs, 25,* 1231–1236.

Lather, P. (1991). *Getting smart: Feminist research and pedagogy within the postmodern.* New York: Routledge.

Lather, P. (1993). Fertile obsession: Validity after post-structuralism. *The Sociological Quarterly, 34,* 673–694.

Lather, P. (2007). *Getting lost: Feminist efforts toward a double(d) science.* Albany: State University of New York Press.

Lather, P., & Smithies, C. (1997). *Troubling the angels: Women living with AIDS.* Boulder, CO: Westview.

Lewin, L. (1993). *Lesbian mothers.* Ithaca, NY: Cornell University Press.

Lewin, L. (1998). *Recognizing ourselves: Ceremonies of lesbian and gay committment.* New York: Columbia University Press.

Lewin, L. (2009). *Gay fathers: Narratives of family and citizenship.* Chicago: University of Chicago Press.

Lincoln, Y. S. (1993). I and thou: Method, voice, and roles in research with the silenced. In D. McLaughlin & W. G. Tierney (Eds.), *Naming silenced lives: Personal narratives and processes of educational change* (pp. 20–27). New York: Routledge.

Lincoln, Y. S. (1997). Self, subject, audience, text: Living at the edge, writing at the margins. In W. G. Tierney & Y. S. Lincoln (Eds.), *Representation and the text* (pp. 37–55). Albany: State University of New York Press.

Lincoln, Y. S. (2005). Institutional review boards and methodological conservatism: The challenge to and from phenomenological paradigms. In N. K. Denzin & Y. S. Lincoln (Eds.), *The SAGE handbook of qualitative research* (3rd ed., pp. 165–182). Thousand Oaks, CA: Sage.

Lincoln, Y. S., & Guba, E G. (1985). *Naturalistic inquiry.* Beverly Hills, CA: Sage.

Llewelyn, S. (2007). A neutral feminist observer? Observation-based research and the politics of feminist knowledge making. *Gender and Development, 15,* 299–310.

Lorber, J. (1994). *Paradoxes of gender.* New Haven, CT: Yale University Press.

Lubelska, C., & Mathews, J. (1997). Disability issues in the politics and processes of feminist studies. In M. Ang-Lygate, C. Corrin, & M. S. Henry (Eds.), *Desperately seeking sisterhood: Still challenging and building* (pp. 117–137). London: Taylor & Francis.

Luft, R. E., & Ward, J. (2009). Toward an intersectionality just out of reach: Confronting challenges to intersectional practice. *Advances in Gender Research. Special Volume: Intersectionality, 13,* 9–37.

Lykes, M. B. (1989). Dialogue with Guatemalan Indian women: Critical perspectives on constructing collaborative research. In R. Unger (Ed.), *Representations: Social constructions of gender* (pp. 167–184). Amityville, NY: Baywood.

Lykes, M. B. (1994). Whose meeting at which crossroads? A response to Brown and Gilligan. *Feminism and Psychology, 4,* 345–349.

MacLure, M. (2009). Broken voices, dirty words: On the productive insufficiency of voice. In A. Y. Jackson & L. A. Mazzie(Eds.), *Voice in qualitative inquiry: Challenging conventional, interpretive, and critical conceptions in qualitative research* (pp. 98–113). New York: Routledge.

Madison, D. S. (2005). *Critical ethnography: Methods and performance.* Thousand Oaks, CA: Sage.

Madison, D. S. (2006). Staging fieldwork/performing human rights. In D. S. Madison & J. Hameva (Eds.), *The SAGE handbook of performance studies* (pp. 397–418). Thousand Oaks, CA: Sage.

Majumdar, A. (2007). Researching South Asian women's experiences of marriage: Resisting stereotypes through an exploration of "space" and "embodiment." *Feminism and Psychology, 17,* 316–322.

Mamo, L. (2007). *Queering reproduction: Achieving pregnancy in the age of technoscience.* Durham, NC: Duke University Press.

Manning, K. (1997). Authenticity in constructivist inquiry: Methodological considerations without prescription. *Qualitative Inquiry, 3,* 93–116.

Martin, E. (1999). The woman in the flexible body. In A. E. Clarke & V. L. Olesen (Eds.), *Revisioning women, health, and healing: Feminist, cultural, and technoscience perspectives* (pp. 97–118). New York: Routledge.

Mauthner, M., Birch, M., Jessop, J., & Miller, T. (2002). *Ethics in qualitative research.* Thousand Oaks, CA: Sage.

Mauthner, N., & Doucet, A. (1998). Reflections on a voice-centered relational method: Analyzing maternal and domestic voices. In J. Ribbens & R. Edwards (Eds.), *Feminist dilemmas in qualitative research: Public knowledge and private lives* (pp. 119–146). Thousand Oaks, CA: Sage.

Maynard, M. (1994). Race, gender, and the concept of "difference" in feminist thought. In H. Afshar & M. Maynard (Eds.), *The dynamics of "race" and gender: Some feminist interventions* (pp. 9–25). London: Taylor & Francis.

Mazur, A. G. (2002). *Theorizing feminist policy.* Oxford, UK: Oxford University Press.

Mazzei, L. A. (2003). Inhibited silences: In pursuit of a muffled subtext. *Qualitative Inquiry, 9*, 355–366.

Mazzei, L. A. (2004). Silent listenings: Deconstructive practices in discourse-based research. *Educational Researcher, 33*, 26–34.

Mazzei, L. A. (2009). An impossibly full voice. In A. Y. Jackson & L. A. Mazzei (Eds.), *Voice in qualitative inquiry: Challenging conventional, interpretive, and critical concepts in qualitative research* (pp. 45–62). New York: Routledge.

Mazzei, L. A., & Jackson, A. Y. (2009). Introduction: The limit of voice. In A. Y. Jackson & L. A. Mazzei (Eds.), *Voice in qualitative inquiry: Challenging conventional, interpretive, and critical concepts in qualitative research* (pp. 1–13). New York: Routledge.

McCall, L. (2005). The complexity of intersectionality. *Signs, 30*, 1771–1800.

McKenna, W., & Kessler, S. (1997). Comment on Hawkesworth's "Confounding gender": Who needs gender theory? *Signs, 22*, 687–691.

Meekosha, H. (2005). *Body battles: Disability, representation, and participation.* Thousand Oaks, CA: Sage.

Mendez, J. B., & Wolf, C. L. (2007). Feminizing global research/globalizing feminist research. In S. N. Hesse-Biber (Ed.), *Handbook of feminist research: Theory and practice* (pp. 651–662). Thousand Oaks, CA: Sage.

Mendoza, B. (2002). Transnational feminisms in question. *Feminist Theory, 3*, 295–314.

Merlis, S. R., & Linville, D. (2006). Exploring a community's response to Lesbian domestic violence through the voices of providers: A qualitative study. *Journal of Feminist Family Therapy, 18*, 97–136.

Mertens, D. B. (2009). *Transforming research and evaluation.* New York: Guilford.

Messer-Davidow, E. (2002). *Disciplining feminism: From social activism to academic discourse.* Durham, NC: Duke University Press.

Mezey, N. J. (2008). *New choices, new families: How lesbians decide about motherhood.* Baltimore, MD: Johns Hopkins University Press.

Mihesuah, D. A. (2003). *American indigenous women: Decolonization, empowerment, activism.* Lincoln: University of Nebraska Press.

Miller, T., & Bell, L. (2002). Consenting to what? Issues of access, gate-keeping and 'informed' consent." In M. Mauthner, M. Birch, J. Jessop, & T. Miller (Eds.), *Ethics in qualitative research* (pp. 37–54). New York: Routledge.

Mohanty, C. (1988). Under Western eyes: Feminist scholarship and colonial discourses, *Feminist Review, 30*, 60–88.

Mohanty, C. (2003). *Feminism without borders: Decolonizing theory, practicing solidarity.* Durham, NC: Duke University Press.

Moore, M. R. (2008). Gendered power relations among women: A study of household decision making in Black, lesbian stepfamilies. *American Sociological Review, 73*, 335–336.

Morgen, S. (2006). Movement-grounded theory: Intersectional analysis of health inequities in the United States. In A. Schulz & L. Mullings (Eds.), *Race, class, gender, and health* (pp. 394–423). San Francisco: Jossey-Bass.

Morris, M. (1998). *Too soon, too late: History in popular culture.* Bloomington: University of Indiana Press.

Morse, J. (2005). Ethical issues in institutional research, *Qualitative Health Research, 15,* 435–437.

Morse, J. (2006). The politics of evidence, *Qualitative Health Research, 16,* 395–404.

Morse, J. (2007). Ethics in action: Ethical principles for doing qualitative health research, *Qualitative Health Research, 17,* 1003–1005.

Naples, N. A. (1996). A feminist revisiting of the insider/outsider debate: The 'outsider phenomenon' in rural Iowa. *Qualitative Sociology, 19,* 83–106.

Naples, N. A. (2002a). The challenges and possibilities of transnational feminist praxis. In N. A. Naples & M. Desai, M. (Eds.), *Women's activism and globalization: Linking local struggles and transnational politics* (pp. 267–282). New York: Routledge

Naples, N. A. (2002b). Changing the terms: Community activism, globalization, and the dilemmas of traditional feminist praxis. In N. A. Naples& M. Desai (Eds.), *Women's activism and globalization: Linking local struggles and transnational politics* (pp. 3–14). New York: Routledge.

Naples, N. A. (2007). Standpoint epistemology and beyond. In S. N. Hesse-Biber (Ed.), *Handbook of feminist research: Theory and praxis* (pp. 579–589). Thousand Oaks, CA: Sage.

Narayan, U. (1997). *Dislocating cultures: Identities and third world feminism.* New York: Routledge.

Nash, J. C. (2008). Re-thinking intersectionality. *Feminist Review, 89,* 1–15.

O'Leary, C. M. (1997). Counteridentification or counterhegemony? Transforming feminist theory. In S. J. Kenney & H. Kinsella (Eds.), *Politics and standpoint theories* (pp. 45–72). New York: Haworth Press.

Olesen, V. L. (1975). Rage is not enough: Scholarly feminism and research in women's health. In V. L. Olesen (Ed.), *Women and their health: Research implications for a new era* (DHEW Publication No. HRA-3138, pp. 1–2). Washington, DC: U.S. Department of Health, Education and Welfare, Public Health Service.

Olesen, V. L. (2005). Early millennial feminist qualitative research: Challenges and contours. In N. K. Denzin & Y. S. Lincoln (Eds.), *The SAGE handbook of qualitative Research* (3rd ed., pp. 235–278). Thousand Oaks, CA: Sage.

Olesen, V. L., & Clarke, A. E. (1999). Resisting closure, embracing uncertainties, creating agendas. In A. E. Clarke and V. L. Olesen (Eds.), *Revisioning women, health and healing: Feminist, cultural studies and technoscience perspectives (355–357).* New York:Routledge.

Ong, A. (1995). Women out of China: Traveling tales and traveling theories in postcolonial feminism. In R. Behar & D. Gordon (Eds.), *Women writing culture* (pp. 350–372). Berkeley: University of California Press.

Parrenas, R. S. (2008). *The force of domesticity: Filipina migrants and globalization.* New York: New York University Press.

Petersen, A. (2006). An African-American woman with disabilities: The intersection of gender, race and disability. *Disability and Society, 21,* 721–734.

Phoenix, A. (1994). Practicing feminist research: The intersection of gender and "race" in the research process. In M. Maynard & J. Purvis (Eds.), *Researching women's lives from a feminist perspective* (pp. 35–45). London: Taylor & Francis.

Phoenix, A., & Pettynama, P. (2006). Intersectionality [Special issue]. *European Journal of Women's Studies, 13*(3).

Pillow, W. S. (2003). Confession, catharsis, or cure. The use of reflexivity as methodological power in qualitative research. *International Journal of Qualitative Studies in Education, 16,* 175–196.

Preissle, J. (2007). Feminist research ethics. In S. N. Hesse-Biber (Ed.), *Handbook of feminist research: Theory and praxis* (pp. 515–534). Thousand Oaks, CA: Sage.

Priyadharshini, E. (2003). Coming unstuck: Thinking otherwise about "studying up." *Anthropology and Education Quarterly, 34,* 420–437.

Prins, B. (2006). Narrative accounts of origins: A blind spot in the intersectional approach? *European Journal of Women's Studies, 13,* 277–290.

Puar, J. K. (1996). Resituating discourses of "Whiteness" and "Asianness" in northern England: Second-generation Sikh women and constructions of identity. In M. Maynard & J. Purvis (Eds.), *New frontiers in women's studies* (pp. 125–150). London: Taylor & Francis.

Randall, M. (2004). Know your place: The activist scholar in today's political culture. *SWS Network News, 21,* 20–23.

Rapp, R. (1999). *Testing women, testing the foetus: The social impact of amnio-centesis in America.* New York: Routledge.

Reid, C., Tom, A., & Frisby, W. (2008). Finding the "action" in feminist participatory research. *Action Research, 4,* 315–322.

Renzetti, C (2005). Editor's introduction. *Violence Against Women, 11,* 839–841.

Rice, C. (2009). Imagining the other? Ethical challenges of researching and writing women's embodied lives. *Feminism & Psychology, 19*(2), 245–266.

Richardson, L. (1993). Poetics, dramatics, and transgressive validity: The case of the skipped line. *The Sociological Quarterly, 34,* 695–710.

Richardson, L. (1997). *Fields of play: Constructing an academic life.* New Brunswick, NJ: Rutgers University Press.

Richardson, L. (2000). Introduction: Assessing alternative modes of qualitative and ethnographic research: How do we judge? Who judges? *Qualitative Inquiry, 6,* 251–252.

Risman, B. (2004). Gender as a social structure: Theory wrestling with activism, *Gender & Society, 18,* 429–450.

Rohrer, J. (2005). Toward a full-inclusion feminism: A feminist deployment of disability analysis. *Feminist Studies, 31,* 34–63.

Rupp, L. J., & Taylor, V. (2003). *Drag queens at the 801 cabaret.* Chicago: University of Chicago Press.

Saavedra, C. M., & Nymark, E. D. (2008). Borderland-Mestija feminism, The new tribalism. In N. K. Denzin, Y. S. Lincoln, & L. T. Smith (Eds.), *Handbook of critical and indigenous methodologies* (pp. 255–276). Thousand Oaks, CA: Sage.

Scheper-Hughes, N. (1983). Introduction: The problem of bias in androcentric and feminist anthropology. *Women's Studies,19,* 109–116.

Scheurich, J. J., & Foley, D. (Eds.). (1997). Feminist poststructuralism [Special issue]. *International Journal of Qualitative Studies in Education, 10*(3).

Scott, J. (1991). The evidence of experience. *Critical Inquiry, 17,* 773–779.

Scott, J. (1997). Comment on Hawkesworth's "Confounding Gender." *Signs, 22,* 697–702.

Schulz, A., & Mullings, L. (Eds.). (2006). *Race, class, gender, and health.* San Francisco: Jossey-Bass.

Segura, D. A., & Zavella, P. (2008). Introduction: Gendered borderlands. *Gender & Society, 22,* 537–544.

Seigfried, C. H. (1996). *Pragmatism and feminism: Reweaving the social fabric.* Chicago: University of Chicago Press.

Shields, S. A. (2008). Gender: An intersectionality perspective. *Sex Roles, 59,* 301–311.

Shim, J. K. (2000). Bio-power and racial, class, and gender formation in biomedical Knowledge production. In J. J. Kronenefield (Ed.), *Research in the sociology of health care* (pp. 173–95). Stamford, CT: JAI Press.

Skeggs, B. (1994). Situating the production of feminist ethnography. In M. Maynard & J. Purvis (Eds.), *Researching women's lives from a feminist perspective* (pp. 72–92). London: Taylor & Francis.

Smith, D. E. (1987). *The everyday world as problematic.* Boston: Northeastern University Press.

Smith, D. E. (1992). Sociology from women's experience: A reaffirmation. *Sociological Theory, 10,* 88–98.

Smith, D. E. (1993). High noon in textland: A critique of Clough. *The Sociological Quarterly, 34,* 183–192.

Smith, D. E. (1997). Telling the truth after postmodernism. *Symbolic Interaction, 19,* 171–202.

Smith, D. E. (2005). *Institutional ethnography: A sociology for people.* Walnut Creek, CA: AltaMira Press.

Smith, D. E. (2006). *Institutional ethnography as practice.* Lanham, MD: Rowan & Littlefield.

Smith, D. E. (2009). Categories are not enough. *Gender & Society, 23,* 76–80.

Smith, L. T. (1999). *Decolonizing methodologies: Research and indigenous peoples.* London: Zed Books.

Smith L. T. (2005). On tricky ground: Researching the native in an age of uncertainty. In N. K. Denzin & Y. S. Lincoln (Eds.), *The SAGE handbook of qualitative research* (3rd ed., pp. 85–107). Thousand Oaks, CA: Sage.

Smith, S. G. (1997). Comment on Hawkesworth's "Confounding Gender." *Signs, 22,* 691–697.

Spivak, G. C. (1988). Subaltern studies: Deconstructing historiography. In G. C. Spivak, *In other worlds: Essays in cultural politics* (pp. 197–221). London: Routledge.

Stacey, J. (1988). Can there be a feminist ethnography? *Women's Studies International Forum, 11,* 21–27.

Stacey, J. (1998*). Brave new families: Stories of domestic upheaval in late twentieth century America.* Berkeley: University of California Press.

Stacey, J. (2003). Taking feminist sociology public can prove less progressive than you wish. *SWS Network News, 20,* 27–28.

Standing, K. (1998). Writing the voices of the less powerful. In J. Ribbens & R. Edwards (Eds.), *Feminist dilemmas in qualitative research: Public knowledge and private lives* (pp. 186–202). Thousand Oaks, CA: Sage.

Stewart, A. J., & McDermott, C. (2004). Gender in psychology. *Annual Review of Psychology, 55,* 519–544.

Stout, N. M. (2008). Feminists, queers, and critics: Debating the Cuban sex trade. *Journal of Latin American Studies, 40,* 721–742.

St.Pierre, E. A. (1997a). Guest editorial: An introduction to figurations—a post-structural practice of inquiry. *International Journal of Qualitative Studies in Education, 19,* 279–284.

St.Pierre, E. A. (1997b). Methodology in the fold and the irruption of transgressive data. *International Journal of Qualitative Studies in Education, 19,* 175–179.

St.Pierre, E. A. (2009). Afterword: Decentering voice in qualitative inquiry. In Y. Jackson & L. A. Mazzei (Eds.), *Voice in qualitative inquiry: Challenging conventional, interpretive, and critical conceptions in qualitative research* (pp. 221–236). New York: Routledge.

Tellez, M. (2008). Community of struggle: Gender, violence, and resistance on the U.S./ Mexican border. *Gender & Society, 22,* 545–567.

Thapar-Bjorkert, S., & Henry, M. (2004). Reassessing the research relationship: Location, position, and power in fieldwork accounts. *International Journal of Research Methodology, 7,* 363–381.

Thayer, M. (2001). Transnational feminism: Reading Joan Scott in the Brazilian Sertao. *Ethnography, 2,* 243–271.

Tregaskis, C., & Goodley, D. (2005). Disability research by disabled and non-disabled people: Towards a relational methdology of research production. *International Journal of Social Research Methodology, 8,* 363–374.

Trinh, T. M-ha. (1989). *Woman, native, other: Writing post-coloniality and feminism.* Bloomington: University of Indiana Press.

Trinh, T. M-ha. (1992). *Framer framed.* New York: Routledge.

Valentine, K. B. (2006). Unlocking the doors for incarcerated women through performance and creating writing. In D. S. Madison & J. Hameva (Eds.), *The SAGE handbook of performance studies* (pp. 309–324). Thousand Oaks, CA: Sage.

Warner, L. R. (2008). A best practices guide to intersectional approaches in psychological research. *Sex Roles, 59,* 454–463.

Weber, L. (2007). Future directions of feminist research: New directions in social policy—the case of women's health. In S. N. Hesse-Biber (Ed.), *Handbook of feminist research: Theory and praxis* (pp. 669–679). Thousand Oaks, CA: Sage.

Weeks, K. (2004). Labor, standpoints, and feminist subjects. In S. G. Harding (Ed.), *The feminist standpoint theory reader* (pp. 181–195). New York: Routledge.

Welton, K. (1997). Nancy Hartsock's standpoint theory: From content to "concrete multiplicity." In S. J. Kenney & H. Kinsella (Eds.), *Politics and feminist standpoint theories* (pp. 7–24). New York: Haworth Press.

West, C., & Zimmerman, D. (1987). Doing gender. *Gender & Society, 1,* 125–151.

Weston, K. (1991). *Families we chose: Lesbians, gays, kinship.* New York: Columbia.

Williams, B. (1996). Skinfolk, not kinfolk: Comparative reflections on identity and participant observation in two field situations. In D. Wolf (Ed.), *Feminist dilemmas in field work* (pp. 72–95). Boulder, CO: Westview Press.

Wolf, D. (1996). *Feminist dilemmas in fieldwork*. Boulder, CO: Westview Press.

Wolf, M. (1992). *A thrice-told tale. Feminism, postmodernism, and ethnographic responsibility*. Stanford, CA: Stanford University Press.

Yuval-Davis, N. (2006). Intersectionality and feminist politics. *European Journal of Women's Studies, 13,* 193–209.

Zavella, P. (1996). Feminist insider dilemmas: Constructing ethnic identity with Chicana informants. In D. Wolf (Ed.), *Feminist dilemmas in field work* (pp. 138–159). Boulder, CO: Westview Press.

Zimmerman, M. K., Litt, J. S., & Bose, C. E. (2006). *Global dimensions of gender and care-work*. Stanford, CA: Stanford University Press.

8

The Sacred and Spiritual Nature of Endarkened Transnational Feminist Praxis in Qualitative Research[1]

Cynthia B. Dillard and Chinwe Okpalaoka

I. Sankofa (Go Back to Fetch It)[2]

History is sacred because it is the only chance that you have of knowing who you are outside of what's been rained down upon you from a hostile environment. And when you go to the documents created inside the culture, you get another story. You get another history. The history is sacred and the highest, most hallowed songs in tones are pulled into service to deliver that story (Latta, 1992).

REVISITING "PARADIGMS"

Several years ago, responding to James J. Scheurich and Michelle D. Young's (1997) *Educational Researcher* article, a number of researchers presented sessions at national meetings, wrote papers, and responded to the challenge inherent in Scheurich and Young's rather provocative title, "Coloring Epistemologies: Are

Our Research Epistemologies Racially Biased?"[3] Among other writings, Cynthia Dillard's (2006a) modest contribution to this paradigm talk became a chapter in her book, *On Spiritual Strivings: Transforming an African American Woman's Academic Life*. In this chapter, as in the aforementioned discussions, she explored the cultural, political, and spiritual nature of the entire conversation about paradigms and the way that the swirling assumptions and conclusions about their proliferation were mostly carried out at a level of abstraction (and distraction), absent any examination of the ways that racism, power, and politics profoundly shape our research and representations, especially as scholars of color. She spoke to how such exclusion

> brings a particularized paradox for scholars of color as we seek to imagine, create and embrace new and useful paradigms from and through which we engage educational research . . . [as] there are deep and serious implications in choosing to embrace paradigms that resonate with our spirit as well as our intellect, regardless of issues of "proliferation" (Dillard, 2006a, pp. 29–30).

She raised up the all too common absence of Black voices and voices of scholars of color in the discussions of the meanings and outcomes of the "coloring" of epistemologies, a discussion that had been carried out as if we did not exist as subjects within the conversation but solely as objects of it, invisible, silent. However well intentioned this discussion may have been, Black people and our thoughts about paradigms were the focus of the steady and often distorted gaze and descriptions of White researchers.

The part of the discussion that still resonates with Dillard most deeply today—and with many students of qualitative research—is the call for scholars of color to turn our attention and desires away from "belonging" to a particular paradigm (or even to the discussion of paradigm proliferation that still often swirls around us but does not include us), but instead to construct and nurture paradigms that encompass and embody our cultural and spiritual understandings and histories and that shape our epistemologies and ways of being.

We see evidence of the same call echoed throughout the literature on qualitative research. Gloria Ladson-Billings's (2000) handbook chapter, "Racialized Discourses and Ethnic Epistemologies," contrasts the concept of individualism and the elevation of the individual mind prevalent in Western thought with the African notion of *Ubuntu* (I am because we are). This notion of individual well-being that is predicated on the wholeness of the community speaks to the same spiritual and epistemological stance of endarkened feminist epistemology. Ladson-Billings's reference to the necessity of using different discourses and epistemologies, ones that can disrupt Western epistemological discourse and the dominant worldview, can be interpreted as an echo of an endarkened transnational feminism, whose notions of the sacred and the spiritual in research disrupts the Western tendency to bifurcate the mind and the spirit. Furthermore, she suggests that we must research and better understand "well developed systems of knowledge . . . that stand in contrast to the dominant Euro-American epistemology" (p. 258) in order to address the critical questions of the world today. While critical race theory is the framework used by Ladson-Billings and Donner (2005), like the endarkened transnational epistemologies put forward in this chapter, it is part of a larger effort by scholars of color and of conscience to address the ravages of racism and other discriminations and to create a space of freedom for all humanity. It is important also to note that a major revision in Virginia Olesen's Chapter 7 on feminism in this volume included an entirely new overview of endarkened, decolonizing, and indigenous feminist qualitative research and the weighty recognition of the breadth of discourses of feminisms that must be strategically used at this moment. Hence, the need for our exploration of endarkened and transnational feminisms here is an extension of the same need that encouraged Norman Denzin, Yvonna Lincoln, and Linda Tuhiwai Smith to edit the extant *Handbook of Critical and Indigenous Methodologies* (HCIM) (2008). Central to HCIM is the embrace of indigenous and critical research epistemologies that foreground spirituality, including feminist, native, indigenous, endarkened and Black feminist, spiritual, hybrid, Chicana, and border/*mestizaje* among others (see chapters by Cannella & Manuelito, 2008; Dillard, 2008; Meyer, 2008; Saavedra & Nymark, 2008, for examples).

We see in these works gestures toward the sacred nature of science, an idea that Peter Reason (1993) forwarded more than a decade ago. In this work, his call is for researchers to consider how spirituality and the sacred can be brought to bear on pressing human and environmental problems. This chapter is a response to Reason's call. Our attempt here is to examine the complexities of Black and endarkened feminisms and epistemologies, which link the continent of Africa and the African diaspora, bringing discourses of the spiritual and the sacred to bear in this discussion in a way that is fundamental. We also recognize a discussion that is still missing in our examinations of multiple epistemologies and theories of research.

So, this Handbook chapter emerges from a paradigm and worldview that is spirit filled, endarkened, and centered in Blackness and international womanhood. However, with the publication of *On Spiritual Strivings* (2006a), and the global reaction to it, Dillard found herself (echoed by her students) wondering more deeply about the way that knowledge travels and moves in the world, enlarging and engaging the discussions and constructions of what it means to be a Black woman (and thus, what it will mean for *us,* as Black women scholars). As the work continued to travel, new opportunities for dialogue and cooperation also arose, including one with the coauthor of this chapter, Chinwe Okpalaoka, who ascends from Nigeria. As sister scholars, we have begun to recognize not just the spiritual but the *sacred* nature of research that African ascendant women have always done and are continuing to do all over the globe. We believe it is the same sacred and divine energy that has brought us together in this writing.

Some definitions of key terms may be important here. An *endarkened feminist epistemology* (Dillard, 2000, 2006a, 2006b) articulates how reality is known when based in the historical roots of global Black feminist thought. More specifically, such an epistemology embodies a distinguishable difference in cultural stand-point from mainstream (White) feminism in that it is located in the intersection or overlap of the culturally constructed notions of race, gender, class, and national and other identities. Maybe most important, it arises from and informs the historical and contemporary contexts of oppressions and resistance for African ascendant women. From an endarkened feminist epistemological space, we are encouraged to move away from the traditional metaphor of research as recipe to fix a "problem" to a metaphor that centers on reciprocity and relationship between the researcher and the researched, between knowing and the production of knowledge. Thus, Dillard (2000, 2006b) suggests that a more useful metaphor of research from an endarkened feminist epistemological stance is *research as a responsibility,* answerable and obligated to the very people and communities being engaged in the inquiry.

Our use of the term *transnational* is a literal one. We are simply meaning a way of looking at endarkened feminism that is beyond or through (*trans*) the boundaries of nations. But we also believe that such a look brings to bear the possibility of a *change* in our viewpoints as well.

An endarkened feminist epistemology is also an approach to research that honors the wisdom, spirituality, and critical interventions of transnational Black woman's ways of knowing and being in research, with the sacred serving as a way to describe the doing of it, the way that we approach the work. Noting the distinction between spirituality and the sacred is important here. What we mean by *spirituality* is to have a consciousness of the realm of the spirit in one's work and to recognize that consciousness as a transformative force in research and teaching (Alexander, 2005; Dillard, 2006a; Dillard, Tyson, & Abdur-Rashid, 2000; Fernandes, 2003; hooks, 1994; Hull, 2001; Moraga & Anzaldúa, 1981; Ryan, 2005; Wade-Gayles, 1995). However, when we speak of the *sacred* in endarkened feminist its research, we are referring to *the way the work is honored and embraced as it carried out.* Said another way, work that is sacred is worthy of being held with *reverence* as it is done. The idea here is that, as we consider paradigms and epistemology from endarkened or Black feminist positions, the work embodies and engages spirituality and is carried out in sacred ways. Thus, we are using the notions of both spirituality and sacredness to explore more globally the meanings, articulations, and possibilities of an endarkened feminist epistemology and research as sacred, spiritual, and relevant practices of inquiry for Black women on the continent of Africa and throughout her diaspora. Mostly, we are suggesting that both spirituality and the sacred are embedded fundamentally in the very ground of inquiry, knowledge, and cultural production of Black women's lives and experiences and that it is this understanding that helps us to understand the radical activism of Black feminism transnationally. However, as we look back to the earlier articulations of the cultural and spiritual nature and work of paradigms for scholars of color, what is missing is an explicit attention to the epistemologies of Black or endarkened feminism in an interconnected, intersubjective, and transnational way that renders *visible* the work of research as *sacred* work, centered in the spiritual notions constructed by Black women on the continent and in the diaspora.

Whether in the United States, Africa, or elsewhere in the African diaspora, women of African ascent share experiences with some form of oppression characterized and related by our class, race, or gender, by our existence as women. And often, it is some version of or belief in spirit that has allowed us to stand in the face of hostility and degradation, however severe (Akyeampong & Obeng, 2005; Alexander, 2005; Dillard, 2006a, 2006b; hooks, 1994; Hull, 2001; Keating, 2008; Moraga & Anzaldúa, 1981; Walker, 2006). Most arguments that have arisen around similarities and differences in transnational Black women's experience with interlocking oppressions have focused on whether there exists a hierarchy of oppressions for women on the African continent versus in the African diaspora and the issue of appropriate naming of the struggle (Hudson-Weems, 1998b; Nnaemeka, 1998; Steady, 1981; Walker, 1983). This is a discussion we take up later in this chapter.

However, such ground leads us to several questions that guide our examination here. What are the contours of Black or endarkened feminist epistemology and paradigms that emerge from African women's voices and spirits transnationally? What are the tensions, the cultural and historical experiences, diversities, nuances, and relationships that have created visions and versions of Black women's thinking, theorizing, and praxis that include or exclude Black feminism, Africana womanism, and other theoretical frameworks for Black women's thinking and being with and against one another? Where is spirituality in these global discussions, and how does it matter to the work of research? To its methods, methodologies, and representations? Most important, we seek to further explore the profound question—and the equally profound response—put forth by M. Jacqui Alexander (2005) in her groundbreaking work, *Pedagogies of Crossings: Meditations on Feminism, Sexual Politics, Memory, and the sacred*:

> What would taking the Sacred seriously mean for transnational feminism and related radical projects beyond an institutionalized use value of theorizing marginalization? *It would mean wrestling with the praxis of the Sacred.* (p. 326, emphasis added)

Taking the sacred seriously means exploring and creating sacred versions and approaches to research and a critical re-visioning of the very meanings of Black feminist inquiry and paradigms. It means taking up spirituality and the sacred as a place "from which to launch a critique of the status quo" (Wright, 2003, p. 209) from a Black-eyed female gaze.

II. Nyame Nti (Since God Exists)

Spirituality as Necessity: Exploring the Cultural and Historical Landscape of Endarkened/Black Feminist Perspectives of Research in Africa and the Diaspora

> *Everything we engage in our lives is primarily a practice ordered by spirit, or authorized by spirit and executed by someone who recognizes that [she] cannot, by herself, make happen what she has been invited towards (Some, 1994).*

The concepts of intersecting oppressions and domination, although universal in practice, take on varying forms of expression from one society to another (Collins, 2000). Patricia Hill Collins further suggests that the shape of domination changes as it takes on specific forms across temporal, historical, and geographical contexts. The key difference lies in the organization of particular oppressions. Said another way, although contexts of domination might be similar across the globe (in that there is some combination of interlocking systems of oppression), the differences arise in the ways these particular oppressions manifest and the historical roots of said oppressions. The type of clothing that oppression is dressed in (that is, apartheid, colonialism, imperialism, enslavement) may vary. However, they are all systems of oppression, intersecting in various combinations and contexts. Ultimately, Collins (2000) suggests that it is fundamentally about whose knowledge and agenda are front, center, and definitive. However, to think about and work through the differences across the continent and diaspora, we must find our "common agenda," a *transnational* Black feminism.

Collins (2000) was not alone in her clarion call for a transnational Black feminism to confront intersecting oppressions of race, class, gender, and sexuality across the globe. She was joined by many, including Obioma Nnaemeka (1998), a groundbreaking Black feminist scholar from Nigeria. Yet, a closer look at the historically and sociological manifestations of oppression and domination of endarkened or Black feminist thought in the African diaspora reveals a sort of dynamism, a constantly changing nature of oppressions for African ascendant women, very particularly within and across national contexts. For example, although interlocking oppressions of race, class, gender, and sexuality characterize Black women's experiences in parts of the African diaspora, the particular oppression that dominates might differ from one geographical and national context to another. Nnaemeka (1998) speaks of multiple feminisms within the countries of Africa and even between Africa and other continents as an indication of multiplicity of perspectives. She further explains that the multiplicity of perspectives must include cultural and historical forces that have fueled women's movements in Africa. Nnaemeka describes the African feminist spirit as both "complex and diffused" (p. 5):

> The much bandied-about intersection of class, race, sexual orientation, etc., in Western feminist discourse does not ring with the same urgency for most African women, for whom other basic issues of everyday life are intersecting in most oppressive ways. This is not to say that issues of race and class are not important to African women in the continent . . . African women see and address such issues first as they configure in and relate to their own lives and immediate surroundings. (p. 7)

Collins (2000) urges us to think globally when we consider the shared legacy of struggle and oppressions and remember that the experiences of women of African ascent have been shaped by varying forms of domination including slavery and colonialism. The oppression of continental African women cannot be isolated from the persistent consequences of colonialism. In other words, as Nnaemeka (1998) frames it, "to meaningfully explain . . . African feminism, it is . . . to the African environment that one must refer" (p. 9). Likewise, the oppressions of African ascendant women in the diaspora cannot be isolated from the persistent consequences of centuries of enslavement. It is noteworthy that the 1960s were turbulent times for African ascendant people on the continent in the fight for independence and for those in the diaspora engaged in various civil rights movements. While the former fought to gain independence from colonial rulers, the latter marched for the rights of Black Americans, women, the disabled, and other marginalized groups.

We believe that a brief historical look at the roots of Black feminism in the United States and on the continent of Africa may help situate Black women's experiences with oppression on the globe, the ground from which interventions and transformations of research must arise. While we begin this discussion with a brief history of Black feminism, we do not believe that U.S. Black feminism marked the beginning of feminism for women of color all over the world. In fact, there are ongoing critiques of U.S (and European) Black feminisms and the dangers of the cultural hegemony throughout the world, particularly from continental African feminist scholars.[4] Instead, we begin here because of the important role U.S. Black feminism continues to play in global discussions on Black women's experiences with oppression. While the holistic nature of interlocking systems of oppression has not been particular to U.S. Black feminists, it has provided the stage for reconceptualizing new relationships within and between African women's spirits and experiences in the diaspora and the African continent and for shaping research paradigms and methodology as well. And while Black feminists in the U.S. context may have strong understandings of our experiences and struggles as African ascendant women in the United States, we often know precious little of the experiences and struggles of African ascendant women throughout the diaspora and on the continent of Africa.

Given our positionalities, the authors attempt to situate our experiential knowings into this historical survey, speaking directly to the material ways that these histories were experienced and are enacted in our lives: Dillard speaking primarily to experiences with Black feminism in the United States and Okpala-oka speaking primarily to her experiences with Black feminism in Nigeria. This is our attempt to bring our herstories to bear across the globe in ways that allow us to create paradigms across our differences "that resonate with our spirit as well as our intellect, regardless of issues of proliferation" (Dillard, 2006a, p. 29–30) and that highlight the sacred and spiritual embodiment of the praise-song that is our story as Black women everywhere.

U.S. Black Feminism in Brief

BY CYNTHIA DILLARD

I remember being very powerfully influenced by the image of Angela Davis in the 1970s. And it wasn't simply the perfect afro that framed her face like a crown that moved me: It was the powerful sound of her voice as she talked about freedom and truth and Black women's struggles in the United States and beyond. I remember my own desires to be a part of the Black Panther Party, but I wasn't quite of age. However, when I saw those brothers (and an occasional sister) walking into my former elementary school to serve lunches to children who needed them most, that act was transformational for me. I realized in that moment that whatever "Black power" meant, it included the commitment to knowing our history, enacting our culture with spirit, and engaging in social and sacred action on behalf of Black people, especially the young and those most needy.

While my parents were involved with more mainstream Black organizations (the Links and Omega Psi Phi), I became more interested in what they deemed the more "radical" Black organizations. And I was especially interested in the places where Black *women* were organizing, marching, making their voices heard. The National Black Feminist Organization (NBFO) was one of the first Black feminist organizations with an explicit commitment to confronting the interlocking systems of racism, sexism, and heterosexism that plagued Black women in the United States. Emerging in 1973, the organization was also a forceful response to the lack of attention and regard for Black women's experiences within both the women's movement and within Black power movements witnessed above (Hull, Bell-Scott, & Smith, 1982; Wallace, 1982). By 1974, a spin-off group of U.S. Black feminists formed the Combahee River Collective, focusing on a more radical commitment to the oppressions that Black women still faced in the United States. The mission of this group of women, in comparison to the NBFO's, was to confront these complex systems of oppression through a Black feminist *political movement* (Combahee River Collective, 1982). Rather than project themselves as "firsts" or as pioneers of Black feminism, the collective's members historically acknowledged their work as an extension of the earlier work of Black women activists like Sojourner Truth, Harriet Tubman, Frances E. W. Harper, Ida B. Wells Barnett, and Mary Church Terrell, whose intellectual and activist work flourished during the antislavery era (Combahee River Collective, 1982). There was also a very strong commitment to spiritually center the work of the Combahee River Collective, both in the sacred approach to seeing and acknowledging the above Black women ancestors and in setting a purpose and vision that sought to transform the social and political milieu away from oppression and toward equality and justice, particularly for U.S. Black women.

By the early 1970s, we witnessed a critical intervention of theorizing and knowledge production, as Black feminist literature (including anthologies and fiction) began to be published and find their way to bookstores and bookshelves, both in the U.S. and abroad. This was not simply publishing as an economic intervention in the lives and knowledges of Black women: This was a radical intervention, as these literatures fundamentally shifted and shaped the foundations of Black feminist thought and actions. Toni Cade Bambara's *The Black Woman: An Anthology* (1970), Toni Morrison's *The Bluest Eye* (1970), Audre Lorde's *Cables to Rage* (1970), Alice Walker's *In Search of Our Mothers' Gardens: Womanist Prose* (1983), and a reissue of Zora Neale Hurston's *Their Eyes Were Watching God* (1978) are examples of landmark literary texts that defined and theorized the early Black feminist movement in the United States. As an adolescent African American girl, I felt these early works profoundly, as I sought desperately to define what it meant to be both Black and female in the predominately White schooling contexts of my youth. All of the texts we were required to read centered images of White womanhood as virtuous and worthy of emulation. Louisa May Alcott's *Little Women* was the standard by which we were asked to aspire, and watching "The Brady Bunch" was the free time text of the day. But my mother's version of Black womanhood (albeit similarly tethered to homemaking and child rearing as Mrs. Brady) was tied to a simple and explicit truth, manifest in her strict attention to our school lives, homework, and consistent trips to the public library: Education and learning to read the word and the world were the *only* ways to create options for Black women's lives. In her precious free time, my mother read these texts along with me, opening me to a world that in some cases highlighted the harsh realities of her own life as a Black woman, growing up in poverty and during segregation in the United States. In other cases, these words on the page opened something that could exist only in her imagination and our own but that always also existed as *possibilities*. These texts also stirred significant debates and controversies *within* the Black community, especially for Black men, who often resented what they interpreted as direct accusations that they were perpetrators of gender and sexual oppression. Regardless of the consequences, my Mom and I continued to read every story of Black womanhood we could. And I learned how powerful words could be: Black women's literature helped define ourselves for ourselves, and as an oral tradition, it goes back generations. Now, through the voices of Walker, Hurston, and others, as well as the words on the page, we could *see* our definitions and return to them over and over again.

The 1980s brought more radical overtly political texts, responding in part to the birth of woman's studies and specifically Black women's thought and knowledge production "in public." We came to know, through their writings, major Black feminist scholars *and* activists like Gloria (Akasha) Hull, Barbara Smith, and Patricia Bell-Scott, whose co-edited text (Hull, Bell-Scott, & Smith, 1982), *All the Women Are White, All the Blacks Are Men, But Some of Us Are Brave*, became a pioneering text for Black feminist studies across the United States. This relative proliferation of Black feminist writing in the 1980s also included works like Barbara Smith's *Home Girls: A Black Feminist Anthology* (1983) and bell hooks's (1981) *Ain't I a Woman: Black Women and Feminism,* which focused on the impact of sexism on Black women. But these women also began to bring questions and concerns of sexual identities and spirituality within Black feminism to the forefront. Lorde's *Sister Outsider* (1984) spoke directly to the need for integration and wholeness in Black women's multifaceted identities, including our sexualities. Paule Marshall's *Praisesong for the Widow* (1984) brought to the fore the ways that remembering culture and history as a Black woman is truly a transformative act, particularly from a spiritual perspective.

Cherie Moraga and Gloria Anzaldúa's *This Bridge Called My Back: Radical Writings by Women of Color* (1981) was one of the earliest attempts to link the underlying oppressions of women across differences of race, class, sexuality, and culture. Equally important, Anzaldúa brought the scholarship and voices of women of color together in an edited volume that began to speak explicitly about the importance of spirituality, healing, and self-recovery as necessities for women of color across our ethnicities and identities.

The proliferation of scholarship of the 1990s and beyond picked up Anzaldúa's call to recognize the sacred and spiritual ethos of Black and endarkened feminisms. From hooks's (1993) *Sisters of the Yam: Black Women and Self-Recovery* and Bambara's *The Salt Eaters* (1992) to Collins's (1990) landmark, *Black Feminist Thought: Knowledge, Consciousness, and the Politics of Empowerment,* which literally transformed our understandings of gender, race, and class, centering it firmly in the epistemologies and theories of Black womanhood. It is interesting to note that one of the most radical revisions in Collins's second edition of *Black Feminist Thought* (2000) was her explorations of the limits of a Black feminism bounded by nations: The revisions provided direction for how to place U.S. Black feminist thought into coalition with the voices and efforts of African ascendant women worldwide. And whether on the continent of Africa, in the United States, or all of the spaces between, around, and among them both, I see that the creation of Black feminism in the United States is only a part of a living, breathing legacy. As Pearl Cleage (2005) suggests, Black/endarkened feminist thought is *itself* a praise song:

the flesh and blood of our collective dreaming,

[through which] we realize with a knowing deeper than the flow of human blood in human veins

that we are part of something *better, truer, deeper.* (p. 15)

At least part of the "better, truer, deeper" is found in the connections between the Black feminism in the United States and efforts of African feminists on the continent, toward which we now turn.

Black Feminism in Africa in Brief

BY CHINWE OKPALAOKA

While the struggle of U.S. Black feminists in the 1960s included the fight for the rights of women and people of color, Africans on the continent of Africa witnessed a decade that ushered in the end of colonial rule in many African nations. As former colonizers retreated to their countries of origin, newly formed African nations began what has and continues to be an arduous and complicated journey toward independence. Oyeronke Oyewumi (1997) asserts that colonization should not be understood solely in the context of the period of the actual colonization. For many, she suggests, the period of the Atlantic slave trade and colonization "were logically *one* process unfolding over many centuries" (p. xi, emphasis added). This argument is critical to understanding the spiritual connection between African women on the continent and throughout the diaspora, in our knowledge production and in praxis. And as Dillard (2006a) asserts, these connections are *always* present, whether we are conscious of them or not. It is an understanding and embrace of this connection that drew me to Dillard shortly after our first meeting. Soon after I began my doctoral studies, I was introduced to the histories of African Americans and theories about their lived experiences. As Oyewumi (1997) argues above, I quickly identified a connection between me (as "representative" of the sister who never left the continent) and my African American sister ("representative" of those who were enslaved and taken from the continent of Africa). My dilemma, then, was how to gain legitimacy to speak on behalf of women from both sides of the Atlantic Ocean. Was I now estranged from my sister because I did not make that trip with her? Was I no longer a part of her story because we were now divided by history, distance, and experience? Did she not understand that I, too, knew the pain of oppression, albeit in a different form and intensity? That at the same time she was fighting for human rights in the United States, I was fighting to end centuries of oppression that began with slavery and continues today as neocolonialism? It is this connection of struggle and spirit that we speak in this chapter.

Amina Mama (2007) connects the advent of African independence struggles with the emergence of feminist activism in Africa, most notably in Nigeria and Egypt. However, many argue that gender, as a political category, was not necessarily a salient category for women in many African societies, especially in comparison to Black American feminists (Aina, 1998; Oyewumi, 1997; Taiwo, 2003). However, although African nations were beginning the slow process of achieving independence from colonial regimes, women's issues were not foregrounded in this independence struggle. Continental African women quickly learned that the fight for independence did not necessarily place women's rights front and center in the fight for independence. Speaking specifically about Nigerian women, Molara Ogundipe-Leslie (1994) explains that the seeming lack of focus on women's issues postindependence could be explained by the preexistence and availability of economic opportunities for women in precolonial Nigeria. This is echoed by Ifi Amadiume (1987) in her precolonial, colonial, and postindependence analysis of the ways that women enjoyed relative power and influence, which diminished in eastern Nigeria only with the advent of British colonialism and its own versions of gender roles. This study counters the master narrative among Western feminists that portrays African women as having had limited political and economic power in comparison to their male counterparts. Amadiume demonstrates the way that colonialism actually disempowered women by limiting the economic freedom that they enjoyed in precolonial times. We see this echoed in prominent African feminist literature that theorizes women's lives, such as Kenyan Margaret Ogola's (1994) novel, *The River and the Source;* Nigerian Flora Nwapa's (1966) *Efuru;* and Ghanaian writer Ama Ata Aidoo's (1970) collection of short stories, entitled *No Sweetness Here.* Having spent the first 25 years of my life in eastern Nigeria, I witnessed, firsthand, the spirit of enterprise and economic independence that characterized women's efforts at running their households. Traditionally, men were the heads of households, but it was apparent that women were the glue that held the homefront together. I understood, even as a young girl, why many women set up their own businesses, even when said business was a small table strategically placed in front of her home from which she hawked basic household and food items, while remaining within eyesight of her home and children. Although I wondered how much profit the women made from selling such small items, I understood that it was their gesture toward economic independence and empowerment. A woman who depended entirely on her husband for financial help was usually perceived as lazy. So, the struggle for independence for the African woman was not necessarily a struggle for her economic independence, but a struggle for the independence of her local and national community at large. Several scholars claim that the struggle for economic opportunities and the right to work, which characterized the struggles of women in the diaspora and elsewhere, could not easily be applied to women on the continent of Africa (Bray, 2008; Mohanty, Russo, & Torres, 1991; Nnaemeka, 1998; Ogundipe-Leslie, 1994). Instead, it was and continues to be neocolonialism, oppressive regimes, and marriage and cultural norms that we must unpack to understand the African woman's experience with oppression in Africa and her feminisms. Aidoo (1998) and Zulu Sofola (1998) concur that the African woman's burdens of oppression can be traced to both internal influences from sociocultural and patriarchal structures and external influences stemming from colonialism and postcolonial crises of leadership. Aidoo (1998) echoes these sentiments when she states:

> Three major historical factors have influenced the position of the African woman today: Indigenous African social patterns; the conquest of the continent by Europe; and the apparent lack of vision, or courage, in the leadership of the post-colonial period. (p. 42)

Like her African ascendant sisters in the diaspora, the African woman on the continent of Africa has had to fight the voicelessness caused by centuries of domination through slavery, colonialism, and imperialism. She, too, has had to confront intersecting oppressions of racism, sexism, and classism. But the multiplicity of manifestations of the particular set of oppressions that plague women within and outside of the African continent has caused African feminists like Aidoo, Abena Busia, Sofola, and Ogundipe-Leslie to advocate for the consideration of *culture* as a form of oppression for the African woman. According to Ogundipe-Leslie (1994) culture, much more than race, more aptly determines African women's identity. We understand that the three major axes of oppression (race, class, and gender), which may plague Black women in the diaspora (and within and against which we have theorized our versions of feminisms), must be expanded to include oppressive cultural norms; we will avoid thinking of African womanhood in universal terms, a tension that is apparent in many discussions of transnational Black feminisms (Collins, 2000; Guy-Sheftall, 1995; Ogundipe-Leslie, 1994; Omolade, 1994; Oyewumi, 1997; Steady, 1981). Nowhere is this wrestling more apparent than in the naming of what Nnaemeka (1998) calls the "feminist spirit" across the globe, to which we now turn.

CALL ME BY MY TRUE NAMES:[5] NAMING BLACK FEMINISM IN THE UNITED STATES, THE DIASPORA AND THE CONTINENT OF AFRICA

Within African culture, naming is a sacred practice, one that is not only important to the continuation of the group's heritage and work, but also to the purpose and future work of the individual being named. Through this issue of naming, we can begin to see the interconnected nature of Black feminist struggles in the United States with those of Black women throughout the diaspora and the continent of Africa.

Given the too often exclusionary spaces for U.S. Black feminists within the broader conversations of feminism, early Black feminists in the United States began to create names that more carefully honored and described a collective *Black* feminism. Walker (1983) first introduced the term *womanism* into the ongoing debates by White feminists, who seemed to quickly forget that their Black counterparts had been their allies nearly a decade before in the fight for civil rights. According to Walker, a womanist is

> a black feminist or feminist of color . . . a woman who loves other women, sexually and/or nonsexually . . . committed to survival and wholeness of entire people, male *and* female . . . Womanist is to feminist as purple is to lavender." (emphasis in the original, pp. xi–xii)

However, in direct criticism of Walker's definition, Clenora Hudson-Weems (1998a, 1998b) argues that, regardless of where women of African heritage exist, we should not adopt the label of feminist because, in comparison to our Western counterparts, gender is not primary in the struggle for equity and recognition. Hudson-Weems (1995) prefers the term *Africana womanism* to womanism, Black feminism, and African feminism. She believes that Africana womanism more succinctly captures the family centeredness in an African framework, rather than the female centeredness of Western feminism. This also resonates with the stance that many continental African feminists have taken, suggesting the crucial need for Africana men and women to come together to confront all oppression, given what is seen as the interdependency of men and women in equally worthwhile albeit different roles in an African cosmology and worldview (Nzegwu, 2006; Oyewumi, 1997; Richards, 1980). In other words, African ascendant people must take control of our struggles for the sake of collective justice for African people (Hudson-Weems, 1998b). While Hudson-Weems suggests there are strong and fundamental differences between her notion of African womanism and womanism as defined by Walker, one can also argue that her version of naming does at least partly align with Walker's original definition of womanism, in that it includes a commitment "to survival and wholeness of entire people, male and female. Not a separatist [movement]" (Walker, 1983, pp. xi–xii). Hudson-Weems's (1998a) main concern is with the issue of self-naming or what she calls "a reclamation of Africana women through properly identifying our own collective struggle and acting on it" (p. 160). She further believes that the agenda of the Africana woman must be "shaped by the dictates of their past and present cultural reality. No one can be accurately defined outside of one's historical and cultural context" (Hudson-Weems, 1998b, p. 450). She goes on to claim that Africana scholars are sometimes forced to identify as feminists, to either gain legitimacy in the academy or because of a lack of a more appropriate framework that is suitable for their particular experiences. However, Busia (1993), in speaking of the need to negotiate multiple and transnational identities, calls for a more fluid, layered, and particular naming that more aptly describes the crossing of national and international boundaries in the act of naming self and other. Busia typifies the sort of complexity and dynamism within which Black women in Africa and in the diaspora wrestle, in her self-identification as

> a Ghanaian-born poet, educated in the United Kingdom, teaching in the universities of the United States of America (p. 204) . . . [or] as scholar, as poet, as Black, as female, as African, as an exile, as an Afro-Saxon living in Afro-America. (p. 209)

These arguments over naming Black feminism are not simply about the act of naming: They are also about defining and constructing the boundaries and possibilities for relationships *across* Black feminisms, across racial, tribal, ethnic, and national differences, as well as advocating for fundamental *human* rights. In her well-known text, *The Black Woman Cross-Culturally,* Filomina Steady (1981) called for a redefinition of concepts, perspectives, and methodologies that position the transnational Black feminist researcher as an advocate for basic *human* rights throughout the world and not solely an advocate for women's rights or the rights of those in her local community. We hear echoes of that same call throughout this chapter, of African ascendant feminist acknowledgment of the oneness of male and female energy in the struggle against oppression (Wekker, 1997). These arguments are also spiritual in nature, seeing African feminism as a standpoint on human life from "a total, rather than a dichotomous and exclusive perspective" (Steady, 1981, p. 7). Steady goes on to echo a common cosmological concept in African thought that "for African women, the male is not 'the other' but part of the human same. Each gender constitutes the critical half that makes the human whole. Neither sex is totally complete in itself to constitute a unit by itself" (p. 7).

hooks (1994) welcomed these contestations in naming, perspectives, positions, and language, seeing these confrontations as less about naming and more about how these "differences [mean] that we must change ideas about how we learn" (p. 113). She continues, suggesting that "rather than fearing conflict [in naming], we have to find ways to use it as a catalyst for new thinking, for growth" (p. 113). Walker (2006) also cautions against arguments that suggest a lack of unity of purpose and proffers an alternative "combined energy" through which we can "scrutinize an oncoming foe" (p. 4). According to Walker (2006), this coming together has the potential to "rebalance the world" (p. 4) and, in the case of these contestations, help us refocus on the task before us. This task—whether historical or contemporary— requires us to remember that the struggle for injustice, regardless of geographical location, must include *an awareness of the specific historical and cultural contexts within which oppressions are taking place* in order to identify effective frameworks with which to do the necessary work to dismantle them.

The rumblings of dissatisfaction with naming and creating an organized and collective transnational Black feminist response to oppression continue today. Led by activist scholars and writers such as Steady, Collins, and Beverly Guy Sheftall, Black feminists across the globe are troubling the boundaries of the definition of feminism to describe differences in African ascendant women's experiences with racial, sexual, class, and cultural oppression. This stands to produce what Steady (1996) has called

> a more inclusive brand of feminism through which women are viewed primarily as human beings and not simply women . . . [that] emphasizes the totality of human experience and [is] optimistic for the total liberation of humanity . . . African feminism is *humanistic* feminism. (p. 4, emphasis added)

This holistic view of the African woman, in relation to her community, echoes precolonial African practices and values regarding the physical as well as the spiritual well-being of the community. Therefore, in contrast to the Western tendency to dichotomize the material and the spiritual, male and female, the emotional and logical, a transnational African feminism merely reflects an age-old concept of a human oneness or human wholeness, where the male is not the enemy but a coparticipator in the struggle for human survival. It is important to note that this concept of oneness existed prior to the European invasion of the continent of Africa and defines the nature of relationships and life both histori-cally and contemporarily. Consequently, the African spiritual concept of com-munal well-being is more highly valued than the individualism that marks Western feminist thought. This was at least part of the tension that existed between African American feminist scholars and White American feminist scholars as well. We argue here that, whether conscious of this African moral value as a carryover from cultural ways of being and ways of thinking prior to the trans-Atlantic slave trade, the pursuit of the well-being of the whole on both the continent and in the African diaspora as a means of meeting the needs of the individual and the community is a spiritual concept. Although the spiritual concept of communal wholeness and wellness prevalent in African feminism sharply contradicts the historical split between the spiritual and material so pervasive in the academy, it has been a critical part of Africana and Black feminist thought historically and continues to be pushed to the fore by scholars like Alexander (2005), Dillard (2006a, 2006b), Guy-Sheftall, (1995), hooks, (2000), Hull, (2001), and Oyewumi, (1997), to name a few.

Thus, like sisters in the diaspora, continental African women scholars have not escaped the tensions present within and among African feminist scholars in defining the connections, however contentious, between versions and visions of Black feminism on the continent and in the diaspora. The well-known Ghanaian feminist writer and activist Aidoo (1998) has been criticized primarily by continental African women scholars for identifying as a feminist. Like the struggles of Black women in the United States, the accusations have to do both with the issue of naming and the critique at the epistemological level that the term *feminism* is a Western construct and that African women should seek empowerment through their own self-naming. The premise of the argument is that the historical realities of Western feminism do not mirror the reality of the continental African woman's historical struggles, particularly as they relate to the sufferings and current realities during and after colonialization. This argument mirrors the one made by Hudson-Weems (1995) about the need to marshal more appropriate terminology to capture Black women's experiences in the diaspora. Aidoo's defense, similar to that of her Sierra Leonean counterpart Steady, is that all men and women are feminists if they believe that the struggle for liberation for all Africans cannot be isolated from the struggle for the well-being of the African woman. Here we see again echoes of the communal versus the individual or the collective versus the self, fundamental to an African-centered cosmology.

While this discussion is by no means complete, the ethos and spirit of transnational Black feminist thought is clear: Black feminist scholars have *always* talked back to the exclusion of Black women's experiences in feminist research, paving the way for more global and diasporic conversations about Black women and the specialized angle of visions that we bring to the question of knowledges, knowledge production, and the practices of research. The call for a naming and marshalling of Black feminism arises from a place—epistemologically, spiritually, paradigmatically—that both acknowledges and addresses the complex intersections of culture, race, class, sexualities, nation, and gender in Black women's experiences and in a way that is historically and sufficiently grounded in African ascendant ways of knowing and being. This call is reminiscent of one made nearly two centuries earlier by Anna Julia Cooper, one of only two Black women to address the Pan African Congress organized by W. E. B. DuBois in 1919 in Paris, France. An acclaimed forerunner of Black feminism in the United

States and abroad, Cooper (1892) cautioned against the expectation within Black communities generally and White feminist communities as well that the Black woman be required to fracture her identity by uplifting her gender identity over race or class. Instead, the work was and is about establishing linkages with African ascendant women globally in the struggle for elimination of all oppressions, wherever Black women are. It is about finding the sacred ground between us.

III. Nkyimkyim (Devotion to Service and Willingness to Withstand Hardship): The Ethos of an Endarkened Transnational Feminism

Re-member what is dark and ancient and divine within yourself that aids your speaking. As outsiders, we need each other for support and connection and all the other necessities of living on the borders . . . The oppression of women knows no ethnic nor racial boundaries, true, but that does not mean it is identical within those boundaries. (Lorde, 1984, p. 69–71)

Our politics initially sprang from the shared belief that black women are inherently valuable, that our liberation is a necessity not as an adjunct to somebody else's but because of our need as human persons for autonomy . . . We realize that only people who care enough about us to work consistently for our liberation are us . . . we have a very definite revolutionary task to perform, and we are ready for the lifetime of work and struggle before us. (Combahee River Collective, 1982)

The quotations above speak volumes to the possibilities of both living and creating spaces for epistemologies and methodologies that arise from the Black or endarkened feminist voices gathered here, including those voices representing multiple forms of migration to the far reaches of globe, those who have transitioned to the spirit world, and those yet to come. What we are suggesting here is that a more globally attentive Black or endarkened feminism and its methodologies would be less about traditional academic notions of research practices and more about a sort of radical spiritual activism that encompasses the collective diversity of Black women's knowings and doings, that defines and describes our collective *ethos*, particularly given that previous definitions of *Black feminism, womanism, Africana womanism,* or *Third World feminism* may no longer hold as bridges (if they ever did) across our differences in paradigms, practices, and purposes. We have also come to know that whatever descriptions and definitions of transnational or global Black feminisms *are,* they must necessarily be "simultaneously historically specific and dynamic, not frozen in time in the form of a spectacle" (Mohanty, 1991, p. 6). That what fundamentally defines and shapes an "in common" ethos and experience of Black women in the world across culture, ethnicity, national affiliation, sexual affinity, economic class and condition, and other forms of identity can be articulated by two core experiences of African ascendant women wherever you find us on the globe. These may seem both obvious and common sense, given the body of literature around Black/African/Africana feminism. However, this is our attempt to make explicit two salient knowings which all Black women experience our lives.

1. Black women work and live within a context of struggle against systems of oppression and exploitation, both large and small.

2. Black women work and live within a context of spirituality and the sacred, holding beliefs in something larger than ourselves.

Such spiritual consciousness is what enables us as Black women to both work against that which oppresses and to find strength and sometimes even joy in the process of the work as well.

This is our collective ethos or spirit as African ascendant women. What is needed is an approach to research and inquiry that honors the wisdom, spirituality, and critical interventions of Black women's ways of knowing and being, with spirituality and sacredness being central to the work. But what is the nature or character of an endarkened feminist approach to research that can work within and against these struggles, that can transcend our present differences, and that embraces spirituality and the sacred nature of inquiry? What might we need to consider and question as we think (and feel) our way into and toward epistemologies and methodologies that might be useful wherever we find ourselves on this globe? That is the focus of this final section.

Section IV. Funtummireku-Denkyemmireku (We Have a Common Destiny, a Unity Through Diversity)

Sacred Practice, Sacred Dialogues: Some Considerations for an Endarkened Transnational Feminist Methodology

An important component of African indigenous pedagogy is the vision of the teacher [and researcher] as a selfless healer intent on inspiring, transforming, and propelling students to a higher spiritual level. (Hilliard, 1995, pp. 69–70)

Sacredness and spirituality are central to endarkened feminism. From Cooper's (1892) advocacy for the well-being of the African American community, to Steady's (1996) call for a feminism that attends to the total liberation of humanity. From Walker's (1983) definition of womanism, which includes a commitment to the survival and wholeness of entire people, male and female, to hooks's (1994) concept of the basic interdependency of life. From these voices, we can clearly see both the expectation and the relative requirement that endarkened feminist scholars bring a spiritual vision and sacred practice to bear within whatever version of Black feminism we might ascribe to. Similar to hooks (1994) and Walker (1983), Dillard (2006a) asserts that "a spiritual life is first and foremost about commitment to a way of thinking and behaving that honors principles of inter-being and interconnectedness" (p. 77). This suggests that bringing sacredness and spirituality to bear in any exploration of an endarkened transnational feminist methodology is not a frivolous exercise: It is a radical response to the need for an approach to research that honors the wisdom, spirituality, and critical interventions of transnational Black women's ways of knowing and being in research. We note again that the distinction between spirituality and the sacred is important here, particularly as it relates to research. Again, what is meant by *spirituality* is to have a consciousness of the spiritual in one's work, recognizing the ways that consciousness can transform research and teaching. However, the *sacred* in endarkened feminist research refers to *the way the work is honored and embraced as it carried out.* Said another way, work that is sacred is worthy of being held with *reverence* as it is done.

Recently, our department offered the first doctoral seminar in education on Black feminist thought. In addition to other goals, the course was designed to be a space where an endarkened and transnational feminist epistemology and pedagogy (Dillard, 2006a, 2006b) would be created, engaged, and experienced. It was about enacting a radical humanism as intervention in higher education, about becoming more fully human in all of our variations as African ascendant women (who made up the entire class). However, we were a very diverse group of Black women, representing identities, histories, and cultural affiliations that enriched our ability to engage the discussion of Black feminisms and endarkened epistemologies not simply with our minds but embodied in our methodology as well. Nationally, we had deep roots in the United States, Japan, Ghana, Nigeria, and Kenya. Economically, we had experienced the economic range from poverty to middle- and upper middle-class wealth. We had migratory and immigration experiences that included a third of the class growing up in countries outside the United States and "becoming" citizens of the United States in adolescence, with the other two thirds having grown up in the United States (in the Pacific Northwest, the South, the North, and in both rural and urban environments). We spanned the continuum of sexualities and partnering. Most important, we were deeply committed to ourselves and to doing our work *as Black women* in the academy.

One of the first assignments in the class was a creative autobiography, where we shared stories of who we are and why we are.[6] The course reading list represented Black and endarkened feminisms that were transnational and historical, as well as multiple in genre including films, poetry, visual art, letters, narrative, research studies, and other course syllabi. This corpus is what Bell-Scott (1994) calls *life notes*. Many of these readings are represented in the bibliography of this chapter; others were suggested by the students and faculty as the course progressed. Our weekly class sessions were mostly dialogues about the readings and short presentations about content. As we were preparing this chapter (a text that we desired at the time of the class but could not find in the literature), the class became a space to engage what bell hooks and Cornel West (1991) call critical affirmation, the humanizing process of critique that "cuts to heal not to bleed."[7] More than that, we found ourselves raising questions and critique that explicitly showed us the difficulty of talking across our different versions of Black womanhood, even given our common "texts" and deep commitments to dialogue as sacred praxis. As the course continued, we began to see more clearly the nature and character of an endarkened transnational feminist dialogue as we engaged with each other. We also experienced the tensions and intelligibilities that still existed between us, despite our good intentions and deep commitments to dialogue. We also had the opportunity to engage in a cross-class dialogue with other doctoral students enrolled in a qualitative course on feminist methodologies that was being offered at the same time. These interactions further exposed the tensions and challenges of such a dialogue, particularly the racialized spaces of feminisms, which often exclude feminisms of color (and certainly African ascendant feminisms) from the consciousness of White researchers.

What would it take to productively enter into these tensions and differences? And could explicating the character of such a dialogue help us to speak to what an endarkened transnational feminist methodology in research might be (especially given our new understandings of the history, culture, and contestations within and among African ascendant feminisms)? A methodology that would be "historically specific and dynamic" (Mohanty, 1991)? One that would be a useful way forward in the spirit of sacred praxis that Alexander (2005) called for?

The following section [Table 8.1] is our attempt to share what we learned *and* some questions we learned to raise, as authors, as members of the course, and as researchers and sisters of the yam.[8] We hope it is not seen as a checklist to legitimate one's identity or research position ("I do these things and now I'm an endarkened transnational feminist researcher!"). Instead, we see it as an offering to the research

Table 8.1   Engaging Transnational Endarkened Feminist Research: Some Considerations and Questions

Considerations for Endarkened Transnational Feminist Research	Some Relevant Questions for the Researcher
On the meaning of African womanhood . . .	
Seeks to examine the multiple intersections of oppressions of Black women relationally *and* historically	What is or was going on here/there? What is or was my/our relation to the lives of Black women here/there?
Sees the way that temporality shapes relative relationships between and among versions of Black womanhood, personhood	Whose story will I tell and from what time period of "African womanhood?" How do I struggle with the tension of the African "continent" and the "diaspora" and their relative and multiple meanings? Have I dealt with questions of the timing (and manner) of im/migrations and the relationship to "authenticity" and naming oneself "African"?
Seeks to know Black women's experiences, contributions, cultures, and "feminisms" in all of their varieties/versions	What do I know about African ascendant woman? How did I gain that knowledge and what would enrich my understanding of specific versions of Black womanhood or endarkened feminisms? How can this knowledge get in the way of my seeing and understanding the vision and version of African ascendant feminism under study?
Embodies responsibility and respect, different than the cult of womanhood	How have I prepared to study the lives of Black women differently than I would for other women? What would show that I respect the particularities of her understandings and embodiment of cultural norms, geographies, and traditions?

(Continued)

Considerations for Endarkened Transnational Feminist Research	Some Relevant Questions for the Researcher
On the sacred nature of experience . . . [9]	
Seeks to recognize multiple experiences outside of one's own	In what ways does the story I'm hearing (or the text I'm reading) map on to my experience and knowings? In what ways is it different? How do I hold those differences as sacred (with reverence), without judgment or denial in their difference?
Recognizes that you can never be the "expert" on another's experience and, thus, must move yourself out of the way to make room for the liberation of others	What does their experience *mean* to them? Can I *hear* and *imagine* the depth of the meaning of their experiences and empathize without trying to "save" another? What does their story mean to me and what emotions/ memories does it evoke? How do my emotions mediate (or distort) *their* intended meaning?
On recognizing African community and landscapes . . .	
Shares the need for alliance and reliance: *I am because we are*	Where are the recognitions and engagements in this work of an endarkened womanhood that moves between and even beyond nation, culture, sexualities, economic class, language, and so on?
Recognizes the dynamic and shifting landscapes and configurations of identity and social location of groups	How does what I *thought* I knew about this individual/ group match what I am hearing from engagements with him/her/them? Where are the places and people who could provide disconfirming data? Have I sought this out?
Is committed to knowing one another's stories through sustained relationship for the purposes of bettering conditions that may not mirror our own	Can I rest in that place where it is not all/always about me? Are humility, sacrifice, and selflessness at the center of my desire to "know"?

Considerations for Endarkened Transnational Feminist Research	Some Relevant Questions for the Researcher
On engaging body, mind, and spirit . . .	
Makes *space* for mind, body, and spirit to be a part of the work	How have I sought knowledge at a level of intimacy and wholeness (beyond the mind), at the level of the senses, the sensual, and the spiritual?
	What questions have I asked of myself and another that move toward connections of our spirit?
	What would happen if I "went there?"
Is reciprocal, as every person is both teacher and taught, changing as we know the other and the other knows us	In what ways are my views of research shifting as a result of my research?
	What "lessons" have I learned from others in this inquiry? What are the lessons they've learned from me?
	When someone reads this work, how will they know that I approached this project with reverence?
Requires radical openness and vulnerability	In what ways have I "shown up" for this inquiry?
	How am I hiding in fear of what I am, what I don't know or misunderstand, or who the other is or what they know?

community of the ways that an endarkened transnational feminist methodology may have the potential to shape a more reverent and sacred approach to inquiry that transcends our differences, our feminisms, and our lives.

These considerations and questions suggest that, as we work to live and theorize from and through endarkened transnational epistemologies, we must also shift our gaze and engagement to embrace a more sacred (reverent) understanding of our relationships with and in endarkened spaces of womanhood and feminisms. We must go beyond employing or engaging our methodologies: We must *be* differently, asking relevant (and reverent) questions of our practice and of ourselves. Some considerations are discussed in brief here.

On the meaning of African womanhood. Endarkened transnational research acknowledges that the lives of African ascendant women are intertwined and interconnected, given our shared legacy of oppressions on the African continent and in the African diaspora. This awareness does not discount the ways that temporality shapes Black women's experiences

(Okpalaoka, 2009). Neither does this awareness discount the notion that there are variations of feminisms that reflect the varied nuances of oppression manifested in women's specific historical, cultural, and geographical locations. The disruption of African ascendant peoples' lives through enslavement, colonization, and apartheid across temporal and geographical boundaries only serves to connect us across these boundaries. A respect for the particularities of Black women's understandings and embodiment of cultural norms, geographies, and traditions must be reflected in the research and work of inquiry.

On the sacred nature of experience. At the core of Black feminism (Collins, 2000; Steady, 1996) and endarkened feminism (Dillard, 2006a) is the recognition of the expertise that Black women acquire through our lived experiences and specific to our lived conditions. An approach to endarkened transnational feminist research is one in which the researcher and the researched are engaged in a mutually *humbling* experience, where each understands our limitations in speaking *for* the other. An endarkened transnational feminist epistemology and methodology recognizes that there are multiple experiences outside of one's own. Therefore, the role of researcher as expert will serve only to hinder the liberation of those with whom we engage in research and the cultural and spiritual knowledge that is inherently valuable to both of us as human and spiritual beings.

On recognizing African community and landscapes. The South African concept of *Ubuntu* ("I am because we are") and the Ghanaian (Akan) concept of *Funtummireku-denkyemmireku* ("We have a common destiny") embody the need to recognize the powerful and omnipresent role of community from an endarkened transnational perspective. Contrary to Western thought that seeks to elevate the individual above the community, researchers committed to an endarkened transnational feminist praxis are also committed to knowing another's stories through both telling one's own and through the sustained relationship that such dialogue requires. From this standpoint, our work as researchers has as part of its purpose to make better conditions that may not mirror our own. In other words, while we recognize the specifics of the oppressions within and amongst African ascendant women, as long as some form of oppression is present within our collective reality, we all must engage in the struggle for freedom from oppression and full humanhood. We are in a collective struggle for liberation regardless of the specifics of our conditions. An endarkened transnational feminist praxis works beyond self to recognize the dynamic and shifting landscapes and configurations of identity and social location of groups.

On engaging body, mind, and spirit. Endarkened transnational feminist research is research that makes space for mind, body, and spirit to be a part of the work. It invites the whole person of the researcher and the whole person of the researched into the work, knowing that the mind, body, and spirit are intertwined in their functions of maintaining the well-being of the individual and community. The place of the sacred in endarkened and transnational feminisms requires radical openness, especially on the part of the researcher, who understands deeply that her or his humanity is linked with that of the people with whom he or she studies. The act of sharing with those who have been silenced and marginalized is a spiritual task that embodies a sense of humility and intimacy. Furthermore, a sense of reciprocity is fundamental from this epistemological space, a sense that the researcher and the researched are changed in the process of mutual teaching and learning the world together.

As we end this chapter, two things are clear. First, this exploration of endarkened transnational feminisms affirms the sacred praxis of Black women on the continent and throughout the diaspora. This chapter is our contribution to the collective legacy of struggle and spirit, to "write all the things I should have been able to read" (Walker, 1983, p. 13). However, this exploration of endarkened transnational feminisms also points to the ways that the paradigms and epistemologies that have been marshaled in qualitative research have still not answered the deeper, spiritual questions that undergird many cultural phenomenon, the persistent social problems of equity and justice, the difficulties of community and solidarity, and the complex nature of identity and personhood.

Given an African cosmology and epistemology, the authors strongly resist attempts to predict the "future" of the field of Black/endarkened feminist thought, as past, present, and future are implicated and embraced in our current existence, not as separate but as part of the same. As we have examined the history of Black feminisms on both sides of the water to arrive at a place where we believe a more transnational endarkened feminism is a necessity, one thing is clear: That attention to epistemologies and praxis that also center the spiritual and sacred nature of qualitative research are the necessary way forward.

Notes

1. The coauthors would like to acknowledge the "sisters of the yam" who were participants in the first *Black Feminist Thought* course in the School of Teaching and Learning at The Ohio State University: Charlotte Bell, Tanikka Price, Detra Price-Dennis, Jacquie Scott, Samatha Wahome, and Ann Waliaula, for their very thoughtful feedback on drafts of this chapter, as well as their willingness to help us answer Alice Walker's call to write the texts that we wish we could read. We are grateful and honored by your wisdom and love. The coauthors would also like to acknowledge Norm Denzin and Yvonna Lincoln for their thoughtful reviews of this chapter.

2. In honor to the long traditions of proverbs in the African and African diasporic communities, we introduce each section of this chapter with an adinkra symbol from Ghana and its corresponding proverb, which represents the focus of the section. For further reading on the language of adinkra symbols, see Willis (1998).

3. "Coloring epistemologies" was a descriptive termed used by Scheurich and Young (1997) for the ways that traditional research epistemologies were being created; centered with/in identity markers such as race, culture, class, gender, national origin, and religion; and marshaled in research projects, primarily by people of color. Tyson's (1998) response in *Educational Researcher* critiques this notion on the basis of its unexamined assumptions and implicit racist implications. The idea of "paradigm proliferation" was an extension of the same argument, that is, that paradigms represented what is known and upheld as legitimizing knowledge in research. Thus, the discussion of proliferation of paradigms (again particularly given that they are being advanced by people of color) continued to also advance the same racist assumptions. See Dillard (2006b) for an examination and critique of the paradigm proliferation.

4. See Oyewumi (2004) *Conceptualizing Gender: Eurocentric Foundations of Feminist Concepts and the Challenge of African Epistemologies* for an in-depth discussion of the expansion of Euro/American feminism and its imperialistic outcomes for a one-sided radicalization of knowledge production, the dismissal of African realities, and consequent distortion of the human condition. See also Steady (2004), *An Investigative Framework for Gender Research in Africa in the New Millennium,* for her critical study of the ways that corporate globalization (led by the United States and Europe) and the persistence of Eurocentric concepts and paradigms continue to shape one-dimensional examinations of Africa and African women.

5. This is a borrowed title from Thich Nhat Hanh's (1999) book of the same name.

6. See Dillard (1994, 1996) for in-depth discussions of the pedagogical power of creative autobiography within teacher education, particularly for people of color.

7. See Wright (2003) for an excellent example of critical affirmation and Dillard (2003) for an explanation and response to that critical affirmation.

8. bell hooks used this as the title for her 1993 book, in which she names her Black women's support group by this name saying: "I felt the yam was a life-sustaining symbol of black kinship and community. Everywhere black women live in the world, we eat yam. It is a symbol of our diasporic connections. Yams provide nourishment for the body as food yet they are also used medicinally—to heal the body" (p. 13). The sisters in the Black feminist thought course also referred to ourselves by this name, in the spirit of solidarity and life-affirming connections to the African continent and diasporic communities we were connected to and responsible for.

9. Experience has and continues to be a space of contestation, particularly for poststructural scholars. As example, Jackson and Mazzei (2008) argue for the need for experience in autoethnography "that acknowledges the constraints of 'one' telling, that theorizes the ethics of such tellings, and that works the limits of the narrative 'I'" (p. 299), seeking instead a deconstructive autoethnography that puts experience under deconstruction, that confronts experience as questionable, incomplete, and problematic "rather than as a

foundation for truth" (p. 304)." The authors further speak of the need, in a deconstructive autoethnography, to engage "a critique of the *relations of power* in the production of meaning from experience" (p. 304, emphasis in original). In this need to critique the relations of power, we see Jackson and Mazzei's call for a different sort of autoethnography (and by extension, qualitative research generally) as useful and important. However, even in their call for a critique of power, the framing of experience remains something that is strikingly singular and somewhat personal (even in their notion of a performative versus narrative "I"). This is counter to African-centered understandings of experience as *collective*, sacredly imbued with a connected spirituality to all that exists past, present, and future. As Dillard (2006b) suggests, we remain in agreement with Lubiano's (1991) notion that an African feminist "post" position must "be politically nuanced in a radical way, focusing on such differences and implications especially in moments of oppositional transgressions" (p. 160). Dillard goes on to suggest that one way that the African American presence in postmodernism can offer a critique is to engage in an alternative cultural discourse in keeping with the spirit of an African ethos. Hence, our notion of experience here is centered in the African notions of the collective, spiritual, and sacred.

References

Aidoo, A. A. (1970). *No sweetness here and other stories.* Harlow, UK: Longman.

Aidoo, A.A. (1998). The African woman today. In O. Nnaemeka (Ed.). *Sisterhood: Feminisms and power from Africa to the diaspora.* Trenton, NJ: Africa World Press.

Aina, O. (1998). African women at the grassroots. In O. Nnaemeka (Ed.), *Sisterhood: Feminisms and power from Africa to the diaspora.* Trenton, NJ: Africa World Press.

Akyeampong, E., & Obeng, P. (2005). Spirituality, gender, and power in Asante history. In O. Oyewumi (Ed.), *African gender studies: A reader.* New York: Palgrave.

Alexander, M. J. (2005). *Pedagogies of crossing: Meditations on feminism, sexual politics, memory, and the sacred.* Durham, NC: Duke University Press.

Amadiume, I. (1987). *Male daughters, female husbands: Gender and sex in an African society.* London: Zed Books.

Bambara, T.C. (1970). *The Black woman: An anthology.* New York: New American Library.

Bambara, T. C. (1992). *The salt eaters.* New York: Random House. (Original work published 1980)

Bell-Scott, P. (1994). *Life notes: Personal writings by contemporary Black women.* New York: W. W. Norton.

Bray, Y. A. (2008). All the "Africans" are male, all the "sistas" are "American," but some of us resist: Realizing African feminism(s) as an Afrological research methodology. *The Journal of Pan African Studies, 2*(2), 58–73.

Busia, A. P. A. (1993). Languages of the self. In S. M. James & A. P. A. Busia (Eds.), *Theorizing Black feminisms: The visionary pragmatism of Black women* (pp. 204–209). London: Routledge.

Cannella, G. S., & Manuelito, K.D. (2008). Feminisms from unthought locations: Indigenous worldviews, marginalized feminisms, and revisioning an anticolonial social science. In N. K Denzin, Y. S. Lincoln, & L. T. Smith (Eds), *Handbook of critical and indigenous methodologies* (pp. 45–59). Thousand Oaks, CA: Sage.

Cleage, P. (2005). *We speak your names: A celebration.* New York: One World Books.

Collins, P. H. (1990). *Black feminist thought: Knowledge, consciousness, and the politics of empowerment.* New York: Routledge.

Collins, P. H. (2000). *Black feminist thought: Knowledge, consciousness, and the politics of empowerment* (2nd ed.). New York: Routledge.

Combahee River Collective. (1982). A black feminist statement. In G. T. Hull, P. B. Scott, & B. Smith (Eds.). *All the women are white, all the blacks are men, but some of us are brave: Black women's studies.* New York: The Feminist Press.

Cooper, A. J. (1892). *A voice from the South: By a woman from the South.* Xenia, OH: Aldine.

Denzin, N. K., Lincoln, Y. S., & Smith, L. T. (Eds.). (2008). *Handbook of critical and indigenous methodologies.* Thousand Oaks, CA: Sage.

Dillard, C. B. (1994). Beyond supply and demand: Critical pedagogy, ethnicity, and empowerment in recruiting teachers of color. *Journal of Teacher Education, 45,* 1–9.

Dillard, C. B. (1996). From lessons of self to lessons of others: Exploring creative autobiography in multicultural learning and teaching. *Multicultural Education, 4*(2), 33–37.

Dillard, C. B. (2000). The substance of things hoped for, the evidence of things not seen: Examining an endarkened feminist epistemology in educational research and leadership. *The International Journal of Qualitative Studies in Education, 13,* 661–681.

Dillard, C. B. (2003). Cut to heal, not to bleed: A response to Handel Wright's "An endarkened feminist epistemology? Identity, difference, and the politics of representation in educational research". *International Journal of Qualitative Studies in Education, 16*(2), 227–232.

Dillard, C. B. (2006a). *On spiritual strivings: Transforming an African American woman's academic life.* New York: SUNY.

Dillard, C. B. (2006b). When the music changes, so should the dance: Cultural and spiritual considerations in paradigm "proliferation." *International Journal of Qualitative Studies in Education, 19*(1), 59–76.

Dillard, C. B. (2008). When the ground is black, the ground is fertile: Exploring endarkened feminist epistemology and healing methodologies in the spirit. In N. K. Denzin, Y. S. Lincoln, & L. T. Smith (Eds.). *Handbook of critical and indigenous methodologies* (pp. 277–292). Thousand Oaks, CA: Sage.

Dillard, C. B., Tyson, C. A., & Abdur-Rashid, D. (2000b). My soul is a witness: Affirming pedagogies of the spirit. *International Journal of Qualitative Studies in Education, 13,* 447–462.

Fernandes, L. (2003). *Transforming feminist practice: Non-violence, social justice, and the possibilities of a spiritualized feminism.* San Francisco: Aunt Lute Books.

Guy-Sheftall, B. (1995). *Words of fire: An anthology of African-American feminist thought.* New York: The New Press.

Hanh, T. N. (1999). *Call me by my true names: The collected poems of Thich Nhat Hanh.* Berkeley, CA: Parallax Press.

Hilliard, A. G. (1995). *The maroon within us: Selected essays on African American community socialization.* Baltimore: Black Classic Press.

hooks, b. (1981). *Ain't I a woman? Black women and feminism.* Cambridge, MA: South End Press.

hooks, b. (1993). *Sisters of the yam: Black women and self-recovery.* Cambridge, MA: South End Press.

hooks, b. (1994). *Teaching to transgress.* New York: Routledge.

hooks, b. (2000). *All about love: New visions.* New York: William Morrow.

hook, b. (2008). *Belonging: A culture of place.* New York: Routledge.

hooks, b., & West, C. (1991). *Breaking bread: Insurgent Black intellectual life.* Cambridge, MA: South End Press.

Hudson-Weems, C. (1995). *Africana womanism: Reclaiming ourselves* (3rd ed.). Troy: MI: Bedford.

Hudson-Weems, C. (1998a). Africana womanism. In O. Nnaemeka (Ed.), *Sisterhood: Feminisms and power from Africa to the diaspora* (pp. 149–162). Trenton, NJ: Africa World Press.

Hudson-Weems, C. (1998b). Self naming and self definition: An agenda for survival (pp. 450–452). In O. Nnaemeka (Ed.), *Sisterhood: Feminisms and power from Africa to the diaspora* (pp.149–162). Trenton, NJ: Africa World Press.

Hull, A. G. (2001). *Soul talk: The new spirituality of African American women.* Rochester, VT: Inner Traditions.

Hull, G., Bell-Scott, P., & Smith, B. (1982). *All the women are white, all the blacks are men, but some of us are brave: Black women's studies.* New York: The Feminist Press.

Hurston, Z. N. (1978). *Their eyes were watching God.* Urbana: University of Illinois Press.

Jackson, A. Y., & Mazzei, L. A. (2008). Experience and "I" in autoethnography: A deconstruction. *International Review of Qualitative Research, 1*(3), 299–318.

Keating, A. (2008). "I'm a citizen of the universe": Gloria Anzaldúa's spiritual activism as catalyst for social change. *Feminist Studies, 34*(1/2), 53–69.

Ladson-Billings, G. (2000). Racialized discourses and ethnic epistemologies. In N. K. Denzin & Y. S. Lincoln (Eds.), *Handbook of qualitative research* (2nd ed., pp. 257–277). Thousand Oaks, CA: Sage.

Ladson-Billings, G., & Donner, J. (2005). The moral activist role of critical race theory. In N. K. Denzin & Y. S. Lincoln (Eds.), *The SAGE handbook of qualitative research* (pp. 279–302). Thousand Oaks, CA: Sage.

Latta, J. M. (1992). *Sacred songs as history* (Interview with Bernice Johnson Reagon). Recorded August 4, 1992. Washington, DC: National Public Radio Archives, Wade in the Water Program.

Lorde, A. (1970). *Cables to rage*. London: Paul Breman Limited.

Lorde, A. (1984). *Sister outsider*. Freedom, CA: The Crossing Press.

Lubiano, W. (1991). Shuckin' off the African-American native other: What's "po-mo" got to do with it? *Cultural Critique, 18,* 149–186.

Mama, A. (2007). Critical connections: Feminist studies in African contexts. In A. Cornwall, E. Harrison, & A. Whitehead (Eds.), *Feminisms in development: Contradictions, contestations and challenge* (p. 152). London: Zeal Books.

Marshall, P. (1984). *Praisesong for the widow*. New York: E. P. Dutton.

Meyer, M. A. (2008). Indigenous and authentic: Hawaiian epistemology and the triangulation of meaning. In N. K. Denzin, Y. S. Lincoln, & L. T. Smith (Eds.). *Handbook of critical and indigenous methodologies* (pp. 217–232). Thousand Oaks, CA: Sage.

Mohanty, C. T. (1991). Cartographies of struggle: Third world women and the politics of feminism. In C. T. Mohanty, A Russo, & L. Torres (Eds.), *Third world women and the politics of feminism* (pp. 1–50). Bloomington: Indiana University Press.

Mohanty, C. T., Russo, A., & Torres, L. (Eds.). (1991). *Third world women and the politics of feminism*. Bloomington: Indiana University Press.

Moraga, C., & Anzaldúa, G. (1981). *This bridge called my back: Writings by radical women of color*. Watertown, MA: Persephone Press.

Morrison, T. (1970). *The bluest eye*. New York: Vintage Books.

Nnaemeka, O. (1998). *Sisterhood: Feminisms and power—from Africa to the diaspora*. Trenton, NJ: Africa World Press.

Nwapa, F. (1966). *Efuru*. London: Cox & Wyman.

Nzegwu, N. (2006). *Family matters: Feminist concepts in African philosophy of culture*. Albany: SUNY Press.

Ogala, M. (1994). *The river and the source*. Nairobi, Kenya: Focus Publications.

Ogundipe-Leslie, O. (1994). *Re-creating ourselves: African women & critical transformations*. Trenton: NJ: Africa World Press.

Okpalaoka, C. L. (2009). *Endarkened feminism and qualitative research: Colonization and connectedness in Black women's experiences*. Unpublished manuscript.

Omolade, B. (1994). *The rising song of African American women*. New York: Routledge.

Oyewumi, O. (1997). *The invention of women: Making an African sense of Western gender discourses*. Minneapolis: University of Minnesota Press.

Oyewumi, O. (2004). Conceptualizing gender: Eurocentric foundations of feminist concepts and the challenge of African epistemologies. In *CODESRIA, African gender scholarship: Concept, methodologies, and paradigms*. Dakar, Senegal: CODESRIA.

Reason, P. (1993). Reflections on sacred experience and sacred sciences. *Journal of Management Inquiry, 2,* 10–27.

Richards, D. (1980). *Let the circle be unbroken: The implications of African spirituality in the diaspora*. Lawrenceville, NJ: The Red Sea Press.

Ryan, J. S. (2005). *Spirituality as ideology in Black women's film and literature*. Charlottesville: University of Virginia Press.

Saavedra, C. M., & Nymark, E. D. (2008). Borderland-Mestizaje feminism: The new tradition. In N. K. Denzin, Y. S. Lincoln, & L. T. Smith (Eds.), *Handbook of critical and indigenous methodologies* (pp. 255–276). Thousand Oaks, CA: Sage.

Scheurich, J., & Young, M. (1997). Coloring epistemologies: Are our research epistemologies racially biased? *Educational Researcher, 26*(4), 4–16.

Smith, B. (1983). *Home girls: A Black feminist anthology.* New York: Kitchen Table:
   Women of Color Press.

Sofola, Z. (1998). Feminism and African womanhood. In O. Nnaemeka (Ed.), *Sisterhood:
   Feminisms and power—from Africa to the diaspora.* Trenton, NJ: Africa World Press.

Some, M. P. (1994). *Of water and the spirit: Ritual, magic, and initiation in the life of an
   African shaman.* New York: G. P. Putnam.

Steady, F. C. (1981). The Black woman cross-culturally: An overview. In F. C. Steady
   (Ed.), *The Black woman cross-culturally.* Cambridge, MA: Schenkman.

Steady, F. C. (1996). African feminism: A worldwide perspective. In R. Terbog-Penn &
   R. Benton (Eds.), *Women in Africa: A reader* (2nd ed.). Washington, DC: Howard
   University Press.

Steady, F. C. (2004). An investigative framework for gender research in Africa in the new
   millennium. In *CODESRIA, African gender scholarship: Concepts, methodologies, and
   paradigms* (pp. 42–60). Dakar, Senegal: CODESRIA.

Taiwo, O. (2003). Reflections on the poverty of theory. In O. Oyewumi (Ed.), *African
   women and feminism: Reflecting on the politics of sisterhood* (pp. 45–66). Trenton, NJ:
   Africa World Press.

Tyson, C. A. (1998). A response to "Coloring epistemologies: Are our qualitative research
   epistemologies racially biased?" *Educational Researcher, 27,* 21–22.

Wade-Gayles, G. (Ed.). (1995). *My soul is a witness: African-American women's spirituality.* Boston: Beacon.

Walker, A. (1983). *In search of our mother's gardens: Womanist prose.* San Diego: Harvest Books.

Walker, A. (2006). *We are the ones we have been waiting for: Inner light in a time of dark-
   ness.* New York: The New Press.

Wallace, M. (1982). A black feminist's search for sisterhood. In G. T. Hull, P. B. Scott, &
   B. Smith (Eds.). *All the women are white, all the blacks are men, but some of us are
   brave: Black women's studies.* New York: The Feminist Press.

Wekker, G. (1997). One finger does not drink okra soup: Afro-Surinamese women and
   critical agency. In M. J. Alexander & C. T. Mohanty (Eds.), *Feminist geneologies, colonial legacies, democratic futures* (pp. 330–352). New York: Routledge.

Willis, B. (1998). *The Adinkra dictionary: A visual primer on the language of Adinkra.*
   Washington, DC: The Pyramid Complex.

Wright, H. K. (2003). An endarkened feminist epistemology? Identity, difference, and the
   politics of respresentation in educational research. *International Journal of Qualitative Research, 16*(2), 197–214.

9

Critical Pedagogy and Qualitative Research

Moving to the Bricolage

Joe L. Kincheloe, Peter McLaren, and Shirley R. Steinberg[1]

Criticality and Research

Over the past 35 years of our involvement in critical theory, critical pedagogy, and critical research, we have been asked to explain how critical theory relates to pedagogy. We find that question difficult to answer because (1) there are many critical theories; (2) the critical tradition is always changing and evolving; and (3) critical theory attempts to avoid too much specificity, as there is room for disagreement among critical theorists. To lay out a set of fixed characteristics of the position is contrary to the desire of such theorists to avoid the production of blueprints of sociopolitical and epistemological beliefs. Given these disclaimers, we will now attempt to provide one idiosyncratic "take" on the nature of critical theory and critical research in the second decade of the 21st century. Please note that this is our subjective analysis and that there are many brilliant critical theorists who disagree with our pronouncements. We tender a description of an ever-evolving criticality, a reconceptualized critical theory that was critiqued and overhauled by the "postdiscourses" of the last quarter of the 20th century and has been further extended in the 21st century (Collins, 1995; Giroux, 1997; Kellner, 1995; Kincheloe, 2008b; McLaren & Kincheloe, 2007; Roman & Eyre, 1997; Ryoo & McLaren, 2010; Steinberg & Kincheloe, 1998; Tobin, 2009; Weil & Kincheloe, 2004).

A reconceptualized critical theory questions the assumption that societies such as Australia, Canada, Great Britain, New Zealand, and the United States, along with some nations in the European Union and Asia, are unproblematically democratic and free (Steinberg, 2010). Over the 20th century, especially after the early 1960s, individuals in these societies were acculturated to feel comfortable in relations of domination and subordination rather than equality and independence. Given the social and technological changes of the last half of the century, which led to new forms of information production and access, critical theorists argued that questions of self-direction and democratic egalitarianism should be reassessed. Researchers informed by the postdiscourses (e.g., postmodernism, critical feminism, poststructuralism) came to understand that individuals' view of themselves and the world were even more influenced by social and historical forces than previously believed. Given the changing social and informational conditions of late-20th century and early-21st century, media-saturated Western culture (Steinberg, 2004a, 2004b), critical theorists have needed new ways of researching and analyzing the construction of individuals (Agger, 1992; Flossner & Otto, 1998; Giroux, 2010; Hammer & Kellner, 2009; Hinchey, 2009; Kincheloe, 2007; Leistyna, Woodrum, & Sherblom, 1996; Quail, Razzano, & Skalli, 2004; Skalli, 2004; Steinberg, 2007, 2009; Wesson & Weaver, 2001).

PARTISAN RESEARCH IN A "NEUTRAL" ACADEMIC CULTURE

In the space available here, it is impossible to do justice to all of the critical traditions that have drawn inspiration from Karl Marx; Immanuel Kant; Georg Wilhelm Friedrich Hegel; Max Weber; the Frankfurt School theorists; Continental social theorists such as Jean Baudrillard, Michel Foucault, Jürgen Habermas, and Jacques Derrida; Latin American thinkers such as Paulo Freire; French feminists such as Luce Irigaray, Julia Kristeva, and Hélène Cixous; or Russian socio-sociolinguists such as Mikhail Bakhtin and Lev Vygotsky—most of whom regularly find their way into the reference lists of contemporary critical researchers. Today, there are criticalist schools in many fields, and even a superficial discussion of the most prominent of these schools would demand much more space than we have available (Chapman, 2010; Flecha, Gomez, & Puigvert, 2003).

The fact that numerous books have been written about the often-virulent disagreements among members of the Frankfurt School only heightens our concern with the "packaging" of the different criticalist schools. Critical theory should not be treated as a universal grammar of revolutionary thought objectified and reduced to discrete formulaic pronouncements or strategies. Obviously, in presenting our version of a reconceptualized critical theory or an evolving criticality, we have defined the critical tradition broadly for the purpose of generating understanding; as we asserted earlier, this will trouble many critical researchers. In this move, we decided to focus on the underlying commonality among critical schools of thought at the cost of focusing on differences. This is always risky business in terms of suggesting a false unity or consensus where none exists, but such concerns are unavoidable in a survey chapter such as this.

We are defining a criticalist as a researcher, teacher, or theorist who attempts to use her or his work as a form of social or cultural criticism and who accepts certain basic assumptions:

- All thought is fundamentally mediated by power relations that are social and historically constituted;

- Facts can never be isolated from the domain of values or removed from some form of ideological inscription;

- The relationship between concept and object and between signifier and signified is never stable or fixed and is often mediated by the social relations of capitalist production and consumption;

- Language is central to the formation of subjectivity (conscious and unconscious awareness);

- Certain groups in any society and particular societies are privileged over others and, although the reasons for this privileging may vary widely, the oppression that characterizes contemporary societies is most forcefully reproduced when subordinates accept their social status as natural, necessary, or inevitable;

- Oppression has many faces, and focusing on only one at the expense of others (e.g., class oppression versus racism) often elides the interconnections among them; and finally

- Mainstream research practices are generally, although most often unwittingly, implicated in the reproduction of systems of class, race, and gender oppression (De Lissovoy & McLaren, 2003; Gresson, 2006; Kincheloe & Steinberg, 1997; Rodriguez and Villaverde, 2000; Steinberg, 2009; Villaverde, 2007; Watts, 2008, 2009a).

In today's climate of blurred disciplinary genres, it is not uncommon to find literary theorists doing anthropology and anthropologists writing about literary theory, political scientists trying their hand at ethnomethodological analysis, or philosophers doing Lacanian film criticism. All of these inter- and cross-disciplinary moves are examples of what has been referred to as *bricolage*—a key innovation, we argue, in an evolving criticality. We will explore this dynamic in relation to critical research later in this chapter. We offer this observation about blurred genres, not as an excuse to be wantonly eclectic in our treatment of the critical tradition but to make the point that any attempts to delineate critical theory as discrete schools of analysis will fail to capture the evolving hybridity endemic to contemporary critical analysis (Denzin, 1994; Denzin & Lincoln, 2000; Kincheloe, 2001a, 2008b; Kincheloe & Berry, 2004; Steinberg, 2008, 2010, 2011).

Critical research can be understood best in the context of the empowerment of individuals. Inquiry that aspires to the name "critical" must be connected to an attempt to confront the injustice of a particular society or public sphere within the society. Research becomes a transformative endeavor unembarrassed by the label "political" and unafraid to consummate a relationship with emancipatory consciousness. Whereas traditional researchers cling to the guardrail of neutrality, critical researchers frequently announce their partisanship in the struggle for a better world (Chapman, 2010; Grinberg, 2003; Horn, 2004; Kincheloe, 2001b, 2008b).

CRITICAL PEDAGOGY INFORMING SOCIAL RESEARCH

The work of Brazilian educator Paulo Freire is instructive in relation to constructing research that contributes to the struggle for a better world. The research of the authors of this chapter has been influenced profoundly by the work of Freire (1970, 1972, 1978, 1985). Concerned with human suffering and the pedagogical and knowledge work that helped expose the genesis of it, Freire modeled critical theoretical research throughout his career. In his writings about research, Freire maintained that there were no traditionally defined objects of his research—he insisted on involving the people he studied as *partners* in the research process. He immersed himself in their ways of thinking and modes of perception, encouraging them to begin thinking about their own thinking. Everyone involved in Freire's critical research, not just the researcher, joined in the process of investigation, examination, criticism, and reinvestigation—all participants and researchers learned to see more critically, think at a more critical level, and to recognize the forces that subtly shape their lives. Critiquing traditional methods of research in schools, Freire took a critical pedagogical approach to research that serves to highlight its difference from traditional research (Kirylo, 2011; Mayo, 2009; Tobin & Llena, 2010).

After exploring the community around the school and engaging in conversations with community members, Freire constructed generative themes designed to tap into issues that were important to various students in his class. As data on these issues were brought into the class, Freire became a problem poser. In this capacity, Freire used the knowledge he and his students had produced around the generative themes to construct questions. The questions he constructed were designed to teach the lesson that no curriculum or knowledge in general was beyond examination. We need to ask questions of all knowledge, Freire argued, because all data are shaped by the context and by the individuals that produced them. Knowledge, contrary to the pronouncements of many educational leaders, does not transcend culture or history.

In the context of reading the word and the world and problem-posing existing knowledge, critical educators reconceptualize the notion of literacy. Myles Horton spoke of the way he read books with students in order "to give testimony to the students about what it means to read a text" (Horton & Freire, 1990). Reading is not an easy endeavor, Horton continued, for to be a good reader is to view reading as a form of research. Reading becomes a mode of finding something, and finding something, he concluded, brings a joy that is directly connected to the acts of creation and re-creation. One finds in this reading that the word and world process typically goes beyond the given, the common sense of everyday life. Critical pedagogical research must have a mandate to represent a form of reading that understood not only the words on the page but the unstated dominant ideologies hidden between the sentences as well.

Going beyond is central to Freirean problem posing. Such a position contends that the school curriculum should in part be shaped by problems that face teachers and students in their effort to live just and ethical lives (Kincheloe, 2004). Such a curriculum promotes students as researchers (Steinberg & Kincheloe, 1998) who engage in critical analysis of the forces that shape the world. Such critical analysis engenders a healthy and creative skepticism on the part of students. It moves them to problem pose and to be suspicious of neutrality claims in textbooks; it induces them to look askance at, for example, oil companies' claims in their TV commercials that they are and have always been environmentally friendly organizations. Students and teachers who are problem posers reject the traditional student request to the teacher: "just give us the facts, the truth, and we'll give it back to you." On the contrary, critical students and teachers ask in the spirit of Freire and Horton: "Please support us in our explorations of the world."

By promoting problem posing and student research, teachers do not relinquish their authority in the classroom. Over the last couple of decades, several teachers and students have misunderstood the subtlety of the nature of teacher authority in a critical pedagogy. In the last years of his life, Freire was very concerned with this issue and its misinterpretation by those operating in his name. Teachers, he told us, cannot deny their position of authority in such a classroom. It is the teacher, not the students, who evaluates student work, who is responsible for the health, safety, and learning of students. To deny the role of authority the teacher occupies is insincere at best, dishonest at worst. Critical teachers, therefore, must admit that they are in a position of authority and then demonstrate that authority in their actions in support of students. One action involves the ability to conduct research and produce knowledge. The authority of the critical teacher is dialectical; as teachers relinquish the authority of truth providers, they assume the mature authority of facilitators of student inquiry and problem posing. In relation to such teacher authority, students gain their freedom—they gain the ability to become self-directed human beings capable of producing their own knowledge (Kirylo, 2011; Siry & Lang, 2010).

Freire's own work was rooted in both liberation theology and a dialectical materialist epistemology (Au, 2007), both of which were indebted to Marx's own writings and various Marxist theorists. Standard judgments against Marxism as economistic, productivist, and deterministic betray an egregious and scattershot understanding of Marxist epistemology, his critique of political economy, and Marx's dialectical method of analyzing the development of capitalism and capitalist society. We assert that the insights of Marx and those working within the broad parameters of the Marxist tradition are foundational for any critical research (Lund & Carr, 2008); Marxism is a powerful theoretical approach to explaining, for instance, the origins of racism and the reasons for its resiliency (McLaren, 2002). Many on the left today talk about class as if it is one of many oppressions, often describing it as "classism." But class is not an "ism." It is true that class intersects with race, and gender, and other antagonisms. And while clearly those relations of oppression can reinforce and compound each other, they are grounded in the material relations shaped by capitalism and the economic exploitation that is the motor force of any capitalist society (Dale & Hyslop-Margison, 2010; Macrine, McLaren, & Hill, 2009).

To seriously put an end to racism, and shatter the hegemony of race, racial formations, the racial state, and so on, we need to understand class as an objective process that interacts upon multiple groups and sectors in various historically specific ways. When conjoined with an insightful class analysis, the concept of race and the workings of racism can be more fully understood and racism more forcefully contested and as a result more powerful transformative practices can be mobilized. Class and race are viewed here as co-constitutive and must be understood as dialectically interrelated (McLaren & Jarramillo, 2010).

TEACHERS AS RESEARCHERS

In the conservative educational order of mainstream schooling, knowledge is something that is produced far away from the school by experts in an exalted domain. This must change if a critical reform of schooling is to exist. Teachers must have more voice and more respect in the culture of education. Teachers must join the culture of researchers if a new level of educational rigor and quality is ever to be achieved. In such a democratized culture, critical teachers are scholars who understand the power implications of various educational reforms. In this context, they appreciate the benefits of research, especially as they relate to understanding the forces shaping education that fall outside their immediate experience and perception. As these insights are constructed, teachers begin to understand what they know from experience. With this in mind they gain heightened awareness of how they can contribute to the research on education. Indeed, they realize that they have access to understandings that go far beyond what the expert researchers have produced. In the critical school culture, teachers are viewed as learners—not as functionaries who follow top-down orders without question. Teachers are seen as researchers and knowledge workers who reflect on their professional needs and current understandings. They are aware of the complexity of the educational process and how schooling cannot be understood outside of the social, historical, philosophical, cultural, economic, political, and psychological contexts that shape it. Scholar teachers understand that curriculum development responsive to student needs is not possible when it fails to account for these contexts.

Critical teacher/researchers explore and attempt to interpret the learning processes that take place in their classrooms. "What are its psychological, sociological, and ideological effects?" they ask. Thus, critical scholar teachers research their own professional practice. With empowered scholar teachers working in schools, things begin to change. The oppressive culture created in our schools by top-down content standards, for example, is challenged. In-service staff development no longer takes the form of "this is what the expert researchers found—now go implement it." Such staff development in the critical culture of schooling gives way to teachers who analyze and contemplate the power of each other's ideas. Thus, the new critical culture of school takes on the form of a "think tank that teaches students," a learning community. School administrators are amazed by what can happen when they support learning activities for both students and teachers. Principals and curriculum developers watch as teachers develop projects that encourage collaboration and shared research. There is an alternative, advocates of critical pedagogy argue, to top-down standards with their deskilling of teachers and the dumbing-down of students (Jardine, 1998; Kincheloe, 2003a, 2003b, 2003c; Macedo, 2006).

Promoting teachers as researchers is a fundamental way of cleaning up the damage of deskilled models of teaching that infantilize teachers by giving them scripts to read to their students. Deskilling of teachers and the stupidification (Macedo, 2006) of the curriculum take place when teachers are seen as receivers, rather than producers, of knowledge. A vibrant professional culture depends on a group of practitioners who have the freedom to continuously reinvent themselves via their research and knowledge production. Teachers engaged in critical practice find it difficult to allow top-down content standards and their poisonous effects to go unchallenged. Such teachers cannot abide the deskilling and reduction in professional status that accompany these top-down reforms. Advocates of critical pedagogy understand that teacher empowerment does not occur just because we wish it to do so. Instead, it takes place when teachers develop the knowledge-work skills, the power literacy, and the pedagogical abilities befitting the calling of teaching. Teacher research is a central dimension of a critical pedagogy (Porfilio & Carr, 2010).

TEACHERS AS RESEARCHERS OF THEIR STUDENTS

A central aspect of critical teacher research involves studying students so they can be better understood and taught. Freire argued that all teachers need to engage in a constant dialogue with students, a dialogue that questions existing knowledge and problematizes the traditional power relations that have served to marginalize specific groups and individuals. In these research dialogues with students, critical teachers listen carefully to what students have to say about their communities and the problems that confront them. Teachers help students frame these problems in a larger social, cultural, and political context in order to solve them.

In this context, Freire argued that teachers uncover materials and generative themes based on their emerging knowledge of students and their sociocultural backgrounds (Mayo, 2009; Souto-Manning, 2009). Teachers come to understand the ways students perceive themselves and their interrelationships with other people and their social reality. This information is essential to the critical pedagogical act, as it helps teachers understand how they make sense of schooling and their lived worlds. With these understandings in mind, critical teachers come to know what and how students make meaning. This enables teachers to construct pedagogies that engage the impassioned spirit of students in ways that move them to learn what they do not know and to identify what they want to know (A. Freire, 2000; Freire & Faundez, 1989; Janesick, 2010; Kincheloe, 2008b; Steinberg & Kincheloe, 1998; Tobin, in press).

It is not an exaggeration to say that before critical pedagogical research can work, teachers must understand what is happening in the minds of their students. Advocates of various forms of critical teaching recognize the importance of understanding the social construction of student consciousness, focusing on motives, values, and emotions. Operating within this critical context, the teacher-researcher studies students as living texts to be deciphered. The teacher-researcher approaches them with an active imagination and a willingness to view students as socially constructed beings. When critical teachers have approached research on students from this perspective, they have uncovered some interesting information. In a British action research project, for example, teachers used student diaries, interviews, dialogues, and shadowing (following students as they pursue their daily routines at school) to uncover a student preoccupation with what was labeled a second-order curriculum. This curriculum involved matters of student dress, conformance to school rules, strategies of coping with boredom and failure, and methods of assuming their respective roles in the school pecking order. Teacher-researchers found that much of this second-order curriculum worked to contradict the stated aims of the school to respect the individuality of students, to encourage sophisticated thinking, and to engender positive self-images. Students often perceived that the daily lessons of teachers (the intentional curriculum) were based on a set of assumptions quite different from those guiding out-of-class teacher interactions with students. Teachers consistently misread the anger and hostility resulting from such inconsistency. Only in an action research context that values the perceptions of students could such student emotions be understood and addressed (Hooley, 2009; Kincheloe, 2001a; Sikes, 2008; Steinberg, 2000, 2009; Vicars, 2008).

By using IQ tests and developmental theories derived from research on students from dominant cultural backgrounds, schools not only reflect social stratification but also extend it. This is an example of school as an institution designed for social benefit actually exerting hurtful influences. Teachers involved in the harmful processes most often do not intentionally hurt students; they are merely following the dictates of their superiors and the rules of the system.

Countless good teachers work every day to subvert the negative effects of the system but need help from like-minded colleagues and organizations. Critical pedagogical research works to provide such assistance to teachers who want to mitigate the effects of power on their students. Here schools as political institutions merge with critical pedagogy's concern with creating a social and educational vision to help teachers direct their own professional practice. Anytime teachers develop a pedagogy, they are concurrently constructing a political vision. The two acts are inseparable (Kincheloe, 2008b; Wright & Lather, 2006).

Unfortunately, those who develop noncritical pedagogical research can be unconscious of the political inscriptions embedded within them. A district supervisor who writes a curriculum in social studies, for example, that demands the simple transference of a body of established facts about the great men and great events of American history is also teaching a political lesson that upholds the status quo (Keesing-Styles, 2003; McLaren & Farahmandpur, 2003, 2006). There is no room for teacher-researchers in such a curriculum to explore alternate sources, to compare diverse historical interpretations, or to do research of their own and produce knowledge that may conflict with prevailing interpretations. Such acts of democratic citizenship may be viewed as subversive and anti-American by the supervisor and the district education office. Indeed, such personnel may be under pressure from the state department of education to construct a history curriculum that is inflexible, based on the status quo, unquestioning in its approach, "fact-based," and teacher-centered. Dominant power operates in numerous and often hidden ways (Nocella, Best, & McLaren, 2010; Watts, 2006, 2009a, 2009b).

Traditional researchers see their task as the description, interpretation, or reanimation of a slice of reality; critical pedagogical researchers often regard their work as a first step toward forms of political action that can redress the injustices found in the field site or constructed in the very act of research itself. Horkheimer (1972) puts it succinctly when he argues that critical theory and research are never satisfied with merely increasing knowledge (see also Agger, 1998; Britzman, 1991; Giroux, 1983, 1988, 1997; Kincheloe, 2003c, 2008a, 2008b; Kincheloe & Steinberg, 1993; Quantz, 1992; Shor, 1996; Villaverde & Kincheloe, 1998; Wexler, 2008). Research in the critical tradition takes the form of self-conscious criticism—self-conscious in the sense that researchers try to become aware of the ideological imperatives and epistemological presuppositions that inform their research as well as their own subjective, intersubjective, and normative reference claims. Critical pedagogical researchers enter into an investigation with their assumptions on the table, so no one is confused concerning the epistemological and political baggage they bring with them to the research site.

On detailed analysis, critical researchers may change these assumptions. Stimulus for change may come from the critical researchers' recognition that such assumptions are not leading to emancipatory actions. The source of this emancipatory action involves the researchers' ability to expose the contradictions of the world of appearances accepted by the dominant culture as natural and inviolable (Giroux, 1983, 1988, 1997; Kincheloe, 2008b; McLaren, 1992, 1997; San Juan, 1992; Zizek, 1990). Such appearances may, critical researchers contend, conceal social relationships of inequality, injustice, and exploitation. If we view the violence we find in classrooms not as random or isolated incidents created by aberrant individuals willfully stepping out of line in accordance with a particular form of social pathology, but as possible narratives of transgression and resistance, then this could indicate that the "political unconscious" lurking beneath the surface of everyday classroom life is not unrelated to practices of race, class, and gender oppression but rather intimately connected to them. By applying a critical pedagogical lens within research, we create an empowering qualitative research, which expands, contracts, grows, and questions itself within the theory and practice examined.

THE BRICOLAGE

It is with our understanding of critical theory and our commitment to critical social research and critical pedagogy that we identify the bricolage as an emancipatory research construct. Ideologically grounded, the bricolage reflects an evolving criticality in research. Norman K. Denzin and Yvonna S. Lincoln (2000) use the term in the spirit of Claude Lévi-Strauss (1968 and his lengthy discussion of it in *The Savage Mind)*. The French word *bricoleur* describes a handyman or handywoman who makes use of the tools available to complete a task (Harper, 1987; Steinberg, 2011). Bricolage implies the fictive and imaginative elements of the presentation of all formal research. The bricolage can be described as the process of getting down to the nuts and bolts of multidisciplinary research. Research knowledges such as ethnography, textual analysis, semiotics, hermeneutics, psychoanalysis, phenomenology, historiography, discourse analysis combined with philosophical analysis, literary analysis, aesthetic criticism, and theatrical and dramatic ways of observing and making meaning constitute the methodological bricolage. In this way, bricoleurs move beyond the blinders of particular disciplines and peer through a conceptual window to a new world of research and knowledge production (Denzin, 2003; Kincheloe & Berry, 2004; Steinberg, 2011).

Bricolage, in a contemporary sense, is understood to involve the process of employing these methodological processes as they are needed in the unfolding context of the research situation. While this interdisciplinary feature is central to any notion of the bricolage, critical qualitative researchers must go beyond this dynamic. Pushing to a new conceptual terrain, such an eclectic process raises numerous issues that researchers must deal with to maintain theoretical coherence and epistemological innovation. Such multidisciplinarity demands a new level of research self-consciousness and awareness of the numerous contexts in which any researcher is operating. As one labors to expose the various structures that covertly shape our own and other scholars' research narratives, the bricolage highlights the relationship between a researcher's ways of seeing and the social location of his or her personal history. Appreciating research as a power-driven act, the critical researcher-as-bricoleur abandons the quest for some naïve concept of realism, focusing instead on the clarification of his or her position in the web of reality and the social locations of other researchers and the ways they shape the production and interpretation of knowledge.

In this context, bricoleurs move into the domain of complexity. The bricolage exists out of respect for the complexity of the lived world and the complications of power. Indeed, it is grounded on an epistemology of complexity. One dimension of this complexity can be illustrated by the relationship between research and the domain of social theory. All observations of the world are shaped either consciously or unconsciously by social theory—such theory provides the framework that highlights or erases what might be observed. Theory in a modernist empiricist mode is a way of understanding that operates without variation in every context. Because theory is a cultural and linguistic artifact, its interpretation of the object of its observation is inseparable from the historical dynamics that have shaped it (Austin & Hickey, 2008). The task of the bricoleur is to attack this complexity, uncovering the invisible artifacts of power and culture and documenting the nature of their influence not only on their own works, but on scholarship in general. In this process, bricoleurs act on the concept that theory is not an explanation of nature—it is more an explanation of our relation to nature.

In its hard labors in the domain of complexity, the bricoleur views research methods actively rather than passively, meaning that we actively construct our research methods from the tools at hand rather than passively receiving the "correct," universally applicable methodologies. Avoiding modes of reasoning that come from certified processes of logical analysis, bricoleurs also steer clear of preexisting guidelines and checklists developed outside the specific demands of the inquiry at hand. In its embrace of complexity, the bricolage constructs a far more active role for humans both in shaping reality and in creating the research processes and narratives that represent it. Such an active agency rejects deterministic views of social reality that assume the effects of particular social, political, economic, and educational processes. At the same time and in the same conceptual context, this belief in active human agency refuses standardized modes of knowledge production (Bresler & Ardichvili, 2002; Kincheloe & Berry, 2004; McLeod, 2000; Selfe & Selfe, 1994; Steinberg, 2010, 2011; Wright, 2003a).

Some of the best work in the study of social complexity is now taking place in the qualitative inquiry of numerous fields including sociology, cultural studies, anthropology, literary studies, marketing, geography, media studies, nursing, informatics, library studies, women's studies, various ethnic studies, education, and nursing. Denzin and Lincoln (2000) are acutely aware of these dynamics and refer to them in the context of their delineation of the bricolage. Yvonna Lincoln (2001), in her response to Joe L. Kincheloe's development of the bricolage, maintains that the most important border work between disciplines is taking place in feminism and race-ethnic studies.

In many ways, there is a form of instrumental reason, of rational irrationality, in the use of passive, external, monological research methods. In the active bricolage, we bring our understanding of the research context together with our previous experience with research methods. Using these knowledges, we *tinker* in the Lévi-Straussian sense with our research methods in field-based and interpretive contexts (Steinberg, in press). This tinkering is a high-level cognitive process involving construction and reconstruction, contextual diagnosis, negotiation, and readjustment. Researchers' interaction with the objects of their inquiries, bricoleurs understand, are always complicated, mercurial, unpredictable, and, of course, complex. Such conditions negate the practice of planning research strategies in advance. In lieu of such rationalization of the process, bricoleurs enter into the research act as methodological negotiators. Always respecting the demands of the task at hand, the bricolage, as conceptualized here, resists its placement in concrete as it promotes its elasticity. In light of Lincoln's (2001) discussion of two types of bricoleurs, (1) those who are committed to research eclecticism, allowing circumstance to shape methods employed, and (2) those who want to engage in the genealogy/archeology of the disciplines with some grander purpose in mind, critical researchers are better informed as to the power of the bricolage. Our purpose entails both of Lincoln's articulations of the role of the bricoleur (Steinberg & Kincheloe, 2011).

Research method in the bricolage is a concept that receives more respect than in more rationalistic articulations of the term. The rationalistic articulation of method subverts the deconstruction of wide varieties of unanalyzed assumptions embedded in passive methods. Bricoleurs, in their appreciation of the complexity of the research process, view research method as involving far more than procedure. In this mode of analysis, bricoleurs come to understand research method as also a technology of justification, meaning a way of defending what we assert we know and the process by which we know it. Thus, the education of critical researchers demands that everyone take a step back from the process of learning research methods. Such a step back allows us a conceptual distance that produces a critical consciousness. Such a consciousness refuses the passive acceptance of externally imposed research methods that tacitly certify modes justifying knowledges that are decontextualized, reductionistic, and inscribed by dominant modes of power (Denzin & Lincoln, 2000; Foster, 1997; Kincheloe & Berry, 2004; McLeod, 2000).

In its critical concern for just social change, the bricolage seeks insight from the margins of Western societies and the knowledge and ways of knowing of non-Western peoples. Such insight helps bricoleurs reshape and sophisticate social theory, research methods, and interpretive strategies, as they discern new topics to be researched. This confrontation with difference so basic to the concept of the bricolage enables researchers to produce new forms of knowledge that inform policy decisions and political action in general. In gaining this insight from the margins, bricoleurs display once again the blurred boundary between the hermeneutical search for understanding and the critical concern with social change for social justice (Jardine, 2006a). Kincheloe has taken seriously Peter McLaren's (2001) important concern—offered in his response to Kincheloe's (2001a) first delineation of his conception of the bricolage—that merely focusing on the production of meanings may not lead to "resisting and transforming the existing conditions of exploitation" (McLaren, 2001, p. 702). In response, Kincheloe maintained that in the critical hermeneutical dimension of the bricolage, the act of understanding power and its effects is merely one part—albeit an inseparable part—of counterhegemonic *action*. Not only are the two orientations not in conflict, they are synergistic (DeVault, 1996; Lutz, Jones, & Kendall, 1997; Soto, 2000; Steinberg, 2001, 2007; Tobin, 2010).

To contribute to social transformation, bricoleurs seek to better understand both the forces of domination that affect the lives of individuals from race, class, gender, sexual, ethnic, and religious backgrounds outside of dominant culture(s) and the worldviews of such diverse peoples. In this context, bricoleurs attempt to remove knowledge production and its benefits from the control of elite groups. Such control consistently operates to reinforce elite privilege while pushing marginalized groups farther away from the center of dominant power. Rejecting this normalized state of affairs, bricoleurs commit their knowledge work to helping address the ideological and informational needs of marginalized groups and individuals. As detectives of subjugated insight, bricoleurs eagerly learn from labor struggles, women's marginalization, the "double consciousness" of the racially oppressed, and insurrections against colonialism (Kincheloe & Steinberg, 1993; Kincheloe, Steinberg, & Hinchey, 1999; Kincheloe & Berry, 2004). In this way, the bricolage hopes to contribute to an evolving criticality.

The bricolage is dedicated to a form of rigor that is conversant with numerous modes of meaning making and knowledge production—modes that originate in diverse social locations. These alternative modes of reasoning and researching always consider the relationships, the resonances, and the disjunctions between formal and rationalistic modes of Western epistemology and ontology and different cultural, philosophical, paradigmatic, and subjugated expressions. In these latter expressions, bricoleurs often uncover ways of accessing a concept without resorting to a conventional validated set of prespecified procedures that provide the distance of objectivity (Thayer-Bacon, 2003). This notion of distance fails to take into account the rigor of the hermeneutical understanding of the way meaning is preinscribed in the act of being in the world, the research process, and objects of research. This absence of hermeneutical awareness undermines the researcher's quest for a thick description and contributes to the production of reduced understandings of the complexity of social life (Jardine, 2006b; Selfe & Selfe, 1994).

The multiple perspectives delivered by the concept of difference provide bricoleurs with many benefits. Confrontation with difference helps us to see anew, to move toward the light of epiphany. A basic dimension of an evolving criticality involves a comfort with the existence of alternative ways of analyzing and producing knowledge. This is why it's so important for a historian, for example, to develop an understanding of phenomenology and hermeneutics. It is why it is so important for a social researcher from a metropolitan center to understand forms of indigenous knowledge, urban knowledge, and youth knowledge production (Darder, 2010; Dei, 2011; Grande, 2006; Hooley, 2009; Porfilio & Carr, 2010). The incongruities between such cultural modes of inquiry are quite valuable, for within the tensions of difference rest insights into multiple dimensions of the research act. Such insights move us to new levels of understanding of the subjects, purposes, and nature of inquiry (Gadamer, 1989; Kincheloe & Berry, 2004; Kincheloe & Steinberg, 2008; Mayers, 2001; Semali & Kincheloe, 1999; Watts, 2009a, 2009b; Willinsky, 2001).

Difference in the bricolage pushes us into the hermeneutic circle as we are induced to deal with parts in their diversity in relation to the whole. Difference may involve culture, class, language, discipline, epistemology, cosmology, ad infinitum. Bricoleurs use one dimension of these multiple diversities to explore others, to generate questions previously unimagined. As we examine these multiple perspectives, we attend to which ones are validated and which ones have been dismissed. Studying such differences, we begin to understand how dominant power operates to exclude and certify particular forms of knowledge production and why. In the criticality of the bricolage, this focus on power and difference always leads us to an awareness of the multiple dimensions of the social. Freire (1970) referred to this as the need for perceiving social structures and social systems that undermine equal access to resources and power. As bricoleurs answer such questions, we gain new appreciations of the way power tacitly shapes what we know and how we come to know it.

ONTOLOGICALLY SPEAKING

A central dimension of the bricolage that holds profound implications for critical research is the notion of a critical ontology (Kincheloe, 2003a). As bricoleurs prepare to explore that which is not readily apparent to the ethnographic eye, that realm of complexity in knowledge production that insists on initiating a conversation about what it is that qualitative researchers are observing and interpreting in the world, this clarification of a complex ontology is needed. This conversation is especially important because it has not generally taken place. Bricoleurs maintain that this object of inquiry is ontologically complex in that it cannot be described as an encapsulated entity. In this more open view, the object of inquiry is always a part of many contexts and processes; it is culturally inscribed and historically situated. The complex view of the object of inquiry accounts for the historical efforts to interpret its meaning in the world and how such efforts continue to define its social, cultural, political, psychological, and educational effects.

In the domain of the qualitative research process, for example, this ontological complexity undermines traditional notions of triangulation. Because of its in-process (processual) nature, interresearcher reliability becomes far more difficult to achieve. Process-sensitive scholars watch the world flow by like a river in which the exact contents of the water are never the same. Because all observers view an object of inquiry from their own vantage points in the web of reality, no portrait of a social phenomenon is ever exactly the same as another. Because all physical, social, cultural, psychological, and educational dynamics are connected in a larger fabric, researchers will produce different descriptions of an object of inquiry depending on what part of the fabric they have focused on—what part of the river they have seen. The more unaware observers are of this type of complexity, the more reductionistic the knowledge they produce about it. Bricoleurs attempt to understand this fabric and the processes that shape it in as thick a way as possible (Kincheloe & Berry, 2004).

The design and methods used to analyze this social fabric cannot be separated from the way reality is construed. Thus, ontology and epistemology are linked inextricably in ways that shape the task of the researcher. The bricoleur must understand these features in the pursuit of rigor. A deep interdisciplinarity is justified by an understanding of the complexity of the object of inquiry and the demands such complications place on the research act. As parts of complex systems and intricate processes, objects of inquiry are far too mercurial to be viewed by a single way of seeing or as a snapshot of a particular phenomenon at a specific moment in time.

This deep interdisciplinarity seeks to modify the disciplines and the view of research brought to the negotiating table constructed by the bricolage (Jardine, 1992). Everyone leaves the table informed by the dialogue in a way that idiosyncratically influences the research methods they subsequently employ. The point of the interaction is not standardized agreement as to some reductionistic notion of "the proper interdisciplinary research method" but awareness of the diverse tools in the researcher's toolbox. The form such deep interdisciplinarity may take is shaped by the object of inquiry in question. Thus, in the bricolage, the context in which research takes place always affects the nature of the deep interdisciplinarity employed. In the spirit of the dialectic of disciplinarity, the ways these context-driven articulations of interdisciplinarity are constructed must be examined in light of the power literacy previously mentioned (Friedman, 1998; Kincheloe & Berry, 2004; Lemke, 1998; Pryse, 1998; Quintero & Rummel, 2003).

In social research, the relationship between individuals and their contexts is a central dynamic to be investigated. This relationship is a key ontological and epistemological concern of the bricolage; it is a connection that shapes the identities of human beings and the nature of the complex social fabric. Bricoleurs use multiple methods to analyze the multidimensionality of this type of connection. The ways bricoleurs engage in this process of putting together the pieces of the relationship may provide a different interpretation of its meaning and effects. Recognizing the complex ontological importance of relationships alters the basic foundations of the research act and knowledge production process. Thin reductionistic descriptions of isolated things-in-themselves are no longer sufficient in critical research (Foster, 1997; Wright, 2003b).

The bricolage is dealing with a double ontology of complexity: first, the complexity of objects of inquiry and their being-in-the-world; second, the nature of the social construction of human subjectivity, the production of human "being." Such understandings open a new era of social research where the process of becoming human agents is appreciated with a new level of sophistication. The complex feedback loop between an unstable social structure and the individual can be charted in a way that grants human beings insight into the means by which power operates and the democratic process is subverted. In this complex ontological view, bricoleurs understand that social structures do not *determine* individual subjectivity but *constrain* it in remarkably intricate ways. The bricolage is acutely interested in developing and employing a variety of strategies to help specify these ways subjectivity is shaped.

The recognitions that emerge from such a multiperspectival process get analysts beyond the determinism of reductionistic notions of macrosocial structures. The intent of a usable social or educational research is subverted in this reductionistic context, as human agency is erased by the "laws" of society. Structures do not simply "exist" as objective entities whose influence can be predicted or "not exist" with no influence over the cosmos of human affairs. Here fractals enter the stage with their loosely structured characteristics of irregular shape—fractal structures. While not *determining* human behavior, for example, fractal structures possess sufficient order to affect other systems and entities within their environment. Such structures are never stable or universally present in some uniform manifestation (Slee, 2011; Varenne, 1996). The more we study such dynamics, the more diversity of expression we find. Taking this ontological and epistemological diversity into account, bricoleurs understand there are numerous dimensions to the bricolage (Denzin & Lincoln, 2000). As with all aspects of the bricolage, no description is fixed and final, and all features of the bricolage come with an elastic clause.

Employing a "Method" Within Bricolage: Ethnography as an Example

As critical researchers attempt to get behind the curtain, to move beyond assimilated experience, to expose the way ideology constrains the desire for self-direction, and to confront the way power reproduces itself in the construction of human consciousness, they employ a plethora of research methodologies (Hyslop-Margison, 2009). We are looking at the degree to which research moves those it studies to understand the world and the way it is shaped in order for them to transform it. Noncritical researchers who operate within an empiricist framework will perhaps find catalytic validity to be a strange concept. Research that possesses catalytic validity displays the reality-altering impact of the inquiry process and directs this impact so that those under study will gain self-understanding and self-direction.

Theory that falls under the rubric of postcolonialism (see McLaren, 1999; Semali & Kincheloe, 1999; Wright 2003a, 2003b) involves important debates over the knowing subject and object of analysis. Such works have initiated important new modes of analysis, especially in relation to questions of imperialism, colonialism, and neocolonialism. Recent attempts by critical researchers to move beyond the objectifying and imperialist gaze associated with the Western anthropological tradition (which fixes the image of the so-called informant from the colonizing perspective of the knowing subject), although laudatory and well-intentioned, are not without their shortcomings (Bourdieu & Wacquant, 1992). As Fuchs (1993) has so presciently observed, serious limitations plague recent efforts to develop a more reflective approach to ethnographic writing. The challenge here can be summarized in the following questions: How does the knowing subject come to know the Other? How can researchers respect the perspective of the Other and invite the Other to speak (Ashcroft, Griffiths, & Tiffin, 1995; Brock-Utne, 1996; Goldie, 1995; Gresson, 2006; Macedo, 2006; Myrsiades & Myrsiades, 1998; Pieterse & Parekh, 1995; Prakash & Esteva, 2008; Scheurich & Young, 1997; Semali & Kincheloe, 1999; Steinberg, 2009; Viergever, 1999)?

Although recent confessional modes of ethnographic writing, for example, attempt to treat so-called informants as "participants" in an attempt to avoid the objectification of the Other (usually referring to the relationship between Western anthropologists and non-Western culture), there is a risk that uncovering colonial and postcolonial structures of domination may, in fact, unintentionally validate and consolidate such structures as well as reassert liberal values through a type of covert ethnocentrism. Fuchs (1993) warns that the attempt to subject researchers to the same approach to which other societies are subjected could lead to an "'othering' of one's own world" (p. 108). Such an attempt often fails to question existing ethnographic methodologies and therefore unwittingly extends their validity and applicability while further objectifying the world of the researcher. Foucault's approach to this dilemma is to "detach" social theory from the epistemology of his own culture by criticizing the traditional philosophy of reflection. However, Foucault falls into the trap of ontologizing his own methodological argumentation and erasing the notion of prior understanding that is linked to the idea of an "inside" view (Fuchs, 1993). Louis Dumont fares somewhat better by arguing that cultural texts need to be viewed simultaneously from the inside and from the outside.

However, in trying to affirm a "reciprocal interpretation of various societies among themselves" (Fuchs, 1993, p. 113) through identifying both transindividual structures of consciousness and transsubjective social structures, Dumont aspires to a universal framework for the comparative analysis of societies. Whereas Foucault and Dumont attempt to "transcend the categorical foundations of their own world" (Fuchs, 1993, p. 118) by refusing to include themselves in the process of objectification, Pierre Bourdieu integrates himself as a social actor into the social field under analysis. Bourdieu achieves such integration by "epistemologizing the ethnological content of his own presuppositions" (Fuchs, 1993, p. 121). But the self-objectification of the observer (anthropologist) is not unproblematic. Fuchs (1993) notes, after Bourdieu, that the chief difficulty is "forgetting the difference between the theoretical and the practical relationship with the world and . . . imposing on the object the theoretical relationship one maintains with it" (p. 120). Bourdieu's approach to research does not fully escape becoming, to a certain extent, a "confirmation of objectivism," but at least there is an earnest attempt by the researcher to reflect on the preconditions of his or her own self-understanding—an attempt to engage in an "ethnography of ethnographers" (p. 122). As an example, critical ethnography, in a bricolage context, often intersects—to varying degrees—with the concerns of postcolonialist researchers, but the degree to which it fully addresses issues of exploitation and the social relations of capitalist exploitation remains questionable. Critical ethnography shares the conviction articulated by Marc Manganaro (1990):

> No anthropology is apolitical, removed from ideology and hence from the capacity to be affected by or, as crucially, to effect social formations. The question ought not to be if an anthropological text is political, but rather, what kind of sociopolitical affiliations are tied to particular anthropological texts. (p. 35)

This critical ethnographic writing faces the challenge of moving beyond simply the reanimation of local experience, an uncritical celebration of cultural difference (including figural differentiations within the ethnographer's own culture), and the employment of a framework that espouses universal values and a global role for interpretivist anthropology (Silverman, 1990). Criticalism can help qualitative researchers challenge dominant Western research practices that are underwritten by a foundational epistemology and a claim to universally valid knowledge at the expense of local, subjugated knowledges (Peters, 1993). The issue is to challenge the presuppositions that inform the normalizing judgments one makes as a researcher.

Although critical ethnography (Hickey & Austin, 2009) allows, in a way conventional ethnography does not, for the relationship of liberation and history, and although its hermeneutical task is to call into question the social and cultural conditioning of human activity and the prevailing sociopolitical structures, we do not claim that this is enough to restructure the social system. But it is certainly, in our view, a necessary beginning (Trueba & McLaren, 2000). Clough (1998) argues that "realist narrativity has allowed empirical social science to be the platform and horizon of social criticism" (p. 135). Ethnography needs to be analyzed critically not only in terms of its field methods but also as reading and writing practices. Data collection must give way to "rereadings of representations in every form" (p. 137). In the narrative construction of its authority as empirical science, ethnography needs to face the unconscious processes on which it justifies its canonical formulations, processes that often involve the disavowal of oedipal or authorial desire and the reduction of differences to binary oppositions. Within these processes of binary reduction, the male ethnographer is most often privileged as the guardian of "the factual representation of empirical positivities" (Clough, 1998).

Critical research traditions have arrived at the point where they recognize that claims to truth are always discursively situated and implicated in relations of power. We do not suggest that because we cannot know truth absolutely, truth can simply be equated with an effect of power. We say this because truth involves regulative rules that must be met for some statements to be more meaningful than others. Otherwise, truth becomes meaningless and, if that is the case, liberatory praxis has no purpose other than to win for the sake of winning. As Phil Carspecken (1993, 1999) remarks, every time we act, in every instance of our behavior, we presuppose some normative or universal relation to truth. Truth is internally related to meaning in a pragmatic way through normative referenced claims, intersubjective referenced claims, subjective referenced claims, and the way we deictically ground or anchor meaning in our daily lives. Carspecken explains that researchers are able to articulate the normative evaluative claims of others when they begin to see them in the same way as their participants by living inside the cultural and discursive positionalities that inform such claims.

While a researcher can use, as in this example, critical ethnography (Willis, 1977, 2000) as a focus within a project, she or he, as a bricoleur (Steinberg, 2011) employs the additional use of narrative (Janesick, 2010; Park, 2005), hermeneutic interpretation (Jardine, 2006a), phenomenological reading (Kincheloe, 2008b), content analysis (Steinberg, 2008), historiography (Kincheloe, 2008b), autoethnography (Kress, 2010), social media analysis (Cucinelli, 2010; Kress, 2008; Kress & Silva, 2009), anthropology (Marcus & Fischer, 1986), quantitative analysis (Hyslop-Margison & Naseem, 2007), and so on; and the bricoleur creates a polysemic read and multiple ways of both approaching and using research. The bricolage, with its multiple lenses allows necessary fluidity and goes beyond a traditional triangulated approach for verification. The lenses expand the research and prevent a normalized methodology from creating a scientistic approach to the research. Bricolage becomes a failsafe way in which to ensure that the multiple reads create new dialogues and discourse and open possibilities. It also precludes the notion of using research as authority.

Clearly, no research methodology or tradition can be done in isolation; the employment of the bricolage transcends unilateral commitments to a singular type of research. In the face of a wide variety of different knowledges and ways of seeing the universe, human beings' confidence in what they think they know collapses. In a countercolonial move, bricoleurs raise questions about any knowledges and ways of knowing that claim universal status. In this context, bricoleurs make use of this suspicion of universalism in combination with global knowledges to understand how they have been positioned in the world. Almost all of us from Western backgrounds or non-Western colonized backgrounds have been implicated in some way in the web of universalism (Scatamburlo D'Annibale & McLaren, 2009). The inevitable conflicts that arise from this implication do not have to be resolved immediately by bricoleurs. At the base of these conflicts rests the future of global culture as well as the future of multicultural research and pedagogy. Recognizing that these are generative issues that engage us in a productive process of analyzing self and world is in itself a powerful recognition. The value of both this recognition and the process of working through the complicated conceptual problems are treasured by bricoleurs. Indeed, bricoleurs avoid any notion of finality in the resolution of such dilemmas. Comfortable with the ambiguity, bricoleurs as critical researchers work to alleviate human suffering and injustice even though they possess no final blueprint alerting them as to how oppression takes place (Kincheloe & Berry, 2004; Steinberg, 2011).

TOWARD A CRITICAL RESEARCH

Within the context of multiple critical theories and multiple critical pedagogies, a critical research bricolage serves to create an equitable research field and disallows a proclamation to correctness, validity, truth, and the tacit axis of Western power through traditional research. Employing a rigorous and tentative context with the notions presented through Marxist examinations of power, critical theory's location and indictment of power blocs vis-à-vis traditional noncritical research methodologies, a critical pedagogical notion of emancipatory research can be located within a research bricolage (Fiske, 1993; Roth & Tobin, 2010). Without proclaiming a canonical and singular method, the critical bricolage allows the researcher to become participant and the participant to become researcher. By eschewing positivist approaches to both qualitative and quantitative research (Cannella & Steinberg, 2011; Kincheloe & Tobin, 2009) and refusing to cocoon research within the pod of unimethodological approaches, we believe critical theory and critical pedagogy continues to challenge regularly employed and obsessive approaches to research.

Note

1. Thanks to Dr. Michael Watts, a local, for his suggestions and critique of this chapter.

References

Agger, B. (1992). *The discourse of domination: From the Frankfurt School to postmodernism.* Evanston, IL: Northwestern University Press.

Agger, B. (1998). *Critical social theories: An introduction.* Boulder, CO: Westview.

Ashcroft, B., Griffiths, G., & Tiffin, H. (Eds.). (1995). *The post-colonial studies reader.* New York: Routledge.

Au, W. (2007). Epistemology of the oppressed: The dialectics of Paulo Freire's theory of knowledge. *Journal for Critical Education Policy Studies, 5*(2). Available at http://www.jceps.com/index.php?pageID=article&articleID=100

Austin, J., & Hickey, A. (2008). Critical pedagogical practice through cultural studies. *International Journal of the Humanities, 6*(1), 133–140. Available at http://eprints.usq.edu.au/4490/

Bourdieu, P., & Wacquant, L. (1992). *An invitation to reflexive sociology.* Chicago: University of Chicago Press.

Bresler, L., & Ardichvili, A. (Eds.). (2002). *Research in international education: Experience, theory, and practice.* New York: Peter Lang.

Britzman, D. (1991). *Practice makes practice: A critical study of learning to teach.* Albany: SUNY Press.

Brock-Utne, B. (1996). Reliability and validity in qualitative research within Africa. *International Review of Education, 42,* 605–621.

Cannella, G., & Steinberg, S. (2011). *Critical qualitative research: A reader.* New York: Peter Lang.

Carspecken, P. F. (1993). *Power, truth, and method: Outline for a critical methodology.* Unpublished manuscript, Indiana University.

Carspecken, P. F. (1999). *Four scenes for posing the question of meaning and other essays in critical philosophy and critical methodology.* New York: Peter Lang.

Chapman, D. E. (Ed.). (2010). *Examining social theory: Crossing borders/ reflecting back.* New York: Peter Lang.

Clough, P. T. (1998). *The end(s) of ethnography: From realism to social criticism* (2nd ed.). New York: Peter Lang.

Collins, J. (1995). *Architectures of excess: Cultural life in the information age.* New York: Routledge.

Cucinelli, G. (2010). *Digital youth praxis and social justice.* Unpublished doctoral dissertation, McGill University, Montréal, Québec, Canada.

Dale, J., & Hyslop-Margison, E. J. (2010). *Paulo Freire: Teaching for freedom and transformation.* Dordrecht, the Netherlands: Springer.

Darder, A. (2010). Schooling bodies: Critical pedagogy and urban youth [Foreword]. In Steinberg, S. R. (Ed.), *19 urban questions: Teaching in the city* (pp. xiii–xxiii). New York: Peter Lang.

Dei, G. (Ed.). (2011). *Indigenous philosophies and critical education.* New York: Peter Lang.

De Lissovoy, N., & McLaren, P. (2003). Educational "accountability" and the violence of capital: A Marxian reading. *Journal of Education Policy, 18,* 131–143.

Denzin, N. K. (1994). The art and politics of interpretation. In N. K. Denzin & Y. S. Lincoln (Eds.), *Handbook of qualitative research.* Thousand Oaks, CA: Sage.

Denzin, N. K. (2003). *Performative ethnography: Critical pedagogy and the politics of culture.* Thousand Oaks, CA: Sage.

Denzin, N. K., & Lincoln, Y. S. (2000). Introduction: The discipline and practice of qualitative research. In N. K. Denzin & Y. S. Lincoln (Eds.), *Handbook of qualitative research* (2nd ed.). Thousand Oaks, CA: Sage.

DeVault, M. (1996). Talking back to sociology: Distinctive contributions of feminist methodology. *Annual Review of Sociology, 22,* 29–50.

Fiske, J. (1993). *Power works, power plays.* New York: Verso.

Flecha, R., Gomez, J., & Puigvert, L. (Eds.). (2003). *Contemporary sociological theory.* New York: Peter Lang.

Flossner, G., & Otto, H. (Eds.). (1998). *Towards more democracy in social services: Models of culture and welfare.* New York: Aldine.

Foster, R. (1997). Addressing epistemologic and practical issues in multimethod research: A procedure for conceptual triangulation. *Advances in Nursing Education, 20*(2), 1–12.

Freire, A. M. A. (2000). Foreword. In P. McLaren, *Che Guevara, Paulo Freire, and the pedagogy of revolution.* Boulder, CO: Rowman & Littlefield.

Freire, P. (1970). *Pedagogy of the oppressed.* New York: Herder and Herder.

Freire, P. (1972). *Research methods.* Paper presented at a seminar on Studies in Adult Education, Dar es Salaam, Tanzania.

Freire, P. (1978). *Education for critical consciousness.* New York: Seabury.

Freire, P. (1985). *The politics of education: Culture, power, and liberation.* South Hadley, MA: Bergin & Garvey.

Freire, P., & Faundez, A. (1989). *Learning to question: A pedagogy of liberation.* London: Continuum.

Friedman, S. (1998). (Inter)disciplinarity and the question of the women's studies Ph.D. *Feminist Studies, 24*(2), 301–326.

Fuchs, M. (1993). The reversal of the ethnological perspective: Attempts at objectifying one's own cultural horizon: Dumont, Foucault, Bourdieu? *Thesis Eleven, 34*(1), 104–125.

Gadamer, H.-G. (1989). *Truth and method* (2nd rev. ed., J. Weinsheimer & D. G. Marshall, Eds. & Trans.). New York: Crossroad.

Giroux, H. (1983). *Theory and resistance in education: A pedagogy for the opposition.* South Hadley, MA: Bergin & Garvey.

Giroux, H. (1988). Critical theory and the politics of culture and voice: Rethinking the discourse of educational research. In R. Sherman & R. Webb (Eds.), *Qualitative research in education: Focus and methods.* New York: Falmer.

Giroux, H. (1997). *Pedagogy and the politics of hope: Theory, culture, and schooling.* Boulder, CO: Westview.

Giroux, H. (2010). *Zombie politics and the age of casino capitalism.* New York: Peter Lang.

Goldie, T. (1995). The representation of the indigenous. In B. Ashcroft, G. Griffiths, & H. Tiffin (Eds.), *The post-colonial studies reader.* New York: Routledge.

Grande, S. (2004). *Red pedagogy: Native American social and political thought.* Lanham, MD: Rowman & Littlefield.

Gresson, A. D., III. (2006). Doing critical research in mainstream disciplines: Reflections on a study of Black female individuation. In K. Tobin & J. Kincheloe (Eds.), *Doing educational research.* Rotterdam, the Netherlands: Sense Publishers.

Grinberg, J. (2003). "Only the facts?" In D. Weil & J. L. Kincheloe (Eds.), *Critical thinking: An encyclopedia.* New York: Greenwood.

Hammer, R., & Kellner, D. (2009). *Media/cultural studies: Critical approaches.* New York: Peter Lang.

Harper, D. (1987). *Working knowledge: Skill and community in a small shop.* Chicago: University of Chicago Press.

Hickey, A., & Austin, J. (2009). Working visually in community identity ethnography. *International Journal of the Humanities, 7*(4), 1–14. Available at http://eprints.usq.edu.au/5800/

Hinchey, P. (2009). *Finding freedom in the classroom: A practical introduction to critical theory.* New York: Peter Lang.

Hooley, N. (2009). *Narrative life: Democratic curriculum and indigenous learning.* Dordrecht, the Netherlands: Springer.

Horkheimer, M. (1972). *Critical theory.* New York: Seabury.

Horn, R. (2004). *Standards.* New York: Peter Lang.

Horton, M., & Freire, P. (1990). *We make the road by walking: Conversations on education and social change.* Philadelphia: Temple University Press.

Hyslop-Margison, E. J. (2009). Scientific paradigms and falsification: Kuhn, Popper and problems in education research. *Educational Policy, 20*(10), 1–17.

Hyslop-Margison, E. J., & Naseem, A. (2007). *Scientism and education: Empirical research as neo-liberal ideology.* Dordrecht, the Netherlands: Springer.

Janesick, V. (2010). *Oral history for the qualitative researcher: Choreographing the story.* New York: Guilford.

Jardine, D. (1992). The fecundity of the individual case: Considerations of the pedagogic heart of interpretive work. *British Journal of Philosophy of Education. 26*(1), 51–61.

Jardine, D. (1998). *To dwell with a boundless heart: Essays in curriculum theory, hermeneutics, and the ecological imagination.* New York: Peter Lang.

Jardine, D. (2006a). On hermeneutics: "What happens to us over and above our wanting and doing." In K. Tobin & J. L. Kincheloe (Eds.), *Doing educational research* (pp. 269–288). Rotterdam, the Netherlands: Sense Publishers.

Jardine, D. (2006b). *Piaget and education.* New York: Peter Lang.

Keesing-Styles, L. (2003). The relationship between critical pedagogy and assessment in teacher education. *Radical Pedagogy, 5*(1). Available at http://radicalpedagogy.icaap .org/content/issue5_1/03_keesing-styles.html

Kellner, D. (1995). *Media culture: Cultural studies, identity, and politics between the modern and the postmodern.* New York: Routledge.

Kincheloe, J. L. (1998). Critical research in science education. In B. Fraser & K. Tobin (Eds.), International handbook of science education (Pt. 2). Boston: Kluwer.

Kincheloe, J. L. (2001a). Describing the bricolage: Conceptualizing a new rigour in qualitative research. *Qualitative Inquiry, 7*(6), 679–692.

Kincheloe, J. (2001b). *Getting beyond the facts: Teaching social studies/social sciences in the twenty-first century* (2nd ed.). New York: Peter Lang.

Kincheloe, J. (2003a). Critical ontology: Visions of selfhood and curriculum. *JCT: Journal of Curriculum Theorizing, 19*(1), 47–64.

Kincheloe, J. L. (2003b). Into the great wide open: Introducing critical thinking. In D. Weil & J. Kincheloe (Eds.), *Critical thinking: An encyclopedia.* Santa Barbara, CA: ABC-CLIO.

Kincheloe, J. L. (2003c). *Teachers as researchers: Qualitative paths to empowerment* (2nd ed.). London: Falmer.

Kincheloe, J. L. (2004). Iran and American miseducation: Coverups, distortions, and omissions. In J. Kincheloe & S. Steinberg (Eds.), *The miseducation of the West: Constructing Islam.* New York: Greenwood.

Kincheloe, J. L. (2007). *Teachers as researchers: Qualitative paths to empowerment.* London: Falmer.

Kincheloe, J. L. (2008a). *Critical pedagogy primer* (2nd ed.). New York: Peter Lang.

Kincheloe, J. L. (2008b). *Knowledge and critical pedagogy.* Dordrecht, the Netherlands: Springer.

Kincheloe, J. L., & Berry, K. (2004). *Rigour and complexity in educational research: Conceptualizing the bricolage.* London: Open University Press.

Kincheloe, J. L., & Steinberg, S. R. (1993). A tentative description of post-formal thinking: The critical confrontation with cognitive theory. *Harvard Educational Review, 63,* 296–320.

Kincheloe, J. L., & Steinberg, S. R. (1997). *Changing multiculturalism: New times, new curriculum.* London: Open University Press.

Kincheloe, J. L., & Steinberg, S. R. (2008). Indigenous knowledges in education: Complexities, dangers, and profound benefits. In N. K. Denzin, Y. S. Lincoln, & L. T. Smith, (Eds.), *Handbook of critical and indigenous methodologies.* Thousand Oaks, CA: Sage Publishing.

Kincheloe, J. L., Steinberg, S. R., & Hinchey, P. (Eds.). (1999). *The post-formal reader: Cognition and education.* New York: Falmer.

Kincheloe, J. L., & Tobin, K. (2009). The much exaggerated death of positivism. *Cultural Studies of Science Education, 4,* 513–528.

Kirylo, J. (2011). Paulo Freire: *The man from Recife.* New York: Peter Lang.

Kress, T. (2010). Tilting the machine: A critique of one teacher's attempts at using art forms to create postformal, democratic learning environments. *The Journal of Educational Controversy, 5*(1).

Kress, T., & Silva, K. (2009). Using digital video for professional development and leadership: Understanding and initiating teacher learning communities. In I. Gibson et al. (Eds.), *Proceedings of Society for Information Technology & Teacher Education International Conference 2009* (pp. 2841–2847). Chesapeake, VA: Association for the Advancement of Computing in Education (AACE).

Leistyna, P., Woodrum, A., & Sherblom, S. (1996). *Breaking free: The transformative power of critical pedagogy.* Cambridge, MA: Harvard Educational Review.

Lemke, J. L. (1998). Analyzing verbal data: Principles, methods, and problems. In B. Fraser & K. Tobin (Eds.), *International handbook of science education* (Pt. 2). Boston: Kluwer.

Lévi-Strauss, C. (1968). *The savage mind.* Chicago: University of Chicago Press.

Lincoln, Y. (2001). An emerging new bricoleur: Promises and possibilities—a reaction to Joe Kincheloe's "Describing the bricoleur." *Qualitative Inquiry, 7*(6), 693–696.

Lund, D., & Carr, P. (Eds.). (2008). *Doing democracy: Striving for political literacy and social justice.* New York: Peter Lang.

Lutz, K., Jones, K. D., & Kendall, J. (1997). Expanding the praxis debate: Contributions to clinical inquiry. *Advances in Nursing Science, 20*(2), 23–31.

Macedo, D. (2006). *Literacies of power: What Americans are not allowed to know* (2nd ed.). Boulder, CO: Westview.

Macrine, S., Hill, D., & McLaren, P. (Eds.). (2009). *Critical pedagogy: Theory and praxis.* London: Routledge.

Macrine, S., McLaren, P., & Hill, D. (Eds.). (2009). *Revolutionizing pedagogy: Educating for social justice within and beyond global neo-liberalism.* London: Palgrave Macmillan.

Manganaro, M. (1990). Textual play, power, and cultural critique: An orientation to modernist anthropology. In M. Manganaro (Ed.), *Modernist anthropology: From fieldwork to text.* Princeton, NJ: Princeton University Press.

Marcus, G. E., & Fischer, M. M. J. (1986). *Anthropology as cultural critique: An experimental moment in the human sciences.* Chicago: University of Chicago Press.

Mayo, P. (2009). *Liberating praxis: Paulo Freire's legacy for radical education and politics.* Rotterdam, the Netherlands: Sense Publishing.

McLaren, P. (1992). Collisions with otherness: "Traveling" theory, post-colonial criticism, and the politics of ethnographic practice—the mission of the wounded ethnographer. *International Journal of Qualitative Studies in Education, 5,* 77–92.

McLaren, P. (1997). *Revolutionary multiculturalism: Pedagogies of dissent for the new millennium.* New York: Routledge.

McLaren, P. (1999). *Schooling as a ritual performance: Toward a political economy of educational symbols and gestures* (3rd ed.). Boulder, CO: Rowman & Littlefield.

McLaren, P. (2001). Bricklayers and bricoleurs: A Marxist addendum. *Qualitative Inquiry, 7*(6), 700–705.

McLaren, P. (2002). Marxist revolutionary praxis: A curriculum of transgression. *Journal of Curriculum Inquiry Into Curriculum and Instruction, 3*(3), 36–41.

McLaren, P. (2003a). Critical pedagogy in the age of neoliberal globalization: Notes from history's underside. *Democracy and Nature, 9*(1), 65–90.

McLaren, P. (2003b). The dialectics of terrorism: A Marxist response to September 11: Part Two. Unveiling the past, evading the present. *Cultural Studies <=> Critical Methodologies, 3*(1), 103–132.

McLaren, P. (2009). E. San Juan, Jr.: The return of the transformative intellectual. *Left Curve, 33,* 118–121.

McLaren, P., & Farahmandpur, R. (2003). Critical pedagogy at ground zero: Renewing the educational left after 9–11. In D. Gabbard & K. Saltman (Eds.), *Education as enforcement: The militarization and corporatization of schools.* New York: Routledge.

McLaren, P., & Farahmandpur, R. (2006). Who will educate the educators? Critical pedagogy in the age of globalization. In A. Dirlik (Ed.), *Pedagogies of the global: Knowledge in the human interest* (pp. 19–58). Boulder, CO: Paradigm.

McLaren, P., & Jaramillo, N. (2010). Not neo-Marxist, not post-Marxist, not Marxian, not autonomist Marxism: Reflections on a revolutionary (Marxist) critical pedagogy. *Cultural Studies <=> Critical Methodologies, 10*(3), 251–262.

McLaren, P., & Kincheloe, J. L. (2007). *Critical pedagogy: Where are we now?* New York: Peter Lang.

McLeod, J. (2000, June). *Qualitative research as bricolage.* Paper presented at the annual conference of the Society for Psychotherapy Research, Chicago.

Myrsiades, K., & Myrsiades, L. (Eds.). (1998). *Race-ing representation: Voice, history, and sexuality.* Lanham, MD: Rowman & Littlefield.

Nocella, A. J., II, Best, S., & McLaren, P. (2010). *Academic repression: Reflections from the academic industrial complex.* Oakland, CA: AK Press.

Park, J. (2005). *Writing at the edge: Narrative and writing process theory.* New York: Peter Lang.

Peters, M. (1993). *Against Finkielkraut's la défaite de la pensés culture, post-modernism and education*. Unpublished manuscript, University of Glasgow, Scotland.

Pieterse, J., & Parekh, B. (1995). Shifting imaginaries: Decolonization, internal decolonization, postcoloniality. In J. Pieterse & B. Parekh (Eds.), *The decolonization of imagination: Culture, knowledge, and power*. Atlantic Highlands, NJ: Zed.

Porfilio, B., & Carr, P. (Eds.). (2010). *Youth culture, education, and resistance: Subverting the commercial ordering of life*. Rotterdam, the Netherlands: Sense Publishing.

Prakash, M., & Esteva, G. (2008). *Escaping education: Living as learning within grassroots cultures*. New York: Peter Lang.

Pryse, M. (1998). Critical interdisciplinarity, women's studies, and cross-cultural insight. *National Women's Studies Association Journal, 10*(1), 1–11.

Quail, C. B., Razzano, K. A., & Skalli, L. H. (2004). *Tell me more: Rethinking daytime talk shows*. New York: Peter Lang.

Quantz, R. A. (1992). On critical ethnography (with some postmodern considerations). In M. D. LeCompte, W. L. Millroy, & J. Preissle (Eds.), *The handbook of qualitative research in education*. New York: Academic Press.

Quintero, E., & Rummel, M. K. (2003). *Becoming a teacher in the new society: Bringing communities and classrooms together*. New York: Peter Lang.

Rodriguez, N. M., & Villaverde, L. (2000). *Dismantling White privilege*. New York: Peter Lang.

Roman, L., & Eyre, L. (Eds.). (1997). *Dangerous territories: Struggles for difference and equality in education*. New York: Routledge.

Roth, W.-M., & Tobin, K. (2010). Solidarity and conflict: Prosody as a transactional resource in intra- and intercultural communication involving power differences. *Cultural Studies of Science Education, 5*(4), 807–847.

Ryoo, J. J., & McLaren, P. (2010). Aloha for sale: A class analysis of Hawaii. In D. E. Chapman (Ed.), *Examining social theory: Crossing borders/reflecting back* (pp. 3–18). New York: Peter Lang.

San Juan, E., Jr. (1992). *Articulations of power in ethnic and racial studies in the United States*. Atlantic Highlands, NJ: Humanities Press.

Scatamburlo-D'Annibale, V., & McLaren, P. (2009). The reign of capital: A pedagogy and praxis of class struggle. In M. Apple, W. Au, & L. Armando Gandin (Eds.), *The Routledge international handbook of critical education* (pp. 96–109). New York and London: Routledge.

Scheurich, J. J., & Young, M. (1997). Coloring epistemologies: Are our research epistemologies racially biased? *Educational Researcher, 26*(4), 4–16.

Selfe, C. L., & Selfe, R. J., Jr. (1994). The politics of the interface: Power and its exercise in electronic contact zones. *College Composition and Communication, 45*(4), 480–504.

Semali, L., & Kincheloe, J. L. (1999). *What is indigenous knowledge? Voices from the academy*. New York: Falmer.

Shor, I. (1996). *When students have power: Negotiating authority in a critical pedagogy*. Chicago: University of Chicago Press.

Sikes, P. (2008). Researching research cultures: The case of new universities. In P. Sikes & A. Potts (Eds.), *Researching education from the inside: Investigations from within.* Abingdon, UK: Routledge.

Silverman, E. K. (1990). Clifford Geertz: Towards a more "thick" understanding? In C. Tilley (Ed.), *Reading material culture.* Cambridge, MA: Blackwell.

Siry, C. A., & Lang, D. E. (2010). Creating participatory discourse for teaching and research in early childhood science. *Journal of Science Teacher Education, 21,* 149–160.

Skalli, L. (2004). Loving Muslim women with a vengeance: The West, women, and fundamentalism. In J. L. Kincheloe & S. R. Steinberg (Eds.), *The miseducation of the West: Constructing Islam.* New York: Greenwood.

Slee, R. (2011). *The irregular school: Schooling and inclusive education.* London: Routledge.

Soto, L. (Ed.). (2000). *The politics of early childhood education.* New York: Peter Lang.

Souto-Manning, M. (2009). *Freire, teaching, and learning: Culture circles across contexts.* New York: Peter Lang.

Steinberg, S. R. (2000). The nature of genius. In J. L. Kincheloe, S. R. Steinberg, & D. J. Tippins (Eds.), *The stigma of genius: Einstein, consciousness, and education.* New York: Peter Lang.

Steinberg, S. R. (Ed.). (2001). *Multi/intercultural conversations.* New York: Peter Lang.

Steinberg, S. R. (2004a). Desert minstrels: Hollywood's curriculum of Arabs and Muslims. In J. L. Kincheloe & S. R. Steinberg (Eds.), *The miseducation of the West: Constructing Islam.* New York: Greenwood.

Steinberg, S. R. (2004b). Kinderculture: The cultural studies of childhood. In N. Denzin (Ed.), *Cultural studies: A research volume.* Greenwich, CT: JAI.

Steinberg, S. R. (2007). Cutting class in a dangerous era: A critical pedagogy of class awareness. In J. Kincheloe & S. Steinberg (Eds.), *Cutting class: Socioeconomic status and education.* Lanham, MD: Rowman & Littlefield.

Steinberg, S. R. (2008). Reading media critically. In D. Macedo & S. Steinberg (Eds.), *Media literacy: A reader.* New York: Peter Lang.

Steinberg, S. R. (2009). *Diversity and multiculturalism: A reader.* New York: Peter Lang.

Steinberg, S. R. (2010). Power, emancipation, and complexity: Employing critical theory. *Journal of Power and Education, 2*(2), 140–151.

Steinberg, S. R. (2011). Critical cultural studies research: Bricolage in action. In K. Tobin & J. Kincheloe (Eds.), *Doing educational research* (2nd ed.). Rotterdam, the Netherlands: Sense Publishing.

Steinberg, S. R. (in press). *The bricolage.* New York: Peter Lang.

Steinberg, S. R., & Kincheloe, J. L. (Eds.). (1998). *Students as researchers: Creating classrooms that matter.* London: Taylor & Francis.

Steinberg, S. R., & Kincheloe, J. L. (2011). Employing the bricolage as critical research in science education. In B. J. Fraser, K. Tobin, & C. J. McRobbie (Eds.), *The international handbook of research in science education* (2nd ed.). Dordrecht, the Netherlands: Springer.

Thayer-Bacon, B. (2003). *Relational "(e)pistemologies."* New York: Peter Lang.

Tobin, K. (2009). Repetition, difference and rising up with research in education. In K. Ercikan & W.-M. Roth (Eds.), *Generalizing from educational research* (pp. 149–172). New York: Routledge.

Tobin, K. (2010). Global reproduction and transformation of science education. *Cultural Studies of Science Education, 5.*

Tobin, K., & Llena, R. (2010). Producing and maintaining culturally adaptive teaching and learning of science in urban schools. In C. Murphy & K. Scantlebury (Eds.), *Coteaching in international contexts: Research and practice* (pp. 79–104). Dordrecht, the Netherlands: Springer.

Trueba, E. T., & McLaren, P. (2000). Critical ethnography for the study of immigrants. In E. T. Trueba & L. I. Bartolomé (Eds.), *Immigrant voices: In search of educational equity.* Boulder, CO: Rowman & Littlefield.

Varenne, H. (with McDermott, R. P.). (1996). Culture, development, disability. In R. Jessor, A. Colby, & R. Shweder (Eds.), *Ethnography and human development.* Chicago: University of Chicago Press.

Vicars, M. (2008). Is it all about me? How Queer! In P. Sikes & A. Potts (Eds.), *Researching education from the inside: Investigations from within.* Abingdon, UK: Routledge.

Viergever, M. (1999). Indigenous knowledge: An interpretation of views from indigenous peoples. In L. Semali & J. L. Kincheloe (Eds.), *What is indigenous knowledge? Voices from the academy.* Bristol, PA: Falmer.

Villaverde, L. (2007). *Feminist theories and education primer.* New York: Peter Lang.

Villaverde, L., & Kincheloe, J. L. (1998). Engaging students as researchers: Researching and teaching Thanksgiving in the elementary classroom. In S. R. Steinberg & J. L. Kincheloe (Eds.), *Students as researchers: Creating classrooms that matter.* London: Falmer.

Watts, M. (2006). Disproportionate sacrifices: Ricoeur's theories of justice and the widening participation agenda for higher education in the UK. *Journal of Philosophy of Education, 40*(3), 301–312.

Watts, M. (2008). Narrative research, narrative capital, narrative capability. In J. Satterthwaite, M. Watts, & H. Piper (Eds.), *Talking truth, confronting power: Discourse, power, resistance* (Vol. 6). Stoke on Trent, UK: Trentham Books.

Watts, M. (2009a). Higher education and hyperreality. In P. Smeyers & M. Depaepe (Eds.), *Educational research: Educationalisation of social problems.* Dordrecht, the Netherlands: Springer.

Watts, M. (2009b). Sen and the art of motorcycle maintenance: Adaptive preferences and higher education in England. *Studies in Philosophy and Education, 28*(5), 425–436.

Weil, D., & Kincheloe, J. (Eds.). (2004). *Critical thinking and learning: An encyclopedia for parents and teachers.* Westport, CT: Greenwood.

Wesson, L., & Weaver, J. (2001). Administration-educational standards: Using the lens of postmodern thinking to examine the role of the school administrator. In J. Kincheloe & D. Weil (Eds.), *Standards and schooling in the United States: An encyclopedia* (3 vols.). Santa Barbara, CA: ABC-CLIO.

Wexler, P. (2008). *Social theory in education.* New York: Peter Lang.

Willinsky, J. (2001). Raising the standards for democratic education: Research and evaluation as public knowledge. In J. Kincheloe & D. Weil (Eds.), *Standards and schooling in the United States: An encyclopedia* (3 vols.). Santa Barbara, CA: ABC-CLIO.

Willis, P. E. (1977). *Learning to labour: How working class kids get working class jobs.* Farnborough, UK: Saxon House.

Willis, P. (2000). *The ethnographic imagination.* Cambridge, UK: Polity.

Wright, H. K. (2003a). An introduction to the history, methods, politics and selected traditions of qualitative research in education [Editorial]. *Tennessee Education, 32*(2), 5–7.

Wright, H. K. (Ed.). (2003b). Qualitative research in education. *Tennessee Education, 32*(2).

Wright, H. K., & Lather, P. (Eds.). (2006). Paradigm proliferation in educational research. *International Journal of Qualitative Studies in Education, 19*(1).

Zizek, S. (1990). Beyond discourse analysis. In E. Laclau, (Ed.), *New reflections on the revolution of our time.* London: Verso.

Cultural Studies

Performative Imperatives and Bodily Articulations[1]

Michael D. Giardina and Joshua I. Newman

Cultural studies has always been propelled by its desire to construct possibilities, both immediate and imaginary, out of its historical circumstances. It has no pretensions to totality or universality; it seeks only to give us a better understanding of where we are so that we can get somewhere else (some place, we hope, that is better—based on more just principles of equality and the distribution of wealth and power).

—Lawrence Grossberg, 1997, p. 415

I. Proem

In the first edition of the *Handbook of Qualitative Research*, John Fiske (1994) began his chapter on cultural studies with the following statement: "Cultural studies is such a contested and currently trendy term that I must disclaim any attempt to either define or speak for it" (p. 189). Nearly 20 years later, Fiske's comment about the contested terrain of the field still holds true; today we find multiple, if not competing cultural studies projects at work.[2] In fact, and as if to underscore the multiplicity of formations, the three chapters on cultural studies to appear in earlier editions of the *Handbook* have each taken strikingly varied approaches to the deployment of cultural studies as theory and method: Fiske addressed production and consumption of media texts and audiences; John Frow and Meghan Morris (2000) outlined a largely multiperspectival approach to culture in an ever-evolving, globalizing world; and Paula Saukko (2005) offered an integrative methodological approach to contextual, dialogic, and self-reflexive validity.

The fourth edition continues this evolutionary trend, as our chapter moves in yet another direction, delving largely into the performative imperatives and bodily articulations of cultural studies in an age of increasing uncertainty characterized by, among other major developments: the post-9/11/01 militarization of culture; a war of aggression by imperial Western powers in Iraq and Afghanistan; the further destabilization of the Middle East as brought forth by, among other things, the Israeli/Palestinian conflict; the meltdown of worldwide financial markets and institutions; drastically rising levels of unemployment and widening gaps between the rich and poor; the growing threats of religious fundamentalism and theocratic nationalism; a condition of neoliberal capitalism run wild; and so forth.

In a collectivity of these instances, we especially find "the body" under various forms of duress:

- Assailed by (global) capital's twin logics of overconsumption (think: genetically modified food in a child's Happy Meal) and overproduction (think: corporate accumulation through the exploitation of underprivileged bodies);

- Gradually stripped of its plurality and subjected to homogenizing strategies of the global popular;

- Discursively confined to the frames of heteronormative, patriarchal, xenophobic, White paranoia;

- Increasingly mediated as both an *immanent threat* (e.g., as carrier of influenza or of Jihadist intent) and as *under threat* (e.g., loss of human rights, etc.); and

- Forced to become an apparatus for—and collateral casualty of—war and genocide in such places as Afghanistan, Bosnia, Kashmir, Iraq, Sudan, Zimbabwe, and elsewhere.

Indeed, these are tough times for the body, deeply entangled as it is in the now-banal conditions of (social and material) production and accumulation; enwrapped in the hegemony of a fundamentalist assault on women's rights, equal rights, and social and economic justice; and "enfleshed" (McLaren, 1988) by the spectacle of the fetishized commodity. These developments have brought about an increasingly complex commixture of bodily contact and separation wherein overconsuming bodies of the developed world are perpetually engaged in the spectacles of late capitalism, and yet in ways that alienate the consumer from the bodies residing on the other end of these exploitative chains of interdependence. We need only glimpse at the front pages of our ever-disappearing newsprint to see headlines heralding the latest legal victory for antichoice advocates or giddily proclaiming increased bodily surveillance technologies being deployed at our airports (e.g., controversial full-body X-ray scanners) or advertisements for the latest reality television fare trading in body maintenance (e.g., *Project Runway*), modification (e.g., *The Biggest Loser*), or mastery (e.g., *Man v. Food*).

In light of these bodily discourses and the increasing importance placed on physical cultural forms and their attendant derivations more generally, this chapter offers both an overview of and a new methodological direction for what David Andrews (2008), Andrews and Michael Silk (2011), Jennifer Hargreaves and Patricia Vertinsky (2006), Alan Ingham (1985), and Pirkko Markula and Richard Pringle (2006) among others, have variously identified by the term *physical* cultural studies—that is, an antidisciplinary intellectual domain aimed at understanding "the complex and diverse practices and representations of active embodiment" and the "empirical and political import of cultural physicalities" (Silk & Andrews, in press) in the historical present.[3] To this end, we argue that such a *radically embodied* project can be found within (at least) three generative coordinates: (1) locating the body within cultural studies' articulative and radically contextual politics; (2) parting ways with the allusive embodiments that haunt most poststructuralist imaginings of the textualized corporeal in favor of a "bodily participative" research paradigm whereby active, agentive human bodies (and their flesh politics) are engaged through sometimes messy, sometimes difficult, sometimes dangerous points of corporeal contact; and (3) self-reflexively wrestling with the bodily politics of research performance, the very research act of physical cultural studies itself.

We begin by situating physical cultural studies within broader discussions related to cultural studies, articulation, and contextual analysis. We then move to directly engage with the embodied practice/s of the research act. In so doing, we draw on various contributions to this fledgling field (including some of our own work), especially as related to sporting physicalities, to discuss the promise of bodily participation. In this way, we move to take up the case of the critically reflexive body within cultural studies writ large and how it can best serve the interests of a public pedagogy—and ultimately "as a means for communicating important social understandings, social criticism, and powerful emotion-laden social science research" (Lincoln, 2004, p. 140). We conclude by offering a rejoinder as to the future of [physical] cultural studies.

II. Revisiting the Politics of Cultural Studies

Before moving forward, some history is in order. Cultural studies, in many of the recognizable iterations, has been a mainstay in contemporary academic discourse from at least the mid-1950s to the present. Institutionally speaking, its (Western) beginnings are popularly though not unproblematically traced to the establishment of the Centre for Contemporary Cultural Studies (CCCS) at the University of Birmingham, United Kingdom, in 1964. Founded by Richard Hoggart and later reaching its apex during the leadership of Stuart Hall, the early work of (British) cultural studies at the CCCS is generally looked on, from a theoretical standpoint, as having used "the methods of literary criticism to understand popular and mass culture and to develop criteria for critically evaluating specific texts" (Dworkin, 1997, p. 116). Leading the way were figures such as Hoggart (*The Uses of Literacy,* 1957), Raymond Williams (*Culture and Society,* 1958), and E. P. Thompson (*Making of the English Working Class,* 1963), the three of whom authored what are considered by many to be among the seminal texts of early (British) cultural studies research. Cast as active interventions into understanding a particular crisis of "English" national identity following World War II—specifically, why large segments of the working class chose to align with a particular political ideology that was seemingly at odds with and did not appear to represent so-called traditional working-class values—their work was *inherently* political.[4]

However, and whereas the CCCS under Hoggart focused on everyday lived experiences and transformations of the English working class, the Hall years took (British) cultural studies in a new direction—what he called "Marxism without guarantees" (Hall, 1982)—as he sought to account for the emergence of the New Right within British politics in the second half of the 1970s. As such, Hall's approach focused on the contextual specificities of cultural meanings, relations, and identities within the temporal and spatial boundaries of the object in question. Marking this shift were numerous texts that have become hallmarks in the field, among them *Policing the Crisis: Mugging, the State, and Law and Order* (Hall, Critcher, Jefferson, Clarke, & Roberts, 1978), *The Empire Strikes Back: Race and Racism in 70s Britain* (CCCS, 1982), *There Ain't No Black in the Union Jack: The Cultural Politics of Race and Nation* (Gilroy, 1987), and *Learning to Labor: How Working-Class Kids Get Working-Class Jobs* (Willis, 1977).[5]

Somewhat lost among this historical record, however, as David Andrews and Jon Loy (1993), and later David Andrews and Michael Giardina (2008), remind us, is that cultural physicalities—most notably those related to the sporting body, but also the leisuring body, active body, healthy body, and so on—have long been embedded within the development of the (British) cultural studies tradition. In point of fact, such physicalities have been a recurrent focus of cultural studies research ever since it was discussed within Hoggart's (1957) critique of postwar British working-class culture; the subtitle of Hoggart's book, *The Uses of Literacy: Aspects of Working-Class Life, With Special Reference to Publications and Entertainments*, expresses its implicit focus on popular institutions such as sport. Indeed, Hoggart's literary humanistic approach viewed sporting culture as a popular practice that easily related to the material conditions and experiences of working-class existence:

> At work, sport vies with sex as the staple conversation. The popular Sunday newspapers are read as much for their full sports reports as for their accounts of the week's crimes. Sports conversations start from personalities, often spoken of by their Christian as well as by their surnames, as "Jim Motson," "Arthur Jones," and "Will Thompson": technical details of play are discussed, often to the accompaniment of extraordinary feats of memory as to the history of matches many seasons back. The men talk about individuals whom they know, at least as figures on the field, in situations eliciting qualities they can respect and admire. (p. 91)

In addition, in his landmark study, *The Making of the English Working Class*, E. P. Thompson (1963) would a few years after Hoggart identify numerous physical, leisuring, and sporting practices that contributed to the creation of a coherent English working-class culture within conditions of industrialization. (for more see Andrews & Giardina, 2008, p. 398).

However, as Andrews and Loy (1993) rightfully point out in their authoritative excavation of "sport" from the CCCS's Working Papers in Cultural Studies and Occasional Stenciled Papers series, it was not until cultural studies was institutionalized at the CCCS that "sport-focused cultural studies projects began to appear" (p. 30) in wide circulation and with anything resembling regularity. A sampling of these papers speaks to the location of sport and the sporting/physical body within both the Centre and English culture; for example, we find Chas Critcher's writings on football (1971) and women's sports (1974) as a cultural practice; Paul Willis's studies of motorbike clubs (1971) and women's sports (1974); Rod Watson's (1973) account of public announcements of motor-racing fatalities; John Clarke's writings on football hooliganism vis-à-vis skinheads (1973, 1975); and Roy Peters's (1975) treatise on the television coverage of sport.

The impact of these early inroads was not lost on Toby Miller. Writing in his introduction to *A Companion to Cultural Studies,* Miller (2001) states:

> I recall my excitement when I first saw the cover of the Birmingham Center's *Working Papers in Cultural Studies 4* of 1973 . . . the bottom center-left read like this:
>
> LITERATURE~SOCIETY MOTOR RACING
>
> It seemed natural to me for these topics to be together (as is the case in a newspaper). But of course that is not academically "normal." To make them syntagmatic was *utterly sensible* in terms of people's lives and mediated realities, and *utterly improbable* in terms of intellectual divisions of labor and hierarchies of discrimination. (pp. 12–13, emphasis in original)

From these interventions forward, the corpus of sport/physical cultural studies blossomed—slowly at first, but later with increasing regularity— beginning to shape the field and take it in multiple directions in the early 1980s and into the 1990s (see, e.g., Andrews, 1993; Clarke & Critcher, 1985; Cole & Hribar, 1995; Gruneau, 1985; Gruneau & Whitson, 1993; Jackson, 1992; Tomlinson; 1981; Whannel, 1983). A guiding principle to take from this early work can be summed up in the work of two of the more prolific scholars associated with cultural studies' early formation, Clarke and Critcher. As they posit in *The Devil Makes Work: Leisure in Capitalist Britain* (1985), which focuses on the problematic politics of leisure and popular culture, their primary interest "is not really in 'leisure' itself, it is in what leisure can tell us about the development, structure, and organization of the whole society" (p. xviii). Updating Clarke and Critcher, we would suggest that our primary interest in the *physical* in this physical cultural studies of ours is not really about physical corporealities in and of themselves, but about what they can tell us about the development, structure, and organization of the whole society in the historical present.[6]

III. So What *Is* This *Physical* In Physical Cultural Studies?

In much the same way as the author from whom we liberally re-appropriate our title of this section asked in his article, "What Is This "Black" in Black Popular

Culture?" (Hall, 1993), we start with a question: *What sort of moment is this in which to pose the question of* physical *culture?* Clearly, it is an epoch in which the imperatives of economic growth and corporate-infused democracy in many cases supersedes society's will to ensure the health of its young, its poor, and its suffering; the laboring and leisuring vestiges of the Keynesian welfare state are being slowly eradicated in the pursuit of a "pure" free-market condition; access to spaces of bodily play and health have been colonized and made exclusionary for the purposes of capital accumulation; women's bodies, queer bodies, and Othered bodies of difference are still largely marginalized in most realms of global physical culture; and now, more then ever, the body is subjected to infantilizing, sexualizing, and objectifying disciplinary regimes.

This is an apt description, for definitional purposes at least, but how are we to better understand the ground-level impact of such developments on real people? How are we to better understand—and communicate—a cultural register about, as Arundhati Roy (2001) has so eloquently written, "what it's like to lose your home, your land, your job, your dignity, your past, and your future to an invisible force. To someone or something you can't see" (p. 32)—stories about what it's like to hate and feel despair, anger, and alienation in a world bursting at the seams as it struggles to reinvent itself and its dominant mythologies (see Denzin & Giardina, 2006). How can we come to see more clearly how "understanding is constituted by the cultural experiences embedded in [our] research" (Berry & Warren, 2009, p. 601) acts made meaningful by and through the "dynamic and dialectical relation of the text and body" (Spry, 2001, p. 711)?

Our answer, we believe, is that the best qualitative inquiries of physical culture—those that intercede on antihumane structures, practices, and symbolic acts within cultures of the active body—make use of *both* physical and ideological praxis to, as Ernesto Laclau and Chantal Mouffe (1985) posit, *articulate* the human experience with these broader contextual forces. These connections are meant to highlight "any practice establishing a relation among elements such that their identity is modified as a result of the articulatory practice" (Laclau & Mouffe, 1985, p. 105). Most often situated within Hall's (1996) work, the idea of the metaphoric lorry in conceptualizing the dialectic theory and method of articulation is quite helpful in understanding such a practice:

"Articulate" means to utter, to speak forth, to be articulate. It carries that sense of language-ing, of expressing, etc. But we also speak of an "articulated" lorry (truck): a lorry where the front (cab) and back (trailer) can, but need not necessarily, be connected to one another. The two parts are connected to each other, but through a specific linkage, that can be broken. An articulation is thus the form of the connections that can make a unity of two different elements, under certain conditions. It is a linkage which is not necessary, determined, absolute, and essential for all time. You have to ask under what circumstances *can* a connection be forged or made. (pp. 141–142; emphasis in original)

Or, as Jennifer Daryl Slack (1996) puts it, articulation is *both* that connection between broader contextual formations and the empirical transference we seek to establish and, at the same time, the methodological *episteme* under which we operate. On the articulation of context and practice, and with particular regard to the ways in which practice produces context, Slack writes: "The context is not something *out there, within which practices occur or which influence the development of practices. Rather, identities, practices, and effects generally constitute the very context in which they are practices, identities, or effects*" (p. 125, emphases in original).

Thus is our *physical* cultural studies project not simply an exercise in context mapping or abstracted corporeal cartography, but a method of using the political and politicized body to directly engage and interact with human activity; that is, an articulatory praxis that produces, and is produced by, social, political, and economic context/s. Furthermore, if we are to emerge from the tautological impasses of our structural Marxist forbearers, then we must break free from the determinism of early Marxist-inspired social thought, instead placing value on the idea that the cultures of the body are neither *necessarily correspondent* to the overdetermining structural realm (much like the economic base determining the superstructure) nor *necessarily noncorrespondent* (culture as autonomous from economic relations) (see Hall, 1985; Laclau & Mouffe, 1985). In other words, and rephrasing Andrews (2002), we might say that the structure and influence of the body in any given conjuncture is a product of intersecting, multidirectional lines of articulation between forces and practices that compose the social contexts. The very uniqueness of the historical moment or conjuncture means there is a condition of no necessary correspondence, or indeed noncorrespondence, between physical culture and particular forces (i.e., economic). Forces do determine *givenness* of physical practices; however, their determinacy cannot be guaranteed in advance (p. 116).

While there are no necessary guarantees that the body will be produced in predictable ways, this is not to suggest that the weight of social, political, and economic structures is not always already bearing down on the body. To rework Karl Marx, and later C. Wright Mills (1959), *we make our own cultural physicalities, but not under conditions of our choosing*. To ignore this fundamental dialectic is at once to abstract the body and to depoliticize its existence. Amid the tides of the academic-industrial complex, decontextualized or antidialectic analyses of the body are *made political.* To feign political neutrality is itself a political act, one that bolsters the hegemony of a natural, taken-for-grantedness of the formations of contemporary life—as the radical historian, Howard Zinn (1996), famously reminded us, "you can't be neutral on a moving train." Informed by Richard Johnson's (1987) formulation of (British) cultural studies, Andrews (2008) makes this point clear: "Physical Cultural Studies researchers must remain vigilant in their struggle against 'the disconnection' that will surely occur if we produc[e] studies in which physical cultural forms are divorced from contextual analyses of 'power and social possibilities'" (p. 58). In critically studying the cultures *of* the body, we seek to better understand context *through* bodily practice, as well as the oppressive and liberatory potential of the human body as constrained by contextual forces.

As such, we should strive to produce or elicit a public pedagogy that peculiarizes the banalities of political and politicized bodies. Indeed, by revealing the social constructedness of the historical contexts acting on cultures of the body, those working on/in physical culture should foster critical consciousness among both those individuals whose social, cultural, and economic status is inextricably linked to past cultures of alienation and exploitation and those individuals whose lives continue to be challenged as a result. Ben Carrington (2001) makes this point clear when he laments the depoliticized nature of too much of what passes for [physical] cultural studies today:

> Being able to deconstruct the dialogic processes within a Nike commercial is one thing; connecting them to the exploitative economic production of the shoes themselves in Southeast Asia, through to their consumption in the deprived inner-cities of the West, and the meanings this produces, is quite another, and a process too often not addressed. (p. 286)

Although such pseudo-political, relatively textual work of the kind Carrington critiques may well "teach us about consumer culture, late-capitalism, and identity politics therein" on some general level, as Joshua I. Newman (2008) notes, it nevertheless "fails to engage the dialectics of practice through which these discursive formations are made meaningful, consequential, and powerful" (p. 2), to move beyond a critique of texts to the relationships between texts, contexts, and interventions into the material realities of everyday operations of power.

In aiming to avoid such a pitfall, we actively follow and endorse the Brazilian critical educator Paulo Freire (1970/2006)—whose pedagogical method was a *mélange* of counteroppressive politics and emancipatory education, of classroom instruction and everyday encounters—in cultivating a form of popular education intended to share in the communal practice of raising individual consciousness (*conscientization*) of the political and oppressive regimes acting against the human condition. For Freire, this critical consciousness, or *conscientização*, comes about when individuals develop an epistemological awareness of the ways dialogic, political, and economic structures act on their everyday lives. Such awareness is nurtured through constant dialogue with, and consideration of, the oppressive elements of one's life, and actively imagining and working to make real alternative, egalitarian social formations.

As Norman Denzin and Michael Giardina's (2010) Freirean-inspired volume on qualitative inquiry and human rights helps us to remember, the conduct of qualitative inquiry "is not *just* about 'method' or 'technique,'" but likewise *also* an inherently political project that works toward "making the world visible in ways that implement the goals of social justice and radical, progressive democracy" (p. 14, emphasis in original).[7] In practical terms, this means subscribing to a public pedagogy that is "never neutral, just as it is never free from the influence of language, social, and political forces" (Giroux, 2000, p. 8). The goal here is to foster an engaged social citizenship, in effect a version of what Peter McLaren (2000) refers to as a *revolutionary pedagogy* that

> creates a narrative space set against the naturalized flow of the everyday, against the daily poetics of agency, encounter, and conflict, in which subjectivity is constantly dissolved and reconstructed—that is, in which subjectivity turns-back-on-itself, giving rise to both the affirmation of the world through naming it, and an opposition to the world through unmasking and undoing the practices of concealment that are latent in the process of naming itself. (p. 185)[8]

To wit, the field's principal intermediaries have often professed that only through rigorous, empirical qualitative encounters can we begin to elucidate the complexities of contemporary physical culture (e.g., Andrews, 2008; Andrews & Silk, 2011; Hargreaves & Vertinsky, 2006; Ingham, 1985; Markula & Pringle, 2006; etc.). This much we agree on, and there is an ever-growing body of work along this general plane that speaks to the promise and potential of physical cultural studies.

Jacqueline Reich's (2010) excellent work on the mediated dimensions of early 20th-century American physical culture as embodied by famed fitness guru Charles Atlas (born Angelo Siciliano in Calabria, Italy) is one such example, as she makes meaningful the textual discourses of "body building photography and the creation and marketing of his iconic fitness plan," which allowed for his public transformation from "Italian immigrant to pillar of American masculinity" (p. 450). As a work of cultural history and media analyses, Reich's article provides a lively and revealing critical interrogation of a popular historical figure whose success and celebrity was predicated on his physicality and the meanings ascribed to it through the armatures of fledgling marketing and advertising industries of the day, especially as related to the complex racial politics of immigration. In a related fashion, Shari Dworkin and Faye Linda Wachs (2004) investigated the gendered discourses germane to postindustrial motherhood in their textual analysis of *Shape Fit Pregnancy* (a magazine aimed at "young, intelligent, affluent, and professional" middle-class women); it is a tour de force commentary on the popular and political forces working to shape normative ideals of femininity, success, and healthy bodies narratives at the height of the U.S. health and fitness empowerment boom. Of course, these are just two of a myriad number of works published in recent years (e.g., Aalten, 2004; Atkinson, 2008; Brace-Govan, 2002; Butryn & Masucci, 2009; Chase, 2008; Cole, 2007; Evers, 2006; Francombe, 2010; Fusco, 2006; Grindstaff & West, 2006; Helstein, 2007; Markula, 1995; Metz, 2008; Miah, 2004; Schultz, 2004; Scott, 2010; Thorpe, 2009; van Ingen, 2004; Wedgewood, 2004; Wheatley, 2005; etc.) that have worked to establish a provisional canon for physical cultural studies (see Andrews, 2008, for more on this).

We have elsewhere engaged in a lengthy debate over several of the core tenets of this fledgling field (see Giardina & Newman, in press), breaking in some regard with our contemporaries about both the definitional and historical legacies contained therein. For our purposes here, and more widely applicable to the broader cultural studies universe, let it be sufficient to say that we want to push beyond the mediated, the textual, the corporeally disembodied to a more actively engaged research act—whatever the focus of empirical inquiry—one that does not reduce itself to textual patterns, media representations, and/or grand corporeal narratives or erase the researcher's own body and politics from any empirical discussion (or do some combination of both).

What we are arguing against then, is the abstraction of politically enfleshed bodies, the disappearance of authorial bodies, and the empirical dialectics of the self, which have given way to rhetorical bravado and, in some cases, what reads like educated guesswork. If we want [physical] cultural studies to matter as an intellectual domain—*or at the least, to push the field(s) forward within the pages of this handbook*—we believe that it has to be more than an empty metaphor, a bland descriptor of *any* study focused on *any* object residing in the cultural realm: We do not think it is enough to write and report on bodies and physicality alone *as if* we were in the field of body studies writ large (or sociology of the body, etc.), or simply apply some form of cultural studies inheritance to sites and artifacts of physical culture (which we have seen as a growing trend the last decade). Ours, then, is a project that seeks to *move beyond writing and researching* about *bodies to writing and researching* through *bodies as a principal force of the research act.*[9]

Put differently, we cannot allow [physical] cultural studies to become a discipline of professional *convenience:* It has to mean more than simply critically "reading" an object of culture from a *distance* (e.g., from our couch or in front of our computers; on ESPN, in *Sports Illustrated,* or on *The New York Times* website, etc.).[10] We cannot allow it to suffer from the same ill fate of (sadly, much of American) cultural studies, which—as Michael Bérubé (2009) recently reported in a somewhat disheartening but nevertheless accurate report on its perception within the corporate university—"now means everything and nothing; it has effectively been conflated with 'cultural criticism' in general, and associated with a cheery 'Pop culture is fun!' approach" (n.p.).[11] We cannot stand to see the field abandon the shared promise of a politically engaged, performative field of inquiry in favor of producing academic and economic capital for the sake of doing so (we readily admit that we are not immune to this charge, either). And we cannot ignore the extent to which the fact of the physical, and the study thereof and *through*, is *consequential;* that spatialized and temporalized empirical physicality is still besieged to ever-increasing ends by normative, hegemonic, and sometimes dangerous forces.

Rather, as Denzin (2007b) reminds us, the best of [physical] cultural studies should be conceived of as an emphatically political, *activist-minded* project, a public intellectualism on the order of the kind Noam Chomsky advanced in his 1967 article "The Responsibility of Intellectuals," where he argued that intellectuals (i.e., you) have a moral, ethical, and professional obligation to speak the truth, to expose lies, and to see events in their historical perspective (see also Denzin & Giardina, 2006).[12] To do so, we must think through the "radical implications of cultural politics, the role of academics and cultural workers as oppositional public intellectuals, and the centrality of cultural pedagogy as moral and political practice" (Giroux, 2001, pp. 5–6)—indeed, thinking through the very political dimensions of our research acts. We must seek critical methodologies that "protest, resist, and help us represent, imagine, and perform radically free utopian spaces" (Denzin, 2007b, p. 40)—methodologies that aid us in creating the very worlds we are embedded within, one that is always already performative, ideological, and pedagogical. We must see our pedagogy as a "kind of transformative intellectual practice that can encompass the variegated works of artists and critics, as well as researchers and educators" (Dimitriadis & Carlson, 2003, p. 3). We must, following Roy (2004), "never let a little hunk of expertise carry us off to our lair and guard against the unauthorized curiosity of passers-by" (p. 120), doing instead the opposite: "We must create links. Join the dots. Tell politics like a story. Communicate it. Make it real . . . And refuse to create barriers that prevent ordinary people from understanding what is happening to them" (p. 10).[13] And we must be committed, as Judith Butler (2004) writes in her moral polemic *Precarious Life,* to creating "a sense of the public in which oppositional voices are not feared, degraded, or dismissed, but valued for the instigation to a sensate democracy they occasionally perform" (p. 151).[14]

This is *not* to say, however, that our answers are or should be "determin[ed] in advance," that our politics should serve "as an excuse for not doing the work of coming to a better understanding of the context of struggle and possibility" (Grossberg, quoted in Cho, 2008, p. 121). Rather, and for example, as Freire (1999) expressed in *Pedagogy of Freedom:*

> My abhorrence of neoliberalism helps to explain my legitimate anger when I speak of the injustices to which the ragpickers among humanity are condemned. It also explains my total lack of interest in any pretension of impartiality. I am not impartial or objective; not a fixed observer of facts and happenings. I never was able to be an adherent of the traits that falsely claim impartiality or objectivity. That did not prevent me, however, from holding always a rigorously ethical position. Whoever really observes, does so from a given point of view. And this does not necessarily mean that the observer's position is erroneous. It is an error when one becomes dogmatic about one's point of view and ignores the fact that, even if one is certain about his or her point of view, it does not mean that one's position is always ethically grounded. (p. 22)

In the sections that remain, and keeping the above in mind, we outline one such theoretical and methodological progression for a radically embodied cultural studies project.

IV. Physical Cultural Studies and "Bodily Participation"

If we allow that our (specific) project must be about more than just a topical focus on bodies and physicality (in whatever varied forms they may take, from the active to the inactive), *and* that we should endeavor to adhere in some manner to the best politics and practices of the (British) cultural studies tradition (i.e., antidisciplinary, self-reflective, political, theoretical, and radically contextual; Grossberg, 1997)—then, first and foremost, we would do well to begin thinking of the research *act* of [physical] cultural studies as necessarily being "an embodied activity" (Coffey, 1999, p., 59). For as Amanda Coffey (1999) writes in *The Ethnographic Self,* we must acknowledge the critical extent to which "our body and the bodies of others are central to the practical accomplishment of fieldwork. We locate our physical being alongside those of others, as we negotiate the spatial context of the field" (p. 59). This would seem an obvious point. And yet, as Michele K. Donnelly (2009) reminds us, the very *embodied* practice of one's research act is, paradoxically, most often overlooked, owing perhaps to the seeming "inevitability of the body's role" in conducting qualitative inquiry. Paul Atkinson, Sara Delamont and William Housley (2008) have written at length about avoiding this oversight in ethnography, explaining that

> the very idea of participant observation implies not merely "observation" but also the embodied presence of the ethnographer. Clearly we cannot engage with the social actors we work with without physical copresence; the element of "participation" is a bodily one. (p. 140)

As such, argues Donnelly (2009), "Participation involves making and maintaining space for the researcher in the field: socially, culturally, *and physically*" (p. 4, emphasis added).

To engender significant heuristic pedagogies of the subjugated and transformative body, we need to wield theories, strategies, and epistemologies that account for the minutiae, the variations, and the complex formations of physical culture (*especially those impacting our own bodies within the research act*). Tami L. Spry (2010), drawing on Elyse Pineau's (2000) notion of *performative embodiment,* describes the epistemological necessity of such an engaged research act in this manner:

> We live in our bodies and learn about self, others, and culture through analyzing the performances of our bodies in the world. The performing body is at once a pool of data, a collector of data, and then the interpreter of data in knowledge creation, in the process of epistemology. (p. 160)

The nature of knowing the body is—and always has been—both a politically entangled and dialectically meaningful enterprise. Because of this dynamic, adherents to the demands of a radically embodied project such as ours might do well, after D. Soyini Madison (2009), to

> embrace the body not only as the feeling/sensing home of our being—the harbor of our breath—but the vulnerability of how our body must move through the space and time of another—transporting our very being and breath—for the purpose of knowledge, for the purpose of realization and discovery. Body knowledge, knowledge through the body, is evidence of the present. . . . This is intersubjective vulnerability in existential and ontological order, because bodies rub against one another flesh to flesh in a marked present and where we live on and between the extremes of life and death. (p. 191)

But such an engaged, interventionist, reflexive, reciprocal, and practiced method can sometimes get messy, if not conflicted. For example, Loïc Wacquant (2004), in his widely hailed treatise on boxing culture on the South Side of Chicago during the late 1980s and early 1990s, *Body and Soul: Ethnographic Notebooks of an Apprentice Boxer,* presents his readership with a "carnal sociology" that finds his body coordinating three points of intersection: his flesh-and-blood bodily actions, his internal struggles with training, and his interactions with his trainer and fellow boxers. While serving as a notable early entrant into the pantheon of research *on* physical culture—and most assuredly using his own researcher body as the primary source of knowledge production—Wacquant ignores the politics of representation governing his enfleshed body and the context of his research act/s. In a stinging critique of Wacquant's text, Denzin (2007a) reminds us of this failing when he states,

> His method presumes a reality that is not shaped by cultural mythology, or self-aggrandizing statements. He wants his embodied method to go directly to the real, actual world of the boxer. [But his] carnal sociology *stays* at the level of the body, the white/black male body in the dying throes of a violent sport. This is a sociology that is outside of time, a sociology that some say time has passed by. (pp. 429–430, emphasis added)

By staying wholly at the level of the body, Wacquant's narrative lacks a "reflexive language of critique, and praxis, a way of looking into and beyond the repressive cultural categories of neoliberal capitalism" (p. 430).

Radically embodied cultural studies research, following Gretchen Rossman and Sharon F. Rallis (2003), is necessarily a complicated mélange of the "recursive, iterative, messy, tedious, challenging, full of ambiguity, and exciting" (p. 4). And as we strive to "forge the micro and the macro in a way that does not reduce the local experiences to props of social theories" (Saukko, 2005, p. 345), we must be sensitive to the ways in which our *own* bodies, and our *own* performances, shape the research encounter. But we must *also* be sensitive to the ways our research acts "reproduce a particular order of things that is shaped by the racial and cultural politics of neoliberalism" (Denzin, 2007a, p. 430) and remain cognizant of the wider conjunctural forces impacting the body (from the mediated to the political); it is not an either/or choice.

Scholars of this new generation have, to varying degrees, found themselves aligned with the very philosophical imperatives on offer by Madison and her contemporaries. Take the following three avatars of this direction.

Ashley Mears's (2008) ethnographic account of the New York fashion industry—in which she actively worked as a model during the course of her research—quite explicitly implicates her *researcher body* in the process of constructing a critical interrogation of gender, power, and cultural production. Her "bodily copresence" is necessarily pronounced in the following extract, in which she describes a model line-up and the degree to which the ever-present, critical gaze works "between and within models as they compare their bodies to one another":

> In the runway rehearsal line, the model before me comments as another model walks past, "Her waist is so small!" Standing backstage in our first look—little bikinis—the models scan each other from head to toe, *myself included.* After standing in line for a while, most of us end up folding our arms across our stomachs. Perhaps the others are tired, or bored, *but I do it to cover up.* (p. 438, emphases ours)

Research, for Mears, is not solely about the mechanical process of methodological expression: It is a personal[ized] and internal[ized] journey—a complicated, self-inhabiting one aimed at intervening directly into the conditions of production and consumption that shape, govern, and exploit women's bodies. This is not the work of a casual or detached ethnographer, carefully taking notes so as to catalog and "reproduce" the social world (as if this can be done!). Rather, through active bodily investment in working within and against the hegemonic spaces of the fashion industry, Mears works through her body to better understand the physical and psychic demands of emotional labor on others in the profession and challenge the chilling effects it can have on its most vulnerable purveyors (i.e., young women). As Ron Pelias (2005) makes clear, there is a considered recognition in such an approach "that individual bodies provide a potent database for understanding the political and hegemonic systems written on individual bodies" (p. 420).

In a related manner, Michael's (see Giardina, 2005, 2009) engaged bodily interrogations of transnational movement, power, and politics serve as a useful vivisection of the complex, conflictual, and continually shifting identity performances revealed in and through our fleeting global experiences with one another. Whether brushing up against the hyphenated spatial histories of British colonialism and Asian diaspora in London and Manchester or witnessing rampant expressions of xenophobic nationalism pervading the U.S. popular-public sphere in Yankee Stadium in New York, Michael actively sutured himself and his critique into and through the landscape of global social relations, including his own interpretive bodily interactions of disconnection and reconnection with place, home, and nation. As he reflexively stated at length while writing a stone's throw from the Baltic Sea:

> Yet, strangely, here in a country whose native tongue I can barely speak clearly without mistakenly ordering the wrong food off of a menu [I really thought I said something that came close to sounding like '*Jag skulle lik en hamburgaren och en soda, behaga*'], I ultimately feel oddly connected to the world. Although writing about someone *else's* flexible or hybrid performances of culture and identity has tended to be easy for me, writing about my *own* (dis)articulation with—nee implication in?—such frames generally proves a far different task. But the moment/s are there, in the text, behind the screen, in the performative acts, of coming face to face with my own (trans)nationally unbounded, floating identity in the performances of others who have been materially and representationally Othered (often revealed unintentionally through some form of white privilege, such as passing through an airport security checkpoint unassailed by watchful eyes): On my way "home" from London once, I caught my reflection in a duty-free store mirror. I was wearing a dark blue fleece pullover, jeans, and Swiss-made Bally shoes. No one would have mistaken me for being "an American" unless we spoke to each other . . . and I didn't go on advertising that fact . . . But with a few hours to kill before my flight was scheduled to depart, I ate a bacon cheeseburger and drank a Coors Light at the T.G.I. Friday's restaurant in Heathrow's Terminal 3. "What could be more American than that?" (I thought at the time). (Giardina, 2009, p. 174)[15]

Here we see Michael presenting his life "as mutually and reciprocally co-articulated to the world and the participants in that world" (McCarthy et al., 2007, p. xx). Not only is his own body implicated in the performance of his research act itself, but *through it,* he exposes the "inviolable link between researchers' identities, experiences in the field, and substantive findings" (Joseph & Donnelly, in press). This is very much an explicit attempt to "reinforce the lost arts of humility, self-questioning, deep reflexivity and conversation in research, re-connecting ourselves to the fractured and divided worlds in which we live" (McCarthy et al., pp. xx). It is an attempt, as Carrington (2008) would say, to

> develop a reflexive account of the Self that opens up to critical interrogation of both the researcher's own biography in relation to those studied and the very act of inscribing or narrating that ethnography, the turning of the analytical gaze back on the researcher in an attempt to dissolve or at least problematize subject/object relations within the research process and even that we have a unified, fixed, singular Self. (p. 426)

Invoking Trinh T. Minh-ha (1991), it is an effort to "interrogate the realities our writing represents, to invoke the teller's story in the history that is being written and performed" (p. 188).

A third example is drawn from Donnelly's (2009) work on "women's only-ness" in roller derby, which explicitly ties the notion of placing our bodies within and among the empirical uncertainties of spatial and corporeal practice(s) discussed above all together:

> When beginning my roller derby research, I was keenly aware of *my* body with respect to impression management. I thought carefully about how to dress, how to speak, how to move, where to be, what to be, etc. . . . More problematically, I was initially apprehensive that my own *performing* body would not hold up to the demands of a physically-demanding, if not dangerous, sport. Yet the explicit physical experience of my research act had the unintended consequence of visibly transforming my body into that of someone who skates for several hours every week for a year . . . Importantly, Coffey (1999) identifies that "In certain places taking part in the physicality of the setting may well be part of gaining insight or understanding into that setting." As I began to notice changes to *my* body, I came to notice—and to better understand—comments I had been hearing all along from my research participants about a "derby body," and, specifically, a "derby butt"—it was only in and through *my* body that I was able to make sense of those bodies performing around me. (p. 8, emphases ours)

Donnelly expresses the thorough-going use of knowledge produced by and through *her* researching body to better understand the aperçutive bodily interactions, feelings, and physicalities experienced by her research participants. Acting as what Cornel West (1991) would term a critical moral agent—one who "understands that the consequences of his or her interventions into the world are exclusively political, judged always in terms of their contributions to a politics of liberation, love, caring and freedom" (Denzin & Giardina, 2006)—Donnelly (and Mears, Giardina, and others doing similar work) is not merely presenting an engaging yet anecdotal look at body politics observed during her accounts of derby life. Rather, she illustrates how, for critical agents and provocateurs of cultural studies, "the body is implicated in the roles and relationships of fieldwork both in terms of how our body becomes part of our experience of the field and in the necessity (albeit often implicit) . . . to learn the skills and rules of embodiment in the particular social setting" (Coffey, 1999, p. 73).

By necessarily situating the researcher's physical body in and among bodies—sharing experiences of the physical ways in which we experience fieldwork—we are better able, as the examples above make clear, to elucidate the politics of gender, exclusion/inclusion, and corporeality acting upon and within these spaces of physical culture. In so doing, as Elin Diamond (1996) notes, we enable the incisive critique and reflexive re-evaluation of cultural contexts through one's own subjectivity (a subjectivity that, Kakali Bhattacharya, 2009, notes is "full of contradictions, inconsistencies, tensions, voices, and silences . . . [of] fractured shifts, border crossings, and negotiations between spaces" [p. 1065]). *But to do so ultimately means that the researcher's body (and self-perceptions thereof) is made vulnerable to, and by, the politically iniquitous circumstances into which the body has been thrust.* This we address in the following section.

V. Critical Reflections on the Physical (Cultural Studies) Body

As we put forth in the section above, we believe the best critical analyses of the corporeal are those that envisage the body through both dialectically imaginative techniques and a conscientious, often stifling, self-awareness of researcher and research act (see Langellier, 1999). As such, to convolute our simple social worlds—to excavate the plural dimensions of social life—we need to both make use of *and also reflect on* how our own bodies frame and are framed by the critical cultural analyses we undertake. In other words, we need to locate our vulnerable bodies within spatial praxes and be insatiably reflexive in how that (re)location produces new dimensions, complex relations, and new bodily epistemologies.

Carrington's (2008) work on racialized performativity, reflexivity, and identity is especially instructive of this position, as he interrogates (his own) black masculinity and the differently arrayed and performed iterations of black bodied-ness he experienced during his research on and with a "black" cricket team in Leeds, England (e.g., as a black south Londoner being "read" by his older West Yorkshire teammates as "black British" rather than the "authentic" Caribbean-based identity they saw themselves as holding). In moving to problematize the signification of blackness itself, revealed to us through deeply personal and self-reflexive accounts of his position "in, but not fully of" the particular black cultural space within which he was located during his time as a participant-observer of the cricket club, he acknowledges that the crux of the matter was that:

> I was coming to terms with my own black Britishness. . . . I started to engage those "most personal" aspects of my self; that is, I began to think about what it meant for me to be "black." . . . [M]y experiences in the field were proving difficult as I negotiated field relations in which my blackness was being questioned. The personal diary began to take the form of self-reflexive questions: How black *am* I? Am I *black* enough? What does such a question even mean? (pp. 434–435, emphases in original)

Susanne Gannon (2006), invoking the work of Roland Barthes, might say of Carrington's weighty confessional that his work reveals how "the lived body is a discursive and multiple but very present space where we do not go looking for any 'sacred originary' but for traces and unreliable fragments" (p. 483) through which to "foreground the dialogic relationship between the self and his or her tenuous and particular social/cultural/historical locations" (p. 477). Or, as Coffey (1999) would say,

> [He is] engaged in a practice of writing and *rewriting* the body. This does not only include the writing of *other* bodies, as performers and physical entities of the social world. We are also engaged in responding to and writing our *own* bodies—as well or sick or fit or hurting or exposed or performing. (p. 131, our emphases)

Carrington is not alone in publicly confronting his intersubjective bodily tensions as he works through its embodied politics. Exposing us to a similar dilemma, Silk (2010) unmasks—if not openly questions—his research act in relation to his consuming identity within spectacularized space in Baltimore, Maryland, and the troubles this caused for his self-reflexive, political self:

> How could I live, work, as a supposed academic committed to social justice and overcoming social inequality, in Redwood Towers? How could I

produce work that offered my narrative accounts from a position of comfort, and, of a city whose regeneration favored civic image over improved
citizen welfare? Was writing about this spectacularized consumption space
as I had previously done . . . only serving to glamorize, if not reify, the space,
and conveniently ignoring the most pressing public health and social
issues? Questions abounded. Social justice? For whom? For what purpose?
Whose city was this? Who belonged? Who did not belong? Where did I fit?
Did I fit? Did that even matter? . . . To understand, to expose, to intervene,
I needed to shift—literally, by moving out of Redwood Towers to a row-
house in Baltimore's historic Pigtown community. To do so, however,
involved crossing a street that "friends" and colleagues had warned me
never to go west of—Martin Luther King Expressway. (pp. 5–6)[16]

Jennifer L. Metz (2008) similarly conveys a sense of internal conflict at the use
of her body within her research act. Her inner dialogue, contemplating an
upcoming interview as part of her project on race and motherhood among professional athletes in the Women's National Basketball Association—and her ultimate re-visioning of identity through the performance of her "role" as a member
of the working media, which allowed her to gain access to her participants—is
illustrative:

Arriving at the stadium tonight, members of the media and I enter through
the side gate door, its plain, black steel doors missing the nostalgia-trimmed
ambience of the consuming public's main entrance. Suddenly, I have
become one of the cogs of the pro sport mechanism, and I am always taken
aback by this change. And yet it should not be a surprise. After all, the radio
station I'm stringing for grants me access to [do] the interviews, I have an
audience that calls in to comment on our words, I record trailers for the
interviews, and yet suddenly—at this moment—the vision of myself as
"MEDIA" becomes a reality. How does one *act* as M-E-D-I-A, that corporate organism a great majority of my project seeks to rebuke for its marginalization of my participants as welfare queens and ghetto sisters? (p. 250)

Here Metz places herself not only on the side of her research participants but,
paradoxically, acts on the side of the corporate media to gain access in the first
place. To borrow liberally from Julianne Cheek's (2007) original argument
regarding research strategies for surviving in the neoliberal moment, simply
"understanding the spaces is not enough"; rather, we must ask, "What actions are
we going to take? What positions are we going to adopt? . . . [and] [W]hat positions are there that we might adopt?" (p. 1054). Or, as Cheek puts it, "Unless we

better understand how we are positioned in these spaces, and how we may, in turn, position ourselves, then there is the very real possibility that we will be worked over by the spaces rather than working in them and, *importantly, on them*" (p. 1057, emphasis in original).

Turning again to our own work, we have each endeavored to account for, in sometimes painstaking (and introspectively painful) detail, how our own situated [researching] bodies have forged new cultural dialectics and conjunctures. Joshua's (Newman, in press) self-reflexive account of the rediscovery of his whiteness, his Southern-ness, and his masculinity through (auto)ethnographic engagement with the "New Sporting South," for example, serves as much as an analysis of the seemingly banal nature of Southern sporting fixtures like college football and stock car auto racing as it does as a critical inspection (and introspection) of the performative politics of engaged cultural studies research on the body. As he reflected on his ethnographic fieldwork on the New Sporting South, Joshua became increasingly concerned about how his own Southern, white body—*against his best intentions*—was becoming a site of identity-based power within these spaces.

Consider his fieldnotes addressing the power and politics of whiteness experienced in the early morning hours prior to a University of Memphis/Ole Miss game:

> The tailgating party to the immediate south of where I was located had begun to fraternize with a group I had joined, telling stories and offering predictions on the upcoming game. On his way back from the "pisser," one of the neighboring tailgaters, a middle-aged white man, stopped by our area to speak with us. He said, in a soft, almost timid voice: "Ya'll mind if I tell ya'll a nigger joke?" While I wanted to answer in the negative, I held my tongue and the all-white members of my group agreed that they did indeed want to hear the joke. (Fieldnotes, September 4, 2004)[17]

This is but one example of a number of overt racist offerings Joshua noted during his time at Ole Miss researching Southern whiteness. In this instance, power was productive in the sense that he was able to use it through research outcomes to create new pedagogies of sporting whiteness. But to do this, he had to make himself *visibly invisible*—using his body to gain access to research sites and moments but not forcing his new "self" onto the lived experiences he encountered. It was through encounters such as these that Joshua came to surmise that there was a "visible center" of identity politics at work within these empirical spaces, one that celebrated hetero-patriarchal Southern whiteness as the dominant cultural corporeality. In addition, and despite his own apprehensions toward these dominant cultural politics, he found that he *himself* was becoming part of that visible center. In short, *Joshua was blending his white, Southern, masculine self in with the crowd.* In large part due to his choice of research sites—two sporting spheres most deeply saturated by neo-Confederate forms of unchallenged whiteness (college football at Ole Miss, see Newman, 2010; and later NASCAR, see Newman & Giardina, 2008), and dialoging with the "white reign" that exists within those spaces (Kincheloe, Steinberg, Rodriguez, & Chennault, 1998)—his body became a symbol of conformity amongst thousands of other similarly white bodies. Like most spectators at these events, Joshua did not wear a Confederate flag T-shirt or less subtle race-based signifiers, yet his white skin was cloaked by the "ideological blanket" (Baudrillard, 1983) that always already covers these Southern sporting spaces.

To put it as explicitly as possible, Joshua's white-skinned body—and all of its ideological and phenotypical entanglements made meaningful in the contemporary South—*is inextricably (and inevitably) bound to the conduct of his research acts.* And it is because of these entanglements that those of us seeking to do radically contextual, politically engaged, rigorously empirical, physical cultural studies must remain cognizant of how our bodies articulate with the formations of power that exist within the research space. Although this particular encounter is one of the more problematic of Joshua's ethnographic experiences within that cultural field, the politics of inquiry beg questions such as, if Joshua was not identified within the boundaries of a white, Southern, masculine researcher (i.e., an 'insider'), how would these and other interactions have been different?

The above examples call for and embrace a heightened, re-engaged sense of what Merleau-Ponty refers to as *corporeal reflexivity:* a self-awareness of the researcher as *embodied subject* (see Vasterling, 2003), both a discursive property in the physical world and an agent subjected to the existential structures acting on those discourses. In "reading for the best" of the phenomenologists' work,[18] as Stuart Hall (1986) would put it, we can surmise that Merleau-Ponty's model of *intercorporeality* illuminates the meaning-making processes active within and between bodies and the power-knowledge relations produced within the bodily encounters we seek to better understand (Kelly, 2002). Rosalyn Diprose's (2002) synthetic interpretations of Merleau-Ponty's imperative for corporeal reflexivity are worth quoting here at length:

And while it may seem as if my corporeal reflexivity is already in place before the world or the other, which would allow the imaginary in my body to dominate, it is also the case that it is the other's body entering my field that "multiplies it from within," and it is through this multiplication, this decentering, that "as a body, I am exposed to the world" (Merleau-Ponty, 1973, p. 138). This exposure to the world through the disturbance of the other's body "is not an accident intruding from outside upon a pure cognitive subject . . . or a content of experience among many others but our first insertion into the world and into truth" (ibid. p. 139). (pp. 183–184)

Much like Deleuze's (1988) notion of "the double," discourses of the body produce embodiments: meaningful texts projected out of similarity and difference. We are thus reminded of his famous dictum that identification is the "interiorization of the outside" (p. 98), the connection between the external discourses of identity and the internal definitions of the self. And by suturing our researcher-bodies into cultural fields of bodily texts (through adornment, gesticulation, physicality, musculature, deportment, etc.), we must not only remain aware of how our bodies are intruding on the bodies of others, but also of how we are engaging and producing various "differential processes."

It is at such a moment that we become all the more aware of the dual nature of subjectivity; at once *a subject* with some agency in shaping various experience (such as those in the research field), and yet *subjected to* the power imbedded in our own bodies and our own performances (of past and present). So we do not offer any answers on this front, but only use these reflections on the self, the body, and the politics of reflexivity and articulation to call for a messier, bottom-up qualitative engagement with the body; one that seeks to counter the nomothetic tendencies and "objective" mythologies of modern (sociology's) scientific paradigms with a contemplative method of articulation. In this regard, we defer to Alan Ingham (1997), who, in laying the groundwork for physical cultural studies and attending to its embodied-ethnographic imperative, sharply postulated:

In "physical culture," all of us share genetically endowed bodies, but to talk about physical culture requires that we try to understand how the genetically endowed is socially constituted or socially constructed, as well as socially constituting and constructing. In this regard, we need to know how social structures and cultures impact our social presentation of our "embodied" selves and how our embodied selves reproduce and transform structures and cultures; how our attitudes towards our bodies relate to our self- and social identities. (p. 176)

Make no mistake: While this soulfully naked positionality might bring about risk, discomfort, and uncertainty, that sense of vulnerability and doubt can be empowering (see Stewart, Hess, Tracy, & Goodall, 2009). These uncertainties are produced out of a sense of "belonging" and in this way demand that the researcher reflect on what constitutes the self; what aesthetic, embodied, performative, (auto) biographical discourses have come to be intertwined within the research act. Vulnerability provides a lens through which to understand the tenuous body and conditions that make it unsettled. Furthermore, the vulnerable body gives the (auto)ethnographer perspective—reminding us at once that we inhabit a political body and that we are in the same instance responsible for, and answerable to, our interpretations and representations of others' corporealities (Butler, 2001). Hence, in studying the complex relations of the body, the self, and pedagogy—and representing the self and the Other in just and reflexive ways—we must be aware of, and limit the violence created by, our embodied selves along the way.

VI. CODA: An Inconvenient [Physical] Cultural Studies

A deeply articulative physical cultural studies, to rephrase Carol Rambo Ronai (1992), should engage in a "continuous dialectic of experience" (p. 396); experience that is both constituent and constitutive of context and through which we frame our discursive-constituted selves. Just as we critically interpret the texts produced by various cultural intermediaries, and even though it could get a bit messy, we ourselves must endeavor to locate our *selves* and *our* bodies in the scholarship we produce. Again invoking the work of Ingham (e.g., 1985), we must therefore make use of our bodies to understand how power operates on the body. Furthermore, we must avoid the temptation to mobilize a progressive aesthetic without fully realizing the potential for interceding through constructivist learning and emancipatory narratives. These are not bodies of society (as some sociologists would lead us to believe) but rather bodies *about* society.

If we do indeed agree that a truly articulative physical cultural studies necessarily looks to illuminate—rather than nomothetically generalize or reduce—the messiness of the human experience (and the corporealities thereof), then we need to cultivate investigations of the body *from the ground up*. This, we have suggested, can be done by developing carefully crafted critical dialogue with the authors of embodiment and empirical praxis and by cultivating those performative representations of practice that come through human interaction—through sharing knowledge and experience with other human beings. We need to understand how and why the body is meaningful, as well as "the conditions of emergence," as Butler (2009) terms it, which have made the body meaningful. In short, we must "act as participants and performers in the meanings that we seek to elicit from the subordinated worlds that we try to understand and intervene into, worlds in which we are densely implicated as meaning makers, cultural citizens, and fellow travelers" (McCarthy et al., p. xx).

Notes

1. The authors thank Norman K. Denzin, Yvonna S. Lincoln, David L. Andrews, Michael Silk, Paula Saukko, and Della Pollock for crucial feedback on earlier iterations of this chapter. The authors also thank Michele K. Donnelly, Ryan King-White, Steven J. Jackson, Jennifer L. Metz, Adam Beissel, C. L. Cole, and Mark Falcous for conversations related to this project. Special thanks to Doug Booth, Dean of the School of Physical Education at the University of Otago, New Zealand, for his generous support of this project at a key moment in its development. This chapter draws on and revisits arguments related to Giardina (2005) and Newman (2008). Portions of this chapter, especially Section IV on physical cultural studies and bodily participation, are reprinted from Giardina & Newman (in press) with kind permission of Human Kinetics.

2. Among them, the Birmingham School, Black British cultural studies, Latin American revisions of Birmingham, Australian cultural studies, Black feminist cultural studies, African cultural studies, Canadian cultural studies, and various forms in between that have developed both *de*pendently and *in*dependently of the British tradition (for more see McCarthy et al., 2007).

3. However, as Stuart Hall's (1985) re-reading of Louis Althusser made clear some time ago, these structural formations hold no guaranteed sway over our "knowing bodies" (see Lattimer, 2009). Rather, they can—and most certainly *will*—be contested. If our task within the *Handbook* is to push [physical] cultural studies forward to new frontiers, then our contribution seeks to consider the body logics, "body pedagogics" (Shilling, 2007), and, ultimately, the "new body ontologies" (as Butler, 2009, would have it) of such a project while still in its formative stages.

4. Carrington (2001) likewise reminds us that such a project was philosophically "aimed at popular education for working-class adults . . . in the hope that a genuinely socialist democratic society could be created . . . as a form of political struggle" (pp. 277–278), rather than a solely academic pursuit.

5. Hall (1996) is quick to point out that the various intellectual shifts occurring at the Centre did not come easily and without struggle, especially concerning feminism and the politics of race.

6. Despite the lofty canonical position ascribed to these early texts—as well as the generative movement(s) surrounding the institutionalization and international expansion of cultural studies—it is important to note that they do operate within a specific historical context (i.e., post–WWII Britain) and that a wholesale appropriation of so-called "British" cultural studies has always been problematic because of its explicit sensitivity to that context. As Jon Stratton and Ien Ang (1996) remind us: "We have to recognize that the intellectual practices which we now bring together under the category of 'cultural studies' were developed in many different (but not random) places in the world, and that there were local conditions of existence for these practices which determined their emergence and evolution. It is undeniable that 'Birmingham' has played a crucial role in the growth of the international cultural studies network as we know it today. But there was never just a one-sided and straightforward expansion of British cultural studies to other locations" (p. 374).

7. They continue, pointing to the demands for such a project within the current moment: "This is a historical present that cries out for emancipatory visions that inspire transformative inquiries, and for inquiries that can provide the moral authority to move people to struggle and resist oppression" (Denzin & Giardina, 2010, p. 15).

8. Critical pedagogues maintain that every dimension of schooling and every form of educational practice (from the classroom to the television screen to the sporting arena) are politically contested sites (see Kincheloe & McLaren, 2000). Through its focus on grappling with issues of ethical responsibility and the enactment of democratic ideals of equality, freedom, and justice in the pursuit of positively altering the material conditions of everyday life, physical cultural studies as a form of critical pedagogy therefore acts as a transformative practice that "seeks to connect with the corporeal and the emotional in a way that understands at multiple levels and seeks to assuage human suffering" (Kincheloe, 2004, p. 2) at every level of injustice.

9. This is a play on Clifton Evers's (2006) phrase.

10. Poststructuralism has served us well, but along the way discourse and textuality became the end, rather than the means, toward understanding the human condition.

11. Bérubé (2009) goes on to summarize one prominent view of the current landscape as such: "Anybody writing about *The Bachelor* or *American Idol* is generally understood to be 'doing' cultural studies, especially by his or her colleagues elsewhere in the university. In a recent interview, Stuart Hall . . . gave a weary response to this development, one that speaks for itself: 'I really cannot read another cultural-studies analysis of Madonna or *The Sopranos*.'"

12. As Roy (2003) explains: "The starting premise of Chomsky's method is not ideological, but it *is* intensely political. He embarks on his course of inquiry with an anarchist's instinctive mistrust of power. He takes us on a tour through the bog of the U.S. establishment, and leads us through the dizzying maze of corridors that connects the government, big business, and the business of managing public opinion" (p. 83).

13. Roy (2004) continues, in unsparing terms: "The language of the Left must become more accessible, must reach more people. We must acknowledge that if we don't reach people, it's our failure. Every success of Fox News is a failure for us. Every success of major corporate propaganda is our failure. It is not enough to moan about it. We have to do something about it. Reach ordinary people, break the stranglehold of mainstream propaganda. It's not enough to be intellectually pristine and self-righteous" (p. 147).

14. In the current era of methodological conservatism with respect to growing hostility toward qualitative inquiry in general, and critical scholarship in particular, Lauren Berlant's (1997) words are worth noting: "The backlash against cultural studies is frequently a euphemism for discomfort with work on contemporary culture around race, sexuality, class, and gender. It is sometimes a way of talking about the fear of losing what little standing intellectual work has gained through its studied irrelevance (and superiority) to capitalist culture. It expresses a fear of popular culture and popularized criticism. It expresses a kind of antielitism made in defense of narrow notions of what proper intellectual objects and intellectual postures should be" (p. 265).

15. Miguel A. Malagreca (2007), writing about the borders of geography and desire, strikes a similar chord: "Though I am writing this paragraph almost two years after I started this essay at a café located at the center of Piazza di Spagna, I can still feel the frantic pace of life that inundates that square at any time during the day. . . . Everybody brings to this piazza a share of cultural capital. Tourist guides are meaningless in their anodyne descriptions of this Roman epicenter of wealth and tourism. I let myself be captured by the intoxicating coexistence of parallel cultures, and anti-cultures formed by the lower-class bargaining in small shops, North African and Latin American immigrants selling imitations of fashion items in the streets, and the working girls streetwalking in daylight. I was at home; oh, yes I was" (pp. 92–93).

16. Redwood Towers, located in the heart of downtown Baltimore near Oriole Park at Camden Yards and the Inner Harbor, advertises itself thusly: "Nestled atop eight floors of above-ground parking, The Redwood offers residents breathtaking views, serene surroundings, and exclusive amenities. Whatever you imagined about Baltimore City living, THIS is even better: a 24-hour fitness center, broadband internet access in every apartment, a short walk to the Light Rail, MARC train, Camden Yards, Hippodrome and Inner Harbor, plus our relaxing imaginative skydeck, The Park on Nine. Does it get any better than this? We don't think so either" (http://www.ar-cityliving .com/redwood/).

17. Repeating the "joke" itself does not add anything to the retelling of the situation, which is why we have omitted it from the chapter. Suffice to say, it is not so much that the joke was explicitly racist (which it was) *but that it was viewed as normative and normalized by those telling/listening to it in the space of the ethnography* and that the researcher/researcher body became implicated in its telling by remaining silent.

18. For a more detailed reconciliation of Jean Paul Sartre's idea of being-for-itself and Merleau-Ponty's phenomenological conceptions of self-discovery of fundamental meaning, see Kujundzic and Buschert's (1994) article, "Instruments of the Body." For our

purposes here, let it suffice to oversimplify: the role of the body in each theorist's work is complex, but each acknowledges various relational interdependencies between the body, conceptions of the body, and the physical and ideological worlds.

References

Aalten, A. (2004). "The moment when it all comes together": Embodied experience in ballet. *European Journal of Women's Studies, 11*(4), 263–276.

Andrews, D. L. (2002). Coming to terms with cultural studies. *Journal of Sport & Social Issues, 26*(1), 110–117.

Andrews, D. L. (1993). *Deconstructing Michael Jordan: Popular culture, politics, and postmodern America.* Unpublished doctoral dissertation, University of Illinois at Urbana-Champaign.

Andrews, D. L. (2008). Kinesiology's inconvenient truth and the physical cultural studies imperative. *Quest, 60*(1), 45–60.

Andrews, D. L., & Giardina, M. D. (2008). Sport without guarantees: Toward a cultural studies that matters. *Cultural StudiesóCritical Methodologies, 8*(4), 395–422.

Andrews, D. L., & Loy, J. W. (1993). British cultural studies and sport: Past encounters and future possibilities. *Quest, 45*(2), 255–276.

Andrews, D. L., & Silk, M. (Eds.). (2011). *Physical cultural studies: An anthology.* Philadelphia, PA: Temple University Press.

Atkinson, M. (2008). Exploring male femininity in the crisis: Men and cosmetic surgery. *Body & Society,* 14(1), 67–87.

Atkinson, P., Delamont, S., & Housley, W. (2008). *Contours of culture: Complex ethnography* and the ethnography of complexity. Walnut Creek, CA: AltaMira Press.

Baudrillard, J. (1983). *Simulations.* New York: Semiotext[e].

Berlant, L. (1997). *The queen of America goes to Washington City: Essays on sex and citizenship.* Durham, NC: Duke University Press.

Berry, K., & Warren, J. T. (2009). Cultural studies and the politics of representation: Experienceósubjectivityóresearch. *Cultural StudiesóCritical Methodologies, 9*(5), 597–607.

Bérubé, M. (2009, 14 September). What's the matter with cultural studies? The popular discipline has lost its bearings. *The Chronicle of Higher Education.* Available at http://chronicle.com/article/Whats-the-Matter-With/48334/

Bhattacharya, K. (2009). Negotiating shuttling between transnational experiences: A de/colonizing approach to performance ethnography. *Qualitative Inquiry, 15*(6), 1061–1083.

Brace-Govan, J. (2002). Looking at bodywork: Women and three physical activities. *Journal of Sport and Social Issues, 24*(4), 404-421.

Butler, J. (2001). *Giving an account of oneself.* New York: Fordham University Press.

Butler, J. (2004). *Precarious life: The power of mourning and violence.* London: Verso.

Butler, J. (2009). *Frames of war: When is life grievable?* London: Verso.

Butryn, T., & Masucci, M. (2009). Traversing the matrix: Cyborg athletes, technology, and the environment. *Journal of Sport & Social Issues, 33*(3), 285–307.

Carrington, B. (2001). Decentering the centre: Cultural studies in Britain and its legacy. In T. Miller (Ed.), *A companion to cultural studies* (pp. 275–297). Oxford, UK: Blackwell.

Carrington, B. (2008). "What's the footballer doing here?" Racialized performativity, reflexivity, and identity. *Cultural Studies ó Critical Methodologies, 8*(4), 423–452.

Centre for Contemporary Cultural Studies. (1982). *The empire strikes back: Race and racism in 70s Britain.* London: Routledge.

Chase, L. (2008). Running big: Clydesdale runners and technologies of the body. *Sociology of Sport Journal, 27*(2), 130–147.

Cheek, J. (2007). Qualitative inquiry, ethics, and the politics of evidence: Working within these spaces rather than being worked over by them. In N. K. Denzin & M. D. Giardina (Eds.), *Ethical futures in qualitative research: Decolonizing the politics of evidence* (pp. 99–108). Walnut Creek, CA: Left Coast Press.

Cho, Y. (2008). We know where we're going, but we don't know where we are: An interview with Lawrence Grossberg. *Journal of Communication Inquiry, 32*(2), 102–122.

Clarke, J. (1973). *Football hooliganism and the skinheads* (Centre for Contemporary Cultural Studies Stenciled Occasional Paper Series, No. 42, pp. 38–53). Birmingham, UK: University of Birmingham.

Clarke, J. (1975, Summer). *Skinheads and the magical recovery of community* (Working Papers in Cultural Studies, Nos. 7–8, pp. 99–105). Birmingham, UK: University of Birmingham.

Clarke, J., & Critcher, C. (1985). *The devil makes work: Leisure in capitalist Britain.* London: Macmillan.

Coffey, A. (1999). *The ethnographic self: Fieldwork and the representation of identity.* London: Sage.

Cole, C. L. (2007). Bounding American democracy: Sport, sex, and race. In N. K. Denzin & M. D. Giardina (Eds.), *Contesting empire/globalizing dissent: Cultural studies after 9/11* (pp. 152–166). Boulder, CO: Paradigm.

Cole, C., & Hribar, A. (1995). Celebrity feminism: Nike-style post-Fordism, transcendence, and consumer power. *Sociology of Sport Journal, 12*(4), 347–369.

Critcher, C. (1971). *Football and cultural values* (Working Papers in Cultural Studies, No. 1, pp. 103–119). Birmingham, UK: University of Birmingham.

Critcher, C. (1974). *Women in sport* (Working Papers in Cultural Studies, No. 5, pp. 77–91). Birmingham, UK: University of Birmingham.

Deleuze, G. (1988). *Foucault.* Minneapolis, MN: University of Minnesota Press.

Denzin, N. K. (2003). *Performance ethnography: Critical pedagogy and the politics of culture.* Thousand Oaks, CA: Sage.

Denzin, N. K. (2007a). Book review: Loïc Wacquant *Body & Soul: Notebooks of an Apprentice Boxer. Cultural Sociology, 1*(3), 429–430.

Denzin, N. K. (2007b). *Flags in the window: Dispatches from the American war zone.* New York: Peter Lang.

Denzin, N. K., & Giardina, M. D. (Eds.). (2006). *Contesting empire/globalizing dissent: Cultural studies after 9/11.* Boulder, CO: Paradigm.

Denzin, N. K., & Giardina, M. D. (2010). *Qualitative inquiry and human rights.* Walnut Creek, CA: Left Coast Press.

Diamond, E. (1996). Introduction. In E. Diamond (Ed.), *Performances and cultural politics* (pp. 1–12). New York: Routledge.

Dimitriadis, G., & Carlson, D. (2003). Introduction: Aesthetics, popular representation, and democratic public pedagogy. *Cultural Studies óCritical Methodologies, 3*(1), 3–7.

Diprose, R. (2002). *Corporeal generosity: On giving with Nietzsche, Merleau-Ponty, and Levinas.* New York: State University of New York Press.

Donnelly, M. K. (2009, November). *Women-only leisure activities: Physicality, inevitability, and possibility in embodied ethnography.* Paper presented at the annual conference of the North American Society for the Sociology of Sport, Ottawa, Ontario, Canada.

Dworkin, D. (1997). *Cultural Marxism in postwar Britain: History, the New Left, and the origins of cultural studies.* Durham, NC: Duke University Press.

Dworkin, S., & Wachs, F. L. (2004). "Getting your body back": Postindustrial fit motherhood in *Shape Fit Pregnancy* magazine. *Gender & Society, 18*(5), 610–624.

Evers, C. (2006). How to surf. *Journal of Sport & Social Issues, 30*(3), 229–243.

Fiske, J. (1994). Cultural practice and cultural studies. In N. K. Denzin & Y. S. Lincoln (Eds.), *Handbook of qualitative research.* Thousand Oaks, CA: Sage.

Francombe, J. (2010). "I cheer, you cheer, we cheer": Physical technologies and the normalized body. *Television & New Media, 11*(5), 350–366.

Freire, P. (1970/2006). *Pedagogy of the oppressed.* New York: Continuum.

Freire, P. (1999). *Pedagogy of freedom: Ethics, democracy, and civic courage.* Lanham, MD: Rowman & Littlefield.

Frow, J., & Morris, M. (2000). Cultural studies. In N. K. Denzin & Y. S. Lincoln (Eds.), *Handbook of qualitative inquiry* (2nd ed., pp. 315–346). Thousand Oaks, CA: Sage.

Fusco, C. (2006). Spatializing the (im)proper: The geographies of abjection in sport and physical activity space. *Journal of Sport & Social Issues, 30*(1), 5–28.

Gannon, S. (2006). The (im)possibilities of writing the self-writing: French poststructural theory and autoethnography. *Cultural StudiesóCritical Methodologies, 6*(4), 474–495.

Giardina, M. D. (2005). *Sporting pedagogies: Performing culture & identity in the global arena.* New York: Peter Lang.

Giardina, M. D. (2009). Flexibly global? Performing culture and identity in an age of uncertainty. *Policy Futures in Education, 7*(2), 172–184.

Giardina, M. D., & Newman, J. I. (in press). What is the 'physical' in physical cultural studies? *Sociology of Sport Journal, 28*(1).

Gilroy, P. (1987). *"There ain't no black in the Union Jack": The cultural politics of race and nation.* London: Hutchinson.

Giroux, H. A. (2000). *Impure acts: The practical politics of cultural studies.* New York: Routledge.

Giroux, H. A. (2001). Cultural studies as performative practice. *Cultural StudiesóCritical Methodologies, 1*(1), 5–23.

Grindstaff, L., & West, E. (2006). Cheerleading and the gendered politics of sport. *Social Problems, 53*(4), 500–518.

Grossberg, L. (1997). *Bringing it all back home. Essays in cultural studies.* Durham, NC: Duke University Press.

Gruneau, R. S. (1985). *Class, sports, and social development.* Amherst: University of Massachusetts Press.

Gruneau, R. S., & Whitson, D. (1993). *Hockey night in Canada: Sport, identities, and cultural politics.* Toronto, ON: Garamond Press.

Hall, S. (1982). The problem of ideology: Marxism without guarantees. In B. Matthews (Ed.), *Marx 100 years on* (pp. 57–86). London: Lawrence & Wishart.

Hall, S. (1985). Signification, representation, ideology: Althusser and the post-structuralist debates. *Critical Studies in Mass Communication, 2,* 91–114.

Hall, S. (1986). Gramsci's relevance for the study of race and ethnicity. *Journal of Communication Inquiry, 10*(2), 5–27.

Hall, S. (1993). What is this "black" in black popular culture? *Social Justice, 20*(1–2), 104–115.

Hall, S. (1996). On postmodernism and articulation. In D. Morley & K. Chen (Eds.), *Stuart Hall: Critical dialogues in cultural studies* (pp. 131-150). London: Routledge.

Hall, S., Critcher, C., Jefferson, T., Clarke, J., & Roberts, B. (1978). *Policing the crisis: Mugging, the state, and law and order.* London: Macmillan.

Hargreaves, J., & Vertinsky, P. (Eds.). (2006). *Physical culture, power, and the body.* London: Routledge.

Helstein, M. (2007). Seeing your sporting body: Identity, subjectivity, and misrecognition. *Sociology of Sport Journal, 24*(1), 78–103.

Hoggart, R. (1957). *The uses of literacy: Aspects of working-class life, with special reference to publications and entertainments.* London: Chatto & Windus.

Ingham, A. (1985). From public sociology to personal trouble: Well-being and the fiscal crisis of the state. *Sociology of Sport Journal, 2*(1), 43–55.

Ingham, A. G. (1997). Toward a department of physical cultural studies and an end to tribal warfare. In J. Fernandez-Balboa (Ed.), *Critical postmodernism in human movement, physical education, and sport* (pp. 157–182). Albany: State University of New York Press.

Jackson, S. J. (1992). *Sport, crisis, and Canadian identity in 1988: A cultural analysis.* Unpublished doctoral dissertation, University of Illinois at Urbana-Champaign.

Johnson, R. (1987). What is cultural studies anyway? *Social Text, 6*(1), 38–79.

Joseph, J., & Donnelly, M. K. (in press). Drinking on the job: The problems and pleasure of ethnography and alcohol. *International Review of Qualitative Research.*

Kelly, S. D. (2002). Merleau-Ponty on the body. *Ratio, 15*(4), 376–391.

Kincheloe, J. L. (2004). *Critical pedagogy.* New York: Peter Lang.

Kincheloe, J. L., & McLaren, P. (2000). Rethinking critical theory and qualitative research. In N. K. Denzin & Y. S. Lincoln (Eds.), *Handbook of qualitative research* (2nd ed., pp. 279–313).

Kincheloe, J. L., Steinberg, S. R., Rodriguez, N. M., & Chennault, R. E. (Eds.). (1998). *White reign: Deploying whiteness in America.* New York: St. Martin's Griffin.

Kujundzic, N., & Buschert, W. (1994). Instruments and the body: Sartre and Merleau-Ponty. *Research in Phenomenology, 24*(2), 206–215.

Laclau, E., & Mouffe, C. (1985). *Hegemony and socialist strategy: Towards a radical democratic politics.* London: Verso.

Langellier, K. (1999). Personal narrative, performance, performativity: Two or three things I know for sure. *Text and Performance Quarterly, 19*(1), 125–144.

Lattimer, J. (2009). Introduction: Body, knowledge, words. In J. Lattimer & M. Schillmeier (Eds.), *Un/knowing bodies* (pp. 1–22). Malden, MA: Blackwell.

Lincoln, Y. S. (2004). Perfoming 9/11: Teaching in a terrorized world. *Qualitative Inquiry, 10*(1), 140–159.

Madison, D. S. (2009). Dangerous ethnography. In N. K. Denzin & M. D. Giardina (Eds.), *Qualitative inquiry and social justice* (pp. 187–197). Walnut Creek, CA: Left Coast Press.

Malagreca, M. (2007). Writing queer across the borders of geography and desire. In C. McCarthy, A. Durham, L. Engel, A. Filmer, M. D. Giardina, & M. Malagreca (Eds.), *Globalizing cultural studies: Ethnographic interventions in theory, method, and politics* (pp. 79-100). New York: Peter Lang.

Markula, P. (1995). Firm but shapely, fit but sexy, strong but thin: The postmodern aerobicizing female bodies. *Sociology of Sport Journal, 12*(4), 424–453.

Markula, P., & Pringle, R. (2006). *Foucault, sport, and exercise.* London: Routledge.

McCarthy, C., Durham, A., Engel, L., Filmer, A., Giardina, M. D., & Malagreca, M. (2007). Confronting cultural studies in globalizing times. In C. McCarthy, A. Durham, L. Engel, A. Filmer, M. D. Giardina, & M. Malagreca (Eds.), *Globalizing cultural studies: Ethnographic interventions in theory, method, and policy* (pp. xvii-xxxiv). New York: Peter Lang.

McLaren, P. (1988). Schooling the postmodern body: Critical pedagogy and the politics of enfleshment. *Journal of Education, 170*(3), 53–83.

McLaren, P. (2000). *Che Guevara, Paulo Freire, and the pedagogy of revolution.* Lanham, MA: Rowman & Littlefield.

Mears, A. (2008). Discipline of the catwalk: Gender, power, and uncertainty in fashion modeling. *Ethnography, 9*(4), 429–456.

Metz, J. L. (2008). An interview on motherhood: Racial politics and motherhood in late capitalist sport. *Cultural Studies <=> Critical Methodologies, 8*(2), 248–275.

Miah, A. (2004). *Genetically modified athletes: Biomedical ethics, gene doping, and sport.* London: Routledge.

Miller, T. (2001). Introduction. In T. Miller (Ed.), *A companion to cultural studies* (pp. 1–20). London: Blackwell.

Mills, C. W. (1959). *The sociological imagination.* London: Oxford University Press.

Minh-ha, T. T. (1991). *When the moon waxes red: Representation, gender, and cultural politics.* London: Routledge.

Newman, J. I. (2008). *Notes on physical cultural studies.* Paper presented at the annual conference of the North American Society for the Sociology of Sport, Denver, CO.

Newman, J. I. (2010). *Embodying Dixie: Studies in the body pedagogics of Southern whiteness.* Melbourne, Australia: Common Ground Press.

Newman, J. I. (in press). [Un]comfortable in my own skin: Articulation, reflexivity, and the duality of self. *International Review of Qualitative Research.*

Newman, J. I., & Giardina, M. D. (2008). NASCAR and the "Southernization" of America: Spectactorship, subjectivity, and the confederation of identity. *Cultural Studies⟷ Critical Methodologies, 8*(4), 497–506.

Pelias, R. J. (2005). Performative writing as scholarship: An apology, an argument, an anecdote. *Cultural Studies⟷Critical Methodologies, 5*(4), 415–424.

Peters, R. J. (1975). *Television coverage of sport* (Center for Contemporary Cultural Studies Stenciled Occasional Paper Series 48). Birmingham, UK: University of Birmingham.

Pineau, E. L. (2000). "Nursing mother" and articulating absence. *Text and Performance Quarterly, 20*(1), 1–19.

Reich, J. (2010). "The world's most perfectly developed man": Charles Atlas, physical culture, and the inscription of American masculinity. *Men and Masculinities, 12*(4), 444–461.

Ronai, C. R. (1992). The reflexive self through narrative: A night in the life of an erotic dancer/researcher. In C. Ellis & M. G. Flaherty (Eds.), *Investigating subjectivity: Research on live experience* (pp. 102–124). Thousand Oaks, CA: Sage.

Rossman, G. B., & Rallis, S. F. (2003). *Learning in the field: An introduction to qualitative research* (2nd ed.). Thousand Oaks, CA: Sage.

Roy, A. (2001). *Power politics.* Cambridge, MA: South End Press.

Roy, A. (2003). *War talk.* Cambridge, MA: South End Press.

Roy, A. (2004). *An ordinary person's guide to empire.* Cambridge, MA: South End Press.

Saukko, P. (2005). Methodologies for cultural studies: An integrative approach. In N. K. Denzin & Y. S. Lincoln (Eds.), *The SAGE handbook of qualitative research* (3rd ed., pp. 343–357).

Schultz, J. (2004). Discipline and push-up: Female bodies, femininity, and sexuality in popular representations of sports bras. *Sociology of Sport Journal, 21*(2).

Scott, S. (2010). How to look good (nearly) naked: The performative regulation of the swimmer's body. *Body & Society, 16*(2), 143–168.

Shilling, C. (2007). Introduction: Sociology and the body. In C. Shilling (Ed.), *Embodying sociology* (pp. 2–18). Oxford, UK: Blackwell.

Silk, M. (2010). Postcards from Pigtown. *Cultural Studies⟷Critical Methodologies, 10*(2), 143–156.

Silk, M., & Andrews, D. L. (in press). Physical cultural studies. *Sociology of Sport Journal, 28*(1).

Slack, J. D. (1996). The theory and method of articulation in cultural studies. In D. Morley and K. H. Chen (Eds.), *Stuart Hall: Critical dialogues in cultural studies* (pp. 112–127). London: Routledge.

Spry, T. (2001). Performing autoethnography: An embodied methodological praxis. *Qualitative Inquiry, 7*(6), 706–732.

Spry, T. (2010). Some ethical considerations in preparing students for performative autoethnography. In N. K. Denzin & M. D. Giardina (Eds.), *Qualitative inquiry and human rights* (pp. 158–170). Walnut Creek, CA: Left Coast Press.

Stewart, K. A., Hess, A., Tracy, S. J., & Goodall, H. L., Jr. (2009). Risky research: Investigating the "perils" of ethnography. In N. K. Denzin & M. D. Giardina (Eds.), *Qualitative inquiry and social justice.* Walnut Creek, CA: Left Coast Press.

Stratton, J., & Ang, I. (1996). On the impossibility of a global cultural studies: "British" cultural studies in an "international" frame. In D. Morley & K. Chen (Eds.), *Stuart Hall: Critical dialogues* (pp. 360–392). London: Routledge.

Thompson, E. P. (1963). *The making of the English working class.* New York: Vintage.

Thorpe, H. (2009). Bourdieu, feminism, and female physical culture: Gender reflexivity and the habitus-field complex. *Sociology of Sport Journal, 26*(4), 491–516.

Tomlinson, A. (Ed.). (1981). The sociological study of sport: Configuration and interpretive studies. *Proceedings of Workshop of British Sociological Association and Leisure Studies Association.* Brighton, UK: Brighton Polytechnic.

van Ingen, C. (2004). Therapeutic landscapes and the regulated body in Toronto Front Runners. *Sociology of Sport Journal, 21*(3).

Vasterling, V. (2003). Body and language: Butler, Merleau-Ponty and Lyotard on the speaking embodied subject. *International Journal of Philosophical Studies, 11*(2), 205–223.

Wacquant, L. (2004). *Body and soul: Ethnographic notebooks of an apprentice-boxer.* New York: Oxford University Press.

Watson, R. (1973). *The public announcement of fatality* (Working Papers in Cultural Studies, 4). Birmingham, UK: University of Birmingham.

Wedgewood, (2004). Kicking like a boy: Schoolgirl Australian Rules Football and bi-gendered 'female embodiment. *Sociology of Sport Journal, 21*(2), 140–162.

West, C. (1991). Theory, pragmatisms, and politics. In J. Arac & B. Johnson (Eds.), *Consequences of theory.* Baltimore, MD: Johns Hopkins University Press.

Whannel, G. (1983). *Blowing the whistle: Culture, politics, and sport.* London: Routledge.

Wheatley, E. E. (2005). Disciplining bodies at risk: Cardiac rehabilitation and the medicalization of fitness. *Journal of Sport and Social Issues, 29*(2), 198–221.

Williams, R. (1958). *Culture and society.* London: Chatto & Windus.

Willis, P. (1971). *The motorbike club within a subcultural group* (Working Papers in Cultural Studies, No. 2, pp. 53–70). Birmingham, UK: University of Birmingham.

Willis, P. (1977). *Learning to labor: How working-class kids get working-class jobs.* Farnborough, England: Saxon House.

Zinn, H. (1996). *You can't be neutral on a moving traing.* Boston, MA: South End Press.

Critical Humanism and Queer Theory

Living With the Tensions Postscript 2011 to Living with the Contradictions

Ken Plummer

Failure to examine the conceptual structures and frames of reference which are unconsciously implicated in even the seemingly most innocent factual inquiries is the single greatest defect that can be found in any field of inquiry.

—John Dewey (1938, p. 505)

Most people in and outside of the academy are still puzzled about what queerness means, exactly, so the concept still has the potential to disturb or complicate ways of seeing gender and sexuality, as well as the related areas of race, ethnicity and class.

—Alexander Doty (2000, p. 7)

Research—like life—is a contradictory, messy affair. Only on the pages of "how-to-do-it" research methods texts or in the classrooms of research methods courses can it be sorted out into linear stages, clear protocols, and firm principles. My concern in this chapter lies with some of the multiple, often contradictory assumptions of inquiries. Taking my interest in sexualities/gay/queer research as a starting point and as a tension, I see "queer theory" and "critical humanism" as one of my own tensions. I have tried to depict each and to suggest some overlaps, but my aim has not been to reconcile the two. That is not possible and probably is not even desirable. We have to live with the tensions, and awareness of them is important background for the self-reflexive social researcher.

Social Change and Zombie Research

This discussion should be seen against a background of rapid social change. Although for many, research methods remain the same over time (they just get a bit more refined with each generation), for others of us, changes in society are seen to bring parallel changes in research practices. To put it bluntly, many claim we are moving into a postmodern, late modern, globalizing, risk, liquid society. A new global order is in the making that is much more provisional and less authoritative than that of the past; it is a society of increasing self-reflexivity and individuation, a network society of flows and mobilities, a society of consumption and waste (Bauman, 2000, 2004; Beck, 2003; Giddens, 1991; Urry, 2000).

As we tentatively move into these new worlds, our tools for theory and research need radical overhaul. German sociologist Ulrich Beck, for example, speaks of "zombie categories"; we move among the living dead! Zombie categories are categories from the past that we continue to use even though they have long outlived their usefulness and even though they mask a different reality. We probably go on using them because at present we have no better words to put in their place. Yet dead they are.

Beck cites the example of the concept of "the family" as an instance of a zombie category, a term that once had life and meaning but for many now means very little. I suggest that we could also cite most of our massive research methodology apparatus as partially zombified. I am not a major fan of television, but when I choose to watch a documentary, I often am impressed by how much more I get from it than from the standard sociological research tract. Yet the skills of a good documentary maker are rarely the topics of research methods courses, even though these skills—from scriptwriting and directing to camera movements and ethics—are the very stuff of good 21st-century research. And yes, some research seems to have entered the world of cyberspace, but much of it simply replicates the methods of quantitative research, making qualitative research disciplined, quantitative, and antihumanistic. Real innovation is lacking. Much research at the end of the 20th century—to borrow Beck's term again—truly was zombie research (Beck, 2003).

Table 11.1 suggests some links between social change and social research styles. The background is the authoritative scientific account with standard research protocols. As the social world changes, so we may start to sense new approaches to making inquiries. My concern in this chapter is largely with the arrival of queer theory.

A Reflexive Introduction

How research is done takes us into various language games—some rational, some more contradictory, some qualitative, some quantitative. The languages we

Table 11.1 Shifting Research Styles Under Conditions of Late Modernity

Current Social Changes	Possible Changes in Research Style
Toward a late modern world	Toward a late modern research practice
Postmodern/fragmentation/pluralization	The 'polyphonic' turn
Mediazation	The new forms of media as both technique and data
Stories and the death of the grand narrative	The storytelling/narrative turn
Individualization/choices/unsettled identities	The self-reflexive turn
Globalization-glocalization hybridization/diaspora	The hybridic turn: decolonizing methods (L. T. Smith, 1999)
High tech/mediated/cyborg/post-human	The high-tech turn
Knowledge as contested	The epistemological turn
Postmodern politics and ethics	The political/ethical turn
The network society	Researching flows, mobilities, and contingencies
Sexualities as problematic	The queer turn

use bring with them all manner of tensions. Although they sometimes help us chart the ways we do research, they often bring their own contradictions and problems. My goal here is to address some of the incoherencies I have found in my own research languages and inquiries and to suggest ways of living with them. Although I will draw widely from a range of sources and hope to provide some paradigmatic instances, the chapter inevitably will be personal. Let me pose the key contradiction of my inquiries. (We all have our own.)

The bulk of my inquiries have focused on sexualities, especially lesbian and gay concerns, with an ultimate eye on some notion of sexual justice. In the early days, I used a relatively straightforward symbolic interactionism to guide me in relatively straightforward fieldwork and interviewing in and around London's gay scene of the late 1960s. At the same time, I engaged politically, initially with the Homosexual Law Reform Society and then with the Gay Liberation Front in its early years. I read my Becker, Blumer, Strauss, and Denzin! At the same time, I was coming out as a young gay man and finding my way in the very social world I was studying. More recently, such straightforwardness has come to be seen as increasingly problematic. Indeed, there was always a tension there: I just did not always see it (Plummer, 1995).

On one hand, I have found myself using a language that I increasingly call that of critical humanism, one allied to symbolic interactionism, pragmatism, democratic thinking, storytelling, moral progress, redistribution, justice, and good citizenship (Plummer, 2003). Inspirations range from Dewey to Rorty, Blumer to Becker. All of these are quite old and traditional ideas, and although I have sensed their postmodernized affinities (as have others), they still bring more orthodox claims around experience, truths, identities, belonging to groups, and a language of moral responsibilities that can be shared through dialogues (Plummer, 2003).

By contrast, I also have found myself at times using a much more radicalized language that nowadays circulates under the name of queer theory. The latter must usually be seen as at odds with the former: Queer theory puts everything out of joint, out of order. "Queer," for me, is the postmodernization of sexual and gender studies. "Queer" brings with it a radical deconstruction of all conventional categories of sexuality and gender. It questions all the orthodox texts and tellings of the work of gender and sexuality in the modern world (and all worlds). It is a messy, anarchic affair—not much different from intellectual anarchists or political International Situationists. "Queer" would seem to be antihumanist, to view the world of normalization and normality as its enemy, and to refuse to be sucked into conventions and orthodoxy. If it is at all sociological (and it usually is not), it is gothic and romantic, not classical and canonical (Gouldner, 1973). It transgresses and subverts.

On one hand, then, I am quite happy about using the "new language of qualitative method" (Gubrium & Holstein, 1997); on the other, I am quite aware of a queer language that finds problems everywhere with orthodox social science methods (Kong, Mahoney, & Plummer, 2002). Again, these tensions are very much products of their time (queer theory did not exist before the late 1980s). Yet, retrospectively, it would seem that I have always walked tightropes between an academic interactionism, a political liberalism, a gay experience, and a radical critique.

But of course, as usual, there are more ironies here. Since the late 1980s, I have more or less considered myself "post-gay." So who was that young man from the past who studied the gay world? Likewise, those wild queer theorists have started to build their textbooks, their readers, and their courses, and they have proliferated their own esoteric cultlike worlds that often seem more academic than the most philosophical works of Dewey. Far from breaking boundaries, queer theorists often have erected them, for while they may not wish for closure, they nevertheless find it. Queer theories have their gurus, their followers, and their canonical texts. But likewise, humanists and new qualitative researchers—finding themselves under siege from postmodernists, queer theorists, some feminists, and multiculturalists and the like—have also fought back, rewriting their own histories and suggesting that many of the critiques laid at their door are simply false. Some, like Richard Rorty—the heir apparent to the modern pragmatism of Dewey and James—fall into curious traps: Himself labeled a postmodernist by others, he condemns postmodernists as "posties" (Rorty, 1999). Methodological positions often lead in directions different from those originally claimed.[1]

So here am I, like many others, a bit of a humanist, a bit post-gay, a sort of a feminist, a little queer, a kind of a liberal, and seeing that much that is queer has the potential for an important radical change. In the classic words of interactionism, Who am I? How can I live with these tensions?

This chapter is not meant to be an essay of overly indulgent self-analysis, but rather one in which, starting to reflect on such a worry, I am simply showing tensions that many must confront these days. Not only am I not alone in such worries, but I also am fairly sure that all reflective qualitative inquiries will face their own versions of them, just as most people face them in their daily lives. Ambivalence is the name of the game.

In this chapter, I plan to deal with three interconnected issues raised by qualitative research—all focused on just how far we can "push" the boundaries of qualitative research into new fields, strategies, and political/moral awareness—and how this has been happening continuously in my own work. New languages of qualitative method benefit from new ideas that at least initially may be seen as opposition. This is how they grow and how the whole field of qualitative research becomes more refined. In what follows, I will explore:

- What is critical humanism and how to do a critical humanist method
- What is queer and how to do a queer method
- How the contradictions can be lived through

The Critical Humanist Project

How different things would be . . . if the social sciences at the time of their systematic formation in the nineteenth century had taken the arts in the same degree they took the physical science as models.

—Robert Nisbet (1976, p. 16)

There is an illusive center to this contradictory, tension-ridden enterprise that seems to be moving further and further away from grand narratives and single, overarching ontological, epistemological, and methodological paradigms. This center lies in the humanistic commitment of the qualitative researcher to study the world always from the perspective of the interacting individual. From this simple commitment flow the liberal and radical politics of qualitative research. Action, feminist, clinical, constructivist, ethnic, critical, and cultural studies researchers all unite on this point. They all share the belief that a politics of liberation must always begin with the perspectives, desires, and dreams of those individuals and groups who have been oppressed by the larger ideological, economic, and political forces of a society or a historical moment.

—Denzin & Lincoln (1994, p. 575)

I use the term "critical humanism" these days to suggest orientations to inquiry that focus on human experience—that is, with the structure of experience and its daily lived nature—and that acknowledge the political and social role of all inquiry. It goes by many names—symbolic interactionism,[2] ethnography, qualitative inquiry, reflexivity, cultural anthropology, and life story research, among others—but they all have several concerns at heart. All these research orientations have a focus on human subjectivity, experience, and creativity: They start with people living their daily lives. They look at their talk, their feelings, their actions, and their bodies as they move around in social worlds and experience the constraints of history and a material world of inequalities and exclusions. They make methodological claims for a naturalistic "intimate familiarity" with these lives, recognizing their own part in such study. They make no claims for grand abstractions or universalism—assuming an inherent ambivalence and ambiguity in human life with no "final solutions," only damage limitations— while simultaneously sensing both their subjects' ethical and political concerns and their own in conducting such inquiries. They have pragmatic pedigrees, espousing an epistemology of radical, pragmatic empiricism that takes seriously the idea that knowing—always limited and partial—should be grounded in experience (Jackson, 1989). It is never neutral, value-free work, because the core of the inquiry must be human values. As John Dewey remarked long ago, "Any inquiry into what is deeply and inclusively (i.e., significantly) human enters perforce into the specific area of morals" (1920, p. xxvi). Impartiality may be suspect; but a rigorous sense of the ethical and political sphere is a necessity. Just why would one even bother to do research were it not for some wider concern or value?

What are these values? In the most general terms, critical humanism champions those values that give dignity to the person,[3] reduce human sufferings, and enhance human well-being. There are many such value systems, but at a minimum they probably must include the following:

1. A commitment to a whole cluster of *democratizing values* (as opposed to totalitarian ones) that aim to *reduce/remove human sufferings.* They take as a baseline *the value of the human being* and often provide a number of suggested *human rights*—freedom of movement, freedom of speech, freedom of association, freedom against arbitrary arrest, and so on. They nearly always include the *right to equality.* This commitment is strongly antisuffering and provides a major thrust toward both equality and freedom for all groups, including those with "differences" of all kinds (Felice, 1996).

2. An ethics of *care* and *compassion.* Significantly developed by feminists, this is a value whereby looking after the other takes on a prime role and whereby *sympathy, love,* and even *fidelity* become prime concerns (Tronto, 1993).

3. A politics of *recognition* and *respect*. Following the work of Axel Honneth (1995) and significantly shaped earlier by George Herbert Mead, this is a value whereby others are always acknowledged and a certain level of empathy is undertaken.

4. The importance of *trust*. This value recognizes that no social relationships (or society, for that matter) can function unless humans have at least some modicum of trust in each other (O'Neill, 2002).

Of course, many of these values bring their own tensions: We must work through them and live with them. A glaring potential contradiction, for example, may be to talk of humanistic values under capitalism, for many of the values of humanism must be seen as stressing nonmarket values. They are values that are not necessarily given a high ranking in a capitalist economy. Cornel West has put this well:

In our own time it is becoming extremely difficult for non-market values to gain a foothold. Parenting is a non market activity; so much sacrifice and service go into it without any assurance that the providers will get anything back. Mercy, justice: they are non market. Care, service: non market. Solidarity, fidelity: non market. Sweetness and kindness and gentleness. All non market. Tragically, non market values are relatively scarce. . . . (West, 1999, p. 11)

THE METHODOLOGIES OF HUMANISM

These values strongly underpin critical humanism. In his classic book *The Human Perspective in Sociology*, T. S. Bruyn (1966) locates this humanistic perspective as strongly allied to the methods of participant observation. Elsewhere, I have suggested an array of life story strategies for getting at human experience. The task is a "fairly complete narrating of one's entire experience of life as a whole, highlighting the most important aspects" (R. Atkinson, 1998, p. 8). These may be long, short, reflexive, collective, genealogical, ethnographic, photographic, even auto/ethnographic (Plummer, 2000). Life stories are prime humanistic tools, but it is quite wrong to suggest that this means that the stories only have a concern with subjectivity and personal experience.[4]

Throughout all of this, there is a pronounced concern not only with the humanistic understanding of experience but also with ways of telling the stories of the research. Usually, the researcher is present in many ways in the text: The text rarely is neutral, with a passive observer. Chris Carrington's (1999) study of gay families, for example, makes it very clear from the outset his own location within a single-parent family: "I grew up in a working-poor, female-headed, single parent family. Throughout much of my childhood, in order to make ends meet, my mother worked nights as bar tender. There were periods where she could not get enough hours and our family had to turn to food stamps and welfare" (p. 7). Likewise, Peter Nardi's (1999) study of gay men's friendships is driven by his own passion for friends: "What follows is partly an attempt to make sense of my own experiences with friends" (p. 2). Humanistic inquiries usually reveal humanistic researchers.

Most commonly, as in Josh Gamson's *Freaks Talk Back* (1998) and Leila Rupp and Verta Taylor's *Drag Queens at the 801 Cabaret* (2003), the method employed will entail triangulation—a combination of cultural analysis tools.[5] Here, multiple sources of data pertaining to texts, production, and reception are collected and the intersections among them analyzed. In Rupp and Taylor's study of drag queens, they observed, tape recorded, and transcribed 50 drag performances, along with the dialogue, music, and audience interactions, including photographs and dressing up themselves. They collected data on the performances through weekly meetings of the drag artists and semistructured life histories, and they conducted focus groups on people who attended the performances. In addition, they looked at weekly newspapers (such as the gay paper *Celebrate*) and others to partially construct the history of the groups. Their research has a political aim, humanistic and sociological, and yet queer too, showing that combinations are possible. Enormous amounts of research have been written on all of this (e.g., Clifford & Marcus, 1986; Coffey, 1999; Coles, 1989; Ellis & Flaherty, 1992; Hertz, 1997; Reed-Danahay, 1997; Ronai, 1992).

A further recent example of such work is Harry Wolcott's (2002) account of Brad, the Sneaky Kid. Wolcott, an educational anthropologist, is well known for his methodological writings and books, especially in the field of education. This book started life in the early 1980s as a short journal article on the life story of Brad, a troubled 19-year-old. The story is aimed at getting at the human experience of educational failure, in particular, the lack of support for those who are not well served by our educational systems.

This would have been an interesting life story but an unexceptional one had it not been for all the developments that subsequently emerged around it. What are not told in the original story are the details of how Wolcott met Brad, how he had gay sex with him, and how he got him to tell his life story. Much follows after the original story, which later takes curious turns: Brad develops schizophrenia and returns one night to Wolcott's house to burn it down in an enraged attempt to kill him. This leads to the complete destruction of Wolcott's home and all his belongings (and those of his schoolteacher partner). A serious court case ensues in which Brad is tried and sent to prison. Despite Brad's guilt, Wolcott is himself scrutinized regarding his relationship, his homosexuality, and even his role as an anthropologist. Brad's family is especially unhappy about the relationship with Wolcott, but so are many academics. Ultimately, Brad is institutionalized. Eventually, the story is turned into an intriguing ethnographic play. I have only read the text of the play and not seen it performed. Judging by the text presented here, it comes across as a collage of 1980s pop music, sloganized slides, and a drama in two layers—one about Brad's relationship with Wolcott and another about Wolcott's ruminations, as a professor, on the plights of ethnography.

I mention this study because although it started out as a life story gloss—a simple relaying of Brad's story—because of the curious circumstances that it led to, a much richer and complex story was revealed that generated a host of questions and debates about the ethical, personal, and practical issues surrounding fieldwork. Sexuality and gender were pretty much at the core. It is a gripping tale of the kinds of issues highlighted by all humanistic research. Indeed, within the book a second major narrative starts to appear—that of Harry Wolcott himself. He was always present, of course, but his story takes over as he reveals how he had regular sex with the young man, his partner's disapproval of Brad, and how one night he returns to his house to find a strong smell of oil and Brad screaming "You fucker. I'm going to kill you. I'm going to kill you. I'm going to tie you up and leave you in the house and set the house on fire" (p. 74). Luckily, Harry escapes, but unluckily, his house does not. It goes up entirely in flames, with all of his and his partner's belongings. This may be one of the core dramatic moments in life story telling—certainly an "epiphany"! After that, a major chapter follows that tells of the working of the court and how Wolcott himself is almost on trial.

When the story of Sneaky Kid was first published in 1983, it was a 30-page essay; it has grown into a book of more than 200 pages (Wolcott, 2002). The original article does not tell much about the relationship from which it grew or much of the other background; the book tells much more, but it raises sharply the issue of just how much remains left out. The book serves as a sharp reminder that all social science, including life stories, consists of only partial selections of realities. There is always much going on behind the scenes that is not told. Here we have the inevitable bias, the partiality, the limits, the selectivity of all stories told—but I will not take these issues further here.

The Troubles With Humanism

Although I think humanism has a lot to offer qualitative inquiry, it is an unfashionable view these days: Many social scientists seem to want to turn only to discourse and language. But this discourse is not incompatible with doing this, as it evokes the humanities (much more so than other traditions), widens communities of understanding by dialoguing with the voices of others, and takes a strong democratic impulse as the force behind its thinking and investigating. As a form of imagery to think about social life, this is all to the good. It brings with it the possibility for such inquiry to engage in poetry and poetics, drama and performance, philosophy and photography, video and film, narrative and stories.

Nevertheless, these days humanism remains a thoroughly controversial and contested term— and not least among queer theorists themselves. We know, of course, the long-standing attacks on humanism from theologies, from behavioral psychologies, and from certain kinds of philosophers: There is a notorious debate between the humanist Sartre's *Existentialism and Humanism* and Heidegger's *Letter on Humanism.* More recent attacks have denounced "humanism" as a form of white, male, Western, elite domination and colonization that is being imposed throughout the world and that brings with it too strong a sense of the unique individual. It is seen as contra postmodernism. In one telling statement, Foucault proclaims, "The modern individual—objectified, analyzed, fixed—is a historical achievement. There is no universal person on whom power has performed its operations and knowledge, its enquiries" (1979, pp. 159–160). The "Human Subject" becomes a Western invention. It is not a progress or a liberation, merely a trapping on the forces of power.

This loose but important cluster of positions critical of humanism—usually identified with a postmodern sensibility—would include queer theorists, multicultural theorists, postcolonialists, many feminists, and antiracists, as well as post-structural theorists. Although I have much sympathy with these projects and the critical methodologies they usually espouse (e.g., L. T. Smith, 1999), I also believe in the value of the pragmatic and humanist traditions. How can I live with this seeming contradiction?

Let me look briefly at what the critics say. They claim that Humanists propose some kind of common and hence universal "human being" or self: a common humanity that blinds us to wider differences and positions in the world. Often this is seen as a powerful, actualizing, and autonomous force in the world: The individual agent is at the center of the action and of the universe. This is said to result in overt individualism strongly connected to the Enlightenment project (Western, patriarchal, racist, colonialist, etc.) which turns itself into a series of moral and political claims about progress through a liberal and democratic society. Humanism is linked to a universal, unencumbered "self" and to the "modern" Western liberal project. Such ideas of the human subject are distinctly "Western" and bring with them a whole series of ideological assumptions about the centrality of the white, Western, male, middle-class/bourgeois position; hence, they become the enemies of feminism (human has equaled male), ethnic movements (human has equaled white superiority), gays (human has equaled heterosexual), and all cultures outside the Western Enlightenment project (human here has equaled the middle-class West).

A MORE COMPLEX HUMANISM?

Such claims made against "humanism" demean a complex, differentiated term into something far too simple. Humanism can, it is true, come to mean all of the above, but the term does not have to. Alfred McLung Lee (1978, pp. 44–45) and others have charted both a long history of humanism and many forms of it. Attacks usually are waged at a high level of generality, and specifics of what constitutes "the human" often are seriously overlooked. But, as I have suggested elsewhere, for me this "human being" is never a passive, helpless atom. Humans must be located in time and space: They are always stuffed full of their culture and history, and they must "nest" in a universe of contexts. Human beings are both embodied, feeling animals and creatures with great symbolic potential. They engage in symbolic communication and are dialogic and intersubjective: There is no such thing as the solitary individual. Human lives are shaped by chance, fateful moments, epiphanies, and contingencies. There is also a continuous tension between the specificities and varieties of humanities at any time and place, and the universal potentials that are to be found in all humans. And there is a continuous engagement with moral, ethical, and political issues.

Curiously, it is also clear that many of the seeming opponents of humanism can be found wanting to hold onto some version of humanism after all. Indeed, it is odd that some of the strongest opponents lapse into a kind of humanism at different points in their argument. For instance, Edward Said—a leading postcolonial critic of Western-style humanism—actually urges another kind of humanism, "shorn of all its 'unpleasantly triumphalist weight,'" and in recent work he actually claims to be a humanist (Said, 1992, p. 230; 2003).

Indeed, at the start of the 21st century, there have been many signs that the critique of humanism that pervaded the previous century has started to be reinvigorated as a goal of inquiry. More and more contemporary commentators, well aware of the attacks above, go on to make some kinds of humanist claims. It would not be hard to find signs of humanism (even if the authors disclaimed them!) in major studies such as Nancy Scheper-Hughes's *Death Without Weeping* (1994), Stanley Cohen's *States of Denial* (1999), and Martha Nussbaum's *Sex and*

Social Justice (1999). For me, they are clearly inspired by a version of humanism with the human being at the heart of the analysis, with care and justice as core values, and with the use of any methods at hand that will bring out the story.[6] So whatever the critiques, it does appear that a critical humanism still has its place in social science and qualitative inquiry. But before going too far, we should see what queer theory has to say on all this.

A Queer Project

Queer articulates a radical questioning of social and cultural norms, notions of gender, reproductive sexuality and the family.

—Cherry Smyth (1992, p. 28)

Queer is by definition whatever is at odds with the normal, the legitimate, the dominant. There is nothing in particular to which it necessarily refers.

—David Halperin (1995, p. 62)

Queer theory emerged around the mid-to late 1980s in North America, largely as a humanities/multicultural-based response to a more limited "lesbian and gay studies." While the ideas of Michel Foucault loom large (with his talks of "regimes of truth" and "discursive explosions"), the roots of queer theory (if not the term) usually are seen to lie in the work of Teresa de Lauretis (Halperin, 2003, p. 339) and Eve Kosofsky Sedgwick, who argued that

> many of the major nodes of thought and knowledge in twentieth century Western culture as a whole are structured—indeed fractured—by a chronic, now endemic crisis of homo/heterosexual definition, indicatively male, dating from the end of the nineteenth century. . . . an understanding of any aspect of modern Western culture must be, not merely incomplete, but damaged in its central substance to the degree that it does not incorporate a critical analysis of modern Homo/heterosexual definition. (1990, p. 1)

Judith Butler's work has been less concerned with the deconstruction of the homo/heterosexual binary divide and more interested in deconstructing the sex/gender divide. For her, there can be no kind of claim to any essential gender: It is all "performative," slippery, unfixed. If there is a heart to queer theory, then, it must be seen as a radical stance around sexuality and gender that denies any fixed categories and seeks to subvert any tendencies toward normality within its study (Sullivan, 2003).

Despite these opening suggestions, the term "queer theory" is very hard to pin down (some see this as a necessary virtue for a theory that refuses fixed identity). It has come to mean many things: Alexander Doty can suggest at least six different meanings, as follow. Sometimes it is used simply as a synonym for lesbian, gay, bisexual, transgender (LGBT). Sometimes it is an "umbrella term" that puts together a range of so-called "non-straight positions." Sometimes it simply describes any non-normative expression of gender (which could include straight). Sometimes it is used to describe "non-straight things" not clearly sign-posted as lesbian, gay, bisexual, or transgender but that bring with them a possibility for such a reading, even if incoherently. Sometimes it locates the "non-straight work, positions, pleasures, and readings of people who don't share the same sexual orientation as the text they are producing or responding to." Taking it even further, Doty suggests that "queer" may be a particular form of cultural readership and textual coding that creates spaces not contained within conventional categories such as gay, straight, and transgendered. Interestingly, what all his meanings have in common is that they are in some way descriptive of texts and they are in some way linked to (usually transgressing) categories of gender and sexuality (Doty, 2000, p. 6).

In general, "queer" may be seen as partially deconstructing our own discourses and creating a greater openness in the way we think through our categories. Queer theory must explicitly challenge any kind of closure or settlement, so any attempts at definition or codification must be nonstarters. Queer theory is, to quote Michael Warner, a stark attack on "normal business in the academy" (1992, p. 25). It poses the paradox of being inside the academy while wanting to be outside it. It suggests that a "sexual order overlaps with a wide range of institutions and social ideologies, to challenge the sexual order is sooner or later to encounter these institutions as a problem" (Warner, 1993, p. 5). Queer theory is really poststructuralism (and postmodernism) applied to sexualities and genders.

To a limited extent, queer theory may be seen as another specific version of what Nancy Harstock and Sandra Harding refer to as standpoint theory (though I have never seen it discussed in this way). Initially developed as a way to analyze a position of women's subordination and domination, it suggests that an "opposition consciousness" can emerge that transcends the more taken-for-granted knowledge. It is interesting that hardly any men have taken this position up, but other women—women of race and disability, for example—have done so. Men seem to ignore the stance, and so too do queer theorists, yet what we may well have in queer theory is really something akin to a "queer standpoint."

Certain key themes are worth highlighting. Queer theory is a stance in which

- both the heterosexual/homosexual binary and the sex/gender split are challenged.
- there is a de-centering of identity.
- all sexual categories are open, fluid, and non-fixed (which means that modern lesbian, gay, bisexual, and transgender identities are fractured, along with all heterosexual ones).
- it offers a critique of mainstream or "corporate" homosexuality.
- it sees power as being embodied discursively. Liberation and rights give way to transgression and carnival as a goal of political action, what has been called a "politics of provocation."
- all normalizing strategies are shunned.
- academic work may become ironic, is often comic and paradoxical, and is sometimes carnivalesque: "What a difference a gay makes," "On a queer day you can see forever" (cf. Gever, Greyson, & Parmar, 1993).
- versions of homosexual subject positions are inscribed everywhere, even in heterosexualities.
- the deviance paradigm is fully abandoned, and the interest lies in a logic of insiders/outsiders and transgression.
- its most common objects of study are textual—films, videos, novels, poetry, visual images.
- its most frequent interests include a variety of sexual fetishes, drag kings and drag queens, gender and sexual playfulness, cybersexualities, polyamoury, sadomasochism, and all the social worlds of the so-called radical sexual fringe.

A Queer Methodology?

What are the implications of queer theory for method (a word it rarely uses)? In its most general form, queer theory is a refusal of all orthodox methods—a certain disloyalty to conventional disciplinary methods (Halberstam,1998, pp. 9–13). What, then, does queer method actually do? What does it look like? In summary, let me give a few examples of what a queer methodology can be seen to offer.

The Textual Turn: Rereadings of Cultural Artifacts. Queer methods overwhelmingly employ an interest in and analysis of texts—films, literature, television, opera, musicals. This is perhaps the most commonly preferred strategy of queer theory. Indeed, Michael Warner has remarked that "almost everything that would be called queer theory is about ways in which texts—either literature or mass culture of language—shape sexuality." More extremely, he continues, "you can't eliminate queerness . . . or screen it out. It's everywhere. There's no place to hide, hetero scum!" (Warner, 1992, p. 19). The locus classicus of this way of thinking usually is seen to be Sedgwick's *Between Men* (1985), in which she looked at a number of key literary works (from Dickens to Tennyson) and reread these texts as driven by homosexuality, homosociality, and homophobia. Whereas patriarchy might condemn the former, it positively valorizes the latter (Sedgwick, 1985). In her wake have come hosts of rereadings around such themes. In later works, she gives readings to work as diverse as Diderot's *The Nun*, Wilde's *The Importance of Being Earnest*, and authors such as James and Austen (Sedgwick, 1990, 1994). In her wake, Alexander Doty gives queer readings to mass culture products such as "the sitcom"—from lesbian readings of the sitcoms *I Love Lucy* or *The Golden Girls*, to the role of "feminine straight men" such as Jack Benny, to the bisexual meanings in *Gentlemen Prefer Blondes* (Doty, 1993, 2000). Indeed, almost no text can escape the eyes of the queer theorist.

Subversive Ethnographies: Fieldwork Revisited. These are often relatively straightforward ethnographies of specific sexual worlds that challenge assumptions. Sasho Lambevski (1999), for instance, attempted to write "an insider, critical and experiential ethnography of the multitude of social locations (class, gender, ethnicity, religion) from which 'gays' in Macedonia are positioned, governed, controlled and silenced as subaltern people" (p. 301). As a "gay" Macedonian (are the terms a problem in this context?) who had spent time studying HIV in Australia, he looks at the sexual conflicts generated between the gay Macedonians and gay Albanians (never mind the Australian connection). Lambevski looks at the old cruising scenes in Skopje, known to him from before, that now take on multiple and different meanings bound up with sexualities, ethnicities, gender playing, and clashing cultures. Cruising for sex here is no straightforward matter. He describes how, in approaching and recognizing a potential sex partner as an Albanian (in an old cruising haunt), he feels paralyzed. Both bodies are flooded with ethnic meaning, not simple sexual ones, and ethnicities reek of power. He writes: "I obeyed by putting the (discursive) mask of my Macedonicity over my body" (p. 398). In another time and place, he may have reacted very differently.

Lambevski is overtly critical of much ethnography and wishes to write a queer experiential ethnography, not a confessional one (1999, p. 298). He refuses to commit himself to what he calls "a textual lie," which "continues to persist in much of what is considered a real ethnographic text." Here bodies, feelings, sexualities, ethnicities, and religions all can be left out easily. Nor, he claims, can ethnography simply depend on site observation or one-off interviewing. There is a great chain of connection: "The gay scene is inextricably linked to the Macedonian school system, the structuring of Macedonian and Albanian families and kinship relations, the Macedonian state and its political history, the Macedonian medical system with its power to mark and segregate 'abnormality' (homosexuality)" (1999, p. 400). There is a chain of social sites, and at the same time his own life is an integral part of this (Macedonian, queer, Australian, gay). Few researchers have been so honest regarding the tensions that infuse their lives and the wider chains of connectedness that shape their work.

I find it hard to believe that this is not true for all research, but it is usually silenced. Laud Humphreys's classic *Tearoom Trade* (1970), for example—admittedly, written some 30 years earlier—cannot speak of Humphreys's own gayness, his own bodily presence (though there is a small footnote on the taste of semen!), his emotional worlds, his white middle-classness, or his role as a white married minister. To the contrary, although he does remind the reader of his religious background and his wife, this serves more as a distraction. As important as it was in its day, this is a very different kind of ethnography. The same is true of a host that followed it. They were less aware of the problematic nature of categories and the links to material worlds. They were, in a very real fashion, "naïve ethnographies"— somehow thinking "the story could be directly told as it was." We live in less innocent times, and queer theory is a marker for this.

Scavenger Methodologies: The Raiding of Multiple Texts to Assemble New Ones. A fine example of queer "method" is Judith Halberstam's work on "female masculinity" (1998). Suggesting that we have failed to develop ways of seeing that can grasp the different kinds of masculinities that women have revealed both in the past and the present, she wrote a study that documents the sheer range of such phenomena. In her own work, she "raids" literary textual methods, film theory, ethnographic field research, historical survey, archival records, and taxonomy to produce her original account of emerging forms of "female masculinity" (Halberstam, 1998, pp. 9–13). Here we have aristocratic European cross-dressing women of the 1920s, butch lesbians, dykes, drag kings, tomboys, black "butch in the hood" rappers, trans-butches, the tribade (a woman who practices "unnatural vices" with other women), the gender invert, the stone butch, the female-to-male transsexual (FTM), and the raging bull dyke! She also detects—through films as diverse as *Alien* and *The Killing of Sister George*—at least six prototypes of the female masculine: tomboys, Predators, Fantasy Butches, Transvestites, Barely Butches, and Postmodern Butches (1998, chap. 6).

In introducing this motley collection, she uses a "scavenger methodology. . . [of] different methods to collect and produce information on subjects who have been deliberately or accidentally excluded from traditional studies of human behavior" (1998, p. 13). She borrows from Eve Kosofsky Sedgwick's "nonce taxonomy": "The making and unmaking and remaking and redissolution of hundreds of old and new categorical meanings concerning all the kinds it takes to make up a world" (Sedgwick, 1990, p. 23). This is the mode of "deconstruction," and in this world the very idea that types of people called homosexuals or gays or lesbians (or, more to the point, "men" and "women") can be simply called up for study becomes a key problem in itself. Instead, the researcher should become more and more open to start sensing new worlds of possibilities.

Many of these social worlds are not immediately transparent, whereas others are amorphously nascent and forming. All this research brings to the surface social worlds only dimly articulated hitherto—with, of course, the suggestion that there are more, many more, even more deeply hidden. In one sense, Halberstam captures rich fluidity and diversity—all this going on just beneath the surface structures of society. But in another sense, her very act of naming, innovating terms, and categorizing tends itself to create and assemble new differences.

Performing Gender and Ethnographic Performance. Often drawing upon the work of Judith Butler, who sees gender as never essential, always unfixed, not innate, never natural, but always constructed through performativity—as a "stylized repetition of acts" (1990, p. 141)—much of the work in queer theory has been playing around with gender. Initially fascinated by drag, trans-gender, and transsexualism, and with Divas, Drag Kings, and key cross-genderists such as Del LaGrace Volcano and Kate Bornstein (1995), some of it has functioned almost as a kind of subversive terrorist drag. It arouses curious, unknown queered desires emancipating people from the constraints of the gendered tyranny of the presumed "normal body" (Volcano & Halberstam, 1999). Others have moved out to consider a wide array of playing with genders—from "faeries" and "bears," to leather scenes and the Mardi Gras, and on to the more commercialized/ normalized drag for mass consumption: RuPaul, Lily Savage, and Graham Norton.

Sometimes performance may be seen as even more direct. It appears in the work of alternative documentaries, in "video terrorism" and "street theater," across cable talk shows, experimental artworks, and activist tapes. By the late 1980s, there was a significant expansion of lesbian and gay video (as well as film and film festivals), and in the academy, posts were created to deal with this— along with creation of more informal groupings. (See, for example, Jennie Livingston's film *Paris Is Burning* [1990], which looks at the "ball circuit" of poor gay men and transgenderists, usually black, in the late 1980s in New York City, or Ang Lee's *The Wedding Banquet* [1993], which reconfigured the dominant "rice queen" image).[7]

Exploring New/Queered Case Studies. Queer theory also examines new case studies. Michael Warner, for example, looks at a range of case studies of emergent publics. One stands out to me: It is the details of a queer cabaret (a counterpublic?) that involves "erotic vomiting." Suggesting a kind of "national heterosexuality" that, along with "family values," saturates much public talk, he argues that multiple queer cultures work to subvert these. He investigates the queer counter public of a "garden variety leather bar" where the routines are "spanking, flagellation, shaving, branding, laceration, bondage, humiliation, wrestling—as they say, you know, the usual" (Warner, 2002, pp. 206–210). But suddenly this garden-variety S&M bar is subverted by the less than usual: a cabaret of what is called erotic vomiting.

The Reading of the Self. Most of the researches within queer theory play with the author's self: It is rarely absent. D. A. Miller's (1998) account, for example, of the Broadway musical and the role its plays in queer life is an intensely personal account of the musical, including snapshots of the author as child, with the albums played.

What's New?

As interesting as many of these methods, theories, and studies most certainly are, I suggest that there is really very little that could be called truly new or striking here. Often, queer methodology means little more than literary theory rather belatedly coming to social science tools such as ethnography and reflexivity (although sometimes it is also a radical critique of orthodox social science— especially quantitative— methods). Sometimes it borrows some of the oldest of metaphors, such as drama. Queer theory does not seem to me to constitute any fundamental advance over recent ideas in qualitative inquiry—it borrows, refashions, and retells. What is more radical is its persistent concern with categories and gender/sexuality—although, in truth, this has long been questioned, too (cf. Plummer, 2002; Weston, 1998). What seems to be at stake, then, in any queering of qualitative research is not so much a methodological style as a political and substantive concern with gender, heteronormativity, and sexualities. Its challenge is to bring stabilized gender and sexuality to the forefront of analyses in ways they are not usually advanced and that put under threat any ordered world of gender and sexuality. This is just what is, indeed, often missing from much ethnographic or life story research.

The Troubles With Queer

Responses to queer theory have been mixed. It would not be too unfair to say that outside the world of queer theorists—the world of "straight academia"—queer theory has been more or less ignored and has had minimal impact. This has had the unfortunate consequence of largely ghettoizing the whole approach. Ironically, those who may most need to understand the working of the heterosexual-homosexual binary divide in their work can hence ignore it (and they usually do), whereas those who least need to understand it actively work to deconstruct terms that really describe themselves. Thus, it is comparatively rare in mainstream literary analysis or sociological theory for queer to be taken seriously (indeed, it has taken three editions of this handbook to include something on it, and the so-called seventh moment of inquiry (see Lincoln & Denzin, Epilogue, this volume) has so far paid only lip service to it!). More than this, many gays, lesbians, and feminists themselves see no advance at all in a queer theory that, after all, would simply "deconstruct" them, along with all their political gains, out of existence. Queer theorists often write somewhat arrogantly, as if they have a monopoly on political validity, negating both the political and theoretical gains of the past. Let me reflect on some of the standard objections to queer theory.

First, for many, the term itself is provocative: a pejorative and stigmatizing phrase from the past is reclaimed by that very same stigmatized grouping and had its meaning renegotiated; as such, it has a distinct generational overtone. Younger academics love it; older ones hate it. It serves to write off the past worlds of research and create new divisions.

Second, it brings a category problem, what Josh Gamson (1995) has described as a Queer Dilemma. He claims that there is simultaneously a need for a public collective identity (around which activism can galvanize) and a need to take apart and blur boundaries. As he says, fixed identity categories are the basis for both oppression and political power. Although it is important to stress the "inessential, fluid and multiple sited" forms of identity emerging within the queer movement, he also can see that there are very many from within the lesbian, gay, bisexual, and transgender movement (LGBT, as it is currently clumsily called) who also reject its tendency to deconstruct the very idea of gay and lesbian identity—hence abolishing a field of study and politics when it has only just gotten going.

There are also many radical lesbians who view it with even more suspicion, as it tends to work to make the lesbian invisible and to reinscribe tacitly all kinds of male power (in disguise), bringing back well-worn arguments about S&M, porn, and transgender politics as anti-women. Radical lesbian feminist Sheila Jeffreys (2003) is particularly scathing, seeing the whole queer movement as a serious threat to the gains of radical lesbians in the late 20th century. With the loss of the categories of woman-identified-woman and radical lesbian in a fog of (largely masculinist) queer deconstruction, it becomes impossible to see the roots of women's subordination to men. She also accuses it of a major elitism: The languages of most of its proponents ape the language of male academic elites, and lose all the gains that were made by the earlier, more accessible writings of feminists who wrote for and spoke to women in the communities, not just other academics. Lilian Faderman claims it is "resolutely elitist" and puts this well:

> The language queer scholars deploy sometimes seems transparently aimed at what lesbian feminists once called the "big boys" at the academy. Lesbian-feminist writing, in contrast, had as primary values clarity and accessibility, since its purpose was to speak directly to the community and in so doing reflect change. (1997, pp. 225–226).[8]

There are many other critics. Tim Edwards (1998) worries about a politics that often collapses into some kind of fan worship, celebration of cult films, and weak cultural politics. Stephen O. Murray hates the word "queer" itself because it perpetuates binary divisions and cannot avoid being a tool of domination, and he worries about excessive preoccupation with linguistics and with textual representation (2002, pp. 245–247). Even some of queer theory's founders now worry if the whole radical impulse has gotten lost and queer theory has become normalized, institutionalized, even "lucrative" within the academy (Halperin, 2003).

From many sides, then, doubts are being expressed that all is not well in the house of queer. There are problems that come with the whole project, and in some ways I still find the language of the humanists more conducive to social inquiry.

Queer Theory Meets Critical Humanism: The Conflictual Worlds of Research

> *Conflict is the gadfly of thought . . . a sine qua non of reflection and ingenuity.*
>
> — John Dewey (1922, p. 300)

And so we have two traditions seemingly at serious odds with each other. There is nothing unusual about this—all research positions are open to conflict from both within and without. Whereas humanism generally looks to experience, meaning, and human subjectivity, queer theory rejects this in favor of representations. Whereas humanism generally asks the researcher to get close to the worlds he or she is studying, queer theory almost pleads for distance—a world of texts, defamiliarization, and deconstruction. Whereas humanism brings a liberal democratic project with "justice for all," queer theory aims to prioritize the oppressions of sexuality and gender and urges a more radical change. Humanism usually favors a calmer conversation and dialogue, whereas queer is carnivalesque, parodic, rebellious, and playful. Humanism champions the voice of the public intellectual; queer theory is to be found mainly in the universities and its own self-generated social movement of aspiring academics.

Yet there are some commonalities. Both, for instance, would ask researchers to adopt a critically self-aware stance. Both would seek out a political and ethical background (even though, in a quite major way, they may differ on this—queer theory has a prime focus on radical gender change, and humanism is broader). And both assume the contradictory messiness of social life, such that no category system can ever do it justice.

On a closer look, several of the above differences overlap. Many critical humanisms can focus on representations (though fewer queer theorists are willing to focus on experience). Critical humanists often are seen as social constructionists, and this hardly can be seen as far removed from deconstructionists. There is no reason why critical humanism cannot take the value and political stances of queer theorists (I have and I do), but the moral baselines of humanism are wider and less specifically tied to gender. Indeed, contemporary humanistic method enters the social worlds of different "others" to work a catharsis of comprehension. It juxtaposes differences and complexities with similarities and harmonies. It recognizes the multiple possible worlds of social research—not necessarily the standard interviews or ethnographies, but the roles of photography, art, video, film, poetics, drama, narrative, autoethnography, music, introspection, fiction, audience participation, and street theater. It also finds multiple ways of presenting the "data," and it acknowledges that a social science of any consequences must be located in the political and moral dramas of its time. One of those political and moral dramas is "queer."

But there again, the histories, canons, and gurus of critical humanism and queer theory are indeed different, even though, in the end, they are not nearly as at odds with each other as one could be led to believe. Yes, they are not the same; and it is right that they should maintain some of their key differences. But no, they are not so very different either. It is no wonder, then, that I find that I can live with both. Contradiction, ambivalence, and tension reside in all critical inquiries.

Notes

1. As Dmitri Shalin noted more than a decade ago, "The issues that symbolic interactionism has highlighted since its inception and that assured its maverick status in American sociology bear some uncanny resemblance to the themes championed by postmodernist thinkers" (1993, p. 303). It investigates "the marginal, local, everyday, heterogeneous and indeterminate" alongside the "socially constructed, emergent and plural" (p. 304). Likewise, David Maines (2001) has continued to sustain an earlier argument that symbolic interactionism, by virtue of its interpretive center, finds an easy affinity with much of postmodernism, but because of that same center, has no need for it (pp. 229–233). He finds valuable the resurgence of interest in interpretive work, the importance now given to writing "as intrinsic to method," the concern over multiple forms of presentation, and the reclaiming of value positions and "critical work" (Maines, 2001, p. 325). In addition, as is well known, Norman K. Denzin has been at the forefront in defending postmodernism within sociology/cultural studies and symbolic interactionism, in numerous books and papers (e.g., Denzin, 1989, 1997, 2003).

2. For some, "interactionism" has become almost synonymous with sociology; see Maines (2001) and P. Atkinson and Housley (2003).

3. The liberal, humanist feminist philosopher Martha Nussbaum (1999, p. 41) suggests a long list of "human capabilities" that need cultivating for a person to function as a human being. These include concerns such as "bodily health and integrity" senses,

imagination, and thought; emotions; practical reason; affiliation; concern for other species; play; control over one's environment; and life itself. To this I might add the crucial self-reflexive process, a process of communication that is central to the way we function.

4. In Bob Connell's rich study of *Masculinities* (1995)—a study that is far from being either avowedly "humanist" or "queer"—he takes life stories as emblematic/symptomatic of "crisis tendencies in power relations (that) threaten hegemonic masculinity directly" (p. 89). He looks at four groups of men under crisis— radical environmentalists, gay and bisexual networks, young working-class men, and men of the new class. Connell implies that I do not take this seriously (1995, p. 89). However, even in the first edition of my book *Documents of Life* (Plummer, 1983), I make it quite clear that among the contributions of the life story, it can be seen as a "tool for history," as a perspective on totality, and as a key focus on social change! (pp. 68–69).

5. Or, as Rupp and Taylor call it, "the tripartite model of cultural investigation" (2003, p. 223).

6. Likewise, I can sense a humanism at work in the writings of Cornel West, Jeffrey Weeks, Seyla Benhabib, Anthony Giddens, Zygmunt Bauman, Agnes Heller, Jürgen Habermas, Michel Bakhtin, and many others. Never mind the naming game, in which they have to come out as humanists (though some clearly do); what matters are the goals that they see will produce adequate understanding and social change for the better. In this respect, a lot of them read like humanists manqué.

7. See, for example, *Jump Cut, Screen, The Celluloid Closet, Now You See It?, The Bad Object Choices* collective, and the work of Tom Waugh and Pratibha Parmar.

8. See also Simon Watney's critiques to be found in *Imagine Hope* (2000). Watney is far from sympathetic to radical lesbianism, but his account has distinct echoes. Queer theory has often let down AIDS activism.

References

Atkinson, P., & Housley, W. (2003). *Interactionism.* London: Sage.

Atkinson, R. (1998). *The life story interview.* Thousand Oaks, CA: Sage.

Bauman, Z. (2000). *Liquid society.* Cambridge, UK: Polity.

Bauman, Z. (2004). *Wasted lives: Modernity and its outcasts.* Cambridge, UK: Polity.

Beck, U. (2003). *Individualization.* London: Sage.

Bornstein, K. (1995). *Gender outlaw.* New York: Vintage.

Bruyn, T. S. (1966). *The human perspective in sociology.* Englewood Cliffs, NJ: Prentice Hall.

Butler, J. (1990). *Gender trouble.* London: Routledge.

Carrington, C. (1999). *No place like home: Relationships and family life among lesbians and gay men.* Chicago: University of Chicago Press.

Clifford, J., & Marcus, G. E. (Eds.). (1986). *Writing culture.* Berkeley: University of California Press.

Coffey, A. (1999). *The ethnographic self: Fieldwork and the representation of identity.* London: Sage.

Cohen, S. (1999). *States of denial.* Cambridge, UK: Polity.

Coles, R. (1989). *The call of stories: Teaching and the moral imagination.* Boston: Houghton Mifflin.

Connell, R. W. (1995). *Masculinities.* Cambridge, UK: Polity.

Denzin, N. K. (1989). *Interpretive biography.* London: Sage.

Denzin, N. K. (1997). *Interpretive ethnography: Ethnographic practices for the 21st century.* London: Sage.

Denzin, N. K. (2003). *Performance ethnography.* London: Sage.

Denzin, N., & Lincoln, Y. (Eds.). (1994). *Handbook of qualitative research.* London: Sage.

Dewey, J. (1920). *Reconstruction of philosophy.* New York: Henry Holt.

Dewey, J. (1922). *Human nature and conduct.* New York: Henry Holt.

Dewey, J. (1938). *Logic of inquiry.* New York: Henry Holt.

Doty, A. (1993). *Making things perfectly queer: Interpreting mass culture.* Minneapolis: University of Minnesota Press.

Doty, A. (2000). *Flaming classics: Queering the film canon.* London: Routledge.

Edwards, T. (1998). Queer fears: Against the cultural turn. *Sexualities, 1*(4), 471–484.

Ellis, C., & Flaherty, M. G. (Eds.). (1992). *Investigating subjectivity: Research on lived experience.* London: Sage.

Faderman, L. (1997). Afterword. In D. Heller (Ed.), *Cross purposes: Lesbians, feminists and the limits of alliance.* Bloomington: Indiana University Press.

Felice, W. F. (1996). *Taking suffering seriously.* Albany: State University of New York Press.

Foucault, M. (1979). *The history of sexuality.* Middlesex, UK: Harmondsworth.

Gamson, J. (1995). Must identity movements self-destruct?: A queer dilemma. *Social Problems, 42*(3), 390–407.

Gamson, J. (1998). *Freaks talk back: Tabloid talk shows and sexual nonconformity.* Chicago: University of Chicago Press.

Gever, M., Greyson, J., & Parmar, P. (Eds.). (1993). *Queer looks: Perspectives on lesbian and gay film and video.* New York: Routledge.

Giddens, A. (1991). *Modernity and self-identity.* Cambridge, UK: Polity.

Gouldner, A. (1973). *For sociology: Renewal and critique in sociology today.* London: Allen Lane.

Gubrium, J., & Holstein, J. (1997). *The new language of qualitative research.* Oxford, UK: Oxford University Press.

Halberstam, J. (1998). *Female masculinity.* Durham, NC: Duke University Press.

Halperin, D. (1995). *Saint Foucault: Towards a gay hagiography.* New York: Oxford University Press.

Halperin, D. (2003). The normalization of queer theory. *Journal of Homosexuality, 45*(2–4), 339–343.

Hertz, R. (Ed.). (1997). *Reflexivity and voice.* Thousand Oaks, CA: Sage.

Honneth, A. (1995). *The struggle for recognition: The moral grammar of social conflicts.* Cambridge, UK: Polity.

Humphreys, L. (1970). *Tearoom trade.* Chicago: Aldine.

Jackson, M. (1989). *Paths toward a clearing: Radical empiricism and ethnographic inquiry.* Bloomington: Indiana University Press.

Jeffreys, S. (2003). *Unpacking queer politics.* Oxford, UK: Polity.

Kong, T., Mahoney, D., & Plummer, K. (2002). Queering the interview. In J. F. Gubrium & J. A. Holstein (Eds.), *The handbook of interview research* (pp. 239–257). Thousand Oaks, CA: Sage.

Lambevski, S. A. (1999). Suck my nation: Masculinity, ethnicity and the politics of (homo)sex. *Sexualities, 2*(3), 397–420.

Lee, A. (Director). (1993). *The wedding banquet* [Motion picture]. Central Motion Pictures Corporation.

Lee, A. M. (1978). *Sociology for whom?* Oxford: Oxford University Press.

Lincoln, Y. S., & Denzin, N. K. (1994). The fifth moment. In N. K. Denzin & Y. S. Lincoln (Eds.), *Handbook of qualitative research* (pp. 575–586). Thousand Oaks, CA: Sage.

Livingston, J. (Director), & Livingston, J., & Swimar, B. (Producers). (1990). *Paris Is Burning* [Motion picture]. Off White Productions.

Maines, D. (2001). *The fault lines of consciousness: A view of interactionism in sociology.* New York: Aldine de Gruyter.

Miller, D. A. (1998). *Place for us: Essay on the Broadway musical.* Cambridge, MA: Harvard University Press.

Murray, S. O. (2002). Five reasons I don't take queer theory seriously. In K. Plummer (Ed.), *Sexualities: Critical concepts in sociology* (Vol. 3, pp. 245–247). London: Routledge.

Nardi, P. (1999). *Gay men's friendships: Invincible communities.* Chicago: University of Chicago Press.

Nisbet, R. (1976). *Sociology as an art form.* London: Heinemann.

Nussbaum, M. C. (1999). *Sex and social justice.* New York: Oxford University Press.

O'Neill, O. (2002). *A question of trust: The BBC Reith Lectures 2002.* Cambridge, UK: Cambridge University Press.

Plummer, K. (1983). *Documents of life.* London: Allen and Unwin.

Plummer, K. (1995). *Telling sexual stories.* London: Routledge.

Plummer, K. (2001). *Documents of life 2: An invitation to a critical humanism.* London: Sage.

Plummer, K. (Ed.). (2002). *Sexualities: Critical concepts in sociology* (4 vols.). London: Routledge.

Plummer, K. (2003). *Intimate citizenship.* Seattle: University of Washington Press.

Reed-Danahay, D. E. (Ed.). (1997). *Auto/ethnography: Rewriting the self and the social.* Oxford, UK: Berg.

Ronai, C. R. (1992). A reflexive self through narrative: A night in the life of an erotic dancer/researcher. In C. Ellis & M. G. Flaherty (Eds.), *Investigating subjectivity: Research on lived experience* (pp. 102–124). Newbury Park, CA: Sage.

Rorty, R. (1999). *Philosophy and social hope.* Middlesex, UK: Penguin.

Rupp, L., & Taylor, V. (2003). *Drag queens at the 801 Cabaret.* Chicago: University of Chicago Press.

Said, E. (2003). *Orientalism* (2nd ed.). New York: Cambridge.

Scheper-Hughes, N. (1994). *Death without weeping.* Berkeley: University of California Press.

Sedgwick, E. K. (1985). *Between men: English literature and male homosexual desire.* New York: Columbia University Press.

Sedgwick, E. K. (1990). *Epistemology of the closet.* Berkeley: University of California Press.

Sedgwick, E. K. (1994). *Tendencies.* London: Routledge.

Shalin, D. N. (1993). Modernity, postmodernism and pragmatic inquiry. *Symbolic Interaction, 16*(4), 303–332.

Smith, L. T. (1999). *Decolonizing methodologies: Research and indigenous peoples.* London: Zed Books.

Smyth, C. (1992). *Lesbians talk queer notions.* London: Scarlet Press.

Sullivan, N. (2003). *A critical introduction to queer theory.* Edinburgh: University of Edinburgh Press.

Tronto, J. (1993). *Moral boundaries: A political argument for an ethic of care.* London: Routledge.

Urry, J. (2000). *Sociology beyond societies: Mobilities for the twenty-first century.* London: Routledge.

Volcano, D. L., & Halberstam, J. (1999). *The drag king book.* London: Serpent's Tail.

Warner, M. (1991). *Fear of a queer planet: Queer politics and social theory.* Minneapolis: University of Minnesota.

Warner, M. (1992, June). From queer to eternity: An army of theorists cannot fail. *Voice Literary Supplement, 106,* pp. 18–26.

Warner, M. (1999). *The trouble with normal: Sex, politics, and the ethics of queer life.* Cambridge, MA: Harvard University Press.

Warner, M. (2002). *Public and counterpublics.* New York: Zone Books.

Watney, S. (2000). *Imagine hope: AIDS and gay identity.* London: Routledge.

West, C. (1999). The moral obligations of living in a democratic society. In D. B. Batstone & E. Mendieta (Eds.), *The good citizen* (pp. 5–12). London: Routledge.

Weston, K. (1998). *Longslowburn: Sexuality and social science.* London: Routledge.

Wolcott, H. F. (2002). *Sneaky kid and its aftermath.* Walnut Creek, CA: AltaMira.

Postscript 2011 to Living With the Contradictions

Moving on: Generations, Cultures and Methodological Cosmopolitanism

Ken Plummer

> *Stop worrying where you're going, move on. If you can know where you're going, you've gone. Just keep moving on.*
>
> Stephen Sondheim, *Sunday in the Park with George*

The contradictory tensions of life and research go on and on. This chapter was written about a decade ago, and life and the tensions it raises, while unresolved, have moved on. The tensions of life do not stop coming—and since I wrote this article, other tensions have become more prominent. Some of the puzzles of critical humanism and queer theory, which are now relatively well established as intellectual orthodoxies, have been supplanted for me by the dilemmas posed by two further issues: generation and culture. Moving on, I see the need for the development of generational and cosmopolitan methodologies. In a very brief afterword, let me hint at these ever-expanding tensions.

TRANSGRESSING GENERATIONS

At the heart of my current concerns and tensions is the awareness that I am growing old: All academics do. With this startling revelation has come clear awareness that all intellectual life is (partially, if not primarily) organized through the tensions of generational standpoints—even though this is rarely discussed. Having recently read Randall Collins's (1998) magisterial *The*

Sociology of Philosophies and re-read Karl Mannheim's (1937/1952) classic account of generations, I can see that academic life—like all social life—is bound up with different ages functioning through their generational cohorts and their generational networks of *interaction ritual chains*. Different generations assemble ideas that reach out to that generation; the task of later intellectual generations is always to move beyond the wisdoms of their predecessors. In intellectual life, there is always a premium on "saying something new": This is the way to forge ahead in a new career. Repeating the old stories of earlier research programs will get you nowhere. The 45 years of my own academic tensions have been but a mere blip in the vast cycle of generations of people thinking about the world we live in from many standpoints and contrasting cultures. Our intellectual, political, and research agendas have restricted time-bound concerns. They come and go, and very few ideas survive more than a generation or two. A few— "the classics"—are singled out from the vast pantheons of knowledges and libraries to be celebrated; most are lost forever, often in their own time (and even more so these days, when there is such a flood of academic work). Intellectual generations are both *diachronic* (bound up with intellectual generations that will rarely last more than 30 years) and *synchronic:* They create tensions across the generations at any one moment in time—as the different trainings and world moments come into radical, often conflictual interplay. All this suggests the significance of memory and time: Older ideas will always be replaced by the latest fashion. We need memories of the past even as old ideas are supplanted by the new ones of a new generation. There is a premium on the new-fashioned rather than the old-fashioned. Social life and social research are always lived at the intersectional ties of generations (a fact often overlooked by those theorists who focus usually only on the class, gender, and ethnicity of intersectional theory) (see Plummer, 2010, on all this).

One quick example, from a multitude of possibilities, must suffice. The term *queer* was the word of my childhood and youthful homosexuality, the word of hostility and hatred run rampant. It was a word that my time in the Gay Liberation Front of the early 1970s struggled so hard to resist. I loathed the idea of queer. It was bad news. Twenty years later, it became the flag post of a new generation—decked out in full radical irony. I have had to live with the term and recognize the new position it supposedly represents. But this does not make me happy with it. Recently, in an issue of *GLQ,* the premier queer journal, a leading review article offered a clear sense of how the different appropriations of queer varied by different generations. In a telling interchange between the young Matt Houlbrook, author of the much acclaimed *Queer London* (2005), and Jeffrey Weeks, the well-established author of the path-breaking account, *Coming Out*

(1977), Chris Waters recounts how their different positions in the world radically shaped their contrasting historical interpretations. Houlbrook was only 2 years old when Weeks published his classic work; now, 30 years on, Houlbrook writes his history from a very different stance. This is, of course, as it must inevitably be. Houlbrook describes the homosexual past in "elegiac terms," arguing that in "exploring the history of queer London in the first half of the twentieth century, we should lament possibilities long lost as much as we celebrate opportunities newly acquired" (p. 140). It is precisely this nostalgia for lost possibilities that does not sit well with Jeffrey Weeks, the young radical of the 1970s who is now himself retired. Pressed on his attitude toward this past at a BBC radio discussion, Houlbrook says, "I think I'm going to have to admit being very nostalgic for this lost world," to which Weeks quickly responds, "I think you can only be nostalgic if you didn't live it. . . . Those of us who had the misfortune to live that life until the 1970s don't feel nostalgic about it" (Waters, 2008, p. 141). It seems to me that they lived in different worlds—and this is precisely what the shaping of generations does. In one sense, all of our qualitative researches are the records of successive generational cohorts jostling with each other. And the message is: Always keep your eye on the next generation; things are bound to change again. The stories we tell of social life are bound up with the generations we live in. All social sciences—like all of social life—entail the telling of generational narratives, and with this comes the presence of continuing tensions and even contradiction.

TRANSGRESSING CULTURE

My second, linked concern here is one I have been aware of for a long time. It is the sheer limitations of my own cross-cultural knowledge—the tensions over the differences across cultures and languages we are born into which are the limiting horizons of our thinking and practices. The vast populations of the world in China, India, Muslim cultures, Latin America, and the rest—who speak languages different from mine and live with religions I do not understand—have long been outside of the provinces of much so-called Western social science. Of course, these days we are sophisticated in postcolonial shapings, standpoint theories, and intersectional knowledges. We are aware that there are disturbing differences in our continents of knowledge and a massive arrogance about the localized theories and methods of the West, especially with the limited worldview of the Anglo American west. We have been told off for ignoring "Southern Theory," as Raewyn Connell (1998) rightly puts it. There is so much politically located knowledge that is beyond that of the limited West, and especially the even more limited United States, and yet our books and our researches carry on more or less in linguistic, emotional, and political ignorance of it. My earlier "Western models" of being gay, for example, now look absurdly quaint in the world scheme—the tales of a little White English boy struggling to come out in the swinging 1960s—when read against the almost genocidal plights of gay and lesbian people in, say, Uganda or Iran today.

At the same time, I am so glad to sense a new generation in the making that is developing research and languages that take this seriously and who are working hard to get us beyond the Western fix. Queer theory and critical humanism are simultaneously highly privileged local Western disputes; but they also travel quite well, having become debates in different ways across a wide range of cultures. Still the question now has to be posed: Is a global critical humanism possible—and, even more, is it possible to generate a transnational queer studies? Here we are hurled straight into major debates about the continuously hybridic and emergent character of cultures. The challenge is on as to whether we seek an abstracted universalism from the North over a truly grounded understanding from the grounded analytics of the daily practices of the South? This is personally a massive challenge. I was born a little boy in England, and although I am a little travelled, I do not speak the dialects of other local cultures, nor do I have the idiosyncratic deep wisdoms that their cultures harbor. It is simply wrong for me to pronounce on them. Sadly, the new (mainly Western) languages of internationalism, globalization, and decolonization make me feel increasingly marginal. It is fair to say I found my own cultural and generational voice in the 1960s, and I was able to have my say; but now is either the time to be silent or to quietly assist a new generational process of those billions of voices in the world without privilege who now need to have their own indigenous global say. We westerners babble and babble on with our theories and methods—often extending our own privileges further and further. It may be time for the Western academic party to call it a day.

Again let me give some examples from many. Travis Kong is a Hong Kong-born man, immediately hybridized between the English colony and his Chineseness. He has lived his life at this juncture. But more: He was working class and gay. This did not make life easy for him or for his ability to advance in academic life. His important book, *Chinese Male Homosexualities* (2010), is written at the intersections of an emerging global mosaic of multiple global sexualities and their challenging diversities at the start of the 21st century. There is much to learn from it. His study shows "the complexity of globalization in the kaleidoscopic life of Chinese homosexualities in Hong Kong, London, and China" (p. 8). We are immediately in three different lands with their wildly different histories and symbolic meanings. At the heart of this book are three case studies of what might conventionally be called gay men in three cities: Hong Kong, London, and Guangdong. The men are all in some sense "Chinese" and "gay," but in these very terms lie definitional problems of the mysterious essence. At various times, we enter the worlds of the diasporic and feminized "golden boys," the *tongzhi,* the "money boy," the *memba,* and the "potato." These new worlds have meant the creation of different hybridized gay identities (Kong, 2010). Same-sex sexualities are never cut from the same cloth. A homosexual is not a homosexual is not a homosexual. We have to learn to live with (and love) the varieties, the differences, the hybridic.

His study finds three broad clusters of Chinese men in search of meaning in their sexual lives in worlds of rapid social change, postcolonialism, globalization—and confusion. It tells of emerging new sexual stories in which we find new sexually imagined communities. It is a study, too, of the plurality, multiplicities, and differences of sexualities in the contemporary world—a move right away from any sense that there is one true Chinese sexual way, or indeed any one true sexual way anywhere. Shaped as they may be by familistic Confucian ideals from the past, new sexual identities are under construction, and this book suggests a patchwork of such differences as new identities generate the hybridization of sexualities. One hybridic dimension Kong points out is the queering of the straights and the straightening the queers. Here, too, sexualities are always on the move—across time and space, we find sexscapes, sexual flows, and sexual mobilities: These men transform their lives as they move to spaces full of new possibilities and from the cities of the East to the cities of the West—from communism to capitalism, from rural to global city, from colonialism to postcolonialism.

There is, then, much to savor in Kong's book. It is a study of hybridic sexualities and their refashioning across the globe. And in this, Kong's book joins a newly emerging field of study, in Latin America and in Asia, which looks at the shifting internal and external borders of the sexualities of nations and countries. There has been a recent flourishing of new work by new scholars who reject the presumptions of much Western theorization about queer and gay. The 2005 Asian Queer Studies Conference was emblematic of this when it brought together in Bangkok some 600 academics and activists. It marked a turning point for all this challenging new work. What we are charting here are hybridic and cosmopolitan sexualities in their lived political contexts. Often, as here, this research produces ethnographic work about the complexities and subtleties of grounded lives in specific locations, work that is always much more messy, contradictory, and ambiguous than wider theories or dogmatic positions allow.

There are many other examples, including the growing work on international sex work and trafficking, which suggests large movements of people across the globe for sexual purposes involving money and often coercion and violence. Queer theory and critical humanism have so far not had that much to say on this. There are instead the standard formal studies—usually condemnatory—which give the global statistics of this "horror" provided by global agencies. But there are also growing numbers of accounts that are more sensitive to the multiple meanings emergent within both the cultures of departure and the cultures of arrival—and the struggles here between actors' shifting definitions, their senses of agency, and the constraining and enabling social structures they negotiate. As women (and men, and children) move from their home cultures (and their ambivalent expectations of work, family, sex) to their new host cultures, they have to negotiate new hybridic sexualities. In the work of Kaoru Aoyama (2009), Laura Agustin (2007), Tiantian Zheng (2009), and others, we find their own lives and those of women in tension. Here we find that migrants often make personal choices to travel and work in the sex industry, even as they are part of a dynamic and exploitative global economy. They all are advocates of listening to the voices of the migrant women.

Aoyama, for example, who is from Japan but studied in the United Kingdom, became interested in the women who leave Thailand for the sex industry in Japan. Here she can depict a theme of much recent work: An international world of sex slavery, trafficking, and coercion runs parallel to the needs of migrating women, who find sex work to be a means to support themselves and their families. Her concern is with the multiple complex paths of human agency shaped within changing culture as sex workers struggle in different places and at different times of their lives with different material conditions and different meanings. Aoyama's (2009) study above all is concerned with studying women's human agency, and it is compelling in detailing its empirical complexity. There is no one pattern of agency but multiple routes and sites.

Likewise, Zheng (2009) focused on the ways in which sexuality and sex work are shifting in a post-Mao landscape. Becoming a field worker in the city of Dalian, she closely observed young Chinese women who become karaoke bar hostesses. She interrogated not only their business situation but also their family and earlier backgrounds. Unsurprisingly, her research was far from welcome in China. She discloses some of her many difficulties in conducting such research—not least as she becomes partially engaged in waiting on the men herself, the only acceptable role that would allow her to be present in such bars as a Chinese woman. All this, however, helped her get close to the data, and it becomes another finely observed ethnography, which investigates what goes on in the club, the kinds of roles that the girls have to play, and their lives outside. Patriarchy (or the gender order) and male dominance can be observed at work everywhere, as can the damage being done to the women. Zheng directly links this sex work to patriarchy and masculinity in China as it is in serious postsocialist change. But the stories are more complex than this. The girls are from poor backgrounds, and Zheng shows the sheer poverty and degradation of their village lives—"the wretched living conditions in the countryside" (p. 150): Ironically, damned as these hostesses' city experiences are, they seem a lot better off. At least, they can send money back to their families. So the stories they tell here start to get more nuanced. They rationalize that their work is for the benefit of their family. More: There is real change in their lives. Often they started their city work in the sweatshops but found themselves moving up and beyond—so that they are now furnished with the very clothes made in the sweatshops. Up to a point, the quality of their lives is better, although they remain full of problems. Yet, at the same time, they daily confront the downright objectionable behavior of many of the men with whom they have to deal. Zheng's work joins a growing body of well-researched feminist ethnographies of the international sex work scene. Sex worker sexualities confront and construct hybridities. Like Kong's queer sexualities, sex worker sexualities are not cut from the same cloth. A sex worker is not a sex worker is not a sex worker.

TOWARD METHODOLOGICAL COSMOPOLITANISM

A vast cosmos so stuffed with conundrum.
A muddle of life with its dialogic drift.
An infinity of lists and contradictory cuts.
The bordered boundaries we break beyond.
So here we here are, never to agree?

So let me conclude this short afterthought by suggesting that we need to become *methodological cosmopolitans*. One recent book by Robert Holton (2009) lays out more than 30 positions and debates within the theory of cosmopolitanism, and I cannot go into all this. I most certainly do not mean the elite and exclusive chatter of the sophisticated intelligentsia of urbane intellectual and university life. Rather, I suggest more straightforwardly *a down-to-earth methodological, epistemological, and political stance that dialogues openly with the now massive diversity and fragmentation of the vast enterprise of understanding the complexities of global human social life*—its labyrinths, its "infinity of lists," its "incorrigible pluralities" (Eco, 2009). We need to develop ways to comprehend the truly radically different ways of speaking across cultures and generations and to set them into tolerant, empathetic dialogues with each other.

As I see it, a cosmopolitan methodology needs to dialogue across multiple disciplines, across multiple academic and everyday life conventions, across generations, and across multiple cultures. Methodological cosmopolitanism means both a respect and willingness to listen, learn, and dialogue across the vast array of tensions found in research methods, epistemological stances, theoretical concerns, and political actions across the world. Ultimately, methodological cosmopolitanism links to the wider project of intimate citizenship—it is a phrase to add to the tools we need to understand the diversities of a global flourishing life. Intimate citizenship (Plummer, 2003) has human rights and responsibilities at its core—the rights and responsibilities of citizens to have and lead a good personal life in all their differences and tensions. The challenge is to develop a methodology that can match this task. We will keep moving on.

References

Agustin, L. M. (2007). *Sex at the margins: Migration, labor markets and the rescue industry.* London: Zed.

Aoyama, K. (2009). *Thai migrant sexworkers: From modernization to globalization.* Hampshire, UK: Palgrave.

Collins, R. (1998). *The sociology of philosophies: A global theory of intellectual change.* Cambridge, MA: Harvard University Press.

Connell, R. (2007). *Southern theory: The global dynamics of knowledge in social science.* Cambridge, UK: Polity Press.

Eco, U. (2009). *The infinity of lists.* Bloomsbury, UK: MacLehose Press.

Holton, R. (2009). *Cosmopolitanisms.* Hampshire, UK: Palgrave.

Houlbrook, M. (2005). *Queer London: Perils and pleasure in the sexual metropolis 1918–1957.* Chicago: University of Chicago Press.

Kong, T. (2010). *Chinese male homosexualities.* London: Routledge.

Mannheim, K. (1952). The problem of generations. In *Collected works of Karl Mannheim* (Vol. 5, pp. 276–320). London: Routledge. (Original work published 1937)

Plummer, K. (2003). *Intimate citizenship.* Seattle: University of Washington Press.

Plummer, K. (2010). Generational sexualities, subterranean traditions, and the hauntings of the sexual world: Some preliminary remarks. *Symbolic Interaction, 33*(2), 163–190.

Waters, C. (2008). Distance and desire in the new British social history. *GLQ, 14*(1), 139–155.

Weeks, J. (1977). *Coming out: Homosexual politics in Britain from the nineteenth century to the present.* London: Quartet.

Zheng, T. (2009). *Red lights: The lives of sex workers in postsocialist China.* Minneapolis: University of Minnesota.

12

Asian Epistemologies and Contemporary Social Psychological Research[1]

James H. Liu

Any analysis of Asian epistemologies and their influence on contemporary social psychological research in Asia should begin by situating itself within recent flows of world history where Western science, industry, and political, economic, and military power have dominated the globe. Global forms of both natural and social sciences have had their origins in Western epistemologies and social practices. Social sciences like anthropology, sociology, and psychology all emerged in European societies in the 19th century, which was perhaps coincidentally the peak of Western nationalism and imperialism. Not coincident to this, elements of racism were both implicitly and explicitly embedded within early theories and practices of social science (Smith, 1999). It took the global cataclysm of World War II and all its aftermaths for racism to be put to bed as a legitimate basis for social science theorizing (Cartwright, 1979).

Given this type of "societal anchoring" (Moscovici, 1961/2008) in a particular historical moment where one civilization had apparently achieved ascendancy above all others through a particular formula of success, it is not surprising that social scientists in Asia found themselves in the position of having to react to forces put into motion by Western societies. First, social sciences in Asia (as in Western societies) have been and continue to be poor cousins to natural and physical sciences in terms of funding and visibility concerning national priorities. Second, modernization has provided a master set of discourses and practices whereby importation of Western ideas and practices is taken for granted as necessary to increase national strength and autonomy (see, e.g., Pandey, 2004). Within these overarching frames, following Western universities by importing logical positivism (an epistemology itself borrowed from the natural sciences) as the basis for Asian social sciences occurred largely without debate. Not only epistemology, but the structure and content of Asian social sciences were borrowed wholesale from the West as Asian universities were established throughout the late 19th and 20th centuries. In most disciplines in most countries, the first textbooks were translations of standard texts from North America and Europe.

This was the historical situation, and given continuing disparities in power, prestige, and influence distributed between developed and developing societies, between Western and non-Western scholars, and between English and non-English speakers (Moghaddam, 1989; Moghaddam & Taylor, 1985, 1986), it is not surprising that in the main, Asian social sciences remain for the most part thoroughly situated within Anglo-empiricist global norms, positioning the social sciences within epistemologies, or theories of knowledge, and practices drawn from the natural sciences.

If historical differences in power and prestige between Asia and the West were responsible for the structural foundation and mainline development of Asian social sciences, then the subsequent rise of Asian societies such as Japan, China, India, Taiwan, Philippines, and South Korea as indispensible components of the global economy has served as the impetus for an important counter-movement. This is the rise of Asian epistemologies and Asian forms of psychological knowledge that emphasize cultural differences with the West rather than imitation (Liu, Ng, Gastardo-Conaco, & Wong, 2008). While decidedly less central than the first movement, this countermovement contains potentiality for the future because the world is moving toward both economical integration *and* the distribution of political, military, and economic power across multiple cultural centers.

A Survey of Recent Developments in Psychology

The necessarily simplified introduction provided here sets the platform to launch a focused discussion of how Asian epistemologies have and will influence the theory and practice of psychology and especially social and cross-cultural psychology. Different patterns may be prevalent in other social sciences, like sociology or anthropology. In psychology, cracks in the edifice of borrowing from the West became visible in the 1960s, with the emergence of the subdiscipline of cross-cultural psychology out of shared interest among scholars in both Western and non-Western societies (the latter who frequently began their careers by attaining doctorates in Western universities and then returned home). Its goals were to (1) empirically test the generality and transportability of theories of psychology and (2) develop theories and constructs better suited to explain and predict behavior, cognition, and emotion in non-Western societies (see Berry, Poortinga, Segall, & Dasen, 1992; Ward, 2007). Although initially situated across subdisciplines in psychology, a cross-cultural approach has been most influential in social and personality studies, perhaps as a result of empirical demonstrations of the limitations of the "transport and test" model (e.g., Amir & Sharon, 1987). As time went on, powerful theories began to emerge to account for cross-cultural differences. In the 1980s, the seminal *Culture's Consequences* by Geert Hofstede (1980/2001), with its statistical analysis of survey data from countries around the world, found dimensions of cultural variation that located Western societies' psychological profiles as not universal, but culture-bound syndromes most notably characterized by individualism and low power distance (see Smith & Bond, 1993, for an update of this literature).

This trend of making psychological phenomena contingent on culture through scientific arguments has continued to the present day. Hazel R. Markus and Shinobu Kitayama (1991) famously made virtually all theories in social and personality psychology contingent on the construal of self as independent or interdependent (this making an element of culture into a discrete variable amenable to experimental manipulation). Ongoing published dialogue between North Americans and East Asians, mainly Japanese and then Chinese, has become a major feature of cross-cultural psychology. One example of recent issues that have engaged attention is the question of whether the requirement for positive self-esteem is universal (see Heine, Lehman, Markus, & Kitayama, 1999, versus Brown & Kobayashi, 2003). Recently, the flagship *Journal of Cross-Cultural Psychology* achieved an impact rating of 2.0, marking an unprecedented level of influence according to such indicators,[2] while the *International Journal of Intercultural Relations* has also been an important contributor to the profile of the subdiscipline (with an impact factor of 1.0 in recent years). Perhaps because of this success, social constructionist epistemologies have had little influence on cross-cultural psychology. The majority of its adherents appear content to operate within empiricist practices and scientific discourses that have become the norm in this growing field (for a brief discussion, see Liu et al., 2010; for a comprehensive overview, see Berry et al., 1997).

Following from cross-cultural psychology, the Asian Association of Social Psychology held its inaugural conference in 1995 and established the *Asian Journal of Social Psychology* in 1998. Recently, an influential former editor of the journal wrote that "In a nutshell, AJSP is able to promote research that addresses cultural issues, and the journal seems to have developed a reputation as a "cultural" journal" (Leung, 2007, p. 10). But on the downside, "No obvious theoretical framework comes to mind when one thinks of Asian social psychology. Except for the indigenous psychologists, most Asian social psychologists work on topics that are popular in the West." (Leung, 2007, p. 11). The term *indigenous* in debates in psychology is used to refer to an intellectual movement that arose in reaction to the Western mainstream and seeks to reflect the social, political, and cultural character of local peoples around the world (Allwood & Berry, 2006). This movement has been especially prominent in Asia, as part of an intellectual decolonization (or de-Westernization) of psychology. For the most part, it does *not* refer to a psychology of first peoples, that is, a psychology of aboriginal peoples positioned as minorities within a politically dominant Westernized majority. Linda Waimarie Nikora, Michelle Levy, Bridgette Masters, and Moana Waitoki decried psychology's use of the term indigenous in their vignette on indigenous psychology for Maori, who are first peoples of New Zealand. But they wrote further,

> Terminology aside, the objectives of an indigenous psychology are agreeable: That is, to develop psychologies that are not imposed or imported; that are influenced by the cultural contexts in which people live; that are developed from within the culture using a variety of methods; and that result in locally relevant psychological knowledge. (Nikora, Levy, Masters, & Waitoki, 2004, quoted in Allwood & Berry, 2006, p. 255)

Indigenous psychology movements sprang up in India, Taiwan, and the Philippines in the 1970s and in Korea in the 1980s under the leadership of charismatic leaders that strongly influenced social science agendas in these and other Asian societies (Sinha, 1997). Whereas cross-cultural psychology has been and continues to be strongly influenced by positivist forms of empiricism dedicated to testing the generalizability and applicability of psychological theories to different populations, indigenous psychologies have been more varied in terms of their philosophical, epistemological, and political stands concerning the production and use of social science knowledge. Several overlapping definitions of indigenous psychology have been offered by major Asian protagonists (see Kim, Yang, & Hwang, 2006, or Allwood & Berry, 2006, for overviews). Virgilio Enriquez (1990) described indigenous psychology as a system of psychological thought and practice rooted in a particular cultural tradition, while Uichol Kim and John W. Berry (1993), defined it as "the scientific study of human behavior (or mind) that is native, that is not transported from other regions, and that is designed for its people" (p. 2). Among its more epistemologically and philosophically oriented advocates, David Ho (1998) views indigenous psychology as "the study of human behavior and mental processes within a cultural context that relies on values, concepts, belief systems, methodologies, and other resources indigenous to the specific ethnic or cultural group under investigation" (p. 93). The most influential programmatic developer of indigenous psychology, Kuo-shu Yang (2000) defined it as "an evolving system of psychological knowledge based on scientific research that is sufficiently compatible with the studied phenomena and their ecological, economic, social, cultural, and historical contexts" (p. 245). All the major protagonists agree that indigenous psychology involves knowledge and practice native to or rooted in particular societies and their cultural traditions. They vary in their commitments to global science, on the one hand, and locally informed action on the other.

The differences between Taiwan and the Philippines, where indigenous psychology has been most prolific (each with large regular meetings attended by hundreds of scholars), are instructive as to variations in theory versus practice. Both emerged in the late 1970s under the auspices of a talented, energetic founder capable of mobilizing both people and funding toward the enterprise. While the tenor of their research aims was similar, Enriquez's (1990, 1992) vision differed substantially from Yang's (1999, 2000) with respect to focus of application.

Enriquez was not opposed to natural science epistemologies in principle, but in practice, he thought that they were often inappropriately applied. He wrote extensively about the process of the indigenization of psychological science (Enriquez, 1990), both by adapting Western scientific constructs to the local culture and by developing local systems of psychological knowledge on its own terms (indigenization from without and within). The Philippines has been and continues to be a developing nation, with a current gross national product (GNP) of less than $2,000 U.S. per capita and a transparency rating putting it in the bottom quartile, along with other countries in the world struggling with endemic corruption.

In this societal climate, Filipino indigenous psychology is highly engaged with communities on a myriad of issues, and it is published mainly in Tagalog (the Filipino national language, which is especially dominant in Luzon; see Enriquez, 1992). It has a thriving relationship with other academic disciplines, government ministries, and nongovernment organizations (NGOs), which results in what could be described as participant action-oriented research (McTaggart, 1997) or community-based participatory research (Minkler & Wallerstein, 2003). As such, ethnographic (qualitative field-based) inquiry is its predominant method of choice. Enriquez (1992) refers to this as "indigenization from within." Its outputs are mainly in monographs (e.g., Aguiling-Dalisay, Yacat, & Navarro, 2004) and internal reports for the commissioning agencies, and it uses primarily qualitative methods developed indigenously (see Pe-Pua & Protacio-Marcelino, 2000, for a recent English-language overview). Publications in international journals are rare, but at least as frequent as for works from other developing nations in Southeast Asia.

Filipino indigenous psychology could be described as highly applied, with development focused on content and ethnographic methods (e.g., how to work with illiterate sex workers) without concurrent development of an epistemology grounded in indigenous philosophical traditions. This pattern of focusing on applied research using the local language without taking a strong position on epistemology would be characteristic of much of Southeast Asia, including Indonesia, Malaysia, and Vietnam, but these latter nations would be less coherent in terms of the use of indigenously compatible theory, practice, and methods compared to the Philippines. Most of this work flies under the radar of the international scholarly community as it is published mainly in monographs, funder-mandated reports, and local journals.

Enriquez, the charismatic founder of Filipino indigenous psychology, died in 1994 at age 52, leaving a huge void that has not been filled. Yang, in contrast, has been and continues to be active in shaping Chinese indigenous psychology from Taiwan for more than three decades. In contrast to the Philippines, Taiwanese indigenous psychology has been more consistent with the norms of research practice prevalent in cross-cultural psychology, which are highly empiricist and quantitative but use paper-and-pencil surveys rather than being based on laboratory experiments as in mainstream psychology. Taiwan is a newly industrialized economy, where GNP and living standards are comparable with the lower half of the Organization for Economic Cooperation and Development (OECD). It is also a newly democratizing society, having achieved significant advances in free elections, gender equality, and the development of civil society over the last two decades. This, together with a weak version of the "publish or perish" academic culture prevalent in North America, helps account for an alternative pathway for the development of indigenous psychology taken here compared to the Philippines (see Allwood & Berry, 2006, for a global perspective on this).

Chinese indigenous psychology is internationally one of the more visible among all the indigenous psychologies in the world (see, e.g., Yang, 1999, or Hwang, 2005a, for accounts; see Bond, 1996, for a more cross-cultural approach to Chinese psychology). Chinese indigenous psychology has its own journal, which has been published regularly in Chinese from Taiwan for two decades, and regular conferences are attended by many hundreds of scholars, often involving Mainland China and Hong Kong. In his most ambitious statement, Yang (2000) offers a program of development in indigenous psychology capable of unifying cultural psychology (derived from anthropology; see Cole, 1995), with its commitment to qualitative methods and "human science" epistemologies, and cross-cultural psychology, with its focus on quantitative and "natural science" epistemologies. He views psychology as consisting of a hierarchically organized system of indigenous psychologies:

> Beyond the imperative of indigenization, no other restraints need to be imposed upon activities of indigenous research. . . . Psychologists in any society may legitimately strive to construct an indigenous psychology for their people that is as comprehensive in scope as the current indigenous American psychology. . . . For example, some indigenously-oriented Chinese psychologists have set their hearts on developing an indigenous Chinese psychology comparable to the North American one in scope and depth. (Yang, 2000, p. 246)

It is understandable, given their population size and time-honored philosophical traditions, that Chinese people might have higher expectations for their indigenous psychology than many other peoples.

Most Asian indigenous psychologists in practice prefer particular methods (e.g., Yang is survey oriented, Enriquez was ethnography oriented), but in principle, they do not regard their activities as constrained by methods warranted by a Western form of epistemology. For Yang (2000), who draws liberally from Enriquez's thinking, the key concept is *indigenous compatibility*, defined pragmatically in terms of "empirical study . . . conducted in a manner such that the researcher's concepts, theory, methods, tools, and results adequately represent, reflect, or reveal the natural elements, structure, mechanism, or process of the studied phenomenon embedded in its context" (p. 250). He offers several do's and don'ts rather than a philosophically oriented system to achieving indigenous compatibility. For example,

> Don't uncritically or habitually apply Western psychological concepts, theories, methods, and tools to your research before thoroughly understanding and immersing yourself in the phenomenon being studied.
>
> Don't overlook Western psychologists' important experiences in developing their own indigenous psychologies, which may be usefully transferred to the development of non-Western indigenous psychologies.

Don't think in terms of English or any other foreign language during the various stages of the research process in order to prevent distortion or inhibition of the indigenous aspects of contemplation involved in doing research. (p. 251)

On the other hand,

Do tolerate ambiguous or vague states and suspend decisions as long as possible in dealing with theoretical, methodological, and empirical problems until something indigenous emerges in your mind during the research process.

Do be a typical native in the cultural sense when functioning as a researcher.

Do take the studied psychological or behavioral phenomenon and its sociocultural context into careful consideration.

Do give priority to culturally unique psychological and behavioral phenomena or characteristics of people in your society, especially during the early stages of the development of an indigenous psychology in a non-Western society.

Do base your research on an intellectual tradition of your own culture. (p. 251)

This highly pragmatic approach, rooted in research practices rather than epistemology, can be said to characterize the modal Asian indigenous psychology response to issues involving the social construction of knowledge. Indigenously oriented East Asians in economically developed societies like Taiwan (or Korea and Japan) as a rule have not used theoretical race, gender, or ethics critiques to challenge prevailing empiricist norms for the practice of psychology. Rather, all of these issues have been examined within an overarching empiricist umbrella that favors quantitative but also makes use of qualitative methods.

Kashima (2005) has argued that this approach is deeply rooted in Asian traditions of knowledge, which may give them an advantage in examining questions that fundamentally involve complexity and multiplicity at their very root, like culture. He challenges Clifford Geertz's (2000, p. 197) assertion that "bringing so large and misshapen a camel as anthropology into psychology's tent is going to do more to toss things around than to arrange them in order." Although this is simplifying his argument considerably, Kashima (2005) locates contemporary epistemological struggles between hermeneutic and empiricist schools of thought within a Western dualist ontology that separates mind from matter, human nature from material nature. He claims,

> If we take a view that intentionality is materially realized, meaning is part of a causal chain, and social scientific investigation is also part of complex causal processes, we can adopt a monist ontology, in which human nature is not distinct from, but continuous with, material nature. (p. 35)

Implications of Chinese Epistemologies for Social Psychological Research

Being understandably better versed in Western philosophy than contemporary Chinese philosophy (which until recently has only been available in Chinese), Kashima (2005) states further, "What we need is a monist ontology that is not the materialist ontology of the Enlightenment. It is difficult to speculate what it looks like until some philosophical investigations clarify this" (p. 36). In fact, the great neo-Confucian philosopher Mou Tsung-san (or Zongshan) (1970) used Immanuel Kant, one of the Enlightenment philosophers who contributed to the emergence of Western dualism, as a starting point to develop an autonomous moral metaphysics (see S. H. Liu, 1989a, for an English-language review of neo-Confucianism). While epistemology was not a central concern for ancient Chinese, Mou's work is emblematic of contemporary Chinese philosophers carrying their intellectual inheritances forward into dialogue with Western thinking. Unlike most Western philosophers, Mou allows for the possibility of the "intuitive illumination" of the cognitive mind (i.e., enlightenment in the highest sense), whereas Kant allowed only sensible intuition.

Kant followed from and expanded upon René Descartes' mind-body dualism by formulating a dualism of phenomenon and *noumenon* (thing-in-itself). Kant was convinced that only God has intellectual intuition (noumenon, thing-in-itself), while humans have to rely on sensible intuition (or evidence from the senses). Pure reason can only construct knowledge of the phenomenal world. According to Kant, human beings cannot know things-in-themselves (noumena), and hence, it is impossible for us to have knowledge of metaphysics because this would end in antinomies.[3] Mou, by contrast, reinterprets "intellectual intuition" to mean "intuitive illumination" (following Eastern traditions such as Buddhism, Confucianism, and Taoism) and posits that humans are capable of this, no matter what their faith. He proposes a transcendental dialectic where the mind, while unable to produce acceptable proof of the metaphysical ultimate, nevertheless can realize the thing-in-itself as "thusness" or "suchness," the exact opposite of phenomenal knowledge constructed by the cognitive mind, bound in time and space. Because Mou's transcendental dialectic does not deal with empirically verifiable knowledge, it is similar to Soren Kierkegaard's position that "subjectivity is truth." However, it nonetheless describes a rational process that departs radically from Kierkegaard's irrational approach and hence avoids dualism.

Western Enlightenment thinkers, influenced by Christian traditions, saw the metaphysical ultimate as God and tended to view it (as Kant and Descartes did) as transcending the phenomenal world. For Kant, freedom of the will, immortality of the soul, and existence of God are postulates of practical reason. Following from these, an epistemology emerges consistent with a dualism between mind and matter and a division between natural and human phenomena because for Christians like Descartes and Kant, it was important to maintain their religion as a valid system of knowledge in the face of their own logic and rationality.

As culture's effects are largely implicit, Kashima's (2005) point is that without necessarily being aware of it, contemporary Western social scientists have maintained an unnecessarily sharp division between natural and human phenomena as part of their particular cultural program (see also Kim, 2000): Some carry on with a natural science paradigm in an Enlightenment vein, and others react against this as an affront to human agency and dignity. As most social scientists are not philosophically trained, they have a tendency to translate their cultural ontology into an almost religious commitment on methodological issues that might be described by philosophers as "methodolatry": the conflation of ontological issues with methodology. As Paul Tillich (1951) observes, value must have an ontological basis. The value of scientific observations formalizing sensible intuition compared to the phenomenology and hermeneutics of intuitive illumination cannot be reduced to any formula involving emotive responses or subjective utilities, and it cannot be deduced or induced by any form of logical or empirical proof. Hence, to privilege one set of research practices, which are derived from a particular value system associated with a particular ontology, as providing "the answer" to all the social sciences' contributions to the human condition is methodolatry.

In general terms, Asian philosophical traditions allow for human beings to have the ability to grasp ontological reality, although they may reach radically different conclusions about what this might be. This means that rather than seeing methodology as the solution to problems involving the privileging of different value systems in social science research (methodolatry), Asian implicit theory (or folk beliefs) is based on holism and perpetual change, where "a tolerance of contradiction, an acceptance of the unity of opposites, and an understanding of the coexistence of opposites as permanent, not conditional or transitory, are part of everyday lay perception and thought" (Spencer-Rodgers, Williams, & Peng, 2007, p. 265; see Nisbett, Peng, Choi, & Norenzayan, 2001, for an overview of East Asian holistic thinking). In practical terms, this means that Asian traditions do not privilege scientific methods of observation above the intuitive illumination of the original mind but rather see these as complementary forms of knowing.

Confucian traditions in particular tend to see the metaphysical ultimate as a creative principle functioning incessantly to guide the becoming of worldly phenomena. *Jen* or *Ren* (defined as humanity) is identified with *Shengsheng* (creative creativity) by Song-Ming neo-Confucian philosophers (see S. H. Liu, 1998a, for an extended treatment). It is thus a "moral principle" in the broadest sense of the term, from which continually changing aspects of being in time and space emerge. In the most powerful and complete statement of contemporary neo-Confucian philosophy by Mou Tsung-san, the Kantian dualism between phenomenon (perception of reality) and noumenon (the thing-in-itself) is not accepted. While Mou (1975) is sympathetic to Martin Heidegger's (1977) notion of human beings as *Dasein* (being there), a being in the world, and psychological states like anxiety and care as modes of existence, Mou argued that a phenomenological ontology is capable of giving only a description of human existence and not a value basis. Hence, according to Mou (1975), the best that Heidegger (1977) can achieve is an inner metaphysics and not the transcendent metaphysics that Asian intellectual traditions demand (see S. H. Liu, 1989a, for a more extended version of these arguments, and Bhawuk, 2008a, for contemporary social psychological work following on this theme from Indian philosophical traditions).

Chinese social scientists, like Western social scientists, might not explicitly reference philosophy as they conduct their research, but like Westerners, they have followed their own implicit cultural program, and many have proceeded to conduct research that frequently combines qualitative and quantitative methods and blurs the boundaries between empiricism and hermeneutics. For instance, many indigenous Chinese psychology papers combine quantitative and qualitative methods, and the warp and weft of their papers is the interweaving of Chinese tradition with contemporary mainstream psychology references. A "hot topic" at indigenous Chinese psychology conferences (most of it published in Chinese) has been the relationship between mother-in-law and daughter-in-law, which is fraught with the weight of contending cultural expectations between younger and older generations. Qualitative or quantitative approaches to analyzing surveys, interviews, and ethnographies have been used as acceptable forms of inquiry. Culture is most often *not* the explicit topic of inquiry but rather is embedded within the processes and objects of inquiry.

There are obvious exceptions to these rules. For example, Lee (2004) is a strong advocate of a hermeneutical phenomenological approach to indigenous research on ethnicity in Taiwan, following Heidegger, and feminist scholars in Asia as elsewhere tend to prefer qualitative to quantitative forms of inquiry. However, the most popular text advising social science graduate students on how to do thesis research (Bih, 2005) is completely ecumenical with respect to methodology, advising only that the research method should suit the research question. Having said this, the flagship *Chinese Journal of Psychology,* representing "the establishment" in Taiwan, still favors quantitative research, and as a whole, the university system privileges the contributions of the natural sciences above those of the humanities and social sciences.

For many Asian social scientists, the six statements that Kashima (2005) uses to describe a generic epistemic position on culture and its implications for psychology would be uncontroversial:

1. Culture is socially and historically constructed.

2. People construe themselves using concepts and other symbolic structures that are available.

3. People develop a theory of mind (i.e., a theory of how the mind works) to understand others.

4. People have beliefs about the world, and they act on those beliefs.

5. People engage in meaningful action.

6. Culture is constitutive of the mind. (p. 20)

For indigenous psychologists in particular, the division between human and natural phenomena and the polemics between advocates of different forms of knowledge construction would appear to be problematic. Kashima's (2005) summary seems more like a good starting point than a bone of contention: "To put it simply, the argument is that human agency and self-reflexivity make human society and culture dynamic (i.e., changing over time) and knowledge and human activities historically and culturally contingent" (p. 22). Gergen (1973), for example, treats the historical contingency of psychological phenomena as a call to revolution, whereas Liu and Hilton (2005) see it as grist for their mill. The former sees historical contingency as evidence requiring the overthrow of a methodological hegemony, whereas the latter see it as a description of the operation of human agency and cultural construction through time requiring empirical investigation (Liu & Hilton, 2005) and philosophical reflection (Liu & Liu, 1997).

As Leung (2007) noted, Asian social psychologists have not yet fully capitalized on the relative freedom from methodolatry that their philosophical traditions provide in terms of creating notable breakthroughs. He criticized Asians for their lack of ambition, citing a relative paucity of sustained programmatic research. As the current editor-in-chief of the *Asian Journal of Social Psychology,* I would have to concur: Most of the 200 or so papers submitted to the journal annually lack imagination, consisting to a significant extent of replications and minor variations on a theme established by quantitative research from the United States.

Although indigenous research in Asian social, personality, clinical, cultural, and cross-cultural psychology is still in its formative years, several characteristics would appear to be foundational. The first is the aforementioned lack of preoccupation for translating epistemological concerns into methodological boundaries. The second is an overwhelming concern with social relationships and social interconnectedness. The third is a naturalistic approach to culture as a relatively uncontested element of basic psychology. Liu and Liu (1997, 1999, 2003) describe this as a psychology of interconnectedness.

It remains to be seen whether Asian social psychologists will be able to fulfill the epistemological promise of their philosophical traditions (Ward, 2007). Asian universities, like universities all over the world, privilege the natural sciences and aspire to and internalize standards set by Western universities. They push their faculty to publish in prestigious journals, which are most often controlled by American universities and American or European academics. The Shanghai Jiaotong University's rankings of the best 500 universities in the world, which was constructed for the purpose of providing "objective standards" to aim for in developing a "world class" Chinese university ranked in the top 100 (Beijing University and Tsinghua are aspirants), completely favors the natural sciences and virtually disregards contributions from the humanities and social sciences. Given these circumstances (see Adair, Coelho, & Luna, 2002; Leung 2007; Ward, 2007), it is highly unlikely that Asian academics will be able to produce philosophically and epistemologically autonomous bodies of work. Rather in the near future, global psychology will emerge as a patchwork quilt of pluralistic practices connected to a still-dominant American center (see Liu et al., 2008; Moghaddam, 1989).

Japanese social psychology is a good example of both the variety and constraint in the patchwork quilt. Mainstream Japanese social psychology is thoroughly enmeshed in an empiricist dialogue with American social psychology on epistemic grounds set by North America. While there certainly is a small indigenous psychology movement in Japan (see Behrens, 2004), it does not have the scope or ambition of the movements in Taiwan or the Philippines. Perhaps in reaction to this, recently a dissident faction emerged in Japan challenging the mission of the mainstream on epistemic grounds, constructing arguments that pit quantitative versus qualitative methods and contrast human science with natural science in ways that would be very familiar to qualitative researchers in North America (see Atsumi, 2007; Sugiman, 2006).

Overall, the volume of increase in submissions to *Asian Journal of Social Psychology,* from 168 in 2007 to 182 in 2008 to 210 in 2009 (a 10% increase per annum), and the massive increase in Asian authors in social psychology over the last 10 years—even after controlling for the impact of *AJSP* (Haslam & Kashima, in press)—point to the potential inherent in the region and its peoples. As the methodological and theoretical skills, together with the cultural confidence of Asians, increase following the trend-setting success of their economies, one cannot help but be excited about possible breakthroughs coming out of Asia that pierce the dichotomy between natural science and human science in innovative ways. Hence, it is fitting to close this chapter by providing a brief introduction to a few of the more prominent epistemologically informed projects that have emerged in Asian psychology in recent years.

Three Epistemologically Informed Asian Research Projects

The work of Hong Kong clinical psychologist David Y. F. Ho is unusual in that it is both informed by Chinese philosophy and written in English, making it accessible to international audiences. Two of his more imaginative pieces on Chinese indigenous psychology contain an interpretative analysis of classic Chinese culture stories (Ho, 1998a) and a humorous dialogue between a Confucianist and a clinical psychologist (Ho, 1989) around such culturally loaded terms as *propriety* and *impulse control.* These excursions are underpinned by a serious commitment to what he and his colleagues call methodological relationalism (Ho, Peng, Lai, & Chan, 2001). This is a general conceptual framework for the analysis of thought and action that takes a person's embeddedness in a network of social relations as the fundamental unit of analysis:

> Actions of individuals must be considered in the context of interpersonal, individual-group, individual-society, and intergroup relations. . . . In particular, each interpersonal relationship is subject to the interactive forces of other interpersonal relationships. This consideration introduces the dialectical construct of *metarelation* or *relation of relations.* (Ho, Peng, et al., p. 937)

Two basic analytic units are used in Ho et al.'s (2001) approach to personality and social psychology, person-in-relations (focused on the target person in different relational contexts), and persons-in-relation (focused on different persons interacting within a relational context). The authors' quantitative work attempts to deconstruct the hegemony of person-versus-situation formulations of behavior as "consistent" versus "inconsistent" by introducing an intermediate layer, person-in-relations. They have argued cogently that relationships can transcend the person-versus-situation dichotomy because they are neither intrinsically part of the person nor intrinsically part of the situation; people are situated in a web of relations that help them to navigate through a situation in particular ways (see Ho & Chau, 2009, for an empirical demonstration).

They have also developed a qualitative approach called investigative research (Ho, Ho, & Ng, 2006), arguing that "neither a psychology predicated on methodological individualism nor a sociology based on methodological holism is fully equipped to account for the total complexities involved" (p. 19) in understanding the relationships between individuals in society.

> A social fact, though not reducible to facts about the individual, is nonetheless a fact about the social behaviour of, manifested by, individuals; and a psychological fact is a social fact wherever it refers to behaviour occurring in the presence of others, actual, imagined, or implied. Each contains and is contained by the other. A knowledge of one enhances, and a lack of knowledge of one diminishes, the understanding of the other. (pp. 19–20)

Ho et al. (2006) propose to base their research methodology on two metatheoretical propositions:

> 1. The conceptualization of psychological phenomena is, in itself, a psychological phenomenon. As a metalevel phenomenon, it requires further study.
> 2. The generation of psychological knowledge is culture dependent: Cultural

values and presuppositions inform both the conceptualization of psychological phenomena and the methodology employed to study them. Accordingly, the role of the knowledge generator, given his or her cultural values and presuppositions, cannot be separated or eliminated from the process of knowledge generation. These propositions do not necessarily negate positivism. Rather, they challenge positivism to have greater sensitivity to culture dependence and to broaden its scope of investigation. (p. 22)

At this point, rather than elaborating their epistemological position, they argue for *reflexivity* in applying three "intellectual attitudes germane to investigative research" based on the two presuppositions. These appear to be pragmatic and dialectical, but grounded in realist epistemology:

The first stresses the importance of critically examining the evidence in the truth-seeking process. The second confronts the inherently complex, even deceptive, nature of social phenomena; vigilance against deception is integral to seeking truth. The third sees the recognition of ignorance and knowledge generation as twin aspects of the same process. (p. 22)

Rather than offer any standard techniques or procedures, they describe investigative research as "disciplined, naturalistic, and in-depth," guaranteeing data quality and acting in the service of social conscience.

Ho et al. (2006) advocate *both* the use of reflexivity *and* moving from exploration to confirmation (e.g., from qualitative exposition to quantitative hypothesis testing) as research methods. They state their admiration for good investigative reporting produced by journalists (e.g., in their verification of source information and their dedication to truth seeking), but they do not state in a clear, programmatic way how such journalistic training could be applied to social science research. From the perspective of the Western-trained methodologist, Ho et al.'s (2006) program might not appear sufficiently compelling—it is lacking in details, and the thorny questions of confrontation between truth-value and desire to do good in the process of investigative research are not articulated. But the Asian ontological and epistemological systems described previously can help Western scholars to make sense of this desire and their pragmatic means of achieving it. For Ho, Ng, and Ho (2007), reifying a dividing line between qualitative forms of "human science" and quantitative forms of "natural science" just does not make sense, and they react against this with an almost moral sense of indignation.

For 30 years, Taiwanese social psychologist Kwang-guo Hwang has conducted a research program in indigenous Chinese psychology built on foundations of traditional Chinese theories of knowledge. Whereas Ho could be described as something of a lone wolf, working out an epistemologically sophisticated program of indigenous research in a Hong Kong social science thoroughly entrained by Western paradigms, Hwang has had the good fortune to have spent his career working within and contributing to a highly developed and collaborative indigenous psychology in Taiwan (Hwang, 2005c; Yang, 1999). Whereas Ho's primary dialogue partners are Westerners and Westernized or bicultural Asians, the capstone of Hwang's (2009) work, *Confucian Relationalism: Philosophical Reflection, Theoretical Construction, and Empirical Research,* was written in Chinese and directed toward Chinese social scientists. Because Hwang's prodigious output consists mainly of books written in Chinese whose thrust is theoretical rather than empiricist, the work is almost impossible to do justice to in a few paragraphs. It is possible here only to give a flavor of the work. It should be noted that while Hwang is situated in social psychology, he has read widely in the philosophy of science and the sociology of science, and his writing is clearly directed toward social scientists and not just psychologists.

Hwang's (2005b, 2005c, 2006, 2009) mission is to realize a comprehensive epistemology of social sciences for Chinese (and by extension other non-Westerners) that provides the philosophical foundations for engaging in fruitful dialogue with one another and Westerners. Hwang's project is consistent with Mou's basic premise that different philosophical and cultural traditions provide alternative (and overlapping) ontological bases for constructing the phenomenology of subjective experience and the epistemology of its examination. The foundational statement of his work on Confucian relationalism was a model of face and favor (Hwang, 1987) that analyzed the inner structure of Confucianism for managing social relations and social exchange.

In his book on *Knowledge and Action,* Hwang (1995) argued that Western culture emphasizes the importance of philosophy for pursuing knowledge, whereas Chinese cultural traditions of Taoism, Confucianism, legalism, and martial school are concerned about wisdom for action. Consistent with an approach based on constructive realism (Wallner & Jandl, 2006), Hwang (1995) argues that since psychology's foundations and current practices are grounded in Western philosophy, genuine progress in indigenous psychology comes through constructing a scientific microworld consistent with Western philosophy, while maintaining a comprehensive understanding of the influence of Chinese cultural traditions on the daily life of Chinese people.

To familiarize Chinese social scientists with the major schools of Western philosophical thought influencing social science thinking, Hwang (2006) wrote

The Logic of Social Science in Chinese. Here he recognizes that to construct a coherent scientific microworld, social scientists must not only be able to recognize themselves as fish swimming in a phenomenological sea of cultural constructions, but *they must be able to translate these insights into the systematic forms that scientific microworlds require.* Moreover, these microworlds often share much in common with one another, so that communication and translation of concepts between them is a critical feature of scientific *and* phenomenological insight.

Based on a philosophy of postpositivism, his summary work *Confucian Relationalism: Philosophical Reflection, Theoretical Construction, and Empirical Research* (Hwang, 2009) emphasizes that the epistemological goal of indigenous psychology is the construction of a scientific microworld constituted by a series of theories that reflect both universal human minds in general and the particular mentalities of a given culture. In view of the fact that most theories of Western social psychology have been constructed on the presumption of individualism, Hwang (2009) explained how he constructed the face and favor model (Hwang, 1987) with four elementary forms of social behavior and used it as a framework to analyze the deep structure of Confucianism (Hwang, 2001). Then he illustrated the nature of Confucian ethics in sharp contrast to Western ethics and constructed a series of theories based on relationalism to illuminate social exchange, the concept of face, achievement motivation, organizational behaviors, and conflict resolution in Confucian societies.

Hwang's (2009) project lays out the foundations and issues a call for programmatic development that could generate decades of research in indigenous social science, particularly if in the future mainland Chinese decide to pursue this avenue of research. Students and professors from various places attend his seminars at National Taiwan University. Hwang is primarily a theorist rather than an empiricist, and so this is a slow developing project that is focused on the big picture. We should not expect to see immediate results. Rather, as the Chinese Culture Connection (1987) noted, one of the most salient characteristics of Chinese people is long-term orientation, and in the 21st century, Chinese will need time on the order of decades to work out their response in the social sciences to the foundations and practices laid out by the West.

Recent work from Indian scholars, which draws from their great philosophical traditions to create a metaphysically oriented psychology, is another topic of international interest. According to a recent definitional statement by Ajit K. Dalal and Girishwar Misra (2010),

> More than materialistic-deterministic aspects of human existence, IP (Indian psychology) takes a more inclusive spiritual-growth perspective on

human existence. In this sense no clear distinction is made between psychology, philosophy and spirituality, as conjointly they constitute a comprehensive and practical knowledge or wisdom about human life.

Hence, what appears consistent among Asian scholars drawing from their massive and distinct traditions is a questioning of Western ontology and reconsideration of whether discretely methodological forms of knowing should hold such a privileged position in generating and reifying social science knowledge (Bhawuk, 2008b; Paranjpe, 1984). But there are differences as well. If Chinese philosophical traditions have drawn Chinese social psychologists into thinking about social relatedness and holistic interconnectedness as fundamental ontological postulates, Indian philosophical traditions have a similar pull into the spiritual depths of the phenomenology, epistemology, and practice of Self (*atman*) (Bhawuk, 2003).

Sinha (1933), as cited by Dharm Bhawuk (2008a), described Indian psychology as based on metaphysics. Rather than beginning with Erik Erikson or Sigmund Freud, Indian scholars like Anand C. Paranjpe (1998) begin with Vedic traditions like the Upanishads, which includes such basic tenets as the "truth should be realized, rather than simply known intellectually" (Bhawuk, 2010). According to Bharati (1985, as cited in Bhawuk, 2008a), the self has been studied as "an ontological entity" in Indian philosophy from time immemorial, and far more "intensively and extensively" than in any of the other societies in the East (Confucian, Chinese, or Japanese) or the West (either secular thought or Judeo-Christian-Muslim traditions). The basic methodology is the practice of meditation, and the goal of meditative practices is to uncover the nature of the true self (*atman*), unencumbered by even such a fundamental phenomenological unity as time (Bhawuk, 2008a; Rao & Paranjpe, 2008). Even the basic dividing line between the knower and the known cannot be maintained if the meditative practices of Indian philosophy are accepted as an important and valid form of knowledge. In marked contrast to Chinese philosophers' tendency to maintain distinctions (*li-i-fen-shu,* one principle, many manifestations) while seeking for unity (*tien-ren-ho-i,* heaven and humanity in union; see S. H. Liu, 1989b, or Liu & Liu, 1999), Indian philosophers have plumbed the very depths of knowing to collapse even basic polarities such as good and evil or being and nonbeing under the glare of intuitive illumination.

The contemporary Indian psychology movement appears to be in the process of constructing a psychology of self that is simultaneously a practice of self-realization. Bhawuk has gone so far as to propose a general methodology for translating classic Indian scriptures into psychological models of theory and practice:

> For example, in the second canto of the *Bhagavad-Gita* a process of how desire and anger cause one's downfall is presented. The sixty-second verse delineates this process by stating that when a person thinks about sense objects, he or she develops an attachment to it. Attachment leads to desire, and from desire anger is manifested. The sixty-third verse further develops this causal link by stating that anger leads to confusion (*sammoha*) or clouding of discretion about what is right or wrong, confusion to bewilderment, to loss of memory or what one has learned in the past, to destruction of *buddhi* (i.e., intellect or wisdom) to the downfall of the person or his or her destruction. (Bhawuk, 2010)

Even a cursory reader of Bhawuk's work will recognize that the phenomenological layer of concepts described in Indian psychology are not only distinct from comparable Western concepts, but also systematic and compelling, once their internal logic is discerned. Bhawuk does not appear to privilege any Western forms of empiricism or phenomenology in terms of validating or providing an understanding of this system. Similarly, advocates of transcendental meditation were quite happy for Western scientists to measure them during meditation and find that their oxygen consumption and heart rate decreased, skin resistance increased, and electroencephalographs showed changes in frequencies suggesting low stress (Bhawuk, 2008b; see Rao & Paranjpe, 2008, for a more detailed review). This scientific knowledge did not change the subjective practice and goals of transcendental meditation one bit.

Bhawuk's (2008a, 2010) models are entirely theoretical at this point: In Hwang's (2006, 2009) terms, they represent a translation of the philosophical microworld of Indian philosophy into a psychological microworld of relationships between variables: How this translation will then impact on the cultural macroworld of the practice of Indian religions by lay people or inspire qualitative or quantitative investigation is anyone's guess. It is mind-boggling to realize that one of the most profound statements on the consequences of anger and desire on the human condition, known and practiced for millennia as part of the root philosophy of one of the world's great cultures, has only recently made its entry into the psychological literature (see Bhawuk, 1999, 2008a). Bhawuk (2010) carefully situates his construction of psychological models within the context of his daily meditative practices and as part of his family life. The dualism of qualitative versus quantitative methodologies never comes up as an issue in his writing. His quest is to expand the boundaries of science, not divide it into analytical portions circumscribed by methodological differences that seem almost quaint beside the monumental questions of being and nonbeing, time and permanence, probed by Indian philosophy (Bhawuk, 1999).

By comparing Indian culture with the culture of science, Bhawuk (2008b) argued that science itself has a culture, which is characterized by tenets like objectivity, impersonalness, reductionism, and rejection of the indeterminate. He cautioned that, as cultural or cross-cultural researchers, we need to be sensitive to the fact that science also has a culture, and our research might benefit from adopting worldviews, models, questions, and methods that are characteristic of indigenous cultures, especially those of non-Western origin. Bhawuk stressed the need for crossing disciplinary boundaries and recommended that we go beyond multiple-method and use multiparadigmatic research strategies to understand various worldviews in their own contexts. A team of researchers from various academic disciplines can help us find linkages across disciplines and paradigms.

Conclusion

While each of the three programs reviewed above is exceptional, they should be situated within the greater flows of history and institutional practices that characterize social science research in Asia. Ho, Hwang, and Bhawuk mobilize the intellectual capital inherent in their cultures to innovate original solutions to perennial problems in social science. The first two are senior scholars toward the final phase of their careers, whereas the third is a senior scholar in his prime; none of them is under survival pressures in terms of career development. The far more typical submission to *Asian Journal of Social Psychology* or other major culture-oriented journals in psychology is a replication of a Western model with minor variations, the primary justification for which is "no data from (fill in the country) has to their knowledge been collected to test this model." Social psychological research in Asia can be characterized by tension between scholars living within a phenomenological layer of cultural constructions as a visible part of their everyday life, and producing English-language publications that are devoid of such meaningful content and dedicated toward the pragmatics of career advancement according to top-down standards imported from the "best" (read Western) universities.[4]

The pockets of innovation cited here have not changed the overall institutional climate favoring natural science research and practices in Asia, nor have they touched the publications prestige gradient, where English language (JCI/SSCI) journals are valued above local language outputs.[5] Asian social psychologists appear highly pragmatic in carving out their careers amid a disjuncture between their subjective experiences and dominant institutional practices (see Adair et al., 2002, for bibliometric evidence of the massive extent of Western dominance of the published literature in psychology, and Haslam & Kashima, in press, for challenges to this trend).

Some researchers working with qualitative paradigms in Western institutions have made highly conscious, sometimes ethical choices in working with particular methodologies. At best, their work reflects the polish and cohesiveness of intellectual rigor. At worst, it dissolves into hair-splitting methodolatry and promotion of group interests using methodology as a means of academic combat. Researchers in Asian institutions seem typically to be more pragmatic, at worst, sublimating their phenomenological experiences into whatever methodological paradigm is dominant and can be used to promote self-advancement and, at best, developing late in their careers an ecumenical and innovative orientation toward methodology. To change the shape of this gradient, it would be necessary for there to be more collaboration and communication between open-minded Westerners with influence on international journals and Asian scholars with a passion for probing the depths of their cultural resources and expanding the breadth of their disciplinary practices (see Liu et al., 2008). In this process, bicultural members of the Asian academic diaspora have and will continue to play a major role (Liu & Ng, 2007).

In the interim, Asian scholars working pragmatically in disciplines not of their cultural making can operate at the margins to adopt an alternative system of meaning for reconciling the disjuncture between their phenomenological experience of the world as a cultural construction and their professional judgment of how to best further their careers. To illustrate with personal experience, early in my career, I would sometimes write quantitative descriptive papers without hypotheses and be forced into a hypothetico-deductive model by international journal editors. At this point in mid-career, I have internalized mainstream psychological discourses to such an extent that writing in such a mode requires little effort and has significant benefits. But in terms of meaning, I regard the hypothetico-deductive model in psychology as a post-hoc explanatory model rather than as a universal model of prediction and control. This is not to deny there might be a deep structure that underlies human psychology, but even where it exists, this deep structure can find expression only through interactions with the phenomenological layer of subjective experiences, which is mediated by culture's concepts and an institutional layer of societal governance. Therefore, I treat all statements of causality in psychology as contingent on the phenomenological and institutional layer operating in the situation at the time of survey or experiment administration. In my own papers, I articulate this symbolic layer of meaning with great detail, and I tend to be cautious about other more careless statements of universality. In some sense, I do treat social psychology, in Kenneth Gergen's (1973) famous phrase, as history (Liu & Hilton, 2005; Liu & Liu, 1997), but I do not see how privileging qualitative methodology over quantitative methodology or vice versa solves the problem of the historical and cultural contingency of human behavior. When I write for quantitative journals, I follow their dominant discourses and practices for communicating how the phenomenological layer of culture conditions individual behavior, emotion, and cognition; when I write for qualitative journals, I do the same thing (Liu & Mills, 2006). I view methodologies as no more and no less than different prisms through which the objects of inquiry are refracted and communicated. In terms of their relative strengths, qualitative research is useful for telling us the *what* of a phenomenon, and quantitative research the *how much, how prevalent,* and *under what conditions is it causal.*

Putting these together, Liu and Sibley (2009) advocate four steps in the interweaving of qualitative and quantitative methods to describe and prescribe national political cultures.

1. Ascertaining the symbolic landscape through open-ended survey methods that give an overview of the major historically warranted symbols prevalent in a society; this may include quantitative analysis techniques and representative samples but must involve open-ended inquiry.

2. Describing the discursive repertoires that make use of political symbols in everyday talk through various institutionally mediated channels; this may involve archival analysis, interview, or focus group methods; the key is to examine naturalistic discourse for thematic content.

3. Operationalizing symbolic representations such as legitimizing myths or ideologies by converting naturally occurring talk to quantitative scale measures or experimental conditions; making maximum use of empiricist techniques to make causal inferences.

4. Moving from representation to action using both empirical findings and personal reflexivity as resources; applying findings from social science with a full awareness of their conditional and contingent nature when giving policy advice.

As the editor of a journal, I am open to either or both modes of communication (Liu, 2008), but I believe that a researcher must understand the internal logic of each prism to be able to blend and transcend their influences. I see the ultimate arbitrator of methodology as value, and I see value as having an onto-logical status that precedes rather than being derived from epistemology. The two research values I subscribe to besides truth value (see Liu & Liu, 1999) are (1) indigenous compatibility (Yang, 2000)—to what extent does the research reflect the phenomenology of cultural and institutional systems from which observations were derived, and (2) practical value—to what extent does the research provide subjective utility to academic *and* lay communities in which the researcher resides. I believe the future for Asian social psychology, to paraphrase Tomohide Atsumi (2007), is to fly with the two wings of scientific inquiry and practical utility. In the latter area, I hope that an Asian social psychology unen-cumbered by dualism will be able to make substantial breakthroughs in the future (Liu, Ng, et al., 2008; Liu & Liu, 2003).

In conclusion, S. H. Liu (1989a) summarizes the methodological advice of Hsiung Shih-Li, another eminent neo-Confucian philosopher (and a teacher of Mou Tsung-san) as follows:

> The scientific way of thinking has to posit an external physical world as having an independent existence of its own. From a pragmatic point of view this procedure is perfectly justifiable. But it has the danger of hyposta-tizing functions into ontological substances and hence committing a meta-physical fallacy. In order to guard against the natural tendency of man to fall into such a naïve attitude, philosophy has to adopt two important methodological procedures. In the first place, we have to appeal to a spe-cific analytical method which purports to destroy all attempts to identify phenomenal functions with ontological principle itself by finding out all the contradiction or absurdities involved in such untenable metaphysical conjectures. (p. 25)

On this first point, qualitative researchers have done well, constructing a phalanx of *posts* to deconstruct naïve attempts to reify natural science models in human science. But Hsiung's second point is more radical and cuts right to the heart of what it means to be a social scientist and a human being:

> This is exactly what the Buddhist philosophy has done in attempting to sweep away phenomena in order to realize the ontological depth of all beings. However, in adopting these negative procedures of the Buddhist philosophy one is tempted to emphasize only the silent aspect of the onto-logical principle and neglect its creative aspect. In the second place, there-fore, we have to appeal to a specific method of inner illumination. It is only

through such illumination that we are able to realize the infinite creative power of the ontological principle. (p. 25)

The great Asian philosophical traditions of both China and India recognize the possibility of both sensible intuition and intuitive illumination. They converge in both providing theories of not only knowledge but also practice. Indian philosophers have delved most deeply into the nature of self, and contemporary Indian psychologists have developed this into a body of knowledge with both theoretical and practical implications. Chinese philosophers have synthesized Indian philosophical insights (particularly those of the Buddhists) to develop a moral metaphysics that leads directly to a psychology of ethical social relations. While these are early days in the development of indigenous psychologies, there is hope for the future as the 21st century unfolds. The twin scourges of the end of cheap oil and the continuation of global warming will likely require a more practically oriented social science (see Liu et al., 2009), particularly in developing societies where these challenges will be felt most keenly. In the critical transition period between a fossil fuel-driven global economy and a mixed energy economy, there is the possibility that the epistemological breakthroughs in Asian philosophy may be translated into concrete practices of social science, where quantitative and qualitative methods are used hand in glove to assist societal development and creating global consciousness. In their summary of open-ended survey data from 24 societies on representations of world history, Liu et al. (2009) commented, "if there is a lay narrative of history, it might be that out of suffering comes great things" (p. 678). Conversely, even if the sky does not fall down, it may still be useful to work on the margins to connect the centers of an increasingly interconnected world of parallel and distributed cultural values (Liu, 2007/2008).

Notes

1. The author wishes to acknowledge the generous comments made by Dharm Bhawuk, K. K. Hwang, Isamu Ito, and Shu-hsien and An-yuan Liu on previous drafts of this chapter; thanks also go to Norman Denzin and Alison Jones for incisive and helpful reviews.

2. While there is considerable debate about the value of such indices, an impact rating in the 2s is comparable to top journals in anthropology and approaches those for sociology, whereas an impact factor of 1 or higher is very respectable (impact factors less than 1 are less prestigious).

3. *Antimonies* are fundamental contradictions between two sets of laws, each of which are reasonable given their premises.

4. Asian education systems emphasize rote learning, and Asian-educated scholars often do not realize that *pure* rote learning (i.e., replication without innovation) is not valued in most international journals.

5. It is more, not less difficult for Asians who have learned English as a second language to publish in international *qualitative* compared to *quantitative* journals. A bibliometric study on international social psychology publications by Haslam and Kashima (in press) reported that the *Journal of Cross Cultural Psychology, International Journal of Intercultural Relations, Asian Journal of Social Psychology,* and *Journal of Social Psychology* were the most popular outlets for Asian authors: All of these are predominantly quantitative in orientation, though AJSP also publishes qualitative papers and the other two culture-oriented journals have had recent special issues on qualitative forms of inquiry.

References

Adair, J. G., Coelho, A. E. L., & Luna, J. R. (2002). How international is psychology? *International Journal of Psychology, 37*(3), 160–170.

Aguiling-Dalisay, G. H., Yacat, J. A., & Navarro, A. M. (2004). *Extending the self: Volunteering as Pakikipagkapwa.* Quezon City: University of the Philippines, Center for Leadership.

Allwood, C. M., & Berry, J. W. (2006). Origins and development of indigenous psychologies: An international analysis. *International Journal of Psychology, 41*(4), 243–268.

Amir, Y., & Sharon, I. (1987). Are social psychological laws cross-culturally valid? *Journal of Cross-Cultural Psychology, 18*(4), 383–470.

Atsumi, T. (2007). Aviation with fraternal wings over the Asian context: Using nomothetic epistemic and narrative design paradigms in social psychology. *Asian Journal of Social Psychology, 10,* 32–40.

Behrens, K. Y. (2004). A multifaceted view of the concept of *Amae:* Reconsidering the indigenous Japanese concept of relatedness. *Human Development, 47*(1), 1–27.

Berry, J. W., Poortinga, Y. H., Pandey, J., Dasen, P. R., Saraswathi, T. S., & Kagitcibasi, C. (1997). *Handbook of cross-cultural psychology* (2nd ed.). Boston: Allyn & Bacon.

Berry, J. W., Poortinga, Y. H., Segall, M. H., & Dasen, P. R. (1992). *Cross-cultural psychology: Research and applications.* Newbury Park, CA: Sage.

Bharati, A. (1985). The self in Hindu thought and action. In A. H. Marsella, G. DeVos, & F. L. K. Hsu (Eds.), *Culture and self: Asian and Western perspectives.* New York: Tavistock.

Bhawuk, D. P. S. (1999). Who attains peace: An Indian model of personal harmony. *Indian Psychological Review, 52*(2/3), 40–48.

Bhawuk, D. P. S. (2003). Culture's influence on creativity: The case of Indian spirituality. *International Journal of Intercultural Relations, 27*(1), 1–22.

Bhawuk, D. P. S. (2008a). Anchoring cognition, emotion, and behavior in desire: A model from the *Gita.* In K. R. Rao, A. C. Paranjpe, & A. K. Dalal (Eds.), *Handbook of Indian psychology* (pp. 390–413). New Delhi, India: Cambridge University Press.

Bhawuk, D. P. S. (2008b). Science of culture and culture of science: Worldview and choice of conceptual models and methodology. *The Social Engineer, 11*(2), 26–43.

Bhawuk, D. P. S. (2010). Methodology for building psychological models from scriptures: Contributions of Indian psychology to indigenous & global psychologies. *Psychology and Developing Societies.*

Bih, H. D. (2005). *Why didn't teacher tell me?* (in Chinese). Taipei: Shang-yi Publishers.

Bond, M. H. (Ed.). (1996). *The handbook of Chinese psychology.* Hong Kong: Oxford University Press.

Brown, J. D., & Kobayashi, C. (2003). Motivation and manifestation: Cross-cultural expression of the self-enhancement motive. *Asian Journal of Social Psychology, 6,* 85–88.

Cartwright, D. (1979). Contemporary social psychology in historical perspective. *Social Psychology Quarterly, 42*(1), 82–93.

Chinese Culture Connection. (1987). Chinese values and the search for culture-free dimensions of culture. *Journal of Cross-Cultural Psychology, 18,* 143–164.

Cole, M. (1995). Socio-cultural-historical psychology: Some general remarks and a proposal about a meso-genetic methodology. In J. V. Wertsch, P. del Rio, & A. Alvarez (Eds.), *Sociocultural studies of mind* (pp. 187–214). Cambridge, UK: Cambridge University Press.

Dalal, A., & Misra, G. (2010). The core and context of Indian psychology, *Psychology and Developing Societies.*

Enriquez, V. (1990). *Indigenous psychologies.* Quezon City, Philippines: Psychological Research & Training House.

Enriquez, V. G. (1992). *From colonial to liberation psychology: The Philippine experience.* Manila, Philippines: De La Salle University Press.

Geertz, C. (2000). Imbalancing act: Jerome Bruner's cultural psychology. In C. Geertz (Ed.), *Available light* (pp. 187–202). Princeton, NJ: Princeton University Press.

Gergen, K. J. (1973). Social psychology as history. *Journal of Personality and Social Psychology, 26,* 309–320.

Haslam, N., & Kashima, Y. (in press). The rise and rise of social psychology in Asia: A bibliometric analysis. *Asian Journal of Social Psychology.*

Heidegger, M. (1977). *Basic writings from* Being and Time *(1927) to* The Task of Thinking *(1964)* (D. F. Kell, Ed. & Trans.). New York: Harper and Row.

Heine, S. H., Lehman, D. R., Markus, H. R., & Kitayama, S. (1999). Is there a universal need for positive self-regard? *Psychological Review, 106,* 766–794.

Ho, D. Y. F. (1989). Propriety, sincerity, and self-cultivation: A dialogue between a Confucian and a psychologist. *International Psychologist, 30*(1), 16–17.

Ho, D. Y. F. (1998). Filial piety and filicide in Chinese family relationships: The legend of Shun and other stories. In U. P. Gielen & A. L. Comunian (Eds.), *The family and family therapy in international perspective* (pp. 134–149). Trieste, Italy: Edizioni LINT.

Ho, D. Y. F., & Chau, A. W. L. (2009). Interpersonal perceptions and metaperceptions of relationship closeness, satisfaction, and popularity: A relational and directional analysis. *Asian Journal of Social Psychology, 12,* 173–184.

Ho, D. Y. F., Ho, R. T. H. H., & Ng, S. M. (2006). Investigative research as a knowledge-generation method: Discovering and uncovering. *Journal for the Theory of Social Behavior, 36*(1), 17–38.

Ho, D. Y. F., Peng, S. Q., Lai, A. C., & Chan, S. F. F. (2001). Indigenization and beyond: Methodological relationalism in the study of personality across cultural traditions. *Journal of Personality, 69*(6), 925–953.

Ho, R. T. H, Ng, S. M., & Ho, D. Y. F. (2007). Responding to criticisms of quality research: How shall quality be enhanced? *Asian Journal of Social Psychology, 10*(3), 277–279.

Hofstede, G. (2001). *Culture's consequences* (2nd ed.). Thousand Oaks, CA: Sage. (Original work published 1980)

Hwang, K. K. (1987). Face and favor: The Chinese power game. *American Journal of Sociology, 92,* 944–974.

Hwang, K. K. (1995). *Knowledge and action* (in Chinese). Taipei: Psychological Publisher.

Hwang, K. K. (2001). The deep structure of Confucianism: A social psychological approach. *Asian Philosophy, 11*(3), 179–204.

Hwang, K. K. (2005a). From anticolonialism to postcolonialism: The emergence of Chinese indigenous psychology in Taiwan. *International Journal of Psychology, 40*(4), 228–238.

Hwang, K. K. (2005b).The necessity of indigenous psychology: The perspective of constructive realism. In M. J. Jandl & K. Greiner (Eds.), *Science, medicine, and culture* (pp. 284–294). New York: Peter Lang.

Hwang, K. K. (2005c). A philosophical reflection on the epistemology and methodology of indigenous psychologies. *Asian Journal of Social Psychology, 8*(1), 5–17.

Hwang, K. K. (2006). Constructive realism and Confucian relationism: An epistemological strategy for the development of indigenous psychology. In U. Kim, K. S. Yang, & K. K. Hwang (Eds.), *Indigenous and cultural psychology: Understanding people in context* (pp. 73–108). New York: Springer.

Hwang, K. K. (2009). *Confucian relationalism: Philosophical reflection, theoretical construction, and empirical research* (in Chinese). Taipei: Psychological Publisher.

Kashima, Y. (2005). Is culture a problem for social psychology? *Asian Journal of Social Psychology, 8,* 19–38.

Kim, U. (2000). Indigenous, cultural, and cross-cultural psychology: A theoretical, conceptual, and epistemological analysis. *Asian Journal of Social Psychology, 3,* 265–288.

Kim, U., & Berry, J. W. (Eds.). (1993). *Indigenous psychologies: Research and experience in cultural context.* Newbury Park, CA: Sage.

Kim, U., Yang, K. S., & Hwang, K. K. (Eds.). (2006). *Indigenous and cultural psychology: Understanding people in context.* New York: Springer.

Lee, W. L. (2004). Situatedness as a goal marker of psychological research and its related methodology. *Applied Psychological Research*, 22, 157-200. (in Chinese, published in Taiwan).

Leung, K. (2007). Asian social psychology: Achievements, threats, and opportunities. *Asian Journal of Social Psychology, 10,* 8–15.

Liu, J. H. (2007/2008). The sum of my margins may be greater than your center: Journey and prospects of a marginal man in the global economy. *New Zealand Population Review, 33/34,* 49–67.

Liu, J. H. (2008). Editorial statement from the new editor. *Asian Journal of Social Psychology, 11,* 103–104.

Liu, J. H., & Hilton, D. (2005). How the past weighs on the present: Social representations of history and their role in identity politics. *British Journal of Social Psychology, 44,* 537–556.

Liu, J. H., & Liu, S. H. (1997). Modernism, postmodernism, and neo-Confucian thinking: A critical history of paradigm shifts and values in academic psychology. *New Ideas in Psychology, 15*(2), 159–177.

Liu, J. H., & Liu, S. H. (1999). Interconnectedness and Asian social psychology. In T. Sugiman, M. Karasawa, J. H. Liu, & C. Ward (Eds.), *Progress in Asian social psychology* (Vol. 2, pp. 9–31). Seoul, Korea: Kyoyook Kwahaksa.

Liu, J. H., & Liu, S. H. (2003). The role of the social psychologist in the "Benevolent Authority" and "Plurality of Powers" systems of historical affordance for authority. In K. S. Yang, K. K. Hwang, P. B. Pedersen, & I. Daibo (Eds.), *Progress in Asian social psychology: Conceptual and empirical contributions* (Vol. 3, pp. 43–66). Westport, CT: Praeger.

Liu, J. H., & Mills, D. (2006). Modern racism and market fundamentalism: The discourses of plausible deniability and their multiple functions. *Journal of Community and Applied Social Psychology, 16,* 83–99.

Liu, J. H., & Ng, S. H. (2007). Connecting Asians in global perspective: Special issue on past contributions, current status, and future prospects of Asian social psychology. *Asian Journal of Social Psychology, 10*(1), 1–7.

Liu, J. H., Ng, S. H., Gastardo-Conaco, C., & Wong, D. S. W. (2008). Action research: A missing component in the emergence of social and cross-cultural psychology as a fully inter-connected global enterprise. *Social & Personality Psychology Compass, 2*(3), 1162–1181.

Liu, J. H., Paez, D., Slawuta, P., Cabecinhas, R., Techio, E., Kokdemir, D., et al. (2009). Representing world history in the 21st century: The impact of 9–11, the Iraq War, and the nation-state on the dynamics of collective remembering. *Journal of Cross-Cultural Psychology, 40,* 667–692.

Liu, J. H., Paez, D., Techio, E., Slawuta, P., Zlobina, A., & Cabecinhas, R. (2010). From gist of a wink to structural equivalence of meaning: Towards a cross-cultural psychology of the collective remembering of world history. *Journal of Cross-Cultural Psychology, 41*(3), 451–456.

Liu, J. H., & Sibley, C. G. (2009). Culture, social representations, and peacemaking: A symbolic theory of history and identity. In C. Montiel & N. Noor (Eds.), *Peace psychology in Asia.* Heidelberg, Germany: Springer.

Liu, S. H. (1989a). Postwar neo-Confucian philosophy: Its development and issues. In C. W. H. Fu & G. E. Spiegler (Eds.), *Religious issues and interreligious dialogues.* New York: Greenwood Press.

Liu, S. H. (1989b). Toward a new relation between humanity and nature: Reconstructing t'ien-jen-ho-i. *Zygon, 24,* 457–468.

Liu, S. H. (1998). *Understanding Confucian philosophy: Classical and Sung-Ming.* Westport, CT: Greenwood.

Markus, H. R., & Kitayama, S. (1991). Culture and self: Implications for cognition, emotion and motivation. *Psychological Review, 98,* 224–253.

McTaggart, E. (1997). *Participatory action research: International contexts and consequences.* Albany: State University of New York Press.

Minkler, M., & Wallerstein, N. (Eds.). (2003). *Community-based participatory research for health.* San Francisco: Jossey-Bass.

Moghaddam, F. M. (1989). Specialization and despecialization in psychology: Divergent processes in the three worlds. *International Journal of Psychology, 24,* 103–116.

Moghaddam, F. M., & Taylor, D. M. (1985). Psychology in the developing world: An evaluation through the concepts of "Dual Perception" and "Parallel Growth." *American Psychologist, 40,* 1144–1146.

Moghaddam, F. M., & Taylor, D. M. (1986). What constitutes an "appropriate psychology" for the developing world? *International Journal of Psychology, 21,* 253–267.

Moscovici, S. (2008). *Psychoanalysis: Its image and its public.* Cambridge, UK: Polity. (Original work published 1961)

Mou, T. S. (1970). Hsin-t'i yu hsing-t'i [Mind and human nature] (in Chinese). In *Philosophy East and West* (Vol. 20). Taipei: Cheng Chung Press.

Mou, T. S. (1975). *Phenomenon and the thing-in-itself* (in Chinese). Taipei: Student Book.

Nikora, L. W., Levy, M., Masters, B., & Waitoki, M. (2004). Indigenous psychologies globally—A perspective from Aotearoa/New Zealand. Hamilton, New Zealand: University of Waikato, Maori & Psychology Research Unit.

Nisbett, R. E., Peng, K., Choi, I., & Norenzayan, A. (2001). Culture and systems of thought: Holistic versus analytic cognition. *Psychological Review, 108*(2), 291–310.

Pandey, J. (2004). *Psychology in India revisited: Development in the discipline: Vol. 4. Applied social and organizational psychology.* New Delhi: Sage.

Paranjpe, A. C. (1984). *Theoretical psychology: The meeting of East and West.* New York: Plenum Press.

Paranjpe, A. C. (1998). *Self and identity in modern psychology and Indian thought.* New York: Plenum Press.

Pe-Pua, R., & Protacio-Marcelino, E. (2000). Sikolohiyang Pilipino [Filipino psychology]: A legacy of Virgilio G. Enriquez. *Asian Journal of Social Psychology, 3,* 49–71.

Rao, K. R., & Paranjpe, A. C. (2008). Yoga psychology: Theory and application. In K. R. Rao, A. C. Paranjpe, & A. K. Dalal (Eds.), *Handbook of Indian psychology* (pp. 163–185). New Delhi: Cambridge University Press.

Sinha, D. (1997). Indigenizing psychology. In J. W. Berry, Y. H. Poortinga, & J. Pandey (Eds.), *Handbook of cross-cultural psychology* (pp. 130–169). Boston: Allyn & Bacon.

Smith, L. T. (1999). *Decolonizing methodologies.* London: Zed.

Smith, P. B., & Bond, M. H. (1993). *Social psychology across cultures* (2nd ed.). New York: Harvester Wheatsheaf.

Spencer-Rodgers, J., Williams, M. J., & Peng, K. P. (2007). How Asian folk beliefs of knowing affect the psychological investigation of cultural differences. In J. H. Liu, C. Ward, A. Bernardo, M. Karasawa, & R. Fischer (Eds.), *Progress in Asian social psychology: Casting the individual in societal and cultural contexts.* Seoul, Korea: Kyoyook Kwahasaka.

Sugiman, T. (2006). Theory in the context of collaborative inquiry. *Theory and Psychology, 16,* 311–325.

Tillich, P. (1951). *Systematic theology* (Vols. 1–3). Chicago: University of Chicago Press.

Wallner, F., & Jandl, M. J. (2006). The importance of constructive realism for the indigenous psychologies approach. In U. Kim, K. S. Yang, & K. K. Hwang (Eds.), *Indigenous and cultural psychology: Understanding people in context* (pp. 49–72). New York: Springer.

Ward, C. (2007). Asian social psychology: Looking in and looking out. *Asian Journal of Social Psychology, 10,* 22–31.

Yang, K. S. (1999). Toward an indigenous Chinese psychology: A selective review of methodological, theoretical, and empirical accomplishments. *Chinese Journal of Psychology, 4,* 181–211.

Yang, K. S. (2000). Monocultural and cross-cultural indigenous approaches: The royal road to the development of a balanced global psychology. *Asian Journal of Social Psychology, 3,* 241–264.

13

Disability Communities

Transformative Research for Social Justice

Donna M. Mertens, Martin Sullivan, and Hilary Stace

The purpose of the present Convention is to promote, protect and ensure the full and equal enjoyment of all human rights and fundamental freedoms by all persons with disabilities, and to promote respect for their inherent dignity.

—Article 1, UN Convention on
Rights of Persons With Disabilities, 2006

If all the disability research conducted from the late 19th century had been carried out with the above article as its guiding principle, then, we would suggest that the lot of disabled people would be qualitatively and quantitatively so much better today. It was not until the advent of the disability rights movement (DRM) on both sides of the Atlantic in the late 1960s that the basic humanity of "the disabled" began to be recognized and they became either "disabled people" or "people with disability."

As "the disabled," terrible things have been done to this group in the name of science; they were imprisoned in nursing homes, surgically mutilated, sterilized, lobotomized, euthanized, shocked into passivity, placed in chemical and physical straitjackets, denied education, denied employment, and denied meaningful lives (see Braddock & Parrish, 2001; Linton, 1998; Morris, 1991; Sobsey, 1994). Most of these procedures were done with the best of intention; they were the product of cutting-edge scientific research of the day into the cause and cure of disability. As the objects of this research, "the disabled" became dehumanized conditions, categories, and examples to be cured, ameliorated, or cared for in institutions, rather than human beings to be loved, cherished, and nurtured in their families and communities.

Following the examples set by antiracist, feminist, and gay rights movements of the 1960s, disabled people throughout the Western world began to organize to challenge the oppressive stereotypes that blighted their lives. In this chapter, we illustrate how social research has been complicit in fostering oppressive stereotypes of disabled people and suggest ways to do nonoppressive disability research.

Reconceptualizing Disability, Rethinking Methodology

In both the United States and the United Kingdom, the intellectual underpinnings of the DRM were provided by what became known globally as "the social model of disability." In the United States, Hahn (1982) described this as a sociopolitical approach in which disability is regarded as a product of interactions between individual and environment. Later, Hahn (1988) went on to say that this perspective could guide research viewing disabled citizens as an oppressed minority. Indeed, in the United States the minority model of disability (see Fine & Asch, 1988) is more commonly referred to than the social model of disability. Albrecht (2002) explains this with reference to the tradition of American pragmatism, which promoted the linking of arguments for civil rights for disabled people with a minority group approach rather than providing a comprehensive theoretical explanation for disability as in the United Kingdom. For Albrecht, American pragmatism can be summarized as "the practical consequences of believing in a particular concept or social policy" (2002, p. 21); other American citizens who experienced prejudice and discrimination on the basis of visible differences—age, ethnicity/race, gender—had successfully fought for their civil rights by adopting a minority group model that had allowed them to present a united front in their struggle. If it worked for these minorities, why would it not work for disabled American citizens of whom, by 1986, many felt constituted a minority group in the same sense as "Blacks" or "Hispanics" (Hahn, 2002, p. 173)?

In the United Kingdom, the social model was largely developed by Mike Oliver (1982, 1990), following the *Fundamental Principles of Disability* booklet published by the Union of the Physically Impaired Against Segregation (UPIAS) in 1976. Here, the separation of impairment and disability lies at the heart of UPIAS's analysis of disability and, subsequently, the social model. For UPIAS, people have impairments and disability is the negative social response to impairment in terms of the exclusion of impaired people from the political, economic, and social organizations of their communities. According to Shakespeare and

Watson (2001), this redefinition of disability changed the consciousness of people with disability. Disability no longer resided in their bodies or minds; it was framed as a problem of social oppression and disabled people described themselves as an oppressed minority. For example, Groce (1985/2003) conducted a retrospective anthropological study of a community on Martha's Vineyard, Massachusetts, that had a high level of genetic deafness. The deaf people who lived there at that time did not live in a disabling society because everyone learned to use sign language. A person in a wheelchair is only disabled if there is no cut in the sidewalk or no elevator in a multistory building.

When discussing complex concepts such as disability, it is not unusual for language-based challenges to surface. In disability studies, the terms impairment and disability are subject to such challenges. Members of disability communities seek to make clear the difference between an inherent characteristic of a person and the response of society to that characteristic. Hence, in the New Zealand Ministry of Health's (2001) governmental documents and the United Nations' (2006) Convention on the Rights of People With Disabilities, we find the following definitions that provide an explanation of this separation.

> Disability is not something individuals have. What individuals have are impairments. They may be physical, sensory, neurological, psychiatric, intellectual or other impairments. Disability is the process which happens when one group of people create barriers by designing a world only for their way of living, taking no account of the impairments other people have. . . . Our society is built in a way that assumes that we can all move quickly from one side of the road to the other; that we can all see signs, read directions, hear announcements, reach buttons, have the strength to open heavy doors and have stable moods and perceptions. (New Zealand Ministry of Health, 2001, p. 1)

In the United Nations' Convention on the Rights of People With Disabilities, people with disabilities are defined as "those who have long-term physical, mental, intellectual or sensory impairments which in interaction with various barriers may hinder their full and effective participation in society on an equal basis with others (United Nations, 2006, p. 1).

Disability Rights Movement advocates in the United States agree with the importance of making a distinction between an inherent characteristic and the societal response to that characteristic (Gill, Kewman, & Brannon, 2003). In the United States, however, there is more emphasis on persons with disabilities as representing dimensions of diversity in society. People with disabilities are "hindered primarily not by their intrinsic differences but by society's response to those differences" (Gill et al., p. 306). Rather than saying they have "an impairment," disability rights advocates self-define as "disabled and proud" (Triano, 2006).

With this radically new self-perception came disability activism as disabled people began to mobilize for equal citizenship in the United States (Anspach, 1979), the United Kingdom (Campbell & Oliver, 1996), and Canada, Europe, Australia, and New Zealand (Barnes, Oliver, & Barton, 2002), and to demand their right to be economically and socially productive rather than exist in a state of forced dependency on welfare, charity, and good will (Scotch, 2001).[1]

The social model was the polar opposite to the hegemonic individual medical model of disability that had dominated conventional wisdom and created a state of dependency for people with disability. The medical model characterized disability as a personal problem for which individuals ought to seek medical intervention in the hope of cure, amelioration, or care. Such medicalized perceptions are underpinned by personal tragedy theory (Oliver, 1990), which casts disabled people as the tragic victims of some terrible circumstance or event and who, rightfully, need to be pitied. Moreover, it created a climate of "aesthetic and existential anxiety" (Hahn, 1988), in which disability and disabled people were to be avoided at all costs.

In Britain, the first disability studies course, The Handicapped Person in the Community, was offered by the Open University in 1975. Vic Finkelstein, a founding member of UPIAS, was key in its development. Each year more and more disabled people were involved in the production of course materials and by the time it closed in 1994, it had been renamed The Disabling Society to reflect its wider content (Barnes et al., 2002). In the United States, a similar link between disability activism, the academy, and the emergence of disability studies exists. Following the 1977 White House Conference on Handicapped Individuals, which brought disability rights activists and academics together, the first disability studies course was offered in the United States (Pfeiffer & Yoshida, 1995). It was in the area of medical sociology, focused on living with a disability, and its main tutor was a disabled person. In 1981, disabled sociologist Irving K. Zola founded the *Disability Studies Quarterly* and cofounded the U.S.-based Society for Disability Studies. Twelve disability studies courses were taught in U.S. institutions at the time; within five years, the number had almost doubled to 23 (Pfeiffer & Yoshida, 1995, p. 482).

With this blossoming of disability studies programs across the United States and the United Kingdom, it was not long before disabled academics and students began asking questions about "the what, how, and who" of disability research

(Sullivan, 2009, p. 72). Oliver (1992) argued that up to that point most disability research was dominated by the individual medical model of disability, which couched disability in terms of functional limitations and individual deficits that needed to be explored in the hope of finding a cure or an explanation as to why people with disability were not participating in their communities. Oliver (1992, p. 104) exemplifies this positivist research with a question taken from a survey of disabled adults that asks, "What complaint causes your difficulty in holding, gripping or turning things?" He contrasts this with an alternative question— "What defects in design of everyday equipment like jars, bottles and tins cause you difficulty in holding, gripping or turning them?" (p. 104)—which paints an entirely different picture.

Oliver (1992) described the challenge to positivist approaches presented by the interpretive paradigm, which sees all knowledge as socially constructed and a product of a particular time and place. From this perspective, disability is a social problem requiring education, attitude change, and social adjustment on the part of both abled and disabled people. While Oliver concedes that the interpretive or constructivist paradigm is an advance on positivism, it does not go far enough as it does not change the relationship between the researcher and the researched/disabled people. He says that in another context this kind of research has been called

> "the rape model of research" (Reinharz, 1985) in that researchers have benefitted by taking the experience of disability, rendering a faithful account of it and then moving on to better things while the disabled subjects remain in exactly the same social situation they did before the research began. (Oliver, 1992, p. 109)

According to Oliver, such research is very alienating for the disabled subjects. He proposed a new paradigm for disability research, the emancipatory paradigm, in which the social relations of research production would be fundamentally changed. The main features of the emancipatory paradigm are similar to the participatory action model of research; they include:

- research is political in nature, rooted in the social model and its focus is on exposing and changing disabling structures to extend the control disabled people have over their own lives;
- the lopsided power relationship between the researcher and the researched is to be redressed by researchers placing their skills at the disposal of disabled people;

- control is now in the hands of people with disability, who can determine the what, the how, and the when of the research process (see Goodley, 2000);

- focus on the strengths and coping skills of people with disabilities, rather than on deficits;

- conduct research that examines the contextual and environmental factors that either facilitate or impede a person with a disability's integration in society (Wright, 1983).

In Doing Disability Research, an edited collection by Colin Barnes and Geof Mercer (1997), a number of researchers reflect upon reconciling the theoretical purity of the emancipatory research paradigm with the practicalities of maintaining intellectual and ethical integrity in their research. Some of the difficulties listed include:

- the majority of funding goes to research based on the individual medical model; hence, little funding is available for participatory and action research;

- while interpretive forms of research may be about improving the existing social relations of research production, they are not about changing them (Oliver, 1992);

- participatory research might increase the input of research subjects into the research process, but control, ultimately, rests with the researcher who is also the one likely to derive the most benefit from the research (Oliver, 1997);

- difficulties arise when applying the emancipatory model to groups with other than physical and sensory impairment, such as psychiatric system survivors (Beresford & Wallcraft, 1997) or people with learning difficulties (Booth & Booth, 1997);

- questions surface about the role of nondisabled researchers (Lunt & Thornton, 1997; Priestly, 1997; Stone & Priestly, 1996) and who owns the research (Priestly, 1997; Shakespeare, 1997).

Other challenges include how to ensure that disabled people are the leaders in research and have maximum involvement in research, and making certain the research is accountable to disabled people (Beazley, Moore, & Benzie, 1997; Frank, 2000). In addition, researchers struggle with the question of integrity of the research. For example, Tom Shakespeare, prominent academic and activist in the British disability movement, contends that he needs to retain choice and control over the process and to "follow my own intellectual and ethical standards, rather than trying to conform to an orthodoxy" (Shakespeare, 1997, p. 185).

In making this statement, Shakespeare reflects the position of many of the contributors to *Doing Disability Research* when trying to deploy the emancipatory paradigm in the field in its purest sense. They had reported having to make some compromises in order to complete their research. These compromises did not mean that the expertise research subjects brought to the project was not acknowledged or drawn upon; rather it meant researchers were guided by the spirit of the emancipatory paradigm rather than adhering rigidly to its principle. Researchers justified, for example, not handing complete control of the process over to their research subjects, by insisting that the theoretical and practical motivation for their research was the social model of disability and, therefore, ethical. This justification, however, rests upon the uncritical acceptance of the social model of disability within disability studies.

In the past decade, critiques of the social model of disability have gathered momentum within disability studies. These critiques are based mainly on feminist and poststructural thought and appear to be creating a self-titled space for their play, critical disability studies (CDS). Helen Meekosha and Russell Shuttleworth (2009) ask, "What's So 'Critical' About Critical Disability Studies?" In this article, they trace the evolution of the term "critical disability studies" in various scholarly articles over the past decade, and observe that "the influx of humanities and cultural studies scholars with their post-modern leanings and decentering of subjectivity during the 1990s, especially in the US, enabled a more self-conscious focus on critical theorizing to take hold in disability studies" (p. 4). This means moving beyond the social model and the binary way of thinking about disability that emerges from the conceptual distinction between impairment and disability. Drawing upon feminism, critical race theory, queer theory, postmodern thought, and postcolonial theory, CDS has set new "terms of engagement" in disability studies:

> The struggle for social justice and diversity continues but on another plane of development: one that is not simply social, economic and political, but also psychological, cultural, discursive and carnal. (Meekosha & Shuttleworth, 2009, p. 4)

This means that CDS will deploy critical theory in a more nuanced and complex exploration of disability in terms of intersectionality; that is, the intersection of disability with the social divisions of gender, race, class, and sexuality. Or, in other words, an account of disability that is embodied, gendered, raced, classed, and sexed.

In a rather devastating critique of the "so-called emancipatory approach" to disability research, Meekosha and Shuttleworth (2009) argue that while it might have democratized the research process,

> The researcher's methodological and theoretical expertise was considered technical skills . . . not critical-interpretive skills in the analysis of interaction, meaning, and the unmasking of ideologies and hierarchies. (p. 8)

So the internal inconsistencies outlined above by researchers deploying the emancipatory research model and the critique offered from CDS raises an important question about the possibility of doing nonalienating disability research: Is there a research paradigm that is able to capture disability as a complex, embodied relationship between people with impairments and their natural and social environments? Yes, there is one: the transformative paradigm.

The Transformative Paradigm in Disability Research

The historical strands of disability research in terms of the disability minority group model and the social oppression model formed the groundwork for the emancipatory paradigm. As Sullivan (2009) notes, the emancipatory paradigm emerged to respond to these models of disability and changed approaches to research in the disability communities to place priority on participatory modes, place power in the hands of those with disabilities, and challenge oppressive research relations. However, several tensions arose in the implementation of the emancipatory paradigm that led to the recognition of the transformative paradigm by some as having potential to address the issues of power and privilege that sustain oppressive conditions for people with disability. The transformative paradigm is a framework of philosophical assumptions that directly engages members of culturally diverse groups with a focus on increased social justice (Mertens, 2009, 2010). The tensions that arose in the emancipatory paradigm are contrasted with the different stance of the transformative paradigm in Table 13.1.

The transformative paradigm provides a framework for research in the disability communities that is more attuned to handling diversity within communities, aims to build on strengths within communities, develops solidarity with other groups that are marginalized, and changes identity politics to a socio-cultural

Table 13.1   Contrasting the Emancipatory and Transformative Paradigms (Mertens, 2009; Sullivan, 2009)

	Emancipatory	**Transformative**
Focus	Focuses exclusively on disability as the central focus	Focuses on dimensions of diversity associated with differential access to power and privilege, including disability, gender, race/ethnicity, social class, sexual orientation, and other contextually important dimensions of diversity
Role of researcher/ participants	Assumes participants are "conscious of their situation and ready to take leadership" (Sullivan, 2009, p. 77)	Team approach; partnerships are formed; capacity building undertaken as necessary
Model of research	Participatory action research; interpretive approaches	Multiple and mixed methods; culturally respectful; supportive of diverse needs
Tone	Sets up an "us" against "them" tone	Acknowledges the need to work together to challenge oppressive structures

perspective. Critical disability theory is one theory that is commensurate with the transformative paradigm. However, the transformative paradigm provides a metaphysical umbrella that covers the intersection of discrimination based on disability and gender, race, ethnicity, age, religion, national origin, indigenous status, immigration, and other relevant dimensions of diversity used as a basis for discrimination and oppression. The encompassing features of the transformative paradigm are explored in subsequent sections of this chapter.

TRANSFORMATIVE PARADIGM: BASIC BELIEF SYSTEMS

Building on the work of Egon Guba, Yvonna Lincoln, and Norman Denzin (Denzin & Lincoln, 2005; Guba & Lincoln, 2005), the transformative paradigm is defined by four basic assumptions: axiology (the nature of ethics), ontology (the nature of reality), epistemology (the nature of knowledge and the relationship between the knower and that-which-would-be known), and methodology (the nature of systematic inquiry). The transformative axiological assumption is given priority as the assumption that provides guidance for the full set of transformative assumptions. It is based on the belief that ethics is defined in terms of the furtherance of human rights, the pursuit of social justice, the importance of cultural respect, and the need for reciprocity in the researcher-participant relationship. Hence, transformative research seeks to challenge the status quo of an oppressive, hegemonic system in order to bring about a more equitable society.

For example, the differential identification of children with disabilities in the United States on the basis of gender and race/ethnicity is viewed through a human rights lens and is suggestive of the need to conduct research that addresses the wider social conditions that explain this situation. Males, especially those from racial and ethnic minority groups, are two times more likely to be identified as having a disability than females (Gravois & Rosenfeld, 2006; U.S. Department of Education, 2004).

The transformative axiological assumption stimulates the recognition of diversity within disability communities and leads researchers to ask such questions as, Are girls from all ethnic groups being underidentified? How are the indicators for various disabilities (e.g., learning disabilities or autism) differently manifested in girls and boys? In members of dominant and minority groups? What are the motivations for parents to have their children identified or not identified? How do these motivations differ based on race/ethnicity? What is the quality of services provided to children who are identified as having a disability and how does this differ on the basis of type of disability, gender, race, or ethnicity? How can diagnostic and referral strategies be adapted to be more culturally fair? How can the quality of special education services be improved to be more responsive to cultural differences among the students? What is the relationship between quality of special education services and success in later life? What is the meaning of using the term special education, which disability advocates have suggested is used to condone exclusion and segregation (Mertens, Holmes, & Harris, 2009; Mertens, Wilson, & Mounty, 2007)? Other researchers who have made contributions at the intersection of gender and disability include Fine and Asch (1988; Asch & Fine, 1992), Doren and Benz (2001), and Rousso (2001).

Ontologically, the transformative paradigm questions the nature of reality as it is defined in the postpositivist and constructivist paradigms. Postpositivists hold that there is one reality that is waiting to be discovered and that can be captured within a specified level of probability. Constructivists' view of reality is that there are multiple socially constructed realities wherein the researcher and researched co-construct meaning. However, the transformative paradigm's onto-logical assumption suggests that there may be one reality about which there are many opinions and that differential access to power influences which version of reality is given privilege (Mertens, 2009, 2010). The researcher then has a respon-sibility to uncover the various versions of reality and to interrogate them to determine which version is most in accord with furthering social justice and human rights. This raises questions about how the researcher becomes compe-tent in each cultural context in order to accurately reveal issues related to oppres-sion and resilience.

This leads to the epistemological assumption that researchers need to have sufficient grounding in the culture of the communities in which they work, as well as recognize the limitations of their grounding, to conduct research in ways that are viewed as credible and useful to members of those communities. For researchers to serve as agents of prosocial change, as is recommended by the American Psychological Association (2002), they need sufficient understanding of the relevant dimensions of diversity to combat racism, prejudice, bias, and oppression in all their forms. The transformative ontological assumption leads to the epistemological stance in which researchers strive for a level of cultural competency by building rapport despite differences, gaining trust of community members, and reflecting upon and recognizing their own biases (Edno, Joh, & Yu, 2003; Symonette, 2009).

Given the focus of the transformative paradigm on the often-overlooked strengths that are found in communities, it comes as no surprise that theoretical lenses that also focus on social justice, human rights, and resiliency are commen-surate with this stance, including, indigenous and postcolonial theories (Barnes, McCreanor, Edwards, & Borell, 2009; Bishop, 2008; Chilisa, 2009; Cram, 2009; Denzin, Lincoln, & Smith, 2008; LaFrance & Crazy Bull, 2009), queer theories (Dodd, 2009), critical race theories (Thomas, 2009), and feminist theories (Brabeck & Brabeck, 2009).

The benefits of combining these theoretical lenses with disability rights theo-ries to research in disability communities are reflected in comments that one of the author's (Mertens) students made after reading about Māori indigenous theories. Heidi Holmes, a Deaf woman who is a member of the American Sign Language community, based her comment on interpretations she made from her readings of Māori academic literature (by nondisabled writers), which she viewed as presenting a homogenous picture of the Māori community because of a lack of mention of disability or deafness or other relevant dimensions of diver-sity (Cram, Ormond, & Carter, 2004; Smith, 2005). She reflects on the need to and benefits of recognizing multiple dimensions of diversity within the Māori community, including disability and deafness.

> What about diversity in the Māori community? Are they all the same? From a Deaf perspective, to what extent do Māori values/culture overlap with the Deaf community? There is a sharing of anger, frustration, discrimination, and oppression. . . . What about studying deaf people? Should we come up with different cultural values within the Deaf culture, such as hard of hearing, cochlear implants, oral, little hard of hearing, deaf of deaf, deaf of hearing, etc.? There is no one approach to the group of deaf people like the Māori approach. How's it work with Māori? Are they all the same? (Heidi Holmes, personal communication, February 5, 2006)[2,3]

Recognition of multiple dimensions of diversity is necessary for conducting research in the space that overlaps indigenous and disability and deaf communities.

A point of overlap between indigenous peoples and people with disabilities is evidenced in the adaptation of the Aboriginal Indigenous Terms of Reference (ITR)[4] (Osborne & McPhee, 2000) to research proposed within the American Sign Language community (Harris, Holmes, & Mertens, 2009). The ITR were developed to explicitly recognize

> what the community believes needs to be taken into consideration [when determining the focus of the research], how the issue will be dealt with and any special requirements the community puts on the issue. This way, the community is empowered to determine what the issue is, how it should be dealt with and what things need to be taken into account. The combination of the community's viewpoint and guidelines is what makes up the Indigenous Terms of Reference. (Osborne & McPhee, 2000, p. 4)

The ITR and the adapted terms of reference for the deaf and disability communities are problematic in the sense that they suggest that there is one homogeneous Māori community, disability community, or deaf community. As Harris, Holmes, and Mertens (2009) struggled to decide what to call the community for which they were proposing terms of reference, they were aware of the diversity within the deaf community in terms of such characteristics as race, ethnicity, gender, sexuality, national origin, and religion. However, they were also aware of the dimensions of diversity uniquely associated with the deaf community in terms of use of either an oral or visual communication system. Visual systems include American Sign Language, cued speech, exact signed English, or Pidgin Signed English. They were aware of the use of assistive listening devices such as hearing aids and cochlear implants that are used by some deaf people to enhance their ability to hear sounds. They were also aware of the contentious history between advocates for sign language and those who favor speech and speech reading. Thus, they decided to write the terms of reference, not for the deaf community, but for the American Sign Language community, referring to people whose primary experience and allegiance are with Sign Language,[5] as well as the community and culture of Deaf people. However, researchers who are interested in studying Sign Language communities should always be conscious of the complexity of deaf people and the Sign Language community.

We present here an adaptation of the American Sign Language Community's Terms of Reference (Harris, Holmes, & Mertens, 2009) more broadly defined for research in the disability community. This is offered with an understanding of the tension in discussing communities as homogeneous groups, but the necessity to recognize communities that have been pushed to the margins of society. The Disability Terms of Reference might include

1. The authority for the construction of meanings and knowledge within the disability community rests with the community's members.

2. Investigators should acknowledge that disability community members have the right to have those things that they value to be fully considered in all interactions.

3. Investigators should take into account the worldviews of the disability community in all negotiations or dealings that impact the community's members.

4. In the application of disability communities' terms of reference, investigators should recognize the diverse experiences, understandings, and ways that reflect their contemporary cultures.

5. Investigators should ensure that the views and perceptions of the critical reference group are reflected in any process of validating and evaluating the extent to which Disability communities' terms of reference have been taken into account.

6. Investigators should negotiate within and among disability groups to establish appropriate processes to consider and determine the criteria for deciding how to meet cultural imperatives, social needs, and priorities. (Adapted from Harris, Holmes, & Mertens, 2009, p. 115)

These Disability Terms of Reference lead to methodological implications consistent with the transformative paradigm. The transformative methodological assumption emanates from the previously described assumptions and brings focus to the contextually relevant dimensions of diversity and engagement with members of the disability community. Research in the transformative paradigm is a site of multiple interpretive practices. It has no specific set of methods or practices of its own. This approach to research draws on several theories, methods, and techniques. Quantitative, qualitative, or mixed methods can be used; however, the inclusion of a qualitative dimension in methodology is critical in order to establish a dialogue between the researchers and the community members. Mixed methods designs can be considered in order to address the community's information needs. However, the methodological decisions are made with a conscious awareness of contextual and historical factors, especially as they relate to discrimination and oppression. Thus, the formation of partnerships with researchers and disability communities is an important step in addressing methodological questions in research.

Overall, the transformative paradigm provides a useful framework for addressing the role that researchers play when dealing with issues related to oppression, discrimination, and power differences. The transformative paradigm places central importance on the dynamics of power inequalities that have been the legacy of many members of disability communities with regard to whose version of reality is privileged. The transformative epistemological assumption raises questions about the nature of relationships among researchers in terms of who controls the investigation, especially when it is conducted by a team of members and nonmembers of disability communities. Transformative methodological assumptions encourage researchers who are interested in investigating a topic within a disability community to follow research guidelines developed by the community itself. The transformative axiological assumption puts issues of social justice and human rights at the forefront of decision making with regard to research in disability communities.

Examples of Research That Transforms the Lives of People With Disabilities

Many examples of transformative research reveal the potential to change lives of research participants, as well as to have a transformative effect on the researcher and the wider social context. In this chapter, we use detailed examples of four studies to illustrate research that transforms the lives of those who are pushed to society's margins. Other examples of such research include Abma's (2006) work with patient involvement in research about themselves; Cushing, Carter, Clark, Wallis, and Kennedy's (2009) transformative research with people with disabilities; Horvath, Kampfer-Bohach, and Farmer Kearns's (2005) study of involvement of people who are deaf and blind in research; Kroll, Barbour, and Harris's (2007) use of focus groups with people with disabilities; Rapaport, Manthorpe, Moriarty, Hussein, and Collins's (2005) work with advocacy research with people with disabilities; Ryan's (2007) work in Australia conducting qualitative research with people with disabilities; collaborative research by MacArthur, Gaffney, Kelly, and Sharp (2007) promoting the agency and voice of disabled children in the New Zealand mainstream school setting; and initiatives such as focus group work in Christchurch, New Zealand, led by young adults with Down syndrome, on transitions from school to post school including work and independent living (Gladstone, Dever, & Quick, 2009).

Court Access With Deaf and Hard of Hearing People

Mertens (2000) conducted a study of court access for deaf and hard of hearing people in the United States that was guided by an advisory board deliberately chosen to reflect the relevant dimensions of diversity in the deaf and hard of hearing communities in terms of hearing status, mode of communication (American Sign Language, speech reading), and use of assistive listening devices (cochlear implants, hearing aids), as well as position in the court (deaf judges, deaf and hearing attorneys who work with deaf clients, interpreters, judicial educators, and police officers who work on cases involving the deaf community).

Based on the transformative paradigm's assumptions, data collection began with discussions between the researcher (Mertens) and members of the advisory board in terms of how to get an accurate picture of the challenges faced by deaf and hard of hearing people in court. This led to a decision to use focus groups to collect data from deaf and hard of hearing people's experiences in court that reflected relevant dimensions of diversity in the deaf and hard of hearing communities, as well as the appropriate accommodations needed to support effective communication.

One focus group included hearing and deaf co-moderators, American Sign Language interpreters, and court reporters, who used real-time captioning to display what was being said (signed) during the focus group on big TV screens in the room. The group also included a deaf and blind woman with an interpreter who signed into her hands so she could feel the communication, as well as a deaf man with a low level of literacy who did not understand sign language as a language. In his case, a deaf interpreter used some signs combined with pantomime and gestures to convey the questions being asked by the moderator. In order to provide appropriate supports, the researcher needs to have a deep understanding of the diversity within the community and what is needed to provide support for meaningful and effective communication.

This level of support was necessary in order to ascertain the experiences of diverse deaf and hard of hearing individuals to serve as a basis for judicial training that would lead to plans to improve court access for the targeted population. The researcher used data from each stage of the study to inform decisions about research methods in subsequent stages. Hence, meetings with the advisory board constitute a qualitative data collection moment; focus group data were analyzed after each one to determine if gaps were still evident in terms of relevant dimensions of diversity. Subsequently, participant observation and quantitative surveys were used to collect data on the effectiveness of the training for judicial teams that included judges, judicial educators, and deaf or hard of hearing advocates from each state. Transformative aspects of this study include the conscious inclusion of the diverse voices of the deaf and hard of hearing people as the starting point, provision of appropriate supports for effective communication, critical reflection on missing voices throughout the process, involvement of the deaf and hard of hearing people in the development and implementation of the training, and formation of teams to prepare plans for increasing accessibility of their courtrooms that included deaf and hard of hearing persons.

As a point of contrast, when Mertens was invited to present about this study in the United Kingdom, a faculty member in the audience stated that they did not have problems like that in Britain. In fact, they had recently had a student do her dissertation on the same topic; she sent a survey form to all the courts to ask if they had interpreters. All the courts wrote back saying that they did have interpreters.

Teacher Training for Deaf Students With Disability

Mertens, Holmes, and Harris (2008) conducted an evaluation of a teacher training program that used a transformative cyclical approach. The teacher training program at Gallaudet University was designed to prepare teachers of color and/ or who were deaf or hard of hearing to teach deaf or hard of hearing students who had an additional disability. In keeping with the transformative paradigm, Mertens used her knowledge of the diversity within the deaf community to assemble a team of researchers who represented relevant dimensions of diversity, including individuals who were hearing, deaf, and hard of hearing (who used a cochlear implant). This team read through program documents such as the funding proposal and seven years of annual reports. They did not assume that they understood which issues would be of importance, rather, they asked for and received permission to conduct observations at a reflective seminar being held for program graduates.

These qualitative data were used as a basis for developing interview questions for use with the seminar participants. To accommodate differences in communication, the hearing and hard of hearing researchers interviewed the hearing and hard of hearing teachers using speech; the deaf researchers interviewed the deaf teachers using American Sign Language. The use of a transformative lens led to the identification of the participants' concerns about their preparation for oppressive conditions that they encountered in their early job placements and the adequacy of their preparation for students who reflected dimensions of diversity, such as choice of communication mode, home language, and type of additional disability. These data were used to develop a quantitative online survey to determine if program graduates who did not attend the seminar had similar experiences.

Being aware of the critical dimensions of diversity relevant in this context, the researchers identified challenges the new teachers encountered with their students, such as home languages other than English or children coming to school with no language at all. They also reported experiences of marginalization and other educators' low expectations for the deaf students. The data that follow are from fieldnotes, interviews, and the online survey. They illustrate the new teachers' challenges and serve as a basis for potential changes in teacher preparation programs that resulted from the use of a cyclical transformative approach.

Low expectations and marginalization. When I graduated, I thought I was ready to teach. Then the principal gave me my list of students and my classroom and just washed his hands of me. You're on your own. The principal did not require me to submit weekly plans like other teachers because he thought I'd only be teaching sign language. But I told him, I'm here to really teach. We (my students and I) were not invited to field day or assemblies. That first year really hit me—so I changed schools and this one is definitely better. Now I'm in a school where people believe that deaf students can learn. (Graduate student fieldnotes, May 2007)

Diversity in the student body. My students are under 5 years old and they come with zero language and their behavior is awful. They can't sit for even a minute. Kids come with temper tantrums and run out of the school building. I have to teach these kids language; I see them start to learn to behave and interact with others. My biggest challenge is seeing three kids run out of school at the same time. Which one do I run after? One kid got into the storm drain. I'm only one teacher and I have an assistant, but that means there is still one kid we can't chase after at the same time as the other two. (Program graduate interview, May 2007)

The quantitative data from the online survey revealed that only a few graduates reported having a mentor from Gallaudet (13%). About half reported having a mentor in their own school during their first year of teaching (47%). The interview questions combined quantitative data from the survey and qualitative data from the interviews and fieldnotes. The combined data reflect the new teachers feeling a lack of the support needed to address the challenges they encountered.

The data from the interviews, fieldnotes, and surveys were presented to the program faculty and staff at the cooperating schools that had served as sites for student teachers. University faculty also were asked to respond to the issues raised by their recent graduates. They expressed concern about the need to recognize the conditions into which their graduates move and include that as part of the teacher preparation curriculum. The university faculty also were moved to action to provide ongoing support for the new teachers.

As a result of reviewing the study's findings, the Gallaudet Department of Education established an online student teaching seminar during the Fall 2007 semester. That semester, the seminar was taught concurrently with the student teaching experience in an online format using the *Black Board* delivery system. The initial feedback from the student teachers was extremely positive. The Department of Education decided to offer the online seminar for all program graduates as well as student teachers from all concentration areas, not just to students in the multiple disabilities program. The goal of the online seminar is to offer ongoing support from not only a faculty member, but also from other new teachers and students located across the country. The transformative cycle was complete when the study's findings related to the need to better prepare new teachers to respond to diversity in students and work against oppression, resulted in the development of the online seminar that brought together students and faculty from different concentration areas in a way that enhances their early teaching experiences.

Spinal Cord Injury Research in New Zealand

Transformative research in other parts of the world includes that of Martin Sullivan and colleagues (Derrett, Crawford, Beaver, Fergusson, Paul, and Herbison), who are currently undertaking research in New Zealand on the first two years of spinal cord injury (SCI) and the transition from spinal unit to community. The aims of the research are (1) to explore how the interrelationship(s) of body, self, and society shape the life chances, life choices, and subjectivity of a cohort of people with SCI; and (2) to investigate how entitlement to rehabilitation and compensation through the Accident Compensation Commission (ACC)[6] affects socioeconomic and health outcomes. Most of the team have SCI and have been developing their own research skills through their participation in this project. The research utilizes a transformative parallel design using quantitative and qualitative methods concurrently. Quantitative material will be collected in three structured interviews with all participants recruited over a two-year period. The first interview is at 4 months following SCI. This is a face-to-face interview undertaken by the trained, onsite interviewers (who themselves have a SCI) prior to participants' discharge from the spinal unit. The second and third structured follow-up interviews will be undertaken by telephone at 12 and 24 months after SCI. The timing of these interviews complies with international recommendations for follow-up times in injury outcome studies (van Beeck et al., 2005).

These three structured interviews are designed to collect factual evidence on the "what" of the world SCI people inhabit: their life chances, attitudes, health status, support services, work and income, personal and social relationships, and life satisfaction, as this constitutes the framework in which they create their subjectivity. Two qualitative, face-to-face interviews with a subsample of 20 participants explore in greater depth the meanings participants now attach to these phenomena and how these phenomena and meanings are shaping their life choices and subjectivity. On the advice of advocacy groups made up of ex-patients of the spinal units, these qualitative interviews will be held at 6 and 18 months after discharge from the spinal units for specific reasons: At 6 months, the person ought to be settled in at home with alterations complete and the necessary personal supports in place to be thinking about venturing out into the broader world if she or he has not already done so. At 18 months, any neurological recovery that was going to occur would have occurred and the person will be thinking, "So this is it for the rest of my life." Inferences derived from facts and personal perspectives will be triangulated to enrich understandings of what actually happens to SCI people in the first two years postinjury.

At the time of writing (August 2009), recruitment is complete and the second round of quantitative interviews has begun. The questionnaire being used repeats a number of questions from the first interview and includes a new set of questions on issues such as what has changed for participants since the first interview, their use of and satisfaction with support services in general and with personal assistants and ACC in particular. These later questions are yielding some interesting data that will be followed up in depth in the second qualitative interview.

Preliminary analyses suggest that participants are so newly paralyzed that most of their energy is directed at their personal situation of learning to live with new bodies and new lives. Notwithstanding, we have had a high response rate to this study as most want to contribute their experience in order to improve or transform the lot of all people with SCI.

Deinstitutionalization

In Melbourne, Australia, academics Patsie Frawley and Christine Bigby (Robertson, Frawley, & Bigby, 2008) challenged the research power dynamic by partnering with a person with intellectual disability, Alan Robertson, as a researcher on a project requiring lived expertise of institutionalization, which Robertson had. The evaluation of a large deinstitutionalization project into smaller residential community accommodation required a researcher with an astute understanding of what constituted "homeliness" in this context. Robertson and Frawley visited the homes and Robertson conducted interviews with the residents. Robertson instructed Frawley, as his research assistant, what to photograph, including indications of inappropriate furniture and fittings and lack of personal belongings. Frawley was responsible for transcribing the tapes and finding a suitable place in the community to use as their office as Robertson was uncomfortable in the university setting. Robertson has traveled to conferences around Australia to report on the research, which was published in easy-to-read "plain language" as "Making Life Good in the Community: When Is a House a Home?"

Predictions

The Disability Rights Movement and the transformative paradigm intertwine to suggest new criteria for interpretive approaches to research with people with disability. First, a focus on social justice suggests a need for a redistribution of resources in terms of who is supported for research and under what conditions. Second, the United Nations declaration that opened this chapter illuminates the need for a focus on human rights in terms of both individual and group dignity. Third, research with disability communities needs to be based on appropriate cultural engagement that takes into account the diversity of cultural and ethnic settings in which these communities exist as well as the diversity found within those communities.

This shift in criteria leads to predictions of what the field of disability research will look like in 10 years. Research conducted using the transformative paradigm illustrates the benefits of the use of mixed methods; we predict that this approach will become the norm in transformative disability research and disabled people will be increasingly rewritten in terms of resilience and purposive subjectivity.

Political struggles will increase between those who seek cure and those who identify as disabled, Aspie,[7] People First,[8] Deaf,[9] neuro-diverse[10]: This struggle has implications for the type and funding of research. For example, there is a debate raging between those who seek a cure for autism (such as Generation Rescue) and those who claim autism is nothing more than a variant of the human condition and are proud to claim their status as a cultural minority (such as the Autistic Self Advocacy Network [ASAN], 2011). While the former valorize neuro-typicality and seek a cure for autism, the latter valorize neuro-diversity, embrace it, and seek inclusion, respect, and equity.

There is bound to be increasing tension between these two groups. One is extremely powerful with high-profile celebrities fronting, while behind the scenes powerful interests fund their efforts. What the other lacks in resources, it makes up with passion, global Internet networks, and the righteousness and justice of their cause. In the meantime, ASAN (www.autisticadvocacy.org) is calling for quality-of-life-type research to be done with them as part of their struggle for inclusion. Significantly, it is linking more and more with other groups of disability activists. This means that over the next decade some hard decisions have to be made over what type of research is done and which is funded; this is likely to be intensely political. Will it be scientific research into the genetics of autism or even interventions that lack any scientific evidence base in search of a "cure"? Or will it be transformative research done with networks such as ASAN, seeking their expertise on research proposals and mentoring? What needs to change for this to happen? Currently, the research process itself is political and even the research application and ethical approval processes are inaccessible to many of those with impairments: for example, those with vision or intellectual impairment.

However, times are changing. The U.S. government's powerful Interagency Autism Advisory Committee now has autistic members to provide expertise and advice on research. In another victory in the battle of "who speaks for me?"— one of those invited to address an IAAC subcommittee was a nonverbal autistic woman who is also a prolific writer and poet. She learned to type, and, thereby, to communicate with words, using the augmentive communication method known as "facilitated communication" (FC), whereby a facilitator supports the hand or arm of a person using some kind of keyboard.

Although not the inventor of FC, Douglas Biklen's name has been associated with it over the last two decades and his 2005 book *Autism and the Myth of the Person Alone* includes the personal narratives of several autistic people who do not use the spoken word for communication. Through FC, they have found not only their written voice but have also challenged the neuro-typical cultural assumptions of the "aloneness" of autism. Yet FC incites fury among many academics and behaviorist psychologists, who believe the facilitator produces the works and thus FC is fraudulent and exploitative of the autistic participants. The fact that many autistic individuals such as Australian Lucy Blackman have gone on from FC to type independently and dispute their lack of agency does not sway the critics of FC (Blackman, 1999).

Disability culture is also threatened by the eugenic potential of developments in genetic and other technology. Unless disabled people in all their diversity win transformative research power, we predict that by 2100 the human race will have become boringly neuro-typical and genetically homogenous after generations of genetic manipulations in pursuit of some mythical "norm" (Alper et al., 2002; Parens & Asch, 2000). We hope the sentiments of Article 1 of the UN Convention on Rights of Persons With Disabilities, with which we began this chapter, prevail in 2100 and that humanity is increasingly eccentrically, creatively, and interestingly neuro-diverse.

Pedagogic Challenges

We need to rethink who are the experts on lived experience of disability, and therefore who should be the teachers and researchers. Christopher Newell (2006; Goggin & Newell, 2005), who died in his prime in 2008, was an Australian medical ethicist, priest, and disability activist who personified a transformative pedagogic approach. He began his working life in a sheltered workshop and ended up as an associate professor lecturing medical students in ethics. When he was unwell, he would often lecture his students from his hospital bed, which he would get wheeled into the lecture theater in the Hobart Hospital. He let his students see him at his most vulnerable and disabled so as to challenge them to respect the humanity of the disabled people they would meet in their professional lives. Christopher was an academic activist to the core. He was also an Anglican priest who chose not to take the high road but trod the back roads and byways where he befriended, counseled, and supported the abandoned, destitute, and lonely—many who were disabled people. His raison d'être was "moving disability from other to us"—a task he struggled to inculcate in the consciousness and public life of Australia (Newell, 2005).

As more people with impairments, including intellectual impairments, assert their rights and expectations to attend tertiary education, the academy will have to rise to the challenge. Trinity College Dublin enrolls students with intellectual impairment in a mainstream undergraduate course. Using a buddy system, the students also attend electives in any other Trinity College course of their choosing (O'Brien et al., 2008).

Such initiatives challenge the tenets of academia and lead to such questions as whether a PhD dissertation in plain language or sign language would be acceptable or even desirable? Should more value be placed on grey literature websites, blogs, and personal stories for those who may not use an academic paradigm? What about language? Who will have power over acceptable usage? How will disabled people—including those with intellectual impairment—be represented on editorial boards of academic journals and other publications? What about access to research funding? As mentioned above, the application process and deliberation process will have to become much more attuned to the needs of disabled researchers.

Many nonverbal disabled students—some previously institutionalized—have successfully attained tertiary qualifications, but there are challenges to finding the appropriate support. Barriers—physical and attitudinal—will need to be removed by universities. Role models are required. But most significant for change will be transformative research led and mentored by disabled people themselves. Linton (2006) urges researchers in the field of disabilities to be cognizant of the value brought by inclusion of many types of people with disabilities. She notes that war veterans who return with disabling conditions have critically important perspectives that can inform research decisions. By combining forces, the issues of equity and discrimination as they relate to disability rights can be brought to greater visibility for researchers, policy makers, and legislators in the areas of employment, mobility, health care, education, transportation, and the arts.

Conclusion

Thirty years ago, the institutionalization of disabled children and adults was the norm and debates were emerging about intelligence and whether disabled children required education. These arguments are still current in many countries. Thirty years on from now there could be two possible scenarios. We are at a crossroads whereby we can go down the path of technology, genetics, further politicization of research, and the domination of research agendas by treatment and cure rather than good living. Or disability could be welcomed in from the margins to the center where, say, the possibilities for the deployment of technology to support disabled people having a good life are researched from within a transformative paradigm in which disabled people, in all their diversity, act as the guides and mentors of the research process. If we achieve this, then the UN Convention on the Rights of Persons With Disabilities will, indeed, be a living document.

The pathway to full realization of human rights and social justice for people with disability is not smooth. A history of oppression and neglect has to be overcome. The transformative paradigm provides a way of thinking about the enduring consequences of this history, as well as a way forward through the conduct of research viewed as an instrument in the struggle. Heterogeneity within the disability communities leads to issues that will not be easily addressed. Challenges remain with regard to the role of nondisabled researchers and how they can work respectfully with disabled people to further the goal of social transformation. Partnerships can be difficult to begin and maintain; however, much strength is gained by bringing those with and without disabilities together. The transformative spirit can be viewed as a positive force to guide those who walk this path.

Notes

1. For additional information about the history of the disability rights movement, see the University of California, Berkeley, oral history website (2010) at http://bancroft .berkeley.edu/collections/drilm/index.html.

2. This quote first appeared in Mertens, 2009, p. 209.

3. The authors wish to thank Kirsten Smiler for bringing to our attention the work of Mason Durie and his colleagues at the Research Centre for Māori Health & Development at Massey University (http://www.massey.ac.nz/~wwwcphr/restph.htm). Since 1994, they have

conducted Best Outcomes for Māori: Te Hoe Nuku Roa, a longitudinal study of Māori households (http://www.tehoenukuroa.org.nz/). This survey is designed to examine the diversity within the Māori community. Smiler's MA thesis focuses on issues of language and identity for Māori members of the New Zealand Deaf community (Smiler, 2004; Smiler & McPhee, 2007); she has an undergraduate degree in Māori studies. She is in the process of conducting her PhD dissertation research on successful interventions with deaf Māori and their families (http://www.victoria.ac.nz/hsrc/projects/maori.aspx).

Adrienne Wiley (2009) of Johns Hopkins University has written one of the few research papers on Māori experience of disability—an evaluation of Objective 11 of the New Zealand Disability Strategy, which promotes the participation of disabled Māori.

4. The Indigenous Terms of Reference (ITR) were developed by the faculty and staff of the Centre for Aboriginal Studies at Curtin University in Perth, Australia. Osborne and McPhee (2000) note that the original concept of the ITR "is attributed to Lilla Watson (1985), a Queensland Murri woman, who developed the concept Aboriginal (or Murri) Terms of Reference to among other things describe an Indigenous worldview and context for Indigenous cultural and social recognition" (p. 2). The Centre for Aboriginal Studies, Curtin University, adopted aspects of the concept and developed them into an area of competence within an undergraduate Community Development and Management course from 1990.

5. The capitalization of the term Sign Language signifies a cultural group similar to African American or Jewish.

6. In 1974, New Zealanders gave up their right to sue for compensation following an accident in exchange for a no-fault compensation system funded from levies on employers, wages, motor vehicle registration, and petrol. It is administered centrally by the Accident Compensation Corporation (ACC) and includes a cash lump sum, all costs associated with hospitalization, rehabilitation, aides, appliances, home and workplace alterations, personal care, continence and medical supplies, and home support; earnings-related compensation (80% of earnings at time of accident) are paid during the period of rehabilitation (or for the rest of a person's working life in the case of SCI) and a suitably modified motor vehicle. All people in New Zealand, including visitors, are covered by ACC. People who get their SCI through congenital or illness-related causes are covered by the far less generous and means-tested Disability Support Services through the Ministry of Health.

7. Many people with Asperger's syndrome refer to themselves as Aspies.

8. People First is the international name of the self-advocacy organization of people with intellectual disability.

9. People who identify as Deaf do not see themselves as disabled but as members of a linguistic minority. They use sign language and refer to themselves as culturally Deaf. Some of the people who are hard of hearing or hearing impaired and use hearing aids, cochlear implants, and try to talk, describe themselves as deaf and disabled.

10. In the literature, people with autism are referred to as having autism spectrum disorder while people without autism are described as neuro-typical. People on the

spectrum who object to being defined as having a disorder, have adopted the term neuro-diverse (see Robertson, 2010) as a less offensive descriptor.

References

Abma, T. A. (2006). Patients as partners in a health research agenda setting: The feasibility of a participatory methodology. *Evaluation in the Health Professions, 29,* 424–439.

Albrecht, G. L. (2002). American pragmatism: Sociology and the development of disability studies. In C. Barnes, M. Oliver, & L. Barton (Eds.), *Disability studies today* (pp. 18–37). Cambridge, UK: Polity.

Alper, J. S., Ard, C., Asch, A., Beckwith, J., Conrad, P., & Geller, L. (Eds.). (2002). *The double-edged helix: Social implication of genetics in a diverse society.* Baltimore: Johns Hopkins University Press.

American Psychological Association. (2002). *Ethical principles of psychologists and code of conduct.* Washington, DC: Author. Available at http://www.apa.org/ethics/code/index.aspx

Anspach, R. (1979). From stigma to identity politics: Political activism among the physically disabled and former mental patients. *Social Science & Medicine, 13*(A), 765–773.

Asch, A., & Fine, M. (1992). Beyond pedestals: Revisiting the lives of women with disabilities. In M. Fine (Ed.), *Disruptive voices: The possibilities of feminist research* (pp. 139–172). Ann Arbor: University of Michigan Press.

Autistic Self Advocacy Network (ASAN). (2011). *About the Autistic Self Advocacy Network.* Available at www.autisticadvocacy.org

Barnes, C., & Mercer, G. (Eds.). (1997). *Doing disability research.* Leeds, UK: The Disability Press.

Barnes, C., Oliver, M., & Barton, L. (Eds.). (2002). *Disability studies today.* Cambridge, UK: Polity.

Barnes, H. W., McCreanor, T., Edwards, S., & Borell, B. (2009). Epistemological domination: Social science research ethics in Aotearoa. In D. M. Mertens & P. G. Ginsberg (Eds.), *Handbook of social research ethics* (pp. 442–457). Thousand Oaks, CA: Sage.

Beazley, S., Moore, M., & Benzie, D. (1997). Involving disabled people in research: A study of inclusion in environmental activities. In C. Barnes & G. Mercer (Eds.), *Doing disability research* (pp. 142–157). Leeds, UK: The Disability Press.

Beresford, P., & Wallcraft, J. (1997). Psychiatric system survivors and emancipatory research: Issues, overlaps and differences. In C. Barnes & G. Mercer (Eds.), *Doing disability research* (pp. 67–87). Leeds, UK: The Disability Press.

Biklen, D. (2005). *Autism and the myth of the person alone.* New York: New York University Press.

Bishop, R. (2008). Te Kotahitanga: Kaupapa Māori in mainstream classrooms. In N. K. Denzin, Y. S. Lincoln, & L. T. Smith (Eds.), *Handbook of critical & indigenous methodologies* (pp. 285–307). Thousand Oaks, CA: Sage.

Blackman, L. (1999). *Lucy's story: Autism and other adventures*. London: Jessica Kingsley Publishers.

Booth, T., & Booth, W. (1997). Making connections: A narrative study of adult children of parents with learning difficulties. In C. Barnes & G. Mercer (Eds.), *Doing disability research* (pp. 123–141). Leeds, UK: The Disability Press.

Brabeck, M. M., & Brabeck, K. M. (2009). Feminist perspectives on research ethics. In D. M. Mertens & P. G. Ginsberg (Eds.), *Handbook of social research ethics* (pp. 39–53). Thousand Oaks, CA: Sage.

Braddock, D. L., & Parish, S. L. (2001). An institutional history of disability. In G. L. Albrecht, K. D. Seelman, & M. Bury (Eds.), *Handbook of disability studies* (pp. 11–68). Thousand Oaks, CA: Sage.

Campbell, J., & Oliver, M. (1996). *Disability politics: Understanding our past, changing our future*. London: Routledge.

Chilisa, B. (2009). Indigenous African-centered ethics: Contesting and complementing dominant models. In D. M. Mertens & P. G. Ginsberg (Eds.), *Handbook of social research ethics* (pp. 407–425). Thousand Oaks, CA: Sage.

Cram, F. (2009). Maintaining indigenous voices. In D. M. Mertens & P. G. Ginsberg (Eds.), *Handbook of social research ethics* (pp. 308–322). Thousand Oaks, CA: Sage.

Cram, F., Ormond, A., & Carter, L. (2004). *Researching our relations: Reflections on ethics and marginalization*. Paper presented at the Kamehameha Schools 2004 Research Conference on Hawaiian Well-being, Kea'au, HI.

Cushing, L. S., Carter, E. W., Clark, N., Wallis, T., & Kennedy, C. H. (2009). Evaluating inclusive educational practices for students with severe disabilities using the program quality measurement tool. *Journal of Special Education, 42*, 195–208.

Denzin, N. K., & Lincoln, Y. S. (Eds.). (2005). *The SAGE handbook of qualitative research* (3rd ed.). Thousand Oaks, CA: Sage.

Denzin, N. K., Lincoln, Y. S., & Smith, L. T. (2008). *Handbook of critical & indigenous methodologies*. Thousand Oaks, CA: Sage.

Dodd, S.-J. (2009). LGBTQ: Protecting vulnerable subjects in *all* studies. In D. M. Mertens & P. G. Ginsberg (Eds.), *Handbook of social research ethics* (pp. 474–488). Thousand Oaks, CA: Sage.

Doren, B., & Benz, M. (2001). Gender equity issues in the vocational and transition services and employment outcomes experienced by young women with disabilities. In H. Rousso & M. Wehmeyer (Eds.), *Double jeopardy: Addressing gender equity in special education*. Albany: SUNY Press.

Edno, T., Joh, T., & Yu, H. C. (2003). *Voices from the field: Health and evaluation leaders on multicultural evaluation*. Oakland, CA: Social Policy Research Associates.

Fine, M., & Asch, A. (1988). Disability beyond stigma: Social interaction, discrimination, and activism. *Journal of Social Issues, 44*(1), 3–21.

Frank, G. (2000). *Venus on wheels*. Berkeley: University of California Press.

Gill, C. J., Kewman, D. G., & Brannon, R. W. (2003). Transforming psychological practice and society. *American Psychologist, 58*(4), 305–312.

Gladstone, C., Dever, A., & Quick, C. (2009, August 26–27). *"My Life When I Leave School" Transition Project: Self-determination and young intellectually disabled students in the transition from school to post school life*. Paper presented at the From Theory to Practice: Knowledge and Practices Conference, the 6th annual conference of the New Zealand Association for the Study of Intellectual Disability, Hamilton, New Zealand.

Goggin, G., & Newell, C. (2005). *Disability in Australia: Exposing a social apartheid*. Sydney, Australia: University of New South Wales Press.

Goodley, D. (2000). *Self-advocacy in the lives of people with learning difficulties*. Buckingham, UK: Open University Press.

Gravois, T. A., & Rosenfield, S. A. (2006). Impact of instructional consultation teams on the disproportionate referral and placement of minority students in special education. *Remedial and Special Education, 27*, 42–52.

Groce, N. E. (2003). *Everyone here spoke sign language*. Cambridge, MA: Harvard University Press. (Original work published 1985)

Guba, E. G., & Lincoln, Y. S. (2005). Paradigmatic controversies, contradictions, and emerging confluences. In N. K. Denzin & Y. S. Lincoln (Eds.), *The SAGE handbook of qualitative research* (3rd ed., pp. 191–216). Thousand Oaks, CA: Sage.

Hahn, H. (1982). Disability and rehabilitation policy: Is paternalistic neglect really benign? *Public Administration Review, 43*, 385–389.

Hahn, H. (1988). The politics of physical differences: Disability and discrimination. *Journal of Social Issues, 44*(1), 39–47.

Hahn, H. (2002). Academic debates and political advocacy: The US disability movement. In C. Barnes, M. Oliver, & L. Barton (Eds.), *Disability studies today* (pp. 162–190). Cambridge, UK: Polity.

Harris, R., Holmes, H., & Mertens, D. M. (2009). Research ethics in sign language communities. *Sign Language Studies, 9*(2), 104–131.

Horvath, L. S., Kampfer-Bohach, S., & Farmer Kearns, J. (2005). The use of accommodations among students with deaf-blindness in large-scale assessment systems. *Journal of Disability Policy Studies, 16*, 177–187.

Kroll, T., Barbour, R., & Harris, J. (2007). Using focus groups in disability research. *Qualitative Health Research, 17*, 690–698.

LaFrance, J., & Crazy Bull, C. (2009). Researching ourselves back to life: Taking control of the research agenda in Indian country. In D. M. Mertens & P. G. Ginsberg (Eds.), *Handbook of social research ethics* (pp. 153–149). Thousand Oaks, CA: Sage.

Linton, S. (1998). *Claiming disability: Knowledge and identity*. New York: New York University Press.

Linton, S. (2006). *My body politic*. Ann Arbor: University of Michigan Press.

Lunt, N., & Thornton, P. (1997). Researching disability employment policies. In C. Barnes & G. Mercer (Eds.), *Doing disability research* (pp. 108–122). Leeds, UK: The Disability Press.

MacArthur, J., Gaffney, M., Kelly, B., & Sharp, S. (2007). Disabled children negotiating school life: Agency, difference, teaching practice and education policy. *International Journal of Children's Rights, 15*(1), 99–120.

Meekosha, H., & Shuttleworth, R. (2009). What's so "critical" about critical disability studies? *Australian Journal of Human Rights, 15*(1), 47–75.

Mertens, D. M. (2000). Deaf and hard of hearing people in court: Using an emancipatory perspective to determine their needs. In C. Truman, D. M. Mertens, & B. Humphries (Eds.), *Research and inequality* (pp. 111–125). London: Taylor & Francis.

Mertens, D. M. (2009). *Transformative research and evaluation.* New York: Guilford.

Mertens, D. M. (2010). *Research and evaluation in education and psychology: Integrating diversity with quantitative, qualitative, and mixed methods* (3rd ed.). Thousand Oaks, CA: Sage.

Mertens, D. M., Holmes, H., & Harris, R. (2008, February). *Preparation of teachers for students who are deaf and have a disability.* Presentation at the annual meeting of the Association of College Educators of the Deaf and Hard of Hearing, Monterey, CA.

Mertens, D. M., Holmes, H., & Harris, R. (2009). Transformative research and ethics. In D. M. Mertens & P. G. Ginsberg (Eds.), *Handbook of social research ethics* (pp. 85–102). Thousand Oaks, CA: Sage.

Mertens, D. M., Wilson, A., & Mounty, J. (2007). Gender equity for people with disabilities. In S. Klein et al. (Eds.), *Handbook for achieving gender equity through education* (pp. 583–604). Mahwah, NJ: Lawrence Erlbaum.

Morris, J. (1991). *Pride against prejudice.* London: Women's Press.

Newell, C. (2005). Moving disability from other to us. In P. O'Brien & M. Sullivan (Eds.), *Allies in emancipation: Shifting from providing service to being of support.* Melbourne: Thomson/Dunmore.

Newell, C. (2006). Representation or abuse? Rhetorical dimensions of genetics and disability. *Interaction, 20*(1), 28–33.

New Zealand Ministry of Health. (2001). *New Zealand disability strategy.* Wellington, NZ: Author.

O'Brien, P., Shevlin, M., O'Keeffe, M., Kenny, M., Fitzgerald, S., Espiner, D., & Kubiack, J. (2008, November 24–26). *Opening up a whole new world: Students with intellectual disability being included within a university setting.* Paper presented at the 43rd Australian Society for the Scientific Study of Intellectual Disabilities Conference, University of Melbourne, Australia.

Oliver, M. (1982). A new model of the social work role in relation to disability. In J. Campling (Ed.), *The handicapped person: A new perspective for social workers?* London: RADAR.

Oliver, M. (1990). *The politics of disablement.* Basingstoke, UK: Macmillan.

Oliver, M. (1992). Changing the social relations of research production? *Disability, Handicap & Society, 7*(2), 101–114.

Oliver, M. (1997). Emancipatory research: Realistic goal or impossible dream? In C. Barnes & G. Mercer (Eds.), *Doing disability research* (pp. 15–31). Leeds, UK: The Disability Press.

Osborne, R., & McPhee, R. (2000, December 12–15). *Indigenous terms of reference* (ITR). Presentation at the 6th annual UNESCO-ACEID International Conference on Education, Bangkok, Thailand.

Parens, E., & Asch, A. (Eds.). (2000). *Prenatal testing and disability rights.* Washington, DC: Georgetown University Press.

Pfeiffer, D., & Yoshida, K. (1995). Teaching disability studies in Canada and the USA. *Disability & Society, 10*(4) 475–495.

Priestley, M. (1997). Who's research? A personal audit. In C. Barnes & G. Mercer (Eds.), *Doing disability research* (pp. 88–107). Leeds, UK: The Disability Press.

Rapaport, J., Manthorpe, J., Moriarty, J., Hussein, S., & Collins, J. (2005). Advocacy and people with learning disabilities in the UK: How can local funders find value for money? *Journal of Intellectual Disabilities, 9,* 299–319.

Reinharz, S. (1979). *On becoming a social scientist.* San Francisco: Jossey-Bass.

Robertson, A., Frawley, P., & Bigby, C. (2008). *Making life good in the community: When is a house a home? Looking at how homely community houses are for people with an intellectual disability who have moved out of an institution.* Melbourne, Australia: La Trobe University and the State Government of Victoria.

Robertson, S. M. (2010). Neurodiversity, quality of life, and autistic adults: Shifting research and professional focuses onto real-life challenges. *Disability Studies Quarterly, 30*(1).

Rousso, H. (2001). *Strong proud sisters: Girls and young women with disabilities.* Washington, DC: Center for Women Policy Studies.

Ryan, J. (2007). Learning disabilities in Australian universities: Hidden, ignored, and unwelcome. *Journal of Learning Disabilities, 40,* 436–442.

Scotch, R. K. (2001). *From good will to civil rights.* Philadelphia: Temple University Press.

Shakespeare, T. (1997). Researching disabled sexuality. In C. Barnes & G. Mercer (Eds.), *Doing disability research* (pp. 177–189). Leeds, UK: The Disability Press.

Shakespeare, T., & Watson, N. (2001). The social model of disability: An outdated ideology? In S. N. Barnarrt & B. M. Altman (Eds.), *Exploring theories and expanding methodologies: Where are we and where do we need to go?* (pp. 9–28). Greenwich, CT: JAI.

Smiler, K. (2004). *Maori deaf: Perceptions of cultural and linguistic identity of Maori members of the New Zealand deaf community.* Unpublished master's thesis, Victoria University of Wellington, New Zealand.

Smiler, K., & McKee, R. L. (2007). Perceptions of "Maori" deaf identity in New Zealand. *Journal of Deaf Studies and Deaf Education, 12*(1), 93–111.

Smith, L. T. (2005). On tricky ground: Researching the native in the age of uncertainty. In N. K. Denzin & Y. S. Lincoln (Eds.), *The SAGE handbook of qualitative research* (3rd ed., pp. 85–108). Thousand Oaks, CA: Sage.

Sobsey, D. (1994). *Violence and abuse in the lives of people with disabilities: The end of silent acceptance?* Baltimore: Brooks.

Stone, E., & Priestly, M. (1996). Parasites, pawns and partners: Disability research and the role of non-disabled researchers. *British Journal of Sociology, 47*(4), 699–716.

Sullivan, M. (2009). Philosophy, ethics and the disability community. In D. M. Mertens & P. G. Ginsberg (Eds.), *Handbook of social research ethics* (pp. 69–84). Thousand Oaks, CA: Sage.

Symonette, H. (2009). Cultivating self as a responsive instrument: Working the boundaries and borderlands for ethical border crossings. In D. M. Mertens & P. G. Ginsberg (Eds.), *Handbook of social research ethics* (pp. 279–294). Thousand Oaks, CA: Sage.

Thomas, V. G. (2009). Critical race theory: Ethics and dimensions of diversity in research. In D. M. Mertens & P. G. Ginsberg (Eds.), *Handbook of social research ethics* (pp. 54–68). Thousand Oaks, CA: Sage.

Triano, S. (2006). Disability pride. In G. Albrecht (Ed.), *Encyclopedia of disability* (Vol. 1, pp. 476–477). Thousand Oaks, CA: Sage.

Union of the Physically Impaired Against Segregation (UPIAS). (1976). *Fundamental principles of disability* [Booklet]. London: Author.

United Nations. (2006). *Convention on the rights of people with disabilities.* New York: Author.

United States Department of Education. (2004). *Twenty-sixth annual report to Congress on the implementation of the Individuals With Disabilities Act* (Vol. 2). Washington DC: Author.

University of California, Berkeley. (2010). *The disability rights and independent living movement.* Available at http://bancroft.berkeley.edu/collections/drilm/index.html

van Beeck, E., Larsen, C. F., Lyons, R., Meerding, W. J., Mulder, S., & Essink-Bot, M. L. (2005). *Draft guidelines for the conduction of empirical studies into injury-related disability.* Amsterdam: Eurosafe (European Association for Injury Prevention and Safety Promotion). Available at http://www.eurosafe.eu.com/csi/catalogus.nsf/c1af8 df8ec2b154bc12570b500682709/62760ac72216e50ac12570d60036ccc9/$FILE/ ER-285.pdf

Watson, L. (1985, July 8–11). *The establishment of aboriginal terms of reference in a tertiary institution.* Paper presented at the Aborigines and Islanders in Higher Education: The Need for Institutional Change National Conference, Townsville, Australia.

Wiley, A. (2009). At a cultural crossroads: Lessons on culture and policy from the New Zealand Disability Strategy. *Disability and Rehabilitation, 31*(14), 1205–1214.

Wright, B. A. (1983). *Physical disability: A psychosocial approach.* New York: Harper & Row.

Part III

The Future of
Qualitative Research

And so we come to the end, which is only the starting point for a new beginning, the contested future. Several observations have structured our arguments to this point. The field of qualitative research continues to transform itself. The changes that took shape in the first decade of this new century are gaining momentum, even as they confront multiple forms of resistance. A new generation is making its presence felt. Scholars trained in the postmodern and experimental moments take for granted what early generations fought to establish.

The indigenous, gendered, narrative turn has been taken. Foundational epistemologies, what Schwandt (2007) calls epistemologies with the big E, have been replaced by post-postconstructivist, hermeneutic, feminist, poststructural, pragmatist, critical race, and queer theory approaches to social inquiry. Epistemology with a small e has become normative, displaced by discourses on ethics and values, conversations on and about the good, and about the just and moral society.

Qualitative inquiry is under assault from three sides. First, on the *political right,* are the methodological conservatives who are connected to neoconservative governmental regimes. These critics support evidence-based, experimental methodologies, or mixed methods. This stance consigns qualitative research to the methodological margins. Second, on the *epistemological right,* are neotraditionalist methodologists who look with nostalgia at the golden age of qualitative inquiry. These critics find in the past all that is needed for inquiry in the present. Third, on the *ethical right*, are mainstream, biomedical scientists and traditional social science researchers who invoke a single ethical model for human subject research. The ethical right refuses to engage the arguments of those researchers who engage in collaborative, consciousness raising, empowering inquiry.

Qualitative researchers in the seventh and eighth moments must navigate between these three oppositional forces, each of which threatens to deny the advances in qualitative research over the past three decades. These critics do not recognize the influences of indigenous, feminist, race, queer, or ethnic border studies. We need to protect ourselves from these criticisms. We also need to create spaces for dialogue and public scholarly engagement of these issues.

The chapters in this volume collectively speak to the great need for a compassionate, critical, interpretive, civic social science. This is an interpretive social science that blurs both boundaries and genres. Its participants are committed to politically informed action research, inquiry directed to praxis, and social change. Hence, as the reformist movement called qualitative research gains momentum, its places in the discourses of a free democratic society become ever clearer. With the action researchers, we seek a disciplined set of interpretive practices that will produce radical democratizing transformations in the public and private spheres of the global postcapitalist world. Qualitative research is the means to these ends. It is the bridge that joins multiple interpretive communities. It stretches across many different landscapes and horizons, moving back and forth between the public and the private, the sacred and the secular.

Paradigm shifts and dialogues have become a constant presence within and across the theoretical frameworks that organize both qualitative inquiry and the social and human sciences. The move to standpoint epistemologies has accelerated. No one any longer believes in the concept of a unified sexual subject, or indeed, any unified subject. Epistemology has come out of the closet. The desire for critical, multivoiced, postcolonial ethnographies increases as capitalism extends its global reach.

We now understand that the civic-minded qualitative researcher uses a set of material practices that bring the world into play. These practices are not neutral tools. This researcher thinks historically and interactionally, always mindful of the structural processes that make race, gender, and class potentially repressive presences in daily life. The material practices of qualitative inquiry turn the researcher into a methodological (and epistemological) *bricoleur*. This person is an artist, a quilt maker, a skilled craftsperson, a maker of montages and collages. The interpretive *bricoleur* can interview; observe; study material culture; think within and beyond visual methods; write poetry, fiction, and autoethnography; construct narratives that tell explanatory stories; use qualitative computer software; do text-based inquiries; construct *testimonios* using focus group inter-views; and even engage in applied ethnography and policy formulation.

It is apparent that the constantly changing field of qualitative research is defined by a series of tensions and contradictions, as well as emergent under-standings. These tensions and understandings have been felt in every chapter in this volume. Here, as in previous editions, we list many of them for purposes of summary only. They take the form of questions and assertions:

1. Will the performance turn in qualitative inquiry lead to performances that decolonize theory, and help deconstruct that global, postcolonial situation?

2. Will critical, indigenous interpretive paradigms, epistemologies, and pedagogies flourish in the eighth moment?

3. Will critical, indigenous interpretive paradigms, epistemologies, and peda-gogies lead to the development and use of new inquiry practices, including coun-ternarratives, autoethnographies, cultural poetics, and arts-based methodologies?

4. Can indigenous qualitative researchers take the lead in decolonizing the academy?

5. Will the emphasis on multiple standpoint epistemologies and moral philoso-phies crystallize around a set of shared understandings concerning the contributions of qualitative inquiry to civil society, civic discourse, and critical race theory?

6. Will the criticisms from the methodological, political, and ethical con-servatives stifle this field?

7. Will the performance turn in ethnography produce a shift away from attempts to represent the stream of consciousness and the world of internal meanings of the conscious subject?

8. How will feminist, communitarian, and indigenous ethical codes change IRBs? Will the two- and three-track IRB model become normative?

9. Will a new interpretive paradigm, with new methods and strategies of inquiry, emerge out of the interactions that exist between the many paradigms and perspectives we have presented in this volume?

10. How will indigenous, ethnic, queer, postcolonial, and feminist paradigms be fitted to this new synthesis, if it comes?

11. Will the postmodern, anti-foundational sensibility begin to form its own foundational criteria for evaluating the written and performed text?

12. When all universals are gone, including the postmodern worldview, in favor of local interpretations, how can we continue to talk and learn from one another?

There are no definitive answers to any of these questions. Examined from another angle, the 12 questions listed above focus on the social text, history, politics, ethics, the Other, and interpretive paradigms more broadly.

Into the Future

The chapter by Judith Preissle (Chapter 14) reflexively moves qualitative inquiry into the future. In so doing, she draws on her own experiences of more than 40 years as a qualitative researcher and teacher. (She established QUALRS-L, a listserv discussion group on qualitative research, in 1991.) She uses multiple metaphors—bramble bush, tapestry, umbrella, confederacy—to describe this sprawling discourse. It has multiple roots—like a bramble bush. It is like a tapestry, with many different threads, colors, and patterns. It is like an umbrella in that it covers a variety of traditions. It is also like a confederacy in the Native American Iroquois manner—it extends across time and space; its membership is fluid.

She reads qualitative research's future through the lens of these metaphors, seeing a future that will be more just, more free, more open to alternative perspectives, and more secure. She imagines a world where young scholars will bring new understandings of critical inquiry into the classroom and into their written work.

Right and Left Pole Activist Methodologies[1]

Eisenhart and Jurow (Chapter 15) enter this pedagogical space. They review the current literature on qualitative pedagogy, and offer extended discussion of the two-semester Introduction to Qualitative Research course required of all entering doctoral students in the College of Education at the University of Colorado, Boulder.

They reinforce the argument that the literature on teaching qualitative research continues to reflect the 1980 paradigm disputes. With Phillips (2006), they see two pedagogical camps, or two poles on a continuum, a right pole and a left pole. On the right pole are the traditionalists who view methods as objective tools. Traditionalists focus their teaching on questions of design, technique, and analysis. This is "qi" in small letters.

As expected, the experimentalists are on the left pole; this is QI in big letters! Those on the left pole take a more avant garde, activist view of method and pedagogy. They adopt a subjective, interpretive approach to inquiry. They concentrate on method as praxis, or method as a tool for social action. Performance ethnographers, action researchers, and community organizers are all in the left pole group. They want to change the world by creating texts that move persons to action. They want texts that move from personal troubles to public institutions. They want to teach students how to do this.

There is a third pole; this is the space of social justice. Right- and left-pole methodologists can be united around social change issues. Traditional methodologists, like left-pole activists, can teach students how to do ground-level social justice inquiry. This is inquiry that is indigenous, collaborative, and community-based.

This initiative combines pedagogy and methodology to

- Help clarify competing definitions of a social problem;
- Collect and use narratives, life stories, statistics, numbers, and facts to expose the limits of official ideologies and to dramatize the extent of injustice operating in a crisis situation;
- Isolate points of intervention;
- Suggest alternative moral points of view;
- Articulate questions concerning "how," not "why" the problem was created;
- Connect personal troubles with public issues;
- Secure multiple instances of injustice through interview, observation, archives, and personal experience;
- Collaborate with community members to produce and perform ethnodramas that dramatize the situations that have been uncovered;
- Interpret and publicize audience feedback.

In these and other interpretive ways, traditional and experimental interpretive methods can be combined in projects that are committed to advancing social justice agendas. More is involved, as elaborated below.

Teaching to the Left Pole for Bricoleurs

Eisenhart and Jurow (Chapter 15) observe that teaching to the left pole involves more then technique. It centers on postmodern epistemological, philosophical principles, including the politics of knowing, as well as issues surrounding objectivity, performance, reflexivity, writing and the first-person voice, complicity with the Other, ethics, values, and truth. In order to travel to the place of the experimental text, students obviously need instruction in a large literature that has traditionally not been regarded as central to methodology. This is qualitative research that is messy, performative, poetic, political, and reflexive. It is autoethnographic, inquiry shaped by the call to social action, by a commitment to undo pedagogies of oppression.

So conceived, there are three attitudes to be enacted, or goals to be pursued. First, teaching, understood as critical pedagogy, is the practice of making the political and the ideological visible through the act of performance itself. Teaching is a performative act. Second, this act is an invitation for students to use their own experiences as vehicles for pushing back against structures of racial, sexual, and class oppression, an invitation to become agents in their own biographies.

Third, in order to realize the first two goals, students become autoethnographers, authors of dramas about their own lives. This performance format presumes that all playwrights are ethnodramatists (Saldaña, 2005, p. 33). This is emancipatory theatre, critical performance ethnography for the oppressed, a theatre that exposes the lies we tell one anther about race and ourselves.

At the same time, students on the left pole need instruction on right-pole methodologies. Critical scholars need to, at some point in their careers, be deeply immersed in the methodological classics of their discipline. They need to know how to interview, do fieldwork, work in archives, do participant observation, write autoethnography, do case studies, engage the various forms of participatory action research (PAR), do focus groups, and write grounded theory. As *bricoleurs*, they need all of these methodologies in their social action tool kit. Traditional qualitative research can be used as a tool to leverage social change. This can happen when participation, action, experience, and inquiry are joined under a critical format.

Language is a key. If new forms of social text are created, then new voices are heard—the voices of change, the voices of resistance. Research is thereby connected to political action. Systems of language and meaning and paradigms of knowing are changed. When this happens, the world changes.

The collapse of foundational epistemologies has led to emerging innovations in methodology. These innovations reframe what is meant by validity. They have shaped the call for increased textual reflexivity, greater textual self-exposure, multiple voicing, stylized forms of literary representation, and performance texts. These innovations shade into the next issues, surrounding representation.

Representational issues involve how the other will be presented in the text. Representational strategies converge with a concern over the place of politics in the text. We can no longer separate ideology and politics from methodology. Methods always acquire their meaning within broader systems of meaning, from epistemology to ontology. These systems are themselves embedded in ethical and ideological frameworks as well as in particular interpretive communities. Our methods are always grafted into our politics.

Scientific practice does not stand outside ideology. As argued in the first and second editions, a poststructural social science project seeks its external grounding not in science, but rather in a commitment to post-Marxism, and an emancipatory feminism. A good text is one that invokes these commitments. A good text exposes how race, class, and gender work their ways into the concrete lives of interacting individuals.

We foresee a future where research becomes more relational, where working the hyphen becomes easier, and more difficult, for researchers are always on both sides of the hyphen. We also see a massive spawning of populist technology. This technology will serve to undermine qualitative inquiry as we know it, including disrupting what we mean by a stable subject (Where is the cyberself located?). The new information technologies also increase the possibilities of dialogue and communication across time and space. We may be participating in the reconstruction of the social sciences. If so, qualitative inquiry is taking the lead in this reconstruction.

Finally, we predict that there will be no dominant form of qualitative textuality in the seventh and eighth moments; rather, several different hybrid textual forms will circulate alongside one another. The first form will be the classic, realist ethnographic text, redefined in poststructural terms. We will hear more from the first-person voice in these texts. The second hybrid textual form will blend and combine poetic, fictional, and performance texts into critical interventionist presentations. The third textual form will include *testimonios* and first-person (autoethnographic) texts. The fourth form will be narrative evaluation texts, which work back and forth between first-person voices and the *testimonio.* These forms will be evaluated in terms of an increasingly more sophisticated set of local, indigenous, anti-foundational, moral, and ethical criteria.

Variations on these textual forms will rest on a critical rethinking of the notion of the reflexive, self-aware subject. Lived experience cannot be studied directly. We study representations of experience: stories, narratives, performances, dramas. We have no direct access to the inner psychology and inner world of meanings of the reflexive subject. The subject in performance ethnographies becomes a performer. We study performers and performances, persons making meaning together, the how of culture as it connects persons in moments of co-creation and co-performance.

History, Paradigms, Politics, Ethics, and the Other

Many things are changing as we write our way out of writing culture, and move into the eighth moment of qualitative research. Multiple histories and theoretical frameworks, when before there were just a few, now circulate in this field. Today, foundationalism and postpositivism are challenged and supplemented by a host of competing paradigms and perspectives. Many different applied action and participatory research agendas inform program evaluation and analysis.

We now understand that we study the Other to learn about ourselves, and many of the lessons we have learned have not been pleasant. We seek a new body of ethical directives fitted to postmodernism. The old ethical codes failed to examine research as a morally engaged project. They never seriously located the researcher within the ruling apparatuses of society. A feminist, communitarian ethical system will continue to evolve, informed at every step by critical race, postcolonial, and queer theory sensibilities. Blatant voyeurism in the name of science or the state will continue to be challenged.

Performance-based cultural studies and critical theory perspectives, with their emphases on moral criticism, will alter the traditional empiricist foundations of qualitative research. The dividing line between science and morality will continue to be erased. A postmodern, feminist, poststructural, communitarian science will move closer to a sacred science of the moral universe.

As we edge our way into the twenty-first century, looking back, and borrowing Max Weber's metaphor, we see more clearly how we were trapped by the twentieth century and its iron cage of reason and rationality. Like a bird in a cage, for too long we were unable to see the pattern in which we were caught. Co-participants in a secular science of the social world, we became part of the problem. Entangled in the ruling apparatuses we wished to undo, we perpetuated systems of knowledge and power that we found, underneath, to be all too oppressive. It's not too late to get out of the cage. Today, we leave that cage behind.

And so do we enter, or leave, the eighth moment, moving into an uncertain future.

Note

1. This section reworks material in Denzin (2010, pp. 55–57).

References

Denzin, N. K. (2010). *The qualitative manifesto.* Walnut Creek, CA: Left Coast Press.

Phillips, D. C. (2006). A guide for the perplexed: Scientific educational research, methodolatry, and the gold versus platinum standards. *Educational Research Review, 1*(1), 15–26.

Saldaña, J. (2005). *Ethnodrama.* Walnut Creek, CA: AltaMira Press.

Schwandt, T. C. (2007). *Qualitative inquiry* (3rd ed.). Thousand Oaks, CA: Sage.

14

Qualitative Futures

Where We Might Go From Where We've Been

Judith Preissle[1]

In the early 1980s, coming off some success in publishing journal articles on qualitative research methods, my colleague Marki LeCompte and I put together a prospectus for a qualitative research methods book in education and sent it to two publishers. An editor at one of them expressed an interest that led to two editions of the text (Goetz & LeCompte, 1984; LeCompte & Preissle, 1993) and a Spanish translation (Goetz & LeCompte, 1988). From the other, we received a polite refusal accompanied by a vitriolic review of our material that ended with the assertion that no one would be doing qualitative research anymore. The reviewer said that qualitative research had been a frivolous endeavor, its time had come and gone, and the projected manuscript would have no market.

I begin my consideration of the future of qualitative research with this cautionary tale because what is ahead of us is always uncertain, some of our expectations will not be met, and some of what happens is rarely anticipated. Although my undergraduate preparation in history convinced me that the present and future reflect the past, that reflection is itself based in hindsight and is partly made up of what was not expected. Furthermore, scholars and academics awake each day to make their worlds—to teach, study, and write with the confidence that what they are creating from the past and the present will contribute to scholarship in the coming years. The nature of research and publication are such that we are always engaged now in preparation for later, and later may be a year, 5 years, or 50 years away.

In this chapter, I base projections for and speculations about the future of qualitative research on three sources. First is my own individual experience of 40 years of doing and teaching qualitative research. Second is the view that experience provides of the history and development of qualitative research methods and design. Third is the work of emerging scholars along with other expert projections of qualitative futures (e.g., Loseke & Cahill, 1999a, 1999b; Denzin & Lincoln's commentaries in previous handbooks, 1994, 2000, 2005; and such). The emphasis is on what changes and what remains the same in practicing qualitative scholarship and how we even recognize the difference. Finally, my focus is on the future of research practice and methodology rather than on broader social and economic trends, although my projections assume that globalization, technical upheavals, and cultural strife will not succumb to apocalypse.

In this material, I consider the dangers of prognostication, as illustrated in the anecdote that begins the chapter, and I acknowledge that my own relationship with the future has been ambivalent. Engagement in the present generally has distracted me from envisioning what is to come. Consequently, I review some of these relevant "presents" that have culminated in my professional history as a qualitative methodologist in the United States. Understanding our present and future based on the concrete experiences of individuals has multiple, overlapping traditions in qualitative scholarship: life history research (e.g., R. Atkinson, 1998; Goodson & Sikes, 2001; Langness & Frank, 1981), biographical and autobiographical work (e.g., Bertaux, 1981; Goodson & Walker, 1991; Kridel, 1998; Okely & Callaway, 1992), narrative representations of experience (Hatch & Wisniewski, 1995; Hinchman & Hinchman, 1997; Josselson & Lieblich, 1993; Polkinghorne, 1988), and autoethnography (Ellis, 2009; Reed-Danahay, 1997). Feminists have contributed illuminating accounts of their lives as scholars (Reinharz, 1979/1984; Richardson, 1997), a practice arguably pioneered earlier in the 20th century by fieldworkers such as Malinowski (1967/1989) and Mead (1972). What follows is less detailed than autoethnography and less comprehensive than life history. They are anecdotes from an academic memoir, they are intended to illuminate a past and project a future, and they invite readers to reflect on their own similar and different experiences with scholarship.

Jude's History

Many children grow up confident of what they want to be and do for a living. My only vision was to be independent. No one was more surprised than I was when practicing education became even more important than achieving and maintaining independence.

BECOMING AN EDUCATOR

In 1962, when I was an undergraduate at Grinnell College in Iowa, my father began pressing me for my plans for independence—a livelihood to support arriving at adulthood. He assured me that my ideas of taking the civil service exam and working for the U.S. federal government in some capacity would lead me nowhere. He said most policy analysts were projecting large reductions in government workers for the coming years. This conversation occurred before John Kennedy was assassinated; before Lyndon Johnson assumed the presidency; and before Johnson's Great Society programs initiated an expansion, rather than a contraction, in the federal government workforce. My father's mistaken ideas may account for my skepticism about my own and anyone else's abilities to project the future, including the qualitative research future.

What routes other than civil service and law make sense for undergraduates majoring in history? My father pressed for teaching certification so I would have "something to fall back on." Having settled for a history major because an anthropology degree was not available at my college at that time, I feared education would take me even further afield from my interest in studying cultures. Reginald Archambault (1963), a Dewey scholar who taught education at Grinnell during those years, set me straight. Archambault introduced his students to Dewey's formulation of the teacher as a mediator between "the child and the curriculum": the teacher who studies child and subject matter to engage the child in learning about the world. This was a life-changing revelation for me. I myself had had few experiences of such teachers. My assumption had been that these gifted individuals were just "born" with those talents. I had not realized that people could learn to become progressive educators if they set themselves that goal. That became my goal.

In the following years, I brought the scientific approach to history taught at Grinnell together with some preparation in English and later study of anthropology at the University of Minnesota to a career teaching social studies and language arts to 12-year-olds. Most of those years, the social studies I taught was an experimental anthropology curriculum developed as one of the federally funded Project Social Studies programs, part of the broader effort by the U.S. government to reform precollegiate curriculum in mathematics, science, language, and social studies. Studying anthropology at the university and studying the youngsters in my classes provided an orientation to doing research deeply lodged in *practice* framed by *theory.*

My own instructors in history, anthropology, and some sociology were insistent on addressing the tensions in these fields between a science and a humanities orientation to conducting research. These scholars represented the different perspectives as sources of creative thought stimulating new insights and methods of study. My education courses, however, presented a much narrower view of scholarship: The ideal taught while I was pursuing graduate study from 1966 to 1975 was experimental design, with survey research a sorry second choice. The proper subject of such scholarship was the improvement of public education in the United States. The research I completed for a master's degree was a quasi-experimental comparison of two approaches to teaching about minority groups in the United States. Although the instruments I used indicated significant differences in results, I never published the study because my observations of the two approaches made me skeptical of those results. At the time, I had no idea of how to combine those observations into a formal report of the research. Three more years of graduate study began to address that limitation.

BECOMING AN ETHNOGRAPHER

Ethnographic activity was something I understood early on as a graduate student as occurring at some other remote time and place. I read widely in the cultural anthropology and qualitative sociology literature of research done in the past by people who had become experts in the present when I was reading them. Like my earlier history curriculum, this fieldwork literature was dominated by Western scholars, Europeans and North Americans, but their purview was global rather than centered on the North Atlantic. Even so, the global world was interpreted from Western frameworks.

I read Margaret Mead, Howard Becker and his colleagues, and anyone offering qualitative analyses in my field of education: Elizabeth Eddy, Estelle Fuchs, Jules Henry, Lou Smith, George and Louise Spindler, and Harry Wolcott. All of these scholars were established researchers at the time, and some had much good work ahead of them—although Henry died in 1969 while I was teaching junior high school full-time and studying for a master's degree part-time. Nevertheless, these people were reporting work done in the 1960s and before, some of it outside the United States, and most were individuals I would later meet. For someone from a family with little experience of higher education, much less scholarship, these direct, face-to-face encounters with practicing researchers made fieldwork accessible and possible.

My first formal experiences doing qualitative research were interviews with rural children about their views of city life and close observations of youngsters and their novice teachers whom I was supervising. Trying to bring fieldwork and other qualitative endeavors into my own present was an effort. What I read about had been done in the past. My instructors in education who had ongoing research projects were running surveys or experiments. The anthropologists and qualitative sociologists with whom I studied were between field projects, and I did not begin to meet students returning from their own fieldwork until late in my doctoral career. Just bringing qualitative scholarship from other people's pasts into my present felt audacious. The future, my own or that of qualitative research, was the last thing on my mind. Of course, an education is supposed to be preparation for the future, but it did not help that being a full-time graduate student was lots of fun and something I found myself reluctant to give up.

However, it was 1972, and I had to make a decision about a dissertation. The future was intruding on the present. Just what was I preparing to do? Who was I intending to be? I decided that I wanted to be the Margaret Mead of education in the United States. Although many of the people I was reading had conducted qualitative studies in U.S. schools, the daily lives of teachers and youngsters in classrooms in Western nations had been documented only in incomplete fragments. What I wanted to do was reveal the rich complexities of what goes on among teachers and students as they interact to teach and learn. Maturing in the midst of the U.S. civil rights movement and the succeeding second wave of feminism radicalized many of us in an occupation otherwise characterized by conventionality (Lortie, 1975). As noted previously, I had taught middle grades children from 1965 to 1971, and I team–taught the last 4 of those 6 years. My colleagues and I had made changes every year in an attempt to improve our students' experiences, but as a teacher educator I saw a gap—a rupture—between the changes educational policy makers and innovators planned and what went on in classrooms. Part of my motivation to contribute to what I envisioned as an ethnology of schools and classrooms was to inform the public, the politicians, and educational researchers of what goes on among teachers and students—"the good, the bad, and the ugly." I thought we should learn how things *are* before we intervene to make things as they *ought to be*. I had seen my own well-intentioned efforts to challenge the status quo lead to mixed results.

After several false starts, I conducted for a dissertation study what I called, after Burnett (1973), a microethnography of a third-grade classroom in the rural Midwest (Goetz, 1975). The ethnology has and has not happened. My teacher, Judith Friedman Hansen, did draw on my dissertation and other educational ethnographies for her 1979 synthesis of educational anthropology. LeCompte and I attempted a chapter-length educational ethnology about a decade later

(1992). Most importantly, however, the growth in qualitative research studies in education across its subfields has been such that a single synthesis, one ethnology, is no longer feasible. What we have attained by the first decade of the 21st century is the possibility of many different ethnologies of education. We not only know more about how teachers and students experience schooling, but we also have more detailed accounts of the effect on these experiences of race, ethnicity, gender, class, religion, ability, citizenship status, and sexual orientation.

As for me, my projected career in teacher education and even in educational anthropology was diverted elsewhere. What characterized the abandoned career was its preoccupation with schooling and education in the United States, as much of my initial reading indicated. What characterized the developing career, however, was a continuing ambivalent relationship with the future. I learned to plan ahead for the next hurdle and then to formulate goals for the next year, but long-term planning remains a challenge because I continue to enjoy the present so much.

BECOMING A QUALITATIVE METHODOLOGIST

In 1975, I took a position in elementary social studies education at the University of Georgia. The faculty believed my dissertation experience and preparation in anthropology were sufficient for developing and offering the first qualitative course to be taught at the university, and that was part of my assigned load. Now, four decades later, I teach qualitative research full-time for a graduate certificate program housed in a college of education, but serving programs across the university. Those enrolled in the program come from all parts of the globe, with some qualitative research classes composed of predominantly international students. Over this period, my instruction and scholarship have been enriched by a year's study in philosophy, by the necessity to keep reading across the social and professional sciences to address my students' concerns, and by the adventure of exploring studies of education elsewhere. Examples of these have been Willis's (1977) critical ethnography of working-class males in the United Kingdom, the inspired work on gender regimes in Australia by Kessler and her colleagues (Kessler, Ashendon, O'Connell, & Dowsett, 1985), and the exploration of schooling and child labor in India by the Dutch anthropologist Nieuwenhuys (1994).

By the middle of the 1980s, other faculty members assumed my responsibilities in social studies teacher education as the student demand for qualitative courses grew from one course to many courses. Although I continue to research and write on topics in educational anthropology, my recent instructional assignment has been almost entirely devoted to the Qualitative Research Program at the University of Georgia. The irony is that I myself never took a course in qualitative research. To the extent that such material was available at Indiana University and most other research institutions in the mid-20th century, it was embedded as a brief topic in courses like the sociological research methods I did take or in anthropological field methods courses focusing on such crucial tasks as acquiring a new language on site.

SUMMARY

Our futures as qualitative practitioners depend in part on decisions each of us makes in the present(s). Each qualitative scholar has a unique history developed over time from particular experiences, although many methodologists of my generation also came to their expertise through variant routes. My particular stance on qualitative research reflects a practice–theory balance acquired as a classroom teacher and an interdisciplinary orientation developed from framing social sciences in liberal arts environments.

Our futures as qualitative practitioners also require visions of what we hope to accomplish and why. I have summarized some of my own hopes in the preceding pages. These hopes are more likely to be achieved if they are articulated. What changes and what stabilities do we intend, expect, and care about? Who are we working with to make these things happen? What are we bringing from our pasts to create our presents and our futures? I turn next to considering the past of qualitative research activity.

Qualitative Research's History

The history of any scholarly subject is the accumulated histories of the people who create and contribute to the subject. The multiple histories of qualitative research are grounded in the practices of those who work from and study qualitative traditions. These histories are specific to times, places, and disciplinary fields. They contribute to the confusion and aggravation experienced by many who expect the research methods and design they study to be conceptually clear, well-organized, and rationally sensible.

In this section, I draw from and summarize material published elsewhere (Preissle, 2006) about what it means to be a qualitative researcher and do qualitative work. In attempting to synthesize an interdisciplinary specialty with contributions from scholars around the world, I organize the discussion with two different metaphors. These draw attention to different facets of qualitative methodologies and are my attempts to make sense of such a complex area of study. The first metaphor, the *qualitative confederacy,* represents the community of qualitative practitioners and theorists. The second metaphor, the *qualitative tapestry,* represents what we produce or make as we practice and theorize. I begin by discussing who we methodologists are.

THE QUALITATIVE CONFEDERACY

To the extent that people have been watching, listening, asking, and collecting material (Wolcott, 1992) to understand and interpret the world within considered frameworks, they have been doing qualitative research for millennia. Herodotus and Thucydides in Greece and Sima Qian in China left accounts of studying and interpreting the world and even assessing the quality of the information they gathered. What is more recent is documenting these activities in detail, reflecting on the purposes they serve, and connecting the acts with the thinking that directs and is directed by engagement with the world. If the acts and activities are methods, then the reflections are the methodology (see Lather, 1992). Qualitative methodology has been invented, reinvented, and borrowed around the world and in many substantive fields of study. It is based on conceptually framed records of our direct sensory experiences of the world, reported so as to preserve as much of that experience as possible. Qualitative methods are practiced in most social and behavioral sciences, across the professional fields such as education, social work, clinical study, law, library science, health and medicine, and in journalism and the humanities. Figure 14.1 represents a third metaphor, the *bramble bush* of disciplinary roots, stems, and branches contributing to qualitative methods and methodologies.

This bramble bush of qualitative research is sometimes referred to as an *umbrella* term that encompasses the variety of traditions involved, but I prefer to consider qualitative methods and methodologies as a *confederation* of practitioners who share a commitment to theoretically and conceptually formulating an engagement with the world that produces vivid descriptive accounts of human experience. This is confederacy in the Native American Iroquois manner: periodic gatherings of equals to discuss matters of common concern characterized by extended discussion and by candid, but amiable disagreements. The confederacy extends across time and space from the ancients and into the future we envision. Its membership is fluid as new scholars are inducted into the work

Figure 14.1   The Qualitative Disciplinary Bramble Bush

The Qualitative Bramble Bush of Disciplinary Sources
Concept by Judith Preissle, drawn by Jane Link

and even as thinkers long dead may be newly recognized for their contributions to qualitative methodologies. Viewed also as a bramble bush, the confederacy clumps into fields of study that draw, borrow, or rob from one another in sometimes prickly fashion.

THE QUALITATIVE TAPESTRY

Most social science and professional disciplines have some tradition of qualitative methods, although the methodologies may be more recent. In sociology, anthropology, and history, where the methods can be traced to the origins of the fields, qualitative methods and methodology are deeply integrated with content. Conversations about *how* are intertwined with conversations about *what*. The subject matter and the research method implicate each other such that they may be difficult to separate. Anthropologists, for example, customarily assume that an ethnography is a study of a group's culture. In contrast, other social scientists may use the term as a synonym for fieldwork or qualitative research generally.

This appears to be what is meant by ethnography in the title of the periodical, *Journal of Contemporary Ethnography*. Even in considering what may be generic approaches like interviewing, many scholars begin with what they want to learn and how others have studied it. The research question, the subject matter, and the theoretical frameworks clearly direct the research design in these situations.

The earliest fieldwork manual I have encountered is the French *philosophe* Degérando's (1800/1969) guide for French sailors on how to properly study the indigenous peoples they would encounter in their explorations of the South Coast of Australia (Preissle, 2004). However, what qualitative methodologists now consider classic texts are likewise concerned with *how* to study *what*. Later in the 19th century, the English sociologists Harriet Martineau (1838/1989) and Beatrice Webb (1926) documented the social lives of ordinary people in the United States and Great Britain. The Polish-American Florian Znaniecki's 1934 discussion of analytic induction focuses on discovering sociological categories and theories, as does Glaser and Strauss's 1967 qualitative text. Powdermaker (1966), Williams (1967), and Wax (1971) all offered guidelines for fieldwork directed to the anthropological study of cultures (see also Mead & Métraux, 1953/2000). Bloch's discussion (1953) of observation, composed in France under the 1940s German occupation, is qualified as historical observation and the particular problems posed for historians of observing human "tracks." During this same period, as Riessman (2008) emphasizes, what has become the qualitative research methodology of narrative analysis was being explored in language and literature studies. My point here is that the history of qualitative research is in part tied to scholars from around the world who practice specific disciplines and fields of study.

From relatively early on in the history of qualitative research methodology, however, more interdisciplinary approaches developed. One example is John Dollard's (1935) anthology of exemplary life histories with a discussion of how the life history should be developed. He draws not only from across the social sciences, but also from the humanities. Dollard, trained in sociology and cited generously in anthropology, later turned to psychology in what became a thoroughly interdisciplinary career. This contrasts with the approach taken by Gottschalk, Kluckhohn, and Angell (1945) in discussing personal documents in research; their treatment is organized by the three disciplines the three scholars represent: history, anthropology, and sociology. Some scholars have worked both within and across disciplines. The English sociologist John Madge, whose academic preparation was in architecture and economics, wrote both about interdisciplinary social science practice (1953) and about sociology as a scientific practice (1962). By the middle years of the 20th century, disciplinary and interdisciplinary treatments of observation (e.g., Adams & Preiss, 1960), interviewing (e.g., Merton, Fiske, & Kendall, 1956), case study approaches (e.g., Foreman, 1948), and fieldwork (e.g., Junker, 1960) were providing the beginning literature of what would become qualitative research methodologies. Adler and Adler (1999) discuss this diversification of participation in what they call the "ethnographers' ball," and Wolcott (2009) illustrates some of the diversification with his tree of qualitative practices (see Figure 14.2).

Threaded, with something like an occasional metallic glint, through the mid-century literature—disciplinary and interdisciplinary—were epistemological challenges to the objectivist-realist or positivist premises of most methodological scholarship. Smith (1989, 1993) and others (e.g., Heshusius & Ballard, 1996) have offered accounts of some of these challenges. Smith and Heshusius (1986) detail, for example, the disagreements among German scholars at the turn of the 20th century between the hermeneutically oriented Wilhelm Dilthey (1883/1989) and the more empirically oriented Max Weber (1903–1917/1949) about whether the physical and the social world can and ought to be studied with similar assumptions. Smith and Heshusius themselves concluded that they cannot and ought not. Phenomenology, reformulated by another German scholar, Edmund Husserl (1893–1917/1999), from earlier philosophical ideas to provide what he hoped would be a foundation for the empirical sciences, was transformed by later continental thinkers into alternatives to positivist thinking (e.g., Berger & Luckmann, 1966; Schutz, 1962) that form the roots of current-day constructionism. By the last decade of the 20th century, reflection on epistemological and ontological assumptions had become central issues in the various methodological traditions. My colleague Linda Grant and I, for example, have discussed some of the different epistemological approaches underlying observation (Preissle & Grant, 2004), and we attempted to represent this graphically (see Figure 14.3).

Having introduced the metaphor of a tapestry for qualitative methodologies, where some of the threads are metallic for philosophies and others are organic materials for methods, I turn to colors to represent purpose. Purposes are, of course, tied to both reflecting-theorizing-philosophizing and practicing-acting-doing, but purposes are also riddled with priorities and values. To weave purpose into this tapestry, I borrow Lather's 1992 framework, itself an elaboration of research purposes formulated by the German philosopher and sociologist Jürgen Habermas (1973). This borrowing of ideas to build different ideas is one of the functions of the intellectual communities of practice I am claiming here. So one purpose for (or color of) inquiry is to find out how the world works and what is going on in it. I think of it as the Pandora impetus, and it appears to be strong in the human species. People want to know, and people value knowing for its

Figure 14.2   Portraying Qualitative Research Strategies Graphically

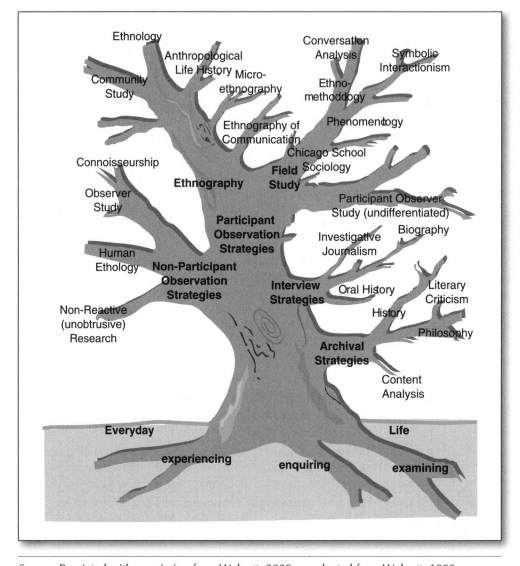

Source: Reprinted with permission from Wolcott, 2009, as adapted from Wolcott, 1992.

own sake. People pass along what they know and do not know as gossip, rumor, assertions, speculations, claims. As the Pandora myth indicates, knowledge, misinformation, and disinformation can be dangerous, but people still seek to *understand*.

Figure 14.3 Philosophies and Fieldwork Conduct

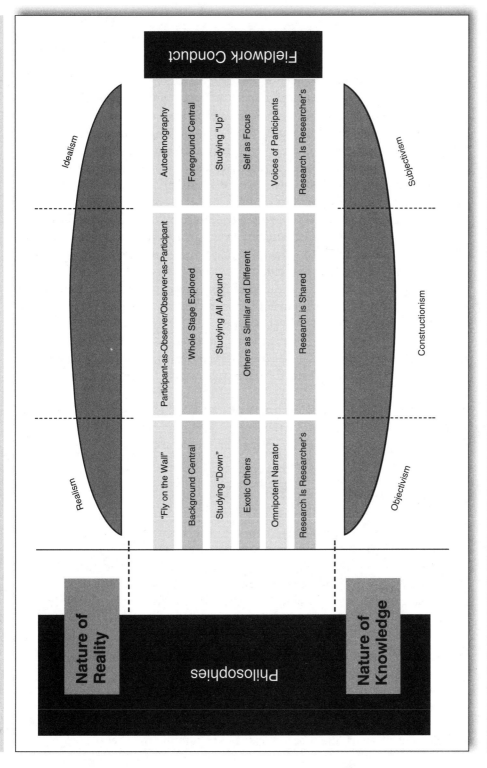

Source: Reprinted with permission from Preissle and Grant (2004).

Note: Philosophical framework adapted from Crotty, M. (1999). *The Foundations of Social Research: Meaning and Perspective in the Research Process.* London: Sage.

For some people, understanding how things are is a stepping-stone to the future, to *predicting* what is to come and to controlling how things will be. For other people, the priority is to improve human experience, to *emancipate*. Freeing people from pain, suffering, abuse, and oppression is another age-old desire, associated especially with the practice of the world religions. Secular emancipation, however, developed with modernism: Marxism, feminism, race-consciousness, and postcolonialism. Secular emancipation is grounded in assumptions about human equity, about distributions of power and resources, and about the potential for communities directed by deliberative choice rather than by traditions and ideologies. Whereas predicting and understanding have often been associated with disinterest and neutrality, emancipating is fueled by care (see, for example, He & Phillion, 2008). Care for others has been inextricably tied to qualitative research traditions, motivating, for example, Beatrice Webb's (1926) observations among the urban poor in Great Britain and Harriet Martineau's (1838/1989) investigations of 19th-century United States.

Lather (1992) extends Habermas's three categories of predicting, understanding, and emancipating to include a fourth: *deconstructing*. Deconstruction seeks "to produce an awareness of the complexity, historical contingency, and fragility of the practices we invent to discover the truth about ourselves" (p. 88). Although drawing from philosophical explorations and arguments, analysts add reflections on language and on the particularities of time and space when they deconstruct human experiences, arguments, and knowledge claims.

SUMMARY

I am combining two organizing metaphors here to represent qualitative research. One is that of a confederation. I have proposed that the various methodological approaches we call qualitative form a confederation of methods and methodologies. What does this mean? What are the constituent parts? I believe we are made up of networked communities of scholarly practice—intellectual communities. Most of us are members of several such communities, so the groups are fluid and highly permeable and they have overlapping memberships. Unlike geographically identified disciplinary groups such as the American Educational Research Association (AERA) or the Hong Kong Sociological Association, the qualitative methodology confederation is made up, for example, of focus group practitioners, field study researchers, phenomenological researchers, constructivist-constructionist scholars, and poststructural feminists. Just as important are the international composition and global context of this scholarship. We are communities because we share a scholarly practice that we communicate about with one another through books, through journal articles, among professional networks formed initially in face-to-face situations like classrooms, in subgroups at professional conventions such as the International Congresses of Qualitative Inquiry, and across the increasingly diverse venues offered by the Internet: listservs, online journals, blogs, social networking sites, and such. We meet and debate, we read and write back to one another, we engage both our deceased colleagues and those still living, and we change our practices as a result of these encounters. We learn some new ideas from an Internet discussion group, reformulate them as we talk about them to colleagues we meet face to face, try them out in publications directed to completely different audiences, and respond to challenges posted on someone's blog.

The second metaphor to represent the history of qualitative research is the tapestry of practice, frameworks, and purposes. Although some scholars work a thread or two in any particular project, most recent scholarship draws self-consciously from mixes of color, metals, and organic materials in constructing single studies and designing careers of many studies. As I talk to people whose initiation to qualitative research was a social science or the arts or practitioners' self-study, I am struck by how we all associate that initiation with normal qualitative research, with a qualitative practice somehow more authentic than what we later encounter. That is the hold of the past on us.

My goal in juxtaposing the history of qualitative research with my own scholarly history is to prompt all qualitative researchers and methodologists to reflect on our educations and developments as human beings who pursue knowledge and understanding and to connect ourselves to the communities in which we practice. Each of us entered into a world made by predecessors, but we make and remake that world as we live in/on/through it. Each individual experience is different, depending on who we are, where we have been educated, and how we have developed our practice. The particularities of time and space may make our challenges specific to now, but we continue to share facets of those challenges with those predecessors and will surely pass along similar issues to our successors. Our networked communities of practice, our global confederacy, live across time. I turn now from past to future.

Looking Into/Toward/For Qualitative Research Futures

Having discussed some varied paths scholars have taken to the qualitative, through purpose, method, and philosophy, in this section of the chapter I reflect on my own and others' projections of where these communities of qualitative practice may be going. Although many science fiction stories represent people living in a future not much differently from how they live in a present, the images I propose are less static. I believe people live *into* futures, much like falling into water. They live *toward* their futures, as if driving to destinations. Scholars especially live *for* their futures: planning, studying, and reporting in cycles intended to accumulate something they may consider knowledge or understanding. What I have borrowed here from science fiction and fantasy are the ideas of multiple, alternative futures. First, people clearly project different ideas of what is to come, even in an intersubjective world. Second, people recall different pasts and experience different presents, so even similar projections may vary significantly.

Here is an example. Some years ago, I listened to several former leaders of a large professional organization describe the current state of their field of study and project what they would like to see happen next. Some talked about the intimacy, intensity, and productivity of the organization's past. Others described the opposite experience. They talked about struggling to get their work represented in an alien and rejecting environment until more recently when the organization had become more diverse and hence more welcoming. The first group projected a future allowing them to return to their past. The second group embraced the present and projected a future allowing them to continue it. Neither group considered an inclusive future: a future welcoming a variety of activities and open even to what is not yet envisioned.

Such a future requires that scholars recognize how porous are their intellectual traditions and how much they are members of multiple, overlapping associations and traditions. I have conceptualized qualitative scholars as a confederacy, not just because I believe the metaphor fits how we are currently operating, but also because it is an image I endorse. In a recent commentary (Freeman, deMarrais, Preissle, Roulston, & St.Pierre, 2007), for example, on standards for qualitative research, my colleagues and I at the University of Georgia strongly advocated for control of standards to be as local as possible. We urged communities of practice, however they define themselves, to begin developing standards tailored to, for example, narrative analysis, social phenomenology, and poststructural feminist interviewing. Some of these will be shared across traditions because of common membership and similar approaches, but standards formulated by practicing scholars are likely to be both more applicable to what people are doing and more amenable to change as new conditions and understandings warrant.

A clear disadvantage of local determination is duplication and confusion. Common language for our practices and shared meanings for ideas may promote better understanding. Certainly a discourse available and accessible to all has its advantages, and I am not mandating a cacophony here. I have contributed to and benefited from discussions of such hegemonic terms as *validity.* I have no objection to the idea of *truth,* for example, so long as truth can be singular or plural and relative to the community practicing it. The problem is that the meaning of constructs such as validity and truth is rarely unitary. In some respects, that is why they are so powerful. Recognizing the different meanings and examining how their facets play out across situations permit flexibility, creativity, and adapting to the particulars of research situations (for an example of this, see Scriven's 1972 treatment of objectivity and subjectivity). What my colleagues and I stressed in our commentary on standards (Freeman et al., 2007) was that most methodologies from a variety of persuasions used the term validity, but their discussions of what *constitutes* validity were richly informed by scholars proposing substitute language.

A task that we as qualitative scholars have, going forward, is to propose the words and ideas we are going to draw on or draw up to communicate about our practice. What are we going to preserve and what are we going to change? This is important not only for how we communicate among ourselves, but also for how we bring in new scholars and how we reach out to the public.

I have taught qualitative research methods since 1976. Much has changed since that first class. The wealth of methodological materials and examples of qualitative research accumulated since then is remarkable. It is overwhelming. In my program, instructors take seriously a charge to introduce students to the range and variation of qualitative research practices. We may teach our own specialties more confidently, but we are committed to representing respectfully others' traditions. This is a challenge, and some students resist. These students often begin knowing what they want to learn, and it is *not* everything.

We also teach research design informed by theory and epistemology. Intellectual meltdowns by the end of the first month of the first course are common among our students. They press us for singular language, and we resist. Our intention is partly to represent what we know to be the diverse and confusing history of qualitative methodologies; just as important is that these students are the future. To produce and to respond to what is to come, they need as much of the qualitative resources provided by others as we can manage. Many of them develop innovations that surprise their teachers, as I discuss subsequently.

Some of what is to come we can anticipate and plan for, but much of it is neither controllable nor foreseeable. For example, growing up in the 1950s, my parents worried about the effect of the growing popularity of television on the newspapers they read avidly. What actually developed was a more symbiotic relationship where newspapers and television news complemented each other

(Heflin, in press). Who knew then that the actual threat to newspapers would be a technology developed by the military called the Internet (Jones, 2009)?

Another unexpected development is the result of the obesity epidemic in youth. People who grew up in the United States and other western nations in the 20th century have benefitted from improved public health and medical treatment, being assured by health experts that they would live healthier and longer lives than their parents and grandparents. However, such adults alive today may be the last group to enjoy this privilege because of the increased health risks associated with obesity in youth (Olshansky et al., 2005). Although the individual consequences of excess weight have been recognized for many years, many people are shocked to learn that their children may be denied their own longevity. What does this have to do with the future of qualitative research? It is a caution, I believe. At one time, the worry was that the world's food supply would not support the world's population. Agricultural technologies have been used to address that issue, but now the world is faced with two challenges. One is the distribution problem of some people getting too much food and others getting too little. The other is the quality problem of inadequate nutrition and overloads of sugars, fats, and such.

Likewise, throughout most of human history, information and knowledge have been limited. The recent intensification of globalization and other developments have produced what can only be considered a glut of information and knowledge. In the past, people lacked the information necessary to understand one another. In the 21st century, many people are inundated by information, but its quality and distribution, like that of food, are uneven. Misinformation and disinformation circulate as rapidly as reliable information and well-vetted knowledge. Some people have the challenge of too much information, while others are deprived of what they need to know to survive: locations of bombs from wars long over, safe routes home during heavy rains, and so forth. Qualitative scholars rarely begin research with no knowledge or information about what they want to study. The mass media, the Internet, and university libraries and archives provide so much relevant material that the task becomes how to handle it: What is pertinent and what is not? What sources are dependable and which are not? When should we stop browsing the literature and start getting our own data? *When* should we seek *what* information? Does beginning with no review of the literature really prevent biases? Glaser and Strauss (1967), contrary to what is attributed to them, did not prescribe reviewing literature after data gathering; they said only that scholars should think about and weigh the consequences of when literature is to be reviewed (p. 253).

Most, but not all, qualitative research scholars have ready and plentiful access to producing, distributing, and applying knowledge, but these privileges are not universal. As I have suggested, many people lack such access, and this constitutes an ethical challenge to be addressed into the future. However, the democratization of higher education, the increasing participation of professionals in studying and evaluating their own situations, and the social networking and information-sharing software that permits people to make their private lives public—a kind of exhibitionism referred to as *celebritizing*—all function to widen access. In a previous consideration of the future, for example, I speculated about whether increasing numbers of people will become researchers of their own lives, activities, and experiences (Preissle, 1999). As insiders to our own organizations, activities, and communities, how will we address the ethics of exposing others as we expose ourselves? Likewise, how may this break down the boundaries between the ivory tower of academia and the so-called real world if everyone can learn and practice the creation of knowledge? On the one hand, people gain access to what has been the domain of the experts, and they can make the knowledge they want and believe to be useful. On the other hand, what is produced or learned may be of uneven quality and may serve questionable purposes. Already the hegemony of government-supported research (Lather, 2010) has been challenged by funds for research provided by philanthropic foundations, by nongovernmental organizations, and by a variety of special interest groups (e.g., deMarrais, 2006).

Qualitative scholars of all varieties and housed both inside and outside academia are challenged and pressed by technological developments, such as those I have just described, that permit a constant data stream documenting people's lives. On the one hand, the ease and accessibility of audio and video recording devices and the simplicity of reproducing and storing the records may seem like a qualitative dream come true. On the other hand, ordinary people may have means to create their own ethnographies if they can learn to document and interpret their own lives and distribute those accounts on Internet sites like YouTube. Alternatively, ordinary people may be even more reluctant to want their privacy threatened by such records. For example, the local school district where my university is located had for several years a ban on video recording for research purposes because of the threat to student privacy. However, presuming we have willing participants and no such restrictions, our recording technology presents other issues such as how to use the material ethically, how to analyze mountains of audio and video files, and how to interpret the recorded life.

In another example of a technological challenge, for many years now, people new to qualitative inquiry have posed the same question on QUALRS-L, the list-serv discussion group on qualitative research that I founded in 1991. They want to know what technology will automatically transcribe their audio files so that they do not have to suffer the tedium of manual transcription or the cost of hiring it out. The answer to that question has not changed in 10 years. Transcription software must be trained to particular voices, cannot easily handle records with two and more voices, and must be carefully vetted for inevitable inaccuracies. Furthermore, the better the software, the more expensive it is. I believe these answers are changing, but I am myself surprised that this is taking so long.

What has surprised me even more has been a proposal by a former student (Markle, 2008) to give up transcription altogether for what he proposes is an analysis of the audio record that is much closer to the interview experience. Using software developed for music editing, Markle shows how to generate an analysis in text that accompanies the audio record. I think of the audio file sound as the music and the analysis as lyrics, but the lyrics are an analysis of the spoken language, and they are layered so that any segment of conversation may have multiple lyrics that comment on the talk. Markle argues that the digital sound file is a more accurate and complete record of what was said than any written transcription can provide and that transcription is unnecessarily time consuming. Furthermore, the music editing software permits scholars to embed portions of an audio or video record right into research manuscripts. Voices of participants would be heard rather than just read. Markle notes that transparency, for those who value it, is improved because data are closer to what the researcher experienced.

Another surprise I have experienced recently is how novice scholars are challenging, even transgressing, epistemological and theoretical boundaries. Most methodologists have little difficulty with the idea of mixing methods of data selection, collection, and analysis, and the recent reinvigoration of mixed methodology is a testament to this acceptance (Greene, 2007). In their classic formulation of research epistemologies, for example, Guba and Lincoln (1994) say, "both qualitative and quantitative methods may be used appropriately with any research paradigm" (p. 105), but caution that "a resolution of paradigm differences can occur only when a new paradigm emerges that is more informed and sophisticated than any existing one" (p. 116). As I have noted previously, however, others argue for a more-or-less complete incommensurability among paradigms. My own position is far less doctrinaire. I have even been accused by some of philosophical schizophrenia. Research approaches are mental models that we formulate for our study of the world. Although I value coherence, consistency, and other such elements under some circumstances, I also believe that innovation and creative problem solving often mean finding ways of putting things together that convention has separated.

One such example comes from another student in the program where I teach. Van Cleave (2008) positions herself as a post-humanist scholar who deconstructs how qualitative interviewing is commonly presented in a variety of introductory texts. She cites many of the questionable assumptions about shared interviewer–respondent meanings and intentions so brilliantly criticized by Scheurich (1997). Then she makes the audacious move of applying Schacter's (2001) cognitive and neuroimaging research on memory, especially what he calls false memory, to raise additional crucial questions about the content of what people report in interviews. She uses clearly postpositivist research work to support her posthumanist claims about how we ought to make sense of interview data. Van Cleave affirms the value of the interview while she insists on reinterpreting what the content might mean: Interviews ought not to be considered true representations of human experience, but rather representations of human sense making.

Another such paradigm-challenging study, by my colleague Chávez (2004), combined analyses of molecular genetics and brain functioning, psychometrics, and phenomenological interviewing to establish links among genetic profiles, neurological activity, and creativity. Now practicing psychotherapy in the United States, Chávez is a Mexican psychiatrist who studied 40 well-known scholars and artists, 30 psychiatric outpatients, and 30 healthy but not famous individuals to demonstrate consistent associations among these three elements. Chávez, an accomplished pianist and poet, brings an eclectic stance to the humanities, the sciences, and the human study she pursues. She and many of her generation of scholars appear little affected by "the repeated, and indeed long-standing, tensions between scientific and interpretive inquiry, between realist and experimental texts, between [the] impersonal and experiential" (P. Atkinson, Coffey, & Delamont, 1999, p. 470). Behar's (1999) observation that "ethnography is reinvented with every journey" (p. 477) projects a future in which research itself may be reconceptualized with every endeavor. Reconceptualization occurs for method, for design, for methodology, for theory, and for philosophy. St.Pierre (2010), for example, is challenging the construct of qualitative itself in her projections for a post-qualitative scholarship.

Conclusion

Our futures are *serial.* They are composed of events particular to each of us in the coming years, decades, and centuries. Denzin and Lincoln's formulation of change over time in qualitative research is an example of chronological history moving into a serial future: sequential moments. These are "the traditional (1900–1950); the modernist or golden age (1950–1970); blurred genres (1970–1986); the crisis of representation (1986–1990); the postmodern, a period of experimental and new ethnographies (1990–1995); [and] postexperimental inquiry (1995–2000)" (2000, p. 2). These six were succeeded by "the methodo-logically contested [seventh moment] (2000–2004) . . . of conflict, great tension, and, in some quarters, retrenchment [and] . . . the eighth moment (2005–) . . . confront-ing the methodological backlash associated with 'Bush science' and the evidence-based social movement" (2005, p. 20). Denzin and Lincoln emphasize differences in their formulation. When Margaret Mead (1962) cautioned that adults are always immigrants to the present, she too was emphasizing the differences between what we have become accustomed to and what we must now and in the future adjust to. Mead's is also a serial understanding of time.

Hammersley (1999) objects to this serial analysis. He disagrees with the time divisions, seeing similarities rather than differences between some periods, and he posits our futures as *recurrent* rather than serial, worrying that the dogma of positivism has been replaced with new dogmas. Others may view the evidence-based eighth moment as another recurrence, an attempt to return to the mod-ernist or golden age, when the federal government funded large scientific projects to solve poverty, racism, and educational inequities. However, different views of time and the future illuminate different understandings of human experiences. Recurrent conceptualizations of time have their own issues:

> All the turning that has been done over the past thirty years—the interpre-tive turn, the linguistic turn, the constructionist turn, the rhetorical turn, the narrative turn. Indeed, all this turning makes a person dizzy. . . . But isn't life itself uncertain, contingent, and paradoxical? Aren't human beings steeped in ambiguity and contradiction? (Bochner & Ellis, 1999, p. 488)

What are the alternatives to viewing the future through serial, recurrent, or chaotic prisms? My preference is to incorporate them all into *recursive* visions of what is to come that concede the unexpected but recognize both what is new and what is the same old experience. We plan for a future that is somewhat recogniz-able. We plan for a future we want to make more just, more free, more secure than our presents and pasts. We prepare our students for the varieties of prac-tices called qualitative methodologies while urging them to think and do beyond these practices.

Note

1. Judith Preissle has also published as Judith Preissle Kasper and Judith Preissle Goetz.

References

Adams, R. N., & Preiss, J. J. (Eds.). (1960). *Human organization research: Field relations and techniques.* Homewood, IL: Dorsey Press and the Society for Applied Anthropology.

Adler, P. A., & Adler, P. (1999). The ethnographer's ball—revisited. *Journal of Contemporary Ethnography, 28*(5), 442–450.

Archambault, R. D. (1963). Introduction. In R. D. Archambault (Ed.), *John Dewey on education: Selected writings* (pp. xiii–xxx). New York: Modern Library.

Atkinson, P., Coffey, A., & Delamont, S. (1999). Ethnography: Post, past, and present. *Journal of Contemporary Ethnography, 28*(5), 460–471.

Atkinson, R. (1998). *The life story interview.* Thousand Oaks, CA: Sage.

Behar, R. (1999). Ethnography: Cherishing our second-fiddle game. *Journal of Contemporary Ethnography, 28*(5), 472–484.

Berger, P. L., & Luckmann, T. (1966). *The social construction of reality: A treatise in the sociology of knowledge.* Garden City, NY: Doubleday.

Bertaux, D. (Ed.). (1981). *Biography and society: The life history approach in the social sciences.* Beverly Hills, CA: Sage.

Bloch, M. (1953). *The historian's craft.* New York: Random House.

Bochner, A. P., & Ellis, C. S. (1999). Which way to turn? *Journal of Contemporary Ethnography, 28*(5), 485–499.

Burnett, J. (1973). Event description and analysis in the microethnography of urban classrooms. In F. A. J. Ianni & E. Storey (Eds.), *Cultural relevance and educational issues* (pp. 287–303). Boston: Little, Brown.

Chávez, R. A. (2004). *Evaluación integral de la personalidad creativa: Fenomenología, clínica y genética (Integral evaluation of the creative personality: Phenomenology, clinic and genetics).* Unpublished doctoral dissertation, Facultad de Medicina, National Autonomous University of Mexico UNAM, Mexico City.

Degérando, J.-M. (1969). *The observation of savage peoples* (F. C. T. Moore, Ed. & Trans.). Berkeley: University of California Press. (Original work published 1800)

deMarrais, K. (2006). The haves and the have mores: Fueling a conservative ideological war on public education. *Educational Studies, 39*(3), 203–242.

Denzin, N. K., & Lincoln, Y. S. (1994). Introduction: Entering the field of qualitative research. In N. K. Denzin & Y. S. Lincoln (Eds.), *Handbook of qualitative research* (pp. 1–17). Thousand Oaks, CA: Sage.

Denzin, N. K., & Lincoln, Y. S. (2000). Introduction: The discipline and practice of qualitative research. In N. K. Denzin & Y. S. Lincoln (Eds.), *Handbook of qualitative research* (2nd ed., pp. 1–28). Thousand Oaks, CA: Sage.

Denzin, N. K., & Lincoln, Y. S. (2005). Introduction: The discipline and practice of qualitative research. In N. K. Denzin & Y. S. Lincoln (Eds.), *The SAGE handbook of qualitative research* (3rd ed., pp. 1–32). Thousand Oaks, CA: Sage.

Dilthey, W. (1989). *Introduction to the human sciences* (R. A. Makkreel & F. Rodi, Eds.). Princeton, NJ: Princeton University Press. (Original work published 1883)

Dollard, J. (1935). *Criteria for the life history, with analyses of six notable documents.* Freeport, NY: Books for Libraries Press.

Ellis, C. (2009). *Revision: Autoethnographic reflections on life and work.* Walnut Creek, CA: Left Coast Press.

Foreman, P. B. (1948). The theory of case studies. *Social Forces, 26*(4), 408–419.

Freeman, M., deMarrais, K. D., Preissle, J., Roulston, K, & St.Pierre, E. A. (2007). Standards of evidence in qualitative research: An incitement to discourse. *Educational Researcher, 36*(1), 25–32.

Glaser, B. G., & Strauss, A. L. (1967). *The discovery of grounded theory: Strategies for qualitative research.* Chicago: Aldine.

Goetz, J. P. (1975). *Configurations in control and autonomy: A microethnography of a rural third-grade classroom.* Unpublished doctoral dissertation, Indiana University, Bloomington.

Goetz, J. P., & LeCompte, M. D. (1984). *Ethnography and qualitative design in educational research.* New York: Academic Press.

Goetz, J. P., & LeCompte, M. D. (1988). *Etnografia y diseno cualitativo en investigacion educative* (A. Ballesteros, Trans.). Madrid, Spain: Morata.

Goodson, I., & Sikes, P. (2001). *Life history research in educational settings: Learning from lives.* Buckingham, UK: Open University Press.

Goodson, I., & Walker, R. (1991). *Biography, identity and schooling: Episodes in educational research.* London: Falmer Press.

Gottschalk, L., Kluckhohn, C., & Angell, R. (1945). *The use of personal documents in history, anthropology, and sociology.* New York: Social Science Research Council.

Greene, J. C. (2007). *Mixed methods in social inquiry.* San Francisco: Jossey-Bass.

Guba, E. G., & Lincoln, Y. S. (1994). Competing paradigms in qualitative research. In N. K. Denzin & Y. S. Lincoln (Eds.), *Handbook of qualitative research* (pp. 105–117). Thousand Oaks, CA: Sage.

Habermas, J. (1973). *Theory and practice* (J. Viertel, Trans.). Boston: Beacon Press.

Hammersley, M. (1999). Not bricolage but boatbuilding: Exploring two metaphors for thinking about ethnography. *Journal of Contemporary Ethnography, 28*(5), 574–585.

Hansen, J. F. (1979). *Sociocultural perspectives on human learning: An introduction to educational anthropology.* Englewood Cliffs, NJ: Prentice Hall.

Hatch, J. A., & Wisniewski, R. (Eds.). (1995). *Life history and narrative.* London: Falmer Press.

He, M. F., & Phillion, J. A. (2008). *Personal-passionate-participatory inquiry into social justice in education.* Charlotte, NC: IAP.

Heflin, K. (in press). The future will be televised: Newspaper industry voices and the rise of television news. *American Journalism.*

Heshusius, L., & Ballard, K. (Eds.). (1996). *From positivism to interpretivism and beyond: Tales of transformation in educational and social research (the mind–body connection).* New York: Teachers College Press.

chman, L. P., & Hinchman, S. K. (Eds.). (1997). *Memory, identity, community: The idea of narrative in the human sciences.* Albany: State University of New York Press.

Husserl, E. (1999). *The essential Husserl: Basic writings in transcendental phenomenology* (D. Welton, Ed.). Bloomington: Indiana University Press. (Original work published 1893–1917)

Jones, A. S. (2009). *Losing the news: The future of the news that feeds democracy.* New York: Oxford University Press.

Josselson, R., & Lieblich, A. (Eds.). (1993). *The narrative study of lives.* Newbury Park, CA: Sage.

Junker, B. H. (1960). *Field work: An introduction to the social sciences.* Chicago: University of Chicago Press.

Kessler, S., Ashendon, D., O'Connell, R. W., & Dowsett, G. W. (1985). Gender relations in secondary schooling. *Sociology of Education, 58*(1), 34–48.

Kridel, C. (1998). *Writing educational biography: Explorations in qualitative research.* New York: Garland.

Langness, L. L., & Frank, G. (1981). *Lives: An anthropological approach to biography.* Novato, CA: Chandler & Sharp.

Lather, P. (1992). Critical frames in educational research: Feminist and post-structural perspectives. *Theory Into Practice, 31*(2), 87–99.

Lather, P. (2010). *Engaging science policy: From the side of the messy.* New York: Peter Lang.

LeCompte, M. D., & Preissle, J. (1992). Toward an ethnology of student life in schools and classrooms: Synthesizing the qualitative research tradition. In M. D. LeCompte, W. L. Millroy, & J. Preissle (Eds.), *The handbook of qualitative research in education* (pp. 815–859). New York: Academic Press.

LeCompte, M. D., & Preissle, J. (1993). *Ethnography and qualitative design in educational research* (2nd ed.). New York: Academic Press.

Lortie, D. C. (1975). *Schoolteacher: A sociological study.* Chicago: University of Chicago Press.

Loseke, D. R., & Cahill, S. E. (1999a). Ethnography: Reflections at the millennium's turn—Part 1 [Special issue]. *Journal of Contemporary Ethnography, 28*(5), 437–585.

Loseke, D. R., & Cahill, S. E. (1999b). Ethnography: Reflections at the millennium's turn—Part 2 [Special issue]. *Journal of Contemporary Ethnography, 28*(6), 597–723.

Madge, J. (1953). *The tools of social science.* London: Longmans, Green.

Madge, J. (1962). *The origins of scientific sociology.* New York: Free Press of Glencoe.

Malinowski, B. (1989). *A diary in the strict sense of the term.* Palo Alto, CA: Stanford University Press. (Original work published 1967)

Markle, D. T. (2008). *Beyond transcription: Promoting alternative qualitative data analysis.* Paper presented at the 2008 SQUIG Conference in Qualitative Research, Athens, GA.

Martineau, H. (1989). *How to observe morals and manners.* New Brunswick, NJ: Transaction. (Original work published 1838)

Mead, M. (1962). *Coming of age in America* [Audiotape]. Guilford, CT: Audio-Forum Sound Seminars.

Mead, M. (1972). *Blackberry winter: My earlier years.* New York: Simon & Schuster.

Mead, M., & Métraux, R. (Eds.). (2000). *The study of culture at a distance.* New York: Berghahn Books. (Original work published 1953)

Merton, R. K., Fiske, M., & Kendall, P. L. (1956). *The focused interview: A manual of problems and procedures.* Glencoe, IL: Free Press.

Nieuwenhuys, O. (1994). *Children's lifeworlds: Gender, welfare and labour in the developing world.* London: Routledge.

Okely, J., & Callaway, H. (Eds.). (1992). *Anthropology and autobiography. Association of Social Anthropologists Monograph 29.* London: Routledge.

Olshansky, S. J., et al. (2005). A potential decline in life expectancy in the United States in the 21st century. *New England Journal of Medicine, 352*(11), 1138–1145.

Polkinghorne, D. E. (1988). *Narrative knowing and the human sciences.* Albany: State University of New York Press.

Powdermaker, H. (1966). *Stranger and friend: The way of an anthropologist.* New York: W. W. Norton.

Preissle, J. (1999). An educational ethnographer comes of age. *Journal of Contemporary Ethnography, 28*(6), 650–659.

Preissle, J. (2004, April). *A rhizomposium on neglected figures in qualitative research: Joseph-Marie de Gérando.* Roundtable paper presented at the meeting of the American Educational Research Association, San Diego.

Preissle, J. (2006). Envisioning qualitative inquiry: A view across four decades. *International Journal of Qualitative Research in Education, 19*(6), 685–695.

Preissle, J., & Grant, L. (2004). Fieldwork traditions: Ethnography and participant observation. In K. B. deMarrais & S. D. Lapan (Eds.), *Foundations for research: Methods of inquiry in education and the social sciences* (pp. 161–180). Mahwah, NJ: Lawrence Erlbaum.

Reed-Danahay, D. E. (Ed.). (1997). *Auto/ethnography: Rewriting the self and the social.* Oxford, UK: Berg.

Reinharz, S. (1984). *On becoming a social scientist: From survey research and participant observation to experiential analysis.* New Brunswick, NJ: Transaction. (Original work published 1979)

Richardson, L. (1997). *Fields of play: Constructing an academic life.* New Brunswick, NJ: Rutgers University Press.

Riessman, C. K. (2008). *Narrative methods for the human sciences.* Thousand Oaks, CA: Sage.

Schacter, D. (2001). *The seven sins of memory: How the mind forgets and remembers.* Boston: Houghton Mifflin.

Scheurich, J. J. (1997). *Research method in the postmodern.* London: Falmer Press.

Schutz, A. (1962). *Collected papers 1: The problem of social reality.* (M. Natanson & H. L. van Breda, Eds.). The Hague, The Netherlands: Martinus Nijhoff.

Scriven, M. (1972). Objectivity and subjectivity in educational research. In Lawrence G. Thomas (Ed.), *Philosophical redirection of educational research* (pp. 94–142). Chicago: National Society for the Study of Education.

Smith, J. K. (1989). *The nature of social and educational inquiry: Empiricism versus interpretation.* Norwood, NJ: Ablex.

Smith, J. K. (1993). *After the demise of empiricism: The problem of judging social and educational inquiry.* Norwood, NJ: Ablex.

Smith, J. K., & Heshusius, L. (1986). Closing down the conversation: The end of the quantitative–qualitative debate among educational inquirers. *Educational Researcher, 15*(1), 4–25.

St.Pierre, E. A. (2010, May 29). *Resisting the subject of qualitative inquiry.* Paper presented at the Sixth International Congress of Qualitative Inquiry, University of Illinois, Urbana-Champaign.

Van Cleave, J. (2008). *Deconstructing the conventional qualitative interview.* Paper presented at the 2008 SQUIG Conference in Qualitative Research, Athens, GA.

Wax, R. H. (1971). *Doing fieldwork: Warnings and advice.* Chicago: University of Chicago Press.

Webb, B. (1926). *My apprenticeship* (Vols. 1 & 2). London: Longmans, Green.

Weber, M. (1949). *The methodology of the social sciences.* New York: Free Press. (Original work published 1903–1917)

Williams, T. R. (1967). *Field methods in the study of culture.* New York: Holt, Rinehart & Winston.

Willis, P. E. (1977). *Learning to labour: How working class kids get working class jobs.* Farnborough, UK: Saxon House.

Wolcott, H. F. (1992). Posturing in qualitative research. In M. D. LeCompte, W. L. Millroy, & J. Preissle (Eds.), *The handbook of qualitative research in education* (pp. 3–52). New York: Academic Press.

Wolcott, H. F. (2009). *Writing up qualitative research* (3rd ed.). Thousand Oaks, CA: Sage.

Znaniecki, F. (1934). *The method of sociology.* New York: Farrar & Rinehart.

15

Teaching Qualitative Research

Margaret Eisenhart and A. Susan Jurow

All programs to develop qualitative researchers must grapple with at least seven key questions: What should students be taught about qualitative research? Should explicit instruction in research methods be required? How much of the program should be devoted to methods versus foundational or topic-specific coursework? Should prospective researchers be prepared in one method or several? How should research ethics be covered? How should research competence be assessed? And, how can the curricular goals, whatever they are, be designed into instruction? (See Page, 2001, and Preissle & Roulston, 2009, for some additional questions.)

Answering these questions can be daunting. Qualitative research communities, whether they be sociologists, anthropologists, educational researchers, psychologists, nurses, or others, do not agree on research priorities. Scattered around the world, they do not face the same research problems or questions about their work. Whether they be discipline-, field-, or practice-based, qualitative researchers do not share one approach. Instructors have different areas of expertise, and understandably, they want to teach in ways consistent with their expertise. Yet at least in compulsory research courses, they have a responsibility to prepare students to conduct research on a range of topics, use various research designs, and work with diverse groups. Further, there is always a limited amount of time for courses in a degree program, even less for so-called "methods" courses, and all course activities have to fit, at least generally, the requirements of university schedules and rules. The proverbial pedagogical question can be a harsh master: What is a qualitative research instructor to do on Monday morning? Surprisingly few qualitative researchers have written in any detail about the teaching decisions they make.

In this article, we first present an overview of the literature that bears on teaching qualitative research. Then, we describe in some detail the pedagogical approach we (Eisenhart and Jurow) took to teaching a two-course introduction to qualitative research required of all entering doctoral students in the School of Education at the University of Colorado, Boulder. In the final section, we reflect on what we have achieved and not achieved in our teaching and suggest some directions for future reflections on and studies of teaching qualitative research.

Literature on Teaching Qualitative Research

The literature on qualitative research focuses mainly on how to do research. Numerous books and articles cover processes and procedures for conducting qualitative research. They range from compendia of different traditions, approaches, and techniques (e.g., Creswell, 2002; Denzin & Lincoln, 1994, 2000, 2005; Green, Camilli, & Elmore, 2006; LeCompte, Millroy, & Preissle, 1992; Schensul & LeCompte, 1999); to extended discussions of a single approach, such as grounded theory (Charmaz, 2006; Glaser & Strauss, 1967), ethnography (Agar, 1996; Hammersley & Atkinson, 1995; Wolcott, 2009), qualitative evaluation (Patton, 2002), or participatory action research (McIntyre, 2008); to guides to specialized techniques, such as ethnographic interviewing and participation observation (Spradley, 1979, 1980), discourse analysis (Phillips & Hardy, 2002), qualitative media analysis (Altheide, 1996), interpretive policy analysis (Yanow, 2000), and systematic self-observation (Rodriguez & Ryave, 2002). Others have focused on particular phases of research practice, e.g., Wolcott on analysis and interpretation (1994) and writing up qualitative materials (2008) and Miles and Huberman on data management and analysis (1994). A few have written from the perspective of novices (or students) as they struggled to learn how to do qualitative research (Heath & Street, 2008; Lareau & Shultz, 1996), and a few others, about the relationships that form between qualitative novice and more experienced mentor (Lee & Roth, 2003; Minichiello & Kottler, 2009). Certainly this body of literature, even more extensive than listed here, serves as a basis for what is taught (and the variety of what is taught) as qualitative research, but it rarely focuses on pedagogical approaches or strategies themselves.

Two recent publications, Hurworth's *Teaching Qualitative Research* (2008) and Garner, Wagner, and Kawulich's *Teaching Research Methods in the Social Sciences*

(2009), directly address this lack of attention to pedagogy. Finding little guidance in the literature to answer her questions about how to teach qualitative research, Hurworth conducted case studies in qualitative research classes in seven Australian and English universities. Garner et al., concerned about the lack of information about how to teach both qualitative and quantitative research methods, compiled articles from researchers around the world in hopes of stimulating the development of a "pedagogical culture in research methods education." In both cases, the authors were shocked at how little has been written on this topic.

Not surprisingly, what literature there is on teaching qualitative research reflects the divide that has fractured the qualitative research community since the 1980s—the divide between those who take a more conventional social science view of methods and concentrate (at least in what they write about teaching) on research designs (case study, ethnography, narrative research, etc.) and techniques (participant observation, open-ended interviewing, etc.) and those who take a more critical or "avant garde" view and concentrate on epistemological and ontological principles.

Phillips (2006) caricatures this divide as two poles of a continuum—a right pole and a left pole. In Phillips's view, researchers at the right pole want to do "rigorous" qualitative research—research that is systematic and accessible to scrutiny by others, and they believe that such research can be done. This pole has also been referred to as "conventional social science," "Old Guard," "modernist," and "scientific." At this end of the continuum, clearly specified, transparent "methods" are what are critically important. This is "qi" in small letters (as labeled by the left pole)—where the focus is on methods per se, almost always multiple methods, for gathering and analyzing or interpreting qualitative data that can serve as evidence for warranted knowledge claims.

The left pole views all research as inherently subjective; therefore, it cannot be and should not try to be systematic and transparent in the style of conventional social science. The point of qualitative research is to lead readers or listeners to understand their taken-for-granted worlds in a new light that is generally sympathetic to the plight of nondominant groups and critical of dominant forms of privileging. In consequence, the left pole is highly skeptical of conventional ways of doing, talking, and thinking, including the conventional ways of doing research. This pole is also referred to as "nonscientific," "postmodern," "discursive" (where different discourses are put into conversation with each other, e.g., a dominant and nondominant one), the "linguistic turn in social science" (where texts, rather than actions, are the object of study), or a "moral discourse" (where morality-in-context is stressed, and universal morality is usually denied). At this end of the continuum, what's important is the force with which a researcher confronts or undermines the taken-for-granted and the status quo. This is "QI" in capital letters (again, as labeled by the left pole), where the focus is on making a statement, telling a story, initiating an action, or catalyzing a movement that promotes "social justice" by putting diverse voices in "conversation" with each other. This position implies at least a different *use* of methods and the materials ("data") derived from them, if not new methods themselves.

TEACHING TOWARD THE RIGHT POLE

Qualitative research instructors who lean toward the right pole tend to write about ways to teach conventional qualitative methods and conventional social science habits of mind.[1] Prior to 1990, most qualitative research instructors leaned in this direction. In 1992, Webb and Glesne published results of interviews and questionnaires from 75 qualitative research instructors and reviews of 55 course syllabi from colleges and schools of education in the United States. They reported that most instructors aimed to develop an appreciation for social science theories and an understanding of how qualitative methods have been used in conventional social science. Common methodological issues addressed were finding a site, identifying appropriate research questions, taking fieldnotes and conducting an interview, keeping a research journal, doing data analysis, coding, finding patterns or themes, and writing a research report.

Keen (1996), for example, recommended an approach outlined by sociologists Lofland and Lofland (1995):

[We] outline a constellation of "thinking topics" that enable students to focus on patterns of social interaction and social organization in the setting. These topics are a set of conceptual categories that identify a series of units of analysis, beginning with the micro and moving progressively toward the macro. They include practices, episodes, encounters, roles, relationships, groups, organizations, social worlds, and lifestyles or subcultures. With the thinking topics in hand, students can begin to transform themselves from general spectators into theoretical observers and can identify a variety of practices, roles, relationships, groups . . . in the setting. . . . To further facilitate the development of analysis, we also introduce coding. . . . We discuss how to use the thinking topics we've identified as coding labels to create a coding scheme, which is to be used in organizing and sorting the data (Lofland and Lofland, 1995, 186–193). . . . To lay the final foundations for our theory construction, and to further focus the gathering of data, the last two weeks of participant observation are accompanied by investigating the relationships between the various units of analysis we've identified through asking questions of the data. To facilitate this process, [we] present eight basic questions for social analysis of the thinking topics: type, frequency, magnitude, structure, process, cause, consequence, and agency of the participants involved (1995, 123–148). (as quoted in Keen, 1996, pp. 170–171)

In 2008, Hurworth, troubled by still-limited information about teaching qualitative research, reviewed what she could find (see her Chapter 2 for a useful review and her Chapter 12 for a list of resources) and then conducted her own intensive case studies of seven qualitative research courses at Australian and English universities. One of her major findings from the literature is that while authors often list what they include in their courses (finding a site, identifying research questions, etc.), they almost never discuss their curriculum design or pedagogical decisions (Keen was apparently an exception). She writes,

Often authors just list what they include [in their courses].... [T]here is little indication of how [they] have made or evaluated their choices. It has been a matter of "This is what I do." Therefore, any curriculum issue tends to be trivialised or glossed over. For example, when questioned about how he devised his course, [one author] just said somewhat naively: "The topics I teach are similar to those in any qualitative or field methods course." (p. 159)

From her observations of the seven courses, Hurworth (2008) found six topics commonly included in the curriculum (although to varying degrees): examinations of particular qualitative methodologies (ethnography, case study, etc.), discussions of paradigm differences (positivist, interpretivist, etc.), components of research design and a research proposal, participant observation, interviewing, and fieldwork practices (gaining rapport and entry, etc.). Other topics, including document analysis, data analysis, credibility and rigor, ethics, history of qualitative research, writing about results, and the use of qualitative methods in multiple methods designs, were covered in some but not all of the courses and usually received rushed and minimal attention at the end of the course.

One clear finding from both reviews and surveys (Webb & Glesne [1992] and Hurworth [2008], spanning 1990–2007) is the common use of a research project as a frame for teaching qualitative research. Webb and Glesne found that 39 of the 55 syllabi they collected required a major piece of qualitative research and

6 more required mini-projects. They suggest that doing a research project leads students to important insights about qualitative research:

> The act of doing qualitative research forces most students to question their own assumptions. Observing and interviewing puts students in close contact with the experiences of others. They soon learn that the research methods serve as guides for intelligence, not as a technical substitute for thought. The act of data analysis rids most students of the naïve assumption that the data will somehow speak for themselves and that researchers can avoid interpreting what they have seen and heard. (pp. 776–777)

Hurworth also found that in most courses students are expected to conduct some kind of research project, and the project counted for 50–75% of the course grade.

In fact, the student research project seems to have become a "signature pedagogy" of qualitative research courses. This term was coined by Shulman (2005) to describe characteristic

> types of teaching that organize the fundamental ways in which future practitioners are educated for their new professions. In these signature pedagogies, the novices are instructed in critical aspects of the three fundamental dimensions of professional work—to *think*, to *perform*, and to *act with integrity*." (p. 52, italics original)

Examples of signature pedagogies include the case dialogue method of teaching in law schools, bedside teaching on daily clinical rounds in medical education, and—we would add—the small-scale research project in qualitative research education.

Others have noted the pedagogical advantages of having students conduct qualitative research projects. Preissle and Roulston (2009) write that "practical engagement in field-related exercises and authentic research activities is integral" to qualitative research courses (p. 16). Strayhorn (2009) suggests that engaging students in authentic research activities is the most appropriate pedagogy for developing higher-order cognitive skills such as application of concepts and strategies to new situations, analysis, synthesis, and evaluation. In fact,

> [A] consensus has emerged that qualitative methods are best taught through "hands-on practice" (Blank 2004), "active learning techniques" (Crull and Collins 2004), "real-world" research (Potter, Caffrey, and Plante

2003), or "learning-by-doing" (Rifkin and Hartley 2001). Evidence specific to teaching qualitative methods shows that experiential pedagogies enhance students' enjoyment of learning (Rohall, Moran, Brown and Caffrey 2004); heighten students' awareness of the complexity of research choices and the philosophies that inform them (Hopkinson and Hogg 2004); impress on students that qualitative research is a process shaped by the particular social context in which it unfolds (Winn 1995); impart to students specific skills such as in-depth interviewing (Roulston, deMarrais, and Lewis 2003); give students confidence in applying qualitative research techniques (Walsh 2003); and help students appreciate the value of qualitative research (Rifkin and Hartley 2001). (Raddon, Nault, & Scott, 2007, n.p.)

TEACHING TOWARD THE LEFT POLE

Those who lean toward the left pole tend to stress teaching about critical or postmodern epistemological principles and habits of mind. These discussions center on beliefs, values, and ethics rather than research design or techniques. Lather (2006),[2] for example, argues that teachers of research should concentrate on the "politics of knowing and being known" and the "logics of inquiry and philosophies and histories of knowledge" (p. 47). She offers a pedagogical approach that challenges conventional assumptions about the world and how researchers can know it. Her approach focuses on five *aphorias* (impasses or complications) that expose students to the messiness, inconclusiveness, and partiality of current research practice: aphorias of objectivity (How can any researcher truly be objective?), complicity (How can any researcher avoid making research political?), difference (How can any researcher avoid static categorizations of difference?), interpretation (How can researchers deal with differences in constructions of reality among participants, social groups, researchers, and stakeholders?), and legitimization (Who has the authority to make and evaluate knowledge claims in the face of multiple, sometimes competing claims, and what are the effects of this exercise of power?). Lather's pedagogical intent is not to produce answers to these questions but to explore them for what they teach about the limits of research practice and the multiple ways of producing and being produced by research.

Somewhat similarly, Preissle and deMarrais (2009) discuss five key principles that guide their qualitative methods instruction. These principles include responsiveness (qualitative researchers must interact with and respond appropriately to research participants), reflexivity (qualitative researchers must study themselves studying topics, participants, and settings), recursiveness (qualitative researchers must work back and forth across the phases of research, such that data collection leads to refined research questions and more informed data collection, etc.), reflectivity (qualitative researchers should bring multiple concepts and theories from various disciplines to bear on collected materials in order to understand the data), and contextual (qualitative researchers assume that settings, participants, time, and place are integral to understanding human experience and behavior).

Phillips (2006) and others (e.g., Atkinson, Coffey, & Delamont, 2003) have criticized both left and right poles for their excesses—for example, researchers on the left who accuse those on the right of being closet positivists, having physics envy, or selfishly wanting to preserve the status of social scientists as experts, and those on the right who accuse those on the left of being wild-eyed radicals, extreme relativists, incoherent theorists, and shrill critics of everything. Arguments focused on the extremes have tended to drown out the voices of those in the middle. As Phillips writes,

> Situated in the middle of the continuum are a variety of moderate or temperate positions. . . . [H]ere research is seen as a fallible enterprise that attempts to construct viable warrants or chains of argument that draw upon diverse bodies of evidence and that support any assertions that are being made. (p. 17)

Phillips continues, and we agree,

> The most that reasonably can be expected is that research results ought to be *constrained* by the evidence [a major concern of those on the right]; and that evidence indicating differential harms and benefits ought to be given due weight [a major concern of those on the left]. . . . [Further, it has] to be acknowledged that *without* careful observation, testing, measurement, construction of ingenious apparatus, designing questionnaires, making models, doing calculations, drawing implications, playing hunches, and so forth, scientific inquiry (however characterized) would not be able to get off the ground. (pp. 22, 24, emphasis original)[3]

We find ourselves near the middle of Phillips's (2006) continuum with respect to our teaching of qualitative research methods, and more toward the right than the left. On the one hand, we require that students engage in specific activities to scaffold their introduction to the practices of qualitative research, and we teach specific skills and techniques that qualitative researchers have conventionally used. On the other hand, we encourage certain interpretive dispositions (habits of mind) that we believe are central to the practice of qualitative research. In the following section, we describe our approach.

Qualitative Research in Education at the University of Colorado, Boulder

The qualitative methods courses we teach are framed by a larger faculty-led initiative, begun in 2002, to strengthen the doctoral program as part of the Carnegie Foundation's Initiative on the Doctorate (www.carnegiefoundation .org/previous-work/professional-graduate-education). The reform was motivated in part by faculty concern that the doctoral curriculum had been virtually unchanged for 10 years and partly by national concerns about the quality of PhD graduates in education research (Burkhardt & Schoenfeld, 2003; Lagemann, 2000; Neumann, Pallas, & Peterson, 1999; Schoenfeld, 1999). Our School of Education is known for teacher education and graduate programs that emphasize research-based classroom practice, research methodology, and educational policy. The special character of the school is its shared commitment to equal educational opportunity, diversity, research-based reform, and collaborative research (http://www.colorado.edu/education). When first implemented in the late 1980s, our existing doctoral program had been ahead of many others in its requirements for coursework in foundational issues in educational research and in both quantitative and qualitative research methods. But over time, concerns had mounted about the datedness of some course content, the balance and extent of training in qualitative and quantitative methods, and the link between research and practice.

As we reviewed other schools' programs and debated alternatives, we returned again and again to the idea of a common core. Although our survey of highly ranked schools of education showed that few required common courses for all doctoral students, the faculty decided that establishing a common core was desirable for three interconnected reasons: (1) Many of our doctoral students are former teachers and lack a discipline-based research background from their undergraduate or master's preparation, i.e., they enter our program with little or no previous research training; (2) prior experience as teachers and lack of research training sometimes produce students who are skeptical of the importance of research for educational improvement—in some cases, this skepticism leads to a rift between students primarily interested in research and those with teaching or activist orientations; and (3) students' inconsistent patterns of course taking were hampering our ability to offer advanced courses (because almost every course included some novices).

A faculty committee set out to design a core set of courses that would establish a common language and shared discourse about education research; present common norms and standards for the conduct of education research; and build an intellectual and methodological foundation for advanced, specialized coursework. After months of discussion, the committee settled on a concrete proposal for the core: a set of courses to be required for all entering doctoral students in the school and taken as a cohort. It would include two 2-semester courses in the "big (or foundational) ideas" of education and educational research, two 2-semester courses in quantitative methods, and two 2-semester courses in qualitative methods. One course of each type (one big ideas course, one quantitative course, one qualitative course) would run concurrently each semester of the students' first year. (See Page, 2001, for a description of a similar program design at the University of California, Riverside.) One additional core course in multicultural education was scheduled for the first semester of the second year. In making this proposal, we were doubling the research methods courses required (from one course to two in each methodology), but by incorporating required material from old courses with new material in the core courses, we were able to eliminate some old courses and hold the total increase in required courses to only one. See Figure 15.1 for an overview of the new course design.

The new core went into effect in the fall of 2004 with a first-year cohort of 16 students. Although surprised by the existence of a core when they arrived on campus, the students were mostly enthusiastic about the new courses. At the beginning of the semester, several students commented that they were thrilled to have a clear program of study laid out for them and were eager to begin. Since then, the new courses have received mostly good reviews from both students and faculty.

TEACHING QUALITATIVE RESEARCH BY DOING REAL RESEARCH

The qualitative courses were further constrained by Eisenhart's decision, made in 2006, to organize the first of the two-course qualitative sequence around a "real" research and outreach project, the Learning Landscapes Initiative (LLI), which was already underway. LLI is a collaborative project of community groups,

Figure 15.1 Overview of the New Doctoral Program at the University of Colorado, Boulder

YEAR ONE: THE CORE	
First Semester	**Second Semester**
Big Ideas: Perspectives on Classroom Teaching and Learning (3 hrs)	Big Ideas: Education Research and Social Policy (3 hrs)
Qualitative Methods I (3 hrs)	Qualitative Methods II (3 hrs)
Quantitative Methods I (3 hrs)	Quantitative Methods II (3 hrs)
Specialty Seminar (1 hr)	Specialty Seminar (1 hr)

YEAR TWO: INTERMEDIATE

First Semester	**Second Semester**
Multicultural Educ (3 hrs)	Specialty Area Courses/Advanced Methods Courses (3 or 6 hrs)
Specialty Area Courses/Advanced Methods Courses (3 or 6 hrs)	

YEAR THREE: INTERMEDIATE/CAPSTONE

First Semester	**Second Semester**
Specialty Area Courses/Advanced Methods Courses/Capstones (3 or 6 hrs)	Specialty Area Courses/Advanced Methods Courses/Capstones (3 or 6 hrs)

school leaders, and university faculty to build new playgrounds at schools in Denver (Brink & van Vliet, 2004). Architects, landscapers, urban planners, and community members have designed, raised money for, and built new playgrounds at 48 elementary schools since 1998; efforts to redo all the city schools' playgrounds continue. The new playgrounds include age-appropriate play structures, artwork, grassy playing fields, and gardens. The new playgrounds replaced aging ones that had old or unsafe equipment and surfaces. Research accompanied the opening of the new playgrounds; the original LLI research team studied how the redesigned playgrounds affected children's physical activity levels and the community's pride and involvement with the school.

Although Eisenhart was committed to the context of LLI as the starting point of her pedagogy for the first-semester course, she also wanted the students to gain experience formulating their own small-scale research projects. Thus, for the final assignment in her class, she asked students to develop a new study based on their experience of LLI. They were required (by institutional review board [IRB] constraints) to conduct their research at LLI schools (if studying children or schools), but they could choose the topic. The new topics became the focus of students' "real" research in Jurow's second-semester course.

The decision to locate students' research projects in the context of LLI and its participating schools was inspired in large part by our commitment to a social practice theory of learning (Bourdieu, 1977; Lave & Wenger, 1991; Wenger, 1998). From this perspective, in order to learn something new, novices must engage in authentic "practices" of a new field while receiving guidance and support from experts and context. The practices of a field, as we refer to them here, are the activities in which regular participants in the field engage and that direct them to perceive the world related to that field in a particular way. Through gradually increased participation in activities with the continuing guidance of more experienced participants and the social organization of the context, novices are expected to learn techniques, strategies, and perspectives for engaging appropriately in the field. In our courses, students had opportunities to participate in activities that were part of an ongoing research endeavor in the actual context of that endeavor, receive feedback on their skills from experts, share their findings with a research team and community members, and eventually take on responsibilities related to conducting qualitative research. Students' research experiences were intended to be "authentic" in the sense that they would have "use value" (by contributing to a community of research practice) as well as "exchange value" (by contributing to course requirements and earning a grade).

From this perspective, novices (here: first-year doctoral students in education) encountered a pedagogy of qualitative research that we (two experienced qualitative researchers) structured, consciously and unconsciously (via our dispositions), as a means of teaching and learning qualitative research. Our decision to organize the courses around a real research project was extraordinarily consequential for the learning environment. Demands of entrée, rapport, ethics, communication, scheduling, observing, interviewing, and reviewing literature for research about children on playgrounds and in elementary schools provided much of the structure for topic coverage and sequence in class, as well as for class assignments and deadlines.

By structuring student participation in these aspects of a real research project, we hoped to cultivate dispositions that we value in qualitative researchers. We hoped students would grasp the distinctiveness of qualitative research, particularly its commitment to learn from participants' perspectives, values, and context through open-ended and flexible inquiry. We hoped they would see that research methods should be used to answer specific research questions (and not simply because one likes or dislikes a method). We hoped they would come to appreciate the importance of careful analysis and thoughtful interpretation of qualitative materials. We hoped they would appreciate how qualitative methods can reveal unexpected insights about people and places thought to be known or understood already.

We also hoped to cultivate ethical dispositions consistent with good research practice. Because students would be observing young children on school playgrounds; interviewing teachers, students, and parents; and using the material they collected and analyzed to make presentations and contribute to LLI, their behavior and activities had to meet the requirements for research with human subjects, including those of the university's institutional review board. Although it can be useful for students to prepare their own IRB materials as part of a class project, we did not want to delay the start of the research; thus, Eisenhart filed the IRB materials, contacted the schools, and received approval before the beginning of the first semester course.[4] During class time, she shared the IRB materials with the students and reviewed ways of minimizing risk: obtaining consent and assent, maintaining confidentiality, refraining from direct involvement except in an emergency, reporting problems and results, and being clear and honest about research purposes with everyone involved.

The decision to focus the students' activities in these ways also was made on pedagogical and logistical grounds, based on past experience. Both instructors had previously taught qualitative research methods in which students chose their own sites and research questions from the start. Although this approach has the advantage of allowing students to select a research topic based on interest, in our experience it also meant that students proceeded at different paces and had different needs at any given time during the course. This situation made it impossible to match class topics and discussion with students' immediate research needs (see also Keen, 1996).

OVERVIEW OF THE QUALITATIVE RESEARCH METHODS SEQUENCE

In the two-course qualitative sequence, students were introduced to qualitative methods in the first course and revisited these ideas as they completed their own research in the second course. Both courses were framed by a view of interpretive, qualitative research as it developed in cultural anthropology and fieldwork sociology. Students read books and articles focused on qualitative research design and interpretation (e.g., Michael Agar's *The Professional Stranger* [1996], Joseph Maxwell's *Qualitative Research Design* [2004], and Phil Carspecken's *Critical Ethnography in Educational Research* [1996]) and book-length ethnographic studies (e.g., Barrie Thorne's *Gender Play* [1993] and Annette Lareau's *Unequal Childhoods* [2003]). As students read and discussed these texts in class, they simultaneously engaged in supervised fieldwork.

In the first semester, teams of students conducted observations and interviews at nine Denver playgrounds to understand children's social experiences during recess. (Details on the project and the students' work will be discussed later.) Students coded and reconstructed their data and wrote short technical reports on their results. Drawing on their experiences in the field and in class, students (individually or in pairs) developed proposals for small-scale studies they would complete in the second-semester course.

In the second course (taught by Jurow), students focused more on the interpretive and critical epistemology of qualitative research; read additional exemplars of qualitative research; and studied texts on how to collect, organize, and analyze data. As in the first semester, the students completed course readings as they conducted supervised fieldwork. Course readings and assignments were coordinated with and to some extent developed in response to students' research activities. Students participated in workshop-style discussions focused on data collection and analysis strategies as well as emergent research dilemmas. Toward the end of the semester, students created posters to share their research in a School of Education poster session where they received feedback from faculty and other students. Building on their posters, they wrote final research papers in which they presented their studies.

ACTIVITIES, SKILLS, AND DISPOSITIONS OF QUALITATIVE RESEARCH

In this section, we discuss the activities we arranged, the skills we hoped students would develop, and the dispositions we wanted to cultivate. Although we discuss activities, skills, and dispositions separately for analytic ease and clarity, in both theory and practice these features overlap and interrelate.

Research Activities

The central activities that we organized for the students included (1) activities for answering (and later developing) research questions with qualitative data,

(2) activities for communicating about research, and (3) activities for making social and cultural comparisons.

Answering research questions with qualitative data. To help students understand how qualitative research methods are used to answer research questions, Eisenhart organized students' early project work around a set of research questions. Rather than asking students to enter the field with no particular focus, which can quickly lead to student frustration, or to develop their own, which is difficult for most novices, Eisenhart structured the students' fieldwork so they would experience (rather than design) qualitative research questions and the kinds of data that can answer such questions. The questions she proposed complemented the LLI's ongoing work. While LLI focused on comparing old and new playgrounds in terms of quantified measures of children's physical activity level, Eisenhart's research questions focused on comparing old and new playgrounds in terms of social behavior. She provided the students with three research questions to begin their research:

1. What kinds of social interactions—among children and between children and adults—take place on the playground?

2. How do these interactions vary depending on gender and ethnicity?

3. Why do these patterns of social interaction occur; i.e, what is a credible explanation for the patterns observed?

She emphasized that the students' contribution to LLI would come in providing tentative answers to these questions for the LLI research team. The three research questions then framed the first-semester readings; class discussions; and assignments on observation, interviewing, and analysis—the main research skills emphasized in the course sequence (described in more detail under "skills" below). Students' observations, interviews, analysis and write-up of their first-semester fieldnotes and transcripts were directed toward providing answers to the three questions.

Eisenhart's questions focused the students' attention on local interactions and encouraged them to interpret the interactions in terms of social and cultural significance. She hoped that the form and focus of the questions, as well as the content of the answers, would serve as a guide to the kinds of qualitative research questions that students would want to ask and be able to answer in their second-semester projects. For the most part, though focused on a range of topics, students in the second semester proposed research questions about participants' social experiences and how these were constrained and afforded by interactional, societal, cultural, and personal dimensions of their lives. Some of the research questions students asked included the following: "What are African American and Mexican American fifth graders' perceptions about race?" "What kinds of interracial interactions do boys and girls have on the playground?" "What meanings/ messages might be conveyed to the jumpers through lyrics in jump rope songs?" "What influences formation of a child's identity on the playground?" and "Are home and school separate spheres with respect to the acquisition and valuing of cultural capital?" Sub-questions to these primary questions allowed students to identify and investigate patterns and variations in the children's playground interactions.

Communicating qualitative research. In order to help students learn how to share their research with others, both Eisenhart and Jurow organized opportunities for students to talk and write about qualitative research. Lave and Wenger (1991) point out that for newcomers to a community of practice, "the purpose is not to learn *from* talk . . . it is to learn *to* talk" (pp. 108–109, emphasis original).

In our courses, talk *about* qualitative methods was frequent and took the form of mini-lectures and class discussions about conducting a study. In both courses, students read, discussed, and critiqued book-length ethnographies. In the first semester, Eisenhart divided the class in half for key readings twice during the first semester: once when each half read portions of a methods text (Agar, 1996, or Carspecken, 1996) and once when each half read an ethnography (Lareau, 2003, or Carter, 2005). Students were given study questions focused on key ideas in each book and came to class prepared to describe their book to those who had not read it. Discussions in which students focus on a text to identify themes and offer critiques are what doctoral students do in most of their courses. This is a valuable form of discourse, allowing students to develop a shared language for communicating, but it does not allow students to engage directly in trying out their own strategies for discussing and justifying qualitative work.

Both instructors also created opportunities for students to practice talking and writing *as* qualitative researchers. At the end of the first course, students wrote technical reports that addressed Eisenhart's research questions; these reports were sent to the LLI researchers. Toward the end of the second semester, students were required to be presenters in a schoolwide poster session. Prior to the session, students developed short written and verbal descriptions of their studies for the poster session. They considered what their most intriguing finding was, what was important about their results, and what still puzzled them. Explaining their study at the poster session verbally positioned students as qualitative researchers in the eyes of the wider school community.

In Jurow's second-semester class, the students' final course papers followed a standard format for publishing qualitative research with an introduction, conceptual framework, literature review, methods section, results, discussion, and conclusion. Jurow encouraged the students to revise their course papers for presentation at conferences and possible publication. Six of the students took this advice and presented their findings in a symposium at the 2008 American Educational Research Association (AERA) meetings.

These multiple and genuine opportunities for talking about and sharing qualitative research were purposefully designed into our courses. Students developed common language for discussing and evaluating qualitative research (others' and their own) and for positioning themselves as qualitative researchers. They also developed an expectation to share the stories, patterns, and potential implications of their qualitative research findings with audiences beyond their immediate peers and instructors.

Social and cultural comparisons. LLI allowed us to organize students' research experiences to encourage comparison of data in and across sites. In the first semester of the 2006–2007 and 2007–2008 doctoral cohort, students (n = 12/each cohort) were divided into three groups of four. Each group was assigned three schools to study: one with an old playground, one with a recently developed new playground, and one with an older new playground. Each student was required to conduct six observations with fieldnotes, thus assuring that each group had 24 sets of fieldnotes spanning three playgrounds. To write the technical report in which they identified and tried to explain patterns they had observed, the students needed to work together to organize, analyze, and develop shared interpretations of their data from across the three sites. Further, in class discussions of the research process and emerging results, students had to consider the findings and interpretations of those who had worked at different sites.

In the second semester, when students chose their own research topics, opportunities for comparison across sites shifted. Students were no longer required to work together at their field sites, although the majority chose to do so.[5] Jurow designed classroom activities to capitalize on the fact that students were studying and facing similar issues at the playground sites. She required students to comment on each others' emerging analyses using standards for evaluating qualitative research that had been previously discussed in class. She purposefully paired individual students/groups that had something in common to read and comment on each others' preliminary claims. Students were then encouraged to consider their emerging interpretations in light of data that others had collected or conceptual frameworks that others were using. These class activities were meant to deepen students' understandings of what was happening in and across playground sites. They also aimed to help students review their peers' analyses of social and cultural patterns in critical and constructive ways.

The LLI group research project with its multiple playground sites enabled us to emphasize the value of social and cultural comparison in qualitative research. For example, students came to consider how different schools' views and policies on diversity affected children's interracial interactions, how playgrounds with spare play structures versus those with more elaborate structures affected the kinds of games children could play and with whom they played, and how children's arguments were resolved differently when peer mediators were present and when they were not. When students in prior years had conducted individual research studies at sites of their own choosing, the possibility for such comparison was limited. In the context of the LLI group research project, students had to look beyond their own data and their own sites in order to answer research questions and complete assignments. We also found that collaboration happened frequently and organically as students learned about each other's work.

Qualitative Research Skills

In the context of the three central activities, we assigned readings, held class discussions, and made assignments to encourage students to develop particular skills that we think necessary (though not sufficient) for doing qualitative research. We focused on having students learn to collect data through relatively unobtrusive methods; write fieldnotes; conduct interviews; and interpret these data by coding, narrating, and reconstructing the material collected. Students practiced these techniques as they collected data to answer research questions (first Eisenhart's and then their own) in the context of the LLI project.

In the first semester, students focused on practicing observational and fieldnote skills. They were required to conduct an open-ended, then a focused, and then a structured observation (each student conducted a minimum of six observations). Fieldnotes from each observation type were turned in to the instructor for feedback on amount of detail, level of concreteness, and likelihood of contributing answers to the research questions that she posed to them.

Using their own fieldnotes and those of two other students who had observed at different playground sites (for a total of 24 fieldnote observations from three sites), student teams began data analysis. Eisenhart introduced students to two different approaches to data analysis: Spradley's (1979, 1980) coding by domain and Carspecken's (1996) reconstructive analysis. Following Spradley, she asked students to develop a coding scheme based on the research questions (e.g., kinds of interactions, ways of displaying gender), and then to add codes that emerged from the data. Each team developed its own scheme, applied it to its observation data, and then received feedback from the instructor on its coding.

Building on these codes, Eisenhart then used readings on Carspecken's (1996) "reconstructive analysis" to encourage interpretations of the patterns. Carspecken focuses his analytic approach on identifying "meaning fields" in interactions, i.e., all possible meanings that any actor could give to an interaction, and then considering the social and historical "horizons of meaning" that give substance to the meaning fields. For example, in a playground interaction in which a girl hits a boy, the analyst identifies meaning fields by speculating about what this interaction could mean to all the actors. From the perspective of the girl, it could mean she likes the boy, so she hits him to show affection; or, she hates the boy, so she hits him to express distaste, and so on. From the perspective of the boy, it could mean that the girl likes him and wants to get his attention; or, the girl is mad at him, and so forth. Once salient meaning fields have been identified, then the analyst considers the logic or narrative that binds the fields together (Do these interactions/meaning fields represent the social norm for children's gender relations in this community or something new and different? Do these interactions/meaning fields represent a historical legacy of gender relations or something new and different?). This approach, which involves systematically considering multiple observations of interactions and their potential meanings for different participants in an activity, allows the analyst to identify which interpretations or meaning fields capture most completely the logic of the actions. The intention behind using Carspecken's approach was to give the students a concrete means for developing a social and cultural analysis of their observations.

Drawing on their own interests and what they were learning through participation at their sites during the first semester, students were asked to develop their own research foci for the second-semester course. To help them locate their interests in the literature, Eisenhart had each student identify 10 relevant sources, read and briefly annotate each source, and then post the results on the class discussion board for all to share. When it came time to write the conceptual framework for the second-semester proposal, students were advised to consult the annotated list, choose three to four primary sources to focus their research interests, and use these to propose a tentative conceptual framework for their own study.[6] The students then wrote research proposals in which they articulated their emerging conceptual framework, research questions, and study design.

Students thus entered the second semester with some foundational knowledge of qualitative research, some strategies for collecting and analyzing data, and a sense of prior research on their research topic. As in the first semester, students began their studies by conducting observations at their sites. This allowed them to develop a sense of what was happening in the local context, what had changed since the first semester (if they were studying the same site), or how this site differed from the one they had studied in the first semester. With this orienting information, students were expected to refocus their research question (if necessary) and then complete initial interviews with site participants who might shed light on or extend their observations.

It was both expected and acceptable for students to modify their research foci in the second semester. In one case, a student who was interested in studying children's interracial interactions switched playground sites from the first to the second semester so that she could conduct her study at a school that had greater numbers of children from different racial groups. At her new site, she quickly noted that the children used what she described as "sophisticated language to talk about race." Her curiosity about the children's language use led her to expand her original research focus from looking only at the children's playground interactions to include an analysis of the children's participation in a character education program run by the school. In other cases, students who ended the first semester with a particular research focus changed their research questions altogether after noticing practices that they found more personally, theoretically, or practically compelling at their sites in the second semester. For example, a pair of students initially interested in how children use rules on the playground shifted their study to messages about gender norms and romantic relations conveyed in jump rope rhymes. This shift allowed the students to narrow what they felt was too broad of a focus to a topic on which they could gather more specific and richer data. In line with authentic qualitative research practices, students were encouraged to view their research investigations not as set in stone, but as responsive to their interests, what they learned from their fieldwork, and their efforts to collect usable data.

In the second semester, the students engaged in approximately 8 weeks of fieldwork. During this time, they also participated in class discussions and activities that increased their skill at writing fieldnotes, designing interview protocols, conducting interviews, and interacting with study participants.

Building on their first-semester experiences with data analysis, in the second semester, students were introduced to a further variety of approaches to thinking about qualitative data analysis. All the course readings emphasized an inductive approach, but were selected to offer the students a range of complementary techniques to make sense of their data (e.g., grounded theory, thematic analysis). As students read about approaches to analyzing data, they wrote about their emerging understandings of their data. Following an interpretive approach to qualitative research methods, a focus of the students' writing was on understanding children's interpretations of actions within their meaning systems. There were a number of analytic writing assignments in the second-semester course: a series of short memos written while students collected their data, a rough and then a final poster draft, and a rough and then a final course paper. In addition to receiving feedback from Jurow on their emerging analyses and writing, peers critiqued each other's writing, and faculty and students at the schoolwide poster session provided feedback on students' work. Through this repeated process of feedback and critique, students often reconsidered original ways of framing their studies, identified the need for additional conceptual tools, and refined their research foci.

The students' approaches to analysis, writing, and presentation of findings were developed in relation to professional standards for sharing qualitative research in education. Students read and referred back to texts including the American Educational Research Association's (2006) standards for reporting empirical research as they reviewed research articles and ethnographies in class. Jurow and the students used the standards to have critical and grounded discussions about issues such as the links among the conceptual framework, the research design, and the interpretations; the adequacy of evidence presented in a text; and the validity of a study's findings. Jurow encouraged the students to use the AERA recommendations as a shared framework for evaluating their own and each other's research posters and papers. In this way, the class developed a common vocabulary for discussing and debating the strengths and weaknesses of qualitative studies.

In summary, we intended for students to learn and practice skills related to participant observation, interviewing, interpreting, and writing up analyses in our courses. Although we focused on these foundational skills for doing qualitative research, our commitment to social practice theory led us to believe that students would learn more than this through their engagement in the LLI group research project. Indeed, this was the case. Students faced ethical issues at their sites related to ensuring children's safety and rights, needed to revise their research questions in light of the data they collected, and shifted their research roles as they came to value children as active participants rather than simply objects of research. As these kinds of problems emerged out of the students' research, we discussed them in class, read texts related to them, and helped students develop skills for managing them in real-time research contexts.

Dispositions for Qualitative Research

In addition to the specific activities we scaffolded and the skills we taught, we wanted our students to develop a set of dispositions, or a more general sense of "how to do" qualitative research. One disposition we certainly hoped to encourage was a commitment to careful and systematic qualitative research. Our attention to the detail of conventional qualitative skills, designs, and sequencing was intended to support this goal. But this was not the only disposition we wanted to nurture in our students. We also hoped they would develop commitments to open-ended and flexible inquiry that leads to new insights about what research participants care about and mean by their actions; a reflective stance on one's subjectivity and position as a researcher (and other social identities), including their effects on research questions, design, and outcomes; and ethical behavior in the conduct of research.

We used several strategies to encourage open-endedness and flexibility. Eisenhart presented observations as proceeding from general guidelines such as "what's happening here" to more focused and then structured observations, where each successive type is developed from the preceding one. She presented reconstruction (following Carspecken, 1996) as a process of identifying and considering many possible interpretations and only then deciding on and justifying "final" interpretations. When students began their own research in the second semester, Jurow emphasized that they should think about their study proposals as resources for thinking about what they would do in the field as opposed to using a script. She recommended that students set aside their proposals for the first few visits to the site so that they could familiarize themselves with the current happenings at the site and how these might affect their research plans. These early observations typically led to a refocusing or sometimes a complete change of students' research questions or data collection strategies. As a case in point, a pair of students, who had regularly observed girls and boys playing foursquare during their first-semester fieldwork, did not see as many mixed-gendered interactions during the second semester. As a result, the students revised their research question from one focused on gender differences to one that considered how children negotiate rules. This was a more appropriate question to ask given what the children were doing, and it required the students to rethink their conceptual framework, their research questions, and the purpose of their observations and interviews.

Also in the second semester, students read Erickson's (1986) chapter in which he introduces the concept of a natural history of inquiry. This method assumes that qualitative research will take turns that one cannot predict at the start, and from these turns, one will learn new things about the topic under study, but mostly one will learn about him- or herself as a researcher. To illustrate this idea, students read qualitative studies (e.g., Whyte's 1955 book, *Street Corner Society*) in which the researcher wrote about the development of his or her research and the unexpected directions the inquiry took based on early data analysis, relationships with participants, challenges in getting access to a particular site, funding and time constraints, and changing commitments related to the purpose of the research.

Throughout both semesters, the students were asked to keep track of how what they were learning affected the course of their project. One student, with some experience doing experimental and survey research, thought that he should not interact with the children on the playground because it would taint his data. Over the course of a few weeks, however, he started to realize that he would get a much deeper understanding of what the children were dealing with by talking and playing with them. This student began engaging with the children, who were eager to have his attentions, and this allowed him to see that they were not passive objects of gender socialization, but active agents in making sense of themselves as gendered beings.

By talking with students explicitly about the value of being responsive to study participants' experiences, we tried to convey that this was a desirable quality for a qualitative researcher to have. By reading qualitative studies in which an unplanned-for refocusing of the research study was prominent in the author's account, we wanted students to see that this was not a disreputable practice. Further, when students needed to refocus their projects, we tried to use these as "teachable moments" to discuss how to decide on appropriate changes to conceptualizing the research project, methods of data collection, and the approach to analysis.

In order to cultivate a reflective stance in our students, we created occasions for them to share stories about their field experiences in class and in writing so that they could consider the ethical, social, and personal dimensions of their research. Some former teachers shared that it was hard for them to watch passively as children acted cruelly to one another on the playground. Should they intervene or not? If so, what kinds of interventions might be good ideas or bad ideas? Others who had been teachers found that they took a decidedly more active role in their research with the children because of their former experiences. Was this good or bad? Some students struggled with how their involvement with students might bias their data; others worried that their failure to interact with students might bias their data. In one situation, student researchers learned about the possibility of criminal behavior at school. What should they do? Should they report the allegation or protect their sources? Who was likely to be harmed and in what ways? Was it ethical to continue to conduct research at this school? Was it ethical to continue to use these data or not? How could they finish the course if they could not continue at the school or use the data?

These professional, ethical, and personal issues were explored throughout the courses in readings, in-class writing, and whole-class discussions. As part of a workshop-style format, Jurow asked two students to talk about problems or questions they were facing in their research as part of every class session. The volunteers talked about their struggles and how they affected their relationships in the field, approaches to data collection and analysis, and their opinions about the import of their research. These discussions were organized as opportunities for students to consider their values, experiences, and commitments alongside their positions as women, men, and members of different cultural communities. Students were invited to reflect on their subjectivities and the reasons they were asking the questions they asked, the perspectives they wanted to investigate or make known, and the purposes of their research beyond fulfilling a course requirement. Subjectivities were examined not as an end in themselves, but as part and parcel of doing qualitative research.

Summary

Consistent with Lave and Wenger, our pedagogy of research emphasized novices' exposure to and participation in authentic research practice—doing the actual work, for the purposes of contributing to an ongoing research project (as well as completing class work), in hopes of nurturing valued dispositions of qualitative inquiry. The pedagogical decisions we made were intended to give students access to and practice with conventional qualitative skills of data collection, analysis, write-up, and presentation, and to encourage them to develop a "sense of the game" of qualitative research.

STUDENT RESPONSES TO OUR TEACHING

Although we did not systematically collect data about our students' responses to our teaching, we do have some evidence of their learning in our courses (see Jurow & Eisenhart, in preparation, for a more detailed discussion). In general, most of the students kept up with the readings, participated in class discussions, and followed the guidelines for setting up and conducting their research projects. Along the way, they had lots of questions and concerns, especially about the LLI project. Some did not want to spend so much time doing research, even for practice, on playgrounds. As they began the observations, they worried about not being able to record everything, not being able to figure out what was going on because they couldn't hear or understand what the children were saying. As the observation data came in and they started preliminary analysis, they worried that their fieldnotes did not contain anything interesting, that the instructions had not been clear enough for them to know how to "do it right." We took these concerns, which are typical of novice qualitative researchers, to suggest that the students were trying to engage with the tasks we set forth.

All the students engaged in some practices associated with qualitative research and tried to get better at them. These practices included taking responsibility for developing a research focus, collecting and analyzing some data, writing and presenting results, collaborating with others to do research, and using discourses of qualitative research. As the students worked on getting better at qualitative research—and they did get better—they also encountered difficulties that stalled their progress. Some challenges were due to the nature of qualitative research; more were due to time constraints imposed by the course structure and organization. Data analysis and interpretation proved especially challenging for all of them (see also Keen, 1996). Our efforts to scaffold students' access to strategies for analysis and interpretation were not sufficient, in the time period we had, to overcome students' lack of experience with conceptual frameworks as used in qualitative studies and with the skills and traditions of qualitative analysis and interpretation.

The students' responses suggest that participating in the qualitative course sequence led them to recognize some of the skills and dispositions associated with being a qualitative researcher. The responses also show the students' ability to use the discourse of qualitative research emphasized in our courses. And, they reveal the possibility of multiple learning trajectories. Some students began to think of themselves as qualitative researchers before the end of the courses. Others needed more experience and greater responsibility. Interestingly, among all the things the students did in the context of our pedagogy of qualitative research, the defining feature of being a qualitative researcher, to them, was being able to analyze qualitative data, arguably the thing they struggled with the most and for which we think they most needed more time.

Conclusion

Clearly our approach to teaching qualitative methods is only one of many approaches that might be taken. Our courses were constrained by the fact that they are compulsory courses for graduate students, many of whom have had limited research experience. They also were constrained by our need to contribute to a core curriculum that groups together all new students in the School of Education, regardless of their specialty area or interest, for introductory methods training. They also were constrained by our theoretical interest in social practice theory as a useful guide to teaching research and our previous dissatisfaction with class-initiated research projects in which each student chose his or her own topic and site.

The pedagogical approach we took in this teaching context was to organize much of our two-course sequence in terms of an ongoing research project to which our students contributed. This allowed us to engage in a form of recursive instruction in which we introduced and then spiraled back to strategies and techniques for observing, participating, interviewing, collaborating, analyzing, interpreting, writing up, and presenting qualitative research. It enabled the class as a whole to progress through all the phases of qualitative research in two semesters. It highlighted the value of collaborations and cross-site comparisons in qualitative research and built a community of researchers—including students and faculty from two universities, as well as teachers, administrators, students, and parents from nine urban schools—with some shared knowledge, language, and experience.

But it did not do everything. We did not systematically introduce all types of qualitative research (e.g., case study, ethnography, grounded theory). We did not encourage a necessarily activist approach to qualitative research (e.g., critical, antiracist, participatory action). We left the students on their own to learn qualitative data analysis software if they wanted. Hopefully, the students developed a foundation on which these things can and will be added.

We also did not do as much as we could have to study our students' learning in our courses. We kept journals about our teaching, collected some student journals, evaluated student assignments, surveyed students at the end of each course, and organized focus group discussions (in which we did not participate) after the completion of our courses in an effort to collect information about the students' learning. Although useful, this information was not systematically collected or analyzed.

Perhaps most salient given other articles in this handbook, we did not spend much time on epistemological debates about positivism vs. interpretivism, interpretivism vs. constructivism, or critical or postmodern stances on qualitative research.[7] Clearly our pedagogical decisions stressed research practice—student opportunities to design, conduct, and complete a research study and to make them aware of professional standards in relation to which they could evaluate their efforts. Students thus practiced strategies for taking fieldnotes, interviewing participants, analyzing data, and reviewing their own and others' research reports according to conventional standards for reporting empirical research. In this sense, we gravitate toward the right pole, the "qi" end, of Phillips's (2006) continuum and have perhaps compromised our students' ability to participate in the epistemological debates that are so prominent in U.S. educational research circles at this time.

On the other hand, we gave attention to left pole issues, too. We located students' research projects within a group project (the LLI) that was selected, among other reasons, for its affordances for investigating issues of equity. The LLI provided opportunities for investigating the lives of children from racial and linguistic minority backgrounds who have been historically underserved by public schools. By locating the students' research in Denver public schools that served these populations, we wanted our students to recognize the specificity of children's lives and move beyond deficit models of thinking about urban, minority children that are pervasive in educational research. Eisenhart's initial set of research questions provided a concrete way for students to investigate issues related to children's experiences of race and gender on the playgrounds and how these might vary across sites.

Our pedagogical practices, including the readings we selected, the feedback and guidance we gave students on their emerging analyses, and class exercises, were intended to teach students how to collect data systematically and make valid claims *as well as* engage them in discussions of the meaning of the patterns they observed and critiques of these patterns. For instance, when students read Thorne's (1993) *Gender Play* and Lareau's (2003) *Unequal Childhoods,* they considered the researchers' analyses of gender, race, and class hierarchies and discussed issues such as whether the arguments were backed by the evidence provided and if they went far enough in their critiques of present social structures.

Our attention to issues toward the left pole was enhanced because our students were simultaneously taking a first-year course on perspectives on classroom teaching and learning that covered sociocultural perspectives, feminist theory, and critical race theory. In that course, students read studies conducted from these perspectives, and these perspectives in turn influenced how some students framed their research questions, thought about the purposes of their research, and considered their roles as researchers in our courses. We welcomed and capitalized on these connections across courses. Especially in the second-semester course, students' interests in avant garde theories and their implications for how researchers engage with study participants, include participants' voices, and act on what they learn through their research, influenced how we discussed their research practice. For example, when a pair of students who were interested in studying young children's ways of talking about race decided to shift from passive roles as observers to being more involved and directive in their interactions with children on the playground, this was encouraged. Jurow talked with the students about the tensions they felt between advocating for a particular view of race, which came out of their commitment to a critical perspective on race and their own experiences, and understanding and documenting the children's perspectives. These students then had to rethink how they would write up their study and evaluate its validity. Their shift led to a discussion with the entire class around these issues.

In this way, we encouraged students to discuss objectivity, complicity, difference, interpretation, and legitimization as they arose in the context of their research projects and readings. Unlike Lather (2006), we did not make these issues the centerpiece of our teaching, but we could not teach qualitative research without attending to them.

There were also ways in which we did not emphasize right-pole priorities. For example, we gave limited attention to anthropological and sociological theories that have been so important to the development of qualitative research in the disciplines. In a previous version of our school's qualitative research offerings, doctoral students were required to take at least one theory-oriented course in anthropology or sociology. They could choose from courses in the Anthropology or Sociology Departments, or a course in Anthropology and Education or Sociology of Education offered by the School of Education, and they had to complete this course before they could enroll in Ethnographic (or Qualitative) Methods. Under this arrangement, students typically spent one semester learning about discipline-based social science theories and writing a theoretically inspired research proposal for implementation in the second-semester methods course. In the methods course, they conducted a small-scale qualitative study of their own choosing. This course arrangement highlighted the place of social science theory as a precursor to designing a qualitative research study, but gave the students very little time to actually practice doing research. At the time, we offered no other courses in qualitative methods.

Another omission was the lack of attention to research designs employing multiple methods. This has been of special concern to the students in our program, who complain that both qualitative and quantitative researchers tout the value of multiple methods but do not teach how to do it. Our position has been that in order to use multiple methods effectively, students must first learn the strengths and weaknesses of specific traditions or designs. Our position would be more tenable if our program offered a subsequent course in multiple methods (which is now in development), although we will face resistance to adding another even quasi-required methodology course to the curriculum.

In our doctoral program, once students have taken our two courses, further coursework and practice in qualitative research is optional. We hope that students will take more advanced qualitative courses before beginning their (qualitative) dissertations, or work with professors on qualitative research projects. We hope that our faculty colleagues advise them to do so. Some students do take more courses and have opportunities for additional practice. But others will conduct and complete qualitative dissertations with no further methodological training.

The practice-oriented project work that was so consequential for our pedagogy was demanding for both the students and for us. Hours outside of class went into setting up the project work; designing the components; conducting the studies; providing individual feedback; doing revisions; and developing posters, final papers, and AERA presentations. But following the development of the students' work over time and listening to them talk about their experiences have been gratifying. They have had opportunities for practice, advice, critique, and revision. They have struggled with issues that are important to us in qualitative research: how to open yourself to perspectives and possibilities different from your own, how to find out about meaning and context, how to think through and rethink a research design, how to grasp and represent the complexity of social and cultural phenomena, how to position oneself in a research study, and how to collaborate and compare so as to go both deep and wide in a research study. At this point, we do not know whether attentiveness to these issues can be taught and learned in other ways, nor do we know what else could be achieved with other pedagogical strategies. We hope that our intentions, successes, and failures will inspire other qualitative researchers to do more research and writing about their teaching intentions, their pedagogical strategies, and their students' learning.

Notes

1. In saying that these instructors focus on method, we do not mean that they have a formulaic or recipe-like approach to teaching methods, as has sometimes been assumed.

2. Lather is talking specifically about educational research, in which she includes both "qualitative" and "quantitative" research.

3. Atkinson, Coffey, and Delamont (2003) take a somewhat different position with respect to what they call "classic" or "Old Guard" ethnographers—those whose careful work during 1950–1970 in sociology and anthropology served to more clearly articulate

the methodological approaches used by qualitative researchers, versus "avant garde" or "critical" or "postmodern" ethnographers who came to have more and more influence from 1980 on. Their main point is that classic ethnographers laid the groundwork for the avant garde and thus the sharp distinction between the two groups is inaccurate and misleading. They do not see a paradigm shift but an evolution of the field in which the issues have become more complex and the answer strategies more diverse.

4. In our experience, the semester time needed to secure IRB approval for students' individual projects substantially limits time for students to practice other aspects of research. Also, because individual approvals can take different amounts of time—some are approved quickly while others take weeks—the instructor's ability to schedule class topics and activities to match students' progress is compromised.

5. Thirteen of 24 students collaborated with at least one other person for their second-semester research project. Others (11 of 24) worked on their own, but 4 of them chose to collect data as a "quasi-team" at one school site (i.e., they shared fieldnotes, transcripts, and a survey that they all used to answer their own research questions).

6. In our courses, we make a distinction between a literature review and a conceptual framework. We define the literature review as a summary of important previous research; we define the conceptual framework as a skeletal structure for organizing or guiding a new study (Eisenhart, 1991). We expect students to use the results of the literature review, in conjunction with guidance from theoretical perspectives, to develop a conceptual framework. Because developing a conceptual framework takes time and is difficult, Eisenhart shortened the process in her course.

7. We should note that our students do have other opportunities to cover this material in their coursework. One of the other core courses, Perspectives on Teaching and Learning, gives considerable attention to critical, feminist, and postmodern perspectives. Another course that is not required but many students take, Philosophical Issues in Educational Research, also covers this material in depth.

References

Agar, M. (1996). *The professional stranger: An informal introduction to ethnography.* San Diego, CA: Academic Press.

Altheide, D. L. (1996). *Qualitative media analysis.* Thousand Oaks, CA: Sage.

American Educational Research Association. (2006). Standards for reporting on empirical social science research in AERA publications. *Educational Researcher, 35*(6), 33–40.

Atkinson, P. A., Coffey, A., & Delamont, S. (2003). *Key themes in qualitative research.* Walnut Creek, CA: AltaMira Press.

Blank, G. (2004). Teaching qualitative data analysis to graduate students. *Social Science Computer Review, 22*(2), 187–196.

Bourdieu, P. (1977). *Outline of a theory of practice.* Cambridge, UK: Cambridge University Press.

Brink, L., & van Vliet, W. (2004). *If they build it, will they come? An evaluation of the effects of the redevelopment of inner-city school grounds on the physical activity of children.* Denver: University of Colorado.

Burkhardt, H., & Schoenfeld, A. (2003). Improving educational research: Toward a more useful, more influential, and better-funded enterprise. *Educational Researcher, 32*(9), 3–14.

Carspecken, P. (1996). *Critical ethnography in educational research.* New York: Routledge.

Carter, P. (2005). *Keepin' it real: School success beyond black and white.* Oxford, UK: Oxford University Press.

Charmaz, K. (2006). *Constructing grounded theory: A practical guide through qualitative analysis.* Thousand Oaks, CA: Sage.

Creswell, J. W. (2002). *Research design: Qualitative, quantitative, and mixed methods approaches* (2nd ed.), Thousand Oaks, CA: Sage.

Crull, S. R., & Collins, S. M. (2004). Adapting traditions: Teaching research methods in a large class setting. *Teaching Sociology, 32*(2), 206–212.

Delgado-Gaitan, C. (1993). Researching change and changing the researcher. *Harvard Educational Review, 63*(4), 389–411.

Denzin, N. K., & Lincoln, Y. S. (Eds.). (1994). *Handbook of qualitative research.* Thousand Oaks, CA: Sage.

Denzin, N. K., & Lincoln, Y. S. (Eds.). (2000). *Handbook of qualitative research* (2nd ed.). Thousand Oaks, CA: Sage.

Denzin, N. K., & Lincoln, Y. S. (Eds.). (2005). *The SAGE handbook of qualitative research* (3rd ed.). Thousand Oaks, CA: Sage.

Eisenhart, M. (1991). Conceptual frameworks for research circa 1991: Ideas from a cultural anthropologist; implications for mathematics education researchers. *Proceedings of the thirteenth annual meeting of psychology of mathematics education, North America* (pp. 202–219). Blacksburg, VA: Psychology of Mathematics Education.

Erickson, F. (1986). Qualitative methods in research on teaching. In M. Wittrock (Ed.), *Handbook of research on teaching* (3rd ed., pp. 119–161). New York: Macmillan.

Garner, M., Wagner, C., & Kawulich, B. (Eds.). (2009). *Teaching research methods in the social sciences.* Burlington, VT: Ashgate.

Glaser, B. G., & Strauss, A. L. (1967). *The discovery of grounded theory: Strategies for qualitative research.* New York: Aldine.

Green, J. L., Camilli, G., & Elmore, P. B. (2006). *Handbook of complementary methods in education research.* Mahwah, NJ: Lawrence Erlbaum.

Hammersley, M., & Atkinson, P. (1995). *Ethnography: Principles in practice* (2nd ed.). London: Tavistock.

Heath, S. B., & Street, B. V. (with Mills, M.). (2008). *Ethnography: Approaches to language and literacy research.* New York: Teachers College.

Hopkinson, G. C., & Hogg, M. K. (2004). Teaching and learning about qualitative research in the social sciences: An experiential learning approach amongst marketing students. *Journal of Further and Higher Education, 28*(3), 307–320.

Hurworth, R. E. (2008). *Teaching qualitative research: Cases and issues.* Rotterdam, The Netherlands: Sense.

Jurow, A. S., & Eisenhart, M. (with Eyerman, S., Gaertner, M., Roberts, S., Seymour, M., Spindler, E., & Subert, A.). (2011, manuscript in preparation). *Learning to be a qualitative researcher in education.*

Keen, M. F. (1996). Teaching qualitative methods: A face-to-face encounter. *Teaching Sociology, 24,* 166–176.

Lagemann, E. C. (2000). *An elusive science: The troubling history of education research.* Chicago: University of Chicago Press.

Lareau, A. (2003). *Unequal childhoods: Class, race, and family.* Berkeley: University of California Press.

Lareau, A., & Shultz, J. (1996). *Journeys through ethnography: Realistic accounts of fieldwork.* Boulder, CO: Westview.

Lather, P. (2006). Paradigm proliferation as a good thing to think with: Teaching qualitative research as a wild profusion. *Qualitative Studies in Education, 19*(1), 35–57.

Lave, J., & Wenger, E. (1991). *Situated learning: Legitimate peripheral participation.* Cambridge, UK: Cambridge University Press.

LeCompte, M. D., Millroy, W. L., & Preissle, J. (Eds.). (1992). *Handbook of qualitative research in education.* New York: Academic Press.

Lee, S., & Roth, W.-M. (2003). Becoming and belonging: Learning qualitative research through legitimate peripheral participation. *Forum: Qualitative Sozialforschung [Forum: Qualitative Social Research]* [Online serial], *4*(2). Available at http://www.qualitativeresearch.net/index.php/fqs/article/view/708

Lofland, J., & Lofland, L. (1995). *Analyzing social settings: A guide to qualitative observation and analysis.* Belmont, CA: Wadsworth.

Maxwell, J. (2004). *Qualitative research design: An interactive approach* (2nd ed.). Thousand Oaks, CA: Sage.

McIntyre, A. (2008). *Participatory action research: Qualitative research methods series, 52.* Thousand Oaks, CA: Sage.

Miles, M. B., & Huberman, M. A. (1994). *Qualitative data analysis: An expanded sourcebook* (2nd ed.). Thousand Oaks, CA: Sage.

Minichiello, V., & Kottler, J. A. (2009). *Qualitative journeys: Student and mentor experiences with research.* Thousand Oaks, CA: Sage.

Neumann, A., Pallas, A., & Peterson, P. L. (Eds.). (2008, July). Investment in the future: Improving education research at four leading schools of education: Campus experiences of the Spencer Foundation's Research Training Grant Program [Special issue]. *Teachers College Record, 110*(7).

Page, R. N. (2001). Reshaping graduate preparation in educational research methods: One school's experience. *Educational Researcher, 30,* 19–25.

Patton, M. Q. (2002). *Qualitative evaluation and research methods* (3rd ed.). Thousand Oaks, CA: Sage.

Phillips, D. C. (2006). A guide for the perplexed: Scientific educational research, methodolatry, and the gold versus platinum standards. *Educational Research Review, 1*(1), 15–26.

Phillips, N., & Hardy, C. (2002). *Discourse analysis: Investing processes of social construction.* Thousand Oaks, CA: Sage.

Potter, S. J., Caffrey, E. M., & Plante, E. G. (2003). Integrating service-learning into the research methods course. *Teaching Sociology, 31,* 38–48.

Preissle, J., & deMarrais, K. (2009, May 23). *Qualitative pedagogy: Teaching ethnography and other qualitative traditions.* Paper presented at the fifth international congress of qualitative inquiry, University of Chicago, Urbana-Champaign.

Preissle, J., & Roulston, K. (2009). Trends in teaching qualitative research: A 30-year perspective. In M. Garner, C. Wagner, & B. Kawulich (Eds.), *Teaching research methods in the social sciences* (pp. 13–21). Surrey, UK: Ashgate.

Raddon, M., Nault, C., & Scott, A. (2007, August 11). *"Learning by doing" revisited: The complete research project approach to teaching qualitative methods.* Paper presented at the annual meeting of the American Sociological Association, New York. Available at http://www.allacademic.com/meta/p182602_index.html

Rifkin, S. B., & Hartley, S. D. (2001). Learning by doing: Teaching qualitative methods to health care personnel. *Education for Health, 14*(1), 75–85.

Rodriguez, N., & Ryave, A. L. (2002). *Systematic self-observation.* Thousand Oaks, CA: Sage.

Rohall, D. E., Moran, C. L., Brown, C., & Caffrey, E. (2004). Introducing methods of sociological inquiry using living-data exercises. *Teaching Sociology, 32*(4), 401–407.

Roulston, K., deMarrais, K., & Lewis, J. (2003). Learning to interview: The student interviewer as research participant. *Qualitative Inquiry, 9*(4), 643–668.

Schensul, J. J., & LeCompte, M. D. (1999). *The ethnographer's toolkit.* Walnut Creek, CA: AltaMira Press.

Schoenfeld, A. (1999). The core, the canon, and the development of research skills: Issues in the preparation of education researchers. In E. C. Lagemann & L. S. Shulman (Eds.), *Issues in education research: Problems and possibilities* (pp. 166–202). San Francisco: Jossey-Bass.

Shulman, L. S. (2005). Signature pedagogies in the disciplines. *Daedalus, 134*(3), 52–59.

Spradley, J. P. (1979). *The ethnographic interview.* New York: Holt, Rinehart & Winston.

Spradley, J. P. (1980). *Participant observation.* New York: Holt, Rinehart & Winston.

Strayhorn, T. L. (2009). The (in-)effectiveness of various approaches to teaching research methods. In M. Garner, C. Wagner, & B. Kawulich (Eds.), *Teaching research methods in social sciences* (pp. 119–130). Burlington, VT: Ashgate.

Thorne, B. (1993). *Gender play: Girls and boys in school.* New Brunswick, NJ: Rutgers University Press.

Walsh, M. (2003). Teaching qualitative analysis using QSR NVivo. *The Qualitative Report, 8*(2), 251–256. Available at http://www.nova.edu/ssss/QR/QR8-2/walsh.pdf

Webb, R. B., & Glesne, C. (1992). Teaching qualitative research. In M. D. LeCompte, W. L. Millroy, & J. Preissle (Eds.), *The handbook of qualitative research in education* (pp. 771–814). San Diego, CA: Academic Press.

Wenger, E. (1998). *Communities of practice: Learning, meaning, and identity.* Cambridge, UK: Cambridge University Press.

Whyte, W. F. (1955). *Street corner society: The social structure of an Italian slum* (4th ed.). Chicago: University of Chicago Press.

Wolcott, H. F. (1994). *Transforming qualitative data: Description, analysis, and interpretation.* Thousand Oaks, CA: Sage.

Wolcott, H. F. (2008). *Writing up qualitative research* (3rd ed.). Thousand Oaks, CA: Sage.

Yanow, D. (2000). *Conducting interpretive policy analysis.* Thousand Oaks, CA: Sage.

Epilogue

Toward a "Refunctioned Ethnography"

Yvonna S. Lincoln and Norman K. Denzin

> *If the Industrial Age was built on people's backs, and the Information Age on people's left hemispheres, the Conceptual Age is being built on people's right hemispheres. We've progressed from a society of farmers to a society of factory workers to a society of knowledge workers. And now we're progressing yet again—to a society of creators and empathizers, pattern recognizers, and meaning makers.*
>
> —D. H. Pink (2005, n.p.)

And so it is we come to another punctuation point in the history of qualitative research and qualitative methods. The changes in even the past 6 years since the third edition of *The SAGE Handbook of Qualitative Research* have been enormous, and they are markers along the trajectory of qualitative and interpretive histories that these mature and new authors have written here. The "pattern recognizers" and "meaning makers" have not, despite considerable denigration, disparagement, and deprecation from some parts of the positivist camp, lost any particular ground, unless it is in funding. And even there, mixed methods proposals have frequently won the day (and the external funding).

We are at an interesting crossroads. On the one hand, qualitative methods as a field has been able to propose methods far beyond those of original fieldwork experts and texts (e.g., McCall and Simmons's [1989] original textbook, wherein they proposed that all fieldwork rested in interviewing and observation). So, for instance, methodologists have been prompt to adapt their methods to emerging technologies and to explore what kinds of data about social life emerge when they examine cultural artifacts—particularly the artifacts of popular culture—or what kinds of data are created by online communities. On the other hand, methodologists have also interrogated deeply classical methods, such as interviewing, and how such methods work at the intersections of race, class, gender, and nationality/hybridity. Our understandings about, for example, interviewing as well as observation is far more nuanced, sophisticated, and sensitive than it was even 20 years ago. There are several such profound changes in the field. This epilogue will cover a number of the more important, including the turn to social justice; the turn, in interpretive work, to critical stances; the rise of mixed methods; the possibilities for cumulating knowledge and understanding for qualitative research; and the upcoming struggle to design even more contemporary methods that address the effects of late capitalism and its reshaping of economies, cultural structures and mores, and social life across the global community.

Social Justice

A mere two decades ago, only a handful of scholars were talking about the impact of their work on issues of social justice, by which they meant the ability of social science to be put to policy objectives with the purpose of redressing a variety of historically reified oppressions in modern life: racism, economic injustice, the "hidden injuries of class," discrimination in the legal system, gender inequities, and the new oppressions resulting from the restructuring of the social welfare system to "workfare." Today, many scholars, positivists and interpretivists alike, purposefully direct their own research toward uncovering such injustices, exposing how historic social structures reify and reinvent discriminatory practices, and proposing new forms of social structures that are less oppressive. The turn toward social justice, of course, is directly linked with the turn toward more critical stances in interpretation and representation (Cannella & Lincoln, 2009; Denzin, 2009, 2010; Denzin & Giardina, 2006, 2007, 2008, 2009).

The Turn to Critical Stances

The call for more critical stances in interpretive inquiry is not new (Lather, 1986, 1991, 1992, 2004, 2007); it has a long history, marching alongside qualitative researchers like a gentle moral conscience on the road trip to somewhere, destination unknown. However, until qualitative researchers were able to understand the connection between social science writ broadly and the quest for better policy, for a more just and democratic society, for a more egalitarian distribution of goods and services, critical perspectives were, in some cases, simply a companion, not a conjoined voice. That has changed.

While it is the case that not all qualitative researchers aim for social justice explicitly—some being focused on simply describing some phenomenon, or helping to create deep *verstehen* of some hitherto unexplored situation—it is the case that many now ask themselves what the outcomes of their research will produce in terms of more extended equality and less domination and discrimination (Mertens, 1998). Ruth Bleier (1984, 1986) makes a similar point: With resources for social science extremely limited, can we afford to engage in such scientific work without having it embody some larger social purpose, principally the amelioration of some social ill? She observes that

> Science is a powerful tool for good as well as for evil, for *emancipation* as well as for exploitation. How scientists use their time and talent, their training at public expense, their *public research funds, and the public trust are not matters to be brushed aside lightly.* Many fascinating research problems wait for attention. Residing, as we do, inside a universe filled with enigmas, many of which lend themselves to research approaches congenial to our personal styles, many with applications beneficial to segments of society that are due for some benefits, how do we justify working on research whose applications threaten to be deeply destructive of natural resources, of human life, of the dignity and self-respect of a racial or ethnic or gender group? (Bleier, 1986, p. 35, emphasis added)

This sense that something is owed back for the education and its privileges that scholars enjoy, but also that there are serious issues to which attention should be turned—issues which bear a strong relationship to redistributing the benefits of society more equitably—is a feeling that has come to full flower at the millennium. However much critics and disparagers of qualitative research criticize interpretive work as "advocacy" or as arguably political—since all knowledge is ultimately political—it is unlikely that issues of social justice, or the more equal distribution of goods and services, or the elimination of discrimination and injustice, will go away. How can we ever return to our former naivete? We know too much, we understand too deeply, to go back now.

Mixed Methods

Nowhere can the theoretical and methodological tumult of the last decade be seen more clearly than in the crucible of mixed methods. As we wrote in the introduction to this volume, we—the two of us—share some misgivings about the paradigmatic (epistemological, ontological, axiological) state of mixed methods research *at this point in time.* The second edition of Tashakkori and Teddlie's *The*

SAGE Handbook of Mixed Methods in Social and Behavioral Research (2010) deals with multiple issues that we and others have raised (Teddlie, personal correspondence, 2009), including epistemological concerns. We are uncomfortable with the stance that some have taken that epistemology doesn't matter. We feel strongly that such a declaration essentially negates the work of dozens (if not hundreds) of feminist theorists; critical theorists; race and ethnic studies theorists; queer and other "embodied" theorists; as well as theorists of postcolonialism, hybridities, borders, Latino/a and Latino critical studies, and others. Epistemology matters. Standpoint matters. Each of these things—one philosophical, one embodied and sociocultural—gives meaning and inflection to both the beginning (the research question) and the ending (the findings) of any inquiry. To deny their influence is to miss most of the major debates of the last quarter-century of qualitative research and indeed, the social sciences more broadly. The apotheosis of mixed methods at the expense of epistemology debates and ontological concerns appears to us to be misplaced, given the attention devoted to the careful plumbing of these issues and the delicate, razor-edged exploration of their implications by scholars for many decades.

Pragmatism may not, either, be the answer to the ontological, epistemological, and axiological concerns raised by the gentle voices of dissent. As we point out, too, the pragmatism that has been captured thus far is neither the classical pragmatism of Peirce or William James, nor is it the revised neopragmatism of Rorty or Habermas. A deep revision of the paradigmatic claims for the foundations of mixed methods seems to us to be called for at this time.

The original criticisms of mixed methods research seem to endure. While no classical methodologists appear to have anything particular against the possibility of mixing methods (see, for instance, Guba & Lincoln, 1981, 1989; Lincoln & Guba, 1985), it is with the caveat that such mixing should be done under the aegis of a single paradigm, such that the ontological, epistemological, and axiological concerns are coherent and resonant. Indeed, there are times when both kinds of data can illuminate different aspects of the same phenomenon so that a sharper and bolder picture emerges. Until such time as the paradigmatic issues are resolved, however, we welcome the ongoing debate and trust that the new mixed methods journal *(Journal of Mixed Methods Research)* will contribute clarity and strength to the conversation.

The Cumulation of Qualitative Knowledge

One of the many myths surrounding qualitative research is that policy formulation utilizing such research is either difficult or impossible (Lincoln, in progress).

Frequently dismissed as "anecdotal" by its detractors, qualitative research has often turned inward, addressing its own community of believers, who choose their own, less global, more locally focused means to effect social change. The major issue appears to be that of aggregating data, much as quantitative researchers rely on meta-analytic techniques for discovering strands of data and meaningful findings that can be "translated" into policy arguments. Aggregation, or cumulation of findings, is not a technique (or set of techniques) often taught or even discussed in doctoral research preparation, so it is not surprising that even qualitative researchers can and do accept the myths about non-aggregatability. There are, however, possibilities for cumulating and aggregating qualitative data, and there are techniques for secondary analyses of data that are beginning to be more widely known (Heaton, 2004), and there are historical efforts—developed for and utilized by the federal government—at case study aggregation analysis (Lucas, 1972, 1974). There are additional techniques being suggested that parallel quantitative meta-analytic techniques. Both secondary analyses and meta-analytic techniques are being made possible by computer-aided archival of data; such large-scale storage permits comparisons of data, reusing and "reworking" of qualitative data in a fraction of the time it might have taken a decade ago, and permits the kinds of comparisons of findings that allow policy construction. An exploration of these options, with a direct focus on their applicability for policy purposes, is the centerpiece of new and future efforts at addressing the cumulation issue.

Navigating the Contemporary

Perhaps the most serious current issue confronting qualitative inquirers is generating a contemporary history and ethnography of the rapid changes characterizing the global community today. Davis and Marquis (2005) comment that "we are constantly reminded that we live in a world in which large organizations have absorbed society and vacuumed up most of social reality" (p. 332), and in which "MNCs [multinational corporations] dominate the world economy (and thus society) through their concentrated control of capital. It hardly seems a fair fight, as large organizations continue their drive to vacuum up whatever is left of social life." Davis and Marquis are not the only observers to note this phenomenon. Perrow (1991) commented on the same issue more than a decade earlier, and closer to this year, Faubion and Marcus (2009) and Westbrook (2008) addressed the same issues of contemporariness. Michael Fischer's (2009) powerful foreword to the Faubion and Marcus volume lays out a project of enormous scope: a beginning set of dialogues that "do not satirize older anthropologies and instead build upon, and extend into a new era, a recursive set of intellectual conversations and experiments" (p. ix), including their ability to guide readers into "the mediations of guarded, packaged, and traded elusive information" that serve to help us "understand the structure of the circuits as [well as] to challenge or guesstimate the veracity in the information packets" (p. viii). Much of the six dissertations reported on in this "Rice project" (dissertations completed at Rice University under the direction of Marcus and Fischer, with particular foci in mind) have to do with faked data (from informants), "made-up statistics and corruption stories" (p. viii) emanating from fieldwork projects, principally in postcolonial settings, but also in governmental and NGO (nongovernmental organization) environments. We have virtually no ethnographic tools to deal with wide-scale corruption, with seriously faked data, with governmental efforts to "vacuum up" what multinational corporations have not managed to "capture," or with information that is "elusive," deliberately hidden, ethically "unusable" (Hamilton, 2009), treated as corporate intellectual property, or carefully packaged for extra-organizational consumption.

Westbrook (2008), too, argues for an "ethnography of present situations," a "refunctioned ethnography" wherein "critical reflexivity" is operationalized "so that self-consciousness is not merely deployed as a critique of texts and stances after the fact, but is instead a part of the design and performance of anthropological work from the beginning" (p. 111). Westbrook reminds us, as well, of the first great principle of the postmodern: "[R]ather than a description or representation in the ordinary sense, which is in principle replicable, the expressions of ethnography for present situations are *in principle* unique" (p. 65, italics original). The function of these reimagined, repurposed, refunctioned ethnographies of "present situations" is to account for how we chose this future over some other; how we moved from the ravages of modernism to the globalized, late-capitalism neoliberalism sowing its seeds around the globe; and how we can examine the "navigator"—the ethnographer herself—how we examine multiple respondents "in some relation to one another"; and what Westbrook calls "liaisons," or connections, junctures, and nexuses that provide alliance between ethnographers and those who can and will supply the raw data of present-situation ethnographies. Faubion and Marcus (2009) would add to these three ingredients "circuits," or the routes by which information, data, stories, narratives, and other dialogic and textual material flows both around and to the ethnographer—or is prevented from reaching the ethnographer.

The call here is for an ethnography that moves beyond the "sin" and "guilt" of modernity, and that attempts to unravel the complexity of the milieu which is, according to Davis and Marquis (2005), "vacuuming up" social life and social reality. In the call for the practical, the pragmatic, or "what works," we may have lost sight of the fact that we are rapidly losing the means to socially construct *any* worlds, let alone one that is more just, more socially, economically, and culturally equitable.

Conclusion: A Real Epilogue

The foregoing are some of the more troubling reasons we term this fourth edition merely a punctuation point in the history of qualitative methods, not a period, not the end of the page. We have work to do, important work, and we must do it fast and well. While keeping our eyes on issues of social justice, we must also contrive how to represent multiple findings from multiple studies in order to achieve presence and voice at the policy table. We must learn to talk with those who speak quantitatively and those who speak qualitatively, but do so with consonance, coherence, and suasion. We must likewise research and make transparent the changes that are overtaking the world, so that we understand the futures we have chosen and are empowered to choose others if we so wish. Far from being some imaginary endpoint, we are in fact at the edge of a new colonialism, a new era, one that we did not fully choose, and one that we must begin to understand more fully than we have to this point. The only meaningful method for that understanding is a refashioned, refunctioned, repurposed imaginary for ethnography and ethnographers. And that is yet to be invented.

References

Bleier, R. (1984). *Science and gender: A critique of biology and its theories on women.* Oxford, UK: Pergamon Press.

Bleier, R. (Ed.). (1986). *Feminist approaches to science.* Oxford, UK: Pergamon.

Cannella, G. S., & Lincoln, Y. S. (2009). Deploying qualitative methods for critical social purposes. In N. K. Denzin & M. D. Giardina, (Eds.), *Qualitative inquiry and social justice: Toward a politics of hope* (pp. 53–72). Walnut Creek, CA: Left Coast Press.

Davis, G. E., & Marquis, C. (2005, July/August). Prospects for organizational theory in the early twenty-first century: Institutional fields and mechanisms. *Organization Science, 16*(4), 332–343.

Denzin, N. K. (2009). *Qualitative inquiry under fire: Toward a new paradigm dialogue.* Walnut Creek, CA: Left Coast Press.

Denzin, N. K. (2010). *The qualitative manifesto: A call to arms.* Walnut Creek, CA: Left Coast Press.

Denzin, N. K., & Giardina, M. D. (Eds.). (2006). *Qualitative inquiry and the conservative challenge: Confronting methodological fundamentalism.* Walnut Creek, CA: Left Coast Press.

Denzin, N. K., & Giardina, M. D. (Eds.). (2007). *Ethical futures in qualitative research: Decolonizing the politics of knowledge.* Walnut Creek, CA: Left Coast Press.

Denzin, N. K., & Giardina, M. D. (Eds.). (2008). *Qualitative inquiry and the politics of evidence.* Walnut Creek, CA: Left Coast Press.

Denzin, N. K., & Giardina, M. D. (Eds.). (2009). *Qualitative inquiry and social justice: Toward a politics of hope.* Walnut Creek, CA: Left Coast Press.

Faubion, J. D., & Marcus, G. E. (Eds.). (2009). *Fieldwork is not what it used to be: Learning anthropology's method in a time of transition.* Ithaca, NY: Cornell University Press.

Fischer, M. M. J. (2009). Foreword: Renewable Ethnography. In J. D. Faubion & G. E. Marcus (Eds.), *Fieldwork is not what it used to be: Learning anthropology's method in a time of transition* (pp. vii–xiv). Ithaca, NY: Cornell University Press.

Guba, E. G., & Lincoln, Y. S. (1981). *Effective evaluation.* San Francisco: Jossey-Bass.

Guba, E. G., & Lincoln, Y. S. (1989). *Fourth-generation evaluation.* Thousand Oaks, CA: Sage.

Hamilton, J. A. (2009). On the ethics of unusable data. In J. D. Faubion & G. E. Marcus (Eds.), *Fieldwork is not what it used to be: Learning anthropology's method in a time of transition* (pp. 73–88). Ithaca, NY: Cornell University Press.

Heaton, J. (2004). *Reworking qualitative data.* Thousand Oaks, CA: Sage.

Lather, P. (1986). Research as praxis. *Harvard Educational Review, 56*(3), 257–277.

Lather, P. (1991). *Getting smart: Feminist research and pedagogy within the postmodern.* New York: Routledge.

Lather, P. (1992). Critical frames in educational research: Feminist and poststructural perspectives. *Theory Into Practice, 31*(2), 1–13.

Lather, P. (2004). Scientific research in education: A critical perspective. *Journal of Curriculum and Supervision, 20*(1), 14–30.

Lather, P. (2007). *Getting lost: Feminist efforts toward a double(d) science.* Albany: State University of New York Press.

Lincoln, Y. S. (in progress). *Policy from prose: The perfect adequacy of policy formulation from qualitative research.* (Paper accepted for presentation, American Educational Research Association, New Orleans, LA, April 8–12, 2011)

Lincoln, Y. S., & Guba, E. G. (1985). *Naturalistic inquiry.* Thousand Oaks, CA: Sage.

Lucas, W. K. (1972). *The case survey method: aggregating case experience.* Santa Monica, CA: The Rand Corporation.

Lucas, W. K. (1974). *The case survey and alternative methods for research aggregation.* Washington, DC: The Rand Corporation.

McCall, G. J., & Simmons, J. L. (Eds.). (1989). *Issues in participant observation*. New York: Random House.

Mertens, D. M. (1998). *Research methods in education and psychology: Integrating diversity with quantitative and qualitative approaches*. Thousand Oaks, CA: Sage.

Perrow, C. (1991). A society of organizations. *Theory of society, 20,* 725–762.

Pink, D. H. (2005, February). Revenge of the right brain, *Wired.* Available at http://www.wired.com/wired/archive/13.02/brain.html

Tashakkori, A., & Teddlie, C. (2010). *The SAGE handbook of mixed methods in social & behavioral research* (2nd ed.). Thousand Oaks, CA: Sage.

Westbrook, D. A. (2008). *Navigators of the contemporary: Why ethnography matters*. Chicago: University of Chicago Press.

Author Index

Subject Index

community, powerful/omnipresent
role of, 330
definitions of, 308
experience, sacred nature of, 330
feminist methodology, sacred approach to
inquiry and, 326-329, 327-329 (table)
gender roles, women's suppression and,
317-318
hegemonic discourse/dominant worldview,
disruption of, 306-307
intersecting oppressions/domination,
common agenda and, 310-312
multiple identities, negotiation of, 320
naming Black feminism, sacred practice of,
318-323
oppression, male/female struggle
against, 320
oppression, shared experience of, 309, 310,
313-315, 317-318
radical openness, whole-person
involvement and, 330-331
radical spiritual activism, collective Black
women's knowings/doings and,
323-324
sacredness/spirituality in endarkened
feminism and, 307-308, 309, 310,
325-326
silenced voices and, 318
spirituality, transformative consciousness
and, 308, 309, 315
traditional paradigms, reconsideration of,
306-308, 320-321
United States/Black feminist history and,
312-316, 322-323
unity in diversity, common destiny and,
324-326
White American feminist scholarship,
tensions with, 321-322
See also Feminist qualitative research; Race;
Racism
Enlightenment model, 45-46, 47
authoritative academic discourse and,
108-109
autonomy doctrine and, 125-127, 132, 136
emergent vs. transcendent values and, 127
Enlightenment dualisms and, 125-127

facts/subjective values, discontinuity
between, 126
freedom-morality dichotomy and, 125, 126,
127, 140
human personality, cult of, 125-126
individual self-determination and, 126-127
materialism and, 126, 451
metaphysical phenomenon, postulates of
reason and, 452
natural science, prestige of, 126, 452
social physics and, 91-92
universal human being/self and, 417
Epistemology, 26, 189, 507
basic tenets of, 202 (table), 204 (table), 210-
212 (table)
transactional epistemology and, 193
transformative paradigm and, 485
Ethical-political qualitative research
framework, 125
autonomy doctrine and, 125-127, 128, 132
codes of ethics and, 134-136
communitarian philosophy and,
147-149, 151
consequentialist ethics and, 129
different conceptions of good, neutrality
between, 127-128, 140
Enlightenment dualisms and, 125-127
experimental inquiry, modes of, 128-129
exteriority of ethics and, 133-134
fallacy of misplaced concreteness and, 136
feminist communitarian model and,
145-146
human research subjects and, 137-138
inductive experimentalism and, 129
institutional review boards, utilitarian
agenda of, 137-139
interpretive sufficiency goal and, 146-155
language of science, collected truths
and, 132
means-ends dualism and, 129-130,
132, 135
Mill's philosophy of social science and,
128-130, 132
moral discernment and, 150-152
moral reasoning, single-consideration
theory and, 133

⑤SAGE research**methods**

The essential online tool for researchers from the world's leading methods publisher

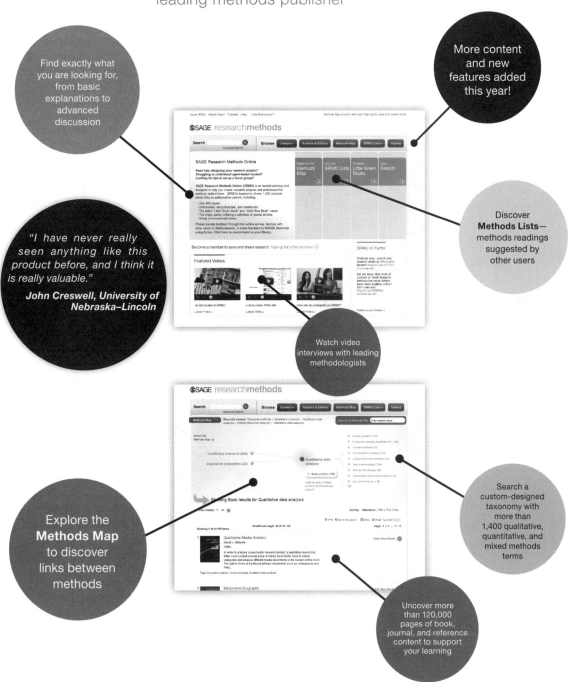

Find exactly what you are looking for, from basic explanations to advanced discussion

More content and new features added this year!

"I have never really seen anything like this product before, and I think it is really valuable."

John Creswell, University of Nebraska–Lincoln

Discover **Methods Lists**— methods readings suggested by other users

Watch video interviews with leading methodologists

Explore the **Methods Map** to discover links between methods

Search a custom-designed taxonomy with more than 1,400 qualitative, quantitative, and mixed methods terms

Uncover more than 120,000 pages of book, journal, and reference content to support your learning

Find out more at
www.sageresearchmethods.com